# Press Law in South Korea

**KYU HO YOUM**

IOWA STATE UNIVERSITY PRESS / AMES

**Kyu Ho Youm,** professor in the Walter Cronkite School of Journalism and Telecommunication at Arizona State University, holds a Ph.D. in journalism from Southern Illinois University–Carbondale. He has served as president of the Southwest Education Council for Journalism and Mass Communication, as head of the Law Division of the Association for Education in Journalism and Mass Communication (AEJMC), and as chair of the Communication Law and Policy Group of the International Communication Association (ICA). On the editorial boards of more than 10 journalism and law journals in the United States and England, he has extensively published about press law in major scholarly journals since 1985. His research and teaching interests are in media law, press freedom theory, international communication, and news writing and reporting.

©1996 Iowa State University Press, Ames, Iowa 50014

⊚ Printed on acid-free paper in the United States of America

First edition, 1996

### Library of Congress Cataloging-in-Publication Data

Youm, Kyu Ho.
    Press law in South Korea / Kyu Ho Youm. — 1st ed.
       p.   cm.
    Includes bibliographical references and index.
    ISBN 0-8138-2327-7 (alk. paper)
    1. Press law—Korea (South)        I. Title.
  KPA3500.Y68   1996
   343.5195099'8—dc20
   [345.19503998]                96-341

To Dr. and Mrs. Harry W. Stonecipher

# CONTENTS

# FOREWORD

The collapse of the Soviet Union and the end of the Cold War ushered in a new era in the comparative study of press laws. The countries formerly dominated by the Soviet Union, including Russia itself, proclaimed themselves republics and began experimenting with democratic processes. These "democracies in transition" feast on the idea of freedom of expression. They celebrate the end of governmental censorship and the arrival of an unregulated market, of ideas as well as other goods.

At the same time, the fledgling democracies are rooted in a legal and political culture which calls for a considerable degree of regulation. The fruit of this tension between the ideal of press freedom and the historical reality of press suppression is the emerging phenomenon of the press in these democracies in transition.

The peculiar condition of the press in democracies in transition is by no means restricted to Eastern Europe or the former territories of the Soviet Union. It is a global phenomenon, extending from Africa to Northeast Asia. South Korea is an excellent case study for those interested in understanding the special position of the press as the transition from an authoritarian regime to a more liberal one takes place.

Indeed, South Korea is different from most democracies in transition, if only because during the Cold War, South Korea inhabited the other side of the divide—the free world. Yet until 1988, South Korea had been anything but a free democracy, and its gradual democratization coincided with the end of the Cold War and has probably benefitted from it.

Like other formerly authoritarian regimes, South Korea faces at least two major and interdependent difficulties as it seeks to transform itself: one legal, the other cultural. Legally, political democratization is typically accompanied by a constitutional commitment to press freedom. There is little doubt that such a normative commitment is of extreme importance in institutionalizing and internalizing democratic values. However, the legal infrastructure is of crucial importance. The criminal code regulating freedom of speech, defamation laws, and rules applying to access to governmental information and to newsgathering may stifle press freedom regardless of the lofty constitutional commitment. Judges unsympathetic to press freedom may interpret the laws in an authoritarian rather than liberal spirit, thus undermining the constitutional commitment.

The political culture is similarly important. How do ordinary men and women interpret the sudden shift in press behavior and press coverage? How does the elite perceive it? Do people still cling to the old distinction between freedom and licentiousness? Are they overwhelmed by the torrent of critical verbosity?; do they find it immoral, anarchic, irresponsible? Or do they take it as a necessary part of their newfound freedom? And what about journalistic ethics? Does ethical journalism find enough fertile ground to grow on in the climate of transition, or is it sacrificed on the altar of the "free marketplace of ideas" where, at least theoretically, anything goes, thereby feeding a popular apprehension of the notion of press freedom?

Professor Kyu Ho Youm's impressive tome on the press law in South Korea provides a wonderful opportunity to explore these issues. It enables the reader to review the various phases of the South Korean republic and the concomitant treatment of the South Korean press during these periods. Its scope provides a model for other scholars in studying press laws of other democracies in transition. More importantly, the book makes the intellectual task of comparison viable by giving us an encyclopedic review of the various aspects of Korean press law in its historical development as well as an updated version of the positive law today.

But there is more to this book. It is the first comprehensive discussion of an Asian press law system. As such, it provides a good, reliable vehicle for those untrained in Asian language to include this important segment in their press law studies. Professor Youm's book brings to the fore such issues as the influence of Confucianism on Korean press law; the influence of the American experience on the same system; whether the South Korean legal system is unique because it has been subjected to Japanese and Continental legal tradition in addition to the Confucian and the American, or whether its press law is a phenomenon quite typical of small, vulnerable countries.

This book is an important contribution to press law studies. It will certainly become an essential reference work for anybody interested in understanding the interaction between the press and the government in any society experiencing a major transformation from authoritarianism to liberalism as well as for anyone interested in press law generally.

Pnina Lahav
Professor of Law
Boston University

# P R E F A C E

The press in South Korea has evolved from a "voluntary servant" to an increasingly "equal contender" in its relationship with its government in recent years. Indeed, it is more accurate to describe the Korean news media as more unrestrained now than ever before. The sweeping change in freedom of the Korean press since 1987 is good testimony to various liberalizing reforms that have characterized a "New Korea." In the context of the traditionally strongman body politic of South Korea, the recent emergence of a free press offers a fascinating case study of how an authoritarian press system has changed to a libertarian system. For those interested in a comparative study of press freedom as a fundamental human right, South Korea is an interesting illustration.

*Press Law in South Korea* examines freedom of the press in South Korea primarily from a statutory and judicial perspective. It also analyzes the constitutional and institutional changes, some of which are still under way, in the Korean press since 1987. The book provides a comprehensive answer to the question of how a free press has been established as a permanent fixture of the sociopolitical and legal system in Korea.

In short, *Press Law in South Korea* is an up-to-date analysis of a number of major legislative statutes, court decisions, and administrative rules and regulations involving the Korean press. Various constitutional and statutory, as well as judicial and administrative, mechanisms relating to the Korean press are scrutinized for their impact on press freedom in that country over the years. Numerous current press issues and concerns are presented throughout the book. The textual approach endeavors to make points about underlying themes and issues through written illustrations.

*Press Law in South Korea* is also intended for those English-reading scholars who are not familiar with Korean law. Chapter 2 is a succinct introduction to both the law and the legal system of South Korea. Its main purpose is to help readers to gain a general understanding of what the Korean law is and where it comes from. The chapter addresses special problems facing readers in studying Korean law in general and Korean press law in particular. It identifies and explains various sources of Korean law and the current judicial system of Korea. Finally, the chapter provides information necessary to find statutory documents and court opinions and includes hints for citation systems on Korean statutes, court decisions, and other legal documents.

While the time frame of *Press Law in South Korea* focuses on the 1948–1994 period, an effort has been made to provide a better historical perspective by exploring the period prior to 1948. In chapter 3, for example, the sociopolitical and legal development of the Korean press from the late 19th century to 1945 are discussed to place the subject in context.

More than anything else, *Press Law in South Korea* aims to fill a void in an international and comparative study of press law by analyzing Korea's legal experience with a wide range of press freedom issues including libel, privacy, national security, obscenity, copyright, access to information, and periodicals, broadcast, and cable television statutes. In addition, the text should serve as a valuable English-language source book on Korean press laws because it synthesizes, in one document, the English texts of the Constitution and several pertinent press statutes of Korea.

*Press Law in South Korea* was written to meet the growing needs of the academic and professional community in the United States and abroad for a book on press law in a democratic South Korea. I hope the book will be useful to students and faculty in journalism, mass communication, political science, history, international studies, and law, and also to professional journalists interested in international reporting for transnational news media and to lawyers working for multinational media organizations.

Parts of chapters 3–8 and 11 of the book appeared in a slightly different version in "A Free Press in South Korea," *Asian Survey* 30 (1990): 312–25, copyright © 1990 by the Regents of the University of California; "Freedom of Expression and the Supreme Court," *Free Speech Yearbook* 31 (1993): 151–73; "Japanese Press Policy in Colonial Korea,"*Journal of Asian History* 26 (1992): 140–59; "Judicial Interpretation of Press Freedom in South Korea," *Boston College Third World Law Journal* 7 (1987): 133–59; "Libel Law and the Press in South Korea: Update," *Occasional Papers/Reprint Series in Contemporary Asian Studies* (1992); "The Libel Law of the Republic of Korea," *Gazette* 35 (1985): 183–96, copyright © 1985 by the Kluwer Academic Publishers; "The Press and National Security," *Asian Profile* 21 (1993): 291–310; "Press Freedom and Judicial Review in South Korea," *Stanford Journal of International Law* 30 (1994): 1–40; "Press Freedom in 'Democratic' South Korea," *Gazette* 43 (1989): 53–71, copyright © 1989 by the Kluwer Academic Publishers; "Press Freedom Under Constraints: The Case of South Korea," *Asian Survey* 26 (1986): 868–82, copyright © 1986 by the Regents of the University of California; "Press Policy of the U.S. Military Government in Korea," *American Journalism* 8 (1991): 161–77; "Right of Reply Under Korean Press Law," *American Journal of Comparative Law* 41 (1993): 49–71; "South Korea: Press Laws in Transition," 22 *Columbia Human Rights Law Review* 22 (1991): 401–35; "South Korea's Experiment with a Free Press," *Gazette* 53 (1994): 111–26, copyright © 1994 by the Kluwer Academic Publishers.

Korean names in this book are given in the Korean name order, family name first. This rule applies especially to the names of the authors of Korean publications. On the other hand, the names of the Korean authors who have published in English are given as they are in their writings. In romanizing Korean titles of books and journal articles as well as the author names of Korean publications, the author has followed the McCune-Reischaur system as noted in "Korean," in *ALA [American Library Association]-LC [Library of Congress] Romanization Tables: Transliteration Schemes for Non-Roman Scripts* 79–93 (1991).

# ACKNOWLEDGMENTS

*Press Law in South Korea* has its genesis in my independent study in 1983 with Dr. Harry W. Stonecipher, a prominent media law scholar, in the School of Journalism at Southern Illinois University–Carbondale (SIUC). During my three-month visit to Seoul in the summer of 1983, Dr. Stonecipher assigned me to do a research paper on freedom of the press in South Korea. My independent study project was derived from Dr. Stonecipher's previous suggestion that I consider writing about press freedom in Korea for my Ph.D. dissertation, not about American media law, which I did a master's thesis on in 1982.

I took up Dr. Stonecipher's idea for my paper with no sense of what would lie ahead. My work on the Korean press freedom paper was more time-consuming and sometimes more frustrating than I had expected. It turned out, however, that I managed to finish a term paper of 270-plus pages during my stay in Seoul. The paper would turn into the foundation of my doctoral dissertation in 1985.

In many ways, *Press Law in South Korea* is the culmination of my 10-year work on Korean press law as a stimulating complement to my primary teaching and research interests in U.S. communication law. Had it not been for Dr. Stonecipher's assignment to me on press freedom in Korea in the summer of 1983, I doubt that I would be doing research on Korean press law, not to mention writing a book on the subject. I dedicate this book to Dr. Stonecipher, now professor emeritus of journalism at SIUC, whose enduring scholarship and "fatherly mentoring" helped me to have a passion for communication law, and to his wife, Helen, for her unceasing support of and interest in my scholarly endeavor since the early 1980s.

I would also like to thank Dr. Douglas A. Anderson, director and Cronkite Endowment Board of Trustees professor in the Walter Cronkite School of Journalism and Telecommunication at Arizona State University, for helping me in numerous ways. He has been exceptionally generous with his advice and encouragement to me on and off campus. As one of the most highly respected journalism and mass communication administrators in the United States, Dr. Anderson has always been willing to go to extra lengths to put me on the path to a better, more rewarding professional life.

Indeed, it was Dr. Anderson who got me thinking more seriously about writing a book as part of my research agenda at Arizona State. In April 1993, he wrote to me in his annual review: "I am particularly pleased ... that you intend to spend a large chunk of time working on your proposed book manuscript. You can't go on—forever—writing a half-dozen articles and a half-dozen papers each year. You have built a tremendous research record in a relatively short career and you are ready for long-term projects like the book." Dr. Anderson, a top-notch First Amendment scholar and an accomplished book author, has been a source of inspiration for me since I joined the faculty of the Cronkite School of Journalism and Telecommunication in 1991.

Special thanks are due to the Institute for Far Eastern Studies (IFES) at Kyungnam University in Seoul for its generous support of my research fellowship during the summer of 1994. During my month-long residency fellowship, I was able to update most of the primary and secondary source materials for this book. I thank especially Dr. Dae-Kyu Yoon, IFES director of planning, and Dr. Su-Hoon Lee, IFES director of international affairs, for their kindness and hospitality. Research for this book was also supported from grants from the National Endowment for the Humanities in Washington, D.C., and from the College of Public Programs at Arizona State University.

Additional thanks go to many Korean government officials who facilitated my access to all of the primary and secondary sources available at the National Assembly Library, the Supreme Court Library, the Constitution Court Library, the Korean Press Institute, and government offices during my research trips to Seoul in 1983, 1991, and 1994. I have also received enthusiastic support and timely direction from Korean scholars, judges, lawyers, and journalists, who are too numerous to be individually acknowledged here. They were kind enough to offer me the benefit of their expertise by commenting on my published articles on Korean press law.

Professor Pnina Lahav of the Boston University School of Law, Professor Manny Paraschos of Emerson College, and Attorney Sandra Coliver, law program director of ARTICLE 19, the International Centre Against Censorship, in London, who have carefully read my manuscript in its early draft, provided fresh insights and advised changes. Especially to Professor Lahav, who has written *Press Law in Modern Democracies: A Comparative Study* (1985), a seminal study of comparative press law in the United States, I owe a special debt of gratitude for encouraging me to keep up my faith in the value of taking a less American-centric approach to research and teaching in media law. She kindly wrote to me in September 1993: "It is very inspiring to have people like you in this country, diligently working on building bridges between their native and adopted countries."

I am also deeply grateful to Ms. Janet Soper, graphic designer senior, at the Publication Assistance Center in Arizona State University's College of Public Programs and her talented staff for their tireless efforts in "cleaning" my book before final printing. They were a delight to work with and were always willing to respond to my often tedious style inquiries. I thank them for their thoughtful contributions to my book.

Finally, I wish to thank my wife, Bokim, for her unending devotion to me and for her unflagging confidence in my career in the United States, and my sons, Harry and Eugene, for cheerfully yielding their PowerBook to me for my work on the book. Without their constant love and understanding, this book would have been impossible.

# PRESS LAW IN SOUTH KOREA

# CHAPTER 1

# South Korea: An Overview

## GEOPOLITICAL AND SOCIAL HISTORY

Korea is a peninsula of about 85,000 square miles, which is roughly equal to the combined areas of New York and Pennsylvania. Located between mainland Asia and Japan, Korea serves as a land bridge connecting continental Northeast Asia with Japan.[1] Because of its geopolitical importance and strategic location, Korea was invaded by its neighboring countries in the north and to the east throughout much of its 2,200-year recorded history. Sung Moon Pae, professor of political science at Bellevue College, claimed, "[F]oreign invasions have been inflicted upon the Korean people on the average at least once every 4.6 years."[2]

From the end of the 16th century to the mid-19th century, Korea deliberately sought isolation from the outside world to avoid being further victimized by foreign countries seeking to expand in Asia. After years of upheaval and uncertainty, Korea became a colony of Japan in August 1910 under the Korean-Japanese annexation treaty, which proclaimed, "[T]he Imperial Government of Japan undertake [sic] the entire government and administration of Korea."[3] It should be noted, however, that in 1905 Japan had already taken control of the diplomatic sovereignty of Korea under a "protectorate treaty."[4] The Government-General created by Japan ruled the Korean people with "absolute power and authority" throughout Japan's 36-year colonial rule.[5] Japan systematically deprived Koreans of their political and economic rights; top colonial government positions in Korea were heavily staffed by Japanese, and the Korean army was disbanded so that the steadily growing Japanese forces could suppress any violent resistance to the militaristic Japanese rule.[6]

Economically, Korea was subjected to drastic restructuring. The Japanese changed currency and introduced their own banking into Korea, which facilitated their control of the Korean economy. Through an eight-year land survey begun in 1910, the Japanese semi-governmental Oriental Development Company effectively

3

expropriated the land of numerous Korean owners.[7] One American authority on Korea has termed Japanese penetration and settlement in colonial Korea "unique" because Western colonialists ruled in Asia with relatively small numbers.[8]

The increasingly repressive Japanese policy was resisted by Koreans in varying degrees. Most dramatic was the nationwide uprising on March 1, 1919, when Koreans boldly declared their independence from Japanese rule.[9] The independence movement was brutally put down by the Japanese police and military.[10] However, the movement had one important repercussion for Koreans as the Japanese Government-General's colonial policy changed from outright suppression to gradual appeasement in an attempt to soothe the outraged anti-Japanese feelings of the Koreans.[11]

From the 1930s through World War II, Japan formulated policies to assimilate Korea economically and socioculturally into its empire. Under these policies, the Japanese colonial government tried to eliminate the cultural identity of the Korean people. It prohibited use of the Korean language at home and schools. Further, it "Japanized" Korean names. One expert on Korea has observed: "This situation was different from that of any other colony in the region. In other colonies, advancement may have required knowledge of the language and culture of the colonizers, but in Korea the indigenous language was prohibited by law. In effect, this was a policy of cultural genocide."[12]

Korea was liberated from Japanese colonial rule in August 1945,[13] when Japan surrendered to the Western Allies at the end of World War II. Koreans gained freedom from Japan, but soon saw their land divided into two halves along the 38th parallel. The division resulted from an agreement between the United States and the Soviet Union to disarm the Japanese armies stationed in Korea. The primarily agricultural and densely populated South was put under U.S. military rule; the more industrial and sparsely inhabited North was governed by the Soviets. After a series of abortive efforts to arrange nationwide elections under the auspices of the United Nations, the general election was held in 1948 in the South only. It created the government of the First Republic of Korea (South Korea) under President Syngman Rhee.

In 1950, two years after the establishment of the South Korean government, the Korean War broke out when communist North Korea invaded the South. It ended with the armistice between the warring parties three years later, in 1953. The unprecedented fratricidal war between the two politically and ideologically opposing sides caused 1.3 million military and civilian casualties in South Korea, and "nearly half of the industrial capacity and a third of the housing in the south were destroyed along with much of the public infrastructure."[14]

During the decade or so following the Korean War, South Korea was sustained largely by U.S. military and economic aid, along with some international assistance. Since the mid-1960s, however, Korea's economy and national defense have progressed rapidly with the successful implementation of six five-year economic development plans since 1962. Having attained self-reliance in almost every area,

Korea is no longer among the less developed countries (LDCs); it is often described as one of the most dynamic "economic miracles" in the world. One Korean-American commentator has noted:

> South Korea stands out as one of few rapidly developing countries. South Korea raised the per capita annual income from less than $100 in 1960 to $6,300 in 1991 as the outcome of the implementation of a series of successive five-year economic development plans. Her canny investment of human and other resources accelerated industrialization and reduced foreign debts through trade expansion. The agony of annual grain shortages and spring famines has been replaced by agricultural surpluses and the rapid rise of grain storage maintenance costs.[15]

When it came to politics based on democratic popular participation, however, South Korea was considerably more backward, taking almost four decades to make the list of "politically developed" nations. A succession of more or less authoritarian regimes more often disregarded than respected political freedom and civil liberties up to the late 1980s. Choi Chang Yoon, chief secretary of the ruling Democratic Liberal Party in South Korea, argued in 1992, "Since its founding in 1948, the Republic of Korea [South Korea] has always professed to be democratic, but in actuality until recently has suffered from a succession of authoritarian governments that seized power in one way or another."[16]

Syngman Rhee, the first President of South Korea, ruled his country for 12 years before being forced out of office and into exile by the April Students Uprising in 1960. His government was generally marked by despotism and political repression, not to mention widespread official corruption. Rhee's ambition for personal power was a contributing factor in his authoritarian politics. He rejected "an elective democracy with various constitutional mechanisms against the arbitrary executive power."[17]

The government of Chang Myon, which replaced the Rhee administration, proved so ineffective as to let extreme social disorder and political terrorism be the norm, not the exception. As Sung-joo Han, a noted authority on Korean politics, pointed out, the less-than-one-year history of the Chang regime attests to "an important problem that many newly developing nations face—namely, their inability to maintain constitutional and democratic political institutions."[18]

The Chang government was toppled in May 1961 by a bloodless military coup led by General Park Chung Hee, who was elected President in late 1963 as the candidate of the now defunct Democratic Republican Party. He was President for more than 16 years until assassinated by his own intelligence chief in October 1979. Compared with the Rhee government, let alone the "most democratic" Chang regime,[19] President Park's administration was much more authoritarian and undemocratic in its response to political criticism. Ruling Korea with an iron hand, Park brooked virtually no dissent from his deeply held political philosophy that "democracy as practiced in the United States, France, and England is not suited to Korea."[20]

The violent death of Park gave many Koreans hope that they would at last have the opportunity to experiment with democracy in the political sense of the term. That hope faded, however, when General Chun Doo Hwan emerged as Korea's new strongman. Assuming the presidency in August 1980, Chun, who had been a loyal protege of the late President-for-life Park, amended the Constitution, which still failed to provide institutional separation of government powers.[21] U.S. Korea observers Jerome Alan Cohen and Edward J. Baker stated in 1991: "The human-rights situation in the Republic of Korea remained as bad or worse during the early years of the Chun Government as in the last year of the Park Government."[22] More recently, constitutional law scholar Kun Yang of Hanyang University in Seoul characterized Chun's Fifth Republic (1980–1987) as the "most blatant dictatorship" in the post-1948 history of South Korea, adding that "[f]reedom of expression was all but non-existent."[23]

In 1987, Roh Tae Woo, while chairman of the ruling Democratic Justice Party (DJP) and a presidential candidate, ushered in an era of open politics with a package of democratic reforms in his June 29, 1987, declaration, issued at a time of worsening anti-government demonstrations. Roh proposed the speedy amendment of the Constitution, allowing for direct presidential elections and a peaceful transfer of power in February 1988; revision of the presidential election law to guarantee freedom of candidacy and fair competition; amnesty for Kim Dae Jung, a prominent dissident leader, and the restoration of his civil rights; freedom for all political prisoners except those accused of treason and violent crimes; maximum promotion and protection of basic rights, including a drastic extension of habeas corpus; freedom of the press, with maximum improvements of the repressive Basic Press Act; local autonomy, including the election of local councils and establishment of municipal and provincial councils and self-government for colleges and universities; guarantees to allow the free and democratic growth of political parties; and bold social reforms aimed at stamping out crime and "deep-seated" corruption.[24] In an editorial on Roh's declaration for a series of democratic reforms in Korea, the *New York Times* noted that Roh brought his country to "the threshold of a remarkable political achievement: the passage ... from backwardness and authoritarianism to prosperity and democratic rule."[25]

During the Sixth Republic, under President Roh (1988–1992), Korea emerged as one of the more advanced democracies in the world. David Steinberg, professor of Korean studies at Georgetown University, asserted that the progress to a more open democracy in Korea was "a product of both the personal and institutional approaches" to the liberalization of Korea's political system since 1987.[26] Donald Gregg, U.S. ambassador to Korea in 1989–1993, described Roh as flexible and open to change, and as "much more relaxed" than his predecessors Park Chung Hee and Chun Doo Hwan.[27] Steinberg pointed out that political pluralism, the growing independence of the judiciary, the vitalized National Assembly, the diminished role of the military in politics and increasing social mobility had contributed substantially to the democratization process during Roh's rule.[28]

The sweeping democratic reforms initiated with Roh's 1987 declaration have continued since Kim Young Sam was elected President in December 1992. "As the first freely elected civilian leader in thirty-two years," stated Seung-Soo Han, the Korean ambassador to the United States, "President Kim's victory was seen as a political watershed for the nation, launching a truly civilian government grounded in unquestioned political legitimacy."[29]

On assuming the presidency in early 1993, Kim initiated unprecedented reforms to create a "New Korea," in which Koreans would live with "clean politics, a transparent government, a more mature, democratic, and just society, and a viable economy that would stand alone, free from government favoritisms."[30] Among the most notable reforms undertaken by Kim during the past two years have been the anti-corruption drive aimed at government agencies and officials, a presidential decree banning anonymous bank accounts, an administrative reform geared toward business deregulation, and political reforms including a March 1994 revision of various statutes on elections, political funds, and the local autonomy system.[31]

Equally important, Kim has neutralized the power of the military in Korean politics. One Korean-born American political scientist has termed Kim's policy of civilian control of the Korean military "thorough, systematic, and deliberate."[32] Kim dismissed a number of senior military officers for their politically oriented activities or for their corruption in promotion and weapons procurements scandals.[33]

President Kim's reforms have been compared to a "quiet revolution" in Korea and have gained enormous popularity among Koreans. More than 90 percent of Koreans who responded to a nationwide poll in September 1993 indicated that they supported Kim's "New Korea" reforms.[34] The year 1994 has been designated by the Kim administration as the "second year of reform," in which "reforms from the bottom" would be pursued as a follow-up to the "reforms from the top" implemented in 1993. The underlying theme of the "reforms from the bottom" approach was "to have the flame of reform spread from the bottom of society upward to meet the one from the top so that the wave of changes may sweep the entire nation."[35]

## PRESS HISTORY

A few semi-newspapers already existed in Korea even before the "Hermit Kingdom" Yi Dynasty was finally opened to the West in the 19th century. *Chobo* (Court Gazette) was first published in 1392 by the royal court "to communicate to the people governmental information such as court announcements, appointments, transfers and dismissals of government officials."[36] In the 16th century, *Chobo* was published by a group of educated civilians and sold to government offices in Seoul and in the provinces. But circulation of *Chobo* was eventually prohibited by royal order on the grounds that "the events in the royal palace should not be known to the common people and ... the secrets of the nation might be leaked to foreigners."[37] Judging from Otto Groth's "universally applicable" criteria for a "true" newspaper[38] (periodical publication, mechanical reproduction, accessibility, timeliness, and various contents with organizational continuity[39]), *Chobo* was far from a functioning newspaper. However, it is generally regarded as the beginning of Korean newspapers.[40]

The first Korean newspaper that generally met the Groth standards was *Hansung Sunbo*, with which the history of modern Korean newspapers is said to have begun.[41] The paper was published every 10 days, starting on October 1 (by the lunar calendar), 1883. Although it carried both domestic and overseas news, its primary function was to publish official government announcements.[42] *Hansung Sunbo* was terminated when, after the Reformist Party's abortive coup of 1884, the conservative opponents attacked the government publication office of Pangmunguk (Office of Culture and Information), which published the paper, and burned the office and destroyed printing presses and other equipment.

In January 1886, the paper was resurrected as a weekly under the name *Hansung Chubo*. In contrast to *Hansung Sunbo*,[43] it used a mixture of Hangul (the Korean alphabet) and Chinese characters. Like its predecessor, however, *Hansung Chubo* did not enjoy a long life; publication ceased when the government publication office closed in 1888, just two years after the first issue of the paper. Although the first two newspapers were short-lived, they contributed significantly to the overall development of the Korean press. Korean journalism historian Chun Chhoe has stated: "[P]ublication of the paper[s] first contributed to introducing the idea of mass communication into Korea. It also marked a turning point in communication which in the past had been limited to decrees from the governors to the governed."[44]

The Koreans were left without a newspaper for the next eight years until 1896, when *Tongnip Shinmun* (Independent News) appeared as the first *private* newspaper in Korea. *Tongnip Shinmun*, which has served as the "guiding spirit" for the Korean press,[45] was published under the editorship of So Jae-pil (Philip Jaisohn) and became the first real newspaper in the modern sense of the word.[46] It first appeared on April 7, 1896, with three of its four pages in Korean and one in English. Published three times a week, the paper was devoted primarily to advocating freedom from foreign dependence, protection of national sovereignty, elimination of class distinctions, and expansion of civil rights.[47] One foreign visitor to Korea in 1897, noting the Fourth Estate role of *Tongnip Shinmun*, wrote: "[*Tongnip Shinmun*] is already fulfilling an important function in unearthing abuses and dragging them into daylight, and is creating a desire for rational education and reasonable reform, and is becoming something of a terror to evil-doers."[48] In 1899, the paper was closed when So was forced to leave for the United States because of internal strife occurring within the royal government of the Yi Dynasty.[49]

Presumably the success of *Tongnip Shinmun* during its three-year existence aroused fresh interest in the press among Koreans. Professor Michael Robinson of the University of Southern California noted: "Early newspapers in Korea were generally in-house publications for officialdom. The *Tongnip Shinmun*, however, had created a precedent for the development of a popular press."[50] Between 1898 and 1899, a number of dailies and weeklies appeared in Korea, including *Hyopsonghoe Hoebo, Kyongsong Shinmun, Taehan Shinbo, Maeil Shinmun, Taeguk Shinmun, Hwangsong Shinmun, Shisa Chongbo, Taehan Maeil Shinbo*, and *Taehan Hwangsong Shinmun*.[51] These papers followed the example of *Tongnip Shinmun* in that their avowed task was "to preserve the national sovereignty" of Korea.[52] What is particularly noteworthy was the emergence in 1898 of Korea's first daily newspaper, *Maeil Shinmun*, edited by Syngman Rhee, who would later become Korea's first President.[53] *Maeil Shinmun* was published half in Korean and half in English.

After the forced annexation of Korea in 1910, several newspapers established at the end of the Yi Dynasty were closed by the Japanese colonial government for their openly anti-Japanese editorial policies.[54] For the next 10 years, Koreans went through the first of the "dark ages" without real newspapers.[55] Although no private newspapers of nationalistic nature were allowed during the dark period, some mouthpieces of the Japanese colonial government appeared: the Korean-language *Maeil Shinbo*, the Japanese-language *Keijo Nippo*, and the English-language *Seoul Press*. Meantime, the numbers of newspapers published by the Japanese sharply increased to a total of 30—16 dailies, four triweeklies, six weeklies, and four monthlies.[56]

A significant turning point in the history of the Korean press occurred with the nationwide independence movement of Koreans against the Japanese colonialists in 1919. The Samil (March 1) Independence Movement led the Japanese Government-General to appease, rather than suppress, Koreans in an effort to accommodate their outraged anti-Japanese sentiments. The policy change of the Japanese colonial government brought into operation two Korean vernacular papers, *Dong-A Ilbo* and *Chosun Ilbo*.[57] In addition, the Japanese expanded opportunities for freedom of the press by issuing 409 publication permits for books and magazines in 1920. By 1925, the number of publication permits had tripled to 1,240,[58] and by 1930, the daily newspapers published in Korea numbered 31, including seven Korean-language papers.[59]

*Dong-A Ilbo* and *Chosun Ilbo*, which started as the first Korean-owned private enterprises since 1910, were permitted to publish on political issues and current affairs. In 1921, *Dong-A Ilbo* introduced a rotary press, the first in Korea. *Chosun Ilbo* first published both a morning and an evening edition in 1924 and was the first Korean newspaper to run a comic strip. In the late 1920s, *Dong-A Ilbo* and *Chosun Ilbo* had circulations of about 40,000 and 18,000, respectively.[60]

Radio broadcasting was first introduced into Korea in February 1927, when Kyongsong (now Seoul) Broadcasting Station started Korean-language broadcasts. The Japanese colonial government strictly regulated broadcasting, which was "perhaps the most tightly controlled" communications medium in Korea "because of the centralized nature of its organization and production."[61] Professors Jong

Geun Kang of Illinois State University and Won Yong Kim of Sungkyunkwan University in Seoul stated in 1994: "Due to the constant surveillance and censorship, Kyongsong Broadcasting Station was unable to schedule its own programming. Furthermore, the station was not allowed to broadcast any matter dealing with Korea's national identities."[62]

In 1940, *Dong-A Ilbo* and *Chosun Ilbo*, then the leading and most independent Korean newspapers, were closed by the Japanese as part of their militaristic oppression of Koreans. The Japanese colonial authorities imposed strict regulations on radio broadcasting, banning Korean broadcasters from producing programs directed at Korean listeners.[63] One commentator observed, "It is difficult to find another colony in the world in which control of the native press is so complete."[64]

After Korea was liberated from 36 years of Japanese colonial rule at the end of World War II, South Korea was temporarily ruled by the U.S. military government while North Korea was occupied by the Soviet Union.[65] During the 1945–1948 rule of the U.S. Army Military Government in Korea (USAMGIK), Koreans had their first real experience with freedom of the press[66] in the "libertarian" sense of the phrase.[67] Professor Bae-ho Hahn of Korea University in Seoul noted, "In a matter of weeks, no fewer than sixty-eight newspapers mushroomed."[68] To cope with communist propagandistic activities and subversive anti-social disorder caused by Korean "yellow journalism," the American military rulers in 1946 promulgated Ordinance No. 88, which provided for registration and licensing of publications, including newspapers.[69] A total of 273 periodicals—57 dailies, 49 weeklies, 13 news agencies, and 154 monthlies and bimonthlies—were published in Korea by September 1946, one year after Korea's liberation.[70]

During American military rule, the USAMGIK Department of Public Information was in charge of regulating radio broadcasting. Programming and other related broadcasting decisions were made by U.S. military advisors, and the Korean Broadcasting System (KBS), which was the only radio station in Korea until 1954, was created by the U.S. military rulers. Radio broadcasting changed in its programming and content under the U.S. military government. Although radio broadcasting was "largely a governmental function," Kang and Kim stated, "radio gradually increased entertainment, educational, and informational programming, based on surveys of audience preferences."[71] In 1948, about 35,000 radio sets were registered with the government.[72]

The founding of the Republic of Korea in 1948, which adopted uncompromising policies against communism, led to a drastic decline of leftist propaganda media in South Korea, and those leftist publications that remained had faded out completely by the time the Korean War broke out in June 1950. Journalism Professor Dong-Chol Kim of Ehwa Women's University in Seoul claimed that the eclipse of the communist journals from South Korea provided a "temporary political lull" for the Korean press. He added: "[T]he Korean press emerged from political party subservience to become a public institution, with a gradual awareness of its duty and obligation to the reading public. They [sic] gradually began to explore the avenues of profit-seeking as private commercial establishments."[73]

The "political lull" truly was temporary in that the sudden outbreak of the Korean War delivered a critical blow to the still unstable newspaper industry in Korea; the war deprived the industry of virtually all newsprint, destroying 76.8 percent of Korea's paper manufacturing facilities.[74] The KBS facilities were also destroyed.

During the war period (1950–1953), the Korean press was subject to strict military censorship, and the Korean press consequently lacked diversity in its contents. Even after the armistice of 1953, the Syngman Rhee regime imposed various restrictions on the Korean press, going so far as to prohibit certain types of news stories from publication by issuing guidelines.[75]

During the Korean War, two special broadcasting systems, the Republic of Korea Army Radio and the American Forces Korea Network (AFKN), had been established in Korea. The ROK Army Radio was to broadcast "informational, educational and entertainment" programs for Korean military personnel, while the AFKN was to provide news, features, and entertainment programs for American military personnel and their dependents in Korea.[76]

The Christian Broadcasting System (CBS), the first privately owned and operated network in Korea, started broadcasting educational and religious programs as well as news and entertainment in 1954. Two years later, the Far East Broadcasting Station was inaugurated to promote evangelical Christianity and to transmit programs to North Korea and other communist countries where missionaries could not be sent.[77] The first *commercial* broadcast station, Munhwa Broadcasting Corporation (MBC), was established in Pusan, Korea's second largest city, in March 1959. MBC was distinguished from CBS in that as a commercial broadcasting station, MBC relied on commercial advertising as its major source of income.[78] In 1954, the number of registered media organizations was 411, including 56 dailies and news agencies, 124 weeklies, and 177 monthlies.[79]

Television broadcasting started in May 1956, when HLKZ-TV was established as a commercial television station in Seoul. Financial difficulties eventually forced HLKZ-TV to merge with KBS-TV, the state-run television station, which was founded in 1961.[80]

During the First Republic period (1948–1960), the Korean press was struggling financially at the same time it faced the government's high-handed media policy. One American journalism professor argued: "The greatest threat to freedom of the press in Korea is not any government control, but economic conditions. Not more than a half dozen newspapers are breaking even financially."[81]

The Second Republic under Chang Myon, the birth of which was brought about by the Students Uprising of April 1960, allowed the Korean press greater freedom than ever before. The largely libertarian press policy of the Chang administration led to "the advent of unprecedented freedom of the press in Korea."[82]

This, however, produced as a side effect the return of the chaotic press conditions of 1945–1946. One 1964 study of the Korean press noted:

> Forty-nine media were launched within 10 days of the enactment of the new law concerning the press registration, including seven dailies, 27 weeklies, one monthly and 14 news agencies. Within three months, numbers of news media increased surprisingly. Compared with those in 1959, dailies increased 51%, weeklies 96%, other publications 31% and news agencies 300%.
> The number of dailies tripled and that of news agencies increased about 20 times by the end of the Chang government.[83]

The Korean news media and periodicals during the Chang era numbered 1,509, including 112 dailies, 274 news agencies, 476 weeklies, 470 monthlies, and 177 others.[84] For better or for worse, the Korean press experienced a freedom that for one year bordered on a *laissez faire* policy, before the Chang regime was overthrown by a military coup d'etat.[85] During the Chang era, Koreans chose private radio stations over the state-run KBS stations for fair and balanced news reporting. "Unlike the newspapers that oftentimes displayed a lack of self-control," stated Korean-broadcasting commentators in 1994, "broadcasters made continuous efforts to protect their independence through fair reporting."[86]

The 1961 military coup, led by General Park Chung Hee, brought to an abrupt halt the unparalleled freedom of the Korean press. The military junta controlled the press through enforcement of various restrictive decrees as part of its campaign to "purify" the Korean press. Under Park, the Supreme Council for National Reconstruction set forth facilities standards for media organizations. These standards were designed "to clean out those phony journalists and press which were catering to defile the sacred freedom of press, and to establish a fresh order in journalism and develop a truly democratic press."[87] A total of 1,200 newspapers, news organizations, and periodicals were closed because of their allegedly substandard facilities. Only 44 dailies, 65 weeklies, 270 monthlies, 34 quarterlies, and 72 miscellaneous publications survived.[88] The junta also arrested as bogus journalists more than 960 reporters, 86 percent of whom were charged with intimidation and blackmail.[89]

On the other hand, MBC, the Dong-A Broadcasting Station (DBS), which was affiliated with *Dong-A Ilbo*, and the Tongyang Broadcasting Company (TBC), affiliated with *Joongang Ilbo* newspaper, began operations in Seoul in 1961, 1963, and 1964, respectively. The military junta under General Park considered broadcasting the "most useful means to give national publicity to the revolutionary cause and to appeal to the people for their cooperation."[90]

Although the Constitution of the Third Republic (1962–1972) provided for a press guarantee similar to that of its predecessors, President Park Chung Hee and his followers often deviated from the letter and spirit of the press freedom clause. Indeed, "the shifts in the fortunes of the press were directly related to the whims of the ruling elite and the changing cross currents of the political situation."[91]

During the period of the Fourth Republic under Park (1972–1979), the Korean press enjoyed freedom only to the extent that the government allowed it. In apparent compensation for the steady decline in their freedom, Korean media focused on their rapid expansion in both financial and industrial terms. During this period, "a trend of sensationalism and an emphasis on soft-news items were evident in media's handling of contents."[92] The increase in total circulation of Korean daily newspapers bore a vivid testimony to the phenomenal expansion of the newspaper industry in the 1970s. As Professor Jae-won Lee of Cleveland State University noted: "The aggregate total circulation in 1970 was about 2.94 million copies a day; there were 44 dailies at that time. The number of dailies declined from that to 37 in 1975 and to 25 in 1980. But at the same time, the size of the aggregate circulation doubled to 5.87 million copies in 1975 and rose to an estimated 6.22 million in 1980."[93]

After Park was assassinated by Kim Chae-kyu, director of the Korean Central Intelligence Agency (KCIA), in October 1979, the Korean press went through a brief period of liberalization before General Chun Doo Hwan, backed by the Korean Army, emerged as an undisputed strongman of Korean politics in May 1980. Chun forced an unprecedented "purification campaign" on the press, forcing a sweeping reorganization of the mass media. More than 700 journalists were dismissed from their print and broadcasting media for various reasons, including being incompetent or anti-government.[94]

Under Chun's purification campaign, 172 publications, including several highly acclaimed opinion journals, were banned "on charges of obscenity and creating social confusion."[95] Professor Jae-won Lee argued: "With the death of such journals, the periodicals specializing in social criticism and political advocacy have disappeared from Korea."[96] Chun also merged six private major news agencies into one—Yonhap News Agency.[97] Yonhap serves the Korean news media as a sole domestic news agency to distribute foreign news to its Korean subscribers. One study of the Korean news agency has concluded: "[T]he gatekeeping function of *Yonhap* is considered to be strong enough to change the international news flow from the world news agencies to Korea.... *Yonhap*'s own news selection and production in its own working system exert a significant gatekeeping function which produces news that is characteristically different from that of the world agencies, thus proving it diminishes the agenda-setting function of world news agencies by the method of independent news selection."[98] Yonhap also collects news at home and abroad on its own by stationing correspondents at major spots around the world and in provincial sections of Korea.[99] Under the structural reorganization of the press in 1980, daily newspapers published in Seoul were prevented from stationing resident correspondents in the provincial areas, and provincial dailies were not allowed to keep full-time correspondents in the capital city of Seoul.

By the end of April 1982, the nationwide dailies printed 72 pages a week, compared with 48 pages in 1980. Korea had 129 weeklies, 755 monthlies, and 559 miscellaneous periodicals.[100] As of 1984, there were 25 daily newspapers in South

Korea—16 general-interest papers, two economic papers, two English-language papers, one sports daily, one Chinese-language paper, and three children's dailies.[101] Six of the general daily papers had a nationwide circulation of more than 700,000 each.[102]

The Fifth Republic under President Chun Doo Hwan (1980–1987), viewing suppression of the press as a crucial element of political power, established systematic control of the news media through daily "press guidelines," some of which were highly specific, for example, directing the press to label anti-government protesters as "procommunist."[103] One Korean-media observer wrote in 1986 that "the hopeless situation facing the Korean press at present will remain in the future unless there is a sweeping change in the Korean sociocultural-political and legal system. Unfortunately, the chances for change are not good as long as President Chun is in power."[104]

The Sixth Republic under President Roh Tae Woo (1988–1992) and the Seventh Republic under President Kim Young Sam (1993–) have been in marked contrast to President Chun's Fifth Republic. The Korean press is flourishing. Indeed, the press is living through "a golden age"[105] largely because of Roh's bold initiative in mid-1987 of political reforms for an open democracy. The Korean media during the past seven years have been freer than ever to criticize the government, address formerly taboo issues, and expand with virtually no restraint.[106]

In July 1987, there were 32 daily newspapers in Korea. By the end of November 1994, a total of 99 daily newspapers were being published in Korea, a more than 200 percent increase since the enactment of the new press law in late 1987.[107] At present, there are 97 radio stations, including 42 FM stations and one short-wave station. A total of 39 television stations are in operation in Korea, and TV broadcasting is in color,[108] color television having been first introduced in 1980. Professor Gwang-jub Han of Howard University stated: "As of January 1994, some 10,000 households are receiving 13 channels including 7 TV channels, 3 FM channels, and 3 information services."[109] Cable television services, provided on an experimental basis since 1991, went into operation in March 1995.[110]

# CHAPTER 2

# The Legal System

The Constitution of South Korea provides for the separation of powers among the three branches of the government. The legislative power is vested in the National Assembly,[1] while the executive power is exercised by the executive branch headed by the President.[2] Courts composed of judges constitute the judicial branch.[3] To all appearances, the Constitution adheres to the principle of checks and balances in government by limiting presidential powers, strengthening the functions of the legislature, and ensuring the independence of the judiciary.[4] However, the turbulent constitutional history of Korean politics up to the mid-1980s cautions against taking the words and phrases of the Constitution at face value.[5] Indeed, "the Korean judiciary ... may not always have been able to live up to the ideals of genuine independence and autonomy."[6] Noting the basic distinction between law in the books and law in reality in all legal systems, constitutional law scholar Dae-Kyu Yoon of Kyungnam University in South Korea stated: "The gap between law and practice is pronounced in Korea too. The establishment of an institution is one thing, yet its efficient operation is another."[7]

## SOURCES OF THE LAW

Freedom of speech and the press has more often been restricted than protected by law in Korea, as has been the case in many other Asian countries. Professor Hahm Pyong-Choon of Yonsei University in Seoul, discussing the sociocultural function of law in Korea from an Asian perspective, wrote: "The law has traditionally been an instrument of ruling and controlling the people in Asia. We have never had a tradition of regarding the law as something for our benefit and protection.... We have always felt fear upon hearing the word 'law.'"[8] Another Korean law commentator views Confucianism as a significant factor in making law a regulatory force in Korea. "In a Confucian society where Confucian doctrine and ethics serve

**15**

as guidelines," Yoon argued in 1990, "law is likely to be a device for enforcing predetermined Confucian norms of authority. Since it is all justification, there is no restraining force."[9]

The most important source of law in Korea,[10] as in other Romano-Germanic "civil-law" systems,[11] is legislation. Korea operates under the comprehensive "Six Codes"—the Constitution, the Civil Code, the Criminal Code, the Code of Civil Procedure, the Code of Criminal Procedure, and the Commercial Code. A prominent legal scholar, Sang Hyun Song, of Seoul National University stated: "The assumption that the code is the exclusive basis for judicial decisions remains very important. This view still dominates Korean study of judicial thinking under the name of conceptual jurisprudence.... [T]he rule of law for every judicial decision must be derived from legislative provisions or what could be read into them."[12]

Of the Six Codes, the Constitution is the "supreme law."[13] Any law that conflicts with the Constitution cannot be enforced; the Constitution prevails. Five other "quasi-constitutional" codes, similar to the Japanese legal system, "purport to a high degree of clarity, authority, and completeness and are the first link in the chain of legalisms uniting the Constitution with concrete cases and policy actions. Each code is meant to provide an outline and comprehensive rules for a major segment of the structure of law."[14]

Other forms of written law in Korea, such as a number of statutes enacted by the National Assembly, are identical in function but not officially classified as codes. Familiarity with the provisions of statutory law is "an important part of Korean legal study and judicial decision-making," according to Professor Song.[15] The Act Relating to Registration of Periodicals (Periodicals Act) and the Broadcast Act are among those statutes affecting the Korean press directly. Presidential decrees, ministerial orders, administrative rules, and court regulations supplement general statutes with detailed enabling procedures.[16] The presidential decrees on implementation of the Periodicals Act and the Broadcast Act typify a kind of "administrative law" in Korea. Regulations of a judicial nature, made by the Supreme Court, include judicial regulations governing the Korean press, such as the Rule on Judgment on Claims for Corrected News Reports promulgated by the Supreme Court in 1988 and revised in 1991.[17]

Compared with the United States, Korea has a smaller body of case law "because litigation is a comparatively rare phenomenon" in Korean society, which has traditionally preferred conciliation to litigation.[18] Although case law is considered "very important," especially in civil and commercial matters, as a means of determining the status of relevant Korean law, case law is not as important as a source of law in Korea as in Anglo-American law.[19] Professor Song explained:

> [A] court is bound primarily by codes and statutes; a judicial decision is nothing but a product of interpretation of codes and statutes; and the judicial decisions per se have no binding effects as precedents for subsequent decisions. A judicial decision is not a theory that states abstract doctrines of law; it is a resolution of a specific and individual dispute. Consequently what binds

subsequent decisions de jure and de fact is how a specific case in question was settled. But *this question is more theoretical than practical.*[20]

Song emphasized that Korean courts are "strongly influenced by the case law, especially those of the Supreme Court," although *stare decisis*[21] is not recognized as a matter of theory in Korean law.[22]

Foreign law is considered by Korean courts "where the Korean law on the point or subject is not well-developed or is unclear."[23] This is especially the case with freedom of speech and the press. Justice Han Pyong-chae of the Constitution Court of Korea told the author in August 1994[24] that in applying the "clear and present danger" doctrine in an Anti-Communist Act case in 1967,[25] he, a district court judge, had relied on the opinion of Justice Oliver Wendell Holmes of the U.S. Supreme Court in *Schenck v. United States.*[26]

The secondary, non-authoritative sources of law in Korea include law text-books and law reviews. Legal commentary is not a primary source of law, but it influences the law to a considerable extent. Professor Song noted, "The views of legal scholars are considered by the courts and sometimes become the law by virtue of being incorporated in legal decisions."[27]

## THE COURTS

The court system in Korea[28] functions on three levels: one Supreme Court; five High Courts; and 13 District Courts with one specialized Family Court at the same level. Courts-martial may be established under the Constitution as "special courts to exercise jurisdiction over military trials"[29] in which the Supreme Court has the final appellate jurisdiction.[30]

### The Supreme Court

The Constitution provides for one Supreme Court as the highest judicial tribunal.[31] As the court of last resort, the Supreme Court reviews cases of final appeal and hears appeals from the judgments or rulings by the high courts or by three-judge appellate divisions of the district courts or the Family Court.[32] Although appeal to the Supreme Court is recognized as "a matter of right" in Korea, the Court may reject the appeal unless it is based on one or more of the statutory grounds for appeal. The Code of Criminal Procedure identifies the following grounds for appeal to the Supreme Court:

1. In case there has been a violation of the Constitution, law, order, or regulation which affected a decision of the court;
2. In case punishment is abolished or changed, or general amnesty has been given after a decision of the court has been rendered;
3. In case there is a reason to request a review; or
4. When regarding those cases for which punishment of death, a life term, or a sentence to hard labor or imprisonment for more than 10

years has been imposed, when the judgment attached was affected by grave mistake of the fact, or when the amount of the punishment is extremely improper.[33]

In civil cases, six grounds for appeal are recognized:

1. In case the court to render judgment has not been constituted in compliance with law;
2. In case a judge, precluded by virtue of law from participating in the judgment, has participated therein;
3. In case provisions relating to exclusive jurisdiction have been contravened;
4. In case there was a defect in the powers of the legal representative or attorney or in the special authority of an attorney for doing litigation acts;
5. In case provisions regarding open oral argument have been violated; or
6. In case a judgment has not been furnished with reasons or there exists inconsistence in the reasoning.[34]

When cases do not fall within the statutory causes for appeal, a dissatisfied party can petition to the Court for review[35] in a similar way that a petition for *certiorari* is filed with the U.S. Supreme Court, asking the Court to review a decision by a federal court of appeals or by a state supreme court.

The Supreme Court of Korea accepts a "jumping appeal," or *piyak sanggo* in Korean, directly carried to the Court against a decision by a single-judge district court or three-judge panel of a District Court in the first instance under unusual circumstances. In the case of criminal litigation, the jumping appeal is allowed "[w]hen the court fails to apply facts which are recognized in the original judgment or where there is an error in the application of laws and ordinances; when the penalty has been abolished or changed or general amnesty has been proclaimed subsequent to the rendition of the original judgment."[36] In civil cases, a jumping appeal can be filed to the Supreme Court against a district court judgment when both parties agree to do so.[37]

The Supreme Court, which consists of 14 justices including the Chief Justice,[38] adjudicates cases either by a petty bench or by a grand bench.[39] The petty bench is composed of three or more associate justices; the grand bench is a collegiate body of more than two-thirds of the justices of the Court, including the Chief Justice.[40] As a rule, cases are assigned to the petty bench for decision only when the participating justices unanimously agree in the decision.[41] The grand bench will rule on the cases:

1. Where it is deemed that any order or regulation is in contravention of the Constitution;
2. Where it is deemed that any order or regulation is contrary to law;

3. Where it is deemed necessary to modify the opinion on the application of the interpretation of the Constitution, laws, orders, or regulation which was formerly decided by the Supreme Court;

4. Deleted (by Law No. 4017, Aug. 5, 1988).

5. Where it is deemed that a trial by Divisions [petty benches] is not proper.[42]

The Supreme Court of Korea received more than 6,350 appeals per year from 1981 through 1990.[43] More recently, about 9,000 cases were appealed to the Supreme Court.[44] In the face of an explosion of often frivolous and abusive appeals,[45] the Supreme Court in April 1994 asked the National Assembly to enact a "Special Act on Appeal Procedures."[46] The Act would allow the Court more discretion in rejecting unmeritorious petitions on civil, domestic, or administrative cases without affording them a full-fledged review.[47]

As already mentioned, Korean courts do not recognize the doctrine of *stare decisis*, as understood and practiced by American courts. As the Court Organization Act states, "Any decision made in a judgment of a higher court shall bind the lower instance *with respect to the case.*"[48] That is, the decisions rendered by the Supreme Court in the exercise of its appellate jurisdictions "form the judicial precedents which are binding upon all other inferior courts."[49] However, a Supreme Court's decision does not have the binding authority of a precedent in later cases of a similar nature.[50] Thus, Professor Dae-Kyu Yoon has characterized the principle of *stare decisis* as "foreign to the civil law tradition" of Korea.[51] But "[i]n practice ... courts are strongly influenced by the case law, especially decisions of the Supreme Court."[52]

Under the current Constitution, the Supreme Court does not have the authority of judicial review, although Korea first adopted the American doctrine of judicial review in 1962.[53] The Constitution Court is empowered to review the constitutionality of any statute "upon the request of the courts."[54] On the other hand, the Supreme Court has the power to determine the "constitutionality or legality of administrative decrees, regulations, or actions when their constitutionality or legality is at issue in a trial."[55]

## The High Courts

Although the High Court on occasion exercises original jurisdiction over cases challenging administrative actions,[56] it is largely the court of intermediary appellate jurisdiction. The High Court reviews judgments of the three-judge panel of a District or Family Court in the first instance as well as appeals against rulings or orders of the three-judge court of a District or Family Court in the first instance.[57] In criminal cases, appeals must be based on grounds stipulated in the Code of Criminal Procedure, as follows:

1. When there is a violation of the Constitution, law, order, or regulation which affected a decision of the court;

2. When the penalty has been abolished or changed, or general amnesty has been proclaimed after the judgment;
3. When the basis for assuming or denying jurisdiction is against the law;
4. When the court which rendered an adjudication was not constituted as prescribed by law;
5. Deleted.
6. Deleted.
7. When a judge who is not supposed to participate in the trial of a case has participated in the trial;
8. When a judge who did not participate in the trial of a case has participated in rendering the judgment;
9. When there has been a violation of the provisions concerning opening of a trial to the public.
10. Deleted.
11. When the reasons are not included in the judgment or when the reason stated is not compatible with the judgment;
12. Deleted.
13. When there exist reasons for applying for renewal of procedure;
14. When the judgment is affected by mistake of fact; and
15. When there exists a reason to find the amount of punishment sentenced unreasonable.[58]

The High Courts in Korea hear and adjudicate cases in panels or divisions designated as criminal, civil, or special, depending upon the nature of the cases involved. The special division handles the administrative cases. Each division is composed of a collegiate body of three judges.[59] One of the judges acts as the presiding judge in rendering the judgment of the division while supervising affairs of the division under the direction of the president of the High Court.[60] District Court judges sometimes may be designated and assigned to the High Court.[61] The High Courts are confronting a growing case load as appeals have increased rapidly over the years. The number of appeals filed with the High Courts rose from 44,375 in 1988 to 67,052 in 1992, an increase of 51 percent.[62]

### The District Courts

The District Courts in Korea try all criminal and civil cases as the courts of general and original jurisdiction.[63] Judicial power of the District Court is exercised either by a single-judge court or by a collegiate body of three judges.[64] The three-judge District Court exercises original jurisdiction over prescribed important cases. The Court Organization Act states:

The District Court and the collegiate court of its Branch shall judge the following cases in the first instance:
1. Cases that the collegiate court itself decides to judge in the collegiate court;

2. With respect to the civil cases, those as prescribed by the Supreme Court Regulations;

3. Cases coming under capital punishment or imprisonment with or without hard labor for a short term or one or more years, excluding those falling under Articles 331 and 332 of the Criminal Code and Articles 2 (1) and 3 (1) and (2) of the Act Relating to Punishment for Violence, etc., and Cases Violating the Military Service Act;

4. Cases of complicity to be judged concurrently with those as referred to in Subparagraph 3;

5. Cases of exclusion or challenge against the judges of District Courts; and

6. Cases coming under the competence of the collegiate court of the District Court under other laws.[65]

The collegiate division of the District Court is vested with the power to exercise appellate jurisdiction in that a ruling or an order of a single-judge District Court is to be appealed to the three-judge panel of the same District Court. The Court Organization Act stipulates:

> The collegiate court of district court shall judge the following cases in the second instance:
> 1. A case of appeal against a judgment of a single judge of the District Court; and
> 2. A case of appeal against a decision or decree of a single judge of the District Court.[66]

Only a judgment, ruling, or order of a three-judge District Court is appealed to the High Court, the court of the second instance.[67] The decision of the three-judge District Court of the second instance is appealed directly to the Supreme Court, not to the High Court.[68]

### The Family Court

The three-judge Family Court is ordinarily a court of the first instance, which is held at the same level as the District Court. It is concerned not only with protecting the legal rights of individual citizens, but also with maintaining the welfare of juveniles and families.[69] The judgment of a single-judge Family Court is appealed to a three-judge Family Court panel as a court of the second instance.[70] The judgment of a three-judge Family Court panel is appealed to the Supreme Court as the court of last resort.[71] Over a five-year period from 1988, district courts in Korea ruled on 585,334 cases in 1992, compared with 477,405 in 1988. Each district court judge decided about 700 cases.[72]

The Constitution provides that trials must be open to the public.[73] Public trials may be closed, however, by the court when publicity is likely to endanger national security, affect public welfare, or disturb social morals.[74] In the court, whether open or closed, no one is allowed to videotape, photograph, or broadcast court proceedings without first obtaining permission of the court.[75]

## FINDING THE LAW[76]

### Statutory Documents
Statutes passed by the National Assembly, a unicameral body, are often designated as "acts." "Law" or "Code" is also used for the title of a piece of legislation enacted by the National Assembly. When a bill is passed by the National Assembly and sent to the executive branch for promulgation, the law is promulgated through publication of its text in the *Official Gazette,* or *Kwanbo* in Korean, of the Korean government.[77] Presidential decrees or ministerial ordinances, which are inferior to statutes in their validity, are issued by the Cabinet or the State Council of Ministers to implement the statutes. They are called "presidential decrees" for the laws or acts in point. They are also published in the *Official Gazette.*

The full text of legislation of all levels promulgated by the Korean government is published in the *Official Gazette.* The *Collection of Laws of the Republic of Korea,* another comprehensive source of laws, decrees, and ordinances published by the Office of Legislation of the Korean government,[78] is brought up to date by loose-leaf supplements, with laws arranged by subject. Private publishing companies publish a collection of the Six Codes and other statutes and important subsidiary legislation in *Compendium of Codes.* One of the most popular commercial compendia of codes in Korea is *Popchon,* a new edition of which is published annually by Hyonamsa in Seoul. The 1994 edition of Hyonam *Popchon* consisted of 5,520 pages and contained more than 1,400 statutes, decrees, ordinances, and rules in force at the end of 1993. The *Law Times*, a weekly legal paper, also publishes new statutes and decrees.

For a virtually complete body of laws, decrees, orders, rules, and court regulations as well as the constitutional provisions on freedom of speech and the press from 1945 to 1981, *Collection of Korean Press Laws, 1945–1981* is an indispensable source. The contents of the volume are not strictly confined to those laws between 1945 and 1981, notwithstanding its title. For example, among the more than 760 press laws and regulations are the Newspaper Law enacted in 1907 by the royal cabinet of the Yi Dynasty and the three ordinances of the U.S. Army Military Government in Korea (USAMGIK) in 1945–1948.

*Broadcasting Handbook* is more selective in that it places special emphasis on laws, decrees, and other regulations governing the broadcasting media in Korea.[79] The 1994 edition of the source book includes the Broadcasting Culture Promotion Act, the Broadcasting Corporation Act and its enforcement decree, and the Broadcasting and Advertising Corporation Act and its enforcement decree.[80]

English-language source materials on Korean statutes are still far from adequate for conducting substantive research on Korean law. Professor Song, who has first-hand experience with the lack of English-language publications on Korean law, stated in 1983: "Up to now English translation of a major portion of the basic Korean legislation, case law and other legal materials is very scarce, although there are isolated cases of translation done by a government agency, business organization or practitioners for their own limited purposes. There is no textbook, commentary, any other reference material or index thereof written in English."[81] This remark is still close to the truth in 1995, especially regarding books and treatises on Korean law. The scarcity of translated literature on Korean law contrasts with the ease of availability of translations of Japanese and Chinese law. Thus, it should come as no surprise that no convention of English citation on Korean statutes and court cases has yet been developed.[82]

Nevertheless, 218 codes and acts have been translated in the three-volume *Laws of the Republic of Korea*. The book, published by the Korean Legal Center in Seoul in 1983, is designed to serve "as a handy reference volume for Koreans who have a need for an accurate English translation of the laws of the Republic [of Korea]."[83] While some of the translations are not as accurate as they should be,[84] *Laws of the Republic of Korea* is a useful source for legal scholars interested in reading Korean statutes in English.

*Current Laws of the Republic of Korea* is another collection of English translations of major Korean statutes. The six-volume publication is distinguished from *Laws of the Republic of Korea* in that *Current Laws* contains 192 important laws *and* some of their enforcement decrees, which *Laws of the Republic of Korea* does not. For example, the English translations of the Copyright Act *and* its enforcement decree are found in *Current Laws* only.[85]

The English translations in the two collections are identical. Some laws are included in both of the publications. For example, the Civil Code and the Criminal Code are translated in both *Laws of the Republic of Korea* and *Current Laws of the Republic of Korea*. Other laws are included only in *Laws of the Republic of Korea* and not in *Current Laws of the Republic Korea*, or vice versa. Although *Laws of the Republic of Korea* contains the National Security Act and the Temporary Act on Fines,[86] *Current Laws of the Republic of Korea* does not. On the other hand, the Periodicals Act and the Broadcast Act are in *Current Laws of the Republic of Korea*, but not in *Laws of the Republic of Korea*.

The Criminal Code, as enacted in 1953, was published in English in *The Korean Criminal Code*.[87] Because the volume was published in 1960 and the Criminal Code was revised in 1975 and 1988, the English version needs updating. But its "Introduction" section is valuable in setting out a comparative analysis between criminal laws of Korea and of several Western nations, including the United States.[88]

The English translations of Korean press statutes such as the Periodicals Act, the Broadcast Act, the Copyright Act, and the Comprehensive Cable Television Broadcast Act appear in *The Korean Press*, published by the Korean Press Institute in Seoul.[89] The annual English report on the Korean press also provides translations of the Press Ethics Code, the Guidelines for Reporting, and the relevant provisions of the Constitution on the press.[90]

### Court Documents

Court opinions are published by the Ministry of Court Administration and by private legal reporting services. The *Collection of Supreme Court Decisions* is the official reporter for decisions of the Supreme Court of Korea. Not all Supreme Court decisions are published in the court reporter,[91] which contrasts with the *United States Reports*. The *Official Gazette of Courts*, a fortnightly publication, is the "quickest means" to obtain Supreme Court opinions.[92] The *Collection of High Court Decisions* is a collection of the important opinions of the High Courts of Korea published since 1973. The opinions of lower court decisions are selectively published in the *Collection of Lower Court Decisions*. The *Digest of Supreme Court Cases*, first published in 1976, is "a handy compendium" for a quick look at the essence of Supreme Court opinions.[93]

Court opinions are also reported in several commercial law reports. The *Monthly Court Case Report* is primarily aimed at printing Supreme Court decisions but often includes decisions of lower courts. Opinions not appearing in the official Supreme Court case report are sometimes found in the *Monthly Court Case Report*. *Law Times* is another quick and ready source of information on the court opinions in all fields. The *General Digest of Court Cases* is a commercial equivalent of the *Digest of Supreme Court Cases*.[94]

The decisions of the Constitution Court are found in a series called *Constitution Court Case Report*. Since it was first published in 1989, nearly 270 important opinions of the Constitution Court have been published in the *Report*. *Official Gazette*, *Law Times*, and *Domestic and Foreign Legal News* provide reprints of the Constitution Court opinions.

There is no court report specializing in press law cases in Korea. Thus, Korean media law does not have a court report analogous to the United States' *Media Law Reporter,* which "reports almost all court cases having a bearing on journalism and communication law" on a weekly basis.[95] According to media law scholar Donald Gillmor of the University of Minnesota, *Media Law Reporter*, published by the National Bureau of Affairs in Washington, D.C., publishes "at least 95 percent of cases that get even to the earliest stages of court proceedings."[96] While not as comprehensive as *Media Law Reporter*, *Press Arbitration Quarterly* is an invaluable resource on court opinions on the press in Korea. The journal, published by the Press Arbitration Commission since 1981, includes the full text of court opinions related to the Korean press from lower courts as well as from the Supreme Court and the Constitution Court. During the past 14 years, almost 100 court cases have been reported in *Press Arbitration Quarterly*. In 1991 and 1995, the Press Arbitration Commission published *Collection of Korean Press Cases*, a reprint of 87 court decisions in libel, privacy, and right of reply cases including two Constitution Court decisions on compulsory apology for libel and on right of reply cases from 1981 through 1992. The Press Arbitration Commission plans to publish the third volume of *Collection of Korean Press Cases* in 1996.

*Newspapers and Broadcasting*, a monthly journal, is not as exhaustive as *Press Arbitration Quarterly* in reporting court opinions. However, court opinions are available much sooner in *Newspapers and Broadcasting*, which appears at the beginning of each month. More often than not, *Newspapers and Broadcasting* publishes excerpts of lengthy court decisions. Court opinions are sometimes found in the *Journalists Association of Korea Newsletter* and the *Korean Newspaper Editors Association Newsletter*. In addition, the *Korean Newspapers and Broadcasting Yearbook* occasionally publishes court opinions involving news media organizations.

There are few case books in Korea "because law students ... usually are not required to have detailed knowledge of judicial doctrine, and in good part because judicial decisions are not the starting point for Korean legal studies."[97] *Case Book on Constitutional Law* by Kim Chol-su is the exception.[98] The book contains 13 court opinions on freedom of speech and the press.[99]

As already noted, court decisions are published selectively in Korea. Some decisions, especially those relating to political and ideological issues, are never published for various reasons. Human rights attorney Pak Won-sun, noting the limitation on access to information on National Security Act cases, has argued that the primary source materials such as court documents, including investigatory records and court opinions, are simply not kept, or ordinary researchers are denied access to the documents.[100] A former Korean judge told the author in July 1994 that his controversial judgment in a 1986 case on an anti-government demonstration was never released even to the parties involved, let alone to the public. In the course of working on this book, the author managed to obtain "slip opinions" in a number of cases through personal contacts. The slip opinions complement the court decisions reported in official and unofficial publications.

## CITING STATUTES AND COURT DECISIONS

Each code or act passed by the National Assembly is assigned a serial number in the order in which it is published in the *Official Gazette* for promulgation. The statutory citations should include the serial number of the law cited. For example, the Periodicals Act is cited as "Law No. 3979 (1987), revised by Law No. 4441 (1991)." If the cited statute has been revised, the statute as most recently revised is referred to throughout this book unless otherwise indicated. The publication in which the law is reprinted or translated is included in the citation. If a translation of the law is available, the translated version is noted in the citation. The Periodicals Act, as revised in 1991, is translated in *Current Laws of the Republic of Korea*. The complete citation to the Periodicals Act should be: "Periodicals Act, Law No. 3979 (1987), revised by Law No. 4441 (1991), *translated in* 4 *Current Laws of the Republic of Korea* 2541–52 (1994)." The citation means that the Periodicals Act, which was passed by the National Assembly in 1987 and revised in 1991, is translated in volume 4 of *Current Laws of the Republic of Korea* at pages 2541–52. The number in parentheses after the page numbers is the date *Current Laws of the Republic of Korea* was updated through its releases. If translations of a law or decree are not available, the citations to the law or decree should include the reprints of the laws and decrees. For example, the Presidential Enforcement Decrees of the Periodicals Act and the Broadcast Act are not yet translated. Accordingly, they are cited as "Presidential Decree of the Periodicals Act, No. 12422 (1988), revised by Presidential Decree No. 13783 (1992), *reprinted in Compendium of Codes* (Korean) 2939–41 (1994)" and "Presidential Decree of the Broadcast Act, No. 12432 (1988), revised by Presidential Decree No. 13842 (1993), *reprinted in Broadcasting Handbook* (Korean) 20–31 (1994)," respectively.

Court case citations in this book provide the names of the parties, the docket number of the case, the name of the court, the date of the decision, and the volume and page numbers of the court report or the periodical where the case is found. The author's citations to Korean court decisions are slightly different from the citation system suggested by Professor Song.[101] To make case citations as similar as possible to U.S. legal citation form, the author identifies the names of the parties, which are rarely given notice by Korean judges or lawyers in citing cases.

For example, the citation "Korean Broadcasting Corp. v. Han Sang-jin, 92 Na 35846, Seoul High Court, Sept. 27, 1994, *Press Arbitration Quarterly* (Korean), Autumn 1994, pp. 161–71" means that the first name in the citation, Korean Broadcasting Corporation, is the party initiating the legal action, whether by filing a complaint or by filing an appeal. The second name refers to the object of the action. 92 Na 35846 is the docket number assigned to the case. The "Na" sign is used to indicate the type of judgment. In Korea, as in Japan, "every judgment is classified according to a category, each of which has its own symbol."[102] The symbol "Na" means that the judgment was rendered by an appellate court in a civil case. The Seoul High Court is the court that heard the case, and the date following the name of the court is the date of the decision. The rest of the citation refers to where the case can be found; in this case, it can be found in the Autumn 1994 issue of *Press Arbitration Quarterly* at pages 161–71.

# CHAPTER 3

# Politics and the Press During the Pre-1945 Period

Journalism scholars John Merrill and Jack Odell, noting the relationship of the press in general and journalism in particular on the one hand to the sociopolitical system on the other, have stated that a nation's journalism mirrors the "political philosophy" in its society.[1] Indeed, it is difficult, if not impossible, to refute such comments[2] on the symbiotic relationship between the press and society. A variety of factors, including illiteracy, per capita income, and daily newspaper circulation, have evidently affected the Korean press over the years.[3] In addition, religion plays an influential role in Korean society. In his 1962 study of religion as a factor affecting press freedom, media law scholar Donald Gillmor pointedly observed: "In spite of the scientific positivism of our modern age, the religious way of thought is deeply imbedded in human consciousness, and to consider it a factor which may or may not affect the development of press and political systems is not beyond the bounds of reason.... When the development of a press system is being considered in toto the religious variable cannot be wisely excluded."[4]

The Korean system of thought has been largely, some would say overwhelmingly, molded by Confucianism in the past several centuries.[5] Confucianism, which has imbued Koreans with a strong sense of duty and responsibility to higher authority, is an Oriental philosophy based on such teachings of Confucius as that people are to follow their leaders, never questioning or challenging their authority.[6] In this way, Confucianism has contributed considerably to the general acceptance of numerous governmental restrictions on the press. The religious factor alone, however, cannot account for various authoritarian features of the Korean press. The influence of religion on press freedom is not as strong as that of non-religious factors such as the historical, legal, and political aspects of Korea.

This chapter examines, from a political perspective, how press freedom has evolved in Korea from the late 19th century through the colonial period of 1910–1945. The post-1945 period is discussed in the next chapter.

## LAST DECADES OF THE YI DYNASTY, 1883–1910

One significant historical, legal, and political influence on the Korean press is related to Japanese colonial rule from 1910 to 1945. Between the publication of *Hansung Sunbo*, the first Korean newspaper, in 1883 and the liberation of Korea from Japan in 1945, numerous political and social vicissitudes unfolded in and around Korea, which was the battlefield between Japan and China in 1894 and between Japan and Russia in 1903. Having won both the Sino-Japanese War and the Russo-Japanese War, Japan annexed Korea as its colony in 1910, when the Yi Dynasty collapsed. During this eventful period of Korean history, the fledgling Korean press underwent various ups and downs.

The concept of human rights is relatively new in Korea, especially in its "liberal" western sense. It was first introduced into Korea in the late 19th century, when Korean reformers sought to transform the Yi Dynasty into a modern constitutional monarchy.[7] When viewed from the adversarial notion of human rights for individuals against the State,[8] human rights rarely have been recognized as essential to a modern body politic in Korea as it has been in other East Asian countries. Professor Vipan Chandra discussed the views of human-rights advocates of the late-19th-century Korea thus:

> They tended to view the value of human rights always from the perspective of the crisis affecting Korea's survival as a nation. The issue of human rights was always presented in terms of its presumed connection with the power and prosperity of the state. The nation's Confucian heritage, which many of the progressives publicly attacked as worthless, was nevertheless implicitly reaffirmed by them in their paradoxical emphasis on the primacy of the state. The state remained the end, and the individual remained the means. Even the most radical of the progressives could not throw off this aspect of their Confucian heritage. They prevented the emergence of that vibrant, creative tension between the individual and the state that has historically been the engine of the development of human rights in Western societies.[9]

The notion of press freedom as a form of human rights first attracted public attention in Korea in the 1890s with the emergence of modern newspapers spearheaded by *Hansung Sunbo*.[10] But even before freedom of the press was recognized as a form of human rights by a limited number of educated Koreans at the turn of the century, the Korean press was already suffering from the harsh reality of foreign domination of Korea.

In its 10th issue on January 30, 1884, *Hansung Sunbo* ran a story on a Korean storekeeper who was fatally shot by a Chinese soldier in Seoul. The story, headlined "Chinese Soldier Commits Crime," said that the Korean store owner had refused to sell medicine to the soldier because he had not paid his overdue bills. This news story led to a strong formal protest from China to the royal government of the Yi Dynasty.[11] Li Hung-chang, Chinese minister of the Northern Ocean, claimed in a letter: "*Hansung Sunbo* is primarily a government bulletin. It is different from the kind of private newspapers, which only indulge in street gossips. The *Hansung Sunbo* story in question is so serious that it cannot be dismissed as a simple mistake."[12] The international controversy over the *Hansung Sunbo* article resulted in the departure of a Japanese consultant to the Korean newspaper.

The *Hansung Sunbo* incident may have been the first case in which an official newspaper of one sovereign nation had its own technical consultant forced out by another country that was displeased with the paper's stories. In this connection, infringement of the freedom of the Korean press in its early days was often imposed upon, not by its own government but by foreign powers, which indicates how strictly the Yi Dynasty in the late 1800s was dominated by other countries.

The closing of *Hansung Sunbo* during the Kapshin coup d'etat in December 1884 also attests to the fact that the newspaper was a victim, not of the government's anti-press repression but of the political strife between two competing factions, the Reformist Party and the Conservatives, within the ruling circle in Korea. The pro-Chinese Conservatives burned Pangmun-guk (Office of Culture and Information), which housed *Hansung Sunbo*. They presumed that *Hansung Sunbo* was the stronghold of the Reformist Party backed by the Japanese government. Journalist Bong-Ki Kim has characterized this attack on the Korean newspaper as the "first violence committed against the press" in Korea.[13]

Press freedom became a more prominent public issue in 1896, when *Tongnip Shinmun* (Independent News) was first published. In its inaugural issue, the newspaper stated in an editorial:

> We will ... tell the people of what the government is doing, and the government of the conditions of the people. If the people know clearly what the government is doing, and also if the government is acquainted with the affairs of the people, nothing but good will come of this communication, removing dissatisfaction and suspicion.... Since we act according to what we believe is right, we will speak out even when government officials err. If we detect corrupt and covetous officials, we will disclose their injustices to the world. Even private citizens who commit lawlessness we will expose and explain in the paper.[14]

Thus, from the very beginning, the first private Korean newspaper proclaimed its intention to advocate and practice press freedom explicitly. This policy statement of *Tongnip Shinmun* in news reporting established "a milestone in the history of upholding the right of the people to be informed."[15]

*Tongnip Shinmun* exposed the corruption and acts of extortion of government officials[16] and attacked growing foreign interference with Korea's internal affairs, while advocating independence of Korea from external forces.[17] In time, the editorial policy of *Tongnip Shinmun* irked Japan and Russia to such an extent that they tried to force publisher So Jae-pil to leave Korea for the United States.[18] After a variety of direct and indirect pressures were exerted against *Tongnip Shinmun*,[19] So returned to the United States in 1898. One year later, his newspaper folded. The forced departure of So from Korea testifies to assorted problems arising from the introduction of press freedom to Korea in the late 19th century. As in the case of oppression against *Hansung Sunbo*, the suppression of *Tongnip Shinmun* originated with foreign forces dissatisfied with the nationalist paper.

The first legal mechanism to affect the Korean press was an imperial edict of the Yi Dynasty in May 1895. The restrictive impact of the primarily postal decree upon the press was limited in that it did not significantly affect production and distribution of newspapers of that day.[20] For example, Article 19 of the decree stipulated that those with articles of mail other than government publications should obtain permission from the Ministry of Agriculture, Commerce, and Industry to use mail service. It further required that every mail matter should have the notice "Authorized by the Ministry of Agriculture, Commerce, and Industry" attached conspicuously to it.[21]

Following the tradition of *Tongnip Shinmun*, several private newspapers intensely criticized the royal government of the Yi Dynasty. The vociferous criticism of the newspapers led the government to consider legal measures to regulate them. In 1899, the government drafted a 33-article bill on press regulations modelled after the 1893 Publication Law of Japan.[22] The bill was opposed by the reformists, who denounced it as suppression of private newspapers.[23] This resistance of the press to the bill was a factor in the bill's failure to be promulgated into law.

Although the royal government of the Yi Dynasty failed to legislate against the press, it did not allow the press to publish stories with complete immunity. One incident involving a simple typographical error illustrates the point: A story published in *Cheguk Shinmun*, a Korean-language newspaper, dealt with the celebration of King Kojong's birthday. It misspelled the word "Manse," or "long live," as "Mangse," or "perdition." For this evidently inadvertent error, the president of *Cheguk Shinmun* was arrested and jailed.[24]

The Japanese victory in the 1904 Russo-Japanese War led to Japan's undisputed supremacy over Korea. To protect the military interests of the Japanese forces, the Japanese commander-in-chief in Korea issued the 19-point "Notification of Military Order," which provided for restrictions on freedom of speech and the press:

> In the case of an offence which falls under one of the following clauses, the principal offender, or an instigator or abettor of the offence, or a person who, though taking no actual part in the offence, is guilty of concealing his knowledge of it, shall according to the circumstances of the case, be punished either by death, imprisonment, banishment or beating. The articles used in the commission of the offence shall be taken and such articles as, from the nature of the offence, are prohibited, shall be confiscated.
>
> 11. Person making false or exaggerated statements prejudicial to the Japanese forces, or spreading false or exaggerated rumours.
> 12. Person who endangers public order by convening meetings or associations, by notifications in newspapers or periodicals, or by other means.[25]

The "Instruction with Regard to Gendarmerie" of the commander further stipulated that "[w]hen it appears that any newspaper or periodical is a menace to peace and order[,] such newspapers shall be suspended or suppressed."[26]

The Advisory Police Board, created in 1906, was authorized to control the Korean press through its power "to examine the draft of each paper or to prohibit the publication of the same if facts were misrepresented or comments made injurious to public peace."[27] The censorship by the Japanese Army and the Japanese-controlled Advisory Police Board of the Korean press is noteworthy in that press censorship in Korea was first imposed by foreigners, not by the Korean government.

In 1907, the Japanese Resident-General, who had already taken lawmaking power from the Korean government, had the Korean royal cabinet promulgate a law regulating newspapers. The Japanese wanted to use the direct press statute to control Korean newspapers that advocated independence and that opposed the impending annexation of Korea to Japan.

The Newspaper Law of 1907,[28] the first of its kind in Korea specifically designed to regulate the press,[29] required obtaining permission of the Minister of Home Affairs and payment of a deposit before a newspaper could be published. The law stipulated: "The publisher of a newspaper is required to receive from the Minister of Home Affairs permission to publish, his application being made through the Police Inspector-General in Seoul, or through a Provincial Governor in the provinces; and 300 *hwan* is to be furnished as a guarantee fund by the publisher but in the case of a newspaper engaging in religious or literary work this guarantee fund is not required."[30] These requirements served as serious restraints on the Korean press in various ways. First, the permission provision accorded a government office full discretion over the establishment of newspapers. Thus, the office approved newspapers likely to follow the government line, while rejecting those critical of authorities. In addition, the deposit requirement was employed as an economic scheme of the government to deprive Koreans without substantial financial backing of any chance to engage in the newspaper business.

The law also provided for prior permission from the Minister of Home Affairs when either publisher, editor, or printer was changed.[31] This provision allowed evaluation or screening of new newspapermen according to the subjective standards of the authorities. In other words, when a person who was going to replace either a publisher or an editor had some conflict with governmental authorities, that person would have a reduced chance of receiving the required permission.

Although the law did not explicitly provide for censorship prior to publication, several provisions had that effect. For example, copies of a newspaper were to be submitted to the Ministry of Home Affairs *before* the newspaper was published.[32] In addition, the following categories of news were prohibited by the law: (1) articles profaning the dignity of the royal family, undermining the Constitution, or detrimental to international amicability;[33] (2) articles distorting crimes or justifying and protecting criminal defendants;[34] and (3) false reports intended to defame others.[35] Furthermore, a qualified prohibition was imposed upon publication of government documents and minutes concerning official secrets[36] and upon news stories of court proceedings.[37]

The Newspaper Law concentrated the power in one government official, the Minister of Home Affairs, to take punitive measures against a newspaper "when it disrupts public peace and violates good custom."[38] Accordingly, the drastic measures provided for in the law could be taken at any time by the government against newspapers that did not meet the extremely ambiguous standards of "public peace" and "good custom." In the case of newspapers published overseas, the home minister could take similar actions.

The penalties of the law included not only suspension of publication but also fines and imprisonment as well as confiscation of equipment and machinery.[39] Such provisions were clearly intended to protect the interests of government rather than to enhance press freedom, which explains why one Korean journalist observed that the law had "the most merciless penalties of all" against the press.[40]

Because the Newspaper Law was primarily aimed at regulating domestic private newspapers, it did not apply to Korean newspapers published overseas and brought into Korea. To close this loophole,[41] the law was revised in 1908, allowing the government to control newspapers from abroad that it considered harmful to public peace or destructive of good custom.[42] Moreover, the revised Newspaper Law provided that a Korean national who sold, transported, or distributed foreign newspapers statutorily proscribed could be fined.[43]

In light of the origin of the Newspaper Law, it is understandable that it had no provision whatsoever regarding protection of the freedom of the Korean press. Legal scholar Hahm Pyong-Choon observed, "Inasmuch as the primary function of the colonial system of law was to safeguard the colonial rule, such a legal system could not ever be 'just' to a populace who was opposed to the colonial rule—no matter how fair and enlightened the legal system might have been in fact."[44]

In 1909, the Resident-General pushed through the enactment of the Publishing Law[45] to control all publications. The law provided penalties of up to three years in prison for publishing seditious material and a fine up to a prescribed amount for publishing anything without prior permission from the Ministry of Home Affairs.[46]

## JAPANESE COLONIAL RULE, 1910–1945

Beginning in 1910, the Japanese Government-General employed the press laws actively to make the Korean press serve as its "forced slave."[47] The first dark period of the Korean press during the Japanese rule[48] started well before 1910 with the Newspaper Law of 1907, which was frequently invoked by the Japanese Resident-General to control Korean newspapers critical of Japanese policy. For example, *Daehan Maeil Sinbo*'s British President, Ernest Thomas Bethel, faced prosecution in April 1908, when his paper reported in large type the assassination by two Korean residents in San Francisco of a former U.S. advisor to the Japanese

Resident-General.[49] The news report resulted in a lawsuit by the Resident-General's office against Bethel on the grounds that the publication allegedly disturbed public order and incited unrest to encourage hostilities between the Korean government and its people. Consequently, Bethel was sentenced to a three-week imprisonment.[50]

During the first 10-year dark period, there was not a single private newspaper in Korea. The only three papers published in Korea were organs of the Japanese colonial government. By contrast, 16 dailies, four triweeklies, six weeklies, and four monthlies were published in Japanese for the Japanese in Korea.[51] This sweeping control by the Japanese Government-General over the Korean press led Koreans to turn to Korean-language newspapers overseas for information. Thus, the incoming overseas Korean newspapers came to serve as valuable sources of information for Koreans.

Not surprisingly, the number and variety of overseas newspapers increased and so did their popularity among their readers in Korea. Recognizing the increasing popularity and influence of these newspapers, the Japanese colonial authorities began to confiscate all such newspapers distributed in Korea. According to statistics, right up to the annexation, there were 255 cases of confiscation of newspapers from abroad, totalling 81,062 sheets.[52]

The press policy of the Japanese colonialists in Korea between 1910 and 1919 was draconian. Several explanations can be cited for such harsh Japanese measures against the Korean press. First, the Japanese considered the Korean press as an impediment to their quick colonization of Korea and viewed it as no more than a harmful entity to Japan's intent to make Korea its docile colony. Second, the factor of the Japanese colonial government personnel contributed to the repressive policy of Japan against the Korean press. The Governors-General's backgrounds and training were military in nature until at least 1920, so the governing style of their administration in Korea was that of military politics. They did not permit any compromise in the enforcement of their policies.

Although the Independence Movement of Koreans in 1919 did not succeed, it brought some pronounced changes in the Japanese policy toward the Korean press in that the newly appointed Governor-General Saito Makoto stated that the then militaristic policy would give way to a cultural policy. The policy change initiated by Saito eventually resulted in the birth of several Korean newspapers, including *Chosun Ilbo* and *Dong-A Ilbo*. This was no doubt a great boon to the Koreans, who had been without their nationalistic vernacular newspapers since 1910. To at least some extent, freedom of the press had been resuscitated in Korea.

In discussing the Japanese motives in permitting the publication of private Korean newspapers, a Korean press historian has argued: "[T]he Japanese government wanted to ingratiate itself with the Koreans by allowing them freedom of speech, the press and the assembly so far strictly prohibited; [T]he Japanese government wanted to get a good grasp of what the Koreans had in mind."[53] It is clearly amiss, therefore, to conclude that the Koreans were finally accorded press freedom as a result of the Japanese modifying their policy in Korea. This was soon evidenced by a number of repressions that these private Korean newspapers had to endure.

About five and a half months after its founding, *Chosun Ilbo* was accused under the Newspaper Law of 1907 of disturbing the public peace and was suspended from publication for one week. The suspension of the paper was precipitated by its August 27, 1920, editorial, which commented on a series of clashes between Koreans and the Japanese colonial police on the occasion of a U.S. congressional visit to Korea. The *Chosun Ilbo* incident was the first act of press oppression on the part of the Japanese authorities since the resurrection of private Korean newspapers in 1920.[54]

As soon as it resumed publication, *Chosun Ilbo* ran an editorial critical of the Japanese suppression of the Korean press. As a result of this criticism, the paper was suspended indefinitely by the Japanese Government-General. *Chosun Ilbo*'s ordeal was not an anomaly. The police bureau of the Government-General confiscated the whole issue of *Dong-A Ilbo*, which had carried an allegedly blasphemous editorial, and suspended the paper indefinitely. The editorial in question ridiculed the so-called Three Divine Wares of Japanese mythology and attacked the Shinto religion of the Japanese. The newspaper also ran serials dealing with Britain's cruelties against the Indian people, which it compared with those of Japan toward Koreans.[55]

In August 1922, notwithstanding the cultural policy of the Government-General of Japan in Korea, the Japanese police bureau chief, announcing the possibility of resorting to additional measures against the Korean press, stated, "Since the press disturbed the public peace by radicalism, the Government-General would from now on regulate the press, not only administratively but also judicially."[56] Without doubt, so far as the judiciary functions in a just and fair manner without interference from the executive branch, judicial regulation generally affords more protection for press freedom than administrative regulation in that it is less arbitrary and affords more procedural safeguards. This comes from "the premise that statutory provisions on criminal punishment are strictly based on the principle of a law-governing country and the judicial independence is fully guaranteed in practical terms."[57]

As it soon turned out, the Japanese colonial government was not interested in providing the Korean press with judicial protection from the arbitrary action of officials in limiting the activities of the Korean press. Instead, it wanted to utilize additional restrictive measures to bolster any ineffective aspects of its existing administrative tactics against the Korean press. The first incident in which the Government-General applied judicial as well as administrative measures against the press took place when *Chosun Ilbo* published an editorial critical of the relations between Korea and Russia. For this, the key staff members of the paper were sentenced to three to four months in jail. Their alleged crime was a violation of the Peace Maintenance Law[58] providing for servitude or imprisonment for entertaining sympathy for communism and anarchy.[59]

The increasingly repressive policy of the Government-General led to the suspension of *Dong-A Ilbo* twice and of *Chosun Ilbo* four times by the mid-1920s. The repeated suspensions by the Japanese authorities apparently paid off in that critical comments and news articles against Japan decreased significantly. The Korean press changed its primarily political and ideological emphasis in news coverage to a more cultural, social, and historical focus. In the seven-year period beginning in 1930, Korean newspapers were less strident in their anti-Japanese criticism. Instead, they concentrated upon cultivating national consciousness and preserving national culture through diverse projects.[60]

The second dark period of the Korean press began with the forced closure of *Chosun Ilbo* and *Dong-A Ilbo* on August 10, 1940. The apparent reasons for their closure were as follows: (1) The Japanese wanted to expedite their war efforts; (2) The Japanese wanted to save newsprint paper, which was direly needed; and (3) The Japanese wanted to create an environment that encouraged Koreans to learn the Japanese language.[61] Without question, however, the closure resulted from the Japanese policy "to exterminate things Korean for more thorough exploitation of Korea."[62] Consequently, all private Korean newspapers were forced out of business.

## SUMMARY AND CONCLUSIONS

Koreans were first exposed to the idea of press freedom, though in a limited way, at the end of the 19th century, when the U.S.-educated So Jae-pil established *Tongnip Shinmun*, the first private newspaper in Korea. What is noteworthy about the early status of freedom of the Korean press is that external rather than domestic factors prevented the freedom from taking firm hold in Korea.

The Newspaper Law of 1907 is a case in point. This first Korean press law, the product of the Japanese colonial policy aimed at circumscribing the Korean press criticism of Japan, epitomizes the repressiveness of a press law. The Japanese authorities employed the law to choke off Korean vernacular newspapers in 1910–1919 by refusing permission to publish *and* to expand freedom of the Korean press in the 1920s by issuing permits to publish.

Professor Kun Yang wrote: "The period of Japanese colonial rule has exerted a more potent influence on present Korean legal development than has the more remote legacy of the Yi dynasty. Especially in the field of public law and criminal law, the legacy from the Japanese rule persists even today...."[63] He added:

> To make the matter worse, even after the First Republic of Korea was established in 1948, the colonial legal system under Japanese rule was maintained in considerable parts, including the Criminal Code and the Civil Code, for a fairly long time until the late 1950s, when new laws were promulgated.
> Even today the vestiges of repressive laws under Japanese imperialism remain alive, particularly in the area of laws of politicosocial control. For example, some remarkable resemblance can be seen between the Law for the

Maintenance of Public Order [Peace Maintenance Law] from the period of
Japanese rule and the National Security Act of today.[64]

Given that the press cannot exist without being influenced by its societal
environment, it would be naive to expect that freedom of the Korean press fared
well during the Japanese colonial period. Its two "dark periods" during the Japanese
colonial rule were ruinous enough to weaken the very foundation of press freedom.
Numerous arrests, confiscations, closures, and political reprisals typified the Japanese rule of Korea and hampered the development of press freedom in Korea. On
the other hand, the Korean press strived to serve as a socioculturally enlightening
institution and managed to provide an outlet, though limited, for Koreans to express
their often suppressed sentiments against the Japanese rulers.

In many ways, the Japanese colonial policy to Korea, which a commentator
has characterized as "totalitarian,"[65] impeded the development of the Korean
press.[66] At the same time, however, it contributed to inculcating in Korean journalists the "spirit of criticism" toward the government.[67] A Korean journalist has
observed: "[T]he better known journalists in Korea after liberation [in 1945] were
those who dared to criticize, oppose, and ridicule the Japanese-controlled government whether in printed or verbal forms. To have been in jail for such daring was
proof of courageous journalism. Indeed, this attitude of opposition did not vanish
with the liberation."[68]

In a similar vein, Professor Jae-won Lee has noted that "[t]he Korean press
has been resilient in its fight against governmental interference. Its fighting spirit
grows out of its tradition of resistance against the unjust colonial government of
the Japanese, and from the influence of Western press practices, especially American."[69]

# CHAPTER 4

# Politics and the Press
# During the Post-1945 Period

In almost every respect, the Korean press, like other societal organizations in the post-1945 era, underwent change. In contrast to the previous decades under the feudal Yi Dynasty and the repressive Japanese colonial government, the press in liberated Korea attained freedom from foreign interference except during the three-year period of the U.S. Army Military Government in Korea (USAMGIK).

## AMERICAN MILITARY GOVERNMENT, 1945–1948

Although in the United States and other Western democracies the right to a free press has long been recognized as "the first right because all the others depend upon it,"[1] this had not been the case in Korea until 1945. Throughout its brief history, beginning during the late 19th century, the Korean press had been typically "authoritarian."[2] Particularly when ruled by the Japanese colonial government in 1910–1945, the Korean press was a captive press operating at the mercy of foreign rulers. This explains in part why the concept of freedom of the press was too alien for Koreans to accept as a basic right when it was first extended by the American military government in 1945. Journalism Professor Jae-kyoung Lee of Ehwa Women's University in Seoul wrote in 1993: "While the notion of the freedom of the press and institutions of democracy have literally evolved hand in hand in the West, the South Korean media have lacked such an institutional foundation. Simply put, the idea of the free press in South Korea was nothing more than a superficial imposition of a foreign idea which completely lacks indigenous institutional support."[3] Professor Wayne Rowland of Southern Illinois University, echoing Lee's view on the transplantation of a free press as a Western concept in Korea, noted in 1958 that press freedom came to Korea before Koreans gained sufficient experience in democratic self-government and other freedoms.[4]

The American military government sought to nurture a political democracy in South Korea modeled after the United States. The State Department declared in August 1946: "[T]the fundamental objectives of occupation policy ... aim, simply, toward ... the eventual reconstruction of political life ... on a peaceful and democratic basis."[5] Thus, it is hardly surprising that Lieutenant General John R. Hodge, commanding general of the U.S. Army forces in Korea, took a "libertarian" stand in proclaiming his military government's policy toward the Korean press shortly after the termination of World War II. At a news conference with Korean reporters on September 11, 1945, he stated: "Since the U.S. troops entered Korea, there now exists in Korea complete freedom of the press. U.S. Army would not interfere with the thought and expression of the Korean people. We could not institute censorship of the press as such. Freedom of the press and of expression should be employed to stimulate public discussion and to articulate the formation of public opinion. U.S. Army would not tamper with reporting activities of the Korean press."[6] He made clear, however, that press freedom would not be absolute. "[I]n case of violation of public security, due measures will be considered," General Hodge said, "I hope I would not face such occasion to resort to this [sic] measures.... I hope this opportunity would be a turning point for the Korean press. I also hope that the Korean press would perform its role as a public leader and articulator of public opinion as most of the American newspapers have done so."[7]

It is clear that the press policy statement of General Hodge reflected the Blackstonian concept of press freedom.[8] While the American military government would impose no *prior restraint* on the Korean press, it would not tolerate violation by the press of laws such as those against breach of the peace and similar acts.

It was one month after General Hodge's proclamation on press freedom that Major General Archibald V. Arnold, the military governor, reaffirmed Hodge's position on a free press in Korea. General Arnold declared: "As long as freedom of speech and the press is permitted, it is possible that foolish and careless stories can be published by inexperienced editors. Nevertheless, these childish acts ... can be dismissed as a matter of nature unless they disrupt law and order and interfere with the orderly administration of the Korean government."[9]

The day before Arnold's statement, the USAMGIK promulgated Ordinance No. 11[10] and its implementation rules to supersede 12 repressive laws of the Japanese colonial government.[11] The Ordinance specifically read, "As of today all the laws and decrees with legal authority shall be rescinded if their judicial and administrative applications result in discriminations because of race, nationality, creeds, or political beliefs."[12] Given that those laws, ordinances, and regulations had been put into force "in pursuance of a [Japanese] policy to suppress the nationalistic aspirations of the Korean people,"[13] Ordinance No. 11 was a "de-Japanizing" process for the Korean press.

The libertarian press policy of the USAMGIK precipitated an explosive increase in the number of newspapers and magazines. There was "a mushrooming of the newspapers of both right and left," according to Professor Sunwoo Nam of the University of Maryland.[14] In the face of the intensifying ideological propaganda war between leftist and rightist papers, the USAMGIK tried to be "strictly neutral" while allowing the Korean press "as much freedom as possible," at least during the early period of its rule.[15] One Korean journalist argued: "Press and radio censorship was exercised on a *voluntary* basis in accordance with the policy of making Korea a free and independent nation. Political neutrality was also maintained. A standing operating procedure was prepared to handle the broadcasting of speeches by all political parties."[16]

Although the American military government often encountered numerous difficulties in facilitating establishment of a civilian government in South Korea, it was determined to create a free but self-regulated press in the mold of the American media. In noting that Koreans regained freedom of the press at the end of World War II after being deprived of it during the Japanese rule, General Hodge expressed his satisfaction with the "good overall record" of the Korean press[17] in striving for the "best tradition of a responsible free press."[18]

In October 1946, affirming his September 1945 pledge to create a free press in Korea, General Hodge said that "it is not intended that censorship of the press be established." He further stated: "The Americans do not fear any presentation of facts. Honest and constructive criticisms of governmental policies based on actual facts are considered helpful and are welcome. In fact, this is one of the functions of a free press."[19] Notwithstanding occasional non-libertarian adjustments of press policy to deal with actual or perceived abuses by the Korean press of its freedom, the basic tenet of the military government's approach toward press freedom in Korea was typically libertarian. As one report on the activities of the USAMGIK noted: "During the three years of American occupation of South Korea, 'freedom of the press' has been the by-word of the Department of Public Information. Lt-General John R. Hodge ... repeated again and again that the press must be kept free. Communist papers must be allowed their place on the newsstands, provided their statements were not libelous."[20]

In connection with this hortatory, if not always actual, commitment of the American military government to a free press in South Korea, the "Proclamation of the Rights of the Korean People," issued on April 5, 1948, by the commanding general of the U.S. forces in South Korea, is noteworthy. It enumerated 11 "inherent liberties" guaranteed by the Bill of Rights of the U.S. Constitution, including those of speech and the press.[21] The Proclamation, however, qualified the exercise of these basic liberties by providing that "they are not inflammatory to the extent of inciting disorder or the overthrow of government."[22]

In the context of the overall libertarian approach of the American military government to its press policy in Korea, one might ask whether the press policy resulted from a firm commitment of the U.S. military rulers to freedom of the Korean press as a basic right of Koreans. If not, did the USAMGIK authorities simply adopt their American press concept as an easy model to experiment with in Korea? Indeed, the Americans came to Korea "without any knowledge of the policy determinants" relating to their transitional rule of Koreans. A Korea expert observed, "Confronted with a strange language and unfamiliar culture, and with no initial conception of the intensity of Korean desires, the Americans were forced to rely upon limited knowledge, ingenuity, and common sense."[23] A close look at the American military government's press policy in Korea indicates how the U.S. libertarian press theory fares in a foreign country amidst authoritarian sociopolitical and ideological impediments rarely compatible with American society.

As noted previously, the *laissez-faire* press policy of the American military government led to "a golden age for Korean newspapers which tended to rouse the people's political interest in the ideologies they leaned toward."[24] It is simplistic to conclude, however, that the emergence of ideological sensationalism in the Korean press stemmed solely from the libertarian press views of the U.S. military government. Given the thesis that "[a]ll press systems reflect the values of the political and economic systems of the nations within which they operate,"[25] it was, to a certain extent, a natural consequence. Amidst the confusion largely precipitated by their sudden liberation from the oppressive colonial rule of Japan, Koreans were impatient to gain independence from any type of foreign dominance. No less important is the fact that Koreans often regarded their newly gained freedom as an unlimited right to indulge themselves in what they could not do—the anything-goes exercise of press freedom to criticize the ruling authorities—during their rule by the Japanese.

Further, the ideological divisions among the "acutely politically conscious" Koreans[26] were intensified by the international developments which in October 1945 culminated in the Moscow agreement on the "four-power trusteeship" of Korea. Political scientist Hakjoon Kim of Seoul National University wrote, "[T]he Moscow agreement on Korea became the crucial issue that divided the political leaders and people throughout the whole of Korea into two opposing and hostile camps: the right-wing nationalist camp that opposed it and the Communist, including the leftist, camp that accepted it."[27]

In an effort to cope with numerous negative side effects of Korean "yellow journalism" upon their administration, the American rulers in October 1945 promulgated Ordinance No. 19, which provided for a registration of newspapers and other publications.[28] The Ordinance stipulated in part: "In order that freedom of speech and freedom of the press may be preserved and safeguarded without being perverted to unlawful and subversive purposes, the registration of every organization engaged in printing of books, pamphlets, papers or other reading materials in Korea south of 38° North Latitude sponsored, owned, directed, controlled, or managed by any natural or juridical person is hereby ordered."[29]

In the meantime, U.S. military authorities took concrete measures to control several intractable newspapers, whether of the left or right. For example, when *Maeil Shinbo*, a leftist newspaper, refused to publish General Arnold's statement denouncing a leftist political organization,[30] it became the target of increasing suppression. As if to teach "a lesson to the south Korean press corps,"[31] the

authorities accused the paper of being communist-controlled. After an investigation[32] found that the paper's accounts were in arrears, the U.S. military government
ordered *Maeil Shinbo* presses to cease.[33] When a rightist paper, *Taedong Shinmun*,
in May 1946 carried an article openly inciting youth to follow the example of Pak
Im-ho, who assassinated a leftist leader, the authorities suspended the paper.[34]
Further, the military tribunal of the government fined *Inchon Shinmun*, a leftist
newspaper, for publication of an allegedly defamatory story about an official of the
Inchon city government.[35]

Obviously out of exasperation over the ever deteriorating sociopolitical
situation in South Korea,[36] the USAMGIK issued Ordinance No. 55 in February
1946 and Ordinance No. 72 in May 1946. According to Professor Bruce Cumings
of the University of Chicago,[37] the two ordinances violated the freedoms guaranteed
by the First Amendment to the U.S. Constitution.[38] While Ordinance No. 55
required registration of political parties,[39] Ordinance No. 72 identified punishable
offenses against the military government, many of which were related to freedom
of association and expression. Among the offenses stipulated in Ordinance No. 72,
for example, were the act of "communicating information which may be harmful
to the security or property of the occupation forces" and any unauthorized forms
of communication "with any person outside of the occupied territory." It further
included: "Publishing, importing or circulating printed, typed or written matter
which is detrimental or disrespectful to the occupying forces; Knowingly making
any false or misleading statement, orally or in writing, to any member of or person
acting under authority of the occupying forces, in a matter of official concern; or
in any manner defrauding, misleading or refusing to give information required by
the Military Government."[40]

Notwithstanding the increasingly tough attitude of the military government
evidenced by Ordinance No. 72, its impact upon the Korean press was not as serious
as initially assumed because it was suspended the following month.[41] The government offered no specific reasons for the suspension, but one commentator surmised
that it was due to criticism from the Korean public.[42]

When the abuse of press freedom continued unabated, the American rulers
resorted to licensing the press, which undoubtedly violated "the most venerated of
all first amendment theories: the prior restraint doctrine."[43] In May 1946, under
Ordinance No. 88, which vested licensing authority in the USAMGIK Department
of Commerce, all newspapers and periodicals were required to acquire licenses and
display them prominently.[44] Although the only reason given for changing from
registration to licensing was the shortage of newsprint, the primary objective of the
licensing ordinance was to regulate the leftist papers, which engaged in the most
vociferous and inflammatory political journalism.[45] This was evident in the fact that
no leftist paper was licensed under the Ordinance.

Although the broadcasting media were less inflammatory than their print
counterparts, the U.S. military government enforced the "Broadcasting Regulation
Rule" to ensure that the media would be used to promote the public interest. The

Rule prohibited stations from broadcasting "unverifiable" news stories and defamatory false reports as well as "titillating, obscene, or blasphemous reports."[46] Journalism scholar Kim Dong-jin of Yonsei University in Seoul said the regulatory actions of the government against the broadcasting stations "were formally modelled after the public interest section of the Communications Act of 1934 in the U.S."[47] He noted, however, that one of the many differences between the two related to programming censorship. "[P]rograms to be broadcasted had to obtain prior permission from the [U.S. military] government," and "[t]he director of Public Information took power to control broadcasting programs...," according to Kim.[48]

Ordinance No. 88 did not result in extermination of the leftist newspapers. The communists "defied the U.S. Military Government by buying the licenses of existing papers to continue publishing leftist papers under different names,"[49] although the Ordinance provided for revocation or suspension of licenses for reasons such as: "The making of any false or misleading statement or omission in the application for a licensee [sic]; Failure to report any change in the information furnished in the application, as ... required."[50] American Korea experts observed in 1950: "In September and October 1946, Military Government suspended publication of all extreme left-wing newspapers and other publications in view of their persistent violation of ordinances regarding the inciting of revolt. Four newspapers were thus shut down and the extreme left was then unable so easily to dispense with [sic] inflammatory propaganda."[51] The Ordinance was invoked by the American military government to ban the publication of *Uri Shinmun* and *Shinmin Ilbo* on the grounds that they published false and misleading statements.

Ordinance No. 88 was not as effective as its proponents had hoped in blocking various actions of the Korean press, which was viewed as abusing its freedom. Consequently, a year later, the USAMGIK took another step backward, further eroding the libertarian press concept. In September 1947, at the strong insistence of the American military governor, the Legislative Council[52] passed a new law regulating newspapers and periodicals, while abolishing Ordinance No. 88. Under this law, primarily designed to address the weaknesses of the abolished Ordinance, the licensing system was retained and the Director of Public Information was empowered to suspend or revoke a license.[53] With respect to the grounds on which the Director could withdraw the license or suspend publication of a newspaper or other publication, Article 6 provided:

(1) If falsity is found in the application papers;
(2) If falsity or negligence is found in reporting as stipulated [by the law];
(3) If the publication is different from the licensed one;
(4) If the publication commits an offense or instigates disturbance of law and order or confuses people by reporting false articles.[54]

Furthermore, publishers and editors could be imprisoned or fined as stipulated by the law.[55] In the face of stiff opposition from the Korean press, the military government backed off by requesting the Legislative Council to reexamine the law.[56] Because the legislative body of the government was dissolved shortly thereafter, the law was shelved until August 1948, when the U.S. military rule ended.

In October 1947, the American military government closed Haebang News Agency for violation of Proclamation No. 2, which forbade the "violation of any proclamation, order or directive" issued under the authority of the Commander-in-Chief of the U.S. Army Forces-Pacific as well as any act to disturb public peace.[57] The USAMGIK stated that the news agency "committed acts to the prejudice of good order and hostile and prejudicial to the life, safety and security of the persons and property of the United States, calculated to disturb public peace and order and prevent the administration of justice, in violation of Proclamation Number 2."[58]

In April 1948, the American military rulers also invoked the Newspaper Law of 1907,[59] one of the suppressive press laws which Japan had forced the Korean royal cabinet to promulgate.[60] The so-called Kwangmu Newspaper Law case[61] arose from an editorial published in *Noryok Inmin*, a communist newspaper. In the editorial, the newspaper praised the mastermind of the communist-inspired attempt of May 1946 to counterfeit currency in Korea while criticizing the prosecutorial authorities of the U.S. military government for demanding severe punishment of those allegedly involved in the counterfeiting. Kim Kwang-su, the publisher of the paper, was tried for the editorial and sentenced to 10 months in prison. On appeal, the Seoul High Court rejected the prosecutor's argument that the Newspaper Law should be applied. The court, noting that the newspaper law was enacted and promulgated by Japan against the will of Koreans, held that the law was invalidated by Ordinance No. 11, section 2.[62] However, the decision was reversed by the Supreme Court of Korea, which ruled that the Newspaper Law was a proper statute enacted by the Koreans' own free will, not one passed by Japan alone to enforce against Koreans.[63] Accordingly, the Court reasoned, "It is self-evident that the law cannot be discriminatory in the sense defined by Ordinance No. 11, section 2."[64]

Under the USAMGIK rule in 1945–1948, South Korea was a society plunging into political chaos after a brief period of celebrating its sudden liberation from Japan's repressive colonial rule.[65] In the daunting task of governing this sociopolitically tumultuous society, the situation turned out far worse than expected for the American military government, which was ill prepared for the task. An American Korea scholar stated, "Hodge had been given almost no policy guidance and had no preparation for the unusually delicate job to which he was assigned."[66] Thus, it is not surprising that the USAMGIK adopted the concept of the libertarian press familiar to the United States, although virtually unknown to Koreans at that time.

One may speculate on what contributed to General Hodge's proclamation of September 1945 on freedom of the Korean press in the context of libertarianism. He may have heeded the proposition: "When one nation endeavors to impose its culture pattern upon that of a people with a very different one and to achieve it in a very brief time, what tools are more worth study than the media of mass communication?"[67] The significance of the policy statement of General Hodge in the very early stage of his government indicates that the dominant leader of the USAMGIK[68] did posit himself on the concept of a free press. The statement presented Koreans with a conceptual seed of libertarian democracy, though not necessarily a procedural one. Professor Chang Yong of Hanyang University in Seoul argued in 1969: "It is indeed true that the USAMGIK brought freedom of the press to South Korea with it. But it is we [Koreans] that did not adopt it as it is."[69]

To a considerable extent, the sociopolitical circumstances unique to the U.S. military rule of South Korea may explain the shift in the USAMGIK approach toward executing its press policy. An American observer of the Korean press during the American military rule said in 1947: "Removal of Japanese restrictions has brought a wide measure of freedom of speech and expression. But the unhappy political situation [in Korea] has not been conducive to the development of objective and well-informed reporters or wise and public-spirited editors."[70] Of course, the basic tenet of the USAMGIK press policy consisted in creating the milieu favorable to a free *and* responsible press. But when the policy often ended up bringing assorted adverse effects on Korean society in general and the military government in particular, the USAMGIK took a number of legal and non-legal measures against the Korean press. Its initial adherence to noninterference with the press, for example, gave way to adoption of restrictive actions to stem the endless practices of partisan journalism.

The military rulers also turned to licensing of newspapers to deal with the inflammatory leftist press although it is debatable to what extent the military government achieved its goal of purging the Korean press of leftist elements through licensing. Journalist Myung Shik Koh wrote: "[T]here is not much evidence that the licensing system, one of the most loathsome restrictions in a libertarian press, caused any restraining effect on the Communist subversive activities. When a newspaper was suspended, the same publisher could start a newspaper anew under a different title with a figurehead publisher. Despite the licensing system, it cannot be denied that the Korean press enjoyed press freedom."[71]

According to a 1988 study of press freedom and socioeconomic development in South Korea, the American military government "sought, without success, to impose Western-style press freedom" in Korea.[72] One illustration of the failure is often associated with the government's attempt to invoke the 1907 Newspaper Law against a leftist newspaper. Journalism historian Choe Chun described the case as a serious policy mistake resulting from the military authorities' ignorance of the history of the law.[73] He asserted: "If the U.S. military government had known how effectively the Japanese colonial rulers had used the law to suppress the Korean press, they would not have applied the law to the Korean press. In short, the United States ... was too unprepared and uninformed about Korea to rule Korea with a military government."[74]

## FIRST REPUBLIC, 1948–1960

The Constitution of the First Republic under President Syngman Rhee, promulgated on July 17, 1948, guaranteed freedom of expression as one of the basic constitutional rights of Koreans. It stipulated: "Citizens shall not be subjected to any restrictions on the freedom of speech, press, assembly and association except as specified by law."[75] The freedom of speech and the press provision of the Constitution was derived from the USAMGIK's "Proclamation of the Rights of the Korean People,"[76] which reflected the basic tenets underlying the Bill of Rights of the U.S. Constitution. However, "[l]egal rules and ideal norms may affect [the observable] behavior, but they rarely describe it fully."[77] In September 1948, the Korean government under Rhee issued a decree to prohibit newspapers from promoting communist-inspired terrorism and subversive activities. The decree proscribed as harmful to the State:

1. Articles that go contrary to the national ideals and policies of the Republic of Korea;
2. Articles that defame the government;
3. Articles that propagate and praise communism and the puppet regime of North Korea;
4. Articles based on fabricated facts and agitating the public generally;
5. Articles that interfere with the relations between the Republic of Korea and other friendly allies and that damage the national prestige of Korea;
6. Articles that, in addition to inciting the people through provocative and radical editorials or reporting, affect the national unity harmfully;
7. Articles that divulge the national secrets detrimental to the security of the Republic of Korea.[78]

In the wake of the communist-led rebellion in Yosu and Sunchon in October 1948, which claimed about 2,700 lives,[79] the National Security Act was enacted in December 1948.[80] The statute made it a crime to form an organization for the purpose of causing a civil disturbance.[81] Under its uncompromising anti-communist policy, the Rhee government restricted newspapers of leftist ideology more systematically than the U.S. military government had done, closing seven newspapers and one news agency between September 1948 and May 1949.[82]

The Rhee regime invoked the USAMGIK Ordinance No. 88 in closing the communist-leaning *Seoul Shinmun* in May 1949, claiming that it violated Article 4[83] in that it carried positive stories about North Korea while ignoring the news on the South Korean government. The spokesman of the Rhee administration argued: "The paper should immediately stop its anti-State approach to news reporting and its notion of newspaper production similar to that of destructive and subversive communist followers. Freedom of the press should not be interpreted as a way to destroy the government."[84] The closing of *Seoul Shinmun* gave rise to a political controversy and finally was taken up by the National Assembly as an issue. Before the National Assembly, the Vice Public Information Director of the Rhee government stated: "The government, from now on, will not permit the publication of newspapers which undermine the existence and development of the Republic of Korea. The government has respected and upheld freedom of the press as guaranteed by Article 13 of the Constitution. It has never deliberately suppressed the press...."[85]

Several more left-wing newspapers were suspended on the basis of having violated Ordinance No. 88 or the Newspaper Law of 1907. One of them was *Hwasong Maeil Shinmun*, which was closed because it published an article allegedly supporting the North Korean formula for national unification. Closure of the paper presumably provided a landmark after which "no article sympathizing with communists appeared in the newspapers in Korea."[86] The increasingly vigorous Korean press was dealt a severe blow when the Korean War broke out in 1950. During the war, several developments bearing upon the freedom of the Korean press unfolded. As is usually the case during war, military censorship was imposed upon all newspapers. In Pusan, the temporary wartime capital of Korea, the Rhee government introduced a bill that was primarily designed to control newspapers and periodicals. The National Assembly, however, voted against the bill. It also rescinded the Newspaper Law of 1907, which was largely a vestige of the former Japanese colonial rule.[87]

When the government party of Rhee manifested its intent to prolong power by amending the Constitution, the Korean press resisted the attempt. To deal with the critical press, Rhee declared martial law and imposed censorship on newspapers on May 26, 1952. Press censorship was lifted the following day—at President Rhee's "special instruction."[88] In the meantime, the Korean press was generally unrelenting in its criticism of the government. Even after the armistice of 1953, the Rhee government did not loosen its shackles on the Korean press. In an October 14, 1954, statement, Rhee set guidelines on restructuring of newspapers in Seoul:

1. Two or three newspapers would be sufficient for the citizens of Seoul;
2. A. The reorganization of newspapers should be carried out through an agreement among publishers or of their own volition;
   B. As an alternative, civic leaders should designate two or three newspapers and sponsor them after consultation among themselves;
   C. Two or three newspapers should be selected through a ballot of Seoul citizens. The other papers not selected should be rejected.[89]

This proposal encountered widespread opposition from the public as well as from the Korean press, and Rhee finally abandoned his attempts to more effectively control the press.[90]

In early 1955, the government made another effort to regulate the usually critical Korean newspapers. This time, it sought to introduce to the National Assembly a "Bill Concerning Temporary Measures for Governing Publications." The bill provided that the Director of Information of the Rhee administration be empowered to revoke the license or suspend publication of periodicals "when they run inflammatory articles disrupting the national security or publish stories that are false, distorting, or violating the law."[91] The strong opposition of the Korean press forced the government to abandon its plan to introduce the bill.

Ordinance No. 88 of the U.S. military government continued to serve as a statutory mechanism for the Korean government to suppress newspapers during the Rhee regime. In 1955, *Dong-A Ilbo* was suspended for a typographical error. In a March 15, 1955, story on the Korea-U.S. oil agreement, the paper used the word "Koere" (puppet) in the headline. "Koere" was a derogatory term generally reserved for referring to the North Korean regime, and it was taboo in South Korea to call the Korean President and his government "Koere." After discovering the error in the news story, the *Dong-A Ilbo* staff promptly sought to correct it, but the government suspended the paper for one month under Ordinance No. 88.[92]

In January 1958, the National Assembly passed two National Assembly election bills with provisions that potentially restricted freedom of the press.[93] The statutes prohibited newspapers, magazines, or other periodicals from publishing "false facts" about candidates that could help them win or lose the election.[94] The statutes contained a clause severely curtailing access to news sources.[95] The new National Security Act[96] promulgated in December 1958 was a restrictive law that the press vigorously opposed while it was being deliberated by the National Assembly. The law was passed unilaterally by the ruling Liberal Party, while opposition party members on strike were forcibly driven out of the National Assembly chamber.[97]

The National Security Act was intended to be an effective legislative mechanism to cope with communists in South Korea. Article 1 stated that the Act aimed at "supplementing the penalties and judicial procedures applicable to associations, groups, or organizations which seek to overthrow the State in violation of the Constitution and to the activities to accomplish their objectives."[98] Article 11 provided that "anyone who detected or collected national secrets or aided and abetted such acts for the purpose of benefitting the enemy shall be subject to the death penalty or penal servitude for life."[99] The law broadly defined "national security" as "political, economic, social, cultural, military, etc., documents, drawings, other materials, facts, or information, which are required to be kept secret for the protection of the State."[100] Moreover, Article 12 declared that those who "gathered information on national politics, economy, society, culture, military forces, for the purpose of benefitting the enemy shall be punished by penal servitude for not less than 10 years."[101] The same penalty applied to the acts of collecting "information on public office, political parties, organizations, or individuals for the purpose of benefitting the enemy."[102]

The National Security Act also provided heavy penalties for vaguely defined criminal activities such as "dissemination of propaganda" relating to the activities of anti-State organizations prohibited under the law. Furthermore, Article 17 stated: "Any person who benefitted the enemy by disturbing the people's minds by openly pointing out or spreading false facts with knowledge of their falsity or openly pointing out or spreading facts in an intentionally distorted way shall be punished by penal servitude for up to five years."[103] Finally, "seditious libel" was provided for as a criminal offense under the National Security Act in Article 22, which stated:

1. Anyone who had openly undermined the prestige of a constitutional organ by holding a meeting or by publishing documents, tape-recorded materials, drawings, or other materials of expression for the benefit of or under the instructions from the associations, groups, or organizations [proscribed by the Act] shall be punished by penal servitude for not more than 10 years.
2. The constitutional organ under the preceding paragraph shall be the President, the Speaker of the National Assembly, and the Chief Justice.[104]

The National Security Act "virtually killed any chance for democratization of politics" in Korea because it deprived Koreans of most of their basic civil rights, according to Andrew C. Nahm, professor of Asian history at Western Michigan University.[105] John Kie-Chiang Oh, a Korean-born American political scientist, of Marquette University, agreed that with the passage of the National Security Act, "most of the democratic civil rights so elegantly [sic] guaranteed in the Constitution of 1948 could be formally and legally crushed."[106]

In 1959, four months after the passage of the National Security Act, which one journalism commentator described as the "most powerful weapon of the government in suppressing freedom of the press,"[107] the Rhee government closed the leading opposition paper, *Kyunghyang Shinmun*. Interestingly, the paper was closed under USAMGIK Ordinance No. 88, not under the newly enacted law. The Korean government cited five alleged criminal offenses of the newspaper, one of which involved a misleading article on President Rhee's news conference. *Kyunghyang Shinmun* challenged the governmental action as being in large part politically motivated. The ensuing fight was characterized by a series of political ups and downs until the paper resumed publication after the overthrow of the Rhee government in April 1960. The *Kyunghyang Shinmun* case was "[t]he most flagrant case of press suppression imposed by [Rhee's] Liberal [Party] regime and one of the most disgraceful scars left upon the Korean press."[108]

## SECOND REPUBLIC, 1960–1961

The Rhee government was replaced by a parliamentary system under Premier Chang Myon. The Students Uprising of 1960 provided a new chapter in freedom of the press in Korea. In contrast to the press in Rhee's days, the Korean press under the Chang government was accorded the kind of freedom found in Western democracies. To begin with, the guarantee of press freedom in the 1960 Constitution differed from that of the First Republic in that the former placed no conditions on freedom at all, while the latter had provided for freedom with numerous qualifications. The new Constitution stated:

> Citizens shall not be subjected to any restrictions on the freedom of speech, and of the press....[109]
>
> Liberties and rights of citizens may be restricted by law only in cases deemed necessary for the maintenance of order and public welfare. In case of such restriction, the essential substance of liberties and rights shall not be infringed. Licensing or censorship in regard to speech and press and permit of assembly and association shall not be recognized.[110]

An American Korea expert, Gregory Henderson, observed that the Constitution of the Second Republic made the basic civil rights of Koreans unconditional, noting that "all 'except as provided by law' escape clauses [were] removed" in reaction to the extensive violations of rights during Rhee's rule.[111] Professors Tscholsu Kim and Sang Don Lee noted that in the course of strengthening the civil liberties provisions of the amended Constitution, "American constitutional theories and court decisions were frequently mentioned in discourse on the Constitution. American constitutional law doctrines ... exerted influence" on the Constitution of the Second Republic.[112]

The Second Republic under Chang allowed the Korean press broader freedom than ever, replacing the old licensing system with a system of registration.[113] The new newspaper registration law superseded the USAMGIK Ordinance No. 88, which had been used off and on by the Rhee regime to suppress the Korean press. Under the new law, a newspaper could be published upon being registered with the government—a process that required no more than essential information about the applicant such as the name of the newspaper, the location of the publication, and the frequency of publication.[114] To expand press freedom even further, the Chang government in June 1960 revised the National Security Act, which had been passed by the Rhee regime in late 1958. The revised statute contained few restrictive provisions for the press.[115] The "evil" provisions of the old National Security Act concerning punishment for seditious libel or crimes of collecting and disclosing vaguely defined national secrets or information were abolished in the revised statute.[116]

The legal changes in favor of press freedom helped the Korean press enjoy the greatest freedom in Korean history. The Koreans in Chang's day were exposed to a freedom bordering on *laissez faire*. A Korean newspaper publisher wrote, "The press especially enjoyed an unprecedented degree of freedom, prestige, and authority—press powers in some cases being absolute."[117] Incidentally, these changes revived the chaotic press situation of 1945–1946. The number of newspapers and periodicals jumped more than twice, to nearly 1,600 from about 600, by April 1961, and these employed some 160,000 reporters.[118] Chin Sok Chong, professor of journalism history at the Hankook University of Foreign Studies, argued, "There was such a confusion of information sources that chaos developed and it became hard to tell fact from rumor."[119]

Accompanying the almost unlimited press freedom were numerous undesirable side effects. While the number of newspapers rapidly increased, their overall quality deteriorated because unqualified, sometimes disreputable, businessmen found that they could exploit the newly found freedom and make easy money as journalists. Some of these "journalists" used their positions to extort sources.[120] Professor John Kie-Chiang Oh wrote:

> Few of the new "publications" had printing facilities and some had no fixed place of business. Many of them never printed a single edition; some distributed a few mimeographed sheets only. Their principal business, and in some instances their only business, was blackmail. Furthermore, it was an open secret that money was flowing into some of these publications from the leftist elements among Korean residents in Japan, who took advantage of the somewhat improved relations between Korea and Japan under the Chang government.[121]

Furthermore, leftist-oriented newspapers reappeared in Korea. *Minjok Ilbo*, for example, advocated what was promoted by communist North Korea as its unification policies.[122] The duration of this unprecedented press freedom was not long. Chang was overthrown in a military coup in 1961.

## THIRD AND FOURTH REPUBLICS, 1962–1979

The downfall of the Chang regime in a military coup led by General Park Chung Hee brought the Korean press one of its darkest periods, which lasted two and a half years, until the Third Republic replaced the military junta in late 1963. From the very beginning, the military junta under Park proclaimed its suppressive policy toward the Korean press. In its Decree No. 1, the junta, first named the Military Revolutionary Committee and later renamed the Supreme Council for National Reconstruction (SCNR), ordered prior censorship of all newspapers and magazine feature articles, comics, cartoons, editorials, photographs, and foreign news.[123] The Decree further prohibited fabrication and dissemination of groundless rumors.[124] Through Decree No. 4, the SCNR warned against publication of news articles that might:

1. benefit the enemy;
2. go contrary to the cause of the Military Revolution;
3. provoke a counterrevolution;
4. be detrimental to public peace and order;
5. damage public opinion;

6. undermine military morale;
7. reveal military secrets;
8. be false and distorted;
9. violate other guidelines relating to the policy of the Supreme Council for National Reconstruction.[125]

Thus, for the Korean press the era of excessive, heady freedom under Premier Chang Myon in 1960–1961 was quickly replaced with a period of fear and intimidation. Months after Park's military rule, Professor Edward W. Wagner of Harvard University argued in his *Foreign Affairs* article: "In South Korea today, 16 years after the United States set out to help instill the art of democratic self-government among its people, we find ourselves in partnership with an openly authoritarian regime.... [T]he United States faces the possibility that Communism may present the impoverished and police-ridden people of the south with an increasingly attractive alternative."[126]

In an effort to "purify" the Korean press, the SCNR drastically restructured the mass media of Korea. In its Decree No. 11, the military revolutionary authorities announced the facilities standards of newspapers and news services, which required that newspapers be published only by those with complete printing facilities for newspaper production and that news services be limited to those with complete wire service facilities for transmission and reception.[127] Under the Decree, the licenses of 834 newspapers were canceled by the Ministry of Public Information, stated Professor John Kie-Chiang Oh, who added, "It should be pointed out that many of the banned papers and news services were financially dubious and had tended to support themselves through blackmail."[128]

Also, the junta made mass arrests of bogus reporters. Between May 25 and June 4, 1960, a total of 283 allegedly fake or corrupt reporters were arrested.[129] Nevertheless, those arrested included a number of innocent genuine reporters whom the military junta considered as undesirable or unacceptable regardless of what criteria were used. These arrests turned out to be a grave threat to press freedom and resulted in an enormous curtailment of normal press activities.[130] These measures of the military authorities were not, however, necessarily criticized by Koreans. Rather, the arrests were considered the price to be paid by the Korean press that "went wild, like a beast suddenly set free" after the collapse of the First Republic in 1960.[131]

In connection with this ordeal suffered by the Korean press during the military junta period, the *Minjok Ilbo* case shows how far the junta went in controlling press freedom. The Revolutionary Court sentenced to death three executives of *Minjok Ilbo* newspaper in August 1961 for advocating political and ideological doctrines similar to those of North Korea, i.e., neutralization of Korea, negotiations with the North Korean communists, exchanges of mail with North Korea, and student meetings between North and South Korea.[132] With appeal of the three condemned denied, the lower revolutionary court's ruling stood.[133] One of the three was executed in December 1961, while the other two were granted a commutation from death sentence to life imprisonment.

To prevent freedom of the press from turning into irresponsible liberty, as had been permitted during the Chang era, the Third Republic under General-turned-President Park Chung Hee emphasized responsibility on the part of the press, while making some exceptions to the enjoyment of press freedom. While Article 18 of the Constitution of the Third Republic (1962–1972) declared that "[a]ll citizens shall enjoy freedom of speech and press, and freedom of assembly and association,"[134] these freedoms were qualified in varying degrees.

> Licensing or censorship in regard to speech and press and permit of assembly and association shall not be recognized. However, censorship in regard to motion pictures and dramatic plays may be authorized for the maintenance of public morality and social ethics;
> The publication standard and facilities of a newspaper and press may be prescribed by law;
> Control of the time and place of outdoor assembly may be determined in accordance with the provisions of law;
> Neither the press nor any other publication shall impugn the personal honor or rights of an individual, nor shall either infringe upon public morality.[135]

As the Minister of Public Information under President Park stated, the constitutional provisions concerning press freedom were intended to accomplish two objectives: (1) to "fortify freedom of the press" and (2) to "prevent defamation and degradation of public ethics through tyranny of freedom of the press."[136] The Third Republic, however, often ignored the press clause, and President Park alternately tightened and loosened his control of the press throughout the 10-year Third Republic.

For a time following the birth of the Third Republic in 1963, the press recovered from two years of stagnation imposed by the military rulers. Koreans witnessed the return of "press-government confrontation" over the issue of how press freedom should be balanced with press responsibility.[137] In the confrontation, the Park government tried to place fetters on the press, but the Korean press often refused to yield to governmental pressures, both direct and indirect. The August 1964 press-government confrontation, which started at the end of 1963, marked the climax of press-government relations. The Park administration enacted the Press Ethics Commission Act in spite of strong opposition from both the press and the public. The Press Ethics Commission Act, which one commentator described as "unacceptable" to the Korean press,[138] aimed at "enhancing the effectiveness of self-regulation by the press and broadcasting."[139] The new law required that certain restrictive provisions be included in the code of ethics for the Korean press.[140] Article 3 listed matters to be stipulated by the code of press ethics thus:

1. Matters relating to guarantee of the national security and public order;
2. Matters relating to respect for the reputation of heads of states at home and abroad;
3. Matters relating to the social responsibility of periodicals and broadcasting;
4. Matters relating to guarantee of the fairness of news reports and commentary;
5. Matters relating to guidance of children and juveniles;
6. Matters relating to respect of human rights;
7. Matters relating to the virtue of family life;
8. Matters relating to guarantee of respect for reputation and privacy of others;
9. Matters relating to guarantee or promotion of social ethics and public morality.[141]

The law further provided that the mass media publish or broadcast the decisions of the Press Ethics Commission.[142] Criminal punishment ranging from penal servitude to fines would be imposed upon those who neglected their statutory obligations as news persons.[143]

When the Press Ethics Commission Act was promulgated, it was strongly criticized. The Park regime discriminated against the five newspaper companies that explicitly or implicitly defied the law.[144] The government took a number of retaliatory measures against the opposing newspapers including *Dong-A Ilbo* and *Kyunghyang Shinmun*. Among the measures were:

1. Subscription of the five papers were stopped by governmental institutions;
2. They were discriminated against in the imported newsprint prices;
3. Advertisement from governmental sources and organizations was not allowed in the five papers, and pressure was exerted to private enterprises not to offer them ads;
4. Restriction of the bank loan and withdrawal of the loan already offered was ordered for them;
5. Restriction in access to news information was imposed upon the five newspapers only.[145]

The press-government crisis over the Press Ethics Commission Act ended when President Park agreed to withhold enforcement of the law.[146] Two Korean journalism scholars stated, "This was an odd situation in which the execution of an enacted law, rather than a legal repeal, was to be withheld as long as the press remained within the bounds specified by the government."[147] According to a 1965 study on press freedom in various countries, the South Korean press was an "intermediate" or "mixed" system with apparent tendencies toward a controlled system under Park.[148]

Park, who ruled South Korea from 1961 until his assassination in 1979, was obsessed with modernizing the country, and he would not tolerate a critical press challenging his grandiose economic plans for Korean self-reliance. The coup was in part a result of Park's concern with the social chaos of the Chang regime, for which he believed the free and "chaotic" press was at least partially to blame.

Park was wary of the abuse of freedom of expression in Korea. In February 1962, he wrote:

> Freedom of thought and speech is not unlimited .... Licentious thought and speech out of the bounds of good sense, and those tending to disrupt national unity, cannot be condoned or tolerated either from moral or legal viewpoints, since they are bound to bring misfortune, instead of progress, to the society and in the end jeopardize the national existence and survival. Let us reflect for a moment how dangerous it would be if Communist imperialism, in the disguise of democracy, made use of the freedom of thought and speech for their propaganda and agitation. Freedom of thought and speech, however fully guaranteed and respected under normal circumstances, cannot be condoned when it threatens to harm the interest of the entire nation and to disrupt the very legal order and social institutions which guarantee it.[149]

Journalism scholar Choe Chong-ho of Yonsei University characterized Park as an early advocate of "development journalism" before the term became popular among Third World journalists.[150] Although the term has numerous shades of meanings, "development journalism" usually posits an active role for a nation's press in promoting a nation's economic and political progress.[151] In a speech before Korean newspapermen in April 1966, Park warned against attacks on the government and urged the press to work with the government in "developing a constructive attitude with which to meet the demands of the new age and the new situation."[152] To accomplish his economic development goals, Park often mobilized the Korean Central Intelligence Agency (KCIA) to conduct extralegal activities, and he invoked a series of emergency decrees to muzzle the press.

While the Constitution of the Third Republic, similar to its predecessors, provided for press freedom in much the same way as the First Amendment to the U.S. Constitution, press freedom in South Korea in terms of practice was somewhat antithetical to that of the United States. As for the contrast between the two press systems, Professor John C. Merrill and two colleagues observed in 1970, "In the U.S. the press may criticize any public official (including the President) and often does so — at times caustically; in Korea the press must be extremely careful of any journalistic barbs cast in the direction of the government."[153]

During the early 1970s, the Korean press fared worse than during most of the '60s. While declaring a state of national emergency in December 1971, Park warned the press against discussing national security issues "in an irresponsible manner."[154] He also urged Koreans to be prepared to reserve their freedoms "in case the worst situations develop."[155] This opened a chapter of Korean press history in which the press was constrained by the government in various ways. From 1972 to 1975,

Park's repression politics reached its highest point since the "worst wartime colonial days."[156] Just before Park initiated the *Siwol Yushin* (October Revitalizing Reforms) in 1972, the government forced the Koreans into a terrorized silence by issuing Martial Law Decree No. 1. The Decree banned "all indoor and outdoor assemblies and demonstrations for the purpose of political activities" and made "speeches, publications, press and broadcasts" subject to censorship.[157] Permission was required for non-political indoor and outdoor assemblies under the Decree, which also prohibited fabrication and circulation of groundless rumors.[158] The policy guidelines of the government for the Decree were more draconian. Under these guidelines, a news blackout was forced on the following:

1. Any article that distorts, defames, or instigates against the purpose of the Declaration of the State of National Emergency of October 17, 1972;
2. Any article that misleads by inciting public opinion and sentiments;
3. Any article that is detrimental to ensuring security of society;
4. Any article that deals with military information;
5. Any article that undermines the morale of military personnel;
6. Any article that is related to duties of the martial law authorities;
7. Any article that is harmful to the national interest.[159]

The government later added four more items to the list, stating that the "decadent trends were not helpful to the accomplishment of the Reforms." Those items banned from coverage by the print and broadcasting media primarily concerned private matters of individuals.[160] This series of decrees or orders contributed greatly to intimidating the press into a frightened silence.

On December 27, 1972, President Park established the Fourth Republic by the "Revitalizing Reforms" Constitution. The revised Constitution provided that "[n]o citizen shall be subject to restriction of freedom of speech and press, or freedom of assembly and association, except as provided by law."[161] Article 32 stated, "Laws which restrict freedoms or rights of citizens shall be enacted only when necessary for the maintenance of national security, order or public welfare."[162] Clearly the Constitution recognized basic rights of Koreans. But the Park regime systematically violated those constitutional norms that on paper it claimed to observe, which "narrowed the differences between the totalitarian north and the supposedly 'free' south in their respect for human rights."[163]

As American newspaper columnist William Cheshire cogently observed, "It is … an immutable principle of modern society that when legitimate protest is throttled and peaceful avenues of disagreement blocked, those with especially strong feelings on emotionally charged issues are sometimes driven toward antisocial behavior."[164] The "Revitalizing Reforms" Constitution was criticized as undemocratic by many Koreans, who staged often violent demonstrations off and on streets. To prevent the anti-government movement from getting out of hand, Park took a series of harsh measures.[165] On January 8, 1974, he issued Presidential

Emergency Measure No. 1, which was primarily intended to eliminate channels of communication among Koreans by muzzling the press. The measure prohibited Koreans from criticizing the Constitution as follows:

> Article 1. It shall be prohibited for any person to deny, oppose, misrepresent, or defame the Constitution of the Republic of Korea;
> Article 2. It shall be prohibited for any person to assert, introduce, propose, or petition for revision or repeal of the Constitution of the Republic of Korea;
> Article 3. It shall be prohibited for any person to fabricate or disseminate false rumors;
> Article 4. It shall be prohibited for any person to advocate, instigate, or propagate any act or acts which are prohibited in Articles 1 through 3 of the present Emergency Measures; or communicate such act or acts to others through broadcasting, reporting, publishing, or by any other means.[166]

When the Park regime in April 1974 outlawed the National Federation of Democratic Youths and Students, which the authorities characterized as an "unlawful underground organization manipulated by the North Korean communists," Park proclaimed Emergency Measure No. 4,[167] which further restricted the already limited press freedom. Emergency Measure No. 4 prohibited "any act to publish, produce, process, distribute, exhibit, and sell papers, books, disks, and other presentations" relating to the Federation and its members. The Emergency Measure also banned any act of inducing, agitating, or propagandizing what was banned by this measure or informing other persons of the banned activities by means of broadcasting, reporting, publishing, or other means.[168]

With the opposition to the "Revitalizing Reforms" Constitution arising, Park issued a series of emergency decrees, of which the ninth, proclaimed in May 1975, proved to be the most drastic use of emergency measures for "safeguarding national security and public order." Decree No. 9 stated:

> Article 1. It shall be prohibited for any person to engage in any of the following acts:
> 1. Fabricating, disseminating false facts, or making false presentation of fact.
> 2. Denying, opposing, distorting, or defaming the Constitution, or asserting, petitioning, instigating, or propagating revision or repeal thereof, by means of assembly, demonstration, or by using mass communication media such as newspapers, broadcasts or news correspondence, or by making documents, pictures, records, or other publications.
> 3. Assemblies, demonstrations, or other activities by students which interfere with politics, with the exceptions of (a) classroom or research activities conducted under guidance and supervision of school authorities, (b) activities conducted with prior approval by

presidents or principals of schools, or (c) other ordinary, nonpolitical activities.

4. Publicly defaming the present Emergency Measures.

Article 2. It shall be prohibited for any person to broadcast, report, or otherwise disseminate publicly the content of an act or acts which violate Article 1 of the present Emergency Measures; or producing, distributing, selling, possessing, or displaying publications the content of which violates Article 1 of the present Emergency Measures.[169]

Further, the Decree made it an offense punishable by a year or more of imprisonment to report, broadcast, or publicize any acts critical of the constitutional structure of the Park regime.

Seven journalists were convicted in a Seoul district court on charges under Decree No. 9 after they had privately published broadsheets reporting the arrests of government critics, student demonstrations, and workers' strikes banned by the Decree.[170] The sale of the monthly *Taehwa* (Dialogue) had been banned because the October 1977 issue violated the Decree, and the managing editor of the magazine was arrested.[171] On suspicion of violating the same decree, the *Minju Chonson* (Democratic Front), the official newspaper of the opposition New Democratic Party, was confiscated and its editor was arrested. The seized edition carried the full text of a speech by Kim Young Sam, the leader of the party, calling on Park to resign from the presidency.[172]

While Park was in power in the 1970s, the KCIA was virtually an omnipotent mechanism with strong arms against the press. It arrested Kim Pyong-ik, president of the Journalists Association of Korea, and four of the Association's leading members after they sent a dispatch to the International Press Institute (IPI) in Zurich and as they were about to send another to the International Federation of Journalists (IFJ).[173] After the *Korea Times*, one of the two English dailies in Korea, published an article by American freelance writer Bernard Wideman criticizing the Park regime, its editor was alleged to have been interrogated and physically abused by the KCIA.[174] The KCIA agents also examined the president and the chief editor of the magazine *Changjo* (Creation), which had run a satirical poem attacking the governmental authorities under President Park.[175]

In 1975, Park revised the Criminal Code to prohibit Koreans from criticizing his government through foreigners or foreign media.[176] A *National Geographic* writer who had just been to Korea reacted to the revision of the Criminal Code: "I was taken aback. If I returned, and some Koreans repeated some of the things they had told me, they could be jailed for seven years."[177] Two American Korea scholars, characterizing the amended Criminal Code as "remarkable," emphasized that the Park regime claimed that it "sought to inform foreign audiences about Korea, that it wished foreign news agencies would report more accurately, and that it welcomed visitors who sought the truth...."[178]

The Park regime used the Anti-Communist Act (since repealed) to punish a leading Korean dissident poet who had published a satirical poem condemning the misuse of power by the governing elite in Korea. Furthermore, the editor and publishers of the magazine *Sasanggye* and the opposition party organ *Minju Chonson*, in which the poem appeared, were all arrested together with the poet on charges of violating the law.[179] In May 1978, two former university professors were each sentenced to three-and-a-half years in prison by a Seoul criminal district court on a similar charge after they published a translated collection of essays about life in China entitled "Dialogue with 800 Million People."[180]

The numerous decrees and measures employed by the Park government contributed to crippling the Korean press. The government also utilized various extra-legal mechanisms to control the press. The confrontation between the government and the press over the Press Ethics Commission Act in 1964 was a good example. Using suppressive tactics, the Park regime forced *Dong-A Ilbo* to stop its reporters from waging "a free press movement" in October 1974. The movement was an "[o]utburst of the journalistic frustration at being muzzled," according to Professor Sunwoo Nam, who once worked as a reporter for *Dong-A Ilbo* in the 1960s.[181] In the "Declaration of Freedom of the Press" issued by about 200 newsmen at the traditionally independent newspaper on October 24, 1974, the Korean reporters stated: "[T]he unprecedented crisis of our society today can only be overcome through the practice of freedom of speech. There can be no reason to suppress freedom of speech.... Freedom of speech is the fundamental task that we must fulfill. It is not a task which can be permitted by the government or granted by the people. We will never kneel to any pressure which comes from the opposition to free speech. We declare that we will do our best to practice free speech."[182] The *Dong-A Ilbo* reporters also resolved to "unite with strength and resolution to oppose all external interference with newspapers, broadcasting, and magazines" and "to reject ... the inspection of Korean Central Intelligence agents."[183]

The aggressive practice of press freedom by *Dong-A Ilbo* reporters in carrying on with their free-press resolutions eventually provoked action by the Park regime to coerce business firms into canceling advertisements. Starting in mid-December 1974, obviously at the behest of the Korean government, virtually all the companies that had traditionally advertised in *Dong-A Ilbo* and its subsidiaries, *Shin Dong-A* monthly and Dong-A Broadcasting Station (DBS), began to withdraw their advertising. By January 1975, the newspaper had lost 98 percent of its advertisers. In the meantime, it had survived on advertisements of encouragement from anonymous readers and on contributions from small groups of concerned sympathizers around the world.[184] During the boycott period, *Dong-A Ilbo* had an increase in its subscription by 200,000.[185] While the reporters as well as editors and publishers vowed never to knuckle under to such indirect governmental control of their press freedom,[186] the Korean government and its strong-arm agency, the KCIA, were too powerful for *Dong-A Ilbo* to challenge for long. In the end, 133 reporters had been dismissed or suspended from the newspaper largely because of their active participation in the free-press movement[187] before the normal flow of advertising returned to the paper.

The impact of the Park regime's repression on *Dong-A Ilbo* was unmistakable. Professor Jae-won Lee of Cleveland State University stated in 1982: "*Dong-A*'s pronounced opposition stance attracted intensive governmental interference in the seventies; this interference took an extensive range of harassment—jailing of reporters, summoning of editors, threatening of advertisers and so on. *Dong-A* was thus systematically shorn of its traditional characteristics, and has now become a newspaper with only a name to remind one of the glories and courage of its past days."[188] The almost decimated Korean press remained timid until the violent death of President Park in October 1979. As one commentator noted, "the shifts in the fortunes of the [Korean] press were directly related to the whims of the ruling elite and the changing cross currents of the political situations."[189]

## FIFTH REPUBLIC, 1980–1987

As John A. Lent, professor of international communication at Temple University, put it, "Suppression has been the standard in regards to the press of *Korea*."[190] Likewise, one Korean-born American scholar compared the Korean press to "a downed person on whose neck a foot of a giant is positioned."[191] Although these two observations were made in 1974 and in 1978, respectively, both were still valid when it came to the Korean press during the Fifth Republic in 1980–1987. After President Park Chung Hee was assassinated in October 1979, the press was given a short period of liberalization until General Chun Doo Hwan took over the civilian government with the backing of the Army in May 1980. Chun carried on what has been called the "biggest purge" in the history of the Korean press,[192] forcing a sweeping structural reorganization of the mass media.

The Constitution of Korea during the Chun era stated that, with regard to freedom of speech and of the press, "[a]ll citizens shall enjoy freedom of speech and the press, and freedom of assembly and association; [n]either speech nor the press shall violate the honor or rights of other persons nor undermine public morals or social ethics. Should speech or the press violate the honor or rights of other persons, claims may be made for the damage resulting therefrom."[193] From all appearances, press freedom in Korea was firmly guaranteed constitutionally as long as the press did not abuse corollary guarantees safeguarding an individual's right to a good name or the preservation of societal morality. As Lent pointed out, however, the constitutional provision can be suspended or dispensed with on a variety of grounds.[194]

The Chun regime enacted the Basic Press Act in December 1980,[195] which was "one of the most restrictive and comprehensive law[s] in capitalistic societies,"[196] providing specifically for the rights and restrictions of the press. Among the rights of the Korean press were those concerning access to public information and protection of news sources.[197] Like most press laws throughout the world, the Korean law was more restrictive than protective of press freedom. More than anything else, it made the press's responsibility a legal requirement per se.[198] This "public responsibility" clause was in accordance with Article 20 (2) of the Constitution. The press law also limited who could be journalists and publishers.

The Basic Press Act was similar to the "Standards for Implementation of the Press Policy," a decree formulated and enforced by the Supreme Council for National Reconstruction in 1962.[199] The former, like the latter, prescribed the standards for publication facilities and in effect functioned as a regulatory force, stunting the growth of existing papers as well as the birth of new papers without a solid financial basis.[200] In one way, however, it differed from the 1962 decree: Separate requirements for different administrative units — i.e., large cities, medium-sized cities, and rural areas, as set forth in the old decree — were not part of the press law. In connection with its registration clause,[201] the law stipulated that the Minister of Culture and Information (MOCI) had the authority to cancel the registration of publications and to suspend them for several reasons, one of which was: "When they *repeatedly and flagrantly* violate the law in encouraging or praising violence or other illegal acts disrupting public order."[202]

The Chun government dealt with some intractable journalists by indirect means rather than by arrest and trial in open court. It engaged the services of the Korean National Security Planning Agency (KNSPA), formerly known as the Korean Central Intelligence Agency (KCIA), the Korean Army Security Command, and other law-enforcement agencies. By law, the duties of the KNSPA were to gather domestic and foreign information on public safety, maintain public safety, and investigate crimes, as provided in the National Security Planning Agency Act.[203] Nevertheless, in practice its range of activities and functions were not statutorily limited during the Chun era. As reported by one Korean-language newspaper in the United States, the case of *Chosun Ilbo* in May 1983 illustrates how far the KNSPA could go in controlling the Korean press during Chun's rule. *Chosun Ilbo*, one of the leading dailies in Seoul, ventured to break a forced silence on the ongoing hunger strike of prominent opposition leader (and now President) Kim Young Sam. When a KNSPA liaison officer attached to the paper learned about it, he battered the political reporter who wrote the news story on the hunger strike. This led the news staff of the paper to refuse to work on the issue that would carry the story.[204]

In 1985, the KNSPA's blatant suppression of the Korean press was a focus of international concern when the agency harassed *Dong-A Ilbo*, one of South Korea's most respected newspapers, for breaking a government news embargo on a "diplomatically sensitive" issue.[205] In its news article, *Dong-A Ilbo* dealt with the August 24, 1985, crash-landing in Korea of a Chinese fighter plane. In its briefing of the Korean press, the Korean government announced that the pilot of the plane would be allowed to defect to Taiwan and that the radio man, who wished to return to China, would be allowed to do so.[206] The paper, in breaking the press embargo on the story, reported that contrary to the official statement of the authorities, South Korean fighter planes had not intercepted the Chinese H-5 bomber when it was entering Korea's territorial air space. Thus, *Dong-A Ilbo* raised serious questions about the adequacy of the Korean military air defense, as noted in the *IPI Report*.[207]

When the story came out, KNSPA Director Chang Se-dong asked the *Dong-A* publisher how the news story was published. Three staff members of the paper, including managing editor Yi Chae-ju, were hauled in for interrogation by the KNSPA agents. During the questioning at the agency, the journalists were beaten up, which the IPI termed "a most distressing sign of intimidation, not only against *Dong-A Ilbo*, but against all the media in South Korea."[208] By using physical violence against the reporters, the Korean government obviously tried to deliver a clear-cut message that those who failed to toe the line set down by the authorities would pay the price. In this instance, *Dong-A Ilbo* did heed the government's warning by strictly holding off on any story about the KNSPA's interference with its freedom.

Korean customs officials served the government off and on as censorial gatekeepers. They forbade both Koreans and foreigners to bring in as well as take out information critical of the Korean government. One American freelance writer, for example, had his photographs confiscated by the customs agents at Seoul's Kimpo International Airport on the grounds that they reflected the "'ugly side' of [South] Korea" and that North Korea might use the pictures to attack its archenemy in the South.[209] The photographs at issue depicted growing labor repression and the Kwangju uprising of 1980. One set of photographs showed Korean human-rights and labor activists who had been "severely beaten by a gang of thugs" while supporting a sit-in by workers protesting a government ban of their union. The second set consisted of photos of Kwangju citizens standing up against the martial law that had been imposed across the nation by General Chun Doo Hwan and the Korean Army.[210]

As in the Park period, suppression of the press was the *modus operandi* of the Chun regime toward the Korean press. Chun used daily "press guidelines" to regulate the media coverage of news events. The government-dictated reporting guidelines were revealed by *Mal* magazine in 1986.[211] *Mal* (Words), an unregistered bimonthly published by a group of banned Korean journalists, described the press guidelines in its special issue on September 6, 1986, as "[i]nstructions to the press, which are sent every day to each newspaper publisher by the Department of Public Information Control (DPIC) of the Ministry of Culture and Information. Using such terms as 'possible,' 'impossible,' and 'absolutely impossible,' the DPIC decides and regulates all details including the form, content, and admissibility of reports about particular incidents, situations and circumstances."[212] *Mal* ran in its September 1986 issue the texts of almost 600 press guidelines issued by the MOCI between October 9, 1985, and August 8, 1986.[213]

Among the guidelines published in *Mal* were:

> Oct. 19, 1985—Not to report ... (3) a total of 15,000 farmers staged demonstrations on 32 occasions this year, the largest resistance movement of farmers since the revolt of the Tonghak Party in 1894, and (4) reports that 95 percent of the people support a civilian government and not a military government.

Oct. 31, 1985—Not to title the report of the International Strategic Research Institute of Britain "South and North Korea Equals in Military Strength" .... To treat stories on the demonstration of Seoul National University students from a critical angle. Not to carry a photograph of [opposition leaders] Kim Dae Jung, Kim Young Sam and Lee Min Woo at today's meeting.

Nov. 4, 1985—Students seized the office of the U.S. Chamber of Commerce and Industry in Korea at the Chosun Hotel and all of them were arrested and taken to police at 1:08 p.m. Not to treat this as a top story. Not to use a photograph. Not to state in the title "Students belonging to the Seoul National University Struggle Committee for National Independence."

Nov. 12, 1985—Regarding the Constitutional Amendment Special Committee, to write "Special Committee" and delete the words "Constitutional Amendment."

Dec. 12, 1985—Not to write stories on the following in the Year-End or New Year special editions.

(1) Outcome of the struggles over the constitution amendment issue; (2) Hasty conclusions or prospects regarding the South–North dialogues; (3) Present state of the opposition circles; (4) Interviews with the two Kims [opposition leaders]; (5) Prospects about the successor in 1988; (6) The questions regarding the TV right on the 1988 Olympics; (7) Various rumors, etc.

Dec. 23, 1985—Not to report the UPI story on the "possibility of the South economy worsening in 1986."

Jan. 8, 1986—Not to report the following statement of Minister of the Unification Board Park Tong Jin in his interview with Japan's Asahi Shimbun—"Since January last year, the North Korean side has been reaching affirmatively to a North–South summit meeting, although it presents a precondition for it."

Jan. 14, 1986—Not to report an AFP dispatch from Washington on a "comparative analysis of human rights conditions in South and North Korea."

Jan. 17, 1986—Not to report on a resolution scheduled to be submitted to U.S. Congress on Jan. 19 calling for the acquittal of opposition leader Kim Dae Jung and restoration of his civil rights.

Jan. 29, 1986—Not to report the fact that the January issue of the New Democratic Front, the organ of NKDP [opposition New Korea Democratic Party], has been banned.

Jan. 31, 1986—Regarding the kidnapping of a South Korean diplomat in Lebanon ... [t]o report the incident in such a way as to create the impression that it was the act of North Korea.

Feb. 2, 1986—To give prominence to Sankei Shimbun's article (a pro-Seoul Japanese newspaper) entitled "North Korea Groundlessly Condemns Team Spirit Maneuvers."

Feb. 14, 1986—Not to report comments by the U.S. State Department on "South Korean government's strong measures against signature collection campaigns for constitutional amendment."

March 14, 1986—To give prominence to the statements on the importance of South Korea's security by Secretary of State Shultz and the Commander of the United States for the Pacific.

March 21, 1986—Guidelines for reporting on North Korea: (1) To use only Naewoe News Agency's reports concerning broadcasts, reports by newspapers and other media of North Korea; (2) Not to use news reports or comments by North Korea's media even indirectly through Japanese newspapers or news agencies. However, when it is considered necessary to quote a foreign report concerning a pressing situation, a consultation should be held in advance with the Culture and Information Ministry. *If a newspaper fails to do so, it is held entirely responsible for it.

March 31, 1986—Statement by dismissed professors ... of Korea University for constitutional amendment—To report it in a short one-column story.

April 7, 1986—About the movement to refuse payment of KBS-TV viewers fees—(1) to play down reports on this movement on a city news page; (2) to report the fact of participation of Catholics in the movement in a one-column story on a city news page.

April 11, 1986—Not to report any more on the movement to refuse payment of KBS-TV fees.

July 1, 1986—To give prominence to the editorial of the Wall Street Journal, dated June 30, which says, "It is difficult to interfere in the democratization of South Korea."

July 12, 1986—To refrain from reporting anything about the sexual torture case against a woman at Puchon Police Station.

July 27, 1986—The U.S. Statement Department expresses regrets over the sexual torture case—Not to report the content of the statement.[214]

The overall sorry status of press freedom in Korea during Chun's rule was summed up as follows by one American journalist: "Normally, citizens here [in South Korea] wouldn't be able to talk openly about government wrongdoing because, while many freedoms exist here, political freedom is not one of them. Likewise, freedom of the press is not a reality, despite being guaranteed in the Constitution. Reporters exercise self-restraint in dealing with sensitive topics, such as criticism of President Chun Doo Hwan."[215]

## SIXTH REPUBLIC, 1988–1992

President Roh Tae Woo (1988–1992), while chairman of the ruling Democratic Justice Party (DJP) and a presidential candidate, ushered in an era of open politics with a package of democratic reforms in his June 29, 1987, declaration, issued at a time of worsening antigovernment demonstrations. He initiated a series of democratic political reforms aimed at breaking Korea's "cycle of authoritarian rule."[216] A number of positive changes subsequently took place in South Korean press-government relations during the Roh era. Some of these resulted in structural changes in the media industry; others were institutional, involving sociopolitical and legal systems affecting the Korean press. The IPI reported in late 1988, "[V]isible and invisible restrictions imposed on the [Korean] press have been abolished in favour of a greater freedom of information and the right of the people to know has been guaranteed."[217]

The Constitution, as revised in October 1987, explicitly prohibits censorship of speech and the press while guaranteeing freedom of expression,[218] which should be a step toward strengthening press freedom in Korea. The Constitution of 1980 did not proscribe prior censorship of expression.[219] On the other hand, the new Constitution, unlike its predecessor of 1980, provides that standards concerning facilities of news services, broadcasting stations, and newspapers should be statutorily set.[220] In his June 1987 declaration, Roh noted the restrictive impact on the press of the Basic Press Act of 1980[221] and suggested that it should "promptly be either extensively revised or abolished and replaced by a different law."[222] The Act was repealed in November 1987 and replaced by the Act Relating to Registration of Periodicals (Periodicals Act)[223] and the Broadcast Act,[224] legislating improvements in several respects.

The legislative reforms initiated by the Roh administration led to revision of the Criminal Code in late 1988, abolishing its "Crime of Slander against the State" clause, which provided for a penalty of up to seven years imprisonment for a Korean national who defamed the State and its constitutional institutions to the foreign press in and outside of Korea.[225] Although the number of criminal convictions under the provision was low compared with other indirect press laws, the seditious libel provision was an effective weapon for Park and Chun in punishing Koreans for expressing antigovernment sentiments to foreign journalists. Its abolition represents another positive development in the South Korean government's avowed intention to "stimulate the constructive criticism of the public" as a foundation for democratic progress.[226] The National Security Act[227] was also revised in May 1991 to curb government abuse by requiring that the law be applied only to achieve its stated objective of preventing anti-State activities. The revision of the controversial National Security Act was the Korean government's legislative response to the Constitution Court's qualified ruling of 1990 on the constitutionality of the Act.[228]

Two American observers pointed out in 1988 that Koreans should be aware of the "indispensability of institutional reforms made possible, but not guaranteed, by the new constitution" to transform their country from a dictatorship to a democracy.[229] Among the institutional reforms affecting press freedom were those that restructured the government through restoration of the checks-and-balances system among the executive branch, the National Assembly, and the courts, which would reduce the likelihood of arbitrary or grossly unjust decisions. In particular, an independent judiciary had long been an urgent concern in Korea: "A powerful judiciary can be the bulwark of a democratic constitution, defending both its integrity (and hence political freedom and due process) and also its preeminence as the source of democratic legitimacy. More generally, the judiciary is the ultimate guarantor of the rule of law, and thus of the accountability of rulers to the ruled, which is a basic premise of democracy."[230]

In connection with the separation-of-powers principle in a functioning democracy, one journalism scholar noted the relationship between press freedom and the independence of courts: "[A] nation's press system is free, not necessarily because of constitutional guarantee ... but because an unintimidated judiciary protects the press against government encroachment."[231] The Korean courts during the Sixth Republic under Roh made visible efforts to ensure that justice was guaranteed in Korea's "highly centralized power structure."[232] This positive development in the status of the Korean judiciary resulted from the opposition-dominated National Assembly and an increasingly outspoken press. The National Assembly confirmed Yi Il-gyu, widely known as a jurist of principle, as the Chief Justice of Korea after rejecting the government's first nominee in the wake of a "judicial crisis"[233] involving vocal demands by more than 300 judges for judicial independence and a restructuring of the Supreme Court.[234] The Korean press devoted extensive coverage to the events and to the judiciary's demands. One Seoul judge stated: "In the past, judges ... resisted the influence of the executive branch ... but it was vain, like standing against a flood. The press was weak, so judges who resigned in protest did not have the power of public opinion to support them. Judges have no power to support themselves. They need public opinion, the press of the whole society, to support an independent judiciary."[235]

In the context of a more independent judiciary and an opposition-dominated National Assembly acting as a balance against the executive branch, it is no wonder that the press control mechanisms of the Chun regime were eliminated or reformed by Roh. The MOCI Bureau of Information Policy (BIP), which during Chun's rule was in charge of issuing numerous daily press guidelines,[236] was abolished[237] and coercive instructions were no longer issued to the press as to what should and should not be reported. The BIP's demise also led to the removal from the news media of government agents who were in charge of overseeing press activities.[238] Finally, the press card system, which permitted only journalists with professional accreditation from the government to be employed in the news media, was repealed.[239] The government's willingness or unwillingness to accredit journalists was used in the past to restrict the press.

As the South Korean government entered a heady period of Korean-style *glasnost* during the Roh rule, the press stretched the limits of freedom. As a result, news coverage of previously taboo subjects became routine. There was little restriction upon media coverage of antigovernment activities, let alone open criticism of President Roh and his party. Most illustrative of the exercise of press freedom was the live TV coverage in 1988 of the National Assembly hearings on the irregularities of the Fifth Republic, inquiring into the corruption and wrongdoing of the Chun administration. One Korean political scientist termed the televised hearings in October–December 1988 "an extraordinary event"[240] that in part represented "an iconoclastic atmosphere of democratization, [where] many of the old values, practices, and institutions were discredited and rejected."[241]

The liberalization under Roh led the Korean news media to change from a docile mouthpiece to an increasingly aggressive entity in line with the changing sociopolitics of South Korea.[242] In fact, change in the degree of press freedom occurred at such a dramatic pace as to make some people wary of possible negative ramifications. The bolder, more enterprising news coverage was, however, far from a complete picture of the changed status of the South Korean media. The explosive expansion of the media industry was another sweeping departure from the past, especially in light of the fact that not a single general interest daily newspaper was registered during the entire term of the Chun administration.[243] The rapid increase in the number of newspapers in 1988 exemplified the government's view of the press in the "era of democracy." By the end of April 1989, a total of 65 daily newspapers were being published in South Korea, more than a 100 percent increase since the enactment of the new press law in late 1987.[244]

The sharp increase in the number of daily newspapers was only part of the overall astonishing expansion of the print media. After June 1987, when Roh proposed expanded press freedom, 3,728 periodicals had been registered by the spring of 1989 with the MOCI for publication—an increase of 1,492.[245] In the past, few applicants had tried to register publications because they expected to be rejected, but now that the new press law required the MOCI to approve registrations as long as applicants satisfied the basic statutory requirements, most of the procedural as well as political obstacles were lifted.

One of the new daily newspapers, *Han-kyoreh Shinmun*, deserves particular attention because it was regarded as a test case of Roh's willingness to accept freedom of the press as indispensable to the new democratic politics of South Korea.[246] The paper, which amassed its original capital of US$7 million from donations during a nationwide campaign, was founded in December 1987 by a group of dissident journalists to rectify the notion that the Korean press "has become [the] private possession of a few people or institutional journalism under the control of political power."[247] The first issue of the paper was published on May 15, 1988, after a lengthy delay in the government's issuance of its registration certificate. The *Han-kyoreh* declared in its code of ethics that it will "serve as a critic of injustice and iniquity and investigate the human rights violations by the political force."

Besides its center-left editorial stance on socioeconomic and political issues, the newspaper is distinctive from others in several respects: It uses *Hangul* (the Korean alphabet) instead of the mixture of Chinese characters and the Korean alphabet that is still prevalent in most daily papers; it strictly prohibits "envelope journalism," the practice of receiving payment for publishing or withholding stories, still openly practiced by a number of Korean journalists[248]; and to demonstrate its structural commitment to defending human rights and the press, the paper maintains "human rights" and "mass media" departments. The human rights department concentrates on coverage of human rights issues in Korea. On the other hand, the mass media department specializes in press-related subjects, ranging from the government press policy to the public's right of access to the media.[249] As the "most critical above-ground" newspaper in Korea,[250] the *Han-kyoreh* had a circulation of 440,000 as of June 1989.[251] On May 15, 1989, it successfully raised a total of US$17.7 million through its nationwide fund-raising campaign aimed at expanding its rather inadequate facilities.[252] Now the *Han-kyoreh* has emerged as a progressive alternative to the largely conservative newspapers that have refrained from criticizing authority.

The restructuring of the print media was the most visible outcome of Roh's press policy, but equally important was the so-called "internal democratization" of the Korean press itself. An increasing number of Korean newspapers recognized that press freedom carries little meaningful value unless it is supported by independence of editorial decision-making from both internal and external pressures. To ensure separation between the editorial department and management, the *Han-kyoreh* and many other newspapers had reporters directly involved in deciding on the overall editorial policy of their newspapers, with managing editors elected by reporters or selected from those recommended by them. The stronger voice of the editorial departments of an increasing number of South Korean newspapers resulted from reactivated labor unions of journalists.[253] The primary *raison d'etre* of the Korean press unions are "to safeguard the right and interests of the unionists and to translate into action the freedom of the press."[254] The new status of the media unions was in stark contrast to the persecution of labor unions during the Park and Chun regimes.[255]

Notwithstanding the positive developments in the Korean press throughout the period of the Roh government, a number of issues arose. Some were seen to be far from new as long dormant issues came out into the open; others were, to a large extent, new in that they were rarely a source of concern to the press. The former related to increasing violence by nongovernmental organizations against certain journalists and publications and the corrupt practices of some journalists. The latter stemmed from a variety of pressures on the press exerted by sociopolitical groups not directly connected with the ruling authorities.

In March 1989, a group of disabled veterans forcibly entered the building of *Kukche Shinmun*, a provincial daily, and injured 20 of its employees after the paper had reported that the Pusan Public Transportation Corporation had awarded several profitable projects to organizations in an arbitrary fashion reminiscent of the Fifth Republic.[256] The veterans were upset by the story because their veterans' village had a contract with the corporation. The incident illustrated how a special interest group might resort to violence in an attempt to silence a paper from reporting on controversial subjects. The physical violence was deplored by the Journalists Association of Korea as "an unprecedented intrusion on press freedom."[257] Korean journalists had also been increasingly subject to attacks by the riot police while covering numerous antigovernment or labor-related demonstrations.

Another issue facing the freer Korean press was the growing incidence of "envelope journalism." According to a Korean Press Institute survey in 1989 of 700 journalists on the question of their professional ethics, 93 percent said they received *chonji*, or monetary gifts, in envelopes from their news sources.[258] *Chonji* journalism in Korea was far from new. As Professor Jae-won Lee stated in 1982: "The majority of journalists have high ethical standards and view the unprofessional activities of some of their colleagues as a disgrace to the profession. Yet receiving payoffs has been a habitual practice with certain reporters for many years."[259] What was noteworthy in recent years is that the public had begun to voice concern about an increasingly blatant abuse of press freedom in total disregard of press responsibility.[260] Consequently, the Roh administration took action to deal with the illegal practice. In March 1989, for example, the Seoul prosecutor's office arrested several reporters for extorting about US$40,000 from more than 20 chemical factory owners in exchange for promising not to expose their alleged violations of an anti-pollution law.[261]

Among the new pressures facing the Korean press was that exerted by public interest organizations with no direct connection to the government. One government official told a Korean newspaper that while the Korean press "is now free from the coercive pressure of the government ... it is not free from the pressure of a particular political organization or interest group. The Korean press is fiercely aggressive in criticizing President Roh Tae Woo and his government. But it is passive in its criticism of the two Kims [opposition leaders Kim Dae Jung and Kim Young Sam]."[262] In a similar vein, an opposition National Assemblyman deplored the "violent" pressure of special interest groups and political organizations on the Korean news media, disrupting autonomous news reporting.[263] Since South Korea has a long history of a timid press that rarely reported on controversial social and political issues, these groups and organizations reacted angrily to a suddenly assertive press.

The dispute between the liberal opposition Party for Peace and Democracy (PPD) and the *Chosun Ilbo* in March 1989 was a case in point. The unparalleled tit-for-tat between the PPD and the country's largest daily newspaper, which attracted attention even from foreign media,[264] resulted from publication of a story in *Chugan Chosun*, a news weekly owned by Chosun Ilbo Company. The weekly reported that during a European tour, several PPD lawmakers accompanying the party president, Kim Dae Jung, behaved in a manner beneath their dignity. Among the rude behaviors reported in the *Chugan Chosun* story were one member of Kim's entourage shouting to Pope John Paul II, "Hey, Can you pose for photographers?"; another walking barefoot during a flight on the European trip; and a third making obscene jokes to an Italian woman.[265] Eight of the lawmakers filed a libel complaint with the Seoul district prosecutor's office, charging that the article "disseminated false facts for no justifiable reasons and damaged the reputational interests" of Kim and the lawmakers.[266] The charge, later dropped, was a criminal offense in South Korea. In a separate civil suit against the *Chosun Ilbo*, the lawmakers sought US$12.8 million in damages and demanded that the newspaper publish an apology.[267] The PPD did not stop with legal proceedings; it also launched a boycott of the *Chosun Ilbo*[268] and prohibited *Chosun* reporters from entering PPD headquarters.[269]

The dispute between the most powerful opposition party and the daily represented a different kind of pressure on the Korean press. Ironically, it also indicated how authoritarian some self-styled "liberal" opposition leaders were in their views about press freedom. The other leading opposition leader (and now President of South Korea), Kim Young Sam, claimed in a 1987 statement that he supported press freedom "as long as the reporters tell the truth," adding that Korean journalists "would probably need 'guidelines' from any new government to help them do their job."[270] For a politician who valiantly strove for freedom of the South Korean press for more than 20 years, Kim Young Sam's remarks sounded like Chun defining the boundaries of press freedom.

## SEVENTH REPUBLIC, 1993–PRESENT

The South Korean press is flourishing these days. Indeed, the press is experiencing "a golden age"[271] largely because of the sweeping democratic reforms that started in mid-1987. The Korean media during the past seven years have been freer than ever to criticize the government, address formerly taboo issues, and expand with virtually no restraint.[272] In July 1987, there were 32 daily newspapers in Korea. By the end of November 1994, a total of 99 daily newspapers were being published in Korea, more than a 200 percent increase since the enactment of the Periodicals Act in late 1987.[273]

The golden era of the Korean press since 1987 is closely linked to the social and political, as well as economic, development of Korean society. There is no doubt that press freedom is a reality in Korea. In his speech at the IPI convention in Budapest, Hungary, in May 1992, Sang Hoon Bang, publisher of the *Chosun Ilbo*, declared: "The political constraints under which the Korean media had to operate during the authoritarian government no longer exist. Today, nobody—neither the President, the military, nor intelligence agencies—is beyond reproach or immune to criticism."[274]

As Korean-press observer David Halvorsen put it in 1992, however, "All the news is not good" so far as the adaption of the Korean press to a changing Korean society is concerned.[275] Halvorsen has argued: "[T]he press is rudely learning that the exercise of freedom is complex. It calls for decisions that editors and reporters never had to make before."[276] As Korea steadily moves toward a liberal democracy, the press will experience a number of changes. The eventual evolution of a free Korean press may lead to an emergence of an "equal-contender" or "antagonist/adversary" relationship between the press and government, depending upon the sociopolitical circumstances.[277] The days in which the South Korean press served as a "voluntary servant" or a "forced slave" may have passed,[278] and in this context there ought to be a soul-searching examination of the new press-government relationship. In South Korea, freedom of the press has been traditionally related to freedom *from* governmental restraints; this passive notion should now be changed to the positive freedom *for* democratizing Korea.

In discussing "journalistic freedom" as distinguished from "press freedom," media scholar John Merrill of the University of Missouri notes that "journalistic freedom concerns a relationship between the journalists working for a news medium and the executives and editors of that news medium, while press freedom concerns a relationship between the press and the government."[279] Law Professor Edwin Baker of the University of Pennsylvania also argues for recognition of legal rules to protect the freedom of press professionals from abridgement by the press owners because "[p]rotection of press personnel may best promote diversity and be most central to the press's obviously vital fourth-estate role—checking abuse by government."[280]

The *Pusan Ilbo* labor strike in July 1988 epitomizes the often volatile relationship between newspaper employees and employers. The strike, which set a precedent for the sociopolitical implications of the press union-management conflict, went beyond traditional labor issues of the newspaper employees. It also related to the employees' demand for a voice in selecting managing editors as part of their editorial independence.[281] The strike ended when the owner of the daily newspaper in Pusan recognized the union's right to recommend three candidates for managing editor for the newspaper management to choose from.[282]

Currently, the Korean press is subject to few direct extra-legal pressures from the government. The Korean government, for example, no longer issues censorial instructions to the press on what and how to report certain news.[283] This is a significant departure from what the government did before 1987. Though the government has now stopped resorting to a blatant form of press censorship, the government continues to exert *indirect* influence on the Korean news media.[284] In their 1991 report on the Korean press, Hans Verploeg, general secretary of the Netherlands Union of Journalists, and Tony Wilton, general secretary of the New Zealand Journalists and Graphic Process Union, claimed that they met many Koreans "who felt there was still a large measure of self-censorship among journalists in the established press, which may be stimulated by corruption or fear of prosecution."[285]

One contributing factor in a corrupt Korean press is the press clubs, commonly known as *kijadan*. The exclusive clubs exist in government ministries, city halls, and police headquarters. They are made up of groups of journalists assigned to cover the same "beat." The press clubs, according to Halvorsen, "have taken it upon themselves to determine who will and will not have access" to news sources of the government.[286] Halvorsen adds that non-club members, "even though representing perfectly legitimate media," are denied access by their peers to news events.[287] The Korean government as a rule channels information through the press clubs. The information is rarely expanded by reporters on their own initiative. Instead of striving for a complete story on the subject of the press release, Korean reporters are often concerned about the possibility that their enterprising reporting might embarrass their complacent peers by making them appear not to be living up to their professionalism.

Further, the challenge to the veracity of the government-provided information in one way or another might lead to "the sting of government disfavor and the humiliation" from other club members because the independent reporter might be perceived to have broken the code of conduct as a club member. This explains, Halvorsen asserts, why "the government statement goes into the newspaper, unchallenged, unquestioned and unfettered."[288]

"Envelope journalism," the practice of a journalist accepting cash gifts in unmarked white envelopes from a news source, is still the rule rather than the exception for the Korean press. More than 90 percent of Korean journalists admitted in a September 1989 survey that they had accepted *chonji* from their news sources for various reasons.[289] Only *Han-kyoreh Shinmun* and the weekly news magazine *Sisa Journal* in Seoul ban the *chonji* practice.

Examples of the notorious *chonji* journalism in Korea,[290] as listed by Halvorsen in his 1992 study of the Korean press, include the following:

The Suso housing scandal payoffs to as many as 80 newsmen allegedly amounted to $750,000, based on another estimate from the prosecution-general's investigation.

A scandal in the Labor Ministry press club in which the club president solicited *chonji* from newsmakers. Estimated "contributions": $85,000.

Nineteen of 21 reporters covering the Health Ministry received $118,000 from their sources in one month.

Reporters reassigned from a news beat to an inside newsroom position get a special inside allowance, *naekun sudang*, to offset the loss of the white envelope. This can range from 25 to 35 percent of their base pay.

A gift of $140, which is 100,000 *won*, is quite common and given at traditional holidays such as Chusok (Korean thanksgiving) and lunar new year.

Some newspapers, established in the frenzy of media growth since enactment of the press freedom law in 1987, are struggling financially and expect their reporters to derive their income from their news sources. They are not front-line newspapers.

While press clubs are the traditional and most profitable repositories of *chonji*, the culture and entertainment beats also have their system. Many art galleries, for example, consider a gift to a reporter to get publicity in the paper another cost of doing business.

A journalist who left a newspaper to take an attractive public relations position with a well-known hotel then learned the primary job was to distribute white envelopes to deserving reporters. The journalist immediately resigned.

*Chonji* never dies, it just changes envelopes. One reporter told of how he customarily received payoffs and would spend some of it buying drinks for his fellow reporters. He would take the rest home to his wife who in turn would take $70 (50,000 *won*), place it inside the cover of a new book, and present it as a gift to the teacher of their son.[291]

Halvorsen, criticizing *chonji* journalism in Korea, rejected some Korean journalists' disingenuous distinction between bribes (solicited payoffs) and gratuities (warm expression of friendship), which include *chonji,* in Korea. He challenged the Korean press, "If accepting money and gifts is such a time-honored custom in Korean journalism, why not share that information with your readers and television viewers?"[292]

A noted Korean journalist, Kwon-sang Park, stated: "[The] increased freedom has not brought the expected increase in quality. The decline in the quality of reporting caused by the media's rapid growth is a major concern: As the number of newspapers and their pages have soared, overextended staffs are unable to pay close attention to accuracy. Sensationalism and biases often creep into their news reporting."[293]

Publisher Bang, of *Chosun Ilbo,* agrees that steep competition among Korean newspapers is forcing them to run "a quantity race," ignoring journalistic quality.[294] As some foreign observers point out, many overstretched Korean journalists suffer the "lack of a certain imaginative quality and flair."[295]

Several restrictive laws have been revised since 1987 in an effort to expand freedom of the press. If the Korean press is to play a positive role by contributing to an informed and politically active electorate in a democracy, however, the government should go further than abolishing or revising suppressive laws; it should establish institutional mechanisms for positively enhancing press freedom. As James Madison, the "father of the Constitution" of the United States, wrote, "A popular Government, without popular information, or the means of acquiring it, is but a Prologue to a Farce or A Tragedy; or, perhaps both."[296] Thus, the freedom of information concept is worth exploring. Access to information should be the rule rather than the exception; there should be as few exemptions as possible and, when needed, they should be specific and justified by the government. The concept would then carry practical meaning for the press in its role of providing the public with information beyond that selectively released by the government.[297]

Closely related to the open records concept is access to sessions of the legislature and other elected bodies, regulatory hearings, and so on. Obviously, if the press is to serve as a watchdog on behalf of the public, reporters ought to be guaranteed some degree of access to the meetings of public bodies. Unfortunately, this has rarely been the case in South Korea. What is needed is a comprehensive "sunshine" statute with carefully crafted exceptions, modeled after the open-meetings laws of the United States.[298] Exceptions for closed meetings ought to be statutorily specified and justified. The adoption of an open meetings law will significantly contribute to the development of democratic politics by making the South Korean government more accessible to people through the press.

As media law scholar Don Pember succinctly put it, "If news and information are the lifeblood of the press, then news sources are one of the wells from which that lifeblood springs."[299] This is especially true of investigative journalism. As the Korean press is shifting from the status of a complacent medium to a more aggressive and inquisitive entity, Korean journalists will more likely explore new issues. If the trend of a feistier Korean press since late 1987 continues, there is a strong possibility that investigative journalism will emerge in South Korea. Among the many issues facing potentially enterprising Korean muckrakers in the days to come will be how to protect their confidential sources. One positive approach to dealing with the issue would be to embrace the shield law concept as more than a sugar-coated phrase, which it was under the Basic Press Act because of its many exemptions.[300] A shield law should have protective mechanisms to give reporters the right to protect their sources, putting the Korean press in a better position to serve the public.

"Relations between the press and the government have been turbulent and explosive in the modern history of Korea. Relations in the future will depend largely on the margin of safety the government feels toward domestic political stability and *perceived* external threats to Korea's security," Professor Jae-won Lee stated in 1982.[301] Lee's commentary on the typical press-government relationship in South Korea prior to 1987 is still well-founded, to a certain extent, even though Korea's authoritarian rule has ended.

Unlike his heavy-handed autocratic predecessors such as Park Chung Hee and Chun Doo Hwan, Kim Young Sam, the first civilian elected President in Korea during the past 30 years, is not likely to resort to extra-legal mechanisms such as brute force, intimidation, or direct interference with the news reporting of the Korean press. Instead, the Korean government most likely will use *legal* means to balance press freedom with other societal interests, including national security and individual reputation. Authorities will invoke various statutes to ensure that "the news media [will] practice prudence against violating human rights or defamation."[302] A crucial issue is when the statutes can be properly employed to rectify wrongs or to protect the asserted governmental interests. When can one know whether the government has a bona fide interest in utilizing statutory mechanisms against the press?

The Korean government's arrest of a news reporter on a libel charge in June 1993 indicates how the Criminal Code could be used to restrict freedom of the press. Chong Chae-hon, a reporter of the *Joongang Ilbo* in Seoul, wrote an allegedly defamatory story about Defense Minister Kwon Young-hae. The story claimed that Kwon was prohibited from leaving the country because he was suspected of taking bribes in connection with a military buildup program of the Korean government.[303] Kwon sued Chong and the four executives of the *Joongang Ilbo*.[304] The Seoul prosecution arrested Chong for an alleged violation of the Criminal Code on libel.[305] The *Joongang Ilbo* retracted the story in its second edition and issued a correction on the front page the next day. The paper acknowledged being "irresponsible" for publishing the story and issued an apology to Kwon.[306] Kwon withdrew his libel complaint against Chong and against the *Joongang Ilbo* management.[307] Under the Criminal Code, only the "express objection" of the alleged defamed person can prevent the defamer from being prosecuted by the State.[308]

Noting that few reporters have been arrested for defamatory falsehoods in Korea in recent years,[309] Professor Yi Kwang-jae of Kyonghee University in Seoul suspected the administration's insensitivity toward the press in taking an unusual criminal libel prosecution against the *Joongang Ilbo*.[310] He said the *Joongang* case revealed the tension between the press and the new administration under President Kim.[311] How would the government have handled Chong and the *Joongang* if the libel episode had happened prior to the democratic reforms of 1987? Without doubt, Chong and the *Joongang* executives would have been hauled into the KCIA or the Korean Army Security Command for brutal interrogation and physical torture. Furthermore, it is highly probable that few Korean news media would have dared to publish articles about the terrifying suppression of Korean journalists by government agencies.

In the context of a free press as a permanent fixture of a democratic Korea, however, the *Joongang* incident is not an ordinary libel complaint. It contains every element of a prosecution for seditious libel, which is fundamentally incompatible with a democratic body politic like South Korea. If the Korean government looks to the incident as a press-taming precedent and jumps at any similar situation in the future, the *libertarian* notion of press freedom in Korea will be called into serious question. This is especially true if Korean courts are not alert to the disguised motives of the government in turning to law for confronting the critical press.

## SUMMARY AND CONCLUSIONS

No matter how the status of press freedom under American military government rule in 1945–1948 is characterized, Koreans in general for the first time experienced a taste of press freedom as part of their daily life. The Korean press had an unprecedented opportunity to participate in a concrete form of press freedom during the period. Consequently, the USAMGIK did help Koreans become aware of what freedom of the press means as a day-to-day right of citizens in a democracy. The unprecedented exposure of Koreans to the Western concept of a free press during the era of the American military rule has contributed enormously to the future sociopolitical development of South Korea.[312]

The American military government strove in principle to cultivate a free press in Korea modeled after the American press. When it came to the actual implementation of its policy, however, the government employed a number of authoritarian mechanisms that often contradicted its own political and ideological commitment to a liberal democracy. In regard to its impact upon the Korean press, Koreans learned to cherish a free press as an ideal from their American rulers. On the other hand, some of the regulatory measures ultimately adopted by the American military government against the Korean press were subsequently abused by the Korean government in the wake of the termination of the USAMGIK.

The American military government's efforts to introduce the American concept of press freedom into South Korea epitomizes a trial-and-error process, illustrating the clash between a foreign-dominated government with a liberal political ideology and a society with little sociocultural and political experience with a free press. Given that the primary *raison d'etre* of the USAMGIK was the task of eventually equipping the Korean people with "a democratic, representative machinery of government,"[313] however, the overall approach of the U.S. military government in Korea toward press freedom was closely related to its various reforms to "democratize" Korean society.[314]

Notwithstanding the widely held opinion that the press during the First Republic under President Syngman Rhee was censored, considerable press freedom was allowed during the first half of Rhee's rule from 1948 to 1960, The largely libertarian status of the Korean press during the early period of the Rhee government was closely related to the then functioning institutionalized separation-of-powers principle in Korea. This is evident in the several unsuccessful attempts by the executive branch under Rhee to legislate against the press.

As the sociopolitical strains on his presidency increased in the late 1950s, however, Rhee became more authoritarian in his relationship with the press, going so far as to enact the repressive National Security Act in 1958 and closing the leading opposition paper, *Kyunghyang Shinmun*. Rhee also invoked the Newspaper Act of 1907, a repressive decree enacted by the Yi Dynasty to deal with newspaper licensing. The end of the 12-year Rhee regime during the Students Uprising of April 1960 resulted, in part, from the continuous struggle between the truculent Korean press and the increasingly authoritarian government under Rhee. In a way, it was natural that the era following the departure of the anti-press regime should have been one of a free press. The Second Republic under Premier Chang Myon might have been a good occasion for press freedom to grow into full bloom, had it not been so short-lived.

According to Frederick S. Siebert's proposition on freedom of the press, "[t]he area of freedom contracts and the enforcement of restraints increases as the stresses on the stability of the government and of the structure of society increase."[315] In all likelihood, Siebert might find that his proposition has had its verity demonstrated by the Korean press vis-à-vis the Korean government in several respects. That is, the Korean press has undergone more and more governmental control as the Korean government has been strained by various stresses both domestic and foreign. However, the Korean case regarding Siebert's general statement shows one or two areas where the statement "can ... apparently work in reverse."[316] The Korean press under the Chang Myon government (1960–1961) was a good example because the press at the time was most active and independent, though there were numerous "stresses on the stability of the government and of the structure of society."

As the history of freedom of the press in Korea indicates, the Korean press had frequently been a target of repression by a succession of dictatorial governments from 1961 to mid-1987. This is explained in part by the fact that most Korean rulers have viewed press freedom as "grants of political favor rather than acceptance of political or civil rights."[317] While in power during the Third and Fourth Republics from 1961 to 1979, President Park Chung Hee resorted to various legal and extra-legal methods to control the Korean press. In the 1970s, the Park administration had the Korean press at its command. Press freedom during the Park era was the epitome of the press theory of authoritarianism underlying "developmental communication."

The nonexistence of a functioning "institutionalized" system of checks and balances in the Korean political system contributed fundamentally to the repression of press freedom by the government. In the face of this undemocratic political structure, the Korean press continuously struggled to get back its freedom from the government until the mid-1980s. This struggle was likened to a "never-ending tug of war," but that analogy did not present a precise picture of the ever deteriorating press situation during the Fifth Republic under President Chun Doo Hwan (1980–1987). The Korean government under Chun completely subjugated its press through a revolutionary reorganization of the mass media in Korea. As a partner in the "new" era, the press often took a safer road toward defining its role as a "voluntary servant." That is, it adjusted itself to the political situation rather than fighting for its freedom.

During the Sixth Republic under President Roh Tae Woo (1988–1992), freedom of the press slowly but steadily became institutionalized as democratization continued in Korea, and there was a strong indication that it was being accepted by the government as an important element of Korean democracy. The democratization process launched by Roh brought about a number of significant developments for the traditionally authoritarian Korean press. The amended Constitution was more explicit than its predecessor in guaranteeing press freedom by enumerating prohibitions against censorship, and the newly enacted Periodicals Act and Broadcast Act were an improvement over the repealed Basic Press Act in limiting government authority to revoke registration of a publication. Equally significant was the revision and abolition of several restrictive statutes such as the National Security Act and the Criminal Code on the crime of anti-State defamation. The International Press Institute years ago noted, however, that "the entirely satisfactory law from the point of view of the press is unfortunately the exception rather than the rule. By and large these [press] laws … contain clauses which are a serious handicap to freedom of expression."[318] The Korean laws serve as a good example. The direct and indirect press statutes in Korea are more often regulatory rather than protective of the news media.

The Korean press under Roh was subject to fewer direct coercive pressures from the government than had been the case during the pre-Roh period. This increasingly salubrious environment largely stemmed from the gradual institutionalization of the separation of powers between the executive branch under Roh, the more assertive National Assembly, and the now emboldened judiciary. Amid the numerous encouraging institutional changes, a new set of issues with which the press must deal was emerging. These included the mushrooming number of newspapers and other publications, the unethical practice of "envelope journalism," and the pressure exerted by special interest groups rather than the government. Further, for the Korean press today, special interests groups, not the government, are often sources of direct and indirect pressure on the press.

The Korean press under President Kim Young Sam of the Seventh Republic (1993–) is facing a different set of problems. Many of the problems do not originate from outside the press, as they did in the old era of the repressive regime. Rather, they arise from inside. In many ways, the internal problems with the Korean press will turn out to be more intractable than the external ones were. As Professor Yu Jae-chon of Sogang University in Seoul stated, "We have achieved the goal of a 'freedom from' but not 'freedom for.'"[319] The growth of the media industry is certainly an indication of the Korean press on the rise, but it does not necessarily mean a better quality of its journalistic work. Press responsibility and ethics demand more sustained attention than ever from Korean journalists.

On the premise that the foremost role of the Korean press is to serve as the watchdog of those in power, the unethical *chonji* practices of many Korean journalists are beneath the dignity of the Korean press as a whole. It takes time and determination for more than a handful of conscientious journalists to eliminate the deep-rooted cultural and social norm of accepting cash gifts as a way of journalistic life in Korea. Professionalism does mandate that Korean journalists place their principled adherence to their code of ethics as impartial and objective conveyers of information above the often irresistible pressure of their social custom.

Finally, the "open marketplace of ideas" concept of press freedom in a democracy repudiates the notion of the *kijadan* system, which hinders, rather than enhances, dissemination of information to the public. Now it is time for the Korean press to launch a vigorous campaign to abolish the *kijadan* system in favor of a more democratic way to facilitate access to news information by all journalists irrespective of their employer, nationality, or medium. In this vein, the Korean press might learn from the decision of the Kasumi Club of Japan to accept AP and Reuters news agencies as its regular members in 1992. An *Asahi Shimbun* reporter stated: "[I]t will be stimulating to have foreign journalists with viewpoints different from those of the Japanese journalists as members. Thus, it appears that having foreign journalists as members in a press club is going to create wholesome tension and stimulation on the both sides of the 'news source' and the club member journalists."[320]

# CHAPTER 5

# Press Freedom
# and the Constitution

Judicial review of legislation constitutes one of the most prominent structural mechanisms in a democracy[1] to ensure a government of law, not a government of men.[2] The value of judicial review evolves from the separation of powers between the executive, legislative, and judicial branches of government, a system that has been recognized as the *modus operandi* of "human rights constitutionalism."[3]

Judicial review is especially crucial for safeguarding the basic freedoms of all citizens. Professor Archibald Cox of Harvard Law School has stated: "[J]udicial review provides better protection for the enduring values that politicians too often neglect and of which the people too often lose sight in the emotional intensity and maneuvering of political conflict, especially in national crises. Individual liberties such as freedom of speech and guarantees of privacy are often in this character."[4]

In South Korea, the constitutionalism characterized by judicial review had been an ideal rather than a reality until the late 1980s. It is little wonder, then, that judicial review was an important issue in the debate over the constitutional amendment of 1987 among those who wished for the "rule of law"[5] in a democratic Korea. In their discussion of the significant American influence upon the constitutional law of Korea, Professors Tscholsu Kim of Seoul National University and Sang Don Lee of Chungang University in Seoul noted: "[I]t is remarkable that so many people in Korea wanted a new Constitution with a strong Bill of Rights, a separation of powers, and judicial review."[6]

Since the current Constitution was adopted in 1987,[7] Korea's politics has moved away from authoritarianism toward libertarianism. The increasingly active and independent Constitution Court[8] epitomizes the blossoming of democracy in Korea. Two commentators on Korean law have argued:

> As of early 1992, barely three years after its establishment, the Constitutional [sic] Court of the Republic of Korea has acquired more significance as an adjudicatory body than many Korean jurists and foreign observers

expected in late 1987 when the Constitution was amended.... As the cases thus far decided illustrate ... the Court has successfully introduced into the Korean political system a new dimension of constitutional review which seems to be strongly supported by the public.[9]

The emergence of judicial review in Korea as "a very significant factor in the guardianship of human rights"[10] is closely related to the expanded freedom of the Korean press in recent years.

This chapter examines how various Korean press laws, which traditionally were more restrictive than protective of the press,[11] have been interpreted by the Constitution Court since 1988. This analysis focuses on the case law of the Constitution Court on the freedom of the Korean press from 1988 through 1994. The first part describes the constitutional and statutory framework of judicial review in Korea. The second part analyzes the Constitution Court's decisions involving Korean press statutes. The third part assesses the impact of judicial review on freedom of the press in Korea.

## JUDICIAL REVIEW: ITS STRUCTURE AND FUNCTIONS

Since achieving independence from Japanese colonial rule in 1945, Korea has provided judicial review in its constitutions. Notwithstanding nine constitutional revisions in Korea, the institution of judicial review has rarely been challenged because "each constitutional amendment has concentrated primarily on the term of the presidency or the executive branch's relationship to the legislative."[12] It is noteworthy, however, that the varying status of judicial review has often reflected the political motives of those behind each of the constitutional amendments.

### Judicial Review System: 1948–1987[13]

The first Constitution of 1948 authorized a Constitution Committee to review a statute "[w]henever the decision of the case depends on the determination of the constitutionality of the law."[14] Only the courts were allowed to request judicial review by the Constitution Committee. Under Article 81, the jurisdiction of the Committee was limited to legislation, while courts had the power to rule on administrative orders or regulations.[15] The Committee comprised the Vice President, five Supreme Court justices, and five lawmakers.[16] A two-thirds majority was required to declare a law unconstitutional.[17]

The Constitution of the Second Republic (1960–1961), which was designed to "prevent abuse of political power and protect civil liberties" to a greater extent than that of the First Republic,[18] provided for the Constitution Court as a standing organ with nine judges. The President, the Supreme Court, and the Senate of the National Assembly were each to appoint three judges.[19] The Constitution Court was an attempt to eliminate the political problems that had undermined the operation of the Constitution Committee under the First Republic.[20] The Constitution prohibited the judges from joining political parties or participating in political activities.[21]

When a case was pending before a court, the parties as well as the court could request judicial review of a statute by the Constitution Court regardless of whether the determination of its constitutionality was a prerequisite to trying the case.

The Third Republic (1962–1972) adopted the American style of judicial review.[22] Article 102 of the Constitution of 1962 provided:

(1) The Supreme Court shall have the power to make final review of the constitutionality of a legislation when its constitutionality is prerequisite to a trial;

(2) The Supreme Court shall have the power to make a final review of the constitutionality or legality of administrative decrees, regulations, or dispositions, when their constitutionality or legality is prerequisite to a trial.[23]

The expansive judicial review power of the Supreme Court under the Constitution led to what one commentator termed "judicial supremacy" in Korea.[24] It was not initially clear whether judicial review was also granted to lower courts. In 1966, however, the Supreme Court ruled that all the courts have the power to determine the unconstitutionality of a legislation regardless of the level of the court. Yet only the Supreme Court can make a final decision about the constitutionality.[25]

Under the Constitution of the Fourth Republic (1972–1980), the Supreme Court no longer had the authority to determine the constitutionality of legislation. The Constitution Committee, which was identical to that of the 1960 Constitution, was resurrected and accorded the power of judicial review. The Committee ruled on a statute at the request of the court when the determination of the statute's constitutionality was a prerequisite to a pending trial.[26] The trial court would request the Committee for a decision through the Supreme Court. While the statute was under review by the Constitution Committee, the trial of the suit would be suspended.[27]

The Constitution of the Fifth Republic (1980–1987) provided for judicial review similar to that under the Fourth Republic, the only difference residing in the conditions governing requests for review. Article 108 of the Constitution of 1980 established that "[w]hen the constitutionality of a law is a prerequisite to a trial, the court, *if it construes that the law at issue runs counter to the Constitution*, shall request a decision of the Constitution Committee, and shall judge according to the decision thereof."[28] Thus, the court possessed the initial power to rule on the constitutionality of a statute being subjected to a trial. If the court held the statute to be constitutional, there would be no further judicial action by the Constitution Committee.

### Judicial Review System: 1987–1994[29]

In 1987, a year of epoch-making political changes for Koreans,[30] the Constitution was amended to bring a pluralistic democracy to Korea.[31] It explicitly prohibited the licensing and censorship of the press, and it guaranteed freedom of expression.[32] It also provided for the direct popular election of the president,[33] who was now limited to one five-year term.[34] The mechanism for separation of powers was also strengthened. For example, the President is no longer allowed to dissolve the National Assembly or to appoint the Supreme Court justices without the consent of the Assembly.[35] Furthermore, the Constitution now states that the National Assembly may "inspect affairs of state or investigate specific matters of state affairs, and may demand the production of documents directly related thereto, the appearance of a witness in person and the furnishing of testimony or statements of opinion."[36]

Judicial independence under the new Constitution of the Sixth Republic was given special attention. Two American specialists in Korean law observed: "Composition of an independent Korean Supreme Court, the appellate court of last resort in political cases, is crucial for future protection of human rights, but there is another judicial organ which, in theory at least, may have an even greater future impact on human rights issues. This is the Constitution Court...."[37] Likewise, the Constitution Court represents "a new dedication [of the Korean government] to constitutionalism—a promise of effective legal protection of fundamental civil, political and economic rights."[38]

Under Article 111 of the Constitution, the Constitution Court "shall adjudicate ... [t]he constitutionality of a law upon the request of the courts."[39] Furthermore, the Constitution Court's jurisdiction is limited to statutes enacted by the National Assembly,[40] while the Supreme Court has more expansive powers that allow it to determine the constitutionality of presidential decrees, ordinances, and other administrative regulations.[41]

Most important, the current Constitution recognizes the power of the Court to adjudicate "[p]etitions relating to the Constitution as prescribed by law."[42] This constitutional provision enables citizens who feel that their rights have been violated to petition the Constitution Court directly for rectification.[43] The implications of the judicial review petitions clause of the Constitution are quite radical: "In a clear departure from the typically passive attitudes of the courts toward constitutional proceedings, this system of petitions signifies a viable and active role the Constitutional [sic] Court is now expected to play."[44]

The Constitution Court Act of 1988 "provide[s] matters necessary for the organization and operation of the Constitution Court and the procedure for its adjudgment."[45] As for the procedure for judicial review, the Constitution Court renders judgment on the constitutionality of a statute upon the request of the court with original jurisdiction over the case.[46] If the request is made by a court other than the Supreme Court, it is referred through the Supreme Court to the Constitution Court.[47]

The Constitution requires that all questions of the constitutional validity of legislation be submitted to the Constitution Court.[48] The request for judicial review may be made by the trial court on its own or at the request of the party involved.[49] The trial court's request depends on whether "the constitutionality of a particular law is doubtful, and the final judgment in the case will be predicated on an application of that law, or if only a portion of the law is of doubtful constitutionality, of the doubtful portion."[50] If the court initially rules the law constitutional, the court may forgo the request by a party for referral to the Constitution Court.

When denied the referral of a constitutional question by the trial court, a party can utilize two avenues for judicial review. On the one hand, the party may either raise its original questions about the constitutionality of the law on appeal to a higher court[51] or may petition directly to the Constitution Court. The Constitution Court Act reads: "If a request ... for adjudgment on whether the law is unconstitutional or not is rejected, the requesting party may request an adjudgment on constitutional petition to the Constitution Court. In this case, the party may not request again an adjudgment on whether it is unconstitutional or not for the same reason in the legal procedure of the case concerned."[52]

Unlike the United States Supreme Court, which exercises discretion in choosing cases to review through the use of writs of *certiorari*, the jurisdiction of the Constitution Court in Korea is mandatory. The Court's jurisdiction, however, is invoked only when the regular courts request review of the constitutionality of legislation.[53] In other words, it is essential that the constitutionality of a law be formulated as a concrete case or controversy for the Court to have adjudication.

## JUDICIAL REVIEW OF PRESS LAWS

As of January 31, 1995, the Constitution Court had adjudicated 1,795 out of 2,265 cases.[54] This is truly extraordinary when viewed against Korea's prior experience with judicial review. No previous Korean judicial body, as noted later in this chapter, can match the number of judgments rendered by the Constitution Court during its existence.

The Constitution Committee during the First Republic (1948–1960), for example, reviewed no more than seven cases.[55] The Constitution Court of the Second Republic (1960–1961) had no opportunity to function at all because of the Constitution's short life.[56] Korean courts, especially lower courts, had a number of opportunities to review the constitutionality of legislation during the Third Republic (1962–1972). However, the Supreme Court was extremely cautious in invalidating a challenged law. Professor Dae-Kyu Yoon has noted, "Only once during the decade did the Supreme Court hand down a decision of unconstitutionality of law, while in the same period it often reversed lower court decisions which held a law unconstitutional."[57] From 1972 to 1987, the Constitution Committee under the Fourth Republic (1972–1980) and the Fifth Republic (1980–1987) rendered not a single decision.[58]

One of the most remarkable aspects of the post-1988 Constitution Court has been its willingness to take on constitutional challenges of a political nature, which were routinely avoided in the past.[59] The Court's decision on the National Security Act[60] in April 1990 is a case in point.

## National Security Act Cases

In reviewing the politically sensitive National Security Act of 1980,[61] the Constitution Court ruled that the Act was "constitutional on condition of proper interpretation."[62] The Act was challenged for the vagueness of Article 7. In an 8-1 decision, the Constitution Court, defining the proper application of the statute, upheld the National Security Act. The Court ruled that the Act would not violate the Constitution if it applied only to "the clear danger of bringing about substantive evils to the State," not to actions unharmful to the security of the State or to the basic order of a liberal democracy.[63] Consequently, so long as there is no substantive evil conferred to the State from conduct or speech, the law has no application. Nor can the security law be enforced under circumstances in which the evil is not clear.[64]

The restriction on the interpretation of the law, the Court argued, was "a natural demand evolving from the preferred position of freedom of expression" under the Constitution.[65] In applying the statute to the specific facts, the Court suggested that courts consider "the proximity between a conduct and its danger to society" and "especially the gravity of the evil" resulting from the dangerous conduct.[66]

In dissent, Justice Pyon Chong-su argued that the National Security Act violated the speech and press guarantees of the Constitution. Because freedom of expression is the "institutional foundation of democracy" and a "singularly important basic right" of citizens under the Constitution, he rejected what he perceived to be the "bad tendency" test of the majority for restriction on expression.[67] Pyon asserted that a criminal law punishing expressions of opinion required the highest degree of definitional precision.[68] The mere tendency of a statement to cause harmful consequences to the State could not be sufficient grounds for invoking the law against the speech. Instead, he stated that the law could be invoked "only when it is proved that the statement may create a clear and present danger of incurring the evils defined by the law (the clear and present danger doctrine)."[69]

Two months later, the Constitution Court affirmed this ruling in a second decision on the National Security Act. In that case, the Court addressed the question of whether the statute could be constitutionally applied to punish possession of books written "for the purpose of helping an anti-State organization."[70] The Court's categorical affirmation of the limited application of the National Security Act indicates that the Court is especially vigilant against the possible abuse by the authorities of the statute's broad and vague restrictions on freedom of the press and speech.

## Military Secrets Protection Act and "Right to Know" Cases

In February 1992, in yet another politically charged case, the Constitution Court reviewed the Military Secrets Protection Act of 1972.[71] As in the National Security Act case, the Military Secrets Protection Act[72] was being challenged as overly vague. Those questioning the validity of the Act had been charged with violating the law by releasing a classified report on national defense.[73] They claimed that the statute, which proscribed the unauthorized gathering and the intentional and negligent disclosure of military secrets, infringed upon their constitutional right to free speech and free press.

The Court upheld the Act insofar as its application is confined to the disclosure of unpublicized military secrets "which are duly marked as classified military information in accordance with a legal procedure and which are substantially valuable enough to create a clear danger to national security, if disclosed."[74] The Court declared that dissemination of information known to ordinary people with average knowledge and experience could not be a violation of the Act.[75]

In balancing the public's right to know against national security interests, the Constitution Court noted that "national security, the maintenance of law and order or ... public welfare" may form the basis for exceptions to basic freedoms and rights unless the restrictions violate the "essential aspect" of these freedoms or rights.[76] The Court went on to recognize the inhibitive effect of ill-defined military secrets protections on press and academic freedom.[77] The overzealous protection of military secrets, the Court warned, would contravene the right to know, which the Court had recognized as an element of speech and press freedom in earlier cases.[78]

The right to know, the Court proclaimed, is necessary to a democratic society for the promotion of individual and social values such as self-fulfillment, the search for truth, participation in political decision-making, and balancing of stability and change.[79] Further, the Court called attention to the "checking value" of the right to know in making the government responsive to people.[80] These higher values of freedom of the press and speech led the Court to conclude that "the boundary of military secrets should be as minimal as necessary to extend the parameters of people's freedom of expression or 'right to know' to a maximum possible degree."[81]

While the Constitution Court's ruling on the Military Secrets Protection Act focused on the right to know, the Court, as previously mentioned, had already addressed the question of access to information in a 1989 case. That case had resulted from the refusal of a county office to grant the petitioner access to public records relating to the title to a forest and other real estate.[82] The Court, while conceding that the right to know was not absolute and might be regulated in the public interest,[83] held that there should be a concrete legal standard to balance the public interest against individual harm caused by such a regulation.[84] The Court enunciated the following standard for access to government information: "The right to know should be broadly accepted if the requester is concerned with the requested information and the release of the information is not harmful to public interests. We are of the opinion that it is indisputable that public information must be mandatorily released to those who have a direct interest in it."[85] In applying this standard to the case, the Court held that the documents in question should have been made available to the petitioner, for they were not classified secrets. The disclosure of the documents would not invade the privacy rights of others; furthermore, no other law barred the release of the documents.[86]

In May 1991, the Constitution Court again ruled on the right to know. This case arose when a prosecutor's office refused to allow a petitioner in a defamation trial to copy the court records in his case.[87] The petitioner claimed that the refusal violated his right to know as guaranteed by the Constitution.[88] In response, the Constitution Court stated that freedom of speech and the press is made possible by a sufficient guarantee of access to information. The Court drew upon the United Nations Universal Declaration of Human Rights of 1948[89] as well as the Constitution for its conclusion that the right to know is "naturally included in the freedom of expression."[90] And under the Court's analysis, the essence of the right to know lies in the "people's right to know about information in the possession of the government."[91]

The Court also considered the "right to liberty" and the "right to petition" as aspects of the right to know. The "liberty" aspect, the Court said, meant "not to be impeded by the government in obtaining access to, collecting, and using information."[92] The "petition" aspect, the Court continued, is the right to petition the government to eliminate restrictions on informational access.[93]

In conclusion, it was held that if release of the requested documents "would not conflict with the fundamental rights of those concerned or violate the national security, maintenance of law and order, and public welfare interest," disclosure of the documents would be a "faithful" execution of the government's duty to guarantee this basic right of its citizens.[94] The Court also brought the right to know within the sphere of the "right of life" as modern society changes to a "high information society."[95] The Court based the right to know on the premise that the quality of life in an information-oriented society would be greatly diminished without access to information.

### Periodicals Act Cases

The constitutionality of the Act Relating to Registration of Periodicals (Periodicals Act)[96] has been challenged three times since 1991. The first Periodicals Act case arose when a Seoul newspaper company challenged the statute's "claim for correction of reports" provisions[97] on the grounds that they violated freedom of the press.[98]

The Court pointed to the two rationales behind the statutory recognition of the "right of reply," a phrase which the Court preferred as conceptually more accurate than the term "correction of reports" as used in the Periodicals Act.[99] First, when an individual's reputation has been injured by a news organization, the Court said, that individual should be given a prompt, appropriate, and comparable means of defense. To counter the effect of the offending article, the right of reply guarantees the injured party an opportunity for defense through the same news organization.[100] Second, the right-of-reply requirement can contribute to the discovery of truth and formation of correct public opinion. Readers often depend on information provided by the news media, and they cannot make a sound judgment until they hear the opposing arguments of the other parties.[101]

The Court looked to several provisions of the Constitution that protect an individual's personality.[102] The Court asserted: "[T]he claim for corrected reports as a right of reply is based on the constitutionally guaranteed right of character. By allowing the injured an opportunity to respond to factual allegations, it protects their right of character."[103] The Court added that the right of reply would make the press more responsible by permitting the injured party to challenge the accuracy of news reports.[104]

Dismissing the petitioner's argument that the reply provisions would violate the "essential aspect" of freedom of the press,[105] the Court emphasized that other constitutional interests, i.e., reputation, privacy, *and* press freedom, were protected by the statutory requirements governing the right of reply.[106] The Court concluded that the reasonable limitations on the right of reply functioned as "a safety mechanism to prevent the unwarranted encroachment on freedom of the press."[107]

The Court cited the following qualifications on the right of reply designed to protect the press: (1) Such reply is limited to statements of facts only, and thus does not affect expression of opinion by the press;[108] (2) The news media can deny the reply request when the injured party does not have a proper interest in the reply, when the contents of the reply are clearly contrary to the facts, or when the reply is only for commercial purposes;[109] (3) The request for reply must be made within one month of the publication of the assertion, or 14 days in the case of daily publications, thereby relieving the media's concern about out-of-date reply requests;[110] (4) The reply is limited to factual information and clarifying statements and cannot contain illegal contents such as libelous or obscene expression, and the length of the reply cannot exceed that of the original story;[111] and (5) The pre-trial requirement for arbitration by the Press Arbitration Commission guarantees an opportunity for a voluntary resolution of the dispute between the parties.[112] The Court also maintained that the reputation or credibility of the news organization is not directly affected by the reply because the reply is published in the name of the injured party, not of the publisher.[113]

The Constitution Court disagreed with the petitioner that the right of reply provision would be a serious violation of the petitioner's right to a trial. Under the Periodicals Act, the media organizations cannot appeal for a stay of execution of a reply judgment. They may object to or appeal the judgment only in accordance with the Code of Civil Procedure.[114] The Court said the right of reply was adopted to provide the injured person with a "prompt recovery of the damaged right" in light of the mass media's powerful capacity for news dissemination. As a result, the Court continued, "the reply is granted once its specified requirements are met, without addressing complicated issues of substantive rights."[115] The Court contended that the underlying purpose of the right of reply was not the search for truth, but the protection of individual reputations and creating a balanced public opinion.[116]

The second Periodicals Act case of the Constitution Court[117] related to the registration provision that requires that periodicals, as defined by the statute, be registered with the Ministry of Public Information (MOPI) before they can be published.[118] The case resulted from the Seoul Criminal District Court's January 1990 request that the Constitution Court review the registration requirement. The parties challenging the Act were being prosecuted for publishing their weekly newspaper without having registered it with the MOPI.[119] In its request to the Constitution Court, the Seoul district court pointed out:

> [G]iven the development of today's printing industry and the varied access to expensive printing equipment through lease, the registration provision imposes excessively stiff registration conditions upon periodicals. These conditions include absolutely requiring that the periodicals possess expensive printing facilities, leaving no alternative means of printing whatsoever. There is a possibility that the provision at issue may be found to violate the essential aspect of freedom of the press. Further, it is possible that the registration system of the press will be in essence as restrictive as the constitutionally prohibited licensing system.[120]

The Constitution Court placed the constitutional issue in a broader perspective by discussing the "essential aspect of press freedom," especially as exercised by the news media. The Court stated that the press freedom clause of the Constitution "protects freedom of the press vigorously" and at the same time "imposes certain duties and responsibilities" on the press to the extent necessary to ensure the sound development of the media.[121] The Court declared that press freedom was "a fundamental right indispensable to the survival and development of a modern liberal democracy" and that "to guarantee the freedom to a maximum possible degree is one of the basic constitutional principles" of a liberal democracy.[122]

The Court acknowledged, however, that freedom of the press can be restricted to protect other constitutionally recognized interests only if its "essential aspect" is not violated.[123] The Constitution permits a statutory requirement that a publisher possess certain facilities. This requirement, according to the Court, was designed to provide an institutional safeguard for the wholesome growth of the press industry and to protect the work environment, welfare, and treatment of media employees as well as their editing and printing processes.[124]

Drawing a distinction between freedom of the press as "an internal essence" and freedom of the press as an institutional entity, the Court stated:

> By confusing the essential aspect of freedom of the press with publication of periodicals which is a means of news reporting, people are likely to claim constitutional rights for the press on the assumption that publication of periodicals is part of press freedom. Freedom of the press under the Constitution represents a guarantee of the contents of expression, which is the internal essence of freedom of the press. It does not necessarily encompass the concrete printing facilities that might be necessary for exercising freedom of the press nor the activities of media owners as businessmen.[125]

In other words, the Court held that news media organizations—as opposed to individuals enjoying their personal freedom of expression—can be regulated as business entities without violating the Constitution. As businesspeople, publishers cannot be exempt from the ordinary laws and regulations of society.

Therefore, "to statutorily require the publisher of a periodical to register with the government must be clearly differentiated from the interference with the essential aspect of freedom of the press."[126] The Court concluded that to censor or meddle in the contents of news reports would violate the internal essence of press freedom, while to impose these requirements on the actual publishing facilities to ensure the proper functioning of the media industry would not.[127] The Court thus ruled that the registration provision was constitutional because its purpose was to enable the MOPI to ensure the stable growth of the media industry, not to allow infringement on the contents of reports and editorials.[128]

In examining the ownership-of-printing-facilities requirement, the Constitution Court agreed with the Seoul district court that a strict interpretation of this requirement—that publishers had to possess their own printing facilities as a prerequisite to registration—would be found to violate the Constitution.[129] Justice Pyon Chong-su criticized the majority opinion for ignoring the similarity between the registration system and the constitutionally prohibited licensing of the news media.[130] He argued that the MOPI is allowed excessive discretion in accepting, rejecting, or delaying registration. Justice Pyon also claimed that the requirement that the MOPI should issue a registration of certificate "promptly" does not prevent the delay and rejection of registrations[131] because the requirement applies only to "when registered," not "when registration forms are submitted."[132] He further took issue with the Court's "constitutional on proper interpretation" approach to the ownership of facilities requirement. He stated that the requirement still discriminated in favor of the haves against the have-nots in their exercise of freedom of the press, thus violating the Constitution's requirement of equality before the law.[133]

On the same day that the Constitution Court decided on the registration requirement case, the Court delivered an opinion on the "delivery of copies" requirement of the Periodicals Act.[134] Article 10 of the Act requires the publishers of a registered periodical to deliver two copies to the MOPI "immediately" after publication.[135] Here the publisher of *Nodong Munhak* (Labor Literature) was fined by the MOPI for not delivering the requisite copies.[136] The publishers challenged the fine in a Seoul district court. The lower court rejected the petitioner's request for referral of the constitutional review of the delivery and fine provisions to the Constitution Court.[137] The district court ruled that the delivery of copies requirement was not a prior restraint on the press because copies were delivered *after* publication.[138]

The Constitution Court, defining the type of press censorship, said: "[The ban on] censorship of speech and the press means the prohibition of prior censorship where the authorities examine the contents of citizens' expressions and then approve or disapprove certain expressions *prior to* their public dissemination."[139] The delivery of copies to the MOPI, the Court ruled, would not constitute press censorship because the contents of the publication were unrelated to the grounds for permitting or banning its circulation.[140]

On the other hand, the Court cautioned that the MOPI would be abusing the delivery provision if its enforcement constituted de facto press censorship.[141] Censorship would result if the MOPI demanded the delivery of copies "before" or "simultaneously with" the circulation of the periodical or if the MOPI, mayor, or governor delayed in issuing certificates of delivery and then punished the periodical on the grounds that it was disseminated without these certificates.[142]

The Court further held that the delivery provision serves the public interest in ensuring the efficient enforcement of the Periodicals Act, which is designed to promote the improvement of the publishing industry.[143] The public benefit from the requirement would outweigh the limits on the publisher's property rights, the Court stated.

### Civil Code on Libel Cases

The Constitution Court in April 1991 ruled on the libel provisions of the Civil Code. Article 764 of the Civil Code authorizes Korean courts, upon the application of the injured party, to order the defaming party "to take suitable measures to restore the injured party's reputation, either in lieu of or together with compensation for damages."[144] The courts have recognized several "suitable" measures for restoring the reputation of the injured party, such as publication of a notice of apology.[145]

The Constitution Court's review of the apology-for-libel requirement[146] started with a libel case in which the plaintiff sued Dong-A Ilbosa, the publisher of the *Dong-A Ilbo* newspaper, for damages and demanded an apology for a story about the plaintiff.[147] Dong-A Ilbosa asked a Seoul district court, prior to ruling on the case, to petition the Constitution Court to review the Civil Code.[148] The publisher claimed that the statutory apology requirement violated the Constitution because it infringed on the newspaper's freedom of conscience[149] and freedom of the press as well.

The Seoul district court rejected the argument, saying that the compulsory apology requirement for defamation would not constitute an "unbearably humiliating psychological violation of moral judgments and freedom of conscience."[150] The court further stated that the Civil Code provision did not contradict the constitutional limitation on freedom of the press because "freedom of the press does not include the right of the news media to publish false information."[151]

The Constitution Court unanimously ruled, however, that the Civil Code was unconstitutional insofar as it required the publication of a notice of apology. In a carefully reasoned opinion, the Court struck down the "unlawful act" provision of the Code as a violation of freedom of conscience and stated that the provision failed to qualify as a restriction of freedoms for public welfare.[152]

The Constitution Court emphasized that the constitutional guarantee of freedom of conscience is separate from that of freedom of religion. The Court interpreted this separate recognition of freedom of conscience as an unambiguous indication that the Constitution prevents the government from interfering with individual value judgments.[153] The Court also stated that freedom of conscience includes both the right not to be forced by the government to express oneself publicly and the right to remain silent on moral judgments.[154] The Court added that "the [freedom of conscience] provision is designed to secure a more complete freedom of spiritual activities as the moral foundation of democracy, which has been indispensable to the progress and development of humankind."[155]

The Constitution Court argued that a compulsory apology forces one to accept a guilt for libel against one's will. The apology violates an individual's freedom of conscience, which includes one's right of silence.[156] The Court observed: "A notice of apology is a person's compulsory expression of mind to the public through the mass media such as newspapers, magazines, etc. It violates the person's freedom of conscience. Although the contents of the apology are specifically dictated by the authorities in the course of judicial proceedings, the public apparently takes them as the person's voluntary expression."[157] Thus, the Court said, the apology requirement undermines the right of individual conscience that underlies the concepts of human dignity and value.[158]

Second, the Constitution Court expressed strong reservations concerning the appropriateness of apology as a means to make good on reputational harm. The Court viewed apologies as an excessive recompense to a plaintiff for that individual's lost good name. Given that an apology is forcibly imposed by the State upon a media organization that may have no desire to apologize and that still believes in the propriety of its report, the apology is similar to "eye for an eye" justice.[159] The Court characterized this strain of retribution justice in libel law as anachronistic and primitive and thus incompatible with the humanitarianism that should be protected in a civilized society.[160] It stated that the forced apology for libel is a punitive sanction derived from ancient law that valued the satisfaction of vendettas.[161] Accordingly, the apology sanction should be limited to criminal law.[162]

Examining the impact of apologies upon the Civil Code, the Court asserted that an "apology is used as a principal means of recovery for libel while it makes damage awards a supplementary decoration of the Civil Code."[163] Consequently, the damage award tends to be so small, the Court said, that the apology measure proves an impediment to the constitutional requirement of just compensation for an injury to one's reputation.[164]

Finally, the Constitution Court addressed the question of whether or not a judicially ordered notice of apology is necessary to promote public welfare. Analyzing the issue from a comparative perspective, the Court said that apology is recognized only in Japan, where arguments against its constitutionality have been "vigorously" raised.[165] The Court noted that the libel laws of several Western countries, including the United States,[166] set forth three alternatives to public apologies under the Civil Code: "(1) publication in newspapers, magazines, etc., of the court opinions on damages in civil libel cases at the expense of the defendant;

(2) publication in newspapers, magazines, etc., of the court opinions against the defendant in criminal libel cases; (3) a notice of retraction of defamatory stories."[167] The Court argued that unlike the compulsory apology requirement for libel under the Korean Civil Code, judicial imposition of these measures would not raise constitutional issues of freedom of conscience or the right of personality.[168]

## IMPACT OF JUDICIAL REVIEW

A Korean constitutional law scholar noted in 1990: "Though it is too early to evaluate the current system, the Constitutional [sic] Court is, so far, the most active body in Korean history of the judicial review system. The Constitutional [sic] Court has shown its readiness to acknowledge the unconstitutionality of legislations and government acts more willingly than any other previous bodies for judicial review."[169]

In a similar vein, the Korean government stated in its human rights report to the United Nations: "[T]he Constitution Court has been performing an important and effective role in checking the abusive acts of the Government, securing the independence of the Judiciary and protecting fundamental rights."[170] Notwithstanding these and other "sanguine" comments on the Constitution Court, however, some experts on Korean law insist that judicial independence in Korea is not adequate when measured against libertarian standards.[171] This is particularly true of the Constitution Court's review of the National Security Act and subsequent amendments to the Act.

The government revised the National Security Act of 1980 in May 1991 in an effort to comply with the Constitution Court's 1990 decision.[172] The revision was not, however, as comprehensive as some human rights groups[173] or the news media in and outside Korea had wished. For example, the *New York Times* argued: "The National Security Law is a vestige of the Korean War and successive dictatorships. Its provisions, though liberalized slightly last year, severely restrict contact with North Korea. And they allow the Government to jail critics they charge with helping the Communist North."[174]

The Constitution Court's decision on the registration provision of the Periodicals Act also carries important long-term implications for the Korean press. The Court's analysis of the "essential aspect" of press freedom will prompt the Supreme Court and lower courts to set a more predictable "definitional balancing" rule[175] to protect free-speech interests.[176] The Court identifies the essence of press freedom with the Blackstonian concept of freedom from prior restraint. In this context, the Court rejects government regulations with respect to the content of the communication. Just as in U.S. First Amendment jurisprudence, content neutrality is now viewed by the Constitution Court as indispensable to the viability of the Korean press as an institution.[177] The notorious pre-1987 "press guidelines" issued by the government to control the style and substance of stories now probably would not withstand the Court's heavy presumption of the unconstitutionality of such content restriction.

By contrast, the Constitution Court concluded that the registration requirements of the Periodicals Act are no more than an administrative mechanism for the Act's efficient operation. The Court's ruling arguably is consistent with its other holdings in that registration of periodicals is not a violation of what the Court considers to be the "essential" aspect of press freedom. As Justice Pyon Chong-su strenuously argued, however, the Court failed to acknowledge the chilling effect of the ambiguity inherent in the registration process. While the Periodicals Act provides that the MOPI "promptly" issue a certificate of registration so long as the minimum registration requirements are met, there is still a possibility that the MOPI may arbitrarily delay processing a registration request.

The Constitution Court's explicit holding against literal interpretation of the facilities requirement of the Periodicals Act will expand the publishing opportunities of many Koreans, who cannot afford to possess their own printing facilities. Undoubtedly, the Court's ruling was a realistic and sensitive response to the criticism that "conditioning approval of a registration upon ownership of costly printing facilities deprives a number of financially weak publishers of the opportunity to exercise press freedom."[178] In compliance with the Court's decision, the Korean government revised the enforcement decree of the Periodicals Act in December 1992.[179] The new decree requires that the MOPI issue certificates of registration to daily and weekly newspapers so long as the papers have leased printing and typesetting facilities.[180]

The Court's notice-of-apology ruling on the Civil Code is potentially significant for the press in connection with the Court's right-of-reply decision on the Periodicals Act. Interestingly enough, freedom of conscience as guaranteed by the Constitution was a primary rationale for the Court's decision to annul the apology provision for libel. Since freedom of conscience resembles the "essential aspect" of press freedom, the Court's resort to conscience is not a surprise. The forced apology, as dictated by government (in this case the court), is an unacceptable variation of official restraint on publishing and strikes at the *internal* freedom of the press.

Publication of court opinions in libel complaints and retraction of libelous stories have already been adopted by Korean courts as alternatives to compelled apologies in defamation rulings. In December 1992, for example, the Seoul Civil District Court ordered a newspaper defendant to publish a notice on the court's decision for the plaintiff in a libel suit.[181] This libel case arose from a story published in *Chugan Chosun* (Chosun Weekly) in October 1991. The story asserted that the plaintiff, then a noted National Assemblyman with a reputation as a lawyer of high integrity and as spokesman for laborers and peasants, was making money unethically and illegally.[182] The court ruled that while the story was published in the public interest, it was not substantially true.[183]

The Korean courts' decisions subsequent to the Constitution Court's invalidation of the apology requirement epitomize a judicial balancing of press freedom with other competing interests, as defined by the Constitution Court.

## SUMMARY AND CONCLUSIONS

The postwar political history of South Korea was a trial-and-error process that finally led to a constitutional democracy in late 1987. Although the rule of law was consistently touted as the underlying principle of the checks-and-balances system of government, it was often nothing more than empty rhetoric. The separation of powers failed to function in reality.

The sweeping sociopolitical and legal reforms in the late 1980s, however, have transformed Korea into a more liberal body politic. Prominent among the reforms were the enhancement of judicial independence and the more systematic protection of human rights under the Constitution of 1987.

The increasingly independent Constitution Court epitomizes an institutional approach by the Korean government toward implementing "human rights constitutionalism." The petition jurisdiction of the Court, unprecedented in the constitutional history of Korea, allows Koreans to turn *directly* to the Court to challenge the constitutionality of government violations of freedom of speech and the press.

The case law of the Constitution Court to date has shaped the important contours of freedom of speech and the press in Korea. First, the "gravity of the evil" test is used to apply the National Security Act. Second, access to public information is a constitutional right as part of freedom of expression. Third, censorship of speech and the press is a constitutional violation of the "essential aspect" of the speech and press freedom. Fourth, the statutory requirement on periodical registration with government is not a violation of press freedom on grounds that it relates to the administrative enforcement of the Periodicals Act, not to the content. And finally, to force a media organization to apologize for libel is a violation of freedom of conscience, but the right of reply under the Periodicals Act is constitutional.

The Constitution Court's forceful posture thus far has wrought notable changes. The National Assembly has revised the National Security Act in the wake of the Court's limited validation of the Act. The Military Secrets Protection Act was also revised in 1993 to rectify the constitutional problems with its application. Further, the Periodicals Act is no longer enforced against potential publishers who do not possess their own printing facilities at the time of their registration.

Judicial review is emerging as one of the most important institutions in a democratic Korea. Indeed, the relationship between judicial independence and the emergence of a free press in Korea since 1988 has been "synergistic."[184] As constitutional law scholar Pnina Lahav has stated, "[T]he judicial awareness of the liberal justifications of a free press and the acceptability of those justifications as part of the legal argument may depend on and be encouraged by the formal constitutional commitment to press freedom."[185]

# CHAPTER 6

# Periodicals and Broadcast Acts

David Halvorsen, an astute Korean-press observer, stated in 1992: "After four years of press freedom, the [Korean] media have gained extraordinary influence in government and with the public. Within the ranks, the issues of responsibility, ethics, balanced reporting, and development of a modern newsroom culture are all experiencing [U.S. Ambassador to Korea Donald P.] Gregg's jack-in-the-box effect."[1] The liberalization of Korean press laws is but one aspect of the overall positive development of the political rights and civil liberties of Koreans since 1987,[2] an opening which has contributed to the evolution of what was traditionally a "partly" free Republic into what is becoming a truly free country.[3]

Roh Tae Woo's proposed reform in the institutional control of the Korean press was implemented by the Korean National Assembly in late 1987.[4] The Korean legislature repealed the Basic Press Act in November 1987, replacing it with two separate laws, the Act Relating to Registration of Periodicals (Periodicals Act)[5] and the Broadcast Act.[6]

In contrast to the Basic Press Act, which was an amalgamation of several press-related laws then on the books,[7] the current press legislation consists of two principal parts that are aimed at the print media and the broadcast media separately. Thus, the structural change in the press laws marks a return to the pre-Basic Press Act era (1963–1979), when the print media and the broadcast media were regulated by different statutes.

These press statutes are viewed as "one of the most meaningful" changes in Korean press policy in recent years.[8] One American specialist in Korean press freedom has characterized the statutory changes as "a legislative improvement—a step forward in the right direction to making the [Korean] government less authoritarian than ever."[9] Some commentators have argued, however, that the laws still tend to be more restrictive than protective of the Korean press.[10] Won-Soon Paeng, an authority on Korean press law, asserts that the new laws bear a similarity to the

Basic Press Act in their restrictions on the press:[11] "Generally speaking, the Act on Registration of Periodicals and the Broadcast Act, which were enacted to supersede the Basic Press Act, both fall far short of our expectations in terms of their essence and are a great disappointment to us.... It is our opinion that the press laws should be enacted afresh after a sufficient study and deliberation by the lawmakers."[12] In a similar vein, a Korean newspaper editorial writer contends that though the Basic Press Act has now been abolished, its "poison provisions" remain scattered among the two new laws.[13]

Essentially the new Korean press laws do to a certain extent illustrate a trend toward, though not a wholesale adoption of, more freedom for the press. In comparison with the now repealed Basic Press Act, the Periodicals Act and the Broadcast Act tend to be less restrictive because they have fewer repressive provisions and more protective procedures for the press. In spite of several positive improvements in the new press laws, however, the laws cannot be said to be truly "libertarian,"[14] for the new print media statute is identical to the old press law in its stifling registration provisions, among other things. Without question, the new law does not permit the Ministry of Public Information (MOPI), formerly the Ministry of Information and Culture (MOCI),[15] as much discretionary power as the old law; still, the MOPI can suspend periodicals for three to six months for violation of any of the statutory requirements.

## PERIODICALS ACT

The objective of the Periodicals Act is noteworthy in representing a subtle but important shift in the notion of press freedom in Korea. Whereas the Basic Press Act focused on the press as an instrument for forming public opinion as defined by the government,[16] the new law is aimed primarily at "striv[ing] for a sound development of the press."[17] Given that the "public responsibility" provision epitomized the regulatory underpinnings of the old law,[18] its deletion from the new law is a notable change.[19] The new law contains no provision for public responsibility of the press.[20] Further, the proscription against the press encouraging or praising illegal acts under the Basic Press Act[21] was not repeated in the Periodicals Act. These omissions suggest that the Korean government is attempting to reverse its authoritarian control of the Korean press.

However, the omission of several libertarian provisions of the Basic Press Act from the new law is inconsistent with the stated purpose of the Periodicals Act. Some of these were purported to promote press freedom, e.g., the right of access to governmental information[22] and the right to protect news sources.[23] Nevertheless, largely because of their numerous vague and overbroad exemptions, neither the informational access provision nor the news source protection clause provided practical value for the press.[24] The right of the press to request information on "matters of public interest," as stipulated by the Basic Press Act, was denied if and

when the furnishing of the requested information had any of the following characteristics:

1. It frustrates or endangers the reasonable performance of one's official duty in progress;
2. It violates the statutory provisions concerning the protection of
   secrets;[25]
3. It clearly infringes upon a greater public interest or a private interest
   that deserves protection.[26]

Pointing out that the exemptions to the the right to obtain information might
"give very wide discretionary powers to government officials to refuse to release
information," a Korean legal scholar suggested that the provision was intended to
withhold information rather than disclose it.[27] The fundamental weakness of the
provision was that it recognized a right to access for the press but denied that right
to the general public. Furthermore, the provision contained few clear-cut procedural
guidelines that the government and the press should follow in applying the provision.[28] Likewise, the exemptions seriously undermined the provision of the Basic
Press Act on protection of news sources.[29] As a result, these purported protections
failed to serve their purpose of ensuring an "open government" by promoting the
people's right to be informed about their government.[30]

As Professor Paeng observed, however, the whole deletion of the informational right and the journalist's right to confidentiality from the new law was "a
matter of great regret."[31] Rather, the libertarian notions of press rights should have
been strengthened under the Periodicals Act in such a way as to make them more
effective by revising the restrictive exemptions of the Basic Press Act.

The Periodicals Act regulates more broadly than did the Basic Press Act in
that the definition of "periodical" now includes publications not within the scope
of the previous law. Any periodical that is published continuously under the same
title more than once a year is regulated by the new periodicals act,[32] whereas under
the Basic Press Act, only those periodicals published "twice or more a year" under
the same title were subject to various statutory requirements.[33] Thus, annual
periodicals were not regulated by the old law, but the new law applies to virtually
all kinds of regular periodicals so far as they are published at least more than once
a year.

In contrast to the Basic Press Act, the new print media law places no limitation
upon the qualification of a journalist. This is an improvement from the Basic Press
Act, which defined a journalist as an employee of a mass media enterprise who was
"professionally" engaged in journalistic activities.[34]

On the other hand, the Periodicals Act is more restrictive than the Basic Press
Act in its provisions governing who is not qualified to be a publisher or editor of a
periodical. The provisions, some of which have been newly added to Article 17 of
the Basic Press Act, prohibit anyone subject to punishment under certain specified
laws, in addition to the Criminal Code, from being eligible for the positions of

publisher or editor of a periodical.[35] As under the previous law, anyone who is not a citizen and resident in Korea is not allowed to publish or edit a periodical under the new law.[36]

Similar to its predecessor,[37] the periodicals statute is designed to ensure as much diversity as possible in the media market.[38] It forbids any person to operate a daily newspaper and a communication or broadcast station concurrently.[39] The new act also prohibits multiple ownership of media properties, whether print, communication, or broadcasting.[40] Further, the new law, as did the Basic Press Act, prohibits certain "large enterprises" from acquiring more than one-half of the outstanding stock issued by a juristic person operating a daily newspaper or communication.[41] The current print media law parallels the Basic Press Act in providing that no media enterprise shall receive financial contributions from foreign sources, except as otherwise provided for by statute.[42] The exemptions involve government-approved contributions from foreign organizations intended to promote education, physical training, religion, charity, or international friendship.[43]

The current Korean press law retains the controversial registration provision of the Basic Press Act. Accordingly, periodicals, as defined by the statute, must be registered with the MOPI before they can be published.[44] Among the registration requirements are identification of the publisher, editor, and printer of the periodical; disclosure of its purpose and contents; the means of dissemination; and the principal objects and areas of publication.[45]

The current press law, however, is more explicit than the old one in specifying the registration process. For example, the new law provides that the MOPI shall "promptly" issue a certificate of registration so long as the minimum registration requirements are met.[46] As a result, the possibility that the MOPI may arbitrarily delay processing the registrations has been diminished considerably. Nevertheless, the length of the processing period is not as specific as it should be to ensure procedural fairness for the Korean press. A case in point is the *Han-kyoreh Shinmun* (One-Nation Newspaper) whose registration took the MOPI three months to process.[47] This center-left daily, founded in late 1987 by a group of previously banned journalists, claimed that the lengthy delay was a "runaround" on the part of the government.[48] On the other hand, the registration provision mandates that any person who has been issued a certificate of registration must publish the registered periodical "within six months (one year in the case of annual and semiannual publication) after it is registered."[49]

The new press act does not allow the MOPI to rescind registration of a periodical by administrative fiat. In the event that the MOPI decides to close a periodical by revoking its registration, it must first obtain a court order enforcing its decision.[50] As a practical matter, this check on executive power is a liberalizing feature of the current press law. The Basic Press Act allowed the former MOCI to close any periodical allegedly violating the law without judicial scrutiny.[51] Equally important is the reduction in the number of grounds for cancellation of a periodical's registration. Although the Basic Press Act allowed the MOCI as many as seven conditions for using its canceling authority,[52] the new law provides for only two: one relating to registration "by deceit or other unlawful means"[53] and the other concerning the publishing of articles which fail "repeatedly and flagrantly" in their purported objectives and contents.[54]

The MOPI can still suspend publication of a periodical for varying periods of time; if it finds that a periodical has violated either of the above two conditions, it can suspend the periodical for up to six months.[55] The press law further authorizes the MOPI to suspend publication for not more than three months if the publisher violates any of the following five grounds: a change in registered matters without governmental approval, disqualification of a publisher or editor, failure to maintain printing facilities, failure to meet any other statutory obligation for publication, or acceptance of financial support from foreign sources.[56] These five grounds, together with the two conditions relating to cancellation of registration of a periodical, constitute the seven previous grounds for suspension in the Basic Press Act. At its heart, then, only the length of suspension is shortened, from a maximum of one year to a period of three to six months. The Korean government still possesses the statutory power to restrict freedom of the press through suspension.[57] Consequently, prior restraint upon the Korean press may be invoked statutorily, contradicting the constitutional provision against violation of the "essential aspect" of the freedoms of Korean people.[58]

In this regard, the *Silchon Munhak* (Practicing Literature) and *Changjak Kwa Pipyong* (Creation and Criticism) episodes are illuminating. The MOCI closed the two critical opinion magazines in 1985. The Korean government charged that *Silchon Munhak*, a quarterly magazine, violated Article 24 (1)-4 of the old press law for carrying articles on sociopolitical issues instead of literature and art as specified at the time of its registration.[59] *Changjak Kwa Pipyong* had its registration revoked[60] because it had allegedly violated Article 24 (1)-2 of the Basic Press Act[61] by specifying its frequency of publication as quarterly, contrary to its registered status as a "non-regular" periodical.[62] The measures of the MOCI against the two magazines considerably confirms the lingering concern of the Korean press about the restrictive power of the MOPI under the Periodicals Act.[63]

The new press law, identical to the Basic Press Act, requires that the publisher of a daily or general weekly newspaper own certain minimum facilities.[64] For example, publishers of Korean-language daily newspapers of general interest must be equipped with rotary presses capable of printing at least 20,000 copies per hour of a minimum four-page tabloid as well as annexed printing facilities as prescribed by the presidential decree.[65]

The facilities requirement, according to its proponents,[66] helps to prevent the Korean press from following the self-destructive path of the mushrooming media in the early 1960s. Indeed, the facilities requirement provision has its genesis in a 1961 decree of the military junta under General Park Chung Hee, enforced to deal with the chaos stemming from the *laissez faire* press policy of the Second Republic (1960–1961).[67] Under that decree, publishing newspapers was permitted only by those with complete printing facilities for the production of newspapers. Similarly, news services were required to have complete wire service facilities for transmission and reception.[68]

Critics point out the restrictive impact of the facilities requirement upon freedom of the Korean press. They argue that by conditioning approval of registrations upon whether a prospective publisher owns the necessary and often costly printing facilities, the law deprives a number of financially weak publishers of their publication opportunities.[69]

The current press law provides for regulation of branch offices of foreign periodicals. The statutory procedure governing the establishment of a branch office of a domestic periodical provides that the person in charge of the registered periodical should "promptly report" to the MOPI.[70] By contrast, any person who wishes to open a branch office of a foreign periodical in Korea is required to obtain "permission" from the MOPI.[71] The MOPI is empowered to cancel this permission for foreign periodicals under certain statutory conditions.[72] One of these conditions is that the foreign periodical not carry news which might "disturb the national Constitution or injure the prestige of the State."[73] This discriminatory regulation of foreign periodicals obviously borrows from the now abolished restrictive provision of the Criminal Code that forbade defamation of the State and its constitutional bodies by Koreans through foreign media.[74] It is noteworthy, however, that the new law does not contain the Basic Press Act provision that stipulated that a branch office of a foreign periodical could be closed when it "disrupts the domestic press."[75] As the law stands, however, the branch office of a foreign periodical is less protected from governmental closure than that of a domestic periodical.

The press law also retains Basic Press Act provisions that recognize the right of individuals who have suffered injury from a published news story to request a correction of the story by way of a "right of reply."[76] The law stipulates: "One who has suffered damage from a factual assertion published by a periodical … may request in writing to the publisher or editor for printing a correction of the reported assertion within 14 days after it is published in a daily newspaper or communication and within one month in the case of other periodicals."[77]

Although it refers to a request, the statute entitles anyone who has been damaged by the print media to recover for his injury through his own reply to the damaging article so long as the published information relates to assertions of facts, not expression of opinion or criticism.[78] The Korean Supreme Court, adopting the German "right of reply" approach in toto, defined the claim for corrected reports thus:

> Contrary to its title [Claim for Correction of Reports] and words, Article 49 of the Basic Press Act provides for a right to request publication of a reply to the reports, not to demand correction of news reports published in periodicals or broadcasts in conformity with their truth. Thus, it is not a prerequisite to the exercising of the right to determine whether the news reports subject to claim for correction should be false. (In this respect, the title, i.e., right to claim for

correction of reports, is not an accurate expression. It should have been named
a claim for a right of reply.)

The significance of this provision ... consists not in requesting correction of the complained-of stories after examining their truth or falsity but in
claiming publication of the allegedly injured party's reply to the stories.[79]

With respect to the procedure for correcting reports, the new press law differs
somewhat from its predecessor. The current law provides that daily newspapers or
weekly periodicals or communications should publish a requested correction not
later than nine days after receiving the request for a correction.[80] The correction
provision does not apply to reports related to the open meetings of the central or
local governments, public organizations, or the public trial proceedings of the
courts,[81] as did the Basic Press Act.

The new press law, like the old, establishes "a press arbitration commission
to deal with claims for correction of disputed factual reports."[82] The commission is
authorized to arbitrate disputes involving requests for corrections and complaints
relating to press infringements of individuals' rights.[83] When arbitration fails to
resolve the dispute, a claim for correction of a challenged report may be taken to a
three-judge district court. However, preliminary action by the arbitration commission is a prerequisite to the judicial decision on the claim.[84] One difference between
the Periodicals Act and the Basic Press Act is that while the new law does not
recognize "preferences" for lawsuits arising from the press activities, the old statute
did.[85]

One significant distinction between the new press law and the Basic Press
Act concerns the claim for a follow-up story to previous reports. While the old law
did not provide for the claim, the new law states: "Any person, who is reported by
a periodical to be under suspicion of a crime or to have been subject to a penal
action, may, when a penal procedure against him is terminated in other than a
conviction, request in writing to the publisher or editor an insertion of an *ex post
facto* report on such facts within one month from the day of termination."[86] This
newly recognized right to the "insertion" of stories subsequent to the termination
of a news event previously mentioned by the news media obviously expands
protection of an individual's reputation at the expense of editorial freedom.[87]

The print media law provides for the punishment of those who violate its
provisions through penal servitude or fine.[88] The statute authorizes imprisonment
for not more than one year or a fine not exceeding 5 million *won* (US$6,250) for
publishing without a governmental certificate of registration, disobeying the
MOPI's suspension of publication,[89] or establishing a foreign publication's branch
office without prior permission from the government.[90] For those who violate the
"disqualification" provisions of the law, a fine of no more than 1 million *won*
(US$1,250) may be imposed by the MOPI.[91] An equivalent fine is authorized for
those who fail to publish a registered periodical within a prescribed period of time[92]
or who fail to report the establishment of a branch office of a domestic periodical.[93]

The new press law differs from its predecessor in its penal servitude provisions for given violations in that the maximum jail term under the new law has been reduced from two years to one, while the fine has been raised from 3 million *won* (US$3,750) to 5 million *won* (US$6,250).[94] Another difference in the two schemes is the deletion of the "concurrent penalties" provision of the Basic Press Act from the new press act. Under its concurrent penalties provision, the Basic Press Act required that when either the representative of a corporate body or its employee committed a statutorily proscribed act, not only the actual violator but also the corporate body or the original actor represented by the violator be punished in accordance with the penal provisions.[95]

## BROADCAST ACT

The primary concern of lawmakers in enacting the new broadcasting law in 1987 was "whether the law guarantees the independence of broadcasting, ensures more diverse programs and a wider participation by the public, and provides the necessary safeguards [to] ensure impartiality."[96] To a certain extent, the Broadcast Act represents progress toward the more autonomous operation of broadcast media. Nevertheless, the Act still fails to serve as a workable framework for safeguarding the media from various forms of political interference.

The purpose of the Broadcast Act is similar to that of the Basic Press Act, except that the "improvement of national culture" is an additional objective of broadcasting.[97] With respect to freedom of broadcast programming, the new law is more explicit than the old in its guarantee of freedom.[98] It parallels the old law in prohibiting outside interference with broadcasting except as authorized by statute.[99] An exhortatory section of the new act enumerates protected broadcast freedoms. The "public responsibility" provisions of the Basic Press Act[100] are retained verbatim in the Broadcast Act. The statute requires that broadcasters respect the dignity of human beings and the democratic fundamental law and order and that they contribute to the democratic formation of public opinion on matters of public concern. The statute prohibits broadcasters from infringing on the reputational interests of individuals or undermining public morality or social ethics.[101] The public-responsibility requirement is in marked contrast to the new periodicals law, which has no such requirements. One explanation for the contrast is that the Korean government views the objectives of the broadcast media in Korean society in the context of the "public function" of broadcasting. The public-responsibility-for-broadcasters provision stipulates that broadcasting should be impartial and objective in news programs, should respect the sentiments and rights of individuals, and should not promote the interests of a particular organization, whether political, social, or religious.[102]

The Broadcast Act provides for the establishment of the Broadcasting Commission as a governing agency of the broadcasting industry. First established under the Basic Press Act,[103] its mission is to ensure "public responsibility, impartiality, and publicness" of broadcasts.[104] The Commission is composed of 12 commissioners appointed for a term of three years[105] by the President.[106] Eight of these commissioners are evenly appointed from among those recommended by the Speaker of the National Assembly and by the Chief Justice of the Supreme Court.[107] The appointment of the commissioners by the President undermines the independence of the Commission. Concern about political influence upon the Commission derives from the fact that the President has discretion to limit commission appointments to his political supporters.[108] In light of the recent restructuring of the Korean government,[109] however, the independence of the Commission may be ensured to a greater extent than in the past. One communications scholar has observed: "A very important difference, one that does not show up in reorganization legislation, between the initial KBC [Korean Broadcasting Commission] and the present one is that the composition of the National Assembly has changed. Because the opposition party now carries more weight in the Assembly, commissioners represent a greater diversity of views than was the case in the past when commissioners normally supported the administration."[110]

The Broadcasting Commission supervises the operation of broadcasting stations by determining basic broadcasting policies[111] and approves or disapproves of the contents of broadcast programming.[112] For example, the Commission has the authority to ensure that certain programs of a broadcasting station may comply with the "public responsibility" requirements of the Act.[113] In meeting its responsibilities, the Commission may establish a "deliberative" committee to assist in its process of reviewing broadcast programs. The membership structure of the deliberative committee under the new law is not as specific as that of the Basic Press Act. The law states only that "[m]embers of the ... committee shall be commissioned by the chairman in the limit of 30 persons."[114] The committee can deliberate various issues arising from the contents of broadcasting programs. Among the issues are whether programming is impartial, promotes free democracy, cultivates national identity, develops national culture, provides proper guidance for children, relates to the purity of family life, or promotes public morality and social ethics.[115]

Under the Broadcast Act, the Broadcasting Commission may employ sanctions to ensure that broadcasting stations observe the statute's requirements. For example, should a station violate the rules, the Commission may order the station to apologize for, correct, clarify, or cancel its violating programs, or it may impose a performance suspension or disciplinary action upon those violators for a period of less than one year.[116] Further, upon receiving the Commission's order, the broadcasting station must broadcast "without delay" the full text of the issues deliberated by the Commission and carry out the order within seven days after receiving the order.[117] In contrast with the Basic Press Act, however, the current broadcasting law provides that alleged violators of the law be given an opportunity to state their opinions about the Commission's order "except in a case where the person concerned or his representative fails to comply with [the current law] without any justifiable reason."[118] While under the Basic Press Act, the MOCI was primarily responsible for enforcing the order of the Commission against a violating station, the new law explicitly empowers the Commission to execute its order.[119] Consequently, the current broadcasting act provides more autonomy for the Commission in exercising its statutory powers over the broadcasting media.

The Broadcast Act is substantially similar to the Basic Press Act in its provisions for operation of broadcasting stations, prohibition of concurrent operation by broadcasting corporations, and proscription against inflow of foreign capital into operation of broadcasting media.[120] The new broadcasting law also lists individuals who are disqualified from being the "head or person in charge of programming" of a broadcasting station.[121]

Unlike the old law, however, the current Broadcast Act requires the payment of television reception fees under the authority of the Broadcasting Commission.[122] The Act also requires that each broadcasting station establish a broadcasting audience committee to provide advice on its broadcasting programs.[123] The new law, compared with the old law, requires the broadcasting station specifically to follow the audience committee's advice about a demand for correction of a program "unless there is any special reason" for rejecting it.[124] The provisions of the Broadcast Act for overseas, educational, and commercial broadcasts are identical to those of the Basic Press Act.[125]

The Broadcast Act deals with establishment of a branch office or station of a foreign broadcasting station in Korea in a manner similar to the Periodicals Act. The MOPI's permission is required of anyone who wishes to establish a branch office or station of a foreign broadcasting station in Korea.[126] The MOPI can cancel the permission on grounds identical to those applicable to the foreign print media in Korea.[127]

The Broadcast Act also recognizes the request by an individual for "right-of-reply" correction of "factual" allegations about him.[128] Like the current print media law, the Act also provides for the claim for publication of stories following on previous news reports about a complaining party.[129] The penal provisions of the current broadcasting statute are different from those of its predecessor so far as the jail terms and the amount of fines are concerned. For example, punishment of up to one year or a fine not exceeding 20 million *won* (US$25,000) will be imposed on:

1. A person who regulates or interferes with the drawing up or making of a broadcasting program ... or the operation of the broadcasting station;
2. A person who violates the provisions of Article 6 (1) or (2) or any order issued under Paragraph (4) of the said Article [operation of broadcasting station];
3. A person who violates the provisions of Article 7 [prohibition of concurrent operation by broadcasting corporation of newspapers];

4. The head of a broadcasting station who receives a contribution of property in contravention of the provisions of Article 8 [prohibition of inflow of foreign capital];
5. A person who violates an order issued under Article 21 (1) [correctional and disciplinary measures];
6. A person who has established a branch office or station of a foreign broadcasting station in the country without obtaining permission under Article 40 (1) [establishment of domestic branch of foreign broadcasting station].[130]

Moreover, a fine of not more than 3 million *won* (US$3,750) can be levied upon those who are statutorily disqualified but take charge of a broadcasting station or of broadcast programming, or upon those who engage in an overseas broadcast without the MOPI's approval, among other acts.[131]

## DISCUSSION AND ANALYSIS

In comparison with the now abolished Basic Press Act, the Periodicals Act is an improvement in one way or another. For example, the new press law tends to be aware of freedom of the press as a fundamental right of Koreans. This is particularly evident in the fact that the law no longer imposes the restrictive notion of "public responsibility" upon the Korean press. No less important is the explicit recognition by the law of judicial check on the MOPI's exercise of its authority to revoke registration of a periodical. Korean courts are expected to protect their press from possible arbitrary termination by the MOPI in view of their growing independence from the executive branch since late 1987.

In spite of the so-called "major reform" in the Periodicals Act,[132] however, the MOPI's power to suspend periodicals for a prescribed period of time may serve as an extraordinary weapon against the press. Indeed, the statutory power should be too reminiscent of the Basic Press Act to effect any meaningful liberalization of Korean press law.[133] Further, the registration provision of the Periodicals Act can be utilized by the Korean government to deny potentially critical publishers of their right of publication.[134] Although several fringe periodicals have thus far claimed to have their applications for registration denied by the MOPI,[135] however, the provision has not yet proved a serious impediment to the rapidly expanding Korean press during these past seven years. The MOPI's attitude to the registration requirement has been remarkably permissive, as clearly evidenced by the explosive growth of the Korean mass media since mid-1987.[136]

The two libertarian features of the Basic Press Act, i.e., journalist's privilege to confidential sources and news media's right to access to information, are notably omitted from the Periodicals Act. Given the reform politics initiated by the Korean government in 1987, they should have been retained for the Korean press after they were substantially revised to make them useful tools for journalistic activities.

Similar to its predecessor, the Periodicals Act recognizes the right of reply to "factual" stories as a remedy to reputational injury. It is noteworthy, however, that the new law requires that the Korean press should publish "*ex post facto* stories" for criminal suspects who were not convicted once the media had published stories about the suspects. This requirement to a large extent interferes with the editorial rights of the Korean press while skewing the balance in favor of those allegedly injured by the initial stories.

All things considered, the Periodicals Act, while representing a step forward in the right direction for freedom of the Korean press in a new era of open politics, is in need of further revision to make it more compatible with the increasingly libertarian body politic of Korea.

As compared with the Basic Press Act, the Broadcast Act is less restrictive from the perspective of governmental interference. Although it still emphasizes the "public responsibility" of the broadcasting media, it guarantees more autonomy to the Broadcasting Commission by strengthening its rights. Under the new law, the MOPI is no longer allowed to supervise the broadcasting stations in Korea. Instead, the Commission is primarily responsible for making *and* enforcing its decisions on the operation of the broadcasting media.

Nevertheless, the Broadcast Act still tends to be more regulatory than deregulatory, especially when it is examined in the context of the Korean government's liberalizing posture since June 1987. One illustration is the prior restraint clause of the Act Relating to the Broadcasting Commission. Though it may be justified in view of the "public mission" concept of broadcasting as stipulated by the law, it obviously violates the explicit constitutional provision prohibiting censorship of the press.

Notwithstanding some positive change in the status and structure of the Broadcasting Commission under the new law, it is still debatable to what extent the autonomy of the Commission has become part of its actual operation as a governing body for the broadcasting media. This is closely related to the composition of the Commission, which makes it structurally vulnerable to outside political influences. There is no institutional procedure for the substantive involvement of the legislature and the judiciary except for recommendations by those two branches.

The "Deliberative Rules"[137] and their application by the Broadcasting Deliberation Committee might also curtail freedom of broadcasting in that some of the rules apply to various vaguely defined subjects. Equally important to Korean broadcasters is the unqualified power of the Broadcasting Commission to impose sanctions upon the violators of these vague and overbroad deliberative rules. No due process provisions are in place for those subject to the "performance suspension or disciplinary punishment" to be meted out by the Commission.

Further, the editorial rights of the broadcasting media most likely will be curtailed by the "*ex post facto* correction" provision of the Broadcast Act, as already noted in the Periodicals Act section. Given the intrusive implications of the provision for the editorial autonomy of news broadcasting, the broadcasting media more often might opt to steer wide of crime stories instead of taking the risk of being burdened by the correction requirement.

All in all, it is not wide of the mark to conclude that these and other provisions of the Broadcast Act turn the new statute into a scheme that is still regulatory for the Korean government against the so-called Fifth Estate of Korea.

## SUMMARY AND CONCLUSIONS

Since mid-1987, when a new era of openness dawned in Korean politics, Korea has undergone a sweeping transition from traditionally strongman rule to an increasingly functional democracy. To a certain extent, the new Korean laws enacted by the Korean National Assembly in late 1987 are a case in point. Nevertheless, they still contain a number of authoritarian provisions undermining the Korean government's promise for a liberal democracy in Korea.

What will be the impact of the new press laws, as written in 1987, upon the Korean press? As an American constitutional law scholar succinctly put it, "[T]he press law of a particular country is not so much determined by the existence of a particular type of constitutional commitment, or by the presence of a special press statute, as by the particular political philosophy which animates it."[138] In the midst of an increasingly functional democracy in Korea, the press laws may prove to be a slight constraint to the press. Indeed, given the fact that direct press laws have caused less serious constraint on the Korean press than a variety of suppressive indirect laws have caused, there is a strong likelihood that the government will resort to some of the more restrictive special laws such as the National Security Act.

Despite these misgivings, however, the Korean press may find itself in a better position to assert its rights now than ever before. The *zeitgeist* sweeping Korea under the new leadership is increasingly evident in the growing judicial activism in Korea. This carries enormous significance for the Korean press in the context of the new press laws in that "[a] court within any democracy, given a healthy and substantive commitment to free speech, can protect the press by conventional methods of statutory interpretation."[139]

# CHAPTER 7

# Access to the Press:
# Right of Reply

The Korean government in 1980, seriously concerned about increasing "press violence" against individuals, adopted the right of "claim for corrected reports"[1] in the Basic Press Act.[2] The statutory right of reply was primarily aimed at providing an expeditious means for individuals to recover from their press-related injury.[3] The now abolished Basic Press Act further stipulated a "press arbitration commission" as a mechanism to enforce the right of reply provisions.[4] The press arbitration commission is "unique"[5] in that there are no such statutory apparatuses in Western Europe, where the right of reply is widely accepted.[6]

What is especially noteworthy about the Korean right of reply was that the statutory concept was wholly imported[7] in 1980 from what was then West Germany. As the Constitution Court of Korea noted in 1991, the right of reply under Korean press statutes has its genesis in the 1964 Land press law (Gesetz über presse) of Baden-Württemberg, Germany.[8]

This chapter examines the right of reply in Korea by exploring two questions. First, what is the statutory framework of the right of reply in Korea as compared with the German press law? Second, how did the Korean courts interpret the right of reply in delineating freedom of the Korean press?

## RIGHT OF REPLY: KOREA AND GERMANY COMPARED

### Korea
The right of reply was first stipulated as the "claim for corrected reports" in the Basic Press Act of 1980.[9] The Periodicals Act and the Broadcast Act,[10] enacted in 1987 to replace the restrictive Basic Press Act, retain the right-of-reply provisions based on the German model.

The right of reply in Korea derives its broad constitutional justification from the notion of individuals' "human worth and dignity" recognized by the Constitution.[11] It is a legislative attempt to provide a concrete apparatus to implement the constitutional mandate that the defamed should be able to vindicate their name.

The Constitution Court of Korea in 1991, upholding the right-of-reply provisions of the Periodicals Act, ruled that the right of reply is based on the constitutionally guaranteed right of character and allows the injured party an opportunity to respond to factual allegations.[12]

The right of reply is also justified by the proposition that it can contribute to the public's discovering truth and forming diverse public opinions. Noting the "one-sided information" gathered by the news media for the public, the Constitution Court stated that the reply requirement could create a more open marketplace of ideas by enhancing the objectivity of news information through the participation of non-media people in forming balanced public opinions.[13] In this vein, the right of reply to a limited degree offers access for the Korean public to the news media.[14]

As noted earlier, the right of reply in Korea is statutorily provided for by the Periodicals Act and the Broadcast Act. Article 16 (1) of the Periodicals Act, using the expression "right of claim for corrected reports," states that any person who is injured by a *factual* statement may request correction of the statement within 14 days after it is published in daily newspapers or within one month for non-daily periodicals.[15]

The parameters of the right of reply are determined by four elements of the statutory provision. The first element is related to the question of who is "[a]ny person" eligible to exercise the right. "Any person" applies not only to natural persons but also to corporate and governmental bodies.[16] Second, what kind of stories are sufficiently injurious to individuals to set the right of response in motion? More often than not, reputational injury and invasion of privacy are involved.[17] Third, the stories should be "factual"; they should not be comments or criticisms in the form of opinions.[18] Adopting the German approach to the right of reply,[19] the "factual" requirement of the Korean law precludes application of the reply clause to subjective opinions of individuals. Finally, the right of reply under Korean law is similar to German press law in that it applies to "periodicals"[20] and "broadcasts"[21] only as respectively defined by the periodicals and broadcast acts. Thus, books and other types of non-regular print and electronic media are exempt from the statutory requirements.

The periodicals and broadcast statutes stipulate the procedures for processing the written requests for reply to harmful stories. The Periodicals Act states that the editor of the daily publication or communication must insert free of charge the replies in the same publication or communication periodical within nine days of its receipt.[22] In the case of non-daily newspapers or periodicals, the editor shall insert the reply "in the following issue the editing of which is not completed" after receipt of the request for reply.[23] Prior to deciding on the reply requests, the media organization is required to immediately consult with the injured person or his representative on the contents of the corrected report and its size, among other considerations.[24]

The Korean press statutes recognize exemptions to claims for corrected reports. That is, the media *may* reject the claim "if the injured person has no proper interest in exercising a claim for a corrected report, or the contents of the claimed corrected report are obviously contrary to the fact, or it aims only at commercial advertisements."[25] This qualification of the right of reply protects press activities from abuse of the right. The burden of proof is on the media in justifying its refusal of the claim for reply.

The Korean press is not subject to the right-of-reply provisions in publishing stories on open meetings of governmental agencies or public organizations or open judicial proceedings.[26] The statutory exemption of corrected reports on governmental and non-governmental open proceedings is analogous to the "fair report privilege" concept recognized in Anglo-American libel law.[27]

The reply, though limited to factual statements, can include a clarification of statements for purposes of explanation. Nevertheless, "illegal contents" such as libelous or obscene expression are prohibited from being published as part of such a reply.[28] The response must be published as a corrected report, not "in a form of readers' contribution" like a letter to the editor. Its space and length cannot exceed that of the article to which the response is sought.[29]

The unique aspect of the Korean right of reply is that it mandates press arbitration commissions "to arbitrate disputes born from claims for corrected reports and [to] deliberate infringements cases" relating to news stories.[30] A request for arbitration of a claim for reply must be filed with the arbitration commission within one month after the story in dispute is published.[31]

When arbitration fails to resolve the dispute, the claim for corrected reports may be taken to a three-judge panel of the district court having jurisdiction over the media defendant.[32] Under Korean press law, preliminary action by the arbitration commission is a prerequisite to any judicial action on the claim.[33]

The Code of Civil Procedure provides for the proceedings applicable to adjudication of claims for correction of reports. That is, the Periodicals Act stipulates that right of reply claims shall be adjudicated in accordance with the provisional measures under the Code of Civil Procedure.[34] If the claim is found to be "well-grounded," the court may order the media to publish the reply as prescribed by a statute.[35]

Current Korean press statutes recognize the claim for a follow-up story to previous reports on a criminal suspect "when a penal procedure against him is terminated in a form other than a conviction."[36] The application of the *ex post facto* claim for correction is limited to the "recovery of one's honor or right."[37]

### Germany

Germany, though one of the countries most strongly committed to a free press,[38] does not have absolute constitutional guarantees of freedom of the press.[39] As far as the constitutional status of the German press is concerned, press interests are "not greater nor less important than the average citizen's."[40]

The right of reply under German law is derived from the basic rights of personality and identity as guaranteed by Articles 1 and 2 of the Basic Law.[41] Further, it is based on Article 5, which reads: "These [speech and press] rights are limited by the provisions of the general laws" including the press law.[42] It is noteworthy, however, that the Basic Law still prohibits the "essential content" of the basic rights from being restricted by application of the general laws.[43]

The right of reply, which one German commentator has described as "central to the rules of the state press laws,"[44] stems from French law. As the legal institution of German law, it was transplanted from the French press law of 1822 into the Baden Press Law of 1831 and then into the Imperial Press Law of 1874 as a demand for "correction."[45] The policy justifications for the right of reply in Germany were not so much to provide the public access to the media as to protect individuals from false defamation.[46] As Helmut Kohl, professor of law at Johann Wolfgang Geothe University, stated, "The underlying legislative rationale has never been to protect the democratic process and public opinion but to safeguard individuals against false press reports."[47]

The German right of reply is regulated by the press law of each individual German state, which details the rights and responsibilities of the press in accordance with the Basic Law. There are more similarities than differences among the various state laws of Germany.[48] The right of reply as stipulated in the press law of Germany's "publishing center," Hamburg,[49] illustrates how right of reply is recognized as a statutory concept at German law.[50]

Under the Hamburg press law, the right of reply is restricted to a statement of fact published in a periodical. The Hamburg press law states: "The responsible editor and publisher of a periodical printed work are obliged to publish the reply of a person or body concerned in a *factual* statement made in the work. This obligation extends to all subsidiary editions of the work in which the statement has appeared."[51] Thus, opinion and subjective expression of value judgments are excluded from the right of reply. The exclusion of subjective opinions from the German right of reply is distinct from the French right, which applies to expressions of both fact *and* opinion.[52] Particularly interesting about the development of the German right of reply is that from its very inception, the right was strictly limited to factual statements.

Every person or authority affected by a statement in the press can request a right of reply. Included in the "deliberately wide" scope of the law are private individuals, associations, companies, and public authorities, both German and foreign.[53] Among the periodical printed works that are subject to the right of reply provisions are newspapers, magazines, and other mass media such as radio, television, and films appearing "at permanent if irregular intervals of not more than six months."[54]

The content of the reply cannot include matters punishable by law such as defamatory charges.[55] Also, the length of the reply must not exceed that of the original statement complained of.[56] If the reply is disproportionately long, the editor and publisher can reject it. The reply must be asserted "immediately and at latest within three months" of the publications.[57]

The Hamburg statute also requires that the reply be published in the next issue if the issue is not yet typeset for printing.[58] It states that the news periodical must publish the reply in the same section of the periodical and in the same type as the challenged statement.[59] In the case of broadcasting media, the reply must be broadcast immediately to the same receiving area and at an equivalent time to the precipitating broadcast.[60] No interpolations or omissions of the reply are allowed under the law.[61] The reply is printed free of charge "unless the text complained of appeared as an advertisement."[62] A letter to the editor cannot be a substitute for the reply. The news medium can publish its own editorial comment on the reply in the same issue so far as it focuses on factual statements.[63]

The Hamburg press law exempts fair and accurate reports of the open proceedings of the three branches of federal government and local and state governments.[64] The rationale of this provision consists in "preventing political opponents from continuing in the press the debate which took place in Parliament."[65] The right of reply is not recognized for purely commercial expression.[66]

If the news media refuse to comply with the reply request, the reply claim can be enforced through an ordinary judicial process.[67] On application of the legitimate complainant, the civil court of the place of the periodical in question may issue a provisional injunction to have the reply published.[68] A German legal scholar has explained: "[T]he press organizations' plea that such injunctions should not be granted without personal consultation was not embodied in the law. An actual civil law trial on the original statement of the publication and the reply cannot be conducted under the press law."[69] Such speedy proceedings are justified because they provide the reply complainants with an opportunity for "immediate reparation."[70] The provisions of the Code of Civil Procedure on obtaining a provisional injunction dictate the court procedure.[71]

## JUDICIAL INTERPRETATIONS

Over a period of 14 years, up to the end of 1994, a total of 54 court decisions resulted from application of right of reply under Korean press law.

### Cases in Which Right of Reply Prevailed

It was not until 1986 that the Supreme Court of Korea ruled on the right of reply as stipulated by the Basic Press Act.[72] In its first ruling on the "claim for corrected reports" provision of the Basic Press Act, the Supreme Court in *An Chae-ran v. Korean Federation of Education*[73] affirmed the lower courts' decisions in favor of the plaintiff. The Court, discussing the *raison d'etre* of the correction claim provision, took issue with the title of the provision, "Claim for Corrected Report." The claim, according to the Court, is not a right to correction by the news media of their challenged stories "in conformity with truth."[74] Instead, the Court held, the statutory claim "is a right for the injured party to request publication of what he claims to be his own reply to the stories."[75] The Court stated *parenthetically* that "claim for a right of reply" would be more accurate than the claim for correction of reports.[76] The Court also said that determining the truth or falsity of the reports in dispute cannot be a prerequisite to the right.[77]

*An Chae-ran* originated when a newspaper owned by the defendant asserted in a story that the plaintiff, a high school principal, fired his vice-principal for allegedly protesting his "improper" instructions.[78] When arbitration did not resolve his complaint about the story, the plaintiff sued the defendant. The Seoul Civil District Court ruled that the defendant should publish the plaintiff's own response to the story unless it had "special excuses" for refusing it.[79] The court reasoned that the defendant presented no proof of the truth of its story precipitating the claim.[80] On appeal, the Seoul High Court affirmed the district court's decision.[81]

The Supreme Court in *Dong-A Ilbosa v. Yi Kyu-hyo*,[82] a 1991 case, followed *An Chae-ran* in ruling that truth or falsity of a story published in *Dong-A Ilbo* newspaper did not bear upon the applicability of the plaintiff's right of reply.[83] The *Dong-A Ilbo*'s story included a disparaging comment by Representative Kim Yong-tae of the ruling Democratic Justice Party, chairman of the Budget and Account Committee of the Korean National Assembly, about residents in North Cholla Province.[84] The story carried the plaintiff's previous statement similar to Kim's remark in a different context.[85]

The Seoul Civil District Court in *Yi Kyu-hyo* agreed with the plaintiff that his statement, as quoted in the story, was not made with the same motive as Kim's,[86] and the out-of-context quotation was not frivolous to his claim. The Seoul High Court upheld the district court's decision in 1990.[87] The Supreme Court, finding no evidence contrary to the plaintiff's challenge to the story, held: "Claim for correct reports is not a right to request correction of the original story…. Rather, it is simply a right to request publication of the response to the story."[88] Further, the Court noted that the right of reply was not affected by the subject matter of the story in question.[89]

Mere repetition of harmful statements about the plaintiff does not place the media outside the requirements of the law. That is, defamatory republication of statements made by a third party can be grounds for a claim for reply because the statements are still considered factual allegations made and adopted by the media as its own.[90] In *World Association for Christian Unification and Spirits v. Korean Christian Information Co.*,[91] the plaintiff charged that the story published in the defendant's media on the basis of a public statement made by a third party defamed his religious organization.[92] The Seoul Civil District Court ruled: "[E]ven though the report is accurate, it does not affect the plaintiff's claim for corrected reports. The right to claim corrected reports under the Basic Press Act is aimed not at correcting inaccurate stories but at providing an opportunity of reply to the injured party. This is designed to obviate the danger of one-sided news reporting and create a correct public opinion."[93]

In a similar vein, when a news organization publishes a story based on police records or a policeman's comments, the story is subject to the statutory claim for reply. In February 1989, the *Han-kyoreh Shinmun* published a story saying the plaintiff held key information about an incident involving her nephew's suicide. The newspaper argued that it could not grant the plaintiff's claim for a reply to the story because her reputation was damaged by the false police records, not by its published story. The Seoul Civil District Court in *Yi Chong-ja v. Han-kyoreh Shinmunsa*[94] disagreed. It held that the defendant's story was a factual statement to which the plaintiff had a right to respond, regardless of where the story originated.[95]

If a news story is not neutral in presenting a raging controversy, the story can constitute a cause for claim for reply. *Joongang Ilbosa v. Ilyo Shinmunsa*[96] arose from newspaper stories on the claim-for-corrected-report dispute between the plaintiff and a milk-producing company in Seoul. The plaintiff asserted that the stories were unbalanced. The Seoul District Court (South Branch) held, with little elaboration, that the plaintiff's argument was "in part justifiable."[97]

The right of reply is applicable to reader-contributed articles. The Seoul District Court in *Myong No-chol v. Chihak Shinbosa*[98] stated that the press law does not differentiate ordinary news stories generated by reporters from stories contributed by readers.[99] The plaintiff claimed that the precipitating story was defamatory in that it depicted him as arrogant and lazy and always seeking influential positions.[100]

At least three cases have focused on the "colloquium" issue under the right-of-reply provisions.[101] In *Joongang Ilbosa v. Chin Pu-ja*,[102] for example, the plaintiff claimed that the "mother's story of experience" published in a defendant's magazine was "of and concerning" her even though she was not specifically named.[103] She asserted that the "mother" in the story was identical to her and could be so recognized by those who knew her and who had read about her son's suicide.[104] Further, she maintained that she had not written the story, let alone been interviewed by the magazine.[105] The Seoul High Court, affirming the lower court's decision, held that the plaintiff was injured by the story and the defendant should publish her response.[106]

A voluntary "correction" published by a news organization after a story has been found erroneous cannot substitute for the plaintiff's right of reply unless the correction is legally sufficient. The Seoul Civil District Court in *Yon Song-man v. Seoul Shinmunsa*[107] concluded that the defendant newspaper's own correction was not comprehensive enough to constitute a response by the plaintiff as guaranteed by the Periodicals Act.[108] The court argued that the size and placement of the correction was less prominent than the original story and that the correction dealt only in part with the story.[109] It ruled, however, that the plaintiff's own draft reply violated the right-of-reply provision in claiming that the defendant had admitted to the falsity of its story and had apologized for it.[110]

The right of reply is also recognized for social organizations, which may not be qualified as juristic persons under the Code of Civil Procedure.[111] In 1983, a

Seoul district court said a small religious association could respond to a defamatory story.[112] Although claim for corrected reports was subject to the procedure for provisional measures under the Code of Civil Procedure, the court stated: "[T]his statutory requirement does not require that the procedure and the issues relating to the status of the parties to the claim be treated in the same way as the strict Code of Civil Procedure. Rather, it recognizes the special right of the injured party to sue the media under the Code of Civil Procedure for the purpose of recovering its interests in a speedy and impartial way."[113] The court added that the qualification of the party for the claim for corrected reports was recognized for a social entity active as a unit of social life, though not a juridical party under the Code of Civil Procedure.[114]

When a dissident leader was misquoted in a news story, he was found to have a right to respond. In *Mun Ik-hwan v. Chosun Ilbosa*,[115] the Seoul Civil District Court held that the defendant newspaper must run the plaintiff's reply to the story that had allegedly misquoted him.[116] The court rejected the defendant's argument, which emphasized the controversial nature of the plaintiff's visit to North Korea and the ambiguity of his quoted statements as well as the deadline pressure to publish the story. The court stated the right of reply did not hinge upon the issue of whether the defendant had an intent to harm the plaintiff's reputation.[117]

In *Hyondae Investment Research Institute v. Cheil Kyongje Shinmunsa*,[118] a Seoul district court ruled in favor of the plaintiff who challenged the story, arguing that it had damaged the good name of the investment company. It claimed that the story falsely identified the plaintiff as an unlicensed company engaging in deceptive business practices.[119] The court held that the "factual" statements about the plaintiff should be subject to a reply demand. It noted, however, that the plaintiff could not respond to the judgmental comment and criticism in the story.[120]

### Cases in Which Right of Reply Failed

In 11 cases to date, Korean courts have ruled that the challenged news stories did not warrant allowing plaintiffs their claim for responses, and they have found several different grounds for denying the right of reply. The Supreme Court in *Kim Tong-yol v. Joongang Ilbosa*,[121] for example, in ruling against the plaintiff, stated that he had failed to meet the "proper interest" requirements under the Basic Press Act. The Court, considering the purpose of the "no proper interest" provision of the law,[122] observed: "Among the cases involving 'no proper interest' [in the claim for corrected reports] is that in which the corrected report does not relate to the essential substance of the original story and only pertains to its insignificant details and so does not contribute to formation of proper public opinions, which the correction provision is primarily aimed at."[123] The Court found few substantial differences between the proposed reply and the original story, notwithstanding some minor discrepancies.

"Direct relationship" should be found between the plaintiff and the complained-of statement in order that the claim for reply may be granted. The Seoul

Civil District Court in *Pasteur Milk Co. v. Joongang Ilbosa*[124] said the plaintiff had no direct connection with the story published in the defendant's newspaper though the story made a specific reference to the plaintiff company's president, Choe Myong-jae.[125] In the story, Choe was depicted as having behaved improperly at a National Assembly inspection hearing. The court emphasized that the inspection focused on a farm owned by Choe and that the story referred to the plaintiff solely to identify Choe more specifically.[126]

Similarly, right of reply cannot be exercised by an organization if the story relates only to the organization's representative as an individual. In *Pyongdong Presbytery of Korean Christian Presbyterian Church v. Tak Myong-hwan*,[127] a 1984 case, the defendant's magazine, *Modern Religion*, said in a story that the president of the presbytery was damaging the reputation of the conservative Christian group by his irreligious behavior.[128] On examination of the story, the Seoul Civil District Court concluded that the statement did not harm the plaintiff. The court further noted that although the story defamed the representative of the plaintiff, it did not necessarily injure the plaintiff as a corollary.[129]

The claim for corrected reports does not apply to commercial expression. The plaintiff in *Tak Myong-hwan v. Christian News*[130] sued the newspaper defendant for running a paid editorial advertisement.[131] He argued that the defendant should publish a corrective advertising.[132] The Seoul Civil District Court in *Tak Myong-hwan* ruled: "[A]dvertisements are the advertiser's statements in the form of the advertiser's private expression run by the press in compliance with the advertising contract, not the factual statements of the press. In addition, there is no principle of equity in that while advertisements are published by the press on the basis of their payment, corrected reports are published free of charge. Consequently, the person who suffers from advertisements cannot respond to the advertisement under the Basic Press Act...."[133] The court suggested that remedies for harmful advertisements could be sought through civil and criminal proceedings.[134]

Criticism and comment as expression of opinion can be grounds for refusing the claim for reply. The Seoul Civil District Court in *Yun Tu-ho v. Presbyterian Association News*[135] said the defendant could refuse to publish the corrected report of the plaintiff.[136] While finding several of the challenged statements in the story true,[137] the court dismissed other statements as expressions of the author's feelings, i.e., opinions, about a meeting the plaintiff had attended.[138] The court did not explain why it concluded the statements were opinions exempt from the right-of-reply requirement.

In ruling on a news story on a libel case involving the plaintiff, the Seoul High Court in *Yi Ui-hyang v. Hankuk Ilbosa*[139] dismissed the plaintiff's appeal from the trial court's ruling. Reasoning that the story was excerpted verbatim from the court opinion, the court relied on Article 49 (7) of the Basic Press Act.[140] It further stated that the plaintiff suffered no damage as a result of the story and that his corrected report was contrary to the truth.[141]

Neither can the right of reply be utilized to protect an author's "moral right" in a work as recognized by the Copyright Act of Korea.[142] The plaintiff in *Kim Yong-so v. Social Development Research Institute*[143] argued that the defendant's publication of his manuscript after revisions, deletions, and additions had been made without his permission had "defamed his reputation and seriously injured his social activities as a Japan expert."[144] The Seoul Civil District Court, rejecting the plaintiff's claim for correction, ruled: "[T]he plaintiff, who was in a primary and active position to make the factual statement subject to claim for corrected reports, is not considered to be directly related to the substance of the statement under discussion. Even though the contents of the statement were changed from their original ones, this is not the kind of circumstances which the Basic Press Act anticipated."[145] However, the court alluded to the possibility that the plaintiff's claim could be adjudicated under the Civil Code or the Copyright Act.[146]

In *Hwang Sang-gi v. Dong-A Ilbosa*,[147] a 1982 case, the Seoul Civil District Court rejected the plaintiff's assertion that he should be allowed to respond to a story. In the story, a scholar reportedly attracted a great deal of attention for making a historical discovery to which the plaintiff claimed to hold a copyright.[148] The court concluded that the plaintiff did not offer concrete evidence for the alleged copyright violation by the defendant. It also said that "publication of a story featuring a scholar taking a similar position to the plaintiff's does not violate his copyright and other rights."[149]

### Cases in Which "Compulsory Performance" Was Ordered

While a court ruling on the right of reply may be objected to or appealed by the media defendant, its execution cannot be suspended.[150] Indeed, the Code of Civil Procedure empowers the court to enforce "compulsory performance" upon the defendant.[151]

For example, when the defendant in *Yi Ui-hyang*[152] appealed to the Seoul High Court a Seoul district court decision on the right of reply without publishing the court-sanctioned plaintiff's response, the Seoul district court issued a compulsory performance order against the defendant newspaper.[153] The newspaper was ordered to publish the plaintiff's reply to the story in question within two days "beginning on the day it received the order." The court held, "If the debtor fails to perform the preceding order within the period specified in the preceding order, it is ordered to pay to the creditor 5 million *won* (US$6,250) a day after the period."[154]

The Seoul Civil District Court also applied the compulsory performance provision when the defendant failed to run the plaintiff's reply to a story after the court had ruled in favor of the plaintiff.[155] Three other cases also resulted in the judicial threat to impose fines on the news media when the media failed to execute the court rulings on the right-of-reply disputes.[156]

## SUMMARY AND CONCLUSIONS

German press law served as a statutory model for South Korea in its enactment of the Basic Press Act in 1980, which adopted the German notion of right of reply. Thus, there are considerable similarities between Korean and German approaches to the right of reply. However, there are also notable differences between the two press laws.

The Korean press law, like the German law, recognizes the right of reply for an aggrieved person to respond to harmful stories in an inexpensive and expeditious way to recover from his reputational injury. At the same time, it provides people with access to the news media in disseminating countervailing information.

Korean and German press laws are identical in that they restrict the right of reply to *factual* statements and in that they both afford a right of reply for any person, whether natural, corporate, or associational. Both Korean and German laws provide for several similar exemptions to the right of reply. The "fair report privilege" to publish stories on governmental and non-governmental open proceedings is a good example.

On the other hand, Korean press law is distinguished from German law in two key respects. One relates to the Korean press arbitration system, which is a prerequisite to a judicial action on reply complaints. German law does not have such a system. The other aspect concerns the *ex post facto* right of reply under Korean law, which provides for the opportunity for reply for those who have not been convicted of suspected crimes reported in the press. German law does not recognize the *ex post facto* replies as such.

Korean courts have ruled on the right of reply on 54 occasions during the years 1981–1994. The rate of success for plaintiffs was nearly 65 percent.[157] The 14-year case law has established various judicial parameters for right of reply. First, opinion advertising, like commercial advertisements, is not covered by the right-of-reply provisions. Second, right of reply does not apply to disputes involving an author's "moral right" to a literary work recognized by copyright law. Finally, the right of reply has been recognized for social organizations though they are not juridical persons under the Code of Civil Procedure.

Notwithstanding its status as a relatively new concept in Korea, the right of reply has now been established as a fact of life for the Korean press and the public. It is profoundly significant that the right-of-reply provision has led to a phenomenal increase in litigation against the Korean press.[158]

# CHAPTER 8

# Libel

Harm to reputation has been a criminal offense or civil wrong in human civilization since the earliest times.[1] But the social and cultural approach to reputation as a value varies from society to society. Professor Robert C. Post elaborates:

> Defamation law would operate differently in a deference society than in a market society. In the latter, reputation is a quintessentially private possession; it is created by individual effort and is of importance primarily to those who have created it. Reputation's claim to legal protection is neither greater nor less than the claim to public protection of similar private goods. The preservation of honor in a deference society, on the other hand, entails more than the protection of merely individual interests. Since honor is not created by individual labor, but instead by shared social perceptions that transcend the behavior of particular persons, honor is "public good, not merely a private possession."[2]

Like the laws of most countries, Korean law prohibits unjustifiable defamation. Unlike the Anglo-American concept of reputation as an individual right,[3] however, the Korean concept is that reputational interests are perceived "in relation to the groups to which they belong."[4] Instead of viewing a defamatory statement as a harm to the "general social relations" of an individual, Koreans consider the statement a "loss of face" to the individual's familial group on the basis of their Confucian tradition.[5] The Confucian concept of defamation is reflected in the administration of the libel law of Korea.

While legal protection against injury of a person's reputation is an "intersubjectively reasonable transcultural goal[] of the law,"[6] the libel law of a society indicates to a large extent how that society views the relative importance of reputational interest vis-à-vis freedom of the press.[7] Press freedom in the United States is protected as a constitutional right, but reputation is not.[8]

118

First Amendment scholar Frederick Schauer has written: "The American approach ... reflects a society in which the press is considered to occupy a much more important role in the resolution of public issues. The press occupies a special position in the American system, a position that accounts for its strong protection against inhibiting defamation laws."[9] By contrast, South Korea does not protect freedom of the press as a transcendent value. The Constitution of Korea makes no preferential distinction subordinating reputation to a free press.

It is widely accepted that American libel law is more favorable to the press than that of any other legal system. Indeed, the media-oriented defamation law of the United States has led an increasing number of libel plaintiffs to sue American media in foreign courts.[10] Despite First Amendment protections, however, "libel has been the principal legal threat" to the freedom of the American press.[11]

Defamation in South Korea is considered a criminal offense under the Criminal Code[12] and an "unlawful act" under the Civil Code.[13] About 30 civil and criminal libel cases were reported during the 1954–1980 period.[14] Eight of the libel decisions resulted from publications of the Korean press.[15] As noted in a 1971 study of libel laws of Korea and Japan: "A debate on the defenses to libel which are similar to those of Japan is conducted among jurists in Korea. However, the debate remains academic since few libel cases lead to significant court decisions."[16]

In recent years, however, the number of suits against the Korean news media for libel and related complaints has increased rapidly. A total of 99 court rulings reported between 1981 and 1994 resulted from publication of allegedly harmful stories in the news media.[17] Considering that suing the press has been a rarity in Korea for many years,[18] the recent trend toward more legal actions against the media is a significant development.

On the premise that a phenomenal increase in media libel litigation in Korea during the past decade indicates a notable departure from the traditionally timid posture of the Korean public to its often overbearing press,[19] this chapter examines libel law and the press in Korea.

## REPUTATION: CONSTITUTIONAL AND STATUTORY FRAMEWORK

Like other countries,[20] Korea guarantees freedom of speech and the press in its Constitution. On the other hand, the Constitution does place limits on the freedom in that press freedom must be balanced with other societal interests. For example, Article 20 (2) states: "Neither speech nor the press shall violate the honor or rights of other persons nor undermine public morals or social ethics. Should speech or the press violate the honor or rights of the persons, claims may be made for the damage resulting therefrom."[21] Further, an individual's constitutional right to protect his reputation from being injured by the press in Korea is recognized by the constitutional requirement that the State be obligated to assure Koreans of their "human worth and dignity" as part of their "fundamental and inviolable human rights" as individuals.[22]

It was with the enactment of the Criminal Code in 1953 that the individual's reputational right was first recognized statutorily. Article 307 of the Criminal Code imposes sanctions for defamation as follows:

1. A person who defames another by publicly alleging *facts* shall be punished by penal servitude or imprisonment for not more than two years or by a fine not exceeding 15,000 *hwan*;
2. A person who defames another by publicly alleging *false facts* shall be punished by penal servitude or imprisonment for not more than five years or suspension of civil rights for not more than 10 years.[23]

Significantly, the punishment for defamation turns upon whether the allegedly defamatory statement is false.[24]

The Criminal Code expressly distinguishes libel (written defamation) from slander (oral defamation). Slander is prohibited by Article 307. Libel is proscribed by Article 309. Article 309 states:

1. A person who, with intent to defame another, commits the crime of Section (1) of Article 307, *by means of newspaper, magazine, radio, or other publication*, shall be punished by penal servitude or imprisonment for not more than three years or fined not more than 25,000 *hwan*;
2. A person who commits the crime of Section (2) of Article 307, by the method described in the preceding section, shall be punished by penal servitude for not more than seven years or suspension of civil rights for not more than 10 years.[25]

The Criminal Code punishes libel more severely than slander on the grounds that the impact of libel is likely to be more lasting and pervasive than the impact of slander.[26] Furthermore, to constitute criminal libel, publication of the statement must be made "with intent to defame." The requirement of criminal intent is protective of the rights of the press, reflecting a recognition that the press should be punished only if it acts with "malice."[27] However, the criminal intent requirement applies only if the allegedly defamatory statement is truthful. If the statement is false, no showing of criminal intent is required.

Article 310 of the Criminal Code provides an affirmative defense to prosecutions under Articles 307 and 309. Article 310 stipulates that "[i]f the facts alleged under Section (1) of Article 307 are *true and solely for the public interest*, the act shall not be punishable."[28] Therefore, a defendant is immune from liability if the statements attributed to him are true *and* made in the public interest. Since the "true and solely for the public interest" defense may be used whether or not the defamatory statement was made with intent to defame, the "intent to defame" clause is of little practical value to the press as a possible defense to defamation.

The Criminal Code also permits a criminal action for a falsehood that defames the dead.[29] Article 308 provides: "A person who defames a dead person by publicly alleging *false facts* shall be punished by penal servitude or imprisonment for not more than two years or fined not more than 25,000 *hwan*."[30] However, a defamatory statement about the dead that is truthful is not actionable under the Criminal Code. Prosecution for defamation of the deceased can be initiated only by complaint.[31] Conversely, prosecution for defamatory crimes under Articles 307 and 309 do not require a complainant. Only the "express objection" of the alleged defamed can prevent the defamer from being prosecuted by the State.[32]

As distinguished from personal libel, "trade libel"[33] is recognized as a crime in Korea. Article 313 of the Criminal Code states that "[a] person who injures the credit of another by circulating false facts or through fraudulent means shall be punished by penal servitude for not more than five years or by a fine not exceeding 25,000 *hwan*."[34] Also, it is a criminal offense to "interfere with the business of another" by the method described in Article 313.[35]

In Korea, the Civil Code also protects individuals from defamation. Although the Criminal Code is largely intended to ensure the social interests in public peace and order, the Civil Code is primarily aimed at safeguarding the rights of individuals to their reputations. The Civil Code provides victims of defamation with two possible means of redress. First, Article 751 authorizes monetary compensation for damages resulting from the defamation thus:

1. A person who had injured another person, his liberty or reputation ... shall make compensation for any other damages arising therefrom as well as damages in the property;
2. The court may order the compensation under the preceding section paid by periodical payments and may order a reasonable security furnished in order to ensure the performance of such obligation.[36]

Second, Article 764 authorizes the court, upon the application of the injured party, to order the defamer "to take suitable measures to restore the injured party's reputation, either in lieu of or together with compensation for damages."[37] Korean courts have recognized several "suitable" measures for restoring the reputation of the injured, such as retraction of the defamatory statement or publication of a notice of apology.[38] Courts can also issue injunctions against publishing the challenged libelous material when it is justifiably requested by the complainant.[39]

The duration of the statute of limitation for criminal libel actions in Korea is three years for truthful defamation to five years for false defamation. Libel of the dead has a three-year time limitation.[40] The limitation period for libel actions under the Civil Code is three years.[41]

## JUDICIAL INTERPRETATIONS

In libel litigation, the penal law has often been invoked in Korea. Media law scholar Paeng Won-sun wrote: "First, it has been a prevailing opinion in Korean society that a man who has injured another's reputation should be subject to penal punishment as part of retributive justice. Second, it has not been a tradition in Korea that infringement on the good name of another person ought to be recompensed for in terms of monetary damages."[42]

### Libel Litigation Before 1980

The first reported defamation case came to the Supreme Court of Korea in 1955, when it overruled the decision of the Seoul High Court in *State v. Yi Kang-sun*.[43] This case stemmed from the allegation of the defendant that the plaintiff was a communist who killed many people during the Korean War. The lower court held the statement nonactionable on the grounds that it was *unintentional*. The Supreme Court disagreed, noting that the specific facts mentioned by the defendant were sufficient to be defamatory of the plaintiff.[44] The Court focused on the contents of the allegedly defamatory statement. On the other hand, the lower court looked at the question of whether the defendant had the "intent to defame" in making the allegation. The *Yi Kang-sun* case is noteworthy in that neither the Supreme Court nor the Seoul High Court correctly applied the relevant libel law. That is, the Supreme Court placed more emphasis on the specificity of the facts in question than the truth of the statement, and the Seoul High Court misinterpreted Article 309 (1) of the Criminal Code when it applied the "intent to defame" clause to a case involving private individuals, not the mass media.

In 1960, the Supreme Court ruled on a group libel by focusing on the identification issue of libel. The case of *Yi Chong-yol v. State*[45] concerned a magazine article on the people of Cholla Province. The article was critical in a disparaging way. The complainant was referred to as an epitome of the Cholla people. On the question of whether the article could constitute a group libel, the Court held that it could not because of its lack of specificity in identifying the defamed group. The Court stated, however, that the article libeled the complainant as mentioned in it. In ruling that the publication was defamatory, the Court applied Articles 307 and 309 of the Criminal Code and sentenced the defendant to a one-year imprisonment. This judicial reasoning shows how the Court deals with the issue of "specificity" concerning the "target" of defamation in a large group of people.

In *Ko Chong-hun v. State*,[46] a criminal libel case of 1962, the Supreme Court held that the evidentiary truth of a defamatory statement must be proved by the defendant to be exempt from liability for libel. The Court rejected the defendant's argument that he made the statement complained of with good motives and for the public purpose. The origin of the case was the news conference the defendant held with Korean and foreign journalists. During the conference, he claimed that the controversial Cho Pong-am spy case was framed by the government in collaboration with what was then the Korean Counter-Intelligence Corps (KCIC). The allegation of the defendant was published in several newspapers in Korea, and those mentioned by the defendant argued that it violated their reputations.[47] By requiring that truth should be established with substantial evidence, the *Ko Chong-hun* case illustrates how heavy the burden of proof is on the part of the libel defendant. In connection with the proceedings of the case, it is interesting that the newspapers which ran the precipitating statement were not prosecuted for libel. Consequently, the originator of libel, not the conveyor of a libelous statement, was primarily liable for the defamation in Korea in the 1960s.

The Supreme Court in *Song Un v. State*[48] ruled on a case involving a news article. The newspaper story reported that the police had violated the civil rights of a girl suspected of prostitution for keeping her under custody as a prostitute suspect. The writer, knowing his statement to be untrue, contended that the girl was highly virtuous. The policemen involved argued that the story libeled them because it damaged their standing as law-enforcement officers. The Taejon District Court agreed and sentenced the defendant to a six-month imprisonment.[49] The prosecutor then appealed to the Supreme Court, contending that the defendant's sentence was not lengthy enough. The Supreme Court agreed and held that the status of the defendant as a newspaper reporter and the effect of his allegedly inaccurate publication should be duly weighed in determining the duration of imprisonment for a criminal violation. Consequently, the reporter was sentenced to a 10-month term.[50]

"Fair comment and criticism" was rejected as a libel defense in Korea in 1969. The Seoul Criminal District Court in *State v. Kwon Ho-yon*[51] held that a review of a Korean history book was actionable under the Civil Code since it exceeded the constitutional protection of freedom of the press. The Supreme Court affirmed the ruling of the lower court on the ground that the defendant's comments on the book were designed to defame the author of the book.[52]

In a 1969 civil libel case, *Yi Hi-yong v. Ilsin Pharmaceutical Co.,*[53] the Seoul Civil District Court ruled that the defendant should publish a notice of apology for defamation, in addition to paying damages arising from its libelous publication. In passing upon the liability of the defendant for the publication of a defamatory advertisement in a newspaper, the court held that the damage payment alone was not sufficient to compensate the plaintiff for his reputational injuries. Noting that the plaintiff was the leading authority on urinary diseases in Korea, the court held that the best possible way for Yi to recover his damaged reputation as a professional was through the defendant's publication of an apology in the same newspaper in which the original statement had appeared.[54] It seems that *Yi Hi-yong* was the first reported libel case in which a Korean court applied the Civil Code for a defamatory publication.

When a defamatory letter is written in the public interest, its writer is not subject to liability. In *State v. Kye Yong-sun,*[55] for example, the Seoul Criminal District Court ruled for the defendant, who claimed in a letter that Kye Hwa-sun, who was responsible for compiling the defendant's family history, took a bribe from printers. The court stated: "The defendant, as chairman of the Family-History Compiling Committee, wrote the letter to members of the General Council of Families in an effort to bring to light rumors regarding the committee through investigation of wrongdoings allegedly perpetrated by the committee members. This was done only for the public interest. Therefore, it is not to be punished under the law."[56] The reasoning of the court largely focused on the "public interest" aspect of the letter, while not addressing the question of whether the letter was true *and* also for the interest of the public.

Truth was accepted as a complete defense for libel of the dead in a 1972 libel case. The Supreme Court in *Yi Pyong-hak v. State*[57] held that the allegedly libelous inscription on a tombstone was nonactionable because the substance of the epitaph was most likely true in light of the available historical evidence.[58] The case started with an epitaph, which read: "The two descendants of the late Chong Pal-gul, who served a king of the Yi Dynasty as vice minister, murdered Yi Kyu-hyong...." It was claimed that the epitaph defamed the deceased Chong.[59]

The "publication" requirement[60] in a libel case can be met if a letter has a possibility of wide dissemination beyond the addressee.[61] The publication element in a slander (oral defamation) case is less strictly interpreted than in written defamation.[62] In slander cases, Korean courts take special note of the circumstances in considering whether there was an actionable "publication" of defamation. In *Yom Tong-ho v. State*,[63] a 1966 slander case, the Supreme Court emphasized that the defendant's defamatory statement was heard by policemen, who were required to keep confidential what was transpiring within the police station. Thus, the Court stated that the statement was not yet published to others and thus was nonactionable.

A Korean National Assemblyman was charged with and found guilty of criminal defamation of President Park Chung Hee of Korea when he expressed his opinions on Park. In *Chang Chun-ha v. State*,[64] the Supreme Court found that Representative Chang, then a member of the now dissolved opposition New Democratic Party, infringed upon President Park's right to a good name. The Court again ruled against a man who allegedly slandered President Park because his remark was not both true and in the public interest.[65] While agreeing with the defendant that his statement was intended for justifiable ends, the Court still held him liable because it was not truthful. These and similar decisions involving criticism of the presidency foster the conclusion that prosecutions and convictions for defamation were politically motivated in the 1970s.

### Libel Litigation After 1980

Although the Civil Code has more often been used in libel cases since 1981 than in the 1960s and 1970s, the Criminal Code is still invoked. The Criminal Code has been applied in at least 11 media libel cases. *State v. Chang Kon-sop*,[66] a 1989 Supreme Court decision, demonstrates the application of the Criminal Code to defamation. This case arose from publication in a monthly magazine of a picture provided by Chang. The picture was used to falsely show airborne paratroopers who allegedly killed civilians during the Kwangju Uprising of 1980.[67] The Seoul District Court, sentencing Chang to 18 months in jail, ruled that the defendant offered the picture to the magazine "with intent to defame" those in the picture as murderers of civilians.[68] The Seoul High Court reduced the jail sentence to 10 months.[69] The Supreme Court affirmed the high court's decision in toto.[70] In applying the Criminal Code, the Supreme Court agreed with the lower courts that the defendant had aimed at injuring the reputation of those in the picture.[71]

While trade libel was at issue in two libel cases under the Criminal Code in the past five years, neither of the actions involved a media organization as a party, although the precipitating libelous statements were published in the press. One of the cases arose when a university professor criticized Poly Ethylene Wrap, a food packing material, for containing cancerous substance. The Seoul District Court (East Branch) ruled in *State v. Ko Yong-su*[72] that the professor interfered with the sale of Poly Ethylene Wrap because her comment led to publication in the news media of false information on the packing material. The court noted that the publication hurt the manufacturing business of Poly Ethylene Wrap in violation of Articles 313 and 314 of the Criminal Code.[73] The professor was sentenced to a 10-month jail term, which was suspended for two years.

In recent years, the Civil Code, as compared with the Criminal Code, has been utilized in an overwhelming number of libel cases. Nearly 74 percent of the media libel cases in 1981–1994 have been adjudicated under the Civil Code.[74] In applying the Civil Code, Korean courts have set forth several new libel law parameters.

*Newsweek, Inc. v. Kwon Sun-jong*[75] is one of the most recent libel decisions adjudicated under the Civil Code. In this 1994 case, three Korean women sued Newsweek, Inc. in a Seoul district court for publication of an allegedly defamatory cutline together with a picture of them.[76] In their action against *Newsweek*, they demanded 100 million *won* (US$125,000) each in damages for defamation and invasion of privacy.[77] Judge Pak Si-hwan of the Seoul Civil District Court ruled that *Newsweek* violated the plaintiffs' right of reputation and privacy. He ordered *Newsweek* to pay each of the plaintiffs 30 million *won* (US$37,500) damages.[78] In March 1994, the three-judge appellate division of the Seoul Civil District Court affirmed Judge Pak's ruling, but it reduced the damage award to 20 million *won* ($25,000) for each plaintiff.[79]

In *Yi Ui-hyang v. Dong-A Ilbosa,*[80] a 1984 civil libel case, the Seoul Civil District Court enunciated a new defense for libelous stories on public matters. The court ruled, "It constitutes no unlawful act for a newspaper to publish a defamatory story for a public interest when the newspaper has a sufficient reason to believe it to be true."[81] The court stated that the "sufficient reason" requirement is met when the newspaper has the provable source or evidence for its belief in the truth of the article.[82] In recognizing the news media's reasonable belief in the truth of a libelous story as a ground for avoiding liability, the Seoul court argued that to ask the press for an extraordinary level of certainty in its belief of truth of its news reports would interfere with its proper function as an expeditious channel of information. An excessive desire to protect an individual's right to reputation from infringement of the press, the court noted, should not chill freedom of the press, which is the "foundation of democratic politics."[83]

Four years later, the Supreme Court of Korea expanded the media defendant's state of mind defense to criminal libel. The Supreme Court in *Hakwonsa v. Yi Il-jae*[84] held: "Under the *Criminal* and the Civil Codes, when an injury to a person's reputation relates to a matter of public concern and is only for the public interest, verification of the defamatory statement justifies the injury. Further, even when there is no proof as such, *the defamation cannot constitute an unlawful act if the defamer has sufficient reasons for believing his statement to be true.*"[85] The Court, affirming the lower court's ruling against Hakwonsa, concluded that the magazine publisher had no good reason for believing the memoir about Yi because prior to publishing the memoir, Hakwonsa made no effort whatsoever to check on the defamatory allegations.[86] The Court further stressed that publication in a monthly magazine of the complained of article did not have the same time constraints as a daily newspaper article, and thus the defendant should have taken time to verify the memoir before publication.[87] In *Hakwonsa*, the Court has recognized a distinction between the "hot news" and the news with little deadline pressure. That is, while absence of deadline pressure at the time of publication of defamatory information makes a media organization more accountable, news that requires immediate dissemination does not necessarily do so.[88]

When a defamatory story is based on hearsay, the defendant's assertion of "belief" in its truth does not stand to reason. In *Kim Song-hi v. Yi Kap-sop*,[89] a 1989 libel case, for example, the Seoul High Court affirmed the trial court's ruling against the media defendant because the defendant published the disputed story relying on unfounded gossip about the unwed plaintiff's alleged affair with a married man.

A Seoul district court in *Yi Tu-sik v. Tak Myong-hwan*[90] ruled that "colloquium,"[91] or that the words are spoken "of and concerning" the plaintiff, was not established when the plaintiffs claimed that they were emotionally distressed by an allegedly defamatory statement in a book published by the defendant. The statement claimed that the plaintiffs' deceased mother had an "unusual relationship" with the Rev. Sun Myung Moon of the Unification Church when her husband was seriously ill.[92] The court, characterizing reputation as "a high degree of individual character," reasoned that the statement did not name the plaintiffs implicitly or explicitly.

On the other hand, the Seoul High Court in *Sin Hyon-sun v. Kukmin Ilbosa*,[93] a 1991 media libel case, stated that the plaintiff's family members were entitled to damages for a libelous article about their father even though they were not directly implicated in the story. The court said that because of their relationship with the subject of the article, as his children they suffered emotional pain.[94] The court concluded that the defendant did not take proper care in checking on the story.

Although not as extensive as Anglo-American libel law,[95] Korean law now recognizes the "fair report privilege"[96] as a defense for libelous publication of governmental records. A good illustration is a 1988 case, *Kwak Chol-am v. State*.[97] The Seoul Civil District Court ruled: "In reporting on a suspected crime of the plaintiff, other defendants [i.e., six newspaper companies] relied on the official announcement of the Seoul Police Department.... They believed the defamatory false information on the plaintiff to be true and they had sufficient ground for their belief. Accordingly, we cannot find that the defendants were intentional or negligent in libeling the plaintiff."[98] The court, while dismissing the suits against the media organizations, held that the State must pay 10 million *won* (US$12,500) in damages for the plaintiff's reputational injury.[99]

For the first time in the history of Korean libel law, fair comment and criticism was accepted as a libel defense in 1990. The Seoul District Court (South Branch) in *Labor Union of Munhwa Broadcasting Corp. v. Dong-A Ilbosa*[100] held that derogatory reviews or comments are justifiable and protected as freedom of criticism so long as they concern matters of public interest, irrespective of whether they are "objectively proper" or acceptable to a majority of people in society.[101] The court stated: *"The comment should not be an exposé of an individual's private life unrelated to his public activities or an attack on his personal character. Further, the opinion about him need not be objectively correct; it is lawful if it is subjectively believed to be appropriate. Even though the comment is not neutral, and is so partisan as to be one-sided, or the words and tone are violent and harsh enough to damage its subject in his social esteem, it cannot be dismissed as unfair."*[102]

As a general rule, a public apology had until 1991 been recognized by Korean courts as a "suitable" way for the defamed to vindicate their reputation. In *Kwon In-suk v. Seoul Munhwasa*,[103] for instance, a Seoul district court in 1991 ordered Seoul Munhwasa Company to issue a public notice of apology for publication of a libelous excerpt from the plaintiff's memoir on the widely publicized policeman's sexual abuse of her.[104] The court contended that without paying attention to the contents of the memoir as a whole, the defendant spotlighted only the isolated passages of the memoir along with "sensational" obscene pictures.[105] The court also argued that the defendant was or could be aware of the defamatory impact of its publication on the plaintiff.[106]

*Kwon In-suk* is distinguished from other libel cases[107] in that the former resulted in only a compulsory public apology in the press against the media defendant while the latter involved an apology *and* payment of damages. *Kim Song-hi v. Dong-A Ilbosa*[108] typifies libel cases in which the plaintiff sues for both damages and an apology from the defendant. This 1990 media case started when *Yosong Dong-A*, a monthly magazine, published a story on a libel case involving the plaintiff.[109] The story was based on interviews with the writer of another story which the plaintiff had claimed to be defamatory in a previous libel case. The Seoul High Court, affirming the Seoul district court's decision, found no reasonable ground for the asserted belief of *Yosong Dong-A* in the complained of story.[110] The court stated that the magazine did little to verify the story and was negligent of its obligation to interview the plaintiff.[111] The court ordered the defendant to pay 10 million *won* (US$12,500) in damages and to publish an apology for the story.[112]

In connection with public apology as a possible "suitable measure" under the Civil Code, *Kim Song-hi v. Dong-A Ilbosa* ended in a Constitution Court's ruling on the Civil Code. In April 1991, the Constitution Court ruled unanimously that the Civil Code was unconstitutional insofar as the Code applies to a notice of apology.[113] The Court held that the "unlawful act" provision of the Code violated the Constitution on freedom of conscience and freedom for public welfare.[114]

## IMPACT OF LIBEL LAW

In a study of the decisions of the Korean Press Ethics Commission from 1961–1980,[115] Professor Yu Jae-chon of Sogang University in Seoul concluded that media violations of citizens' reputational rights in Korea resulted from the sensationalism of news reporting, the unprofessional practices of news reporters, and the journalists' lack of consciousness of law and professional ethics.[116] He also noted that the legal and ethical issues facing the Korean press are in part ascribable to the usual tendency of the defamed to forgo suing the media.

Obviously aware of the "do-nothing" attitude of most libel victims in Korea, one Korean law commentator argued in 1985 that "Korean news media will remain relatively free from libel litigation though the press may be subject to severe nonlegal and political restraints more characteristic of an authoritarian government."[117] He considered three sociopolitical fac rs in speculating on the limited impact of libel law on the Korean press.

First, he called attention to the still pervasive influence of Confucian ethics in Korea, which "place[s] harmony and conciliation before legal battle" as a way to resolve disputes among individuals.[118] Second, the traditional perception of many Koreans who view the press as "too powerful to challenge" tends to be a strong incentive against suing the news media for libel, whether real or perceived.[119] Finally, he contended that Koreans rarely expect their courts to be institutionally competent to exercise their rule-of-law authority in ruling on their claims. The Korean judiciary, which has been traditionally controlled by the executive branch,[120] was viewed as being unduly influenced by the ruling class, including media organizations.[121]

However, the explosive increase in media libel actions in Korea in recent years leaves the above commentator's observations in doubt. There are several possible explanations for the recent strong tendency for Koreans to sue their media organizations. To a large extent, the unprecedented changes in the media industry as well as in the body politic of Korea since mid-1987 are directly related to the increasingly litigious Korean society.

Yi Hye-bok, president of the Korean Journalists Club in Seoul, reported in his 1990 study that there had been an explosion in the number of claims for press arbitration since mid-1987,[122] when the Korean government initiated several liberalizing measures to expand press freedom. In discussing the rapidly growing number of complaints to the press arbitration committees, Yi pointed out positive and negative aspects of the changing relationship between the press and the public. Of the positive side of the issue, he said: "[O]ur citizens' consciousness [of rights] has enormously risen. In the past, people were so intimidated by the power of the news media that they dared not assert their rights against the media although they had their rights violated by the media. At present, however, they claim their rights openly enough to confront the press."[123] Yi also attributed the growing number of press arbitration cases to a declining sense of professional ethics among Korean journalists. Because of their anxiety concerning a shrinking audience as a result of the expanded media industry, Yi argued that the Korean media tend to deviate from the "right path of journalism."[124] He also maintained that the rapidly growing media industry, facing a lack of professionally trained journalists, hire less-qualified people.[125] As a result, the overall quality of journalistic work has suffered, often precipitating complaints against the press.

In the context of the press arbitration system under the Korean press statutes since 1980, the right-of-reply litigation has brought about libel cases on similar grounds and for different purposes. More often than not, plaintiffs in right-of-reply actions sue the media for damages for reputational injury under the Civil Code. For example, *Yi Ui-hyang* was a case that involved both right-of-reply claims under the press statutes[126] and damages for libel under the Civil Code. Thus, there is now a reasonable likelihood that the Korean media can be subject to two different suits for the same news stories.

Equally important is the improved status of the Korean courts as a more independent branch in the midst of an increasingly functional democracy since 1988. Now Koreans have become more fully aware of the likelihood that Korean courts are no longer dominated by the "established leadership" in Korea in their judicial proceedings. Illustrative of the change was the increasingly frequent invocation by the courts of the right of judicial review.

In November 1988, the Supreme Court of Korea ruled that portions of the Act for the Protection of Society violated the Constitution and referred the matter to the Constitution Court for final determination.[127] The Supreme Court's ruling marked the first time since 1972 that it had struck down any laws. More significantly, the Court questioned the validity of the Act for the Protection of Society, which had been held constitutional by the courts nine times since it was enacted in 1980.[128]

One month after the Supreme Court ruling, the Seoul High Court ruled that Article 3 of the Act on Assembly and Demonstration was unconstitutionally vague and overbroad in that it prohibits "assembly or demonstration which shall be greatly feared to cause social unrest."[129] Chief Judge Yi Il-yong of the Seoul High Court held: "Our Constitution provides that freedom of assembly and association may be restricted by law only when necessary for national security, the maintenance of law and order or for public welfare. The Constitution, however, prohibits the essential aspect of the freedom from being restricted even when the restriction is justifiable. In this context, the current law on assembly and demonstration is feared to violate the essential aspect of the citizens' freedom of assembly and association."[130] This was further unmistakable testimony to the increasing independence of the Korean courts. In the past, laws on political rights or civil liberties had almost never been subject to judicial challenge.[131]

In another case pointing to the gradual restoration of judicial authority, a military court in October 1988 convicted military officers accused of assaulting a newspaper editor for publishing a negative story about the Korean military. The fact that a military court ruled against military officers was seen as a major break-through. The case involved publication of a newspaper article titled "Military Culture Should Be Eradicated," which argued that a military culture still pervaded South Korea despite President Roh Tae Woo's promises for democratic reforms.[132] The military court held in October 1988 that the assault on the newspaper's editor caused a social controversy and undermined the trust and prestige of the military among the people.[133]

Korean libel law, as applied by courts in the past 14 years, has impacted on both the press and the general public. On the one hand, libel jurisprudence indicates that the courts recognize the institutional function of the press as the cornerstone of democracy in Korea. Now the media can utilize the "reasonable belief in truth," the "fair report privilege," or "fair comment and criticism" in claiming protections from libel actions. These newly recognized libel defenses indicate a more liberal approach of the courts to accommodating the conflict between the press and the individual.

Media organizations, however, still often lose libel actions. Between 1981 and 1994 the courts ruled against the media in 34 of 42 libel cases. That is, the rate of success for libel plaintiffs was nearly 81 percent during the past 14 years. There is no question that the possibility of court action against the media is more of a reality now than in the past. As a result, the Korean press has indicated a tendency to be "more prudent" in dealing with the kind of stories that it published casually or routinely in the past.[134]

Another notable development in the libel explosion in Korea in the 1980s relates to the long-term impact of the rejuvenated libel law on the psyche of Koreans. The dramatic changes in the law have awakened the reluctant public to the legal mechanisms to employ against the media organization. This is consider-ably due to the wide publicity entailing media libel and related cases involving politicians and others of fame or notoriety. Consequently, Koreans have become more conscious of their reputation as a constitutional and statutory right.

## SUMMARY AND CONCLUSIONS

Korean courts have ruled on a growing number of libel claims in recent years. The courts, however, have yet to find a clear-cut, definitional approach to balancing freedom of the Korean press with the interests of individuals' reputations. As compared with pre-1980 libel rulings, recent case law on libel indicates that Korean judges are more sensitive to the value of a free press in an increasingly democratic Korea. For example, the news media's reasonable belief in the truth of a defamatory story is now accepted as grounds for exempting the story from liability. Also, Korean courts have established the "fair report privilege" as a defense for publication of a defamatory falsehood based on government documents. Opinion, as distinguished from factual statements, is now protected from libel suits if it concerns subjects of public interest.

The compulsory apology requirement under the Civil Code is no longer accepted as a means of vindicating an injured reputation. It is especially noteworthy that the Constitution Court invalidated the apology requirement largely on the basis of the freedom of conscience provision of the Constitution.

The libel explosion in the past decade has brought about notable changes in the function of the Korean press. It has led Korean journalists to more carefully handle their potentially defamatory stories. From a legal perspective, the growing libel litigation has offered a soul-searching opportunity for Korean courts to define press freedom vis-à-vis reputation in a new sociopolitical context. Consequently, the debate on libel defenses in Korea is no longer as academic as it was 20 years ago. Finally, dramatic changes in the libel law have impacted on the awareness of Koreans of their rights to such an extent that they are now more likely to assert their rights than ever before. All in all, the changes indicate that the law of libel probably will remain an area of increasing litigation in Korea.

# CHAPTER 9

# Seditious Libel

Anthony Lewis, a First Amendment commentator, stated in 1991 that seditious libel typifies the methods that tyrannical governments use "to insulate themselves from disagreement."[1] Seditious libel is "political criticism that threaten[s] to diminish respect for the government, its laws, or public officials."[2] It is distinguished from "sedition," which is defined as concrete and specific acts to overthrow the government by force or violence. "In many countries," however, "this distinction is ignored."[3] In South Korea, which has proclaimed itself as a liberal constitutional democracy since 1948, seditious libel was punished as a crime up to late 1987. In this context, some commentators often questioned whether Korea was a democracy, especially when the government suppressed political activists, alleging that their criticism was defamation of the State.

This chapter looks at seditious libel in conflict with freedom of expression in Korea. It examines the now abolished "anti-State defamation" provision of the Criminal Code and other related issues.

## CRIMINAL CODE ON "ANTI-STATE DEFAMATION"

In March 1975, the Korean government under President Park Chung Hee revised the Criminal Code and made it a crime to defame the State.[4] As a ranking member of the ruling Democratic Republican Party told the *New York Times*, the legislation aimed to "clear up 'flunkeyism'—meaning a tendency to depend on foreign power to influence domestic politics."[5] Article 104-2 of the Criminal Code read:

> 1. Any Korean national who endangers or is assumed to endanger the security, interests, or the prestige of the Republic of Korea by defaming or insulting the Republic of Korea or the governmental bodies established under the Constitution, or by distorting the facts

about them or by circulating false facts or in any other way, outside of the country shall be punished by penal servitude or imprisonment for not more than seven years;

2. Any Korean national who commits such acts as prescribed in the preceding paragraph by use of foreigners or foreign organizations inside of the country shall be punished in the same way as in the preceding paragraph.[6]

The Criminal Code had been often criticized for infringing on freedom of speech and the press. One Korean-law commentator, characterizing it as "undoubtedly a remnant of the authoritarian control" of freedom of expression in Korea, wrote in 1989: "To punish citizens for voicing disagreement with the ruling authorities is incompatible with the kind of liberal democracy propounded by Roh [Tae Woo] in 1987. This law should be repealed as soon as possible to put the sociopolitical and legal system of Korea in line with the democratic politics of Korea under President Roh."[7]

The seditious-libel clause was unconstitutionally vague or overbroad, or both. What was the "prestige" of Korea that the Criminal Code sought to protect? "Prestige" is defined as "[a] person's high standing among others; honor or esteem."[8] Did it mean the standing of Korea as a sovereign state among the nations of the world? Was it different from the "reputation" of Korea in terms of how Korea was viewed by foreigners? In connection with "by defaming ... the Republic of Korea or the governmental bodies ..." in the Code, it is accepted that there was little distinction between the "prestige" and "reputation" of Korea under the law.[9] However, could Korea possess a reputational interest as a legal entity? Equally important, what was "Korea" as referred to in the statute? In the context of the international prestige of Korea, "Korea" could have been interpreted as a political system as a whole; that is, it could not have been applied to a statement about only a part of Korea.[10]

The "insulting" of Korea was not clear at all. It is not difficult to envision that many Koreans of ordinary intelligence must have guessed at its meaning and differed as to how it applied. Indeed, "insulting" was used together with "defaming" in the Criminal Code. Were the two terms used synonymously? Or did the terms have different meanings? As the Code stipulates, defamation and insults are recognized separately and distinctly. Defamation is a more serious felony than insulting under Korean law.[11] The Supreme Court of Korea distinguished defamation from insults as follows: "Defamation requires an injury to reputation through a statement of specific facts damaging the social standing of an individual. On the other hand, insults undermine an individual's social standing through an expression of an *abstract judgment* or *contemptuous feelings* toward the individual. Defamation carries a heavier penalty than insulting."[12]

The statutory and judicial distinctions between defamation and insults in Korean law are of profound significance. Indeed, they are conceptually analogous to American law. Insulting expression is ordinarily not actionable in the United States because it is "no more than either an idle comment or the venting of the speaker's or writer's emotions and therefore does not reflect adversely on the plaintiff's reputation."[13]

While the Korean law has consistently differentiated libel from insults, the Criminal Code made the two one and the same in criminalizing anti-State defamation. This leads to the conclusion that the word "or" in "defaming or insulting" was used as a conjunctive rather than as a disjunctive. If that conclusion is untenable, there still remains a question of whether the "insulting" of Korea could constitute a crime as prescribed in the Code. Professor Namgung Ho-gyong of Seoul National University doubts the possibility, adding that insults as a crime could not be applied to a juristic person, an organization, or a nation because the term related to the reputational *feelings* of the insulted party. Again, the U.S. law on the distinction between defamation and invasion of privacy bears on the problems inherent in the "insulting" clause of the Criminal Code of Korea. In American law, "[u]nlike actions for defamation, suits for invasion of privacy can be brought only by individuals. Neither corporations, associations, nor partnerships have 'feelings' or a right to personal privacy...."[14]

What constitutional organs would fall into the category of "governmental bodies established by the Constitution"? According to Professor Yu Ki-chon of Seoul National University, among the protected governmental bodies were the President, the executive branch, the National Assembly, the judiciary, the Constitution Committee, the Board of Audit and Inspection, and the Central Election Management Committee, but not the administrative agencies such as the Ministry of Home Affairs, the Ministry of Justice, mayors, heads of counties, etc., established in accordance with statutes.[15] Nevertheless, the vagueness of "governmental bodies" still remains. Would the Criminal Code have been applied to defamation of the President as a natural person, not as the head of state? Let's assume that a visiting Korean wrote a letter to the editor of the *Washington Post* to the effect that President Park Chung Hee was the "most brutal dictator" in the 4,000-year history of Korea. This comment clearly relates to Park as the President of Korea and would be most likely to precipitate the application of the anti-State defamation clause to the Korean visitor's statement if the law were aimed at preventing libelous criticism of the Presidency itself. To borrow Professor Namgung's illustration,[16] however, what would have happened to another Korean who called President Park an " inveterate playboy" who frequently engaged in sex orgies with young girls in the Blue House? This disparaging reference to Park has little to do with his status as a public figure but a great deal to do with Park as a natural person. Would the caustic comment on the natural-person conduct of Park have been a crime under the law? The answer should be, "Probably not." This stems partially from the inherent vagueness of the "defaming or insulting" of the President, as already discussed.

The vagueness problem is also found in the "distorting the facts" basis for seditious libel. In what way and to what extent should a fact have been "distorted" in order for the Criminal Code to be invoked? Was it supposed to mean a *substantial and material* alteration of the facts, not a slight or trivial exaggeration, that might have resulted in placing the government in an unfavorable light? Was the distortion limited only to the negative portrayal of Korea? Or did it cover even positive but false allegations relating to Korea? The "distorting the facts" could have been applied in one way or the other, even though negative distortions of the facts were far more likely to be punished by the law.[17]

The "or in any other way" phrase of the Criminal Code must be a catchall for an indeterminate number of kinds of expressions about the Korean government, in addition to defamation, insults, distortion of facts, or dissemination of false facts. It definitely carried the danger of prohibiting too much because any mode of expression could fit into the "in any other way" of committing criminal acts. This was often the case with the application of the Anti-Communist Act and the National Security Act.[18]

The first paragraph of Article 104-2 targeted Koreans abroad. By contrast, the second paragraph was aimed at Koreans within Korea. Professor Namgung said that as a matter of practicality, the second paragraph of Article 104-2 was more likely to be applied than the first paragraph because investigation of the crime of anti-State defamation could not be conducted in foreign countries if the violators refused to return to Korea in the face of possible prosecutions.[19] The most controversial part of the second paragraph focused on the interpretation of the vague phrase "by use of foreigners or foreign organizations." Was it a prerequisite to application of the law that foreigners or foreign news media should commit the defamatory acts against Korea inside the country? Or was it already a violation of the law when Koreans defamed or insulted Korea *to* foreigners within Korea although foreigners did not engage in the proscribed acts at all? In other words, could "by use of foreigners or foreign organizations" and "to foreigners or foreign organizations" be used interchangeably? When the Supreme Court of Korea ruled in two anti-State defamation cases, the Court was confronted with the issue of how to apply "by use of foreigners or foreign organizations" to the facts involved.[20]

Until December 1988, when it was abrogated as part of the democratic political and legal reforms in Korea,[21] the anti-State defamation clause had not been invoked as often as had been initially expected. Nevertheless, the infrequent application of the seditious libel clause does not necessarily indicate that the clause did not function at all.[22] Professor Namgung argued, "The clause worked as the sword of Damocles well enough against making contacts with foreign news media, foreign organizations, or foreign press as an outlet for expression or as a political means under the circumstances in which the Korean press was thoroughly controlled [by the government]."[23] Illustrative was the prosecution of a Korean student leader in 1987 for criticizing the Korean government during an interview with the *New York Times* in Seoul. The student was quoted as saying to the *Times*, "The fascism in Korea is directly related to Hitler's Nazism."[24] He was arrested on charges of slandering the State by making "undesirable" statements to the *Times* and other foreign reporters in Korea.[25] He was sentenced to four years in jail but was released soon after serving "only a small portion of his sentence."[26]

Other similar seditious libel crimes are prescribed by the Criminal Code of Korea. For example, the Code prohibits Koreans from defaming foreign heads of state visiting Korea. Article 107 states: "A person who insults or defames the sovereign of a foreign country … shall be punished by penal servitude or imprisonment for not more than five years."[27] Under the Code, insulting or libeling foreign diplomats in Korea may result in an imprisonment or penal servitude of up to three years.[28] Profaning and defamation of the national flag is also a crime in Korea. The Criminal Code states:

> A person who damages, removes, or stains the national flag or the national emblem for the purpose of insulting the Republic of Korea shall be punished by penal servitude or imprisonment for not more than five years, suspension of qualifications for not more than 10 years, or a fine of not more than 25,000 *hwan*;[29]
> A person who defames the national flag or the national emblem for the purpose mentioned in the preceding Article shall be punished by penal servitude or imprisonment for not more than one year, suspension of qualifications for not more than five years, or a fine of not more than 10,000 *hwan*.[30]

Similarly, it is statutorily forbidden to "profane" a foreign national flag or emblem as a way of insulting the foreign country.[31]

## JUDICIAL INTERPRETATIONS

During the 1975–1988 period, when anti-State defamation was a crime under the Criminal Code, two cases involved alleged violations of Article 104-2. *Kim Chol-gi v. State*,[32] a 1983 case, was the first decision of the Supreme Court of Korea on seditious libel as a crime. The case began on July 23, 1982, when Kim Chol-gi, executive director of the Korean Ecumenical Youth Council, circulated 300 anti-government leaflets to about 10 Korean and foreign correspondents in Seoul.[33] In the leaflets, entitled "Our Position on the Control Data Incident," the Ecumenical Youth Council stated:

> [T]he Korean government did nothing about the violence committed during the Control Data incident. Instead, it sympathized with and supported the violence. While the Korean government resorted to every possible means of force in dealing with Korean laborers and citizens, it was powerless and subservient toward a multinational company [i.e., Data Control Co.]. The government maintained the national economy at the expense of starving Korean laborers, and it depended on foreign power instead of the support of the Korean populace.[34]

The Council demanded that the Korean government under President Chun Doo Hwan step down.[35]

A Seoul district court found Kim guilty of violating the Criminal Code and sentenced him to an 18-month prison term. In his appeal to the Seoul Criminal District Court, Appellate Division, Kim argued that what was criticized in the leaflets was the ruling authorities of South Korea, not South Korea itself or the governmental bodies established by the Constitution. He further asserted that criticism of the governmental policy was an exercise of his basic right as a citizen, not an act that endangered or was deemed to endanger the prestige of Korea.[36] The appellate division of the Seoul Criminal District Court in February 1983 held that Paragraph 2 of Article 104-2 of the Criminal Code was designed to prevent foreign disturbance by punishing Korean nationals for using foreigners within Korea to endanger the security, interests, and prestige of Korea by defaming Korea and its constitutional bodies.[37] The appellate court stated, "In order for an act to constitute a crime of anti-State defamation, it is required that a Korean national use a foreigner in Korea *and* the foreigner defame Korea and its constitutional bodies in foreign countries."[38] The court concluded that Kim did not violate the law because there was no proof that the foreign correspondent who received the seditious material from Kim did commit the proscribed act of defaming Korea abroad.[39]

The Seoul District Prosecutor's Office appealed to the Supreme Court for review of the Seoul district court's decision. The petition argued that the decision was based on several misinterpretations of the Criminal Code.[40] First, the Prosecutor's Office stated that the phrase "any Korean national, who commits such acts as prescribed in the preceding paragraph ... inside of the country" in the Code requires that Koreans be the subject of the prescribed acts, not foreigners or foreign organizations, contrary to what the Seoul court held.[41] Second, the Prosecutor's Office maintained that "by use of ..." in the Code should be interpreted as "to" because the main points of the original bill made it clear that "by use of ..." meant "to."[42] Third, the Korean government claimed that "acts as prescribed in the preceding paragraph" did not relate to defamation or insults against Korea in foreign countries, but to distortion of the facts about or circulation of false facts about Korea and its constitutional bodies within Korea.[43]

The Prosecutor's Office pointed out that the legislative intent behind the anti-State defamation clause of the Criminal Code was "completely ignored" by the appellate division of the Seoul district court in ruling against the State. It quoted extensively from the minutes of the National Assembly on the 1975 anti-State defamation bill:

> Judging from their recent speech and behavior at home and abroad, some Koreans do not discard flunkeyism, which is the historical disease of our nation. They are taking an excessively subservient attitude toward foreigners and foreign organizations. Moreover, they not only defame and insult the Republic of Korea and the governmental bodies established under the Constitution, but they also do not hesitate to distort the facts and disseminate the false facts about them.... They so often engage in the kind of speeches and behaviors that are deemed to endanger our independence and security that they create the

circumstances in which the security, interests, or prestige of the State are or are likely to be undermined. In this context, revision of the Criminal Code would root out the chronic flunkeyism of some people by punishing their sycophantic behavior.[44]

The prosecutor emphasized that the primary purpose of the revised Code was to punish the servile behavior of Koreans toward foreigners inside and outside Korea and that the statute would apply to the act of defaming or insulting the governmental bodies *to* foreigners, whether at home or abroad, if such acts harm the national security, interests, and prestige of Korea.[45]

In reversing the lower court's ruling in July 1983, the Supreme Court, sitting en banc, accepted the argument of the Prosecutor's Office in toto. The Court, quoting verbatim the National Assembly's minutes on the proposed revision of the Criminal Code included in the appellant's brief, concluded that notwithstanding the language of the revised Code, "it is clear that Article 104-2 of the Criminal Code was designed to forbid the stipulated acts [committed by Koreans] *to* foreigners or foreign governments."[46] The Court stated that there was no reason for reading the "place of crime" into the two paragraphs of Article 104-2 differently because the reference to "outside the country" in Paragraph 1 and "inside the country" in Paragraph 2 were merely designed to protect the security, interests, or prestige of Korea from abroad.[47] In its 11-2 opinion, the Supreme Court held that Kim's distribution of the anti-government leaflets to foreign journalists constituted the kind of activities proscribed by the law. The Court noted that the print material was to defame the State. The Court remanded the decision to the Seoul Criminal District Court.[48]

Strongly dissenting from the majority, however, Justice Yi Il-gyu argued that the crime of defamation against the State required three elements: (1) The violator of the Code should be a Korean national; (2) The location of the crime should be outside of Korea; and (3) The interests to be protected by the Code should be the public opinion and credibility of Korea and its constitutional bodies in foreign countries. Justice Yi elaborated on his three-prong analysis of the anti-State defamation clause. Foreigners or those with no nationalities could not be criminals under the law and a Korean national's act within Korea could not be punished, according to him. Justice Yi then stated: "Even though foreign journalists reported abroad on a defamatory act against Korea which was committed by a Korean national inside Korea, the act cannot constitute a crime because it was done in Korea. The intent of Paragraph 2 [of Article 104-2] is interpreted in such a way as to punish a Korean national who uses foreigners or foreign organizations within Korea to endanger the security, interest, and prestige of the Republic of Korea abroad."[49]

He also said that because there was no difference between a Korean national's act of defaming the State to foreigners or foreign organizations within Korea and a Korean national's similar act to other Korean nationals, the defamatory act of the Korean national could not be punished under the law.[50] Justice Yi concluded that although Kim defamed the State by taking advantage of foreign correspondents in Korea, he could not be punished under the Criminal Code so long as they did not commit the acts outside of Korea, which endangered or were assumed to damage the security, interest, and prestige of Korea.[51]

Another dissent was filed by Justice Yi Hoe-chang, who criticized the majority of the Court for its "carelessly overextended interpretation" of the law.[52] He agreed with Justice Yi Il-gyu that Article 104-2 was to protect the security, interests, and prestige of Korea and to restrict Korean nationals' acts that might hurt the public image and credibility of Korea and its constitutional organs in foreign countries.[53] Justice Yi Hoe-chang, focusing on the meaning of the "by use of" foreigners or foreign organizations, stated that it should be viewed as "aiding or abetting" foreigners to defame the State.[54] Under the law, according to him, a Korean national's libel against the State could not be penalized, but Koreans' acts of aiding and abetting foreigners to defame the State within Korea might be prohibited under Paragraph 2 of Article 104 "because foreigners' defamatory acts will have a serious danger of affecting the public opinion and trust toward the State abroad."[55]

Justice Yi Hoe-chang took issue with the majority's way of interpreting "by use of" as "to." He asserted that it was an improperly expansive interpretation of the Code, going beyond the legislative intent behind the law.[56] He reasoned:

> We are fully aware of the fact that in today's international society, in which the development of communication and reporting technology is advanced, a Korean national's defamatory act toward the State in Korea may be no less harmful to the public opinion and trust regarding the State and its constitutional bodies than his similar act is abroad. Nevertheless, the Criminal Code targets only anti-State defamation outside the country; it does not aim at anti-State defamation within the country, except in extraordinary circumstances. This significant aspect of the Criminal Code was intended to eliminate the possibility that proscription against anti-State defamation within Korea will restrict the freedom of expression and criticism guaranteed by the Constitution.[57]

Justice Yi Hoe-chang claimed that the majority's holding that using foreigners to do the proscribed acts under Article 104-2 (2) meant doing the acts *to* the foreigners might make the clause inapplicable to a Korean national, who, as an indirect principal offender, aids a foreigner in defaming the State within Korea.[58] He doubted that punishing Korean nationals for defaming the State to foreigners would be more important than punishing Korean nationals for persuading foreigners to libel the State.[59]

The ruling in *Kim Chol-gi* was followed by the Supreme Court in *Kim Pyong-gon v. State*.[60] This 1986 anti-State defamation case resulted from Kim Pyong-gon's alleged distribution to a foreign correspondent in Seoul of a written statement on President Chun Doo Hwan's planned visit to the United States in April 1985.[61] In the statement entitled "Mr. [Chun Doo Hwan's] Planned Visit Should Be

Canceled," the Youth Alliance for Democratization Movement (YADM) said, "The United States should withdraw its support of the current regime because it is a military dictatorship conspiring to stay in power for long and it delays in pardoning and releasing those involved in the U.S. Cultural Center incident in Pusan."[62]

The Seoul Criminal District Court, Appellate Division, affirming the single-judge decision of the same court, held that Article 104-2, paragraph 2, provided not for a crime of aiding and abetting but for the act of committing a crime.[63] The court ruled that the defendant's distribution of the statement at issue to a foreign correspondent endangered the prestige of Korea and was assumed to harm the interests of Korea by insulting or defaming the President or by distorting the facts and disseminating false facts about the President.[64]

Kim appealed the decision of the Seoul Criminal District Court to the Supreme Court, arguing that the statement was a political expression to be protected by the Constitution.[65] The four-justice panel of the Supreme Court disagreed:

> As the defendant claimed, the crime [anti-State defamation] requires an act of defaming a particular constitutional body. A mere expression of political opinions does not constitute the crime. According to the facts reviewed by the court of first instance in a proper manner, the defendant's act of insulting or defaming the President, a governmental body established under the Constitution or of distorting the facts or spreading false facts about him, was assumed to endanger the interests and prestige of Korea. As a result, it met the criminal elements as stipulated in the Criminal Code. We cannot accept the defendant's argument that the statement involved was an expression of the citizens' political beliefs in that it was a protest to the U.S. government against its invitation to the President of Korea and that the statement did not aim at a particular constitutional agency. Indeed, it is clear that the statement exceeded far and above the boundaries of the political freedom of citizens and thus constituted a criminal act of violating the legal interests of protecting the security, interests, and prestige of the State.[66]

## SUMMARY AND CONCLUSIONS

The crime of anti-State defamation, which was prohibited by the Criminal Code from 1975 to 1988, was a statutory tool devised by the Korean government. It was one of numerous legal and extra-legal measures taken by President Park Chung Hee in the 1970s and by President Chun Doo Hwan in the 1980s to silence the outspoken opposition to the government. The anti-State defamation clause of the Korean law was fundamentally antithetical to the notion of a democratic polity, which South Korea had proclaimed itself to be over the years. In his classic statement on seditious libel, Professor Harry Kalven of the University of Chicago Law School stated:

> The concept of seditious libel strikes at the very heart of democracy. Political freedom ends when government can use its powers and its courts to

silence its critics.... [D]efamation of the government is an impossible notion for a democracy. In brief, I suggest that the presence or absence in the law of the concept of seditious libel defines the society. A society may or may not treat obscenity or contempt by publication as legal offenses without altering its basic nature. If, however, it makes seditious libel an offense, it is not a free society no matter what its other characteristics.[67]

In many ways, the seditious libel clause of the Criminal Code was the darkest chapter in the increasingly authoritarian rule of the Korean government for more than a decade beginning in the mid-1970s.

While not as insidious as the provisions on anti-State defamation, the provisions of the Criminal Code that prohibit defamation of those foreign leaders and diplomats who are present in Korea are noteworthy in that they illustrate how sensitive the Korean government is to international criticism, particularly criticism from friendly nations. This is understandable because Korea is highly dependent on its stronger allies in the West. Significantly, though, the provisions have rarely been enforced to date notwithstanding the fact that the presidents and other leaders of the U.S. government have often been subject to defamatory and insulting attacks by dissidents in Korea.

The Supreme Court of Korea is considered to be overly cautious in drawing the parameters of freedom of expression. This is particularly true with respect to the Court's application of the statutes such as the Criminal Code on anti-State defamation. When asked to define the constitutional protection of political expression, the Court offered no more than a cursory observation on the protection of "political opinions." The Court refused to elaborate on what statements would be political opinions not to be punished under the Criminal Code. The Court's strained interpretation of the Code epitomizes the Korean judiciary's approach to allowing the law to play a "subservient role ... to political and social power," rather than seizing "the role of an independent balance to the highly centralized power structure" of the Korean government before 1988.[68] Instead of interpreting the Code as it was phrased, the Court endeavored to divine the intents and purposes of the National Assembly in ruling for the government. The Court's constrictive interpretation of the Code was an inevitable consequence of Park and Chun's authoritarianism, in which political stability as part of "development politics" was a precondition for economic development and national security in Korea.[69]

# Right of Privacy

Privacy, "in practice as well as in concept," has long been recognized as an important element of human history.[1] It is no wonder that privacy has been guaranteed in a number of international agreements on political rights and civil liberties over the years. Article 12 of the United Nations Universal Declaration of Human Rights states: "No one shall be subjected to arbitrary interference with his privacy, family, home or correspondence, nor to attacks upon his honor and reputation. Everyone has the right to the protection of the law against such interference or attacks."[2] But privacy is not easy to define. Justice Hugo Black of the U.S. Supreme Court wrote in 1965, "'Privacy' is a broad, abstract and ambiguous concept."[3]

The conceptual ambiguity of privacy is derived from the fact that the meaning of the word varies from society to society. Professor Franklyn Haiman of Northwestern University observed: "What will be considered presumptuous, intrusive, or embarrassing by an individual depends in large measure on the value which the person's culture places on privacy, and that is a highly variable phenomenon. Not only do primitive cultures tend to have far less concern than modern industrialized societies about individual privacy in general but the specific kinds of behavior that are thought to require seclusion differ from culture to culture."[4] A 1990 comparative study of U.S. and Japanese law on privacy argued that in American society "where individual autonomy reigns supreme," privacy causes of action are limited to the individual about whom the precipitating statement was made; they are not, however, in Japan, where "relationship is the fundamental principle of society."[5]

South Korea is another good example in which culture affects the notion of privacy so as to make it different from the notion of privacy in other countries including the United States. Journalism researcher Jisuk Woo wrote in 1993:

> The meaning and the value of general "privacy" in Korea is [sic]
> different from those in Western countries. Although it is difficult to measure

how much the individual right to privacy is valued compared with other values, there are many examples where an individual's privacy is sacrificed for some other values. For instance, many high schools publicly post students' grades as a strategy to provide students an incentive to improve their grades. Some schools even assign seats in the class according to students' grades. This is very unlikely to happen in Western countries.[6]

In arguing for recognition of privacy as a legal right in American law, Samuel D. Warren and Louis D. Brandeis claimed in 1890, "Instantaneous photographs and newspaper enterprise have invaded the sacred precincts of private and domestic life; and numerous mechanical devices threaten to make good the prediction that 'what is whispered in the closet shall be proclaimed from the house-tops.'"[7] Given that privacy is widely defined as "the *control* we have over information about ourselves"[8] in the context of the "right to be let alone,"[9] privacy and freedom of speech and the press represent "an almost natural conflict: add to one and you subtract from the other."[10] The Supreme Court of Korea held that freedom of expression collides with personal privacy.[11] As Professor Rodney Smolla of William and Mary College wrote, however, the right of privacy and freedom of expression should be looked upon as "jealous siblings." Smolla stated: "[P]rivacy is often an aid to freedom of expression, for a life devoid of any intimacy or quiet contemplation is a life less likely to produce creative or insightful expression. Privacy may thus nurture the expressive side of men and women, by giving them something to say."[12]

The individual's right of privacy to control information about himself emerges as an important issue in Korea. One study has found that Koreans feel strongly that their privacy should be protected by law. Nearly 85 percent of those surveyed indicated that a privacy protection statute should require that:

1. Personal information about an individual should be collected after permission is obtained from the individual;
2. The governmental objective of gathering personal information should be clearly defined and the information should not be misused for purposes other than those originally stated;
3. The specified subject matter of protection of individual privacy should be set forth;
4. Individuals should be allowed access to their own files kept by the government;
5. Individuals should have a right to request government agencies to correct information about them in case it is inaccurate;
6. A supervisory mechanism like a movie review board or a broadcasting deliberation committee should be established;
7. Damages should be allowed for infringement on privacy;
8. Violators of another's right of privacy should be subjected to criminal sanctions.[13]

In this chapter, right of privacy is examined as an interest to be balanced with freedom of the press in Korea. An analysis of the case law as well as the constitutional and statutory framework of privacy in Korea is the primary focus of this chapter.

## CONSTITUTIONAL AND STATUTORY FRAMEWORK

The right of privacy had not been enumerated in the Constitution of Korea until 1980. Nevertheless, Kim Tong-chol, professor of journalism at Ehwa Women's University in Seoul, noted that privacy was protected in Korea as a basic right emanating from various constitutional provisions on citizens' freedoms and liberties.[14] The Constitution of 1980 expressly guaranteed privacy as a right for the first time in the history of Korea since 1948. Article 16 stated: "No citizen shall be subject to violation of privacy."[15] The privacy clause was carried over as Article 17 of the current Constitution amended in 1987, which stipulates that "[t]he privacy of no citizen shall be infringed."[16]

Privacy right is also protected under Article 10 of the Constitution. Article 10 provides: "All citizens shall be assured of human worth and dignity and have the right to pursue happiness. It shall be the duty of the State to confirm and guarantee the fundamental and inviolable human rights of individuals."[17] This clause is another carry-over from the 1980 Constitution.[18] The right to private life is protected by other constitutional provisions. For example, Articles 14 and 16 stipulate "freedom of residence and the right to move at will"[19] and citizens' right to "be free from intrusion into their place of residence."[20] The Constitution also prohibits violation of the privacy of correspondence.[21] Its freedom of expression clause protects privacy by forbidding speech and the press from violating "the honor or rights of others," adding that claims may be made for the injury resulting from violation of the honor or rights of others.[22] Further, privacy is clearly related to the constitutional protection of marriage and family life.[23]

Legislative efforts were reportedly being made to implement the constitutional protection of privacy as a basic right in 1993.[24] Of the current statutory status of privacy in Korea, however, Woo said:

> While the Korean constitution clearly indicates the right to privacy as a fundamental right of human beings, no specified attempt was made to construct an integrated law on privacy. Individual laws in other general areas such as the Libel Law and the Law on the National Governmental Officials, can be applied for the protection of privacy, but they are not targeted directly to privacy protection, nor can they cope with issues arising from the collection and use of personal information in the modern information society.[25]

Articles 750 and 751 of the Civil Code constitute the major statutory basis for proscribing invasion of privacy as an unlawful act in Korea. Article 750 reads, "Any person who causes damage to or inflicts injuries on another person by an unlawful act intentionally or negligently is bound to make compensation for damages arising therefrom."[26] Article 751 states that a person who violates the right of another or "inflict[s] any mental anguish" on another person must pay damages for non-pecuniary injury, irrespective of whether such injury was to the person, liberty, or reputation of another, or to his property rights.[27]

The Civil Code provides for the duration of the statute of limitation for privacy: "The right to claim damages which has arisen from an unlawful act shall elapse by prescription if not exercised within three years from the time when the injured party or his legal representative becomes aware of such damage and of the identity of the person who caused; the same shall apply if 10 years have elapsed from the time when the unlawful act was committed."[28] Other provisions of the Civil Code apply to privacy resulting from space. Article 243 is noteworthy in that it provides for the right of privacy as a notion of space: "If a person constructs, at a distance of less than two meters from the boundary line, a window or veranda which overlooks the inside of other person's house, he shall put a proper screen thereto."[29]

The Criminal Code also protects privacy. Article 316 of the Code makes criminal the opening of sealed letters, documents, or drawings.[30] Article 317 bars professionals including physicians, pharmacists, lawyers, and priests from disclosing secrets of others which come to their knowledge in the course of practicing their professions.[31] Similarly, the privacy of mails is guaranteed by Article 3 of the Postal Services Act, which states: "No postal employee who is, or was once, engaged in the postal services may disclose any private matters concerning the mail which may have come to his knowledge during his tenure of office."[32]

Intrusion into a private home of another is a crime under the Criminal Code. The Criminal Code stipulates: "A person who intrudes upon a human habitation, guarded dwelling house, structure or ship or occupied room shall be punished by penal servitude for not more than three years or by a fine not exceeding 15,000 *hwan*."[33] The Act Relating to Registration of Periodicals Act (Periodicals Act),[34] the Broadcast Act,[35] and the Comprehensive Cable Television Broadcast Act (Cable Television Act)[36] recognize privacy rights. The right of reply provisions of the statutes are applicable to complaints relating to inaccurate news reports which injure the privacy rights of individuals.[37]

The Act on Protection of Personal Information of Government Agencies (Personal Information Act)[38] was enacted by the National Assembly in 1993. It was designed to facilitate the proper execution of official duties and at the same time to safeguard people's rights and interests by providing for matters necessary for protection of personal information processed by computers in government agencies.[39] The statute prohibits the gathering of personal information of individuals which is feared to substantially infringe on their basic human rights such as their political ideology and beliefs unless the subject of the information agrees or other law designates the information as "to be gathered."[40] Under the Act, if government agencies plan to keep personal information files, the agencies are required to notify the Minister of Government Administration of the name, purpose of the files, the matters and their scope recorded in the file, and other relevant information.[41]

However, the notification requirement provision exempts certain personal information files as follows:

1. Containing records on the security of the State, diplomatic secrets, and other matters relating to vital national interests;
2. Containing records on matters relating to investigation of crimes, filing and maintenance of litigation, execution of sentencing, disposition of correction and security, and entry into and departure from Korea;
3. Containing records on matters relating to investigation of tax and customs criminals;
4. Used for test-operation of computers;
5. Containing records to be deleted within one year;
6. Containing information internally processed by the agency in custody of the file;
7. Aimed at the subjects of information who are determined under the Presidential Decree; and
8. Other similar personal information files designated under the Presidential Decree.[42]

While personal information files may not be used for purposes other than those of the agency keeping the files, the law lists several exceptional circumstances, including the accomplishment of official duties of other agencies, criminal investigation and litigation, or trial proceedings.[43] Individuals are allowed access to their personal information files in the government agencies.[44] Nonetheless, access is denied when it results in substantial interference with performance of official duties or when it is deemed to endanger a person's life and body, or damage his property or other interests unreasonably.[45]

## JUDICIAL INTERPRETATIONS

One legal commentator wrote on the judicial interpretation of privacy vis-à-vis reputation in Japan: "Cultural blinders notwithstanding, Japanese conceptions of defamation and privacy are fuzzy. Professor [Shigenori] Matsui has noted the confusion and observes that many plaintiffs, not understanding the distinction, simply allege both defamation and invasion of privacy resulting from the same facts and leave it to the courts to decide which theory is correct. Frequently, the courts add to the confusion by relying on both theories in reaching a decision."[46]

The Japanese approach to the right of privacy through libel law is similar to that of Korean courts. Media Law Professor Paeng Won-sun maintained in 1988 that privacy was recognized as part of reputation in its broader sense.[47] He added that no Korean court had ever ruled on privacy separately from reputation.[48] Kim Sang-yong, professor of law at Yonsei University in Seoul, also argued that "it seems that there has been no court decision" on the Civil Code on invasion of privacy as an unlawful act.[49]

In the past six years, however, several court decisions in Korea have been based on privacy claims, separately from or in addition to reputational injury claims. This, of course, does not necessarily say that Korean courts have made conscious efforts in distinguishing invasion of privacy from defamation, as American courts have done since the early 20th century. The basic differences between invasion of privacy and defamation are recognized in U.S. law:

> Defamation law protects the individual's interest in reputation; it permits compensation for other injury only when a publication *also* results in other personal harm. The requirement that the defamatory statement be false to be actionable permits no redress for invasion by accurate statements of what has been called "the sacred precincts of private and domestic life." Nor can an individual recover in defamation for false statements that injure feelings without at least presumptively injuring reputation.[50]

The law of privacy in Korea has not yet evolved to such an extent that it needs the classification of privacy torts in American law, as developed by Dean William Prosser in 1960. Prosser identified four different types of invasion of privacy: "intrusion," "public disclosure of private facts," "false light in the public eye," and "appropriation."[51] "Intrusion," which overlaps but is distinct from trespass, consists of the violation of one's legally protected "private" space or solitude without one's consent. "Public disclosure of private facts" involves the unreasonable publication of true but embarrassing private facts. "False light in the public eye," which is called "a close cousin of defamation,"[52] is placing an individual in a false light through publication. "Appropriation" is the commercial exploitation of the plaintiff's identity or likeness for the defendant's benefit or advantage. Significantly, one Korean law commentator suggested in 1993 that Prosser's classification of privacy torts would serve as a valuable frame of reference for Korean courts in determining whether an act constitutes a wrongful act under the Civil Code.[53]

Thus far, appropriation has often been a "right of publicity" issue[54] in privacy cases in Korea, while not exactly in the same way it has been in U.S. law. Korean courts have recognized it by way of protecting one's right to one's own likeness, or *chosanggwon* in Korean.[55] *Newsweek, Inc. v. Kwon Sun-jong*[56] was the most recent decision that arose from publication of pictures of three Korean women in the Pacific edition of *Newsweek* magazine.[57] In this 1994 case, the Seoul Civil District Court, Appellate Division, discussed the right of privacy in detail:

> It can be predicted on the basis of our experience that a person of ordinary sensibilities will have unpleasant feelings such as shame and embarrassment and thus have his emotional stability disturbed when a picture of his face and body is taken and the picture is widely disseminated. It is to a person's benefit in life to enjoy living in peace and quiet without undergoing these emotional sufferings. And it is reasonable to conclude that his peaceful life should be protected not only as a matter of morality but it should also be safeguarded *as his legal right of character, given the spirit of the Constitution*

*guaranteeing the human dignity and privacy and secrets of individuals* (this right is conveniently called "chosanggwon"). As a consequence, it constitutes a violation of the right to protect one's own likeness for the defendant to have taken pictures of the plaintiffs without their permission and to have published them in the defendant's magazine for worldwide distribution.[58]

The purpose of recognizing one's privacy right not to have his picture taken is to protect the person from emotional distress resulting from the taking and dissemination of the picture to the public, the Seoul Civil District Court stated.[59] The violation of the privacy right, the court ruled, does not require that the picture should have been taken after an intrusion into one's home. The court rejected *Newsweek*'s argument that the noncommercial use of the picture should be protected from liability. The court said that "limiting the right of privacy to one's identity to a commercial context is unreasonable because it restricts the scope of privacy protection too much."[60] The court held, however: "When it is found that a person's picture was obtained and published because of its nature of public interest and was used for public interest, it is not liable because it does not constitute a wrongful act."[61]

In September 1988, a Seoul district court handed down a decision addressing more directly an invasion of privacy through appropriation in the sense that a person's picture or likeness is used for another's commercial profit with no authorization. The Seoul Civil District Court, Appellate Division, held in *Han Hye-suk v. Lucky Goldstar Trading Co.*[62] that the defendant company and its advertising agency, L G Ad, was liable for 8 million *won* (US$10,000) damages to Han Hye-suk, a popular television actress who appeared in a TV drama on KBS (Korean Broadcasting Service), for their unauthorized use of Han's pictures for commercial gain.[63]

Han signed a contract with the defendants to use her 10 pictures for clothing advertisements of Bando Fashion, owned by Lucky Goldstar. The contract provided that the pictures were to run in the spring and summer 1987 advertising catalogues to be prepared by Bando Fashion. Han's pictures, however, were published in a number of women's magazines for advertisements for Bando Fashion clothing.[64] Han claimed that publications of her pictures in the magazines violated her right of privacy. The Seoul Civil District Court agreed, holding: "The defendants' unauthorized use of the plaintiff's pictures for magazine advertising was a violation of the plaintiff's right to protect her pictures from being used for purposes other than those originally agreed. Thus, the defendants are liable to the plaintiff for her emotional damage as a result of their wrongful act."[65]

Four months earlier, a Seoul civil district court in *Kim Kyong-ae v. Seoul Advertising and Planning Co.*[66] ruled against the plaintiff's claim for damages for an appropriation. The plaintiff, formerly a commercial model and now a housewife, claimed that the defendant had published for newspaper advertising of Yongdong Department Store an illustration of a woman in Korean traditional costume, which was similar to her photograph previously published in the cosmetics brochure put out by the Pacific Chemical Company in Seoul.[67] She argued that the defendant was liable to her for her psychological pain and her financial loss because of the defendant's violation of her right in using her picture for commercial advertisements without her permission.[68]

The appellate division of the Seoul district court first examined the scope of a person's privacy right to be protected from being commercially exploited by others. The court ruled that an individual's right to his likeness protects the unique qualities of his likeness by prohibiting the unauthorized use of it for commercial or noncommercial ends.[69] While it does not distinguish between a photograph and an illustration, the court held, "because a person's right to protect his own likeness consists in securing the person's outer appearance from its unjustifiable commercial use, the complained of likeness can fall into the coverage of the tort only when ordinary people can immediately recognize who it represents."[70] Applying this standard for determining the presence of a privacy violation in the case, the Seoul district court concluded that the plaintiff's privacy right was not violated by the defendant's publishing the illustration in question for commercial advertising. The court held that notwithstanding a similarity between the defendant's illustration and the plaintiff's photograph in their contents and shapes, the face of the woman in the illustration "cannot be viewed as representing that of the plaintiff or her unique features."[71] The court stated that the illustration, even though based on the plaintiff's photograph, could not violate the plaintiff's privacy.

Article 751 of the Civil Code was applied by the Supreme Court of Korea in an intrusion case. Although the case did not involve freedom of expression issues, the Court's interpretation of Article 751 is illustrative of how intrusion becomes a violation of privacy. *Ko Chong-hi v. Chon Ki-hwa*[72] arose from the defendant's illegal entry into the bedroom of the plaintiff for the purpose of raping her. The Supreme Court held that the defendant must pay damages to the plaintiff for "interrupting" her life and for "disturbing" her emotional security. The Court reasoned that judging from the good sense of social life, it was clear that the defendant committed a wrongful act.[73] The Court further ruled that the defendant was also liable to the plaintiff's husband for the emotional injury he caused in the course of intruding into his bedroom.

## SUMMARY AND CONCLUSIONS

Privacy has rarely been a pressing concern in Korea as a legal right, though it has been given attention in Korea in varying degrees over the years. Since 1980, however, privacy has been expressly protected as a constitutional right. Of course, it had already been statutorily recognized as an important societal interest. Invasion of privacy, for example, is punished as a crime or a wrongful act under the Criminal and Civil Codes. Also, several press statutes such as the Periodicals Act and the Broadcast Act contain provisions on privacy.

More recently, the Korean government has devised several legal mechanisms on privacy relating to personal information in the age of computer technology. The Act on Protection of Personal Information of Government Agencies (Personal Information Act) is a good example. The Act reflects the worrisome impact of computers on personal privacy as the specter of "Big Brother" becomes more and more a reality. "When government gathers and stores personal information," as one American media law commentator noted recently, "it has a concomitant duty to ensure the privacy of that information."[74] The Korean statute on privacy is designed to protect Koreans' right of privacy to control information about themselves. However, it tends to emphasize release more than withholding of personal information because it provides for numerous exceptions to prohibition of access to the information. Jisuk Woo pointed out: "The value of 'free flow of information' or 'freedom of expression' is ... very likely to be valued more than that of individual privacy, because in the long history of oppression of the mass media and the freedom of expression, the value of free flow of information may be considered 'the most important value' yet to be achieved in Korea."[75]

To date, court decisions on invasion of privacy in Korea have been far and few between. It is only in recent years that Korean courts had an occasion to rule on privacy as a legal right. Nevertheless, it is clear that Koreans are more conscious of their right to privacy and are more willing to sue when they feel their privacy is violated by the press. Although Korean courts have yet to develop the kind of privacy law that American courts have developed in the past 100 years, they have accepted the "right of publicity" in the context of appropriation. Importantly, Korean courts have accepted "public interest" as a possible defense against liability for "right of publicity" privacy invasion.

# CHAPTER 11

# National Security

Since 1987, when the Korean government embarked on a series of sweeping sociopolitical and legal reforms, South Korea has emerged as one of the most democratic Asian nations in the sense of participatory politics. "[P]erhaps the strongest evidence of progress toward democratization," as one Western journalist in Korea put it, "is that no one talks about democracy" during the presidential election of December 1992.[1] Likewise, Sang Hoon Bang, publisher of *Chosun Ilbo*, an influential daily newspaper in Seoul, claimed: "Before democracy was restored in 1987, newspapers were suppressed by authoritarian regimes. Freedom of the press was almost completely lost. Today, the Korean press enjoys an unprecedented amount of freedom, which is the most crucial element of democracy."[2]

Freedom of the press, however, does not exist as an absolutely impregnable right; it must be balanced with other important social values. National security is one of them. As Justice Felix Frankfurter of the U.S. Supreme Court observed in 1951, security of the government from violent overthrow is a "substantial enough interest" of the government to limit freedom of expression, for "if a society cannot protect its very structure ... it must follow that no subordinate value can be protected."[3] The Supreme Court of Korea also stated that the Constitution of Korea guarantees freedom of expression as a limited right in that the freedom may be restricted for the security of the State, the maintenance of order and public welfare unless its essential element is violated.[4]

The Korean government has in varying degrees restricted freedom of the Korean press on the grounds that it should be reconciled with the national security emergencies facing the country. The uniqueness of South Korea as a divided nation confronting the ever-belligerent North Korean communists across the Demilitarized Zone (DMZ) explains in part why national security has been an interest inferior to none in the hierarchy of sociopolitical values in the country since the Korean War of 1950–1953.[5] During his visit to South Korea in January 1995,

General John Shalikashvili, chairman of the U.S. Joint Chiefs of Staff, characterized the situation on the Korean Peninsula as "tense and dangerous."[6] One American scholar on Korea noted, "The threat faced by the Republic [South Korea] is a very real and serious one, notwithstanding its exploitation for domestic political purpose. North Korea has made no secret of its hostility toward the South Korean regime...."[7] Nevertheless, the Korean government cannot have *carte blanche* to use national security in limiting the constitutionally guaranteed freedom of speech and of the press at the slightest threat—real or imagined.

This chapter examines the conflict between freedom of expression and national security interests in Korea by exploring how national security is statutorily defined and judicially interpreted as a societal interest for restricting freedom of speech and the press.

## CONSTITUTIONAL AND STATUTORY FRAMEWORK

As in the past, the current Constitution of Korea contains a provision that empowers the government to restrict all constitutional guarantees, including freedom of the press. Article 35 states: "The freedoms and rights of citizens may be restricted by law only when necessary for national security, the maintenance of law and order or of public welfare."[8] In accordance with the constitutional provision for the legislative power of the government, the Korean government has enacted and enforced a number of laws and regulations restrictive of freedom of speech and the press.[9] Some of the laws and regulations have directly dealt with freedom of the press. The Act Relating to Registration of Periodicals (Periodicals Act),[10] the Broadcast Act,[11] and the Act on Import and Distribution of Foreign Periodicals (Foreign Periodicals Act)[12] are cases in point. Others bear on the press in an indirect way.

The Periodicals Act enumerates several conditions for which the Ministry of Public Information (MOPI) can use its suspending authority,[13] but none of them directly relates to national security interests. The statute, however, prohibits anyone who is subject to punishment under the National Security Act and other specified laws from being a publisher or editor of a periodical.[14] The broadcast law is identical to the Periodicals Act in its disqualification provisions, which enumerate certain individuals who are not eligible to be the "head or person in charge of programming" of a broadcasting station.[15]

Under the Foreign Periodicals Act, the Ministry of Culture and Sports can take comprehensive measures against foreign periodicals that the Korean government finds may "subvert the constitutional system of the State or undermine the public security and customs" of Korea.[16] The government can order them suspended from sale or their contents deleted[17] and retract the permit for distribution of the periodicals.[18]

Numerous restrictive special laws and regulations combined with the traditionally authoritarian political culture had undoubtedly contributed to constraining press freedom in South Korea until recent years. The ruling authorities had long employed the repressive laws to perpetuate a cowed press up to 1987. Typical of the special laws are the National Security Act[19] and the now abolished Anti-Communist Act.[20]

When the National Security Act was first enacted in 1948,[21] it was directed at "anti-State activities" posing a danger to the national security of Korea and thus was intended to ensure the security of the State and the freedom of citizens. The law, however, was used by the Korean government "not only against espionage or sabotage, but also to control and punish domestic dissent, such as the publication of unorthodox political commentary, art, or literature, on the ground that such expressions benefitted an 'antistate organization.'"[22] More often than not, the law had been employed by past governments to protect "political security" interests.[23]

The Anti-Communist Act, another special law relating to national security in Korea, was enacted shortly after the military coup d'etat led by General Park Chung Hee in 1961. It was "[p]erhaps the single most important law in terms of its widespread political effect" and "perhaps the greatest articulated threat to the educated groups."[24] The law provided for hard labor for up to seven years for any person who praised, encouraged, or sided with or "through other means" the activities of anti-State organizations or their members or foreign communist organizations.[25] As U.S. critics pointed out: "The only requirement for conviction under the Anti-Communist Law was that the conduct in question be deemed to have benefitted an anti-state organization. No subjective intention on the part of the actor to aid such an organization need be proved."[26]

The Kim Song-hwan episode in October 1966 illustrates the impact on the Korean press of the Anti-Communist Act as a legal and non-legal means of coercion. Cartoonist Kim's comic strip published in the September 22, 1966, issue of the *Dong-A Ilbo* newspaper was alleged to have benefitted North Korea in violation of the Act "because it instigated the people to entertain class consciousness by means of encouraging them to have the feeling of hatred for business tycoons."[27] In the comic strip, Kim's hero, while reading a newspaper, said, "Now, war has been declared against the Zaibatsu Republic," and a nearby A-frame carrier commented, "Don't they need recruit volunteers, sir?" The prosecution claimed that Kim's comic strip focused on public indignation at the smuggling by business tycoons.[28]

The 1980 National Security Act, which incorporated various provisions of the Anti-Communist Act, provided:

> Any person who has benefitted the anti-State organization by praising, encouraging, or siding with or through other means the activities of the anti-State organizations or their members or the person who had been under instruction from such organizations shall be punished by penal servitude for not more than seven years;
> Any person who has, for the purpose of committing [the above actions], produced, imported, duplicated, kept in custody, transported, disseminated,

sold, or acquired documents, drawings, and any other similar means of expression shall be punished by the same penalty as set forth in each paragraph.[29]

The National Security Act was revised in May 1991[30] to "control anti-State activities which endanger the national security, so that the safety of the State as well as the existence and freedom of the citizens may be secured."[31] The 1991 revision of the National Security Act was the Korean government's legislative action subsequent to the Constitution Court's qualified ruling[32] of 1990 on the constitutionality of Article 7 of the Act.[33] The revised National Security Act is designed to curb governmental abuse by requiring that the law's interpretation and application "be done within the necessary minimum for the accomplishment of the [law's] purpose...."[34] Stipulating that the law "should not be interpreted excessively or should not limit unreasonably the human rights of citizens secured by the Constitutional law,"[35] the Act mandates a narrow judicial interpretation.

Under the new National Security Act, "anti-State organization" is defined as "an association or group within the territory of the Republic of Korea or outside of it, organized for the purpose of assuming a title of the government or disturbing the State."[36] The revised provision does not penalize contact with communist organizations or governments in countries other than North Korea. The National Security Act of 1980 was also revised so that acts of praising, encouraging, publicizing, or showing sympathy for an anti-State organization will be punished only when committed with the knowledge that it will endanger national security and survival and the free and democratic basic order. Article 7 of the revised statute stipulates:

(1) Any person who has, *with the knowledge* that he might endanger the existence, security of the State or the basic order of free democracy, praised, or encouraged or propagandized or sided with the activities of an anti-State organization, its member or a person who had been under instruction from such organization, or who has propagandized, instigated a disturbance of the State shall be punished by penal servitude for a term not exceeding seven years;

(2) Deleted;

(3) Any person who has organized an association which purports to commit the actions as stipulated in Paragraph 1 or has participated in such an association shall be punished by penal servitude for not less than one year;

(4) Any person who has, as a member of the association as mentioned in Paragraph 3, fabricated or disseminated false facts concerning such matters that might cause social disorder shall be punished by penal servitude for not less than two years;

(5) Any person who has, for the purpose of committing the actions as stipulated in Paragraph 1, 3 or 4, produced, imported, duplicated, kept in custody, transported, disseminated, sold or acquired documents, drawings, and other similar means of expression shall be punished by the same penalty as set forth in each paragraph.[37]

The current National Security Act further requires that punishment of acts of giving or receiving goods or money to or from a member of an anti-State organization, or communicating with a member of an anti-State organization or someone acting under its instructions, or escaping from or to the territory of an anti-State organization be based on the "scienter" proof on the part of the accused.[38]

While the revised National Security Act helps to eliminate the "possibility of infringement of human rights" of Koreans by limiting the scope of its application,[39] its amendments are still considered ineffective in that they are "vague and inhibit the ordinary citizen's understanding under the constitution of what is in fact prohibited."[40]

The Constitution of Korea accords the President power to issue executive orders "[i]n case of major hostilities affecting national security ... only when it is required to preserve the integrity of the nation, and it is impossible to convene the National Assembly."[41] Furthermore, Article 52 of the Constitution provides for the power of the President to proclaim martial law to "maintain the public safety and order by mobilization of the military forces in time of war, armed conflict or similar national emergency."[42] Under extraordinary martial law, special measures may be taken with respect to freedom of speech, the press, assembly, and association,[43] as well as other matters relevant to the enforcement of martial law.[44] The martial law authorizes the martial law commander appointed by the President "to take whatever special measures arising from military necessities concerning ... speech, the press" where an extraordinary martial law is enforced.[45]

As discussed above, the Foreign Periodicals Act regulates foreign publications. Nevertheless, the law is not the only statutory device of the Korean government dealing with foreign periodicals. Also indirectly affecting the press is the Customs Act.[46] Article 146 provides that no "books, publications, drawings, films, phonographic records, video works, sculpture and other items of similar nature that will either disturb the national constitutional order or harm public security or custom"[47] or that "will reveal confidential information of the Government or are used for intelligence activities" shall be imported or exported.[48] Any person who violates the provisions of the Customs Act regarding foreign publications is subject to at least one year in prison or fine of up to 20 million *won* (US$25,000).[49]

## JUDICIAL INTERPRETATIONS

### Anti-Communist and National Security Acts Cases: 1948–1980

The National Security Act of 1948 and the Anti-Communist Act of 1961 were applied in a number of cases arising from freedom of expression issues until 1980, when the two laws were combined into a new National Security Act. Especially the much criticized Anti-Communist Act when in force in the sixties and seventies was invoked against the Korean press on several occasions. In interpreting the special laws, however, Korean courts were wary of the possible adverse impact of the legislation upon press freedom in Korea, where there was a "pronounced" gap between law and practice.[50]

In *State v. Choe Sok-chae*,[51] for example, the Supreme Court of Korea in 1956 affirmed the ruling of the Taegu High Court for Choe Sok-chae, editor-in-chief of *Taegu Maeil Shinmun*, who was charged with violating the National Security Act of 1948. The Court held that Choe's critical editorial on a government policy was to offer a constructive suggestion for the authorities, not to help North Korean communists.[52] This case involved Choe's editorial, "Don't Use Students as a Tool," on the authorities' mobilization of young students for a series of government-sponsored rallies against the communist nationals supervising the cease-fire of the Korean War.[53] Choe pointed to the harmful impact of the rallies on primary and secondary school children.[54] The editorial was quoted by Pyongyang Radio in North Korea for propaganda. Human rights lawyer Pak Won-sun, an authority on national security laws of Korea,[55] noted that the courts were independent in ruling against the government in *Choe Sok-choe* without being dictated by the Rhee Syngman regime.[56]

When a scholarly article advocating a proletariat movement in South Korea was published as an expression of opinion, it did not violate the National Security Act. In *Yu Kun-il v. State*,[57] the Seoul District Court held in 1958 that the defendant wrote his article in a Seoul National University journal for a purely academic purpose although the contents of the article seemed to be radical. The court also said the defendant merely expressed his ideas on socialist democracy. The court thus ruled that the defendant was not guilty of violation of the National Security Act.[58]

One year later, the Supreme Court in *Progressive Party v. State*[59] held that the constitutional guarantee of freedom of speech and the press protected the Progressive Party, which adopted as its platform the denial of liberal democracy, nationalization of major industries, and South Korea's peaceful unification with North Korea under its leadership. The Court paid close attention to the intention of the party in discussing the peaceful unification in an affirmative way with no ulterior motives relating to the government of North Korea. The Court significantly recognized the unique value of freedom of *political expression* in a democracy as indispensable to the normal activities of political party members.[60]

In August 1964, a newspaper reporter in Seoul was sentenced to one year in prison for a violation of the Anti-Communist Act, Article 4 (1), of 1961.[61] In *State v. Chu Yong-hyon*,[62] the defendant published a story in *Kyunghyang Shinmun* after listening to Pyongyang Radio from North Korea. "There are millions of people on the verge of starving to death in our country [South Korea]. Our government takes an easygoing attitude, adjusting grain prices.... If relief measures are nothing more than an empty rhetoric, accept and distribute the 2 million bags of rice that North Korea promises to provide for us," the story claimed. "In North Korea jobs are offered to the unemployed. Thus, negotiating with North Korea on the opening of Panmunjom [truce village in the DMZ] is more urgent to us than the South

Korea-Japan conference."[63] Judge Yang Hon of the Seoul Criminal District Court held that the defendant benefitted North Korea by siding with its activities through letting people read his story.[64]

In 1964, Hwang Yong-ju, former president of Munhwa Broadcasting Corporation (MBC) in Seoul, published an article, "Our Firm Determination for a Unified Government in Korea," in the *Saedae* (Generation) magazine. He argued (1) that North and South Korea should be admitted to the United Nations simultaneously; (2) that the United States stationed its troops in South Korea for its own interests; (3) that it was doubtful whether South Korea benefitted from the Okinawa military base of the United States; (4) that North and South Korea should sign a nonaggression treaty and reduce their military forces on an equal basis; and (5) that North and South Korea should start a conference aimed at reducing tensions and relaxing hostilities between them. In *Hwang Yong-ju v. State*,[65] Hwang was charged with a violation of the Anti-Communist Act by benefiting North Korea through his article. He took issue with the constitutionality of the Act for its vagueness and overbreadth.[66] He also claimed that the "clear and present danger" test should be used in restricting freedom of expression and that under this test his article did not create such danger to South Korea.[67]

The Seoul Criminal District Court, rejecting Hwang's argument, held that the theme of Hwang's article was the same as advocated by the communists in North Korea. The court found that the article depicted North Korea as another political regime on the Korean Peninsula, thus negating the basic constitutional principle of South Korea that South Korea was the only legitimate government on the Korean Peninsula. The court further stated that the article damaged the normally amicable relations between South Korea and the United States, creating a favorable environment for North Korea's military revolution.[68] The Supreme Court curtly affirmed the Seoul district court's decision, which did not consider the "clear and present danger" test argued by Hwang.[69] One legal commentator wrote: "In the past, 'intent' was essential in determining the crime of espionage or aiding and abetting the enemy, but as the *Hwang Yong-ju* case indicates, the Supreme Court's position underwent a change: intent was no longer held to be essential; now 'result' was all that counted and was sufficient to constitute a crime of espionage or aiding and abetting the enemy."[70]

A movie director in 1965 violated the Anti-Communist Act when he produced a film, "Seven Lady POWs." The Seoul Criminal District Court in *State v. Yi Man-hi*[71] held that director Yi Man-hi supported the cause of North Korea on the grounds that his movie portrayed North Korean soldiers during the Korean War in a favorable way while emphasizing the negative aspects of the South Korean and American forces.[72]

In December 1966, a Seoul district court in *State v. So Min-ho*[73] used the "clear and present danger" doctrine, as developed by the U.S. Supreme Court,[74] in applying the Anti-Communist Act to statements made by an opposition leader. So Min-ho, chairman of the Democratic Socialist Party, stated on May 27, 1966, "If I come to power, I am willing to confront Kim Il Sung [President of North Korea] through an international organization or at a face-to-face meeting."[75] He also said on April 13, 1966, that the Park Chung Hee regime sent South Korean soldiers to South Vietnam as a means to stay in power and to help domestic and foreign merchants to accumulate capital. So argued: "Is it preposterous for us to carry on with the Vietnam War as a proxy while the United States is responsible for guarding our front line?"[76] Condemning the Park regime's policy of sending South Korean soldiers to South Vietnam as mercenaries, he asked Koreans to "actively participate in and to continuously support" his plan to oppose any further dispatch of Korean soldiers to Vietnam and to demand the quick return of the soldiers to Korea.[77] In a third statement of May 9, 1966, on his party's unification policy, So suggested that there should be an exchange of letters, journalists, athletes, and relatives between North and South Korea.[78]

So claimed that his remark on Kim Il Sung was qualified with "if people want and if it is for the interest of the State" and that it thus should be protected speech in a democratic society like South Korea.[79] The Seoul Criminal District Court disagreed, holding that freedom of speech was not unlimited under the Constitution. The court stated: "It is highly likely that freedom of speech will be used as a pretext for destroying social order. If a statement constitutes a clear and present danger to society, the statement can be restricted for the maintenance of order and public welfare."[80] So's statement did not warrant the application of the clear and present danger principle, the court held, because it resulted in a clear and present danger of undermining South Korea's policy of thwarting the anti-State activities of North Korea.[81]

On the other hand, the Seoul district court in *So Min-ho* held that So's criticism of the Park administration's policy on Korean soldiers in the Vietnam War was protected under the Constitution. The court reasoned that So's motives in criticizing the Vietnam policy were "totally" different from those of North Korea.[82] The court concluded that So opposed Park's policy because he was concerned that South Korea's national defense would be weakened by the dispatch of Korean troops to Vietnam and that South Vietnam was not a suitable battlefield for Korean soldiers in its weather and terrain and that Korean soldiers were discriminated against by other foreign troops.[83]

The Seoul district court in *So Min-ho* applied the clear and present danger doctrine in ruling that So's discourse on the possible North-South Korea exchange did not violate the Anti-Communist Act.[84] So's exchange idea was used by North Korean government as propaganda material on its own unification policy, but the court underscored the fundamental differences between So's idea and that of North Korea. The court elaborated: "The North Korea's exchange proposition is aimed at turning South Korea into a communist nation. By contrast, the objective of the defendant's proposal is to accomplish a democratic unification on the initiative of the Republic of Korea [South Korea] within the framework of the ROK Constitution. Further, So's exchange theory itself is not a clear and currently occurring danger, but was offered as a step for preparation and research on unification."[85]

In 1967, two literary works led to a conflict between press freedom and the Anti-Communist Act. In two separate cases, press freedom prevailed in one and failed in the other. In the first case, *State v. Kim Chun-sik*,[86] the Taejon District Court addressed the problem of how the one-act play entitled "Songaji" allegedly violated the Anti-Communist Act. The court held that "[r]ead as a whole, the radio drama was mainly to depict the psychological discord between a country girl and a city woman, not to focus on encouraging the kind of class struggle advocated by the communists."[87] The play, therefore, could not be viewed to support a cause of action for a crime under the Anti-Communist Act. In a second 1967 case, *State v. Nam Chong-hyon*,[88] however, the Seoul Criminal District Court ruled that the defendant's novel published in a literary monthly was full of expression leading readers to become anti-American. The court, characterizing the anti-American theme of the novel as promoting the cause of the North Korean communists, concluded that the defendant "sided with" North Korea in violation of the Anti-Communist Act.[89]

A Taegu district court in 1967 adopted the "clear and present danger" test in upholding the press in an Anti-Communist Act case. In *Yi Sang-gwan v. State*,[90] Judge Han Pyong-chae ruled that the defendants, who published a news story on an espionage search operation, should be justified in reporting the operation, for their story "did not pose the kind of *present and clear danger* that would irreparably jeopardize" the spy operation under way.[91] Judge Han, who stressed that press freedom could not be curtailed merely on the grounds that anti-communism happened to be a national policy of Korea, stated: "Freedom of the press is most important for survival of a political democracy. Only press freedom can ensure an ideal national consensus for us. It can also protect civil rights from being infringed upon by the government. It contributes to our playing a creative role in our overall national development through its criticism and factual reporting. Indeed, press freedom is a *life-and-death issue* for our democracy."[92]

The *Yi Sang-gwan* case arose from a newspaper article, which said that Yongdok County police began a search for North Korean espionage agents after being alerted to the discovery of several spying devices. *Taegu Maeil Shinmun* published the story notwithstanding the request from the police for a news blackout on the espionage operation. The government argued that the publication assisted North Korea by helping the communist agents to flee. In rejecting the government's arguments, Judge Han observed that first, in spite of the "news blackout" request, the newspaper received no "official written request" from those in a responsible position; second, the information published in the newspaper had been already known to almost every one in the area for a week prior to the publication; and third, there was no evidence indicating that publication of the story was intended to aid North Korea. The ruling of the single-judge district court of Taegu was appealed by the government to the three-judge appellate panel of the same district court. The appellate panel of the Taegu District Court affirmed the decision of Judge Han, without expressing its views on Judge Han's application of the clear and present danger test.[93]

Human rights attorney Pak Won-sun wrote in 1992 that the *Yi Sang-gwan* case was "significant not only because it has accepted the 'clear and present danger theory' which has been established in U.S. case law as a legal standard for restriction of press freedom but it has also discussed precisely the meaning of press censorship under law, recognizing the value of press freedom."[94] The Journalists Association of Korea noted that the whole judicial process in the case marked "a new chapter in the history of the fighting Korean press."[95]

When a *Dong-A Ilbo* reporter published a story claiming that an informant was not paid a cash reward for information on an espionage suspect, the report did not violate the Anti-Communist Act. The Supreme Court in *Chong Ik-chin v. State*[96] held that the reporter did not know that his article could affect the counter-espionage operation or benefit the anti-State organization as prescribed by the law. The Court added that the article clarified possible mishandling of the compensation money to be paid by the government for discovery of a suspected North Korean spy. As in *Yi Sang-kwan*, the Court emphasized that the spy-search operation was widely known to the public well before the publication of the story.[97]

In 1970, one year after *Chong Ik-chin*, the Seoul Criminal District Court in *Kim Che-yol v. State*[98] declared that "[o]nce classified military information is discussed in pubic, it can no longer be categorized as secret. The publication of now unclassified information is not subject to punishment under the Anti-Communist Act and the Military Secrets Act."[99] The *Kim Che-yol* case involved Tongyang News Agency, which reported a three-year combat preparation plan debated at an open meeting of the National Defense Committee of the National Assembly of Korea. The court held that the government's request for a news embargo on the plan was no more than a cooperative understanding between the government and the press. So, the court ruled, "even though the press did not comply with the embargo request, it could not be criminally punished."[100] On appeal, the Supreme Court affirmed the lower court's ruling, stating that the story on the defense budget plan did not establish the reporters' positive intent to serve the interests of North Korea.[101]

In 1972, however, the Supreme Court defined classified state secrets broadly enough to cover virtually everything. The Court in *Yim Chong-jo v. State*[102] held that even though it was already published in newspapers or broadcast over radio and TV, the information, when known to North Korea and found useful to it, was protected as a classified state secret under the National Security Act. The *Yim Chong-jo* decision supports Professor Pnina Lahav's proposition that "if the history of governmental suppression teaches anything, it is that the concept of national security has been quite elastic, and has been used by governments to shelter information that was politically embarrassing or that for some political reason the government did not wish the people to know."[103]

The *Hwang Yong-ju* decision of 1965 was followed by the Seoul Criminal District Court in *State v. So Min-ho*, a 1972 Anti-Communist Act case.[104] The issue in *So Min-ho* was whether freedom of the press and speech would protect the campaign speech of a presidential candidate arguably beyond the established constitutional boundaries. At issue in the case was a speech by So, who proposed that the armed forces of North and South Korea be reduced in proportion to the population of the North and the South to lighten the enormous financial burden of military expenditures placed upon the peoples of the two Koreas. Given that North Korea participated in the armistice conference at Panmunjom and in the International Olympic Games, So also argued, "North Korea is recognized as a legitimate political entity by the world community. Thus, we have to recognize North Korea as such."[105]

The Seoul district court in *So Min-ho* first related the Anti-Communist Act to the "clear and present danger" in applying the law:

> The freedom of speech clause of the Constitution does not allow an unlimited liberty. When it is necessary for the maintenance of order and public welfare, that is, when the contents of a statement pose a clear and present danger to our social order and public welfare, the freedom can be restricted by law. On the basis of this constitutional provision, Article 4 (1) of the Anti-Communist Act is one of those revised statutes to restrict a statement when it brings about a clear and present danger to the social order and public welfare.[106]

The preferred status of political expression under the Constitution, as recognized in the *Progressive Party* case, was given notice. The *So Min-ho* court, however, concluded: "Although the speech in question was made by So in the capacity of a presidential candidate to express his political views, it creates a clear and present danger to social order in that it suggests that North Korea should be recognized as a legitimate sovereignty.... This apparently contributes to enhancing the international prestige of the puppet regime of North Korea."[107]

*Chong Chae-in v. State*[108] contrasts with *So Min-ho* in that the Supreme Court refused to find the defendant's statement illegal under the Anti-Communist Act. In *Chong Chae-in*, the defendant, then a member of the opposition New Democratic Party, denounced the ruling class in South Korea in the same way as a North Korean communist would do. He claimed that the government under President Park Chung Hee was characterized by three criminal elements—injustice and corruption, an attempt at establishing the generalissimo, and a scheme to destroy democracy once and for all. While admitting that some phrases used by the defendant were those frequently adopted by North Korea in attacking South Korea, the Supreme Court held that this did not necessarily mean that the opposition politician attempted to serve the interests of the enemy in the North. The Court rejected the prosecutor's argument that the defendant advocated communism through his vociferous criticism of President Park and his government. The Court considered the defendant's purpose in making the criticism. The defendant wanted to emphasize the weaknesses of the ruling Democratic Republican Party from the perspective of his opposition party, according to the Court.[109]

The Seoul District Court in *State v. Chang Pong-jin,*[110] a 1972 case, held that *Dong-A Ilbo* did not violate the Anti-Communist Act in publishing an article that claimed that some Koreans living near a military base cut up war tanks and sold them as scrap metal for money. The court reasoned that the writer of the article, while he was apparently mistaken in having written the story, did not undermine the overall public confidence in the South Korean Army to the benefit of North Korea.

Under the Anti-Communist Act, it was a crime to listen to North Korean broadcasts and read leaflets disseminated by North Korean authorities. In adjudicating such cases, Korean courts considered the circumstances involved. For example, the intention of the listeners or readers in getting exposed to the North Korean propaganda onslaught was a primary factor in the judgments of the courts. Accidental listening to the North Korean broadcasting denouncing the Park Chung Hee regime was not a violation of the Anti-Communist Act, held the Supreme Court in *Nam Tuk-u v. State*[111] in 1968. The case grew out of an allegation that the defendant heard the broadcast over the radio from North Korea in a coffee shop and he prevented an employee of the coffee shop from turning off the radio. What he and other people heard on the radio was North Korea's virulent attack on the South Korean government action to raise railroad fares. The North Korean radio charged: "The chieftain of Chongwadae [South Korea's presidential mansion in Seoul] residents hiked railroad fares to gain private profits for them."[112] He was indicted for violating the Anti-Communist Act in aiding the activities of anti-State organizations by getting other people in the coffee shop to hear the broadcast from North Korea. The lower court ruled the defendant guilty. On appeal, the Supreme Court remanded the judgment to the original court, stating that the defendant "inadvertently heard the broadcast in question, which indicates that he did not intend to violate the law."[113] In 1975, the Court again reversed the decision of the Extraordinary High Court-Martial, which had found a defendant guilty for merely listening to a North Korean broadcast.[114]

The Supreme Court in another radio-listening case ruled for the defendant involved in an allegedly illegal act of advancing the North Korean interests. The case, *Chang Yong-sik v. State,*[115] concerned a Korean resident from Japan listening to a Pyongyang radio broadcast. Noting that the defendant was not likely to have fully understood the North Korean broadcast, the Court held that there was no reasonable ground for concluding that the defendant intentionally praised or sided with North Korea when he made favorable comments on North Korea.[116] Two years prior to *Chang Yong-sik*, the Supreme Court ruled that the discussion of foreign publications about North Korea did not violate the Anti-Communist Act.[117]

In December 1976, however, the Supreme Court in *Paek Kwang-ok v. State*[118] held that the defendant had violated the Anti-Communist Act when he took notes of what he heard from North Korean broadcasts. The Court observed that the defendant, who had been already won over by an anti-State organization, listened purposely to the North Korean radio and kept notes of the contents of the broadcasts.

Note-taking of the broadcast, the Court held, was clearly tantamount to serving the interests of the enemy. The Court also stated that the illegal act was a violation of the pertinent laws of South Korea, whether it was done in public or in private.[119]

The Anti-Communist Act punished possession of documents, drawings, and other similar means of expression in support of the activities of an anti-State organization. The Seoul Criminal District Court in *Hwang Chong-guk v. State*[120] sentenced to six months in prison a defendant who acquired allegedly seditious literature from North Korea and passed it around among several people without notifying the authorities. The court ruled that the defendant's dissemination of leaflets and books on a South Korean soldier who defected to North Korea was to encourage the subversive activities of North Korea against South Korea.[121]

The possession or purchase of books on socialism or communism was subject to punishment under the Anti-Communist Act although the criminal intent of defendants was required to be proved by the government. The Supreme Court in 1970 affirmed the lower court's decision against the defendant in *Kim Kak v. State*[122] on grounds that the defendant knew that he was prohibited from purchasing or selling the books at issue under the Anti-Communist Act. One year later, the Seoul Criminal District Court in *State v. Kim Chong-nam*[123] ruled that the defendant, in violation of the Anti-Communist Act, knowingly bought several books on socialism and circulated them among his friends, which he was aware would benefit the efforts of North Korea to communize South Korea.

In applying the Anti-Communist Act to the purchase or sale of books on communism and similar ideologies, Korean courts also determined whether the defendant knew that the books would contribute to North Korea's efforts to "brainwash" South Koreans into following communism. The Supreme Court in *Yi Yong-su v. State*[124] ruled the law inapplicable to a university student in economics who bought or checked out the books in question from his school library for the sole purpose of doing academic research, not for anti-State organizations or communist followers abroad.[125] The Court stated that the defendant gathered his research material primarily because it related to the ideology and value system advocated by communist organizations outside South Korea.

The Anti-Communist Act prohibited the act of copying books for propaganda of communist ideology. The Supreme Court in *Han O-su v. State*,[126] for example, interpreted the statute when the defendant was accused of benefiting communists by duplicating a Chinese book on acupuncture. The Court noted that the book, though it primarily dealt with acupuncture as a field of medicine, contained a number of paragraphs extolling Mao Tse-tung, chairman of the Chinese Communist Party. The Court asserted that although he was aware that those with access to the acupuncture book might be affected by its favorable discussion of the Chinese leader, the defendant still copied and sold the book. The Court argued that the act of the defendant contributed to the communists' cause in violation of the law.[127]

Publication of a Korean-language translation of *Dialogue with 800 Million People*, a collection of essays about life in China, originally written by John K.

Galbraith, Harrison Salisbury, Edgar Snow, and other noted Americans, was ruled a violation of the Anti-Communist Act in 1979. In *Yi Yong-hi v. State*,[128] Yi Yong-hi, professor of mass communication in Hanyang University in Seoul, argued in his appeal to the Supreme Court that in finding criminality of a challenged statement, the statement should be read as a whole and in the context relating to its main theme.[129] Nevertheless, the Court's approach was non-contextual and selective in reading the statement under the Act. The Court, affirming the judgment of the Seoul Criminal District Court, held:

> If a person uses a word or phrase that cannot be interpreted in any possible way as praising, encouraging, or siding with the activities of an anti-State organization under the Anti-Communist Act, his statement does not constitute a crime. On the other hand, if he uses a word or phrase in his statement in praising, encouraging, or agreeing with the activities of an anti-State organization, knowing that his statement impresses readers favorably on the anti-State organization, his statement is a crime. It does not matter whether his conclusion may be contradictory and the statement describes the anti-State organization as it is.[130]

The act of praising anti-State organizations was forbidden under the Anti-Communist Act, especially when it was done in public. The Supreme Court's decision in *State v. Kim Che-bong*[131] deserves special notice in that the Court focused on whether the apparently subversive statement was understood by the defendant. This 1970 case related to the English-language statement, "North Korea, Land of the Free," on the jacket made by the defendant on the order of American soldiers in Korea. The jacket was on a display rack at the defendant's dress parlor. The defendant was charged with violating the Anti-Communist Act because he allegedly praised North Korea in public. While acknowledging that the statement on the jacket obviously praised and promoted the activities of the North Korean government, the Supreme Court upheld the lower court's ruling that the defendant did not know the meaning of the English words printed on the jacket.[132]

The "publicity" element of communication under the Anti-Communist Act led the Supreme Court to rule that it was not a crime to write on scratch paper in praise of the works of President Kim Il Sung of North Korea[133] without letting others know of it or to make comments in a private diary favorable to anti-State organizations.[134]

Korean courts often took into account the contexts of various anti-State statements in differentiating between genuinely anti-State expressions as opposed to insults, epithets, name-calling, rhetorical hyperbole, invective, or other verbal abuse. The Seoul Criminal District Court held in 1971 that the defendant's utterance, "Kim Il Sung is better than Park Chung Hee," was not intended to exalt North Korea and thus not culpable under the Anti-Communist Act.[135] The Supreme Court in *State v. Chong Chae-yong*[136] examined the situation in which the defendant asserted that the law of South Korea was "worse than that of the communists."

Noting that the statement was an intemperate comment by the outraged defendant on the way police treated him on suspicion of a traffic violation, the Court held: "It might be far-fetched to conclude that the defendant made the statement as a way to mean, 'The Commies' laws are really good.' Assuming that they are the worst of its kind, the defendant made the statement in the course of expressing his strong feeling about the treatment he received from the police."[137]

In 1973, the Supreme Court followed a similar line of reasoning. In ruling that the Anti-Communist Act would not apply to the defendant's statement: "I am sick and tired of the military drill. I want to skip it. When I go on a sightseeing trip to Panmungak [the observation tower in the truce village of Panmunjom], I'll defect to North Korea," the Court concluded that the defendant expressed his strong disapproval of the rigorous military drill of the Homeland Reserve Forces during the Park regime.[138]

In several cases, the Supreme Court held that the Anti-Communist Act would not apply to statements made under the influence of alcohol. *Chong Ui-yong v. State*[139] involved the statement, "Our government does not do a job of governing people as well as the North Korean government does." The Supreme Court said the statement was not meant to praise North Korea, since it was made by the defendant while arguing with other people at a drinking party. In a similar vein, the Court rejected the government assertion that the Anti-Communist Act would proscribe such statements as "The Commies will not kill all of us [South Koreans] even when another Korean War breaks out"[140] and "It is impossible to make ends meet in South Korea no matter how hard you may work. Let's defect to North Korea, where your hard work pays well."[141] The Court stated that the defendants were drunk at the time of making the statements.[142]

While heated arguments and similar mitigating circumstances justified otherwise criminal statements under the Anti-Communist Act, several Supreme Court cases indicate that favorable thought-out comments on communism could be punishable as a violation of the Act. The defendant in *State v. Yu Kap-chong*[143] claimed, "The Korean War resulted from the combined efforts of the Soviet Union and the United States." The Court stated that the defendant's remark on the Korean War was helpful to North Korea. The Court added that the statement would benefit the propaganda of North Korea against the United States and South Korea.[144] In *Song Su-yong v. State*,[145] the defendant was alleged to have stated: "The purpose of communism is bad. But its means are not bad. My Japanese books say so. Contrary to the general understanding that the scientific management technique discussed in the study of public administration originated from the United States, the truth is that it was first developed by the Soviet Union. The communists' scientific management technique has a great deal for us to learn."[146] The Court held that the defendant's statement to his colleagues at work would foster communism outside of South Korea, which the defendant was fully aware of.[147]

The Supreme Court invoked the Anti-Communist Act in ruling against the defendant in *State v. Kim Tok-song*,[148] a 1974 case. The defendant said: "The Kim

Il Sung regime is governing very well.... Kim Il Sung is doing an excellent job of ruling his people. The Labor Party [of North Korea] is very powerful and is doing well.... North Korea is a better place to live [than South Korea]."[149] In reversing the lower court's decision for the defendant, the Court held that it was clear from the statement that the defendant made the remark with a view to praising the government of North Korea.[150]

### National Security Act Cases: 1980–1994

Since 1980, when the National Security Act superseded the Anti-Communist Act, Korean courts have most often applied Article 7 of the statute to cases involving freedom of expression. The Supreme Court in *Yi Kyu-chol v. State*,[151] the 1986 case, tried to draw a distinction between protected and unprotected expression under the law. Nevertheless, the Court's distinction was more theoretical than practical as a constitutional standard. The Court stated that expression could be protected under the Constitution as long as it was used for the "veritable" purpose of searching for truth, but not when it would benefit an anti-State organization.[152]

In October 1987, the constitutionality of the National Security Act of 1980 was challenged in *Ko Chin-hwa v. State*.[153] The Supreme Court ruled that the law was constitutional as a legal means for South Korea to protect its security and the liberties of its citizens while thwarting North Korea from engaging in subversive activities aimed at communizing the South.[154] The Court in *Ko Chin-hwa* defined "benefiting anti-State organizations" under Article 7 (1) of the Act: "It is an action whose contents, viewed objectively, may benefit an anti-State organization. The law does not require that the actor should be conscious of a purpose of benefiting the anti-State organization. The criminality requirement under the law is met if a person's act was known to benefit the anti-State organization."[155] The Court found that the defendant violated the law in possessing books which contained contents bearing a similarity with North Korea's propaganda against the South because he was aware that the books would aid North Korea.[156] Dismissing the fact that the books were translated for publication in South Korea, the Court stressed that the defendant possessed the books "not for a purely academic purpose."[157]

The Supreme Court in two cases of 1983 and 1984 applied the National Security Act principle that the defendant's intent to benefit an anti-State organization was not a prerequisite to punishing an expression under the statute if there was a proof of recognition on the part of the defendant that his act would be beneficial to the organization. In *State v. Kim Kwang-il*,[158] the Supreme Court affirmed the Pusan District Court's ruling for the defendant. The Court ruled that the defendant did not praise, advocate, or side with the activities of an anti-State organization when he said: "It seems that millions of Chinese are no longer starving to death in groups in Communist China these days as in the past. It seems that unlike the Soviet Union and Cambodia, there are no executions of millions of people in China."[159] The Court argued that the defendant made a comparison between China and other communist countries quoting literature on China published in South Korea. The

Court also noted that the defendant made the statement at a drinking party when the issue relating to famine and massacre in Cambodia was raised as a topic for conversation.[160]

In *Yu Hyong-u v. State*,[161] however, the Supreme Court rejected the defendant's appeal from the High Court-Martial of the Navy on the grounds that his statement clearly benefitted North Korea. This 1984 National Security Act case involved the statement made by the defendant, a seaman in the Korean Navy:

> I would receive a special promotion and a large cash reward if I defect to North Korea. The gap between the rich and the poor is so wide in our country that the rich remain well off but the poor remain poor. Since things are distributed equally in communist countries, there will be no poverty-stricken people. Listening to North Korean defectors to the South, I think that North Korea is not that impoverished. North Korea's weapons are fairly sophisticated. If weapons are to be manufactured, a heavy industry should be developed; if a heavy industry is developed, it seems that its economy is developed.[162]

The defendant made the statement to the troop information and education personnel in his office.

The Supreme Court held that the defendant's statement was far from "a simple joke or his skepticism or speculations" on North Korea and that it indicated the defendant's advocacy or praise of North Korea's hackneyed propaganda.[163]

The National Security Act, Article 7 (5), of 1980 provided for punishment of any person who has produced, imported, duplicated, possessed, transported, disseminated, sold, or acquired documents, drawings, and other similar means of expression to aid an anti-State organization. The Supreme Court's interpretation of Article 7 (5) in *Kim Sang-myong v. State*[164] carries significant implications for freedom of expression relating to national security issues in Korea in that the Court had a rare occasion to sit en banc in ruling on the provision. Most important, the thoughtful dissenting opinion of three justices of the Court indicates that national security interests would no longer be accepted as an untouchable justification for restricting freedom of speech and the press.

*Kim Sang-myong* resulted from publication of the defendant's article, "United States: For Whom Is the United States?," in the newsletter of his company's labor union and from the defendant's possession of several books which allegedly aided an anti-State organization. The appellate panel of the Masan District Court upheld a trial court's ruling that the defendant has violated the National Security Act because his act benefitted the anti-State organization.[165] In his appeal to the Supreme Court, the defendant claimed that the lower court applied Article 7 of the National Security Act improperly. The lower court's ruling, he argued, contradicted the Constitution Court's interpretation of the law, which requires that his act be punished if it caused a "clear and present danger" to the existence and security of the State and the basic order of free democracy.[166]

The majority of the Supreme Court in *Kim Sang-myong* stated that a crime under Article 7 (5) of the National Security Act is based on the defendant's *purpose* of benefiting an anti-State organization through the means enumerated in the statute. Even when the defendant commits the proscribed acts, knowing them to be beneficial to an enemy, the Court said, the defendant's action does not meet its criminal requirements unless the defendant is proved to have a purpose of aiding the enemy. The Court elaborated on the determination of whether there is a criminal purpose in the defendant's act under the statute: "The purpose of benefiting an anti-State organization ... does not require [the defendant's] positive desire or confirmed recognition; it requires [the defendant's] knowing awareness. The criminal purpose is established when the defendant recognizes that expressive material, objectively considered, contains information in line with North Korea's activities including the anti-South propaganda and incitement and he is aware that the expression may benefit the enemy."[167] Applying the "purpose" test to the facts at hand, the Supreme Court concluded that the defendant's knowing awareness could be presumed if the defendant benefitted North Korea by supporting the North in its subversive activities against the South or if the defendant purchased, possessed, produced, or distributed publications, knowing that they would aid the enemy.[168]

On the other hand, the Court admitted that its previous decisions might have created "a misunderstanding" of national security crimes because they ignored the "purpose" element of the criminal expressions while being overly concerned with the issue of whether the expressions might benefit the enemy. "However," the Court said, "the overall meaning of the decisions in context show that the decisions were based on the crimes of purpose."[169]

Justices Yi Hoe-chang, Yi Chae-song, and Pae Man-un strongly dissented, characterizing the majority's "assertive and aggressive expression" approach as impermissibly vague.[170] Because the majority's standard "is so abstract and ambiguous," the dissenting justices argued, "it is impossible to know what is the proscribed assertive and aggressive expression and what is the limit to freedom of expression and whether the standard is premised from *the preferred position of freedom of expression.*"[171] They could not ascertain whether the majority followed the Court's previous interpretation of the National Security Act or offered a new approach. They placed their uncertainty about the majority's opinion in perspective: "Under the domestic and international circumstances in which national security was underscored over the years, the National Security Act was interpreted in such a way as to give priorities to national security interests rather than to individuals' freedom of expression."[172] Noting that the changing circumstances within South Korea and outside led to a debate over the revision or repeal of the law and that the old National Security Act was similar to the revised one in criminalizing certain types of expressions, the justices suggested that the Court ought to "clarify the regulatory framework of criminal expressions" under the law.[173]

Before setting forth a determination on a criminal act under Article 7 of the National Security Act, the dissenting justices discussed the value of freedom of expression to a democratic Korean society. They stated: "Liberal democracy as our ideology ... recognizes the higher value of individuals as human beings than those of groups. Thus, an individual's freedom to express his opinions contrary to those of the groups or his opponents is an indispensable element of free democracy and its epitomizing symbol. This freedom of expression is crucial as a way for an individual to express his value judgments and also a way to secure a right to actively participate in democratic politics through political decision-making."[174]

The justices invoked the Miltonian "free marketplace of ideas" theory as a sine qua non of freedom of expression. They said that freedom of expression can be a reality only in a society where "the competition of ideas is freely allowed." They continued:

> The existing truth and values of a society evolve to new truth and values through the free competition and challenge of ideas. We recognize this process as a historical development. The evolution of new truth and values results when the existing truth and values are challenged and tested. Instead of automatically rejecting or suppressing worthless or harmful ideas because they are contrary to the existing ideas, we should let them undergo the process of being criticized or eliminated in the free marketplace of competition so that they can lay the foundation of a healthy society. In the current period where mass media are highly developed and organized and the dissemination and formation of ideas is subject to manipulation, there may be arguments to the effect that the libertarian principle of competition does not work as well as it should. Nonetheless, there is no gainsaying that the competition of ideas is essential to the maintenance of a free democratic society.[175]

The justices claimed that the tolerance of expression of views in negation of the existing ideas or value system is to ensure the sound preservation of a democratic society through the competition of ideas. They asserted, however, that freedom of expression cannot be accorded for "acts to destroy the democratic order and system itself" because "such acts are outside the protection of freedom of expression and punishment of the unprotected acts is consistent with the self-defense of free democracy."[176]

In this context, the justices stated that the standard for determining a violation of the National Security Act should be based on the limitation of freedom of expression to protect liberal democracy. They then defined an illegal expressive conduct under the Act as "an expression that threatens the security of the State, that is, an expression that creates a 'concrete and probable danger' that it will destroy the existence and security of the Republic of Korea and the basic order of free democracy."[177] The justices said that application of the National Security Act to a statement should examine two aspects of the statement: (1) the substance of the harm from the statement; (2) the possibility of the harm to society. They explained: "'Concrete and probable danger' means that the substance of the harm violating legal interests is concrete and the likelihood of the legal interests being violated is probable. That the substance of the harm is concrete means that the harm is not abstract but substantive and serious, and the likelihood of the legal interests being harmed means that there is a considerable possibility that legal interests will be harmed."[178]

The justices distinguished protected from unprotected expression under their "concrete and probable danger" test. If a statement merely criticizes the ideology and the basic order of liberal democracy in South Korea and expresses ideas or opinions antithetical to them, its harm may be "concrete" but short of carrying the "probability" of bringing about the harm, they said. "Only when a statement is an active incitement to the violent or illegal overthrow of the existence of the government and the abolition of the fundamental order of our liberal democracy, there is a probability of causing a concrete harm."[179] The justices stated: "It must be an unpleasant attack on the existing order when a person expresses ideas or opinions negating or contradicting the ideology and value of the established order. Nevertheless, unless there is an unusual circumstance in which the person's statement is part of the activities inciting to the abolition of the system of liberal democracy, free democracy demands protection of the statement."[180]

In applying their "concrete and probable danger" doctrine, the dissenting justices identified the critical elements of a criminal expression under Article 7 (1) of the National Security Act of 1980. They first argued that Article 7 (1) forbids two kinds of activities: (1) "benefiting the anti-State organization by praising, encouraging, or siding with ... the activities of the anti-State organizations or their members, or the person who had been under instruction from such organizations," and (2) benefiting the anti-State organizations "through other means." The justices said that the criminal offense of praising, encouraging, or siding with the "activities" of the anti-State organizations is premised on the "anti-State" activities of the organizations. That is, they maintained, "if the activities of the anti-State organizations are not against the State at all, the acts of praising, etc., those activities cannot be anti-State."[181] Praising North Korea's admission to the United Nations and North Korea's cancellation of its nuclear program cannot be an anti-State activity under the National Security Act, according to the justices, because the subjects of praise are not related to anti-State activities against South Korea. The justices emphasized: "It contradicts the underlying premise of the crime under the law to punish every act of praising, encouraging, or siding with the activities of an anti-State organiza- tion *without determining whether the organization's activities are against the State or not.*"[182]

The justices warned, however, against concluding that the National Security Act cannot be used to punish praise or encouragement of the "anti-State" activities of the anti-State organizations irrespective of the criminal nature of the praise or encouragement at issue. They said that although the activities of an anti-State organization may not be serious in their harmful impact on the State, an individual will be punished under the law when he disseminates the activities by way of "exaggerating or embellishing" them because he exacerbates the harm of the original activities to the State.[183] The justices continued:

[U]nder the concrete and probable danger test ... the acts of praising, encouraging, or encouraging the propaganda which the North Korean regime has used for its so-called policy of indirect invasion of the South cannot be a criminal act if it is not established that the acts are *presently* creating a concrete and probable danger of destroying the existence and security of the Republic of Korea and its liberal democratic system. Courts, being carried away by the fact that the acts jibe with the propaganda spread by North Korea, should not presume the acts to be criminal just on the basis of the symbolic danger of the thus far tabooed expression, without establishing whether they pose a concrete and probable danger to the State.[184]

The justices held that the "other means" of benefiting the anti-State organizations is of little significance in that there can be no other types of expression that cannot be included in those enumerated by the statute. They further noted that if "other means" provides for all acts benefiting anti-State organizations in addition to praising, encouraging, or siding with the activities of the organizations, it is unconstitutionally vague because it does not define what act benefits an enemy.[185]

The dissenting justices also dissected Article 7 (5) of the National Security Act. Noting that a person, in violating Article 7 (5), must have a desire and intention to engage in the acts provided for in Article 7 (1), they said that even when he engages in a criminal expression knowing that it is illegal or beneficial to an enemy, he cannot be punished under the law if he cannot be proved to have pursued a purpose of aiding the enemy. However, the justices distinguished dissemination or sale of anti-State material from other acts under Article 7 (5). They claimed: "If a person, with knowledge that the context of his expression relates to an anti-State organization or its activities, disseminates it, his act can become an act of praising, encouraging, or siding with the activities of the anti-State organization. Thus, there may be many cases in which the purpose of praising, encouraging, or siding with the anti-State organization can be presumed from the person's act if the act is not academic research, artistic expression, or public interest."[186]

On the other hand, the presumption of criminality in the dissemination or sale of anti-State material is not applicable to the acquisition or possession of the prohibited material under the law. The justices said that the possession and acquisition of the banned publications is different from their dissemination or sale in their harmful impact on society.[187] They added that a person's acquisition or possession of a forbidden publication, more often than not, is "an outward behavior" of his freedom of thought or freedom of conscience. If the law criminalizes the acquisition or possession of the publication without a strong evidence of benefiting an enemy, the justices asserted, "it is likely to threaten the constitutionally guaranteed freedom of thought and freedom of conscience."[188]

Similar to the required proof of the "anti-State" nature of the challenged expression under Article 7 (1), the justices held that Article 7 (5) should be limited to documents, drawings, or other means of expression that bring about the "concrete and probable danger" of threatening the security of the State and the basic order of free democracy. They also said that expressions cannot be punished if they are no more than a criticism of South Korea. At a minimum, the justices argued, the expressions will be considered to create a concrete and probable danger only when they incite the violent overthrow of the South Korean government.[189]

The dissenting justices found that the defendant in *Kim Sang-myong* did not violate the National Security Act under the "concrete and probable danger" doctrine. First, they concluded that the defendant's possession of the allegedly anti-State book could not be a crime under the law even though he knew that it was pro-North Korea, for he did not intend to benefit the enemy.[190] Second, the justices ruled that the defendant's article was not a criminal expression because it could not meet the "concrete and probable danger" requirements. They said that the overall theme of the article was a description of historical facts, and its contents were clearly false: "While the harm of the article is concrete, we cannot hold that it constitutes a *present and direct* threat to the national security of the Republic of Korea and that there is a considerable likelihood that it will endanger the security of the Republic and its liberal democracy."[191]

The justices characterized the defendant's article as "upsetting." Invoking the "marketplace of ideas" concept of freedom of expression, however, they argued that the article should be protected:

> Because that kind of expression is similar to the propaganda disseminated by the North Korean regime as part of its indirect invasion of the South and has been entirely prohibited [by South Korea] for national security reasons thus far, we more strongly perceive its symbolic danger ... than its actual danger. An expression turns into an object of symbolic danger by making it taboo. It disappears into oblivion because it proves to be false and worthless once it enters the *open marketplace of ideas*. The article at issue in this case may be discomfiting and unpleasant to us now because it challenges our ideology and values. It is our opinion, however, that it is the right path for us to take in liberal democracy to allow the article to be tested in the *competition of ideas* and to eliminate its symbolic danger.[192]

In 1992, the Supreme Court applied the "other similar means of expression" provision of the National Security Act in upholding a lower court's decision against a student dissident. The Court in *Ho Tong-jun v. State*[193] held that the defendant's act of communicating with a student organization in North Korea through interviews with Korean and foreign reporters fell within the prohibited "other similar means of expression" under the statute. The Court dismissed the defendant's argument that his freedom of correspondence under the Constitution should protect his expression and that he was not aware of the response from the North Korean students organization to his interview.[194]

In *Sin Hyon-jun v. State*,[195] the Supreme Court ruled in 1993 that presumption against application of the National Security Act should be the rule and not the exception in cases where scholars possess publications for purely academic use. The Court said that if a person who does scholarly work or needs to acquire knowledge possesses material beneficial to an anti-State organization, "it would be proper either to presume that his possession is for the purpose of academic work or acquisition of knowledge or to reject the presumption that it is to benefit an anti-State organization."[196] The Court added, however, that "there may be no presumption against application of the National Security Act if a person uses scholarly work in engaging in activities which benefit an anti-State organization."[197]

In September 1994, the Supreme Court affirmed the ruling of the Kwangju High Court for two university students who were charged with violating the National Security Act with possession of pro-communist books on communism or sociology.[198] The Court agreed with the lower court that the students kept the books for academic work as political science and sociology majors in college. The Court, however, disagreed with the lower court's reasoning that there was no criminal act on the part of the students because they did not possess, read, or discuss the books to side with North Korea or with a view to benefiting the North.[199] The Court stated that the criminal act of possessing prohibited books under the law did not require proof of the defendants' "purposeful" intent of benefiting an anti-State organization.[200]

As compared with pre-1980 cases, only a few National Security Act cases have involved the Korean press since 1980. Noting the chilling impact of the National Security Act on the Korean press over the years, *Chosun Ilbo* Publisher Sang Hoon Bang stated: "[T]he existence of the National Security Law can still restrict the freedom of thought and press in Korea. The National Security Law is a product of the Cold War, when South Korean communists were punished by that Law. In recent years, however, the National Security Law has been severely criticized for being abused to limit individual freedom. Accordingly, the Law was revised after the democratization [of 1987] and does not have its restrictive power as before."[201]

One of the press freedom cases was *State v. Kim Tae-hong*,[202] widely known as the *Mal* (Word) case. The *Mal* case, which attracted considerable attention from both in Korea and abroad, resulted from the 1986 publication in *Mal* magazine of the Korean government's detailed press guidelines.[203] The underground magazine, published by the Council for Democratic Press Movement (CDPM) in Seoul, an association of banned journalists in Korea, published the texts of hundreds of daily press guidelines issued by the Ministry of Culture and Information between October 19, 1985, and August 8, 1986. In December 1986, three months after the publication in *Mal* of the politically embarrassing press guidelines, the authorities arrested two CDPM officials alleged to have been involved in the publication and also a journalist said to have leaked the guidelines to the CDPM for violating the National Security Act of 1980.

On June 3, 1987, Judge Pak Tae-bom of the Seoul Criminal District Court sentenced two of the defendants to suspended prison terms and set aside a penalty for the third. In finding two defendants guilty of violating the National Security Act, Judge Pak noted that they knowingly possessed the prohibited "subversive" books espousing the revolutionary ideology of North Korea.[204] The judge stated, however, that the defendants were motivated by their "interest in the reality and development" of the South Korean press and thus deserved another opportunity to contribute to society.[205]

In July 1994, the three-judge appellate panel of the Seoul Criminal District Court reversed Judge Pak's decision.[206] The appellate panel relied on the "clear and present danger" doctrine for rejecting application of the National Security Act of 1980. The court stated, "In order to punish the defendants under the National Security Act, the books in the possession of the defendants must create a *clear danger* that their contents will threaten the existence and security of the State and will bring about a substantive harm to the basic order of free democracy."[207] The court continued that "if the contents of the books do not cause a substantive harm to the existence and security of the State or to the basic order of free democracy, or if it is not clear whether they are doing the harm, the defendants cannot be punished" under the law.[208] The court argued that it was "difficult to conclude that the books, read as a whole, create the kind of 'clear danger' as defined previously."[209]

Yi Yong-hi, an editorial advisor to the left-of-center *Han-kyoreh Shinmun* (One-Nation Newspaper), was arrested for attempting a secret visit to North Korea to interview President Kim Il Sung in April 1989 and was charged with a criminal act under the National Security Act of 1980.[210] A single-judge Seoul criminal district court in *State v. Yi Yong-hi*[211] in September 1989 had sentenced Yi to a suspended prison term. Yi, in an appeal to the three-judge appellate panel of the Seoul criminal district court, claimed that the government had infringed on press freedom, adding that his attempt to visit North Korea for a journalistic purpose did not constitute a violation of the National Security Act.[212] In February 1993, the appellate panel rejected Yi's argument, reasoning that freedom of the press, though constitutionally protected, must be balanced against other constitutional provisions.[213] In affirming the lower judge's ruling, the panel stated: "The accused's planned trip [to North Korea] might have jeopardized our national security if it had been exploited by the North Korean government as an opportunity to publicize its position [on South Korea] abroad or if it had created chaos in our North Korea policy by causing disorderly visits to North Korea."[214]

A 1993 decision of the Seoul Criminal District Court, Appellate Division, raised an issue of whether a magazine editor violated the National Security Act in publishing dissident novelist Hwang Sok-yong's travelogue on his visit to North Korea. In *Yi Si-yong v. State*,[215] the defendant, editor-in-chief of *Changjak Kwa Pipyong* (Creation and Criticism) magazine, appealed the judgment of a one-judge trial court. He argued that Hwang's writings did not benefit North Korea. He further asserted that he was not aware that it would be beneficial to North Korea and that he had no intention to benefit North Korea with publication of Hwang's articles.[216] The appellate panel of the Seoul Criminal District Court disagreed, stating that North Korea would benefit from the contents of the travelogue. The court reasoned: "The writings went beyond the author's real-life description of what he saw during his trip to North Korea. Following the writer's subjective intentions, it defames the democratic society of the South. On the other hand, it emphasizes the relative superiority of the North Korean system, ideology, and life, and praises the leadership and self-reliance ideology of President Kim Il Sung of North Korea."[217] The court concluded that the defendant's publication of Hwang's articles on North Korea endangered the security and free democratic system of South Korea and benefitted the North with "forceful and aggressive expressions."[218]

The National Security Act was applied to Korean news media conducting a telephone interview with a South Korean dissident student who was in North Korea in July 1989[219] attending the World Festival of Youth and Students in open defiance of the Seoul government's ban on the trip.[220] The Roh Tae Woo government stated that such interviews would constitute violation of the security act. This and other instances of applying or threatening to apply the security law to the press were ironic in that the government already had decided to revise the law.

Few reported court decisions as of July 1994 involved direct application of the newly revised National Security Act of 1991 to freedom of speech and the press issues. According to a recent report on human rights in Korea, however, the revised statute still threatens to violate freedom of expression in Korea.[221] In a petition to the Constitution Court in early 1995, the Pusan District Court questioned the validity of the revised National Security Act in that it does not differentiate a protected expression of opinions from a prohibited act of violence. The court argues that the "clear and present danger" test should be a guiding principle in applying the security law to freedom of expression cases.[222]

### Martial Law and Emergency Decrees Cases

As discussed above, the Korean press has been subject to restriction by martial laws and emergency decrees. The scope of restriction by these extraordinary measures was far more extensive than other statutory restrictions. The martial law and emergency decrees often had been enforced by the government in an extra-judicial manner without being challenged in court.[223]

Presidential Emergency Measure No. 9, proclaimed in May 1975, for example, prohibited any person from fabricating and disseminating groundless rumors or from diffusing distorted facts. What is noteworthy about the emergency decree in the context of judicial interpretation is that the Supreme Court somewhat narrowed its applications when it held that a person who told only one other person allegedly distorted facts was not guilty of engaging in a disseminating or diffusing act. In *Cho Man-song v. State*,[224] a 1976 case, the Court held that the defendant, in relating distorted facts to a policeman who attempted to arrest him, did not violate the measure.[225]

In ruling in Presidential Emergency Measure cases, the Supreme Court did not always focus upon the question of whether or not false rumors or distorted facts were disseminated to the public. In 1977, the Court in *Chong Hyong-mo v. State*[226] scrutinized the circumstances in which the false or exaggerated facts were circulated. Noting that the defendant was collecting information for the KCIA, the Court held that it found no ground of suspecting that the defendant had made unfounded rumors intentionally. The Court further said: "The alleged facts constituting a violation of the measure ... clearly were provided to the KCIA and came from the defendant's answers to the questions from KCIA agents. Admitting that there may be some falsity or exaggeration in the information provided to the KCIA, it is more to the point to presume that the defendant's act of providing the information to the KCIA is part of assistance in the whole work of the KCIA, which makes policies after a scientific analysis and synthesis of various information."[227]

The defendant in *Son Jin-sok v. State*[228] was charged with violating the emergency measure for stating that the purification of officialdom was mere talk and that official injustice and corruption were pervasive of the President Park Chung Hee government. The defendant made the statement in a cab that other passengers shared with him. The lower court ruled against the defendant. The case was appealed to the Supreme Court, which affirmed the lower court's judgment in 1978. The Supreme Court held, "When the defendant mentioned the groundless rumors in question, he was with three others including the cab driver, in addition to the very person to whom he was primarily interested in talking."[229]

An instructor at a private preparatory school said to his students: "The Revitalizing Reforms Constitution should be abolished." The Kwangju High Court ruled that the statement was a violation of the measure prohibiting criticism of the Constitution. In *Cha Pong-hyon v. State*,[230] the Supreme Court agreed with the decision of the lower court against the defendant, but the Court dismissed the case because the measure had been suspended.[231]

On the other hand, the definition of "groundless rumors" under martial law was expanded by the Supreme Court in *Pak Song-chol v. State*.[232] In this 1981 decision, the Court interpreted "groundless rumors" as not only false statements but also those which exaggerated or distorted the facts. Furthermore, the Court stated, "It is an act of disseminating groundless rumors when you mention them or distribute the books containing them though they have already been known to some people."[233]

## SUMMARY AND CONCLUSIONS

Media law scholar Kim Taek-hwan of the Korean Press Institute noted in his 1993 study of Korean press law that most court decisions on the Korean press under the pre-1987 authoritarian regimes related to national security and military secrets while media cases in recent years more often involved libel and invasion of privacy and the constitutionality of press statutes.[234] Evidence validates Kim's observation in that the National Security Act since 1980 has been much less frequently employed by the Korean government in press freedom cases.

In interpreting press freedom under national security law, Korean courts have failed to establish consistent reasoning in their rulings. Consequently, court decisions have confounded the problem of defining the extent to which the Korean press could expect to be statutorily protected by the courts in exercising its freedom. Professor Pnina Lahav's criticism of Israeli Supreme Court's approach to national security law can apply to the Supreme Court of Korea on press freedom: "[T]he court is not unanimous in its commitment to press freedom.... From the legal standpoint, the court itself is not bound by its precedents, and since it [rarely] sits en banc, it can produce contradictory precedents.... The lower courts are free to choose the precedents that fit their philosophy."[235]

It is noteworthy, however, that in at least half a dozen cases, Korean courts clearly recognized the affirmative function of the press while the courts in general have tended to be narrow in interpreting the constitutional clause on press freedom. The Supreme Court has been overly cautious in drawing the boundaries of freedom of expression. This was particularly noticeable when the Court interpreted the National Security Act and the Anti-Communist Act in politically sensitive cases. The Court, for example, recognized the "preferred position" theory of freedom of expression in the context of political speech in 1959, but the theory has been more or less "the stagecoach ticket inscribed: 'Good for this day only'" for the past 35 years.[236]

The Supreme Court often engages in *ad hoc* balancing in ruling on freedom of expression. As a result, the Court to date has established few constitutional standards of its own. Moreover, the Court has not yet seriously considered adopting the "clear and present danger" test or its variations, as established in the First Amendment law of the United States. Most significantly, however, the three dissenting justices in a 1992 case set forth what they termed the "concrete and probable danger" doctrine as a standard for balancing national security with freedom of expression under the National Security Act. If it is accepted by the Supreme Court in the future, the doctrine, which seems to have its conceptual genesis in the clear and present danger theory, is expected to alter the way the National Security Act has been interpreted over the years.

As compared with the Supreme Court, lower courts have been bolder in experimenting with various free speech or free press theories in ruling on national security restrictions. Several lower courts have been remarkably libertarian in their views on the role and function of the Korean press. The Seoul and Taegu district courts' applications of the "clear and present danger" test in the 1960s are a good example. In recent years, lower courts frequently utilized the test and also the "preferred position" concept in national security cases.

While the National Security Act has been less of a direct threat to the Korean press since 1987, the still-persisting "ideological confrontation" between North and South Korea makes it likely that the controversy over the law will continue. Indeed, the Pusan District Court in January 1995 asked the Constitution Court to review the constitutionality of the National Security Act of 1991, arguing that Article 7 of the Act is too vague and overbroad to protect freedom of expression.[237]

# Selected Problems of Press Law

Major constitutional and legal issues of press freedom in Korea have been examined in the preceding chapters. As comparative legal scholar Lawrence Beer aptly pointed out, however, "[p]roblems of freedom with respect to expression arise in such a wide range of social, political, cultural, and economic contents that their study not only illuminates small areas of public law but also provides a prism of richly tinted color through which to view a country's life."[1] In this chapter, some additional legal problems affecting the Korean press directly and indirectly are discussed. Analysis of the problems, of course, proceeds from a press law premise that "press law plays but one part, and surely not the most important, in determining the degree to which the press carries out the[] two functions [of serving as a public watchdog and imparting information and ideas of public interest]."[2]

## IMPORT AND DISTRIBUTION OF FOREIGN PERIODICALS

"In many countries," ARTICLE 19 reported in 1991, "the circulation of foreign publications is restricted. Ministers can prohibit the sale and distribution of such publications without recourse to judicial proceedings."[3] The Korean government, for example, regulates incoming foreign publications through the Act Relating to Import and Distribution of Foreign Periodicals (Foreign Periodicals Act).[4] The law is aimed at "providing regulations concerning the importation and distribution of foreign periodicals in order to promote the international cultural exchange, to ensure the sound development of publishing culture and to safeguard public law and order, and to maintain the good morals and manners unique to the nation by establishing the proper order on importation of foreign periodicals."[5] However, the practical effect of the law obviously goes further because it often serves as legal pressure to curb the domestic circulation of certain foreign publications.

The Foreign Periodicals Act is noteworthy in that it deals with the importation of foreign publications in a discriminatory way, depending on whether they are for distribution or for sale. In the case of importing periodicals from overseas for *distribution*, a certificate of registration from the Ministry of Culture and Sports (MOCS) is required.[6] On the other hand, a person with the intent to bring in foreign publications for *sale* in Korea should first obtain a recommendation from the MOCS for import.[7]

Pursuant to the Foreign Periodicals Act, the MOCS is empowered to take sweeping measures against the "designated" foreign periodicals under the Presidential Decree or those "feared to disrupt the customs" of Koreans. The designated periodicals, which the Act defines to be "feared to subvert the constitutional system of the State or undermine the public security" of Korea,[8] contain any of the following contents:

1. Denouncing the legitimacy of the Republic of Korea or violating the sovereignty of Korea;
2. Defaming the reputation of the Republic of Korea by discrediting its constitutional organs;
3. Renouncing the liberal democratic system in toto or encouraging or inciting the activities subversive of the system;
4. Advocating, promoting, sympathizing with, publicizing, or inciting the activities of an anti-State organization or its members;
5. Distorting or fabricating important historical facts.[9]

The foreign periodicals which may be subject to restriction for their harmful impact on the Korean custom contain one of the following contents:

1. Violating the sound sex morality by depicting the sexual acts by focusing on a particular part of a body or obscene acts;
2. Feared to induce a criminal behavior by depicting decadent activities or cruel acts such as murder or violence;
3. Inducing use of drugs;
4. Undermining the sound social ethics by depicting the abuse or abandonment of family members, children, women, or elderly people;
5. Deemed to stimulate minors' sexual desire or to harm the cultural education of juveniles;
6. Creating a bad influence on the promotion of the national sentiments or the sound social environment.[10]

The Korean government may not recommend the import of the periodicals or may order them suspended from distribution or their contents deleted[11] and may retract the permit for distribution of the periodicals if the order is violated.[12] Furthermore, importers of foreign periodicals found in violation of the Act may be imprisoned for less than three years or fined not more than 30 million *won* (US$37,500) and the publications in question may be confiscated by the authorities.[13]

Koreans as well as the foreign press are also regulated by the Customs Act.[14] Article 146 states that no books or publications that will "either disturb the national constitutional order or harm public security or custom" shall be imported or exported.[15] It further forbids the import or export of any print or nonprint publications that "will reveal confidential information" about the Korean government or that "are used for intelligence activities."[16] Any person who violates the provisions of the Customs Act regarding prohibited publications is subject to "penal servitude for a fixed period not less than one year or a fine of not more than 20 million *won* (US$25,000)."[17] Additionally, the materials at issue may be confiscated.[18] The Customs Act is less severe with regard to duration of penal servitude than is the Foreign Periodicals Act.

## OBSCENITY AND PORNOGRAPHY

Sandra Coliver, ARTICLE 19's law program director, stated, "In most countries, it is a criminal offence to publish certain kinds of pornographic, obscene and/or other materials which offend public morality."[19] Korea is no exception. Obscenity is a crime under the Criminal Code and other related statutes. The Criminal Code provides:

> A person who distributes, sells, leases, or openly displays obscene literature, pictures, or similar goods shall be punished by penal servitude for not more than one year or by a fine not exceeding 10,000 *hwan;*[20]
>
> A person who, for the purpose of accomplishing the acts of the preceding Article, manufactures, possesses, imports, or exports obscene goods shall be punished by penal servitude for not more than one year or by a fine not exceeding 10,000 *hwan.*[21]

Obscene cartoons relating to children are prohibited by a separate statute. Article 2-2 of the Minors Protection Act[22] prohibits the sale, distribution, possession, or offer of pornographic cartoons, pictures, documents, or recordings to minors.[23] The Act on Registration of Publishers or Printers[24] authorizes the government to cancel registration of publishers or printers on grounds that they are found to have violated public mores and social ethics by publishing obscene or decadent periodicals or cartoons harmful to children.[25]

As far as the statutory crime of obscenity is concerned, Korean courts have taken various approaches in applying the Criminal Code. In *State v. Han Ki-hong*,[26] for example, the Supreme Court held that viewing of pornographic films at a private home would not be an open display and thus was not a violation of the Code. The Court in *Chong In-wi v. State*[27] defined "*openly* displays obscene ... pictures" under the Code as follows: "To display obscene pictures openly means to expose those pictures to the situation where many and unspecified persons can watch them. Accordingly, it is not a crime for a few and specified people to watch them."[28]

In *State v. Yom Chae-man*,[29] the "Revolting Slaves" case, the Supreme Court defined obscenity as "a description vivid and specific enough to excessively stimulate sexual desire or to defy sex morality considerably."[30] The Court observed that the contents of an allegedly obscene publication should be examined as a whole and in context before a determination of criminal obscenity can be properly made.[31] The Court thus limited the crime of obscenity to patently offensive sexual depictions and morally decadent expressions. In 1994, the Seoul Criminal District Court, Appellate Division, in *Ma Kwang-su v. State*,[32] widely known as the "Happy Sarah" case, articulated the most comprehensive definition of obscenity under Korean law. The court stated:

> "Obscenity," which is one of sexual expressions ... conveyed through a concrete medium such as words or pictures for sexual stimulation and satisfaction, means: (1) The depiction or narrative on sex is explicit and detailed, and it glorifies deviant sex; (2) It occupies the principal part of the work; (3) Taken as a whole, it lacks literary, artistic, political, or social value; and (4) It affects the sense of shame and disgust ... on the part of ordinary adults exposed to the material by arousing prurient interests in them. If a work meets this definition, it violates the desirable sexual habit and the good sex morality to be protected by the Criminal Code.[33]

The appellate court argued that just because a novel is called a literary work does not necessarily mean that it should be allowed unlimited freedom of expression so that any type of expression is permitted. The court continued that when the sexual customs and morality of society are violated, the Criminal Code may be used to punish those involved.[34]

In dealing with the commercial use of nude pictures, the Supreme Court in 1970 ruled that manufacturers or dealers of such pictures sold them because they were aware of the obscene nature of the pictures.[35] The Court further held that the standards of obscenity should be objective and not be based on the subjective value judgments of those who deal in the nude pictures.[36] In *State v. Kim Kwi-jin*,[37] a 1978 case, a commodity called "Penis Enlarger" was alleged to be obscene in violation of the Criminal Code. Penis Enlarger was shaped like a cylinder for penises to be inserted. The lower court held that the object was not obscene. The Supreme Court agreed: "Judging from its cylinder-like shape, it does not remind us of the male sexual organs. Indeed, it does not possess anything relating to sex. Thus, the object cannot be categorized as the obscene goods capable of exciting and satisfying sexual desire."[38]

When Pak Sung-hun, author and professor of English literature at Konkuk University in Seoul, portrayed sexual acts in vivid detail in one of his sensational novels in the 1960s, he was found guilty under the obscenity law. In *State v. Pak Sung-hun*,[39] the Seoul Criminal District Court ruled in 1969 that Pak's primary objective in writing his novel in point was to cater to the sexual desire of its readers.

## COPYRIGHT

Since 1948, when the Constitution of the first Republic of Korea was proclaimed, copyright has been consistently recognized as a constitutional right. The Constitution of 1948 did not use the word "copyright" but did provide the basis for it: "All citizens shall have freedom of science and art. Rights of authors, inventors, and artists shall be protected by law."[40] The first copyright statute was enacted in 1957.[41] The current Constitution, amended in 1987, states: "All citizens shall enjoy freedom of learning and the arts. The right of authors, inventors, scientists, engineers, and artists shall be protected by law."[42]

The Copyright Act,[43] which was wholly amended in 1986, protects the right of authors while ensuring the improvement and development of culture in Korea.[44] Copyright protection begins upon the work's creation and extends for 50 years past the death of the author.[45] The copyright on a work created by two or more authors extends through the life of the last author to die plus 50 years.[46] The "work made for hire" is recognized in Korea. The law states that if a person prepares a work within the scope of his employment, the copyright belongs to the employer, not the creator of the work.[47] A work for hire is protected for 50 years after publication.[48] The Korean law recognizes foreigners' copyright to works under treaties Korea has signed with foreign countries.[49]

A wide variety of items can be protected under the Copyright Act. Among those listed in the statute are: (1) linguistic and literary works; (2) musical works; (3) theatrical works; (4) art works; (5) pictorial works; (6) motion pictures; and (7) computer programs.[50] Some works cannot be copyrighted; governmental notices and decrees, judicial, administrative, and legislative, and judicial opinions, and speeches delivered at the public sessions of the National Assembly and city councils are not protected.[51] Titles of books and movies are also not copyrighted. The Seoul High Court ruled in 1991: "A work protected under the current Copyright Act is a creative literary, scholarly, or artistic product of thinking and feelings.... Generally speaking, the title of a work indicates no more than the symbol of the work and it cannot be considered to possess an original thinking and a creative expression of feelings."[52]

As in the U.S. copyright law,[53] the Korean law follows the principle that expressions are copyrightable, while ideas are not. The Supreme Court of Korea held:

> A work under the Copyright Act must be a *creative expression* of thinking and feelings acquired through an individual's efforts. Accordingly, what is protected by the Act is the *creative means of expressing* thinking and feelings to the public by way of speech, language, sounds, or color. Although the contents or ideas expressed ... may be creative and novel in their own way, they ... cannot be copyrightable work and thus cannot be entitled to protection as part of the author's personal or property rights.[54]

After all, what is protected by the Copyright Act is *not ideas but their expressions* and it is limited to the individual aspect of the author's originality. Accordingly, a determination of whether a copyright was violated must be based on the rule that a substantial similarity between the two works at issue should concern their *original expressions.*[55]

The idea-and-expression distinction explains why copyright law does not condition its protection of a work on its contents. Copyright is recognized even where a magazine is considered "immoral" or "illegal."[56]

The Copyright Act recognizes the "fair use"[57] of copyrighted work. The statute restricts the property rights of authors:

> If it is necessary for the judicial proceedings or for internal material for legislative or administrative purposes, any work may be reproduced for such purposes unless it infringes unreasonably on the interest of the author's property right owner in light of the nature of the work and the number of copies and forms of the reproduction;[58]
>
> The released works may be inserted in textbooks to the degree necessary for educational purposes at schools of the level lower than high schools or the equivalent thereto;[59]
>
> In case of reporting current news through broadcasting, motion pictures, newspapers, or other means, any work which is viewed or listened to in the course of such reporting may be reproduced, distributed, performed publicly, or broadcast within the limits proper for such purposes.[60]

The Copyright Act also does not apply to quotations from released works "within the reasonable limit in conformity with fair practice,"[61] to nonprofit public performance and broadcasting,[62] to reproduction for private use,[63] and to reproduction in libraries,[64] among others.[65] The fair use exemptions to copyright, however, do not affect the author's personal right to reputation or privacy.[66]

The Copyright Act protects author's "moral rights"[67] in their work. Article 14 states, "The author's personal right shall belong exclusively to the author himself."[68] The right does not abate with the death of the author.[69] An author whose work is violated can sue to stop the violation and to claim monetary damages. Article 95 provides that "[a]n author may demand a person who has infringed intentionally or negligently on his author's personal right to take measures necessary for the restoration of his reputation instead of or in addition to the compensation for damage."[70] Further, Article 98 makes violation of the author's moral right a crime punishable by imprisonment for up to three years or a fine of not more than 3 million *won* (US$3,750).[71]

In 1994, the Seoul High Court applied the "moral rights" provision of the Copyright Act in *Korean Broadcasting Corp. v. Han Sang-jin.*[72] In his suit, Han Sang-jin, professor of sociology at Seoul National University, complained that his reputation as a scholar was damaged by the unreasonably edited Korean Broadcasting System (KBS) broadcast of his lecture.[73] Han's lecture was taped for a

60-minute segment of the "KBS 21st Century Forum," but it was broadcast with one-third of the lecture deleted.[74]

Prior to suing the Korean Broadcasting Corporation, which owns KBS, Han had asked the Press Arbitration Commission to arbitrate his claim for a reply under the Broadcast Act.[75] He demanded the re-broadcast of his original lecture and a public apology from KBS.[76] KBS, rejecting his claim, argued that editing was a proper right of broadcasters and that Han's demand for an apology would violate the network's freedom of the press.[77] Nonetheless, Han requested that KBS broadcast that it has lost in a libel suit relating to Han's TV lecture, if that was the verdict.[78] KBS in turn responded that because Han had demanded a notice of apology, his libel complaint would violate the freedom of conscience of KBS.[79] The Seoul District Court (South Branch) disagreed. The court held that Han's reputation was damaged and that he should be offered a "suitable" means of recovery for his injury instead of monetary damages, which Han did not claim. The suitable measure for Han, the court ruled, would be for KBS to broadcast statements on the ruling as prescribed by the court.[80]

The media defendant appealed the decision to the Seoul High Court. The court affirmed the lower court's ruling unanimously in September 1994. Chief Judge Pak Yong-sang stated in a carefully reasoned opinion for the court that Han had a right to his TV lecture to demand that it be identical to what he originally prepared.[81] Han's "exclusive" right to his lecture as an author was violated by the defendant's heavy "inconsistent" editing of the lecture, according to Judge Pak.[82] In responding to Han's argument that he lost his scholarly reputation as a result of the KBS program, Pak concluded:

> It would be reasonable to conclude that the defendant's act of deleting part of the plaintiff's work before broadcasting, rather than diminishing his social reputation generally, has affected the conceptual consistency and identity of the middle class theory developed by the plaintiff. Consequently, the defendant's act injured the personal right of the plaintiff as a scholar and author by discrediting his confidence in his theory. Admittedly the plaintiff's standing in the estimation of his professional community has been damaged more or less, but his reputational injury can be included in his claim for loss of his author's personal right.[83]

Noting that the Copyright Act allows an injured party several preventive measures and restorative actions relating to a copyright violation of his work, Judge Pak ruled that Han's demand for KBS's broadcast of the court's decision on his libel suit was a necessary means of being recompensed for his injury under the Act.[84]

Four years earlier, the Supreme Court of Korea rejected the moral rights claim of a photographer. The plaintiff in *Yi Chong-suk v. Yi Chae-gil*[85] claimed that his reputation as a professional photographer was violated when the defendant's magazine published several of the nude pictures of Korean women that he had contributed to a Japanese weekly. The Supreme Court, reversing the Seoul High

Court's ruling,[86] held that the defendant published the pictures in criticizing the Japanese magazine for "misusing" the pictures to stimulate its readers' curiosity and to serve its commercial purpose, which could not constitute a defamation of the plaintiff.[87]

## CABLE BROADCASTING

Cable television broadcasting started in the spring of 1995. The regulatory mechanism of cable television had been devised by the Korean government over the years prior to the operation of cable television. Professor Gwang-jub Han of Howard University placed the policy justifications for regulation of cable television in Korea in perspective: "Korea has not [sic] experience of regulatory evolution in the cable television industry. At the same time, contents of media will no longer be provided without requiring an extra expense and extra time, as we are moving towards the 'pay-per-society.' In other words, the locus of control has been shifting from communication providers to communication consumers as the number of electronic outlets increases."[88]

The Comprehensive Cable Television Broadcast Act (Cable Television Act) of 1991,[89] modeled largely after the Broadcast Act of 1987,[90] is the organic legislation that controls Korean cable broadcasting. The purpose of the Act is "to contribute to the improvement of the national culture and promotion of the public welfare by striving for a sound fostering and development of the comprehensive cable television broadcast and a convenience of users thereof."[91] The law prohibits programming and operation of a cable broadcast station from being interfered with from outside unless statutorily authorized.[92]

The cable broadcasting act prohibits concurrent operation by other cable broadcasting stations, over-the-air broadcasting corporations, or daily newspaper or other media companies.[93] In addition, the law bars business conglomerates from operating cable broadcasting stations.[94] It further states, "Any political party or religious organization supporting or advocating a specified ideology or thought may not operate a comprehensive cable television broadcasting station or hold the stocks or quotas thereof."[95] The cable television law is more sweeping than the Broadcast Act in provisions for qualification of operators of cable broadcasting service[96] and for proscription against inflow of foreign capital into operation of cable broadcasting media.[97] The cable broadcasting law delineates what the Minister of Public Information (MOPI) should consider before issuing a permission to a cable broadcasting applicant through local authorities. Article 7 reads in part:

> If the Minister of Public Information desires to grant a permission [to any person who desires to operate a comprehensive cable television broadcasting station], he shall examine the following matters:

1. Whether the object and contents of the comprehensive cable television broadcast are conformed to the provisions of laws and regulations and they are not detrimental to the interests of the State;
2. Whether the comprehensive cable television broadcast has the regional, social, and cultural necessity and propriety;
3. Whether it contributes to the development of the communities
   through the operation of the comprehensive cable television broadcasting station.[98]

Licenses for cable broadcasting are granted for limited periods of time. The license period is determined by the Presidential Decree of the cable broadcasting statute "in the limit not exceeding five years."[99] Under the Presidential Decree of 1992, cable broadcasting stations are licensed for three years.[100] Prior to renewing broadcast licenses, the MOPI investigates "whether or not the conditions of permission are fulfilled faithfully without violating the Act" *and* "whether or not the furnishing of service by the comprehensive cable television broadcasting stations accepts reasonably the intention of residents in the area concerned."[101] If the MOPI is not satisfied with what it finds, it "shall hear the opinion" of the administrators of local governments on the renewal issue.[102] The law also provides for an opportunity for the cable operator to "state his opinion."[103]

Program providers are required to obtain permission from the MOPI.[104] They must produce up to 20 percent of the broadcasting programs.[105] The import or relay of foreign programs or joint production with foreign programmers requires permission from the MOPI.[106] The MOPI may deny permission for the import or relay of foreign programs:

1. Deemed to violate the basic order of the Constitution or damage the
   prestige of the State;
2. Deemed to undermine the social mores or disturb the social order
   with lewdness, decadence, and violence;
3. Deemed to harm the international amity.[107]

While imported programs cannot exceed 30 percent of total programming,[108] Professor Han states that "the limit has been increased up to 50% in Science, Refinement and Sports channels."[109]

The MOPI is authorized by the Cable Television Act to cancel the license of a broadcasting station or to suspend its operation in part or in its entirety for up to three months.[110] Likewise, program providers are subject to license revocation or suspension by the MOPI on substantially similar grounds.[111] The MOPI can also take sanctions against program providers for supplying programs not included in the designated field or for refusing to provide programs to a cable broadcaster "without any justifiable reason."[112]

The Korean cable act is similar to the 1984 Cable Communications Policy Act[113] of the United States in that it allows public access to cable broadcasting facilities. While not the same as the American law that requires cable systems to set aside channels for "public, educational or governmental use,"[114] the access requirement of the Korean law is designed "to embody the diversity of broadcasting fields and not to be overemphasized in a specified field."[115] The Cable Television Act states:

> The comprehensive cable television broadcasting station shall reserve any channel to be used for any public purpose by the State under the conditions as prescribed by the Presidential Decree;
> The comprehensive cable television broadcasting station may operate a regional channel to transmit any regional information, information on broadcasting programs, official announcement, etc., which are made by itself under the conditions as prescribed by the Presidential Decree;
> No channel of the comprehensive cable television broadcasting station may be lent to, or allowed to be used by, another person onerously or gratuitously.[116]

In programming, cable operators are required to comply with the contents criteria stipulated by the Act and "not to distort the fact," among others.[117]

The Cable Television Act provides for the establishment of the Cable Television Broadcast Commission as a governing agency of the cable broadcasting industry. It is to promote the "publicness and morality" of cable broadcasting and the "qualitative improvement" of its contents.[118] The Commission is composed of seven to 11 commissioners, including a chairman and a vice chairman, appointed by the MOPI.[119] Commissioners are appointed for a term of three years.[120]

The Cable Television Broadcast Commission regulates the operation of cable broadcasting stations. It is responsible for enforcing the programming requirements specified in the Cable Television Act. Article 38 provides in part that the Commission "deliberate and decide ... matters concerning the publicness and morality" of cable broadcasting.[121] The Commission is empowered to approve or disapprove the contents of the broadcasting programs. The Commission, for example, has the authority to decide whether certain programs such as dramatic movies and cartoon films, foreign programs, and advertisements can be broadcast in the context of their relevance to the public responsibility of the cable station.[122]

In meeting its responsibilities, the Commission may establish a deliberative committee to carry out its functions. The Commission can deliberate various issues arising from the contents of broadcasting programs. Article 41 enumerates the contents criteria for the Commission to consider in reviewing the programs:

> Matters concerning the maintenance of the fundamental democratic order and the respect of human rights under the Constitution;
> Matters concerning the sound home life and the proper guidance of children and youths;
> Matters concerning the elimination of lewdness, decadence, and violence and the encouragement of public morality and social ethics;

Matters concerning the prevention of international friendship from being damaged;
Matters concerning the cultivation of the national identity;
Matters concerning the creative development of the national culture;
Matters concerning the impartiality of news and comments;
Matters concerning the measure for correction as prescribed in Article 38.[123]

The request by an individual for correction of *factual* allegations about him is recognized by the Cable Television Act,[124] as in the Broadcast Act and the Periodicals Act. One significant difference between the cable act and the other press statutes on the right of reply is that the former allows 30 days to exercise the right after broadcast of the allegations, while the latter provides a 14-day period. Like the current print and broadcast media law, the claim for *ex post facto* news report is also provided for by the cable statute.[125]

The Cable Television Act provides various penal sanctions for violations of the Act, ranging from a maximum fine of 5 million *won* (US$6,250) for negligence[126] to three years in jail or a fine of up to 20 million *won* (US$25,000) for more serious violations.[127] Punishment of up to one year or a fine not exceeding 10 million *won* (US$12,500) will be imposed on:

1. A person who violates the prohibition of concurrent operation of businesses as prescribed in Article 4 (1) to (4);
2. A person who operates a comprehensive cable television broadcasting station or owns the stocks or quotas thereof, in contravention of the provisions of Article 4 (5) or (7);
3. A person who receives any contribution of property in contravention of the provisions of Article 6 [prohibition of inflow of foreign capital];
4. A person who obtains a permission on change as prescribed in Article 10 (1) by any deceitful or other unlawful manner and operates a comprehensive cable television broadcasting station;
5. A person who operates a comprehensive cable television broadcasting station without obtaining the permission on change as prescribed in Article 10 (1);
6. A person who imports any foreign broadcasting program, relays any foreign broadcast, or produces a broadcasting program jointly with a foreign programmer without obtaining the approval as prescribed in Article 16;
7. A person who regulates or interferes with the programming of a comprehensive cable television broadcast as prescribed in Article 23 (1).
8. A person who sets up a branch office or station in Korea without the permission on change as prescribed in Article 32 (2);
9. A person who violates the order as prescribed in Article 38 (1);
10. A person who produces and distributes any obscene materials which might be remarkably detrimental to the public order and good morals

in contravention of the criteria for deliberation as prescribed in Article 41.[128]

## ACCESS TO INFORMATION

In their analysis of freedom of the press amidst the democratic political reforms of 1987 in Korea, two American journalism scholars proposed: "If the press is to play a positive role by contributing to an informed and politically active electorate in a democracy, the government should go further than abolishing or revising suppressive laws; it should establish institutional mechanisms for positively enhancing press freedom."[129] They criticized the revised press laws for not recognizing right of access to information, which was included in the more restrictive Basic Press Act.[130]

The Constitution Court's recognition in 1992 of the right to know[131] as an integral part of freedom of the press will serve as a sorely needed incentive to institutionalize access to information for the press in Korea as is the case in the United States.[132] Soon after the Court ruled in the Military Secrets Protection Act case in 1992, the Ministry of Defense proposed a revision of the Act.[133] The draft revision reportedly contained a provision requiring "prior cooperation" between the news media and the military in deciding whether to release certain military information.[134] Despite this questionable aspect of the proposed revision, the Korean government's eagerness to follow up on the Constitution Court's ruling is noteworthy. As the *Korea Herald* stated in an editorial: "The free flow of information and the opening up of the military community will help promote popular understanding of, and cooperation with, the armed services in the long run. The Defense Ministry had made the right choice."[135]

In December 1993, the Military Secrets Protection Act was completely revised by the National Assembly.[136] The new statute is a significant improvement of the old one in that it defines military secrets in less broad terms and newly recognizes the public interest in getting access to military secrets. Article 2 of the revised statute defines "military secrets" as "military documents, books, electronic records ... which are unknown to the public and whose contents, if disclosed, would bring about a clear danger to the security of the State and which have been marked or known as military secrets and for whose protection special measures have been taken."[137] The public's right to know about the military secrets is stipulated by the law. Individuals may request the Minister of Defense in writing for release of military secrets.[138] Military secrets may be disclosed "when it is needed to inform the public or when it is deemed to be clearly in the interest of national security."[139] They may also be provided or explained to research institutes if requested for technological development and academic research.[140]

One prime example of Korean society's recognition of the right to know is the "Ordinance on Release of Administrative Information" adopted by the city council of Chongju on July 1, 1992. The purpose of the Ordinance, the first of its kind in Korea, was "to foster a responsible city government for the welfare of the public and the development of a democratic city administration by guaranteeing residents the right to know."[141] Article 3 of the Ordinance states that the enforcement agency is obligated to "actively" release the information specified in the Ordinance. The Ordinance also requires the agency to voluntarily disclose information that the majority of residents need to know as citizens and to comply with information requests.[142]

The Ordinance contains exceptions similar in many ways to those found in the Freedom of Information Act (FOIA) of the United States.[143] Like Exemption 3 of the FOIA,[144] the Ordinance is not applicable to information prohibited by other statutes or ordinances from disclosure.[145] Under the Ordinance, information whose release is "feared" to invade individual privacy is exempted.[146] Furthermore, information relating to the enforcement of administrative policies is not subject to the Ordinance. Falling within this exemption is information about inter-agency or intra-agency decision-making processes, negotiations, personnel decisions, budget matters, litigation, and investigation of crimes relevant to a trial.[147] The exemption is to prevent the disclosure of information from interfering with proper decision-making by the administration.

The Ordinance requires that the agency answer requests for records and documents within 14 days.[148] If the request is not granted, an individual can file an appeal within 30 days.[149] The agency has 10 days to refer the appeal to the Information Release Deliberation Commission. The Commission then has 20 days to rule upon the appeal.[150] The agency is also required to prepare a list of the public records to be "immediately" released for the convenience of the requesters.[151]

The legality of the Ordinance was challenged by the mayor of Chongju.[152] Among the arguments against the Ordinance were the lack of a statutory basis for the Ordinance, overbreadth, and the conflict with requirements of other statutes.[153] The Supreme Court dismissed all of the arguments on several grounds. First, the Court noted that the open records system has long been accepted in many foreign countries and that "it is desirable to have one in our country."[154] Second, insofar as the Ordinance is limited to disclosure of information about the autonomous local administration and not about the delegated responsibilities from the central government, the Ordinance cannot be invalidated merely because it is not based on a national uniform open records law.[155] The Court found the Ordinance's application to be clear in that it was limited to information about the local government.[156] Finally, the Court stated that the Ordinance defined access to information in such a way as to exempt statutorily classified information from disclosure and thus did not violate other laws and regulations.[157]

The Chongju Ordinance, the Supreme Court's ruling on the Ordinance, and the Constitution Court's interpretation of the right to know under the Constitution strongly indicate that Korea is closer than ever to accepting the policy of openness embodied in the FOIA of the United States—"Freedom of information is now the rule and secrecy the exception."[158]

Indeed, a Seoul district court in September 1993 recognized the "people's right to know" as a possible justification for blowing the whistle on government wrongdoing. In *State v. Yi Mun-ok*,[159] an inspector of the Board of Audit and Inspection of the Korean government was accused of violating the Criminal Code[160] by revealing to a Korean newspaper a secret internal report on real estate owned by business conglomerates.[161] The Seoul Criminal District Court asserted that the report released by Yi Mun-ok was neither classified as secret by law nor treated as a secret for political, military, or economic purposes.[162] The court noted that a document, which has never been classified as secret and whose contents do not fall within the boundaries of "substantial secrets," cannot become an official secret under the Criminal Code merely because the document is being internally processed by an administrative agency.[163]

The Seoul district court in *Yi Mun-ok* stated that Yi's disclosure of the report did not affect public confidence in the government, nor did it undermine the credibility of the business groups involved. The court reasoned: "Judging from the *people's right to know*, the alleged state interest in keeping the report from the public did not stem from the objective and general interest of the government, administrative agencies, or the public. Rather, it was derived from the subjective and peculiar perspectives of the banking supervisor or the businesses on the report."[164] The Seoul court's ruling on "whistleblowing" in the context of the right to know constitutes an expansive reading of press freedom, especially given the fact that Korea provides no legal protection for "whistleblowers" as the United States does.[165]

# Table of Cases

An Chae-ran v. Korean Federation of Education, 85 Taka 1973, Supreme Court, January 28, 1986, *Korean Press Cases* 71–74 (1990); *Press Arbitration Quarterly* 6 (Spring 1986): 169–71.

An Chae-ran v. Korean Federation of Education, 84 Ka 1598, Seoul Civil District Court, May 25, 1984, *Korean Press Cases* 64–68 (1990); *Press Arbitration Quarterly* 4 (Winter 1984): 171–73.

An Chae-ran v. Korean Federation of Education, 86 Na 3679, Seoul High Court, August 18, 1987, *Korean Press Cases* 251–55 (1990); *Press Arbitration Quarterly* 7 (Winter 1987): 185–88.

An Chae-ran v. Korean Federation of Education, 86 Kahap 1441, Seoul Civil District Court, August 21, 1986, *Korean Press Cases* 244–50 (1990).

An Chong-hyo v. Korean Literature Promotion Foundation, 83 Kahap 6051, Seoul Civil District Court, July 24, 1984, *Korean Press Cases* 235–41(1990); *Press Arbitration Quarterly* 5 (Spring 1985): 165–68.

An Ho-jun v. State, 73 To 2188, Supreme Court, February 12, 1974, *Supreme Court Decisions* 22(1) (1974): 11–22.

An Mi-ja v. State, 92 To 455, Supreme Court, March 23, 1993, *Official Gazette of Courts*, May 15, 1993, pp. 136–40.

An Pyong-won v. Kyohaksa, 91 Kahap 39509, Seoul Civil District Court, June 5, 1992, *Lower Court Decisions* 2 (1992): 290–301.

Association of Korean Galleries v. Munhwa Broadcasting Corp., 93 Kahap 1107, Seoul District Court (South Branch), December 20, 1993, *Press Arbitration Quarterly* 14 (Summer 1994): 169–74.

Baptist Association for Christian Evangelism v. Ha Yong-jo, 91 Ka 8154, Seoul Civil District Court, October 10, 1991, *Press Arbitration Quarterly* 12 (Spring 1992): 154–55.

Broadcasting Commission v. Korean Advertisers Association, 95 Kahap 1359, Seoul District Court (South Branch), June 15, 1995, *Press Arbitration Quarterly* 15 (Autumn 1995): 167–69.

Broadcasting Producers Association of Korea v. Ilyo Shinmunsa, 95 Kagi 1885, Seoul District Court, July 5, 1995, *Press Arbitration Quarterly* 15 (Autumn 1995): 169–74.

Cha Pong-hyon v. State, 79 To 2391, Supreme Court, December 28, 1979, *Official Gazette of Courts*, February 15, 1980, p. 12506.

Chang Chong-sik v. State, 79 To 1455, Supreme Court, February 22, 1977, *Supreme Court Decisions* 25(1) (1977): 18–24.

Chang Chong-taek v. State, 82 To 2915, Supreme Court, February 22, 1983, *Supreme Court Decisions* 31(1) (1983): 191–95.

Chang Chun-ha v. State, 74 To 1123, Supreme Court, August 20, 1974, *Monthly Court Case Report*, January 1975, p. 93.

Chang Chun-ha v. State, 70 To 704, Supreme Court, May 26, 1970, *slip opinion.*

Chang Kon-sop v. State, 89 No 2338, Seoul Civil District Court, July 14, 1989, *Korean Press Cases* 327–30 (1990); *Press Arbitration Quarterly* 10 (Spring 1990): 165–66.

Chang Yong-sik v. State, 76 To 3446, Supreme Court, December 28, 1976, *Law Times*, February 14, 1977, p. 4.

Cheju Onchon Co. v. Cheju Shinmunsa, 94 Kahap 27, Cheju District Court, June 16, 1994, *Press Arbitration Quarterly* 14 (Autumn 1994): 163–69; *Law Times*, July 28, 1994, pp. 12–13.

Chi Yong-song v. State, 77 No 713, Seoul High Court, *High Court Decisions: Special* (1977): 230–34.

Chin Pu-ja v. Joongang Ilbosa, 86 Ka 28755, Seoul Civil District Court, September 26, 1986, *Korean Press Cases* 121–25 (1990); *Press Arbitration Quarterly* 6 (Winter 1986): 165–67.

Chin Pu-ja v. Joongang Ilbosa, 86 Ta 24988, Seoul Civil District Court, December 18, 1986, *Korean Press Cases* 125–26 (1990).

Chin Pyong-chol v. State, 88 To 1008, Supreme Court, September 27, 1988, *Official Gazette of Courts*, November 1, 1988, pp. 63–64.

Cho Ha-mun v. Yowonsa, 88 Kahap 17151, Seoul District Court (East Branch), April 21, 1989, *Korean Press Cases* 295–301 (1990); *Press Arbitration Quarterly* 9 (Summer 1989): 172–75.

Cho Ku-hyon v. State, 85 To 1629, Supreme Court, October 22,1985, *Official Gazette of Courts*, December 15, 1985, pp. 73–74.

Cho Man-song v. State, 76 To 876, Supreme Court, May 11, 1976, *Monthly Court Case Report*, October 1975, pp. 92–93; *slip opinion.*

Cho Son-gil v. State, 90 To 230, Supreme Court, August 28, 1990, *Supreme Court Decisions* 38(2) (1990): 714–18.

Cho Su-bi v. Yonbang Film Co., 91 Ra 79, Seoul High Court, September 5, 1991, *Lower Court Decisions* 3 (1991): 262–72.

Cho Yong-ju v. State, 78 To 1357, Supreme Court, August 22, 1978, *Law Times*, October 16, 1978, p. 6.

Cho Yong-su v. State, Hyoksang 3, Prosecution Ministry of the Military Revolutionary Government, October 31, 1961, *Korean Press Annual 1968* (1968): 532.

Cho Yun-hwan v. Hankuk Ilbosa, 92 Kadan 58180, Seoul Civil District Court, October 15, 1992, *Press Arbitration Quarterly* 14 (Autumn 1994): 171–73.

Choe Chong-sun v. Munhwa Broadcasting Corp., 89 Ka 8917, Seoul District Court (South Branch), February 20, 1992, *Press Arbitration Quarterly* 12 (Summer 1992): 154–61.

Choe Chong-sun v. Om Hyo-sop, 89 Kahap 13975, Seoul District Court (South Branch), February 20, 1992, *Press Arbitration Quarterly* 12 (Summer 1992): 161–68.

Chon Hong-kyun v. State, 83 To 891, Supreme Court, February 28, 1984, *Supreme Court Decisions* 32(1) (1984): 433–35.

Chong Chae-hong v. State, 82 To 269, Supreme Court, June 8, 1982, *Monthly Court Case Report*, November 1982, pp. 128–29.

Chong Chae-in v. State, 72 To 1730, Supreme Court, September 26, 1972, *Supreme Court Decisions* 26(3) (1972): 16–18.

Chong Chang-jun v. State, 4287 Hyongsang 65, Supreme Court, March 22, 1955, *Supreme Court Decisions* 1 (1950–57): 384–90.

Chong Chin-tae v. State, 83 To 2755, Supreme Court, December 27, 1983, *Official Gazette of Courts*, February 15, 1984, pp. 51–52.

Chong Ha-yon v. Korean Broadcasting Corp., 83 Kahap 7, Seoul District Court (South Branch), October 21, 1983, *Korean Press Cases* 202–208 (1990); *Press Arbitration Quarterly* 4 (Autumn 1984): 176–79.

Chong Hae-kum v. State, 4293 Hyongsang 861, Supreme Court, February 24, 1961, *Supreme Court Decisions* 9 (1961): 25–28.

Chong Hyon-baek v. Korean Broadcasting Corp., 94 Kahap 3123, Seoul Civil District Court (South Branch), *Press Arbitration Quarterly* 15 (Summer 1995): 172–74.

Chong Hyon-baek v. Korean Broadcasting Corp., 95 Na 11261, Seoul High Court, July 12, 1995, *Press Arbitration Quarterly* 15 (Winter 1995): 155–59.

Chong Hyon-baek v. Seoul Broadcasting System, 94 Kahap 3222, Seoul Civil District Court, March 28, 1995, *Newspapers and Broadcasting*, May 1995, pp. 118–19.

Chong Hyong-mo v. State, 76 To 3638, Supreme Court, January 11, 1977, *slip opinion.*

Chong In-wi v. State, 73 To 2178, Supreme Court, October 23, 1973, *Supreme Court Decisions* 21(3) (1973): 25–29.

Chong Kum-taek v. State, 86 To 1429, Supreme Court, September 23, 1986, *Supreme Court Decisions* 34(3) (1986): 528–46.

Chong Myong-su v. State, 92 To 3160, Supreme Court, June 22, 1993, *Official Gazette of Courts*, September 1, 1993, pp. 120–23; *Monthly Court Case Report*, December 1993, pp. 206–10; *Press Arbitration Quarterly* 13 (Autumn 1993): 170–73.

Chong Myong-su v. State, 92 No. 5394, Seoul Criminal District Court, November 17, 1992, *Press Arbitration Quarterly* 13 (Autumn 1993): 174–75.

Chong Pyong-yul v. State, 72 To 687, Supreme Court, May 23, 1972, *Monthly Court Case Report*, July 1972, pp. 82–84.

Chong Ui-yong v. State, 76 To 3603, Supreme Court, December 14, 1976, *Monthly Court Case Report*, May 1975, pp. 84–85.

Dong-A Ilbosa v. State, 89 Honma 160, Constitution Court, April 1, 1991, *Official Gazette*, April 26, 1991, pp. 50–54; *Press Arbitration Quarterly* 11 (Summer 1991): 162–67.

Dong-A Ilbosa v. Yi Kyu-hyo, 90 Taka 25468, Supreme Court, January 15, 1991, *Supreme Court Decisions* 39(1) (1991): 36–42; *Press Arbitration Quarterly* 11 (Spring 1991): 172–74.

Dong-A Ilbosa v. Yi Ui-hyang, 82 Na 4188, Seoul High Court, November 17, 1983, *Korean Press Cases* 50–56 (1990); *Press Arbitration Quarterly* 3 (Winter 1983): 188–91.

F. Hoffman Larosch Co. v. Tonghwa Pharmaceutical Co., 79 Ta 2138, 2139, Supreme Court, February 26, 1980, *Supreme Court Decisions* 28(1) (1980): 112–25.

Hakwonsa v. Yi Il-jae, 85 Taka 29, Supreme Court, October 11, 1988, *Official Gazette of Courts*, November 15, 1988, pp. 30–32; *Korean Press Cases* 224–28 (1990); *Press Arbitration Quarterly* 8 (Winter 1988): 167–70.

Hakwonsa v. Yi Il-jae, 84 Na 1780, Seoul High Court, December 11, 1984, *Press Arbitration Quarterly* 8 (Winter 1988): 170–74.

Ham Sok-hon v. Minister of Culture and Information, 70 Ku 194, Seoul High Court, May 4, 1971, *Law Times*, May 17, 1971, p. 6; *Korean Newspaper Editors Association Newsletter*, May 18, 1971, p. 2.

Ham Un-gyong v. State, 86 To 403, Supreme Court, June 24, 1986, *Supreme Court Decisions* 34(2) (1986): 385–91.

Ham Yun-sik v. Song Ki-hyon, 91 Kodan 8793, Seoul Criminal District Court, September 14, 1992, *Press Arbitration Quarterly* 12 (Winter 1992): 165–66.

Han Chang-u v. Chon Sung-chon, 1959 Haengso 26, Seoul High Court, June 26, 1959, *Korean Press Annual 1968* (1968), p. 515.

Han Chang-u v. Chon Sung-chon, 4292 Haengsang 110, Supreme Court, February 5, 1960, *Korean Press Annual 1968* (1968), p. 528; *Law Times*, February 15, 1960, p. 3.

Han Hye-suk v. Lucky Goldstar Trading Co., 87 Kahap 6032, Seoul Civil District Court, September 9, 1988, *Korean Press Cases* 270–74 (1990); *Press Arbitration Quarterly* 9 (Spring 1989): 173–75.

Hankuk Ilbosa v. Cho Yun-hwan, 93 Ta 36622, Supreme Court, *Press Arbitration Quarterly* 14 (Autumn 1994): 169–71.

Hankuk Ilbosa v. Cho Yun-hwan, 92 Na 36013, Seoul Civil District, June 11, 1994, *Press Arbitration Quarterly* 14 (Autumn 1994): 173–74.

Han-kyoreh Shimunsa v. Yi Chong-ja, 89 Na 30506, Seoul High Court, February 6, 1990, *Korean Press Cases* 161–64 (1990); *Press Arbitration Quarterly* 10 (Autumn 1990): 170–72.

Han O-su v. State, 78 To 2254, Supreme Court, October 31, 1978, *Supreme Court Decisions* 26(3) (1978): 82–85; *Monthly Court Case Report*, April 1979, p. 97

Han Sang-jin v. Korean Broadcasting Corp., 90 Kaham 1404, Seoul District Court (South Branch), May 14, 1992, *Press Arbitration Quarterly* 12 (Summer 1992): 169–72.

Han Sung-hon v. State, 76 To 364, Supreme Court, October 16, 1976, *Law Times*, December 20, 1976, p. 4.

Ho Myong-sun v. Chosun Ilbosa, 94 Kahap 47709, Seoul District Court, May 2, 1995, *Press Arbitration Quarterly* 15 (Autumn 1995): 164–67.

Ho Tong-jun v. State, 92 To 1211, Supreme Court, August 14, 1992, *Supreme Court Decisions* 40(2) (1992): 717–26.

Hong Song-chol v. State, 69 To 1003, Supreme Court, July 29, 1969, *Supreme Court Decisions* 17(2) (1969): 135–36.

Hong Song-dam v. State, 90 To 1586, Supreme Court, September 25, 1990, *Supreme Court Decisions* 38(3) (1990): 353–64; *Monthly Court Case Report,* February 1991, pp. 184–89.

Hwang Chang-yon v. State, 81 To 149, Supreme Court, August 25, 1981, *Official Gazette of Courts*, October 15, 1981, pp. 14313–14.

Hwang Chong-guk v. State, 68 Ko 1080, Seoul Criminal District Court, February 6, 1969, *Law Times*, February 24, 1969, p. 6.

Hwang Chu-hong v. State, 76 To 3905, Supreme Court, February 22, 1977, *slip opinion.*

Hwang Chu-hong v. State, 77 To 2979, Supreme Court, October 10, 1979, *Monthly Court Case Report*, April 1980, p. 113.

Hwang Chun-ung v. State, 89 To 251, Supreme Court, July 24, 1990, *Monthly Court Case Report*, December 1990, pp. 174–76.

Hwang Sang-gi v. Dong-A Ilbosa, 81 Ka 36289, Seoul Civil District Court, October 21, 1982, *Korean Press Cases* 17–21 (1990); *Press Arbitration Quarterly* 2 (Winter 1982): 166–68.

Hwang Sil-gun v. Kyonghyang Shinmunsa, 93 Kagi 3887, Seoul Civil District Court, November 15, 1993, *Press Arbitration Quarterly* 14 (Spring 1994): 169–71.

Hwang Song-mo v. State, 68 To 739, Supreme Court, July 30, 1968, *Law Times*, August 26, 1968, p. 4; September 2, 1968, p. 5.

Hwang Yon-dae v. Cho Kun-tae, 93 Kagi 3786, Seoul District Court, December 11, 1993, *Press Arbitration Quarterly* 14 (Spring 1994): 171–74.

Hyondae Investment Research Institute v. Cheil Kyongje Shinmunsa, 89 Ka 28984, Seoul Civil District Court, May 25, 1990, *Press Arbitration Quarterly* 10 (Winter 1990): 160–63.

Idoho Kendaro v. State, 76 To 720, Supreme Court, May 11, 1976, *Supreme Court Decisions* 24(2) (1976): 5–9; *Official Gazette of Courts*, June 15, 1976, pp. 26–27.

Irand Co. v. Sim Chae-jong, 94 Kahap 2072, Seoul Civil District Court, April 14, 1994, *slip opinion.*

Joongang Ilbosa v. Pasteur Milk Co., 89 Na 7209, Seoul High Court, July 12, 1989, *Korean Press Cases* 152–55 (1990); *Press Arbitration Quarterly* 9 (Autumn 1989): 169–71.

Joongang Ilbosa v. State, 89 Honma 165, Constitution Court, September 16, 1991, *Press Arbitration Quarterly* 11 (Autumn 1991): 169–77.

Joongang Ilbosa v. Ilyo Shinmunsa, 89 Ka 5999, Seoul District Court (South Branch), November 7, 1989, *Korean Press Cases* 175–80 (1990); *Press Arbitration Quarterly* 10 (Spring 1990): 160–62.

Joongang Ilbosa v. Chin Pu-ja, 86 Na 4096, Seoul High Court, March 18, 1987, *Korean Press Cases* 127–31 (1990); *Press Arbitration Quarterly* 7 (Autumn 1987): 173–76.

Kang Chun-ho v. Taehan Songso Konghoe, 90 Kahap 95311, May 29, 1992, *Lower Court Decisions* 2 (1992): 284–90.

Kang Ki-jong v. State, 86 To 456, Supreme Court, May 27, 1986, *Official Gazette of Courts*, July 1, 1986, pp. 38–39.

Kang Sin-ok v. State, 74 To 3501, Supreme Court (en banc), January 29, 1985, *Supreme Court Decisions* 2 (1978–87): 517–82.

Kang Sung-pyong v. State, 69 To 934, Supreme Court, July 22, 1969, *Supreme Court Decisions* 17(2) (1969): 112.

Kim Chae-uk v. State, 80 To 464, Supreme Court, April 22, 1980, *Supreme Court Decisions* 28(1) (1980): 100–106.

Kim Che-won v. State, 4289 Hyongsang 149, Supreme Court, July 13, 1956, *slip opinion.*

Kim Che-yol v. State, 71 To 2264, Supreme Court, February 29, 1972, *Law Times*, March 20, 1972, p. 4.

Kim Chin-kyong v. State, 86 To 1499, Supreme Court, September 23, 1986, *Official Gazette of Courts*, November 15, 1986, pp. 78–79.

Kim Chin-tae v. State, 68 To 1569, Supreme Court, December 24, 1968, *Supreme Court Decisions* 16(4) (1968): 94–97.

Kim Chon v. State, 84 To 1197, Supreme Court, July 10, 1984, *Supreme Court Decisions* 32(3) (1984): 803–12.

Kim Chong-saeng v. State, 82 To 1219, Supreme Court, July 13, 1982, *Supreme Court Decisions* 30(2) (1982): 141–48; *Monthly Court Case Report*, January 1983, pp. 121–24.

Kim Song-hi v. Dong-A Ilbosa, 89 Na 36528, Seoul High Court, May 4, 1990, *Press Arbitration Quarterly* 11 (Summer 1991): 155–62.

Kim Song-hi v. Dong-A Ilbosa, 88 Kahap 31161, Seoul Civil District Court, July 25, 1989, *Korean Press Cases* 301–11 (1990); *Press Arbitration Quarterly* 9 (Autumn 1989): 173–79.

Kim Song-hi v. Yi Kap-sop, 89 Na 8158, Seoul High Court, November 29, 1989, *Korean Press Cases* 284–95 (1990); *Press Arbitration Quarterly* 10 (Spring 1990): 166–73.

Kim Song-hi v. Yi Kap-sop, 88 Kahap 20604, Seoul Civil District Court, January 18, 1989, *Korean Press Cases* 274–84 (1990); *Press Arbitration Quarterly* 9 (Spring 1989): 168–73.

Kim Song-kwi v. Chonbuk Ilbosa, 92 Ka 50, Chonju District Court, October 29, 1992, *Press Arbitration Quarterly* 13 (Autumn 1993): 164–65.

Kim Tae-hong v. State, 88 No 781, Seoul Criminal District Court, July 5, 1994, *slip opinion.*

Kim Tae-hong v. State, 94 To 2379, Supreme Court, December 5, 1995, *slip opinion.*

Kim Tae-su v. State, 68 To 538, Supreme Court, June 18, 1968, *Supreme Court Decisions* 16(2) (1968): 21–27.

Kim Tae-yon v. State, 93 To 2995, Supreme Court, January 11, 1994, *Official Gazette of Courts*, March 1, 1994, pp. 158–60.

Kim To-song v. State, 81 To 2280, Supreme Court, November 24, 1981, *Official Gazette of Courts*, January 15, 1982, p. 37; *Law Times*, December 1, 1981, p. 7.

Kim Tok-hwan v. State, 86 To 1603, Supreme Court, October 14, 1986, *Official Gazette of Courts*, December 1, 1986, pp. 58–59.

Kim Tong-yol v. Joongang Ilbosa, 86 Taka 818, Supreme Court, December 23, 1986, *Korean Press Cases* 118–20 (1990); *Press Arbitration Quarterly* 7 (Spring 1987): 174–76.

Kim Tong-yol v. Joongang Ilbosa, 85 Na 3140, Seoul High Court, February 25, 1986, *Korean Press Cases* 114–18 (1990); *Press Arbitration Quarterly* 6 (Summer 1986): 171–74.

Kim Tong-yol v. Joongang Ilbosa, 85 Ka 20576, Seoul Civil District Court, July 27, 1985, *Korean Press Cases* 106–114 (1990); *Press Arbitration Quarterly* 5 (Autumn 1985): 167–71.

Kim U-ryong v. Journalists Association of Korea, 90 Ka 41568, Seoul Civil District Court, July 19, 1990, *Press Arbitration Quarterly* 10 (Winter 1990): 164–66.

Kim Ui-bang v. State, 4288 Hyongkong, Seoul Civil District Court, February 27, 1955, *Law Times*, April 11, 1955, p. 3.

Kim Yang-gi v. State, 87 To 455, Supreme Court, May 26, 1987, *Official Gazette of Courts,* July 15, 1987, pp. 90–91.

Kim Yong-hi v. Kim Hi-suk, 90 Kahap 15032, Seoul Civil District Court, November 9, 1990, *Press Arbitration Quarterly* 11 (Spring 1991):160–63.

Kim Yong-hwan v. Kangwon Ilbosa, 82 Ka 768, Chunchon District Court, February 9, 1983, *Korean Press Cases* 21–27 (1990); *Press Arbitration Quarterly* 3 (Summer 1983): 167–70.

Kim Yong-kun v. State, 83 To 1520, Supreme Court, October 25, 1983, *Official Gazette of Courts*, December 15, 1983, pp. 92–94.

Kim Yong-so v. Social Development Research Institute, 83 Ka 17754, Seoul Civil District Court, August 26, 1983, *Korean Press Cases* 39–43 (1990); *Press Arbitration Quarterly* 3 (Winter 1983): 180–83.

Kim Yong-suk v. State, 91 To 420, Supreme Court, May 14,1991, *Supreme Court Decisions* 39(2) (1991): 700–702.

Ko Chae-duk v. State, 83 To 3124, Supreme Court, February 28, 1984, *Official Gazette of Courts*, May 1, 1984, pp. 85–86.

Ko Chin-hwa v. State, 86 To 1784, Supreme Court, October 28, 1986, *Official Gazette of Courts*, December 15, 1986, pp. 84–87.

Ko Chong-hi v. Chon Ki-hwa, 4294 Minsang 1028, Supreme Court, March 8, 1962, *Supreme Court Decisions* 10(1) (1962): 184–86.

Ko Chong-hun v. State, 4294 Hyongsang 12, Supreme Court, May 17, 1962, *Law Times*, May 28, 1962, p. 3.

Ko Chun-hwan v. State, 74 To 2189, Supreme Court, October 10, 1978, *Collection of Supreme Court Decisions* 26(3) (1978): 37–42.

Ko Kwang-mun v. State, 71 To 1122, Supreme Court, September 28, 1971, *Supreme Court Decisions* 19(3) (1971): 1–4; *Law Times*, October 11, 1971, p. 4.

Ko Kyong-dae v. State, 87 To 434, Supreme Court, April 28, 1987, *Official Gazette of Courts*, June 15, 1987, pp. 83–84.

Ko Yong-chol v. State, 94 To 348, Supreme Court, April 26, 1994, *Official Gazette of Courts*, June 1, 1994, pp. 188–89.

Korean Broadcasting Corp. v. Han Sang-jin, 92 Na 35846, Seoul High Court, September 29, 1994, *Press Arbitration Quarterly* 14 (Winter 1994): 161–71; *slip opinion*.

Korean Consumer Protection Institute v. Pasteur Milk Co., 91 Kahap 38193, Seoul Civil District Court, December 15, 1992, *Press Arbitration Quarterly* 13 (Spring 1993): 169–77; *Law Times*, February 8, 1993, p. 11.

Korean Council for Guidance and Evangelism of the Handicapped v. Hankuk Ilbosa, 85 Ka 8825, Seoul Civil District Court, June 11, 1985, *Korean Press Cases* 95–101 (1990).

Korean Council for Guidance and Evangelism of the Handicapped v. Hankuk Ilbosa, 85 Na 2457, Seoul High Court, July 14, 1986, *Korean Press Cases* 101–106 (1990); *Press Arbitration Quarterly* 6 (Autumn 1986):169–72.

Korean Electric Wire Corp. Labour Union v. Joongang Ilbosa, 95 Kagi 3524, Seoul Civil District Court, September 30, 1995, *Press Arbitration Quarterly* 15 (Winter 1995): 165–68.

Korean Electric Wire Corp. Labour Union v. Kyonghyang Shinmunsa, 95 Kagi 3525, Seoul Civil District Court, September 30, 1995, *Press Arbitration Quarterly* 15 (Winter 1995): 159–64.

Korean Federation of Education v. An Chae-ran, 84 Na 2524, Seoul High Court, August 16, 1985, *Korean Press Cases* 68–70 (1990).

Korean Housing Management Co. v. Yang Chun-kun, 87 Taka 1450, Supreme Court, June 14, 1988, *Supreme Court Decisions* 36(2) (1988): 34–37.

Korean Munhwa Broadcasting Corp. v. State, 70 Ma 900, Supreme Court, January 29, 1971, *Constitution Committee and Supreme Court Decisions on the Constitution* 2 (1990): 674.

Ku Chan-an v. State, 83 To 2222, Supreme Court, October 11, 1983, *Official Gazette of Courts*, December 1, 1983, pp. 45–46.

Ku Myong-u v. State, 87 To 432, Supreme Court, May 26, 1987, *Official Gazette of Courts*, July 15, 1987, pp. 87–90.

Kuk Yun-gu v. State, 93 To 2445, Supreme Court, August 26, 1993, *Official Gazette of Courts*, December 15, 1993, pp. 69–70.

Kwak Chol-am v. Republic of Korea, 87 Kahap 3739, Seoul Civil District Court, April 29, 1988, *Korean Press Cases* 262–66 (1990); *Press Arbitration Quarterly* 8 (Autumn 1988): 185–87.

Kwak Kwi-ja v. State, 87 To 739, Supreme Court, May 12, 1987, *Official Gazette of Courts*, July 1, 1987, pp. 82–83.

Kwon In-suk v. Seoul Munhwasa, 90 Kahap 15896, Seoul Civil District Court, January 17, 1991, *Press Arbitration Quarterly* 11 (Autumn 1991): 152–55; *slip opinion.*

Kwon Kyong-bok v. State, 91 To 919, Supreme Court, October 22, 1991, *Supreme Court Decisions* 39(4) (1991): 717–21.

Kwon Mun-sun v. State, 82 To 486, Supreme Court, February 8,1983, *Law Times*, March 14, 1983, p. 7.

Kwon Sun-jong v. Newsweek, Inc., 92 Kadan 57989, Seoul Civil District Court, July 8, 1993, *Press Arbitration Quarterly* 13 (Autumn 1993): 168–70; *Newspapers and Broadcasting*, September 1993, pp. 130–31.

Kyonghyang Shinmunsa v. Chu Sun-il, 68 Na 207, Supreme Court, September 29, 1970, *Journalists Association of Korea Newsletter*, October 16, 1970, p. 2; *Korean Newspaper Editors Association Newsletter*, October 23, 1970, p. 6.

Labor Union of Munhwa Broadcasting Corp. v. Dong-A Ilbosa, 89 Kahap 18505, Seoul District Court (South Branch), October 12, 1990, *Press Arbitration Quarterly* 11 (Spring 1991): 164–72.

Ma Kwang-su v. State, 93 No 446, Seoul Criminal District Court, July 13, 1994, *slip opinion.*

Ma Kwang-su v. State, 92 Kodan 10092, Seoul Criminal District Court, December 28, 1992, *Lower Court Decisions* 3 (1992): 393–406.

Mayor of Chongju v. City Council of Chongju, 92 Chu 17, Supreme Court, June 23, 1992, *Collection of Supreme Court Decisions* 40(2) (1992): 511–25; *Newspapers and Broadcasting*, August 1992, pp. 97–98.

Minister of Culture and Information v. Ham Sok-hon, 71 Nu 62, Supreme Court, July 6, 1971, *Supreme Court Decisions* 19(2) (1971): 32.

Mun Ik-hwan v. Chosun Ilbosa, 89 Ka 28545, Seoul Civil District Court, September 22, 1989, *Korean Press Cases* 167–72 (1990); *Press Arbitration Quarterly* 9 (Winter 1989): 181–84.

Mun Pyong-rip v. State, 77 To 1445, Supreme Court, June 28, 1977, *Supreme Court Decisions* 25(2) (1977): 62–64.

Myong No-chol v. Chihak Shinbosa, 87 Ka 40175, Seoul Civil District Court, December 11, 1987, *Korean Press Cases* 131–34 (1990); *Press Arbitration Quarterly* 8 (Spring 1988): 176–77.

Na Song-su v. State, 91 No 3346, Seoul Criminal District Court, September 4, 1991, *Lower Court Decisions* 3 (1991): 372–78.

Nam Tuk-u v. State, 68 To 1118, Supreme Court, October 22, 1968, *slip opinion*; Supreme Court Ruling Card no. 3412.

Namyang Dairy Co. v. Pasteur Flour Milk Co., 91 Ka 116924, Seoul Civil District Court, June 9, 1992, *Press Arbitration Quarterly* 12 (Autumn 1992): 160–64.

Namyang Dairy Co. v. Pasteur Flour Milk Co., 91 Kahap 3081, 91 Kahap 84677, Seoul Civil District Court, June 9, 1992, *Press Arbitration Quarterly* 12 (Autumn 1992): 164–71.

Newsweek, Inc. v. Kwon Sun-jong., 93 Na 31886, Seoul Civil District Court, March 30, 1994, *Press Arbitration Quarterly* 14 (Autumn 1994): 152–56.

Pasteur Milk Co. v. Joongang Ilbosa, 88 Ka 39283, Seoul Civil District Court, January 13, 1989, *Korean Press Cases* 134–46 (1990); *Press Arbitration Quarterly* 9 (Spring 1989): 158–65.

Pasteur Milk Co. v. Joongang Ilbosa, 89 Tagi 1609, Seoul Civil District Court, February 28, 1989, *Press Arbitration Quarterly 9* (Spring 1989): 165.

Pasteur Milk Co. v. Joongang Ilbosa, 88 Ka 43429, Seoul Civil District Court, January 13, 1989, *Korean Press Cases* 147–50 (1990); *Press Arbitration Quarterly* 9 (Spring 1989): 166–67.

Pasteur Milk Co. v. Joongang Ilbosa, 89 Tagi 1608, Seoul Civil District Court, February 28, 1989, *Korean Press Cases* 151 (1990); *Press Arbitration Quarterly* 9 (Spring 1989): 167.

Pasteur Milk Co. v. Kukmin Ilbosa, 92 Kahap 3879, Seoul District Court (West Branch), December 14, 1992, *Press Arbitration Quarterly* 13 (Summer 1993): 170–75.

Preparatory Committee on Formation of the South Side Headquarters of the Pan-National Federation for National Unification v. Seoul Shinmunsa, 92 Kagi 649, Seoul Civil District Court, November 26, 1992, *Press Arbitration Quarterly* 13 (Summer 1993): 153–58.

Progressive Party v. State, 4291 Hyongsang 559, Supreme Court, February 27, 1959, *General Digest of Court Cases: Constitutional Law* 25 (1982): 1:13–14 .

Pu Wan-hyok v. Minister of Culture and Information, 71 Nu 183, Supreme Court, April 25, 1972, *Law Times,* May 8, 1972, p. 4.

Pyo Ul-gyong v. State, 78 To 2243, Supreme Court, December 13, 1978, *Supreme Court Decisions* 26(3) (1978): 131–40.

Pyon Ui-suk v. State, 93 Cho 107, Seoul High Court, July 8, 1993, *slip opinion.*

Pyongdong Presbytery of Korean Christian Presbyterian Church v. Tak Myong-hwan, 84 Ka 35089, Seoul Civil District Court, November 23, 1984, *Korean Press Cases* 91–95 (1990); *Press Arbitration Quarterly* 5 (Summer 1985): 174–76.

Republic of Korea v. Tae Yong, 93 Ta 18389, Supreme Court, November 26, 1993, *Supreme Court Decisions* 41(3) (1993): 302–306.

Sammi Food Industrial Co. v. Community Leaders Foundation of Taegu Catholic Church, 67 Ta 591, Supreme Court, December 26, 1967, *Constitution Committee and Supreme Court Decisions* 2 (January 1990): 668–73.

Seoul Integrated Terminal Co. v. So Sok-won, 82 Ka 19263, Seoul Civil District Court, July 21, 1982, *Press Arbitration Quarterly* 2 (Autumn 1982): 140–41.

Seoul Sillim Elementary School v. Munhwa Broadcasting Corp., 93 Kahap 792, Seoul Civil District Court (South Branch), September 6, 1993, *Press Arbitration Quarterly* 13 (Winter 1993): 164–70.

Sim Han-sik v. State, 87 To 929, Supreme Court, September 22, 1987, *Official Gazette of Courts,* November 15, 1987, pp. 67–69.

Sin Hyon-chong v. Kyonghyang Shinmunsa, 92 Kagi 474, Seoul Civil District Court, September 15, 1992, *Press Arbitration Quarterly* 12 (Winter 1992): 166–68.

Sin Hyon-jun v. State, 92 To 1711, Supreme Court, February 9, 1993, *Official Gazette of Courts,* October 1, 1994, pp. 241–44.

Sin Hyon-sun v. Kukmin Ilbosa, 91 Na 27320, Seoul High Court, September 25, 1991, *Press Arbitration Quarterly* 11 (Winter 1991): 166–70.

Sin Kong-hyon v. State, 82 To 1256, Supreme Court, November 9,1982, *Supreme Court Decisions* 30(4) (1982): 4–6; *Official Gazette of Courts*, January 15, 1983, pp. 129–30.

Sin Sang-bong v. State, 80 To 808, Supreme Court, July 22, 1986, *Official Gazette of Courts*, September 15, 1986, pp. 77–78.

Sin Sang-chol v. State, 70 To 1879, Supreme Court, October 30, 1970, 1 *Supreme Court Cases* 1–2 (1971); *Monthly Court Case Report* 4 (January 1971): 79.

Sin Sok-u v. Chosun Ilbosa, 95 Kahap 41982, Seoul District Court, October 24, 1995, *Press Arbitration Quarterly* 15 (Winter 1995): 168–71.

Sin _____ v. _____ Ilbo (plaintiff and defendant not fully identified), 93 Kahap 91402, Seoul Civil District Court, August 2, 1994, *Newspapers and Broadcasting*, October 1994, pp. 108–109; *Accurate Press*, September 12, 1994, p. 1.

So Sun-un v. State, 91 To 3, Supreme Court, March 12, 1991, *Supreme Court Decisions* 39(1) (1991): 701–706.

So Sung v. State, 71 No 999, Seoul High Court, December 7, 1972, *Monthly Court Case Report*, February 1973, pp. 86–88.

Son Chung-mu v. Seoul Shinmunsa, 93 Na 22236, Seoul High Court, January 21, 1994, *Press Arbitration Quarterly* 14 (Winter 1994): 159–61; *Law Times*, February 21, 1994, p. 11; *slip opinion*.

Son Jin-sok v. State, 78 To 2203, Supreme Court, November 28, 1978, *Official Gazette of Courts*, March 1, 1979, p. 39.

Son Yu-ji v. Cho Yong-pil, 90 Kahap 3961, Seoul Civil District Court, April 17, 1991, *Press Arbitration Quarterly* 11 (Summer 1991): 149–52.

Song Chong-suk v. Journalists Association of Korea, 89 Kahap 51612, Seoul Civil District Court, September 5, 1990, *Korean Press Cases* 312–20 (1990); *Press Arbitration Quarterly* 10 (Winter 1990): 167–72.

Song In-hwi v. State, 73 To 682, Supreme Court, November 26, 1974, *Monthly Court Case Report,* March 1975, p. 89.

Song Min-sok v. State, 82 To 2655, Supreme Court, February 8, 1983, *Official Gazette of Courts*, April 1, 1983, pp. 71–72.

Song Mun-suk v. Korean Broadasting Corp., 94 Kahap 1797, Seoul District Court (South Branch), November 29, 1994, *Press Arbitration Quarterly* 15 (Spring 1995): 169–71.

Song Sok-rae v. State, 83 To 1017, Supreme Court, August 23, 1983, *Supreme Court Decisions* 31(4) (1983): 88–93.

Song Su-yong v. State, 73 To 166, Supreme Court, March 13, 1973, *Monthly Court Case Report,* May 1973, p. 78.

Song Tae-jin v. Nongmin Shinmunsa, 92 Ka 77904, Seoul Civil District Court, November 26, 1992, *Press Arbitration Quarterly* 13 (Winter 1993): 170–73.

Song Un v. State, 4294 Hyongsang 451, Supreme Court, November 16, 1961, *Law Times*, December 11, 1961, p. 3.

Song Un v. State, [no docket number provided], Taejon District Court, March 20, 1961, *Korean Newspaper Editors Association Newsletter*, April 5, 1961, pp. 4–5.

State v. An Song-gun, 71 To 745, Supreme Court, June 22, 1971, *Supreme Court Decisions* 19(2) (1971): 33–35; *Monthly Court Case Report*, September 1971, pp. 101–102.

State v. [appellee not named], 4289 Hyongsang 60, Supreme Court, June 29, 1956, *Supreme Court Decisions* 2 (1950–57): 826–29

State v. Chang Hak-sik, 93 To 1035, Supreme Court, June 22,1993, *Official Gazette of Courts*, September 1, 1993, pp. 131–33.

State v. Chang Kon-sop, 89 To 1744, Supreme Court, November 14, 1989, *Korean Press Cases* 330–31 (1990); *Press Arbitration Quarterly* 10 (Spring 1990): 163–64

State v. Chang Kon-sop, 88 Kodan 8891, Seoul Criminal District Court, March 29, 1989, *Korean Press Cases* 325–27 (1990); *Press Arbitration Quarterly* 10 (Spring 1990): 164–65.

State v. Chang Pong-jin, 72 Kahap 315, Seoul Criminal District Court, September 27, 1972, *Journalists Association of Korea Newsletter*, September 29, 1972, p. 4; October 6, 1972, p. 6.

State v. Cho Tok-son, 77 To 1360, Supreme Court, July 12, 1977, *Law Times*, August 15, 1977, p. 7.

State v. Cho Yon-song, 71 Kohap 836, Seoul Criminal District Court, January 29, 1972, *Monthly Court Case Report*, April 1972, pp. 104–109.

State v. Choe Chang-sop, 4292 Hyonggong 9318, Seoul District Court, March 11, 1960, *Law Times*, April 4, 1960, pp. 3–4.

State v. Choe Chong-gon, 71 To 36, Supreme Court, February 23, 1971, *Monthly Court Case Report*, May 1971, pp. 91–93.

State v. Choe Myong-jae, 92 To 3035, Supreme Court, April 13, 1993, *Official Gazette of Courts*, June 1, 1993, pp. 87–89.

State v. Choe Myong-jae, 90 Kodan 108, Chunchon District Court, February 26, 1991, *Press Arbitration Quarterly* 11 (Summer 1991): 168–71.

State v. Choe Sok-chae, [no docket number provided], Taegu District Court, December 6, 1955, *Korean Press Annual 1968* (1968): 517; Kye Hun-mo, ed., *Korean Press Chronology III, 1951–1955* (1993): 1334–35.

State v. Choe Sok-chae, Hyonggong 832, Taegu High Court, January 27, 1956, *Korean Press Annual 1968* (1968): 517–18; Kye Hun-mo, ed., *Korean Press Chronology III, 1951–1955* (1993): 1335–37.

State v. Choe Sok-chae, 4289 Hyongsang 80, Supreme Court, May 8, 1956, *Korean Press Annual 1968* (1968), pp. 518–19; *Law Times*, June 25, 1956, p. 3; Kye Hun-mo, ed., *Korean Press Chronology III, 1951–1955* (1993): 1337–38.

State v. Chon Kon-su, 76 To 1402, Supreme Court, July 27, 1976, *Supreme Court Decisions* 24(2) (1976): 83–88.

State v. Chon Kum-song, 90 Kodan 7304, Seoul Criminal District Court, December 4, 1990, *Press Arbitration Quarterly* 11 (Summer 1991): 163–64.

State v. Chon Yon-sok, 71 To 165, Supreme Court, April 6, 1971, *Law Times*, April 19, 1971, p. 4.

State v. Chong Bong-yul, 71 No 958, Seoul High Court, January 27,1972, *Monthly Court Case Report*, April 1972, pp. 93–98.

State v. Chong Chae-jung, 94 Kohap 485 and 94 Kohap 1032, Seoul Criminal District Court, November 22, 1994, *slip opinion.*

State v. Chong Chae-yong, 71 To 2022, Supreme Court, December 28, 1971, *Supreme Court Decisions* 19(3) (1971): 78–80.

State v. Chong Chan-u, 67 To 1460, Supreme Court, December 26, 1967, *Law Times*, January 1. 1968, p. 4.

State v. Chong Chong-ho, 70 Ko 18095, Seoul Criminal District Court, November 26, 1970, *Monthly Court Case Report*, February 1971, pp. 84–85.

State v. Kim Che-bong, 71 To 466, Supreme Court, May 24, 1971, *Monthly Court Case Report*, August 1971, p. 95.

State v. Kim Che-yol, 68 Ko 21972, Seoul Criminal District Court, June 15, 1970, *Law Times*, August 17, 1970, p. 6; August 24, 1970, p. 6.

State v. Kim Chol-gi, 83 To 515, Supreme Court (en banc), June 14, 1983, *Supreme Court Decision* 2 (1978–87): 440–55; *Law Times*, June 27, 1983, p. 6; *slip opinion*.

State v. Kim Chong-gang, 64 Ko 12378 and 20387, Seoul Criminal District Court, January 27, 1965, *Law Times*, February 8, 1965, p. 6.

State v. Kim Chong-ho, 73 To 2045, Supreme Court, February 12, 1974, *Monthly Court Case Report*, May 1974, pp. 78–79.

State v. Kim Chong-nam, 70 Ko 45085, Seoul Criminal District Court, February 11, 1971, *Monthly Court Case Report*, April 1971, pp. 78–80.

State v. Kim Chong-u, 77 To 836, Supreme Court, April 26, 1977, *Monthly Court Case Report*, November 1977, p. 102.

State v. Kim Chun-sik, 66 Ko 2067, Taejon District Court, May 18, 1967, *Law Times*, September 11, 1967, p. 6; September 18, 1967, p. 6.

State v. Kim Chun-yon, 64 Ko 5623, Seoul Criminal District Court, August 2, 1965, *Law Times*, August 23, 1965, p. 6.

State v. Kim Chung-hwan, 85 To 588, Supreme Court, May 28, 1985, *Official Gazette of Courts*, July 15, 1985, pp. 94–95.

State v. Kim Chung-tae, 64 Ko 11105, Seoul Criminal District Court, October 28, 1964, *Law Times*, November 2, 1964, p. 6.

State v. Kim Hae-ryong, 72 To 1694, Supreme Court, March 23, 1973, *Monthly Court Case Report*, June 1973, pp. 58–59.

State v. Kim Hi-so, 83 To 2190, Supreme Court, October 25, 1983, *Official Gazette of Courts*, December 15, 1983, pp. 99–100.

State v. Kim In-sop, 81 To 49, Supreme Court, April 10, 1984, *Official Gazette of Courts*, June 1, 1984, p. 97.

State v. Kim Kwang-il, 81 To 1145, Supreme Court, December 27, 1983, *Official Gazette of Courts*, February 15, 1984, pp. 36–37.

State v. Kim Kwang-su, Hyongsang 369, Seoul High Court, April 7, 1948, *Korean Press Annual 1968* (1968): 515.

State v. Kim Kwang-su, Pisang 1, Supreme Court, May 21, 1948, *Korean Press Annual 1968*, pp. 515–16.

State v. Kim Kwi-jin, 78 To 2327, Supreme Court, November 14, 1978, *Supreme Court Decisions* 26(3) (1978): 100–103.

State v. Kim Nam-yong, 82 To 371, Supreme Court, April 27,1982, *Official Gazette of Courts*, July 1, 1982, pp. 36–37.

State v. Kim Pyong-jae, 86 To 1341, Supreme Court, October 14, 1986, *Official Gazette of Courts*, December 1, 1986, pp. 52–53.

State v. Kim Son-wang, 94 Kodan 1165, Taegu District Court, December 23, 1994, *Press Arbitration Quarterly* 15 (Summer 1995): 167–69.

State v. Kim Tae-hong, 87 Kodan 503, Seoul Criminal District Court, June 3, 1987, *Press Guidelines* 230–39 (Council for Democratic Press Movement ed., 1988); *slip opinion*.

State v. Kim Tok-song, 74 To 846, Supreme Court, July 16, 1974, *Monthly Court Case Report*, December 1974, pp. 88–89.

State v. Kim Tok-won, 70 To 1266, Supreme Court, July 21,1970, *slip opinion*.

State v. Ko Chong-hun, 4293 Hyongkong 3959, Seoul District Court, September 20, 1960, *Law Times*, October 10, 1960, p. 3.

State v. Ko Chun-hwan, 73 Kohap 91, Seoul Criminal District Court, April 23, 1973, *Journalists Association of Korea Newsletter*, May 4, 1973, p. 3.

State v. Ko Yong-su, 89 Kodan 3303, Seoul District Court (East Branch), May 16, 1990, *Korean Press Cases* 332–34 (1990); *Press Arbitration Quarterly* 10 (Autumn 1990): 157–58.

State v. Ku Yong-hwa, 75 To 473, Supreme Court, April 25, 1978, *Monthly Court Case Report*, October 1978, p. 85.

State v. Kwon Ho-yon, 67 No 631, Seoul Criminal District Court, January 21, 1969, *Law Times*, January 19, 1970, p. 6; January 26, 1970, pp. 6–7.

State v. Kwon Ki-o, 71 To 743, Supreme Court, June 22, 1971, *Monthly Court Case Report*, September 1971, p. 100.

State v. Kye Yong-sun, 77 Kodan 681, Seoul Criminal District Court, October 5, 1977, *Monthly Court Case Report*, April 1978, pp. 107–108.

State v. Mun Chu-hwi, 69 No 789, Seoul High Court, June 29, 1972, *Monthly Court Case Report*, September 1972, pp. 97–100.

State v. Mun Kyu-hyon, 90 To 1613, Supreme Court, September 25, 1990, *Supreme Court Decision* 38(3) (1990): 364–77.

State v. Nam Chong-hyon, 66 Ko 14198, Seoul Criminal District Court, June 28, 1967, *Law Times*, August 7, 1967, p. 6; August 14, 1967, p. 6; August 21, 1967, p. 6.

State v. Paek Sang-gi, 75 To 982, Supreme Court, November 25, 1975, *Monthly Court Case Report*, February 1976, pp. 70–72.

State v. Paek Yong-chol, 74 To 2183, Supreme Court, May 13, 1975, *Monthly Court Case Report*, August 1975, pp. 63–64.

State v. Pak Chu-sop, 68 To 1825, Supreme Court, February 25, 1969, *Supreme Court Decision* 17(1) (1969): 53–55.

State v. Pak Pok-tok, 76 To 2644, Supreme Court, October 26, 1976, *Law Times*, November 22, 1976, p. 4.

State v. Pak Sung-hun, 69 Ko 27460, Seoul Criminal District Court, December 15, 1969, Kim Chol-su, *Casebook on Constitutional Law* 336 (1981).

State v. Sim Yong-sun, 85 To 2037, Supreme Court, November 26,1986, *Official Gazette of Courts*, January 15, 1986, p. 82.

State v. Sinohara Misato, 94 No 166, Seoul High Court, April 22, 1994, *slip opinion.*

State v. So Min-ho, 67 Ko 10961, Seoul Criminal District Court, April 17, 1972, *Law Times*, May 1, 1972, p. 6.

State v. So Min-ho, 67 No 99, Seoul Criminal District Court, October 17, 1970, *Monthly Court Case Report*, December 1970, pp. 82–84.

State v. So Min-ho, 66 Ko 141, Seoul Criminal District Court, December 27, 1966, *Law Times*, January 9, 1967, p. 6; January 16, 1967, p. 6; January 23, 1967, p. 6.

State v. Son Hak-kyu, 74 To 1236, Supreme Court, July 13, 1976, *Official Gazette of Courts*, September 1, 1976, pp. 17–18; *Monthly Court Case Report*, December 1976, pp. 75–76.

State v. Tak Myong-hwan, 82 Koyak 6184, Seoul District Court (North Branch), July 14, 1982, *Korean Press Cases* 321–22 (1990); *Press Arbitration Quarterly* 3 (Spring 1983): 174–75.

State v. Tak Myong-hwan, 83 Koyak 201, Seoul District Court (North Branch), January 28, 1982, *Korean Press Cases* 323–25 (1990); *Press Arbitration Quarterly* 3 (Spring 1983): 175–76.

State v. U Yang-gu, 71 Kohap 386, 421 and 447, Seoul Criminal District Court, June 29, 1971, *Monthly Court Case Report*, October 1971, pp. 114–19.

State v. Yang Chong-ho, 86 No 6426, Seoul Criminal District Court, December 17, 1986, *Lower Court Decisions* 4 (1986): 447–50.

State v. Yi Chon-su, 91 Kodan 4554, Seoul District Court (South Branch), January 14, 1993, *Press Arbitration Quarterly* 13 (Summer 1993): 168–69.

State v. Yi Ho-yon, 71 To 1414, Supreme Court, September 28, 1971, *Supreme Court Decisions* 19(3) (1971): 14–16.

State v. Yi Ik-sun, 91 Kodan 6158, Seoul Criminal District Court, May 26, 1992, *Press Arbitration Quarterly* 12 (Autumn 1992): 158–59; *Law Times,* July 2, 1992, p. 9.

State v. Yi Ik-sun, 92 No 4099, Seoul Criminal District Court, May 25, 1993, *Press Arbitration Quarterly* 14 (Winter 1994): 156–59.

State v. Yi Ik-sun, 93 To 1732, Supreme Court, September 24, 1993, *Press Arbitration Quarterly* 14 (Winter 1994): 155–56.

State v. Yi Kang-hi, 83 To 2040, Supreme Court, September 27, 1983, *Official Gazette of Courts*, November 15, 1983, pp. 88–89.

State v. Yi Kang-sun, 4287 Hyongsang 36, Supreme Court, April 22, 1955, *Supreme Court Decisions* 1 (1964): 428–29.

State v. Yi Kong-sun, 91 Kodan 4995, Seoul Criminal District Court, November 16, 1993, *Press Arbitration Quarterly* 14 (Summer 1994): 160–65; *slip opinion.*

State v. Yi Man-hi, 65 Ko 2047, Seoul Criminal District Court, December 8, 1965, *Law Times*, January 10, 1966, p. 6; January 24, 1966, p. 6; January 31, 1966, p. 6.

State v. Yi Mong-ui, 91 To 1950, Supreme Court, October 11,1991, *Supreme Court Decisions* 39(4) (1991): 713–16.

State v. Yi Mun-ok, 90 Kodan 3615, Seoul Criminal District Court, September 6, 1993, *slip opinion.*

State v. Yi Sang-du, 76 To 282, Supreme Court, June 26, 1979, *Supreme Court Decisions* 27(2): (1979): 18–22; *Official Gazette of Courts*, September 1, 1979, p. 27.

State v. Yi Sang-gwan, 65 Ko 8762, Taegu District Court, October 18, 1967, *Law Times*, November 6, 1967, p. 6; *Journalists Association of Korea Newsletter*, October 15, 1967, p. 2.

State v. Yi Sang-gwan, 68 No 451, Taegu District Court, November 7, 1969, *Journalists Association of Korea Newsletter*, November 21, 1969, p. 2; *Korean Newspaper Editors Association Newsletter*, November 17, 1969, p. 7.

State v. Yi Sang-gyu, 93 To 1689, Supreme Court, April 26, 1994, *Official Gazette of Courts*, June 1, 1994, pp. 184–86.

State v. Yi Sin-bom, 70 Ko 11034, Seoul Criminal District Court, February 15, 1971, *Monthly Court Case Report*, April 1971, pp. 80–81.

State v. Yi Sok-pyo, 82 To 1930, Supreme Court, February 8, 1983, *Law Times*, March 7, 1983, p. 7.

State v. Yi Song-yong, 74 Kodan 13021, Seoul Criminal District Court, March 28, 1975, *Monthly Court Case Report*, July 1975, pp. 106–107.

State v. Yi Yong-hi, 89 Kodan 3509, Seoul Criminal District Court, September 25, 1989, *slip opinion.*

State v. Yom Chae-man, 74 To 976, Supreme Court, December 9, 1975, *Supreme Court Decisions* 23(3) (1975): 52–57; *Official Gazette of Courts*, February 15, 1976, pp. 27–78.

State v. Yom Chae-man, 71 To 1371, Supreme Court, August 31, 1971, *Supreme Court Decisions* 19(2) (1971): 91–93.

State v. Yu Hyon-mok, 66 Ko 89, Seoul Criminal District Court, March 15, 1967, *Law Times*, May 1, 1967, p. 6; May 5, 1967, p. 6; May 15, 1967, p. 6.

State v. Yu Kap-chong, 70 To 1325, Supreme Court, September 29, 1970, *Monthly Court Case Report*, December 1970, p. 80.

State v. Yu Song-hwan, 91 To 3317, Supreme Court, September 22, 1992, *Supreme Court Decisions* 40(3) (1992): 561–81.

State v. Yun Pyong-rok, 84 To 86, Supreme Court, March 27,1984, *Official Gazette of Courts*, May 15, 1984, pp. 84–85.

Taesong Church v. Tak Myong-hwan, 83 Kahap 2449, Seoul Civil District Court, September 30, 1983, *Korean Press Cases* 195–202 (1990); *Press Arbitration Quarterly* 3 (Winter 1983): 184–88.

Taeyang Development Co. v. Kyongin Ilbosa, 92 Kahap 9602, Suwon District Court, April 20, 1993, *Press Arbitration Quarterly* 13 (Winter 1993): 170–73.

Tak Myong-hwan v. Church Federation News, 84 Ka 34375, Seoul Civil District Court, November 30, 1984, *Korean Press Cases* 86–91 (1990); *Press Arbitration Quarterly* 5 (Summer 1985): 172–74.

Tak Myong-hwan v. Christian News, 84 Ka 34374, Seoul Civil District Court, November 30, 1984, *Korean Press Cases* 82–86 (1990); *Press Arbitration Quarterly* 5 (Spring 1985): 170–73.

Ujin Construction Co. v. Ward Head of Nam-Ku, Inchon City, 88 Nu 9312, Supreme Court, October 24, 1989, *Supreme Court Decisions* 37(3) (1989): 572–74.

Whang Song-mo v. State, 68 To 1772, Supreme Court, March 18, 1969, *Law Times,* May 12, 1969, p. 5.

World Association for Christian Unification and Spirits v. Korean Christian Public Information Co., 83 Ka 9145, Seoul Civil District Court, August 19, 1983, *Korean Press Cases* 31–35 (1990); *Press Arbitration Quarterly* 3 (Autumn 1983): 166–68.

World Association for Christian Unification and Spirits v. Christian News, 83 Ka 9146, Seoul Civil District Court, August 19, 1983, *Korean Press Cases* 35–39 (1990); *Press Arbitration Quarterly* 3 (Autumn 1983): 168–70.

Wonsok Institute v. Uijong Shinmunsa, 89 Ka 1188, Seoul District Court (West Branch), February 20, 1990, *Korean Press Cases* 189–94 (1990); *Press Arbitration Quarterly* 10 (Autumn 1990): 172–75.

Yang Tong-hwa v. State, 86 To 1429, Supreme Court, September 23, 1986, *Supreme Court Decisions* (Korean) 34(3) (1986): 528–46.

Yi Chae-du v. State, 87 To 705, Supreme Court, June 23, 1987, *Official Gazette of Courts*, August 15,1987, pp. 95–96.

Yi Chae-gil v. Yi Chong-suk, 89 Na 32908, Seoul High Court, February 13, 1990, *Lower Court Decisions* 1 (1990): 262–74; *slip opinion.*

Yi Chae-gil v. Yi Chong-suk, 90 Na 48718, Seoul High Court, January 23, 1991, *slip opinion.*

Yi Chang-bok v. State, 98 No 8, Seoul Criminal District Court, April 6, 1995, *slip opinion.*

Yi Chang-hi v. State, 86 To 2683, Supreme Court, September 20, 1968, *Official Gazette of Courts*, June 15, 1993, pp. 49–50; *Monthly Court Case Report*, September 1993, pp. 240–41.

Yi, Chang-jun v. State, 77 To 3984, Supreme Court, March 14, 1978, *Official Gazette of Courts*, May 1, 1978, pp. 29–30; *Monthly Court Case Report*, August 1978, pp. 92–92.

Yi Che-bong v. State, 76 No 11699, Seoul Criminal District Court, February 16, 1977, *Law Times*, March 7, 1977, p. 9.

Yi Chin-kyu v. Na Un-mong, 83 Ka 22003, Seoul Civil District Court, November 25, 1983, *Korean Press Cases* 56–62 (1990); *Press Arbitration Quarterly* 4 (Spring 1984): 179–82

Yi Chin-kyu v. Na Un-mong, 83 Ta 20389, Seoul Civil District Court, January 12, 1984, *Korean Press Cases* 62–63 (1990); *Press Arbitration Quarterly* 4 (Spring 1984): 182.

Yi Chon-su v. State, 93 To 3535, Supreme Court, April 12, 1994, *Press Arbitration Quarterly* 14 (Autumn 1994): 156–57.

Yi Chon-su v. State, 93 No 1025, Seoul Criminal District Court, December 2, 1993, *Press Arbitration Quarterly* 14 (Autumn 1994): 157–63.

Yi Chon-sul v. State, 93 To 3535, Supreme Court, April 12, 1994, *Official Gazette of Courts*, June 1, 1994, pp. 169–70.

Yi Chong-bo v. State, 94 To 237, Supreme Court, August 26, 1994, *Official Gazette of Courts*, October 1, 1994, pp. 250–52.

Yi Chong-ja v. Han-kyoreh Shinmunsa, 89 Ka 11518, Seoul Civil District Court, July 7, 1989, *Korean Press Cases* 156–60 (1990); *Press Arbitration Quarterly* 9 (Autumn 1989): 166–68.

Yi Chong-ja v. Han-kyoreh Shinmunsa, 89 Tagi 11984, Seoul Civil District Court, August 21, 1989, *Korean Press Cases* 160–61 (1990).

Yi Chong-ju v. State, 87 To 1081, Supreme Court, July 21, 1987, *Official Gazette of Courts*, September 15, 1987, pp. 74–75.

Yi Chong-suk v. Yi Chae-gil, 90 Taka 8845, Supreme Court, October 23, 1990, *Supreme Court Decisions* 38(3) (1990): 7–20; *Monthly Court Case Report,* January 1991, pp. 105–109.

Yi Chong-yol v. State, 4293 Hyongsang 244, Supreme Court, November 16, 1960, *Law Times*, December 12, 1960, pp. 3–4; *slip opinion.*

Yi Hak-ki v. Kwangmyong Remicon Co., 92 Ta 42583, Supreme Court, December 8, 1992, *Monthly Court Case Report*, April 1993, pp. 111–13.

Yi Hi-jae v. State, 82 To 744, Supreme Court, June 14, 1983, *Official Gazette of Courts*, August 1, 1983, p. 61.

Yi Hi-yong v. Ilsin Pharmaceutical Co., 68 Ka 11886, Seoul Civil District Court, June 20, 1969, *Law Times*, September 14, 1970, pp. 6–7; September 21, 1970, p. 6.

Yi Ho-yun v. Kim Chin-hwan, 93 Kagi 4057 (previously 93 Kahap 33284), Seoul Civil District Court, September 8, 1993, *Press Arbitration Quarterly* 14 (Autumn 1994): 151–52.

Yi Hwa-bok v. State, 92 To 234, Supreme Court, April 13, 1993, *Official Gazette of Courts*, June 1, 1993, pp. 85–86.

Yi Hwa-yong v. Kimhae Girls High School, 75 Nu 249, Supreme Court, April 27, 1976, *Law Times*, May 10, 1976, p. 4.

Yi Tu-sik v. Tak Myong-hwan, 83 Kadan 7668, Seoul Civil District Court, October 15, 1984, *Korean Press Cases* 241–44 (1990); *Press Arbitration Quarterly* 5 (Spring 1985): 169–70.

Yi Ui-hyang v. Hankuk Ilbosa, 84 Na 3255, Seoul High Court, January 18, 1985, *Korean Press Cases* 78–82 (1990); *Press Arbitration Quarterly* 5 (Summer 1985): 176–78.

Yi Ui-hyang v. Hankuk Ilbosa, 84 Ka 17261, Seoul Civil District Court, July 13, 1984, *Korean Press Cases* 75–78 (1990); *Press Arbitration Quarterly* 4 (Winter 1984): 174–76.

Yi Ui-hyang v. Dong-A Ilbosa, 82 Kahap 4734, Seoul Civil District Court, April 11, 1984, *Korean Press Cases* 229–35 (1990); *Press Arbitration Quarterly* 4 (1984): 174–77.

Yi Ui-hyang v. Dong-A Ilbosa, 82 Ka 27454, Seoul Civil District Court, November 4, 1982, *Korean Press Cases* 44–49 (1990); *Press Arbitration Quarterly* 2 (Winter 1982): 168–71.

Yi Ui-hyang v. Dong-A Ilbosa, 82 Ta 20095, Seoul Civil District Court, December 10, 1982, *Korean Press Cases* 49–50 (1990).

Yi Ui-hyang v. Dong-A Ilbosa, 82 Ta 27454, Seoul Civil District Court, December 10, 1982, *Press Arbitration Quarterly* 2 (Winter 1982): 172.

Yi Yong-hi v. State, 89 No 5990, Seoul Criminal District Court, February 2, 1993, *slip opinion.*

Yi Yong-hi v. State, 85 To 1143, Supreme Court, March 25, 1986, *Supreme Court Decisions* 34(1) (1986): 425–30.

Yi Yong-hi v. State, 78 To 2706, Supreme Court, January 16,1979, *Supreme Court Decisions* 27(1) (1979): 1–6; *Official Gazette of Courts*, May 15, 1979, pp. 36–37.

Yi Yong-su v. State, 82 To 716, Supreme Court, May 25, 1982, *Supreme Court Decisions* 20(2) (1982): 20–27; *Law Times*, June 21, 1982, p. 6.

Yim Chae-jong v. Yun Chong-ran, 93 Kahap 14585, Seoul District Court (West Branch), September 14, 1994, *Press Arbitration Quarterly* 15 (Autumn 1995): 154–56.

Yim Chong-jo v. State, 72 To 1514, Supreme Court, September 12, 1972, *Monthly Court Case Report*, November 1972, pp. 76–77.

Yim Hyong-sin v. Chong Ku-ho, 82 Ka 18633, Seoul Civil District Court, September 3, 1982, *Korean Press Cases* 13–17 (1990); *Press Arbitration Quarterly* 2 (Autumn 1982): 137–39.

Yom Chae-man v. State, 71 No 3610, Seoul Criminal District Court, November 6, 1973, *Official Gazette of Courts*, February 15, 1976, pp. 28–29.

Yom Tong-ho v. State, 66 To 179, Supreme Court, April 19, 1966, *slip opinion.*

Yon Hak-hum v. State, 76 To 2671, Supreme Court, September 28, 1976, *Law Times*, October 18, 1976, p. 4.

Yon Song-man v. Seoul Shinmunsa, 89 Ka 46152, Seoul Civil District Court, December 29, 1989, *Korean Press Cases* 180–85 (1990); *Press Arbitration Quarterly* 10 (Spring 1990): 156–58.

Yon Song-man v. Seoul Shinmunsa, 90 Kahap 35265, Seoul Civil District Court, August 17, 1990, *Lower Court Decisions* 2 (1990): 108–117.

Yon Song-su v. Joongang Ilbosa, 94 Kagi 5463, Seoul Civil District Court, *Press Arbitration Quarterly* 15 (Summer 1995): 169–71.

Yonhap News Agency v. Maeskom Shinmunsa, 92 Kahap 3033, Seoul Civil District Court, July 29, 1992, *Press Arbitration Quarterly* 12 (Autumn 1992): 171–75.

# APPENDIX B

# Table of Statutes

Act on Assembly and Demonstration, Law No. 4095 (1989), revised by Law No. 4408 (1991)
Act on Promotion of Expansion of Access to and Use of Computer Networks, Law No. 3848 (1986), revised by Law No. 4528 (1992)
Act Relating to Import and Distribution of Foreign Periodicals, Law No. 4688 (1993)
Act on Phonorecords or Videos, Law No. 4351 (1991), revised by Law No. 4541 (1993)
Act on Protection of Personal Information in Governmental Agencies, passed by the National Assembly during the 165th session (1993)
Act Relating to Registration, etc. of Periodicals, Law No. 3979 (1987), revised by Law No. 4441 (1991)
Act on Registration of Publishers or Printers, Law No. 904 (1961), revised by Law No. 4541 (1993)
Act on Temporary Measures on Fines, Law No. 216 (1951), revised by Law No. 4296 (1990)
Broadcast Act, Law No. 3978 (1987), revised by Law No. 4441 (1991)
Children's Welfare Act, Law No. 3438 (1981)
Civil Code, Law No. 471 (1958), revised by Law No. 4199 (1990)
Code of Civil Procedure, Law No. 547 (1960), revised by Law No. 4931 (1995)
Code of Criminal Procedure, Law No. 341 (1954), revised by Law No. 4796 (1994)
Comprehensive Cable Television Broadcast Act, Law No. 4494 (1991), revised by Law No. 4737 (1994)
Computer Program Protection Act, Law No. 3920 (1986), revised by Law No. 4712 (1994)
Constitution Court Act, Law No. 4017 (1988), revised by Law No. 4408 (1991)
Court Organization Act, Law No. 3992 (1987), revised by Law No. 4765 (1994)
Copyright Act, Law No. 3916 (1986), revised by Law No. 4746 (1994)
Correspondence Protection Act, Law No. 4650 (1993)
Criminal Code, Law No. 293 (1953), revised by Law No. 4040 (1988)
Customs Act, Law No. 1976 (1967), revised by Law No. 4743 (1994)
Martial Law, Law No. 3442 (1981), revised by Law No. 3993 (1994)
Military Secrets Protection Act, Law No. 4616 (1993)
Minor Offenses Act, Law No. 3680 (1983), revised by Law No. 4369 (1991)
Minors Protections Act, Law No. 838 (1961), revised by Law No. 4351 (1991)

# Constitution of the Republic of Korea

Established on July 12, 1948
Promulgated on July 17, 1948
Amended on July 7, 1952
November 29, 1954
June 15, 1960
November 29, 1960
Wholly Amended on December 26, 1962
Amended on October 21, 1969
Wholly Amended on December 27, 1972
Wholly Amended on October 27, 1980
Wholly Amended on October 29, 1987

## PREAMBLE

We the people of Korea, proud of a resplendent history and traditions dating from time immemorial, upholding the cause of the Provisional Republic of Korea Government born of the March First Independence Movement of 1919 and the democratic ideals of the April Nineteenth Uprising of 1960 against injustice, having assumed the mission of democratic reform and peaceful unification of our homeland and having determined to consolidate national unity with justice, humanitarianism and brotherly love, and

To destroy all social vices and injustice, and

To afford equal opportunities to every person and provide for the fullest development of individual capabilities in all fields, including political, economic, social and cultural life by further strengthening the basic free and democratic order conducive to private initiative and public harmony, and

To help each person discharge those duties and responsibilities concomitant to freedoms and rights, and

To elevate the quality of life for all citizens and contribute to lasting world peace and the common prosperity of mankind and thereby to ensure security, liberty and happiness for ourselves and our posterity forever,

Do hereby amend, through national referendum following a resolution by the National Assembly, the Constitution, ordained and established on the Twelfth Day of July Anno Domini Nineteen hundred and forty-eight, and amended eight times subsequently.

October 29, 1987

## CHAPTER I. GENERAL PROVISIONS

**Article 1**  (1) The Republic of Korea shall be a democratic republic.

(2) The sovereignty of the Republic of Korea shall reside in the people, and all state authority shall emanate from the people.

**Article 2**  (1) Nationality in the Republic of Korea shall be prescribed by law.

(2) It shall be the duty of the State to protect citizens residing abroad as prescribed by law.

**Article 3**  The territory of the Republic of Korea shall consist of the Korean peninsula and its adjacent islands.

**Article 4**  The Republic of Korea shall seek unification and shall formulate and carry out a policy of peaceful unification based on the principles of freedom and democracy.

**Article 5**  (1) The Republic of Korea shall endeavor to maintain international peace and shall renounce all aggressive wars.

(2) The Armed Forces shall be charged with the sacred mission of national security and the defense of the land and their political neutrality shall be maintained.

**Article 6**  (1) Treaties duly concluded and promulgated under the Constitution and the generally recognized rules of international law shall have the same effect as the domestic laws of the Republic of Korea.

(2) The status of aliens shall be guaranteed as prescribed by international law and treaties.

**Article 7**  (1) All public officials shall be servants of the entire people and shall be responsible to the people.

(2) The status and political impartiality of public officials shall be guaranteed as prescribed by law.

**Article 8**  (1) The establishment of political parties shall be free, and the plural party system shall be guaranteed.

(2) Political parties shall be democratic in their objectives, organization and activities, and shall have the necessary organizational arrangements for the people to participate in the formation of the political will.

(3) Political parties shall enjoy the protection of the State and may be provided with operational funds by the State under the conditions as prescribed by law.

(4) If the purposes or activities of a political party are contrary to the fundamental democratic order, the Government may bring action against it in the Constitution Court for its dissolution, and, the political party shall be dissolved in accordance with the decision of the Constitution Court.

**Article 9**  The State shall strive to sustain and develop the cultural heritage and to enhance national culture.

## CHAPTER II. RIGHTS AND DUTIES OF CITIZENS

**Article 10**   All citizens shall be assured of human worth and dignity and have the right to pursue happiness. It shall be the duty of the State to confirm and guarantee the fundamental and inviolable human rights of individuals.

**Article 11**   (1) All citizens shall be equal before the law, and there shall be no discrimination in political, economic, social or cultural life on account of sex, religion or social status.

(2) No privileged caste shall be recognized or ever established in any form.

(3) The awarding of decorations or distinctions of honor in any form shall be effective only for recipients, and no privileges shall ensue therefrom.

**Article 12**   (1) All citizens shall enjoy personal liberty. No person shall be arrested, detained, searched, seized or interrogated except as provided by law. No person shall be punished, placed under preventive restrictions or subject to involuntary labor except as provided by law and through lawful procedures.

(2) No citizens shall be tortured or be compelled to testify against himself in criminal cases.

(3) Warrants issued by a judge through due procedures upon the request of a prosecutor shall be presented in case of arrest, detention, seizure or search: Provided that in a case where a criminal suspect is apprehended *flagrante delicto*, or where there is danger that a person suspected of committing a crime punishable by imprisonment of three years or more may escape or destroy evidence, investigative authorities may request an *ex post facto* warrant.

(4) Any person who is arrested or detained shall have the right to prompt assistance of counsel. When a criminal defendant is unable to secure counsel by his own efforts, the State shall assign counsel for the defendant as prescribed by law.

(5) No person shall be arrested or detained without being informed of the reason therefor and of his right to assistance of counsel. The family, etc., as designated by law, of a person arrested or detained shall be notified without delay of the reason for and the time and place of the arrest or detention.

(6) Any person who is arrested or detained shall have the right to request the court to review the legality of the arrest or detention.

(7) In a case where a confession is deemed to have been made against a defendant's will due to torture, violence, intimidation, unduly prolonged arrest, deceit, etc., or in a case where a confession is the only evidence against a defendant in a formal trial, such a confession shall not be admitted as evidence of guilt nor shall a defendant be punished by reason of such a confession.

**Article 13**   (1) No citizen shall be prosecuted for an act which does not constitute a crime under the law in force at the time it was committed, nor shall he be placed in double jeopardy.

(2) No restrictions shall be imposed upon the political rights of any citizen, nor shall any person be deprived of property rights by means of retroactive legislation.

(3) No citizen shall suffer unfavorable treatment on account of an act not of his own doing but committed by a relative.

**Article 14**   All citizens shall enjoy freedom of residence and the right to move at will.

**Article 15**   All citizens shall enjoy freedom of occupation.

**Article 16**   All citizens shall be free from intrusion into their place of residence. In case of search or seizure in a residence, a warrant issued by a judge upon request of a prosecutor shall be presented.

**Article 17**   The privacy of no citizen shall be infringed.

**Article 18**   The privacy of correspondence of no citizen shall be infringed.

**Article 19**   All citizens shall enjoy freedom of conscience.

**Article 20**   (1) All citizens shall enjoy freedom of religion.

(2) No state religion shall be recognized, and religion and politics shall be separated.

**Article 21**   (1) All citizens shall enjoy freedom of speech and the press, and freedom of assembly and association.

(2) Licensing or censorship of speech and the press, and licensing of assembly and association shall not be recognized.

(3) The standards of news service and broadcast facilities and matters necessary to ensure the functions of newspapers shall be determined by law.

(4) Neither speech nor the press shall violate the honor or rights of other persons nor undermine public morals or social ethics. Should speech or the press violate the honor or rights of other persons, claims may be made for the damage resulting therefrom.

**Article 22**   (1) All citizens shall enjoy freedom of learning and the arts.

(2) The rights of authors, inventors, scientists, engineers and artists shall be protected by law.

**Article 23**   (1) The right of property of all citizens shall be guaranteed. The contents and limitations thereof shall be determined by law.

(2) The exercise of property rights shall conform to the public welfare.

(3) Expropriation, use or restriction of private property from public necessity and compensation therefor shall be governed by law. However, in such a case, just compensation shall be paid.

**Article 24**   All citizens shall have the right to vote under the conditions as prescribed by law.

**Article 25**   All citizens shall have the right to hold public office under the conditions as prescribed by law.

**Article 26**   (1) All citizens shall have the right to petition in writing to any governmental agency under the conditions as prescribed by law.

(2) The State shall be obligated to examine all such petitions.

**Article 27**   (1) All citizens shall have the right to be tried in conformity with the law by judges qualified under the Constitution and the law.

(2) Citizens who are not on active military service or employees of the military forces shall not be tried by a court martial within the territory of the Republic of Korea, except in case of crimes as prescribed by law involving important classified military information, sentinels, sentry posts, the supply of harmful food and beverages, prisoners of war and military articles and facilities and in the case of the proclamation of extraordinary martial law.

(3) All citizens shall have the right to a speedy trial. The accused shall have the right to a public trial without delay in the absence of justifiable reasons to the contrary.

(4) The accused shall be presumed innocent until a judgment of guilt has been pronounced.

(5) A victim of a crime shall be entitled to make a statement during the proceedings of the trial of the case involved as under the conditions prescribed by law.

**Article 28**  In a case where a criminal suspect or an accused person who has been placed under detention is not indicted as provided by law or is acquitted by a court, he shall be entitled to claim just compensation from the State under the conditions as prescribed by law.

**Article 29**  (1) In case a person has sustained damages by an unlawful act committed by a public official in the course of official duties, he may claim just compensation from the State or public organization under the conditions as prescribed by law. In this case, the public official concerned shall not be immune from liabilities.

(2) In case a person on active military service or an employee of the military forces, a police official or others as prescribed by law sustains damages in connection with the performance of official duties such as combat action, drill and so forth, he shall not be entitled to a claim against the State or public organization on the grounds of unlawful acts committed by public officials in the course of official duties, but shall be entitled only to compensations as prescribed by law.

**Article 30**  Citizens who have suffered bodily injury or death due to criminal acts of others may receive aid from the State under the conditions as prescribed by law.

**Article 31**  (1) All citizens shall have an equal right to receive an education corresponding to their abilities.

(2) All citizens who have children to support shall be responsible at least for their elementary education and other education as provided by law.

(3) Compulsory education shall be free of charge.

(4) Independence, professionalism and political impartiality of education and the autonomy of institutions of higher learning shall be guaranteed under the conditions as prescribed by law.

(5) The State shall promote lifelong education.

(6) Fundamental matters pertaining to the educational system, including in school and lifelong education, administration, finance, and the status of teachers shall be determined by law.

**Article 32**  (1) All citizens shall have the right to work. The State shall endeavor to promote the employment of workers and to guarantee optimum wages through social and economic means and shall enforce a minimum wage system under the conditions as prescribed by law.

(2) All citizens shall have the duty to work. The State shall prescribe by law the extent and conditions of the duty to work in conformity with democratic principles.

(3) Standards of working conditions shall be determined by law in such a way as to guarantee human dignity.

(4) Special protection shall be accorded to working women, and they shall not be subjected to unjust discrimination in terms of employment, wages and working conditions.

(5) Special protection shall be accorded to working children.

(6) The opportunity to work shall be accorded preferentially, under the conditions as prescribed by law, to those who have given distinguished service to the State, wounded veterans and policemen, and members of the bereaved families of military servicemen and policemen killed in action.

**Article 33** (1) To enhance working conditions, workers shall have the right to independent association, collective bargaining and collective action.

(2) Only those public officials who are designated by law shall have the right to association, collective bargaining and collective action.

(3) The right to collective action of workers employed by important defense industries may be either restricted or denied under the conditions as prescribed by law.

**Article 34** (1) All citizens shall be entitled to a life worthy of human beings.

(2) The State shall have the duty to endeavor to promote social security and welfare.

(3) The State shall endeavor to promote the welfare and rights of women.

(4) The State shall have the duty to implement policies for enhancing the welfare of senior citizens and the young.

(5) Citizens who are incapable of earning a livelihood due to a physical disability, disease, old age or other reasons shall be protected by the State under the conditions as prescribed by law.

(6) The State shall endeavor to prevent disasters and to protect citizens from harm therefrom.

**Article 35** (1) All citizens shall have the right to a healthy and pleasant environment. The State and all citizens shall endeavor to protect the environment.

(2) The substance of the environmental right shall be determined by law.

(3) The State shall endeavor to ensure comfortable housing for all citizens through housing development policies and the like.

**Article 36** (1) Marriage and family life shall be entered into and sustained on the basis of individual dignity and equality of the sexes, and the State shall do everything in its power to achieve that goal.

(2) The State shall endeavor to protect mothers.

(3) The health of all citizens shall be protected by the State.

**Article 37** (1) Freedoms and rights of citizens shall not be neglected on the grounds that they are not enumerated in the Constitution.

(2) The freedoms and rights of citizens may be restricted by law only when necessary for national security, the maintenance of law and order or for public welfare. Even when such restriction is imposed, no essential aspect of the freedom or right shall be violated.

**Article 38** All citizens shall have the duty to pay taxes under the conditions as prescribed by law.

**Article 39** (1) All citizens shall have the duty of national defense under the conditions as prescribed by law.

(2) No citizen shall be treated unfavorably on account of the fulfillment of his obligation of military service.

## CHAPTER III. THE NATIONAL ASSEMBLY

**Article 40** The legislative power shall be vested in the National Assembly.

**Article 41** (1) The National Assembly shall be composed of members elected by universal, equal, direct and secret ballot by the citizens.

(2) The number of members of the National Assembly shall be determined by law, but the number shall not be less than 200.

(3) The constituencies of members of the National Assembly, proportional representation and other matters pertaining to National Assembly elections shall be determined by law.

**Article 42** The term of office of members of the National Assembly shall be four years.

**Article 43** Members of the National Assembly shall not concurrently hold any other office prescribed by law.

**Article 44** (1) During the sessions of the National Assembly, no member of the National Assembly shall be arrested or detained without the consent of the National Assembly except in case of *flagrante delicto.*

(2) In case of apprehension or detention of a member of the National Assembly prior to the opening of a session, such member shall be released during the session upon the request of the National Assembly, except in case of *flagrante delicto.*

**Article 45** No member of the National Assembly shall be held responsible outside the National Assembly for opinions officially expressed or votes cast in the Assembly.

**Article 46** (1) Members of the National Assembly shall have the duty to maintain high standards of integrity.

(2) Members of the National Assembly shall give preference to national interests and shall perform their duties in accordance with conscience.

(3) Members of the National Assembly shall not acquire, through abuse of their positions, rights and interests in property or positions, or assist other persons to acquire the same, by means of contracts with or dispositions by the State, public organizations or industries.

**Article 47** (1) A regular session of the National Assembly shall be convened once every year under the conditions as prescribed by law, and extraordinary sessions of the National Assembly shall be convened upon the request of the President or one fourth or more of the total members.

(2) The period of regular sessions shall not exceed a hundred days, and that of extraordinary sessions, thirty days.

(3) If the President requests the convening of an extraordinary session, the period of the session and the reasons for the request shall be clearly specified.

**Article 48** The National Assembly shall elect one Speaker and two Vice-Speakers.

**Article 49** Except as otherwise provided for in the Constitution or in law, the attendance of a majority of the total members, and the concurrent vote of a majority of the members present, shall be necessary for decisions of the National Assembly. In case of a tie vote, the matter shall be regarded as rejected.

**Article 50**    (1) Sessions of the National Assembly shall be open to the public: Provided that when it is decided so by a majority of the members present, or when the Speaker deems it necessary to do so for the sake of national security, they may be closed to the public.

    (2) The public disclosure of the proceedings of sessions which were not open to the public shall be determined by law.

**Article 51**    Bills and other matters submitted to the National Assembly for deliberation shall not be abandoned on the ground that they were not acted upon during the session in which they were introduced, except in a case where the term of the members of the National Assembly has expired.

**Article 52**    Bills may be introduced by members of the National Assembly or by the Executive.

**Article 53**    (1) Each bill passed by the National Assembly shall be sent to the Executive, and the President shall promulgate it within fifteen days.

    (2) In case of objection to the bill, the President may, within the period referred to in Paragraph (1), return it to the National Assembly with written explanation of his objection, and request it be reconsidered. The President may do the same during adjournment of the National Assembly.

    (3) The President shall not request the National Assembly to reconsider the bill in part, or with proposed amendments.

    (4) In case there is a request for reconsideration of a bill, the National Assembly shall reconsider it, and if the National Assembly repasses the bill in the original form with the attendance of more than one half of the total members, and with a concurrent vote of two thirds or more of the members present, it shall become law.

    (5) If the President does not promulgate the bill, or does not request the National Assembly to reconsider it within the period referred to in Paragraph (1), it shall become law.

    (6) The President shall promulgate without delay the law as finalized under Paragraphs (4) and (5). If the President does not promulgate a law within five days after it has become law under Paragraph (5), or after it has been returned to the Executive under Paragraph (4), the Speaker shall promulgate it.

    (7) Except as provided otherwise, a law shall take effect twenty days after the date of promulgation.

**Article 54**    (1) The National Assembly shall deliberate and decide upon the national budget bill.

    (2) The Executive shall formulate the budget bill for each fiscal year and submit it to the National Assembly within ninety days before the beginning of a fiscal year. The National Assembly shall decide upon it within thirty days before the beginning of the fiscal year.

    (3) If the budget bill is not passed by the beginning of the fiscal year, the Executive may, in conformity with the budget of the previous fiscal year, disburse funds for the following purposes until the budget bill is passed by the National Assembly:

        1. The maintenance and operation of agencies and facilities established by the Constitution or law;

2. Execution of the obligatory expenditures as prescribed by law; and

3. Continuation of projects previously approved in the budget.

**Article 55** (1) In a case where it is necessary to make continuing disbursements for a period longer than one fiscal year, the Executive shall obtain the approval of the National Assembly for a specified period of time.

(2) A reserve fund shall be approved by the National Assembly in total. The disbursement of the reserve fund shall be approved during the next session of the National Assembly.

**Article 56** When it is necessary to amend the budget, the Executive may formulate a supplementary revised budget bill and submit it to the National Assembly.

**Article 57** The National Assembly shall, without the consent of the Executive, neither increase the sum of any item of expenditure nor create any new items of expenditure in the budget submitted by the Executive.

**Article 58** When the Executive plans to issue national bonds or to conclude contracts which may incur financial obligations on the State outside the budget, it shall have the prior concurrence of the National Assembly.

**Article 59** Types and rates of taxes shall be determined by law.

**Article 60** (1) The National Assembly shall have the right to consent to the conclusion and ratification of treaties pertaining to mutual assistance or mutual security; treaties concerning important international organizations; treaties of friendship, trade and navigation; treaties pertaining to any restriction in sovereignty; peace treaties; treaties which will burden the State or people with an important financial obligation; or treaties related to legislative matters.

(2) The National Assembly shall also have the right to consent to the declaration of war, the dispatch of armed forces to foreign states, or the stationing of alien forces in the territory of the Republic of Korea.

**Article 61** (1) The National Assembly may inspect affairs of state or investigate specific matters of state affairs, and may demand the production of documents directly related thereto, the appearance of a witness in person and the furnishing of testimony or statements of opinion.

(2) The procedures and other necessary matters concerning the inspection and investigation of state administration shall be determined by law.

**Article 62** (1) The Prime Minister, members of the State Council or government delegates may attend meetings of the National Assembly or its committees and report on the state administration or deliver opinions and answer questions.

(2) When requested by the National Assembly or its committees, the Prime Minister, members of the State Council or government delegates shall attend any meeting of the National Assembly and answer questions. If the Prime Minister or State Council members are requested to attend, the Prime Minister or State Council members may have State Council members or government delegates attend any meeting of the National Assembly and answer questions.

**Article 63** (1) The National Assembly may pass a recommendation for the removal of the Prime Minister or a State Council member from office.

(2) A recommendation for removal as referred to in Paragraph (1) may be introduced by one third or more of the total members of the National

Assembly, and shall be passed with the concurrent vote of a majority of the total members of the National Assembly.

**Article 64**  (1) The National Assembly may establish the rules of its proceedings and internal regulations, provided that they are not in conflict with law.

(2) The National Assembly may review the qualifications of its members and may take disciplinary actions against its members.

(3) The concurrent vote of two thirds or more of the total members of the National Assembly shall be required for the expulsion of any member.

(4) No action shall be brought to court with regard to decisions taken under Paragraphs (2) and (3).

**Article 65**  (1) In case the President, the Prime Minister, members of the State Council, heads of Executive Ministries, judges of the Constitution Court, judges, members of the Central Election Management Committee, members of the Board of Audit and Inspection, and other public officials designated by law have violated the Constitution or other laws in the performance of official duties, the National Assembly may pass motions for their impeachment.

(2) A motion for impeachment prescribed in Paragraph (1) may be proposed by one third or more of the total members of the National Assembly, and shall require a concurrent vote of a majority of the total members of the National Assembly for passage: Provided that a motion for the impeachment of the President shall be proposed by a majority of the total members of the National Assembly and approved by two thirds or more of the total members of the National Assembly.

(3) Any person against whom a motion for impeachment has been passed shall be suspended from exercising his power until the impeachment has been adjudicated.

(4) A decision on impeachment shall not extend further than removal from public office. However, it shall not exempt the person impeached from civil or criminal liability.

## CHAPTER IV. THE EXECUTIVE

### Section 1. The President

**Article 66**  (1) The President shall be the Head of State and represent the State vis-à-vis foreign states.

(2) The President shall have the responsibility and duty to safeguard the independence, territorial integrity and continuity of the State and the Constitution.

(3) The President shall have the duty to pursue sincerely the peaceful unification of the homeland.

(4) Executive power shall be vested in the Executive Branch headed by the President.

**Article 67**  (1) The President shall be elected by universal, equal, direct and secret ballot by the people.

(2) In case two or more persons receive the same largest number of votes in the election as referred to in Paragraph (1), the person who receives the largest number of votes in an open session of the National Assembly attended by a majority of the total members of the National Assembly shall be elected.

(3) If and when there is only one presidential candidate, he shall not be elected President unless he receives at least one third of the total eligible votes.

(4) Citizens who are eligible for election to the National Assembly, and who have reached the age of forty years or more on the date of the presidential election, shall be eligible to be elected to the presidency.

(5) Matters pertaining to presidential elections shall be determined by law.

**Article 68** (1) The successor to the incumbent President shall be elected seventy to forty days before his term expires.

(2) In case a vacancy occurs in the office of the President or the President-elect dies, or is disqualified by a court ruling or for any other reason, a successor shall be elected within sixty days.

**Article 69** The President, at the time of his inauguration, shall take the following oath: "I do solemnly swear before the people that I will faithfully execute the duties of the President by observing the Constitution, defending the State, pursuing the peaceful unification of the homeland, promoting the freedom and welfare of the people and endeavoring to develop national culture."

**Article 70** The term of office of the President shall be five years, and the President shall not be reelected.

**Article 71** If the office of the presidency is vacant or the President is unable to perform his duties for any reason, the Prime Minister or the members of the State Council in the order of priority as determined by law shall act for him.

**Article 72** The President may submit important policies relating to diplomacy, national defense, unification and other matters relating to the national destiny to a national referendum if he deems it necessary.

**Article 73** The President shall conclude and ratify treaties; accredit, receive or dispatch diplomatic envoys; and declare war and conclude peace.

**Article 74** (1) The President shall be Commander-in-Chief of the Armed Forces under the conditions as prescribed by the Constitution and law.

(2) The organization and formation of the Armed Forces shall be determined by law.

**Article 75** The President may issue presidential decrees concerning matters delegated to him by law with the scope specifically defined and also matters necessary to enforce laws.

**Article 76** (1) In time of internal turmoil, external menace, natural calamity or a grave financial or economic crisis, the President may take in respect to them the minimum necessary financial and economic actions or issue orders having the effect of law, only when it is required to take urgent measures for the maintenance of national security or public peace and order, and there is no time to await the convocation of the National Assembly.

(2) In case of major hostilities affecting national security, the President may issue orders having the effect of law, only when it is required to preserve the integrity of the nation, and it is impossible to convene the National Assembly.

(3) In case actions are taken or orders are issued under Paragraphs (1) and (2), the President shall promptly notify it to the National Assembly and obtain its approval.

(4) In case no approval is obtained, the actions or orders shall lose effect forthwith. In such case, the laws which were amended or abolished by the orders in question shall automatically regain their original effect at the moment the orders fail to obtain approval.

(5) The President shall, without delay, put on public notice developments under Paragraphs (3) and (4).

**Article 77** (1) When it is required to cope with a military necessity or to maintain the public safety and order by mobilization of the military forces in time of war, armed conflict or similar national emergency, the President may proclaim martial law under the conditions as prescribed by law.

(2) Martial law shall be of two types: extraordinary martial law and precautionary martial law.

(3) Under extraordinary martial law, special measures may be taken with respect to the necessity for warrants, freedom of speech, the press, assembly and association, or the powers of the Executive and the Judiciary under the conditions as prescribed by law.

(4) When the President has proclaimed martial law, he shall notify it to the National Assembly without delay.

(5) When the National Assembly requests the lifting of martial law with the concurrent vote of a majority of the total members of the National Assembly, the President shall comply.

**Article 78** The President shall appoint and dismiss public officials under the conditions as prescribed by the Constitution and law.

**Article 79** (1) The President may grant amnesty, commutation and restoration of rights under the conditions as prescribed by law.

(2) The President shall receive the consent of the National Assembly in granting a general amnesty.

(3) Matters pertaining to amnesty, commutation and restoration of rights shall be determined by law.

**Article 80** The President shall award decorations and other honors under the conditions as prescribed by law.

**Article 81** The President may attend and address the National Assembly or express his views by written message.

**Article 82** The acts of the President under law shall be executed in writing, and such documents shall be countersigned by the Prime Minister and the members of the State Council concerned. The same shall apply to military affairs.

**Article 83** The President shall not concurrently hold the office of Prime Minister, a member of the State Council, the head of any Executive Ministry, nor other public or private posts as prescribed by law.

**Article 84** The President shall not be charged with a criminal offense during his tenure of office except for insurrection or treason.

**Article 85** Matters pertaining to the status and courteous treatment of former Presidents shall be determined by law.

## Section 2. The Executive Branch

### Sub-section 1. The Prime Minister and Members of the State Council

**Article 86** (1) The Prime Minister shall be appointed by the President with the consent of the National Assembly.

(2) The Prime Minister shall assist the President and shall direct the Executive Ministries under order of the President.

(3) No member of the military shall be appointed Prime Minister unless he is retired from active duty.

**Article 87** (1) The members of the State Council shall be appointed by the President on the recommendation of the Prime Minister.

(2) The members of the State Council shall assist the President in the conduct of State affairs and, as constituents of the State Council, shall deliberate on State affairs.

(3) The Prime Minister may recommend to the President the removal of a member of the State Council from office.

(4) No member of the military shall be appointed a member of the State Council unless he is retired from active duty.

## Sub-section 2. The State Council

**Article 88** (1) The State Council shall deliberate on important policies that fall within the power of the Executive.

(2) The State Council shall be composed of the President, the Prime Minister, and other members whose number shall be no more than thirty and no less than fifteen.

(3) The President shall be the chairman of the State Council, and the Prime Minister shall be the Vice-Chairman.

**Article 89** The following matters shall be referred to the State Council for deliberation:

1. Basic plans for state affairs, and general policies of the Executive;
2. Declaration of war, conclusion of peace and other important matters pertaining to foreign policy;
3. Draft amendments to the Constitution, proposals for national referendums, proposed treaties, legislative bills, and proposed presidential decrees;
4. Budgets, settlement of accounts, basic plans for disposal of state properties, contracts incurring financial obligation on the State, and other important financial matters;
5. Emergency orders and emergency financial and economic actions or orders by the President, and declaration and termination of martial law;
6. Important military affairs;
7. Requests for convening an extraordinary session of the National Assembly;
8. Awarding of honors;
9. Granting of amnesty, commutation and restoration of rights;
10. Demarcation of jurisdiction between Executive Ministries;
11. Basic plans concerning delegation or allocation of powers within the Executive;
12. Evaluation and analysis of the administration of State affairs;
13. Formulation and coordination of important policies of each Executive Ministry;
14. Action for the dissolution of a political party;

15. Examination of petitions pertaining to executive policies submitted or referred to the Executive;

16. Appointment of the Prosecutor General, the Chairman of the Joint Chiefs of Staff, the Chief of Staff of each armed service, the presidents of national universities, ambassadors, and such other public officials and managers of important State-run enterprises as designated by law; and

17. Other matters presented by the President, the Prime Minister or a member of the State Council.

**Article 90**  (1) An Advisory Council of Elder Statesmen, composed of elder statesmen, may be established to advise the President on important affairs of State.

(2) The immediate former President shall become the Chairman of the Advisory Council of Elder Statesmen: Provided that if there is no immediate former President, the President shall appoint the Chairman.

(3) The organization, function and other necessary matters pertaining to the Advisory Council of Elder Statesmen shall be determined by law.

**Article 91**  (1) A National Security Council shall be established to advise the President on the formulation of foreign, military and domestic policies related to national security prior to their deliberation by the State Council.

(2) The meetings of the National Security Council shall be presided over by the President.

(3) The organization, function and other necessary matters pertaining to the National Security Council shall be determined by law.

**Article 92**  (1) An Advisory Council on Democratic and Peaceful Unification may be established to advise the President on the formulation of peaceful unification policy.

(2) The organization, function and other necessary matters pertaining to the Advisory Council on Democratic and Peaceful Unification shall be determined by law.

**Article 93**  (1) A National Economic Advisory Council may be established to advise the President on the formulation of important policies for developing the national economy.

(2) The organization, function and other necessary matters pertaining to the National Economic Advisory Council shall be determined by law.

## Sub-section 3. The Executive Ministries

**Article 94**  Heads of Executive Ministries shall be appointed by the President from among members of the State Council on the recommendation of the Prime Minister.

**Article 95**  The Prime Minister or the head of each Executive Ministry may, under the powers delegated by law or Presidential Decree, or *ex officio,* issue ordinances of the Prime Minister or the Executive Ministry concerning matters that are within their jurisdiction.

**Article 96**  The establishment, organization and function of each Executive Ministry shall be determined by law.

## Sub-section 4. The Board of Audit and Inspection

**Article 97**  The Board of Audit and Inspection shall be established under the direct jurisdiction of the President to inspect and examine the settlement of the revenues and expenditures of the State, the accounts of the State and other organizations specified by law and the job performances of the executive agencies and public officials.

**Article 98**  (1) The Board of Audit and Inspection shall be composed of no less than five and no more than eleven members, including the Chairman.

(2) The Chairman of the Board shall be appointed by the President with the consent of the National Assembly. The term of office of the Chairman shall be four years, and he may be reappointed only once.

(3) The members of the Board shall be appointed by the President on the recommendation of the Chairman. The term of office of the members shall be four years, and they may be reappointed only once.

**Article 99**  The Board of Audit and Inspection shall inspect the closing of accounts of revenues and expenditures each year, and report the results to the President and the National Assembly in the following year.

**Article 100**  The organization and function of the Board of Audit and Inspection, the qualifications of its members, the range of the public officials subject to inspection and other necessary matters shall be determined by law.

## CHAPTER V. THE COURTS

**Article 101**  (1) Judicial power shall be vested in courts composed of judges.

(2) The courts shall be composed of the Supreme Court, which is the highest court of the State, and other courts at specified levels.

(3) Qualifications for judges shall be determined by law.

**Article 102**  (1) Departments may be established in the Supreme Court.

(2) There shall be Supreme Court Justices at the Supreme Court: Provided that judges other than Supreme Court Justices may be assigned to the Supreme Court under the conditions as prescribed by law.

(3) The organization of the Supreme Court and lower courts shall be determined by law.

**Article 103**  Judges shall rule independently according to their conscience and in conformity with the Constitution and law.

**Article 104**  (1) The Chief Justice of the Supreme Court shall be appointed by the President with the consent of the National Assembly.

(2) The Supreme Court Justices shall be appointed by the President on the recommendation of the Chief Justice and with the consent of the National Assembly.

(3) Judges other than the Chief Justice and the Supreme Court Justices shall be appointed by the Chief Justice with the consent of the Conference of Supreme Court Justices.

**Article 105**  (1) The term of office of the Chief Justice shall be six years and he shall not be reappointed.

(2) The term of office of the Justices of the Supreme Court shall be six years and they may be reappointed as prescribed by law.

(3) The term of office of judges other than the Chief Justice and Justices of the Supreme Court shall be ten years, and they may be reappointed under the conditions as prescribed by law.

(4) The retirement age of judges shall be determined by law.

**Article 106** (1) No judge shall be removed from office except by impeachment or a sentence of imprisonment or heavier punishment, nor shall he be suspended from office, have his salary reduced or suffer any other unfavorable treatment except by disciplinary action.

(2) In the event a judge is unable to discharge his official duties because of serious mental or physical impairment, he may be retired from office under the conditions as prescribed by law.

**Article 107** (1) When the constitutionality of a law is at issue in a trial, the court shall request a decision of the Constitution Court, and shall judge according to the decision thereof.

(2) The Supreme Court shall have the power to make a final review of the constitutionality or legality of administrative decrees, regulations or actions, when their constitutionality or legality is at issue in a trial.

(3) Administrative appeals may be conducted as a procedure prior to a judicial trial. The procedure of administrative appeals shall be determined by law and shall be in conformity with the principles of judicial procedures.

**Article 108** The Supreme Court may establish, within the scope of law, regulations pertaining to judicial proceedings and internal discipline and regulations on administrative matters of the court.

**Article 109** Trials and decisions of the courts shall be open to the public: Provided that when there is a danger that such trials may undermine the national security or disturb public safety and order, or be harmful to public morals, trials may be closed to the public by court decision.

**Article 110** (1) Courts-martial may be established as special courts to exercise jurisdiction over military trials.

(2) The Supreme Court shall have the final appellate jurisdiction over courts-martial.

(3) The organization and authority of courts-martial, and the qualifications of their judges shall be determined by law.

(4) Military trials under an extraordinary martial law may not be appealed in case of crimes of soldiers and employees of the military; military espionage; and crimes as defined by law in regard to sentinels, sentry posts, supply of harmful foods and beverages, and prisoners of war, except in the case of a death sentence.

## CHAPTER VI. THE CONSTITUTION COURT

**Article 111** (1) The Constitution Court shall adjudicate the following matters:

1. The unconstitutionality of a law upon the request of the courts;
2. Impeachment;
3. Dissolution of a political party;
4. Disputes about the jurisdictions between State agencies, between State agencies and local governments and between local governments; and
5. Petitions relating to the Constitution as prescribed by law.

(2) The Constitution Court shall be composed of nine adjudicators qualified to be court judges, and they shall be appointed by the President.

(3) Among the adjudicators referred to in Paragraph (2), three shall be appointed from persons selected by the National Assembly, and three appointed from persons nominated by the Chief Justice.

(4) The head of the Constitution Court shall be appointed by the President from among the adjudicators with the consent of the National Assembly.

**Article 112** (1) The term of office of the adjudicators of the Constitution Court shall be six years and they may be reappointed under the conditions as prescribed by law.

(2) The adjudicators of the Constitution Court shall not join any political party, nor shall they participate in political activities.

(3) No adjudicator of the Constitution Court shall be expelled from office except by impeachment or a sentence of imprisonment or heavier punishment.

**Article 113** (1) When the Constitution Court makes a decision on the unconstitutionality of a law, impeachment, dissolution of a political party or a petition relating to the Constitution, the concurrence of six adjudicators or more shall be required.

(2) The Constitution Court may establish regulations relating to its proceedings and internal discipline and regulations on administrative matters within the limits of law.

(3) The organization, function and other necessary matters of the Constitution Court shall be determined by law.

## CHAPTER VII. ELECTION MANAGEMENT

**Article 114** (1) Election Management Committees shall be established for the purpose of fair management of elections and national referenda, and dealing with administrative affairs concerning political parties.

(2) The Central Election Management Committee shall be composed of three members appointed by the President, three members selected by the National Assembly, and three members designated by the Chief Justice of the Supreme Court. The Chairman of the Committee shall be elected from among the members.

(3) The term of office of the members of the Committee shall be six years.

(4) The members of the Committee shall not join political parties, nor shall they participate in political activities.

(5) No member of the Committee shall be expelled from office except by impeachment or a sentence of imprisonment or heavier punishment.

(6) The Central Election Management Committee may establish, within the limit of laws and decrees, regulations relating to the management of elections, national referenda, and administrative matters concerning political parties and may also establish regulations relating to internal discipline that are compatible with law.

(7) The organization, function and other necessary matters of the Election Management Committees at each level shall be determined by law.

**Article 115** (1) Election Management Committees at each level may issue necessary instructions to administrative agencies concerned with respect to administrative matters pertaining to elections and national referenda such as the preparation of the pollbooks.

(2) Administrative agencies concerned, upon receipt of such instructions, shall comply.

**Article 116** (1) Election campaigns shall be conducted under the management of the Election Management Committees at each level within the limit set by law. Equal opportunity shall be guaranteed.

(2) Except as otherwise prescribed by law, expenditures for elections shall not be imposed on political parties or candidates.

## CHAPTER VIII. LOCAL AUTONOMY

**Article 117** (1) Local governments shall deal with administrative matters pertaining to the welfare of local residents, manage properties, and may enact provisions relating to local autonomy, within the limit of laws and regulations.

(2) The types of local governments shall be determined by law.

**Article 118** (1) A local government shall have a council.

(2) The organization and powers of local councils, and the election of members; election procedures for heads of local governments; and other matters pertaining to the organization and operation of local governments shall be determined by law.

## CHAPTER IX. THE ECONOMY

**Article 119** (1) The economic order of the Republic of Korea shall be based on a respect for the freedom and creative initiative of enterprises and individuals in economic affairs.

(2) The State may regulate and coordinate economic affairs in order to maintain the balanced growth and stability of the national economy, to ensure proper distribution of income, to prevent the domination of the market and the abuse of economic power and to democratize the economy through harmony among the economic agents.

**Article 120** (1) Licenses to exploit, develop or utilize minerals and all other important underground resources, marine resources, water power, and natural powers available for economic use may be granted for a period of time under the conditions as prescribed by law.

(2) The land and natural resources shall be protected by the State, and the State shall establish a plan necessary for their balanced development and utilization.

**Article 121** (1) The State shall endeavor to realize the land-to-the-tillers principle with respect to agricultural land. Tenant farming shall be prohibited.

(2) The leasing of agricultural land and the consignment management of agricultural land to increase agricultural productivity and to ensure the rational utilization of agricultural land or due to unavoidable circumstances, shall be recognized under the conditions as prescribed by law.

**Article 122** The State may impose, as under the conditions prescribed by law, restrictions or obligations necessary for the efficient and balanced utilization, development and preservation of the land of the nation that is the basis for the productive activities and daily lives of all citizens.

**Article 123** (1) The State shall establish and implement a plan to comprehensively develop and support the farm and fishing communities in order to protect and foster agriculture and fisheries.

(2) The State shall have the duty to foster regional economies to ensure the balanced development of all regions.

(3) The State shall protect and foster small and medium enterprises.

(4) In order to protect the interests of farmers and fishermen, the State shall endeavor to stabilize the prices of agricultural and fishery products by maintaining an equilibrium between the demand and supply of such products and improving their marketing and distribution systems.

(5) The State shall foster organizations founded on the spirit of self-help among farmers, fishermen and businessmen engaged in small and medium industry and shall guarantee their independent activities and development.

**Article 124** The State shall guarantee the consumer protection movement intended to encourage sound consumption activities and improvement in the quality of products under the conditions as prescribed by law.

**Article 125** The State shall foster foreign trade, and may regulate and coordinate it.

**Article 126** Private enterprises shall not be nationalized nor transferred to ownership by a local government, nor shall their management be controlled or administered by the State, except in cases as prescribed by law to meet urgent necessities of national defense or the national economy.

**Article 127** (1) The State shall strive to develop the national economy by developing science and technology, information and human resources and encouraging innovation.

(2) The State shall establish a system of national standards.

(3) The President may establish advisory organizations necessary to achieve the purpose referred to in Paragraph (1).

## CHAPTER X. AMENDMENTS TO THE CONSTITUTION

**Article 128** (1) A proposal to amend the Constitution shall be introduced either by a majority of the total members of the National Assembly or by the President.

(2) Amendments to the Constitution for the extension of the term of office of the President or for a change allowing for the reelection of the President shall not be effective for the President in office at the time of the proposal for such amendments to the Constitution.

**Article 129** Proposed amendments to the Constitution shall be put before the public by the President for twenty days or more.

**Article 130** (1) The National Assembly shall decide upon the proposed amendments within sixty days of the public announcement, and passage by the National Assembly shall require the concurrent vote of two thirds or more of the total members of the National Assembly.

(2) The proposed amendments to the Constitution shall be submitted to a national referendum not later than thirty days after passage by the National Assembly, and shall be determined by more than one half of all votes cast by more than one half of voters eligible to vote in elections for members of the National Assembly.

(3) When the proposed amendments to the Constitution receive the concurrence prescribed in Paragraph (2), the amendments to the Constitution shall be finalized, and the President shall promulgate it without delay.

## ADDENDA

**Article 1**    This Constitution shall enter into force as of the twenty-fifth day of February, Anno Domini Nineteen hundred and eighty-eight: Provided that the enactment or amendment of laws necessary to implement this Constitution, the elections of the President and the National Assembly under this Constitution and other preparations to implement this Constitution may be carried out prior to the entry into force of this Constitution.

**Article 2**    (1) The first presidential election under this Constitution shall be held not later than forty days before this Constitution enters into force.

(2) The term of office of the first President under this Constitution shall commence on the date of its enforcement.

**Article 3**    (1) The first elections of the National Assembly under this Constitution shall be held within six months from the promulgation of this Constitution. The term of office of the members of the first National Assembly elected under this Constitution shall commence on the date of the first convening of the National Assembly under this Constitution.

(2) The term of office of the members of the National Assembly incumbent at the time this Constitution is promulgated shall terminate the day prior to the first convening of the National Assembly under Paragraph (1).

**Article 4**    (1) Public officials and officers of enterprises appointed by the Government, who are in office at the time of the enforcement of this Constitution, shall be considered as having been appointed under this Constitution: Provided that public officials whose election procedures or appointing authorities are changed under this Constitution, the Chief Justice of the Supreme Court and the Chairman of the Board of Audit and Inspection shall remain in office until such time as their successors are chosen under this Constitution, and their terms of office shall terminate the day before the installation of their successors.

(2) Judges attached to the Supreme Court who are not the Chief Justice or Justices of the Supreme Court and who are in office at the time of the enforcement of this Constitution shall be considered as having been appointed under this Constitution notwithstanding the proviso of Paragraph (1).

(3) Those provisions of this Constitution which prescribe the terms of office of public officials or which restrict the number of terms that public officials may serve shall take effect upon the dates of the first elections or the first appointments of such public officials under this Constitution.

**Article 5**    Laws, decrees, ordinances and treaties in force at the time this Constitution enters into force shall remain valid unless they are contrary to this Constitution.

**Article 6**    Those organizations existing at the time of the enforcement of this Constitution which have been performing the functions falling within the authority of new organizations to be created under this Constitution shall continue to exist and perform such functions until such time as the new organizations are created under this Constitution.

# APPENDIX D

# Act Relating to Registration, Etc., of Periodicals

(Law No. 3979, Nov. 28, 1987)
(Amended by Law No. 4183, Dec. 30, 1989)
(Amended by Law No. 4441, Dec. 14, 1991)

## CHAPTER I. GENERAL PROVISIONS

**Article 1** (Purpose) The purpose of this Act is to strive for a sound development of the press by providing for matters concerning periodically published newspapers, communications, magazines and other publications.

**Article 2** (Definition) For the purpose of this Act, (Amended by Law No. 4441, Dec. 14, 1991)

1. the term "periodicals" means newspapers, communications, magazines and other publications which are published continuously under the same title more than once a year;

2. the term "general daily newspaper" means a publication published every day for the purpose of propagating news, comments, public opinion, etc. on political affairs, economy, society, culture, current events, etc.;

3. the term "special daily newspaper" means a publication published every day for the purpose of propagating news, comments, public opinion, etc. on matters limited to a certain field (excluding the political field), such as industry, science, religion, education, physical training, etc.;

4. the term "foreign language daily newspaper" means a general or special daily newspaper published in a foreign language;

5. the term "general weekly newspaper" means a publication published once each week (including those published more than twice a week or month) for the purpose of propagating news, comments, public opinion, etc. on political affairs, economy, society, culture, current events, etc.;

6. the term "special weekly newspaper" means a publication published once each week (including those published more than twice a week or month) for the purpose of propagating news, comments, public opinion, etc. on matters limited

to a certain field (excluding the political field), such as industry, science, religion, education, physical training, etc.;

7. the term "communication" means a transmission and reception carried out, or a publication published, for the purpose of propagating news, comments, public opinion, etc. on domestic or foreign political affairs, economy, society, culture, current events, etc. after concluding a contract of communication with foreign news agencies with permission of a radio station under the Radio Waves Act;

8. the term "magazine" means a publication published periodically under the same title not more than once each month and bound in book form for the purpose of propagating news, comments, public opinion, information, etc. on all fields: political affairs, economy, society, culture, current events, industry, science, religion, education, physical training, etc., or on specified fields;

9. the term "publisher" means a representative publishing periodicals;

10. the term "editor" means a person who is appointed by a publisher and is responsible for the editing of periodicals; and

11. the term "printer" means a person who is appointed by a publisher or enters into a printing contract with a publisher and is responsible for printing periodicals.

**Article 3**   (Prohibition, etc. of Concurrent Operation)

(1) Any daily newspaper (referred to a general or special daily newspaper or foreign language daily newspaper; hereinafter the same shall apply) and a communication shall not be operated concurrently, and operate concurrently a broadcasting station licensed by a radio station under the Radio Waves Act (hereinafter referred to as "broadcast"). (Amended by Law No. 4441, Dec. 14, 1991)

(2) Any person who holds more than one half of the stocks or quotas issued by a juristic person operating a daily newspaper, communication or broadcast (including a case where interrelated enterprises as prescribed by the Presidential Decree hold them) shall not acquire more than one half of the stocks or quotas issued by a juristic person operating other daily newspapers or communications.

(3) Any large enterprise as prescribed by the Presidential Decree or its affiliate shall not acquire more than one half of the stocks or quotas issued by a juristic person operating a daily newspaper or communication.

(4) Of directors of a juristic person operating a daily newspaper or communication (managing partners in case of an unlimited partnership, and partners with unlimited liability in case of a limited partnership), those who are related to one another as prescribed in Article 777 of the Civil Code or wife's blood relatives within the third degree, or who are spouses of lineal descendants, shall not exceed a third of the directors.

(5) In order to confirm the facts as referred to in Paragraphs (1) to (4), the Minister of Public Information may have publishers of daily newspapers and communications furnish necessary material under the conditions as prescribed by the Presidential Decree. (Amended by Law No. 4183, Dec. 30, 1989)

**Article 4**   (Prohibition of Inflow of Foreign Fund) No person may receive a contribution of property under any pretext of donation, supporting fund, etc. from a foreigner, foreign government or organization in order to publish periodicals, except in case of contribution from a foreign organization the object of which is education, physical training, religion, charity and international friendship, and which is approved by the Minister of Public Information. (Amended by Law No. 4183, Dec. 30, 1989)

**Article 5** (In-Service Training)

(1) Publishers shall establish and operate in-service training to improve the ability and quality of employees.

(2) Publishers may establish and operate jointly an organization for in-service training of employees.

**Article 6** (Guarantee of Function)

(1) Publishers shall take measures necessary for improving the working environment, treatment and other welfare of employees according to the spirit of cooperation between labor and management.

(2) Publishers shall protect editing and producing activities of employees.

(3) Any person who desires to publish a daily newspaper, general weekly newspaper or communication shall provide the following facilities: (Amended by Law No. 4441, Dec. 14, 1991)

    1. For a general daily newspaper, a rotary press having the capacity to print a newspaper of double tabloid four-page standard more than twenty thousand copies per hour, and annexed printing facilities as prescribed by the Presidential Decree;

    2. For a special daily newspaper, foreign language daily newspaper or general weekly newspaper, one or more rotary presses and annexed printing facilities as prescribed by the Presidential Decree; and

    3. For a publication of communication, radio communication facilities under the Radio Waves Act.

(4) Any person who desires to publish a special weekly newspaper or magazine which does not fall under Paragraph (3) shall enter into a printing contract with a printing office registered under the Act Relating to Registration of Publishing Companies and Printing Offices.

## CHAPTER II. REGISTRATION

**Article 7** (Registration)

(1) Any person who desires to publish periodicals shall register the following matters with the Minister of Public Information under the conditions as prescribed by the Presidential Decree. The same shall also apply when he desires to modify any of the registered matters, except in cases where the State or local governments publish them, or any organization or institution as prescribed by the Presidential Decree publishes them for the purpose of disseminating them among its members, and only materials for study or commercial advertisements are carried: (Amended by Law No. 4183, Dec. 30, 1989)

    1. Title;

    2. Classification by kind and publication;

    3. Permanent and present addresses, names and dates of birth of publishers, editors and printers (in case where a publisher or printer is a corporation or organization, its title, seat of its principal office, permanent and present addresses, name and date of birth of its representative);

    4. Seat of publishing office;

    5. Types of printing blocks;

    6. Language used;

    7. Object and details of publication;

    8. Method, objects and areas of dissemination; and

9. In case of daily newspapers, general weekly newspapers or communication, corresponding facilities as prescribed in Article 6 (3).

(2) Any person who desires to register a periodical under Paragraph (1) shall specify the classification by publication in matters to be registered according to the following categories:

1. Daily publication (including those published in a day's interval or more than three times each week);
2. Weekly publication (including those published more than twice each week or month);
3. Monthly publication;
4. Bimonthly publication;
5. Quarterly publication;
6. Biannual publication; and
7. Yearly publication.

(3) When a periodical is registered under Paragraph (1), the Minister of Public Information shall promptly deliver a certificate of registration. (Amended by Law No. 4183, Dec. 30, 1989)

(4) Any person who has registered a periodical under Paragraph (1) shall publish the registered periodical within six months (one year in case of biannual or yearly publication) after it is registered.

(5) No periodical the title of which is the same as an already registered periodical, or is so similar that it is easy to be confused with it, shall be registered.

(6) The Minister of Public Information may delegate to the mayor of the Seoul Special City, mayors of direct control cities or provincial governors affairs concerning the registration of periodicals published by an enterprise or an organization the object of which is purely friendship, for the purpose of disseminating only to its members. (Amended by Law No. 4183, Dec. 30, 1989)

**Article 8** (Obligatory Matters to Be Inserted) On periodicals shall be inserted the number and date of registration, title, classification by publication, publisher, editor, printer, publishing office and date of publication, and if there is a number of editors, the name of each editor shall be inserted with the responsible field.

**Article 9** (Disqualification, etc.)

(1) Any person who falls under any of the following subparagraphs shall not be a publisher or editor of a periodical:

1. A person who is not a national of the Republic of Korea;
2. A person who has no domicile in the territory of the Republic of Korea;
3. A person who was sentenced to imprisonment without hard labor or more severe punishment for committing a crime as prescribed in Articles 87 to 90, 92 to 101 of the Criminal Code, Article 5 to 8, 9 (2), 11 to 16 of the Military Criminal Act or Articles 3 to 9 of the National Security Act, and the execution of such punishment is not terminated, or non-execution of it does not become definite, or the period for stay of execution is not terminated; and
4. A person who is subject to execution of a disposition for security under the Social Security Act or disposition for protection under the Social Protection Act.

(2) Any person who is not a juristic person may not publish a daily newspaper, general weekly newspaper or communication of periodicals.

(3) No foreign corporation or organization, or no juristic person or organization in which a person falling under Subparagraph 1 or 2 of Paragraph (1) acts as its representative or exercises the right to vote, may publish periodicals, unless such periodicals are published only for the purpose of disseminating to its members.

**Article 10**   (Delivery of Books)

(1) When a person who made a registration under Article 7 (1) has published a periodical, he shall immediately deliver two copies of the periodical to the Minister of Public Information under the conditions as prescribed by the Presidential Decree. (Amended by Law No. 4183, Dec. 30, 1989)

(2) In the case as referred to in Paragraph (1), if the person who delivered books requests compensation, the State shall make reasonable compensation.

**Article 11**   (Report on Suspension and Discontinuation of Publication)

(1) When a person who made a registration under Article 7 (1) suspends or discontinues the publication of a periodical, he shall promptly report it to the Minister of Public information under the conditions as prescribed by the Presidential Decree. (Amended by Law No. 4183, Dec. 30, 1989)

(2) The suspension of publication as referred to in Paragraph (1) shall be justified, and it shall not exceed the period as prescribed by the Presidential Decree.

**Article 12**   (Request, etc. for Decision on Cancellation of Registration)

(1) If a person who has a periodical registered under Article 7 (1) falls under any of the following subparagraphs, the Minister of Public Information may order a suspension of publication of the periodical during a prescribed period of not more than three months: (Amended by Law No. 4183, Dec. 30, 1989)

  1. When he has published the periodical with matters registered under Article 7 (1) modified at his discretion without having the modified matters registered;
  2. When the publisher (including a juristic person or organization) or editor falls under any of the disqualifications as prescribed in Article 9;
  3. When he fails to maintain facilities as prescribed in Article 6 (3) or (4);
  4. When he fails to maintain an actual result of publication as prescribed by the Presidential Decree; and
  5. When there is a fact that he received a contribution of property in contravention of Article 4.

(2) If a person who has a periodical registered under Article 7 (1) falls under any of the following subparagraphs, the Minister of Public Information may order a suspension of publication of the periodical during a prescribed period of not more than six months or request to the court a decision on cancellation of registration of the periodical: (Amended by Law No. 4183, Dec. 30, 1989)

  1. When there is a fact that he made a registration by deceit or other unlawful means; and
  2. When the contents of the periodical infringes repeatedly and remarkably the registered object and details of publication.

(3) The collegiate court of the district court having the jurisdiction over the general judicial seat of the publisher shall be competent to a trial of the first instance for a request for decision under Paragraph (2). The court shall bring it to trial within three months after receiving the request for decision. The request, examination, trial and other matters necessary for a case concerning decisions on cancellation of registration shall be determined by the Supreme Court Regulations.

(4) The Procedure in Noncontentious Cases Act shall be applicable to cases concerning decisions on cancellation of registration.

(5) If a registration is canceled by a judgment of the court, no person may publish any periodical under the title of the canceled periodical within two years from the date of its cancellation.

**Article 13** (Hearing) If the Minister of Public Information desires to make a disposition for suspension of publication under Article 12 (1) or (2), he shall give in advance the publisher of the periodical or his representative an opportunity to state his opinion under the conditions as prescribed by the Presidential Decree, except in a case where the publisher of the periodical or his representative fails to comply with it without any justifiable reason, or it is impossible to give him an opportunity to state his opinion due to obscurity of his address, etc. (Amended by Law No. 4183, Dec. 30, 1989)

**Article 14** (Establishment of Branch Office, etc.)

(1) When a person who has a periodical registered under Article 7 (1) established a branch office, he shall promptly report it to the Minister of Public Information under the conditions as prescribed by the Presidential Decree. (Amended by Law No. 4183, Dec. 30, 1989)

(2) No branch office may edit and publish any periodical unless it is an overseas branch office and it is approved by the Minister of Public Information. (Amended by Law No. 4183, Dec. 30, 1989)

(3) The provisions of the Act concerning periodicals published by the head office shall be applicable to periodicals published by a person who obtained approval under the proviso of Paragraph (2).

**Article 15** (Establishment of Branch Office, etc. of Foreign Periodicals)

(1) Any person who desires to establish a branch office of foreign periodicals in the country shall obtain the permission of the Minister of Public Information under the conditions as prescribed by the Presidential Decree. (Amended by Law No. 4183, Dec. 30, 1989)

(2) If a person who has obtained the permission under Paragraph (1) falls under any of the following Subparagraphs, the Minister of Public Information may cancel the permission: (Amended by Law No. 4183, Dec. 30, 1989)

   1. When there is a fact that he obtained the permission by deceit or other unlawful means;

   2. When he has violated the terms and conditions of permission, and

   3. When the foreign periodicals carry news which might disturb the national constitution or injure the prestige of the State.

## CHAPTER III. REMEDY FOR INFRINGEMENT

**Article 16** (Claim for Corrected Report)

(1) Any person who is injured by a factual assertion published in a periodical (hereinafter referred to as "injured person") may request in writing an insertion of a corrected report to the publisher or editor within fourteen days after it is published, in case of daily newspapers or communication, and within one month, in case of other periodicals.

(2) The written claim for a corrected report shall be signed and sealed by the injured person or his representative, and his address shall be mentioned therein and the text of the article against which he raises an objection and that of the corrected report which he requests insertion of shall be attached thereto.

(3) The publisher or editor shall, upon receiving a claim for insertion of a corrected report, carry them free of charge in the same periodical within nine days after he receives the claim in case of daily newspapers and periodicals and communication published more than once each week, and in the following issue the editing of which is not completed, in case of other periodicals, after consulting without delay with the injured person or his representative on the contents of the corrected report, size, etc.: Provided that if the injured person has no proper interest in exercising a claim for a corrected report, or the contents of the claimed corrected report is obviously contrary to the fact, or it aims only at commercial advertisement, the insertion of it may be rejected.

(4) Any corrected report shall be limited to factual statements and an explanation necessary for transmitting it clearly, and it shall not include illegal contents.

(5) The contents of a corrected report shall not be inserted in a form of readers' contribution, and the number of words in the text of the corrected report shall not exceed that in the published contents against which an objection is raised.

(6) The provisions of Paragraphs (1) to (5) shall not be applicable to factual articles on an open meeting of the State, local governments or public organizations and a public trial procedure of the court.

**Article 17**  (Press Arbitration Committee)

(1) In order to arbitrate disputes borne from claims for corrected reports and deliberate infringement cases by the contents carried in periodicals, the Press Arbitration Committee (hereinafter referred to as "Arbitration Committee") shall be established.

(2) The Arbitration Committee shall be composed of forty to seventy members, who are commissioned by the Minister of Public Information from among those of learning, experience and high moral repute, but two fifths or more of members shall be recommended by the Minister of the Court Administration from among those having a qualification for judicial officer. (Amended by Law No. 4183, Dec. 30, 1989)

(3) The Arbitration Committee shall assign a chairman and two deputy chairmen, who are elected from among the members, respectively.

(4) The term of the chairman, deputy chairmen and members of the Arbitration Committee shall be three years, respectively.

(5) Any person registered with a political party and public official (excluding those having a qualification for judicial officer and education officials) shall not be members of the Arbitration Committee.

(6) Members of the Arbitration Committee shall perform their duties independently according to law and conscience and shall not be subject to any direction in respect of their duties.

(7) Members of the Arbitration Committee shall be an honorary office: Provided that they may receive allowances and compensation for actual expenses under the conditions as prescribed by the Presidential Decree.

**Article 18**  (Arbitration Procedure, etc.)

(1) Any person who has a claim for a corrected report or the other party may request in writing an arbitration to the Arbitration Committee within one month after the publication in dispute is made (in case as prescribed in Article 16 (1), fourteen days after the corrected report is requested). The provisions of Article 16 (2) shall be applicable to a request for arbitration.

(2) The arbitration shall be effected by an arbitration section consisting of five or less members, and the head of the arbitration section shall be a member having qualification for a judicial officer.

(3) The head of the arbitration section may, if necessary, order a publisher of the periodical which is the object of the arbitration case, to present the expressed material subject to the arbitration or copies thereof, or to investigate evidence necessary for the arbitration.

(4) The head of the arbitration section may demand an attendance of the parties to the arbitration or interested person, and those who are requested to attend, shall attend under the conditions as mentioned in the written demand for attendance.

(5) If person requesting an arbitration fails to attend even after receiving a written demand for attendance under Paragraph (4), he shall be considered to withdraw his request for arbitration, and if the requested person fails to attend twice, he shall be considered to have agreed to carry the corrected report in accordance with the contents for which an arbitration is requested unless he explains that he could not attend due to natural calamity, terrestrial upheaval or other justifiable reasons.

(6) In case where an agreement between parties concerned is realized as a result of the arbitration, and where it is considered to reach an agreement under Paragraph (5), such agreement shall have the same effect as a judicial conciliation.

(7) The arbitration shall be effected within fourteen days after a request for arbitration is received, and if the period expires, the arbitration shall be considered not to have been effected.

(8) The Arbitration Committee shall deliberate matters of infringement by periodicals, and may, if necessary, recommend a correction to the publisher concerned.

(9) The procedure of arbitration, composition method and jurisdiction of the arbitration section, organization of the secretariat, method and procedure of recommendation on correction, allowance of the member of the Arbitration Committee, and other necessary matters shall be determined by the Presidential Decree

**Article 19** (Trial on Case of Claim for Corrected Report)

(1) No claim for a corrected report shall be requested to the court without passing through an arbitration of the Arbitration Committee. The trial on a claim for a corrected report shall be requested to the court within fourteen days from the day on which the arbitration is not effected.

(2) The collegiate court of the district court having the general jurisdiction over the defendant shall be competent for a trial of the first instance on a claim as referred to in Paragraph (1).

(3) The claim as refereed to in Paragraph (1) shall be brought to trial pursuant to the provisions concerning the procedure for provisional measures under the Code of Civil Procedure, and if the claim is deemed well-grounded, the court may order an insertion of the corrected report in such manner as prescribed in Article 16 (3) to (5): Provided that the provisions of Articles 697 and 705 of the Code of Civil Procedure shall not be applicable.

(4) Matters necessary for a trial on case of a claim for a corrected report shall be determined by the Supreme Court Regulations.

**Article 20** (Claim for *Ex post Facto* Report)

(1) Any person who is reported by a periodical to be under suspicion of a crime or to have been subject to a penal measure may, when a penal procedure against him is

terminated in a form other than a conviction, request in writing to the publisher or editor an insertion of an *ex post facto* report on such fact within one month from the day of termination.

(2) The contents of an *ex post facto* report as referred to in Paragraph (1) shall be limited to the extent necessary for the recovery of one's honor or right.

(3) Except as prescribed in Paragraphs (1) and (2), the provisions of this Act concerning the claim for a corrected report shall be applicable to the claim for an *ex post facto* report.

**Article 21** (Subsidy) The State may grant a subsidy to the Arbitration Committee in the limit of the budget.

## CHAPTER IV. PENAL PROVISIONS

**Article 22** (Penal Provisions) Any person who falls under any of the following subparagraphs shall be punished by imprisonment for not more than one year or a fine not exceeding five million Won:

1. A person who violates the provisions of Article 3 (1) to (4);
2. A person who receives a contribution of property in contravention of the provisions of Article 4;
3. A person who publishes a periodical without registering it under Article 7 (1);
4. A person who publishes a periodical in contravention of a disposition under Article 12 (1) or (2), or the provisions of Article 14 (2); and
5. A person who has established a branch office of foreign publication in the country without obtaining permission under Article 15 (1).

**Article 23** (Penal Provisions) Any person who falls under any of the following subparagraphs shall be punished by a fine not exceeding one million Won:

1. A person who falls under any of subparagraphs of Article 9 (1) and has taken office as a publisher or editor; and
2. A publisher who has appointed a person falling under any of subparagraphs of Article 9 (1) as an editor.

**Article 24** (Fine for Negligence)

(1) Any person who falls under any of the following subparagraphs shall be punished by a fine for negligence not exceeding one million Won:

1. A person who was requested to present materials under Article 3 (5) but fails to do so;
2. A person who fails to publish a registered periodical within a period as prescribed in Article 7 (4);
3. A person who fails to insert the obligatory matters to be inserted under Article 8;
4. A person who fails to deliver copies under Article 10 (1);
5. A person who fails to make a report on a suspension or discontinuation of publication under Article 11 (1); and
6. A person who fails to report an establishment of a branch office under Article 14 (1).

(2) The fine for negligence as referred to in Paragraph (1) shall be imposed and collected by the Minister of Public Information under the conditions as prescribed by the Presidential Decree. (Amended by Law No. 4183, Dec. 30, 1989)

(3) Any person who is dissatisfied with a disposition of fine for negligence under Paragraph (2) may raise an objection against the Minister of Public Information within

thirty days from the day on which he is informed of the disposition. (Amended by Law No. 4183, Dec. 30, 1989)

(4) When a person who is subject to a disposition of fine for negligence under Paragraph (2) has raised an objection under paragraph (3), the Minister of Public Information shall immediately notify it to the competent court, which brings the case of fine for negligence to trial under the Noncontentious Case Procedure Act. (Amended by Law No. 4183, Dec. 30, 1989)

(5) If no objection is raised and the fine for negligence is not paid in the period as referred to in Paragraph (3), it shall be collected according to the example of the disposition of national taxes in arrears.

## ADDENDA

**Article 1** (Enforcement Date) This Act shall enter into force as of the date of its promulgation.

**Article 2** (Relation to Other Acts) In case where the Basic Press Act repealed at the time this Act enters into force is applied *mutatis mutandis* or cited in other Act, it shall be considered to apply *mutatis mutandis* or cite this Act with respect to periodicals.

**Article 3** (Interim Measures)

(1) Periodicals registered or approved, or branch offices and the Press Arbitration Committee permitted, reported or established under the Basis Press Act repealed at the time of the enforcement of this Act shall be considered to be registered, approved, permitted, reported or established under this Act.

(2) Any publication which has been published yearly at the time of the enforcement of this Act shall be registered with existing publication appended within three months from the day this Act enters into force.

(3) Any corporation which is established under the special law and which holds more than one half of the stocks or quotas issued by a corporation operating a daily newspaper or communication under the proviso of Article 12 (1) of the Basic Press Act repealed at the time of the enforcement of this Act shall dispose of such holding stocks or quotas so as to conform to the provisions of Article 3 of the Act not later than December 31, 1988.

### ADDENDA (Law No. 4183, Dec. 30, 1989; Government Organization Act)

**Article 1** (Enforcement Date) This Act shall enter into force as of the date of its promulgation. (Proviso omitted)

**Articles 2 to 6 Omitted.**

### ADDENDA (Law No. 4444, Dec. 14, 1991; Radio Waves Act)

**Article 1** (Enforcement Date) This Act shall enter into force as of July 1, 1992. (Proviso omitted)

**Articles 2 to 3 Omitted.**

# APPENDIX E

# Broadcast Act

(Law No. 3978, Nov. 28, 1987)
(Amended by Law No. 4183, Dec. 30, 1989)
(Amended by Law No. 4263, Aug. 1, 1990)
(Amended by Law No. 4441, Dec. 14, 1991)

## CHAPTER I. GENERAL PROVISIONS

**Article 1** (Purpose) This Act aims to strive for the democratic formation of public opinion and the improvement of national culture, and to contribute to the promotion of public welfare by guaranteeing the freedom and public function of broadcasting.

**Article 2** (Definition of Terms) For the purpose of this Act, (Amended by Law No. 4441, Dec. 14, 1991)

1. the term "broadcast" means a transmission of wireless communication operated by a broadcasting station for the purpose of propagating to the general public, news, comments and public opinion on politics, economy, society, culture, current events, etc., and education, music, entertainment, etc.;

2. the term "special broadcast" means a transmission of wireless communication operated by a broadcasting station which is granted permission for carrying out special purposes, such as religious, educational, traffic, weather and overseas broadcast, etc.;

3. the term "broadcasting station" means a radio station giving a broadcast (including a special broadcast) with permission granted under the Radio Waves Act;

4. the term "broadcasting corporation" means a juristic person operating broadcasting station;

5. the term "broadcasting program" means the kind, content, quantity and arrangement of matters to be broadcasted;

6. the term "commercial broadcast" means an onerous broadcast given for the purpose of advertising;

7. the term "person in charge of programming" means a person who is appointed by the head of a broadcasting station and who is responsible for drawing up the broadcasting program; and

8. the term "person in charge of advertisement" means a person who is appointed by the head of a broadcasting station and who is responsible for commercial broadcast.

**Article 3** (Freedom of Broadcast Programming)

(1) The freedom of broadcast programming shall be guaranteed.

(2) No person shall regulate or interfere with the drawing up or making of a broadcasting program or operation of a broadcasting station without complying with the conditions as prescribed by this Act or other laws.

**Article 4** (Public Responsibility of Broadcast)

(1) The broadcast shall respect the dignity and value of human beings and the democratic fundamental order.

(2) The broadcast shall contribute to a democratic formation of public opinion on public matters by means of data collection, news, comments and other ways, and perform its public function by converging harmoniously various opinions of all levels of society.

(3) The broadcast shall not infringe on the honor or right of others or public morality or social ethics.

**Article 5** (Impartiality and Publicness of Broadcast)

(1) News broadcast shall be impartial and objective.

(2) The broadcast shall respect the ethical and emotional sentiments of citizens, and contribute to the propagation of social justice, defense of the fundamental rights of citizens and promotion of international friendship.

(3) The broadcast shall not support or advocate a certain political party, group, interest, belief or thought, except in case where a broadcast permitted for the purpose of a religious mission gives a broadcast according to permitted contents.

(4) The broadcast shall contribute to the harmony of citizens and harmonious development of the State and shall not encourage any discord among social strata and regional groups. (Newly Inserted by Law No. 4263, Aug. 1, 1990)

(5) The broadcast shall spread and disseminate the living information useful for the society, improve the quality of the cultural life of citizens, and contribute to the creative development of the national culture. (Newly Inserted by Law No. 4263, Aug. 1, 1990)

(6) The broadcast shall contribute to a sound family life and proper guidance of children and youth, and its contents shall not encourage the lewdness, decadence, violence, etc. (Newly Inserted by Law No. 4263, Aug. 1, 1990)

## CHAPTER II. OPERATION OF BROADCASTING STATION AND BROADCASTING CORPORATION

**Article 6** (Operation of Broadcasting Station)

(1) No person may hold the stocks or quotas of the same broadcasting corporation including the stocks or quotas held by a person having a special relation as prescribed by the Presidential Decree, in excess of 30/100 of the total stocks or quotas, except in the following cases: (Amended by Law No. 4263, Aug. 1, 1990)

1. Where the State or local government contributes to the broadcasting corporation;

2. Where a corporation established pursuant to a special law holds the stocks or quotas of the broadcasting corporation; and

3. Where the contribution is made to a broadcasting corporation established with a permission for the purpose of a missionary work of a religion.

(2) Notwithstanding the provisions of Paragraph (1), the large enterprises as prescribed by the Presidential Decree, interrelated enterprises and persons having special relation with them may not hold stocks or quotas issued by a broadcasting corporation. (Newly Inserted by Law No. 4263. Aug. 1 1990)

(3) No person holding stocks or quotas in contravention of the provisions of Paragraph (1) or (2) may exercise his voting right on the excess or holding portion. (Newly Inserted by Law No. 4263, Aug. 1, 1990)

(4) The Minister of Public Information may order a person holding stocks or quotas in contravention of the provisions of Paragraph (1) or (2) to take a measure in conformity with the provisions of Paragraph (1) or (2). (Newly Inserted by Law No. 4263, Aug. 1, 1990)

(5) No person other than the State, local government or a juristic person established under the special law or a broadcasting corporation permitted for the purpose of a religious mission shall give any special broadcast.

(6) The head of a broadcasting station shall make a public notice on the status of assets of the broadcasting corporation at the end of each year and submit the particulars thereof to the Minister of Public Information. (Amended by Law No. 4183, Dec. 30, 1989)

**Article 7**  (Prohibition of Concurrent Operation by Broadcasting Corporation)

(1) Any broadcasting corporation shall not operate concurrently any daily newspaper or communication as prescribed in Article 7 of the Act Relating to Registration, etc. of Periodicals.

(2) Directors (managing partners in case of unlimited partnerships and partners with unlimited liability in case of limited partnerships) of a broadcasting corporation who are related to one another as prescribed in Article 777 of the Civil Code shall not exceed a third of the total directors. (Amended by Law No. 4263, Aug. 1. 1990)

**Article 7-2**  (Submission of Materials) The broadcasting station shall, upon a request of the Minister of Public Information, submit related materials necessary for confirming the facts as prescribed in Articles 6 (1), (2) and 77. (This Article Newly Inserted by Law No. 4263. Aug. 1, 1990)

**Article 8**  (Prohibition of Inflow of Foreign Capital) No broadcasting corporation shall receive any financial contribution on the pretext of donation, patronage or others from a foreigner or foreign government or organization, except a contribution from a foreign organization having an object of education, physical training. religion, charity or other international friendship, which is approved by the Minister of Public Information. (Amended by Law No. 4183, Dec. 30, 1989)

**Article 9**  (Disqualification) Any person who falls under any of the following subparagraphs shall not be the head or person in charge of programming of a broadcasting station: (Amended by Law No. 4263, Aug. 1, 1990)

1. A person who is not a national of the Republic of Korea;

2. A person who does not establish his domicile in the Republic of Korea;

3. A representative of a corporation or organization in which a representative of a foreign corporation or organization or a person falling under Subparagraph I or 2 may exercise the right to vote;

4. A person who committed a crime as prescribed in Articles 87 to 90, 92 to 101 of the Criminal Code, or Articles 5 to 8, 9 (2), 11 to 16 of the Military Criminal Act or Articles 3 to 9 of the National Security Act, and sentenced to imprisonment without hard labor or more severe, but the execution of such punishment is not terminated or it is not definite not to be executed, or the period of stay of execution is not terminated; and

5. A person who is in the course of execution of a disposition for social security and probation under the Security and Probation Act or a disposition for social protection under the Social Protection Act.

**Article 10** (In-Service Training)

(1) The head of a broadcasting station shall establish and operate an in-service training system for the purpose of improving the ability and quality of those who are engaged in the broadcast.

(2) The head of a broadcasting station may establish and operate jointly an in-service training organization as prescribed in Article 5 (2) of the Act Relating to Registration etc. of Periodicals.

## CHAPTER III. THE BROADCAST COMMITTEE

**Article 11** (Establishment) In order to maintain public responsibility, impartiality and publicness of a broadcast and to strive for the qualitative improvement of general contents of the broadcast, the Broadcast Committee (hereinafter referred to as "Committee") shall be established. (Amended by Law No. 4263, Aug. 1, 1990)

**Article 12** (Composition, etc.)

(1) The Committee shall be composed of nine members appointed by the President from among the broadcast-related experts and those who are of learning, experience and high moral repute. (Amended by Law No. 4263, Aug. 1, 1990)

(2) Three members of the Committee shall be appointed from among those who are recommended by the Speaker of the National Assembly, and three, from among those who are recommended by the Chief justice of the Supreme Court. (Amended by Law No. 4263, Aug. 1, 1990)

**Article 13** (Chairman, etc.)

(1) The Committee shall assign a chairman and a vice-chairman.

(2) The chairman and vice-chairman shall be elected from among the members.

(3) The chairman shall represent the Committee and take charge of all affairs of the Committee, and if the chairman is unable to carry out his duties by accident, the vice-chairman shall act for him. (Amended by Law No. 4263, Aug. 1, 1990)

(4) The members excluding the chairman and vice-chairman shall be in nonpermanent service. (Amended by Law No. 4263, Aug. 1,1990)

**Article 14** (Term of Member)

(1) The term of the chairman, vice-chairman and members shall be three years, respectively.

(2) If a vacancy occurs among the members, a substitute member shall be appointed under Article 12, and his term of office shall be the remaining term of his predecessor.

**Article 14-2** (Treatment of Members) The position of nonpermanent members shall be honorary: Provided that they may receive the per diem, travel expenses and other actual expenses, under the conditions as prescribed by the Regulations of the Committee. (This Article Newly Inserted by Law No. 4263, Aug. 1, 1990)

**Article 15** (Disqualification of Member) Any person who falls under any of the following subparagraphs shall not be a member:

1. A public official (excluding educational public officials and public officials qualified for judges);
2. A member of a political party under the Political Party Act;
3. A person who is engaged in a broadcasting station or broadcast-related business; and
4. A person who falls under any of subparagraphs of Article 33 of the State Civil Service Act.

**Article 16** (Functional Independence and Status Guarantee of Member)

(1) No member shall be subject to any external direction or interference with respect to his duties during his term of office.

(2) No member shall be dismissed from office contrary to his intention unless he falls under any of the following subparagraphs:

1. Where he is sentenced to imprisonment without hard labor or more severe punishment; and
2. Where he becomes unable to perform his duties due to mental and physical impediment for a long time.

**Article 17** (Function of Committee)

(1) The Committee shall deliberate and decide the following matters: (Amended by Law No. 4183, Dec. 30, 1989; Law No. 4263, Aug. 1, 1990)

1. Matters concerning the basic policy on the operation and programming of broadcasts and commercial broadcasts;
2. Recommendation in the appointment of directors of a broadcasting corporation established under the special law;
3. Matters concerning the research, study and training to improve the contents of broadcast;
4. Matters concerning relations among broadcasting stations and broadcasting categories, joint projects and cooperation;
5. Matters concerning the basic policy of broadcast, and which are requested by the Minister of Public Information;
6. Matters concerning the settlement of complaints of TV audience;
7. Enactment, revision and repeal of the Regulations of the Committee; and
8. Correctional and disciplinary measures as prescribed in Article 21 (1).

(2) The Committee shall deliberate and decide whether or not the contents broadcast by the broadcasting station maintain the impartiality and publicness and fulfill the public responsibility for matters concerning public interests. (Amended by Law No. 4263, Aug. 1, 1990)

(3) In order to make the broadcast contribute to the improvement of the national culture and maintain the impartiality and publicness of its contents, the Committee shall deliberate and decide whether the broadcast is given or not, before the following broadcast materials are broadcasted: (Amended by Law No. 4263, Aug. 1, 1990)

1. Dramatic movies and cartoon films for broadcasting (including video materials, etc.);

2. Broadcasting programs imported from foreign countries (excluding those concerning relay and report of athletic sports, etc.); and

3. Advertising materials which the Korea Broadcasting Advertisement Corporation desires to broadcast by entrusting it to the broadcasting station under Article 15 of the Korea Broadcasting Advertisement Corporation Act.

(4) The Minister of Public Information and the head of the broadcasting station or his entrusted person may attend the Committee to state their opinions. (Amended by Law No. 4263, Aug. 1, 1990)

(5) The Committee may request the broadcasting station to present materials necessary for judging whether or not matters deliberated and decided by the Committee are observed and order the correction of any offense. (Amended by Law No. 4263, Aug. 1, 1990)

(6) The Committee shall submit each year a report on the duties of the Committee to the National Assembly before the commencement of the ordinary session of the National Assembly (Amended by Law No. 4263, Aug. 1, 1990)

**Article 18** (Quorum for Decision) The proceedings of the Committee shall be decided with the attendance of more than two-thirds of all the members, and a concurrent vote of a majority of the members present.

**Article 19** (Deliberative Committee, etc.)

(1) The Committee shall assign the deliberative committee to assist the deliberation of matters falling under subparagraphs of Article 17 (2) and (3). (Amended by Law No. 4263, Aug. 1, 1990)

(2) Members of the deliberative committee shall be commissioned by the chairman in the limit of thirty persons with the consent of the Committee, and matters necessary for the organization and operation of the deliberative committee and the term of members of the deliberative committee shall be determined by the Regulations of the Committee. (Amended by Law No. 4263, Aug. 1, 1990)

(3) The Committee may assign research members to research technically specified affairs under the conditions as prescribed by the Regulations of the Committee.

**Article 20** (Deliberative Rules)

(1) In order to deliberate matters as prescribed in subparagraphs of Article 17 (2) and (3), the Committee shall formulate and announce publicly as the Regulations of the Committee the Rules Relating to Deliberation of Broadcast (hereinafter referred to as "Deliberative Rules"). (Amended by Law No. 4263, Aug. 1, 1990)

(2) The Deliberative Rules as referred to in Paragraph (1) shall include the following matters: (Amended by Law No. 4263, Aug. 1, 1990)

1. Matters concerning the impartiality of news and comments;

2. Matters concerning the extension of free democracy and the respect of human rights;

3. Matters concerning the cultivation of national identity;

4. Matters concerning creative enlightenment and development of national culture;

5. Matters concerning the proper guidance of children and youth;

6. Matters concerning the purity of family life;

7. Matters concerning the extension of the public morality and social ethics;

8. Matters concerning the correctional and disciplinary measures as prescribed in Article 21; and

9. Other matters concerning the function of the Committee as prescribed by this Act.

**Article 21** (Correction and Sanction)

(1) The Committee may order the following correctional and disciplinary measures against the broadcasting station which violates the Deliberative Rules: (Amended by Law No. 4263, Aug. 1, 1990)

1. Apology for the radio and television audience;
2. Revision, explanation or cancellation of the broadcast contents concerned; and
3. Discipline against persons responsible for or related to the broadcasting program or suspension of the production or performance in the limit of one year.

(2) The broadcasting station shall, upon receiving an order under Paragraph (1), broadcast without delay the full text of matters deliberated and decided by the Committee as to the contents of such order, and after carrying out the order within seven days from the day on which it receives the order, report the result to the Committee.

(3) When the Committee desires to order a correction or sanction under Paragraph (1), it shall give in advance the person concerned or his representative an opportunity to state his opinion, except in a case where the person concerned or his representative fails to comply with it without any justifiable reason.

(4) When the Committee has issued an order under Paragraph (1) or received a report under Paragraph (2), it shall promptly notify it to the Minister of Public Information. (Amended by Law No. 4183, Dec. 30, 1989)

(5) Deleted. (by Law No. 4263, Aug. 1, 1990)

**Article 22** (Secretariat)

(1) The secretariat shall be established in the Committee for the purpose of assisting in the affairs of the Committee.

(2) A secretary-general and necessary personnel shall be assigned to the secretariat, and they shall be appointed by the chairman. In this case, the appointment of the secretary-general shall be approved by the Committee.

(3) The organization and operation of the secretariat, the remuneration of personnel and other necessary matters shall be determined by the Regulations of the Committee.

**Article 23** (Regulations of Committee) The chairman may establish the Regulations relating to operation of the Committee through a decision of the Committee.

**Article 24** (Subsidy) The State may grant a subsidy to the Committee in the limit of the budget.

### CHAPTER IV. (Articles 25 To 29) Deleted.
### (by Law No. 4263, Aug. 1, 1990)

### CHAPTER V. MATTERS TO BE OBSERVED BY BROADCASTING STATION

**Article 30** (Audience Committee)

(1) The broadcasting station shall establish the broadcasting audience committee (hereinafter referred to as "audience committee") for the purpose of providing advice on the broadcasting program. (Amended by Law No. 4263, Aug. 1, 1990)

(2) The head of the broadcasting station shall commission members of the audience committee from among those who are representable of the audience in all levels of society through the recommendation of an organization or agency as prescribed by the Presidential Decree. (Amended by Law No. 4263, Aug. 1, 1990)

(3) The audience committee may deliberate matters concerning the broadcasting program excluding the broadcast on the news and present its opinion to the head of the broadcasting station or, if necessary, demand him a correction, according to the result of deliberation. (Amended by Law No. 4263, Aug. 1, 1990)

(4) The head of the broadcasting station shall, upon receiving a demand for correction under Paragraph (3), carry it out unless there is any special reason.

(5) The head of the broadcasting station shall report to the Committee the result of deliberation of the audience committee under Paragraph (3) and matters concerning settlement thereof. (Amended by Law No. 4263, Aug. 1, 1990)

(6) Matters concerning the composition and operation of the audience committee shall be determined by the Presidential Decree (Amended by Law No. 4263, Aug. 1, 1990)

**Article 30-2** (Self-Deliberation) The broadcasting station shall set up an internal organization to deliberate the broadcasting program and deliberate the broadcasting program excluding that pertaining to the news before it is broadcasted. (This Article Newly Inserted by Law No. 4263, Aug. 1, 1990)

**Article 31** (Drawing Up, etc. of Broadcasting Program)

(1) The broadcasting program shall be drawn up so that each field of interest: political, economic, social, cultural, etc. may be expressed harmoniously in a proper ratio.

(2) In drawing up a broadcasting program, the broadcasting station shall include contents of culture or education, news and recreation according to the criteria as prescribed by the Presidential Decree, and make the broadcasting programs harmonize with one another according to their categories: Provided that in drawing up a program of special broadcasting, the principal approved broadcasting matters shall be reflected sufficiently. (Amended by Law No. 4263, Aug. 1, 1990)

(3) In drawing up a broadcasting program, the broadcasting station shall draw it up so that the ratio the broadcasting programs imported from foreign countries occupy in the whole broadcasting program does not exceed such ratio as determined by the Presidential Decree, and the ratio the broadcasting programs made by persons other than the broadcasting station in Korea occupy in the whole broadcasting program exceeds such ratio as determined by the Presidential Decree. (Newly Inserted by Law No. 4263, Aug. 1, 1990)

**Article 32** (Person in Charge of Programming)

(1) The head of the broadcasting station shall appoint persons in charge of programming and advertisement by fields of the broadcasting program and announce publicly their names once or more times every day in the broadcasting hours.

(2) If a person in charge of programming or advertisement is unable to carry out his work, he shall immediately designate his representative to do so.

**Article 33** (Overseas Broadcast)

(1) In drawing up and broadcasting an overseas broadcast or drawing up a broadcasting program to be provided to foreign broadcasting station, it shall be required to have a true appreciation of the Republic of Korea and at the same time to contribute to the improvement of the international friendship and understanding and the promotion of the cultural and economic exchange.

(2) In case where a broadcasting station gives an overseas broadcast under Paragraph (1), it shall prepare periodically each month a plan of the overseas broadcast under the conditions as prescribed by the Presidential Decree and obtain the approval of the Minister of Public Information. (Amended by Law No. 4183, Dec. 30, 1989)

**Article 34** (Educational Broadcast) In drawing up and broadcasting an educational broadcast, those who are the object of the broadcast shall be distinct and the contents shall be drawn up usefully, properly, systematically and continuously, and the program of the broadcast shall be notified in advance to the general public. In this case, if the broadcasting program is in the interest of school education, its contents shall be conformed to the standards of curriculum as determined by laws and regulations relating to school education.

**Article 35** (Commercial Broadcast)

(1) When a broadcasting station gives a commercial broadcast, the station shall indicate or distinguish it so as to be identified as a commercial broadcast.

(2) The time and frequency of the commercial broadcast shall be determined by the Presidential Decree.

(3) The proceeds of the commercial broadcast may be used for the broadcast promoting projects and the culture and arts promoting projects under the conditions as prescribed by the Korea Broadcasting Advertisement Corporation Act. (Amended by Law No. 4263, Aug. 1, 1990)

(4) Deleted. (by Law No. 4263, Aug. 1, 1990)

**Article 36** (Preservation of Broadcasted Particulars) The head of a broadcasting station shall preserve the original or copy of a recording or videotape of published matters for one month after publication.

**Article 37** (Report on Opening of Station, Suspension and Discontinuation of Broadcast) When a broadcasting station is opened or the broadcasting is suspended for more than twenty four hours, or it is discontinued, it shall be reported to the Minister of Public Information under the conditions as prescribed by the Presidential Decree. (Amended by Law No. 4183, Dec. 30, 1989)

**Article 38** (Monthly Report) The broadcasting station shall keep a broadcasting diary and record thereon broadcast contents every day, and submit periodically each month the broadcasting result to the Committee and the Minister of Public Information, respectively, under the conditions as prescribed by the Presidential Decree. (Amended by Law No. 4183, Dec. 30, 1989)

**Article 39** (Establishment of Overseas Branch, etc.) If a broadcasting station having reported its opening under Article 37 desires to establish a branch office or station in a foreign country, it shall obtain the approval of the Minister of Public Information under the conditions as prescribed by the Presidential Decree. (Amended by Law No. 4183, Dec. 30, 1989)

**Article 40** (Establishment of Domestic Branch, etc. of Foreign Broadcasting Station)

(1) Any person who desires to establish a branch office or station of a foreign broadcasting station in the territory of the Republic of Korea shall obtain the permission of the Minister of Public Information under the conditions as prescribed the Presidential Decree. (Amended by Law No. 4183, Dec. 30, 1989)

(2) If a branch office or station or a foreign broadcasting station as permitted under Paragraph (I) falls under any of the following subparagraphs, the Minister of Publics Information may cancel the permission: (Amended by Law No. 4183, Dec. 30, 1989)

1. Where it has obtained the permission by deceit or other unlawful means;

2. Where it has infringed the conditions of permission; and

3. Where it has broadcasted news disturbing the national constitution or injuring the national prestige.

**Article 40-2** (Recommendation on Import of Foreign Broadcasting Program) Any broadcasting station which desires to import broadcasting programs made in foreign countries for broadcasting shall obtain the recommendation of the Minister of Public Information on the import thereof under the conditions as prescribed by the Presidential Decree, except in case of the broadcasting programs as to the news. (This Article Newly Inserted by Law No. 4263, Aug. 1, 1990)

## CHAPTER VI. REMEDY FOR INFRINGEMENT

**Article 41** (Claim for Corrected News)

(1) Any person who is injured by a factual allegation published in the broadcast (hereinafter referred to as "injured person") may request in writing a broadcast of corrected news to the head of the broadcasting station or a person in charge of programming within fourteen days after it is published.

(2) The claim for corrected news shall be signed and sealed by the injured person or his representative, with his address, and accompanied by details of the news in question and a text of the corrected news he requests to broadcast.

(3) The head of the broadcasting station or the person in charge of programming shall, upon receiving a claim for the corrected news, consult immediately with the injured person or his representative on the contents, etc. of the corrected news, and then broadcast it without charge: Provided that if the injured person has no proper interest in exercising such claim for corrected news, or the contents of claiming the corrected news is obviously contrary to the fact, or the claim aims only at a commercial advertisement, such broadcast may be rejected.

(4) The corrected news shall be limited to a factual statement and an explanation necessary for transmitting it obviously, and it shall not include illegal contents.

(5) The number of words in a text of corrected news shall not exceed that of the published text in question.

(6) The corrected news given out by the head of the broadcasting station or the person in charge of programming shall be given out in such a manner that it produces the same effect with the same broadcasting frequency as that by which it was published.

(7) The provisions of Paragraphs (1) to (6) shall not be applicable in case of factual broadcast concerning open meetings of the State, local governments or public organizations, and public trial procedures of the court.

**Article 42** (Application of Other Acts) The provisions of Article 17 to 20 of the Act Relating to Registration, etc. of Periodicals shall be applicable to matters concerning an arbitration of dispute on a claim for corrected news related to a broadcast and a procedure thereof, and matters concerning a decision on a case of claim for corrected news and a claim for *ex post facto* news.

## CHAPTER VII. PENAL PROVISIONS

**Article 43** (Penal Provisions) Any person who falls under any of the following subparagraphs shall be punished by imprisonment for not more than one year or a fine not exceeding twenty million Won: (Amended by Law No. 4263, Aug. 1, 1990)

1. A person who regulates or interferes with the drawing up or making of a broadcasting program under Article 3 (2) or the operation of the broadcasting station;

2. A person who violates the provisions of Article 6 (1) or (2), or any order issued under Paragraph (4) of the said Article;

3. A person who violates the provisions of Article 7;
4. The head of a broadcasting station who receives a contribution of property in contravention of the provisions of Article 8;
5. A person who violates an order issued under Article 21 (1); and
6. A person who has established a branch office or station of a foreign broadcasting station in the country without obtaining permission under Article 40 (1).

**Article 44** (Penal Provisions) Any person who falls under any of the following subparagraphs shall be punished by a fine not exceeding three million Won: (Amended by Law No. 4183, Dec. 30, 1989; Law No. 4263, Aug. 1, 1990)

1. A person who falls under any of subparagraphs of Article 9 and take office as the head of a broadcasting station or the person in charge of programming;
2. The head of a broadcasting station who has appointed a person falling under any of subparagraphs of Article 9 as the person in charge of programming or his representative; and
3. A person who gives an overseas broadcast without obtaining the approval of the Minister of Public Information under Article 33 (2).

**Article 44-2** (Joint Penal Provisions) If a representative of a juristic person, or an agent, serviceman or other employee of a juristic or private person commits an offense as prescribed in Article 43 or 44 with respect to the business of the juristic or private person, the fine as prescribed in the respective Article shall be imposed even on the juristic or private person in addition to a punishment of the offender. (This Article Newly Inserted by Law No. 4263, Aug. 1, 1990)

**Article 45** (Fine for Negligence)

(1) Any person who falls under any of the following subparagraphs shall be punished by a fine for negligence not exceeding three million Won: (Amended by Law No. 4263, Aug. 1, 1990)

1. A person who fails to notify publicly or submit the status of assets of the broadcasting corporation under Article 6 (6);
2. A person who fails to report the result of carrying out deliberated and decided matters under Article 21 (2);
3. A person who draws up a broadcasting program in contravention of the provisions of Article 31 (3);
4. The head of a broadcasting station who fails to publish the person in charge of programming, etc. under Article 32 (1);
5. A person who fails to report the opening of a broadcasting station, suspension or discontinuation of broadcasting under Article 37;
6. A person who fails to make a monthly report under Article 38; and
7. A person who has established a branch office or station in a foreign country without obtaining the approval under Article 39.

(2) The fine for negligence as referred to in Paragraph (1) shall be imposed and collected by the Minister of Public Information under the conditions as prescribed by the Presidential Decree. (Amended by Law No. 4183, Dec. 30, 1990)

(3) Any person who is unsatisfied with a disposition of fine for negligence under Paragraph (2) may raise an objection against the Minister of Public Information within thirty days after he is informed of the disposition. (Amended by Law No. 4183, Dec. 30, 1989; Law No. 4263, Aug. 1, 1990)

(4) If a person who is subject to a disposition of fine for negligence under Paragraph (2) has raised an objection under Paragraph (3) the Minister of Public Information shall promptly notify it to the competent court, which, upon receiving such notification, brings the case of fine for negligence to trial under the Non-Contentious Case Procedure Act. (Amended by Law No. 4183, Dec. 30, 1989)

(5) If no objection is raised and the fine for negligence is not paid within the period as referred to in Paragraph (3), it shall be collected according to examples of disposition of national taxes in arrears.

## ADDENDA

**Article 1** (Enforcement Date) This Act shall enter into force as of the date of its promulgation: Provided that the provisions of Articles 25 to 29 shall enter into force as of January 1, 1989.

**Article 2** (Relation to Other Acts) In case where the Basic Press Act repealed at the time of the enforcement of this Act is applied *mutatis mutandis* or cited in other Acts, it shall be considered to apply *mutatis mutandis* or cite this Act with respect to matters concerning the broadcast.

**Article 3** (Interim Measures)

(1) The Broadcasting Committee as prescribed in Article 11 shall be composed within six months after this Act enters into force, and the Broadcasting Committee and the Broadcasting Deliberative Committee established under the repealed Basic Press Act shall carry out their duties pursuant to the provisions of this Act until the Committee composed under this Act is established.

(2) The broadcasting stations reported, the broadcasting advisory committees established, and domestic branch offices or stations of foreign broadcasting stations permitted under the repealed Basic Press Act at the time of the enforcement of this Act shall be considered to be reported, established or permitted under this Act.

(3) Any branch office or station established in a foreign country at the time of the enforcement of this Act shall be approved within three months after this Act enters into force, so that it is conformed to the provisions of Article 39 of this Act.

(4) Any television receiver set registered under the Korea Broadcasting Corporation Act at the time the provisions of Articles 25 to 29 enter into force shall be considered as a TV set registered under this Act.

(5) Notwithstanding the provisions of Article 6 (1), stocks or quotas owned by a broadcasting corporation established under the special law at the time of the enforcement of this Act, which are issued by other broadcasting corporations, shall be disposed by December 31, 1988.

**Article 4** (Revision of Other Act) Omitted.

## ADDENDA (Law No. 4183, Dec. 30, 1989; Government Organization Act)

**Article 1** (Enforcement Date) This Act shall enter into force as of the date of its promulgation. (Proviso omitted)

**Articles 2 to 6 Omitted.**

## ADDENDA (Law No. 4263, Aug. 1, 1990)

(1) (Enforcement Date) This Act shall enter into force at the expiration of one month after its promulgation: Provided that the revised provisions of Chapter IV (Articles 25 to 29) shall enter into force as of January 1, 1991.

(2) (Composition of Audience Committee) The audience committee as prescribed in the revised provisions of Article 30 shall be composed within thirty days from the enforcement date of this Act.

(3) (Interim Measures Concerning Stock Holding of Broadcasting Corporation, etc.) Any person who holds stocks of a broadcasting corporation at the time of the enforcement of this Act and is not conformed to the holding ceiling, etc. as referred to in the revised provisions of Article 6 (1) or (2) shall not be subject to the revised provisions of Article 6 (1) to (4) in the limit of the stocks held by him.

(4) (Interim Measures Concerning the Composition of Broadcasting Committee) The Broadcasting Committee as referred to in the revised provisions of Article 12 shall be composed within three months from the enforcement date of this Act and the broadcasting committee as referred to in the previous provisions shall perform its function under this Act until the Broadcasting Committee as prescribed by this Act is composed.

## ADDENDA (Law No. 4441, Dec 14, 1991; Radio Waves Act)

**Article 1** (Enforcement Date) This Act shall enter into force as of July 1, 1992. (proviso omitted)

# A P P E N D I X   F

# Comprehensive Cable Television Broadcast Act

(Law No. 4494. Dec. 31. 1991)
(Amended by Law No. 4737, Jan. 7, 1994)

## CHAPTER I. GENERAL PROVISIONS

**Article 1** (Purpose) The purpose of this Act is to contribute to the improvement of the national culture and promotion of the public welfare by striving for a sound fostering and development of the comprehensive cable television broadcast and a convenience of users thereof.

**Article 2** (Definition) For the purpose of this Act,

1. the term "comprehensive cable television broadcast" means a multichannel broadcasting to transmit images (including characters and static pictures), voices, sounds, etc. to receiving persons using cable television telecommunication facilities;
2. the term "comprehensive cable television broadcasting facilities" means the comprehensive cable television broadcasting station facilities and transmission line facilities;
3. the term "comprehensive cable television broadcasting station facilities" means any equipment and facilities installed in a comprehensive cable television broadcasting station for programming, operation and transmission of the comprehensive cable television broadcasting;
4. the term "transmission line facilities" means any line facilities required for transmitting any comprehensive cable television broadcast;
5. the term "comprehensive cable television broadcasting station" means an enterprise which is equipped with the comprehensive cable television broadcasting station facilities, and transmits any comprehensive cable television broadcast after having the broadcasting programs supplied by a person who holds a license for the program supply business;
6. the term "program supply business" means a business supplying any broadcasting programs to the comprehensive cable television broadcasting stations;

7. the term "transmission network business" means a business to install and operate the transmission line facilities;

8. the term "comprehensive cable television broadcasting zone" means a service zone in which a comprehensive cable television broadcasting station furnishes any service of comprehensive cable television broadcast;

9. the term "receiving person" means a person who has entered into a contract of subscription with the comprehensive cable television broadcasting station in order to receive the comprehensive cable television broadcast; and

10. the term "simultaneous retransmission" means to retransmit simultaneously a cable televisionless broadcast of a broadcasting station pursuant to the Broadcast Act without alternating the broadcasting program after receiving such cable televisionless broadcast.

**Article 3** (Policy of Government) In order to attain the purpose of this Act, the Minister of Public Information shall consider a fundamental and comprehensive policy on the comprehensive cable television broadcast.

**Article 4** (Restriction, etc. on Concurrent Operation of Business)

(1) The comprehensive cable television broadcasting station, program supply business and transmission network business shall not be operated concurrently (including holding stocks or quotas thereof; hereinafter the same shall apply), except in case where the Minister of Public Information deems necessary in particular for the technical development of the comprehensive cable television broadcast and standardization thereof, survey of social and economic receptivity, etc., and grants a permission on a comprehensive cable television broadcasting station to a government-invested institution or other public organization as prescribed by the Presidential Decree.

(2) The comprehensive cable television broadcasting stations may not be operated concurrently each other, except in case where a comprehensive cable television broadcasting station is operated additionally in an area as designated by the Minister of Public Information under Subparagraph 2 of Article 8 (3).

(3) The comprehensive cable television broadcasting station and the broadcasting station as prescribed by the Broadcast Act (hereinafter referred to as "cable televisionless broadcasting station") may not be operated concurrently.

(4) The comprehensive cable television broadcasting station and the daily newspaper or communication as prescribed by the Act Relating to Registration, etc. of Periodicals may not be operated concurrently.

(5) Any large enterprise and its interrelated one may not operate a comprehensive cable television broadcasting station or hold the stocks or quotas thereof.

(6) Any political party or religious organization supporting or advocating a specified ideology or thought may not operate a comprehensive cable television broadcasting station or hold the stocks or quotas thereof.

(7) No person may own stocks or quotas of the same juristic person operating the program supply business on news (hereinafter referred to as "news program supply business") of the program supply business, including those owned by a person having such special relations as prescribed by the Presidential Decree, in excess of 30/100 of the total thereof. (Newly Inserted by Law No. 4737, Jan. 7, 1994)

(8) Notwithstanding the provisions of Paragraph (7), no person who falls under any of the following subparagraphs may operate a corporation carrying on the news program

supply business or own stocks or quotas thereof: (Newly Inserted by Law No. 4737, Jan. 7, 1994)

1. Such large enterprises and interrelated ones as prescribed by the Presidential Decree; and

2. Those who own more than 5/100 of stocks or quotas of a broadcasting corporation as prescribed by the Broadcast Act; Provided that in case where the principal corporation of those belonging to the same broadcasting network owns stocks of another broadcasting corporation, such principal broadcasting corporation shall be excluded.

(9) No person who has a special relation with a person who is subject to a prohibition of concurrent operation as referred to in Paragraphs (1) to (5) may own a comprehensive cable television broadcasting station, and no person having a special relation with a person who is subject to a prohibition of operation as referred to in Paragraph (8) may operate a corporation carrying on the news program supply business or own stocks or quotas thereof. In this case, the scope of those having a special relation shall be determined by the Presidential Decree. (Amended by Law No. 4737, Jan. 7, 1994)

(10) Any person who owns stocks or quotas in contravention of the provisions of Paragraphs (1) to (9) may not exercise the voting right on such owned or excessive portion. (Amended by Law No. 4737, Jan. 7, 1994)

(11) Those of directors of a corporation carrying on the news program supply business (in case of an unlimited partnership, the managing partners, and in case of a limited partnership, the general partners), who have a relationship by blood and marriage as prescribed in Article 777 of the Civil Code among them, shall not exceed a third of a total. (Newly Inserted by Law No. 4737, Jan. 7, 1994)

(12) The head of the comprehensive cable television broadcasting station or the representative of a corporation carrying on the news program supply business shall make at the end of each year a public notice on the situation of property of the corporation operating such comprehensive cable television broadcasting station or news program supply business and submit the details thereof to the Minister of Public Information. (Amended by Law No. 4737, Jan. 7, 1994)

**Article 5** (Causes of Disqualification)

(1) The State, local government or any person other than a juristic person may operate a comprehensive cable television broadcasting station, a program supply business and a transmission network business (hereinafter referred to as "comprehensive cable television broadcasting business"). The provision shall also apply to a person for whom two years have not passed after the permission or designation is canceled under Article 21.

(2) No person who falls under any of the following subparagraphs may be a representative, director, auditor, or program director of a juristic person operating a comprehensive cable television broadcasting business:

1. Person who has no nationality of the Republic of Korea;

2. Person who has no address in the Republic of Korea;

3. Person who is minor, quasi-incompetent or incompetent;

4. Person who is declared bankrupt, but not yet reinstated;

5. Person who was sentenced to a punishment heavier than imprisonment without hard labor, for a crime as prescribed in Articles 87 to 90, 92 to 101 of the Penal Code, Articles 5 to 8, 9 (2), 11 to 16 of the Military Penal Code, and Articles 3

to 9 of the National Security Act, and for whom the execution of such sentence is not terminated, or non-execution thereof does not become definite, or the execution stay period is not terminated;

6. Person who is under a security and probational action under the Security and Probation Act, or a protective action under the Social Protection Act;
7. Representative of a foreign corporation or organization; and
8. Representative of a corporation or organization in which a person falling under any of Subparagraphs 1 to 7 holds more than 5/100 of the voting rights.

**Article 6** (Restriction on Inflow of Foreign Capital) No person who operates a comprehensive cable television broadcasting business shall receive any contribution or investment of property on such pretext as contribution, patronage, etc. from any foreigner, foreign government or organization: Provided that in a case of the program supply business (excluding the news program supply business), it is permitted to receive any contribution or investment of property from any foreigner or foreign organization, with the approval of the Minister of Public Information, in the limit not exceeding 15/100 of the total of stocks or quotas owned by the corporation licensed under Article 13. (Amended by Law No. 4737, Jan. 7, 1994)

## CHAPTER II. COMPREHENSIVE CABLE TELEVISION BROADCASTING BUSINESS

**Article 7** (Permission on Comprehensive Cable Television Broadcasting Station)

(1) Any person who desires to operate a comprehensive cable television broadcasting station shall obtain the permission of the Minister of Public Information through the mayor of the Seoul Special City, the mayor of the direct control city, or the provincial governor (hereinafter referred to as "city/province governor") under the conditions as prescribed by the Presidential Decree.

(2) If the Minister of Public Information desires to grant a permission as referred to in Paragraph (1), he shall examine the following matters:

1. Whether the object or contents of the comprehensive cable television broadcast are conformed to the provisions of laws and regulations, and it is not detrimental to the interest of the State;
2. Whether the comprehensive cable television broadcast has the regional, social and cultural necessity and propriety;
3. Whether it contributes to the development of the communities through the operation of the comprehensive cable television broadcasting station;
4. Whether the financial capability is enough to operate the comprehensive cable television broadcasting station; and
5. Whether the installation plan of the comprehensive cable television broadcasting station facilities is reasonable, and conformed to the technical standards as prescribed in Article 33, and it provides a sufficient technical capability to operate the comprehensive cable television broadcasting station.

(3) In examining such manners as referred to in Subparagraphs 2 to 4 of Paragraph (2), the Minister of Public Information shall hear the option of the city/province governor.

(4) In examining such matters as referred to in Subparagraph 5 of Paragraph (2), the Minister of Public Information shall consult with the Minister of Communications.

(5) When the Minister of Public Information has granted the permission as referred to in Paragraph (1), he shall notify it to the head of the administrative agency concerned and the city/province governor.

**Article 8**  (Right to Regional Business)

  (1) In granting a permission as prescribed in Article 7, the Minister of Public Information may vest a right to operate a business exclusively in a specified comprehensive cable television broadcasting zone (hereinafter referred to as "regional business right").

  (2) The comprehensive cable television broadcasting zone as referred to in Paragraph (1) shall be designated and notified publicly by the Minister of Public Information taking into consideration the telecommunication circuit facilities, living circles of residents in the zone, geographical conditions, etc. with priority given to the administrative district, under the conditions as prescribed by the Presidential Decree.

  (3) In vesting the regional business right as referred to in Paragraph (1), the Minister of Public Information may attach to it any condition necessary for,

      1. improving the public interest and offering convenience to receiving persons;

      2. operating additional comprehensive cable television broadcasting station in any area designated by the Minister of Public Information for a balance between areas; and

      3. discharging without fail the permitted matters.

  (4) The Minister of Public Information may collect a fee to the regional business right from the person who is vested such right under Paragraph (1), in the limit of 10 percent of the total annual proceeds, under the conditions as prescribed by the Presidential Decree.

**Article 9**  (Installation of Comprehensive Cable Television Broadcasting Station Facilities, and Inspection on Completion thereof, etc.)

  (1) Any comprehensive cable television broadcasting station which has obtained the permission under Article 7 shall install the comprehensive cable television broadcasting station facilities by the time limit as determined by the Presidential Decree, and undergone the inspection of the Minister of Communications on the completion thereof. This provision shall also apply in case where such installed comprehensive cable television broadcasting station facilities are altered.

  (2) If the comprehensive cable television broadcasting station is unable to install the comprehensive cable television broadcasting station facilities by the time limit as referred to in Paragraph (1) due to any inevitable cause, such as natural disaster, terrestrial upheaval, etc., it may request the Minister of Communications an extension of the time limit for installation of such facilities under the conditions as prescribed by the Presidential Decree.

  (3) When the comprehensive cable television broadcasting station has undergone the inspection of the Minister of Communications on completion of the comprehensive cable television broadcasting station facilities under Paragraph (1), it shall report it without delay to the Minister of Public Information under the conditions as prescribed by the Presidential Decree.

**Article 10**  (Permission on Change)

  (1) If a comprehensive cable television broadcasting station desires to change any of permitted matters, it shall obtain the permission of the Minister of Public Information under the conditions as prescribed by the Presidential Decree: Provided that with respect to insignificant matters as determined by the Presidential Decree, it may be changed after making a prior report to the Minister of Public Information.

  (2) In case where the Minister of Public Information desires to grant a permission on any change under Paragraph (1), if the permitted matters to be changed include any change

in the comprehensive cable television broadcasting station facilities, the matters concerning such facilities shall be consulted with the Minister of Public Information.

(3) When the Minister of Public Information has granted a permission on any change under Paragraph (1), he shall notify it to the head of the administrative agency and city/province governor concerned.

**Article 11**  (Validity Term of Permission) The validity term of a permission on a comprehensive cable television broadcasting station shall be determined by the Presidential Decree in the limit not exceeding five years.

**Article 12**  (Repermission)

(1) If a person who holds a permission on a comprehensive cable television broadcasting station desires to operate it even after the validity term of the permission expires, he shall obtain a repermission of the Minister of Public Information under the conditions as prescribed by the Presidential Decree.

(2) When the Minister of Public Information desires to grant a repermission as referred to in Paragraph (1), he shall examine the following matters in addition to those as prescribed in subparagraphs of Article 7 (2):

  1. Whether or not the conditions of permission are fulfilled faithfully without violating this Act; and

  2. Whether or not the furnishing of service by the comprehensive cable television broadcasting station accepts reasonably the intention of residents in the area concerned.

(3) If it is deemed unreasonable as a result of the examination as referred to in Paragraph (2) to grant a repermission, the Minister of Public Information shall hear the opinion of the city/province governor on matters as referred to in Subparagraph 2 of Paragraph (2).

(4) The Minister of Public Information shall, upon granting a repermission under Paragraph (1), notify it to the head of the administrative agency and city/province governor concerned.

**Article 13**  (Permission on Program Supply Business)

(1) Any person who desires to operate a program supply business shall obtain the permission of the Minister of Public Information through the Comprehensive Cable Television Broadcasting Committee, under the conditions as prescribed by the Presidential Decree. This provision shall also apply in case where he desires to change any permitted matters.

(2) If the Minister of Public Information desires to grant a permission as referred to in Paragraph (1), he shall examine the following matters:

  1. Whether or not the object and contents of the program supply business are contrary to laws and regulations; and

  2. Whether or not the capability to make any broadcasting program more than the rate specified under Article 15 (2) is provided.

(3) In examining matters as referred to in subparagraphs of Paragraph (2), the Minister of Public Information shall hear the opinion of the Comprehensive Cable Television Broadcasting Committee.

(4) In granting the permission as referred to in Paragraph (1), if it is deemed necessary in particular for a harmonious supply of the broadcasting programs, the Minister of Public Information may not apply the provisions of Subparagraph 2 of Paragraph (2)

to those as prescribed by the Presidential Decree, such as government-invested institutions, etc.

**Article 14** (Designation of Broadcasting Program Supply Fields) In granting the permission as prescribed in Article 13, the Minister of Public Information may designate the supply fields of the broadcasting programs so that the specialty and diversity of the supply of broadcasting programs are realized without overemphasizing any specialized field.

**Article 15** (Supply, etc. of Broadcasting Programs)

(1) Any person who has obtained the permission on the program supply business under Article 13 (hereinafter referred to as "program supplier") shall supply a good quality of broadcasting programs to the comprehensive cable television broadcasting stations at a fair and reasonable market price and shall not refuse it without any justifiable reason.

(2) Any program supplier shall make the broadcasting programs more than the specified rate under the conditions as prescribed by the Presidential Decree, except in case of a person who is deemed by the Minister of Public Information, not to be required to provide any capability of producing the broadcasting programs under Article 13 (4).

**Article 16** (Import, etc. of Foreign Broadcasting Programs)

(1) If a program supplier desires to import any broadcasting programs of a foreign country or to relay any broadcast of a foreign country (including the case of relaying reedited one; hereinafter the same shall apply), he shall obtain the approval of the Minister of Public Information under the conditions as prescribed by the Presidential Decree.

(2) If a program supplier desires to produce jointly a broadcasting program with a foreign programmer, he shall obtain the approval of the Minister of Public Information under the conditions as prescribed by the Presidential Decree.

**Article 17** (Designation of Transmission Network Businessman)

(1) Any person who desires to operate a transmission network business shall obtain the permission of the Minister of Communications.

(2) The Minister of Communications shall, upon making a designation as referred to in Paragraph (1), notify it to the Minister of Public Information.

**Article 18** (Installation of Transmission Line Facilities) Any person designated under Article 17 (hereinafter referred to as "transmission network businessman") shall install a transmission line facilities in the broadcasting zone of a comprehensive cable television broadcasting station permitted under Article 7 so as to be used by such broadcasting station.

**Article 19** (Installation, etc. of Facilities by Transmission Network Businessman)

(1) Any transmission network businessman shall, upon receiving a request for installing a transmission line facilities from a comprehensive cable television broadcasting station, install it not later than the time limit as determined by the Presidential Decree and obtain the confirmation of the Minister of Communications on whether such facilities are conformed to the technical standards as prescribed in Article 25 of the Basic Telecommunication Act. This provision shall also apply in case where he changes the installed transmission line facilities.

(2) If a transmission network businessman is unable to install the transmission line facilities up to the time limit as referred to in Paragraph (1) due to any *force majeure*, such as natural disaster, terrestrial upheaval, etc., he may request the Minister of Communications an extension of the time limit for installing the facilities under the conditions as prescribed by the Presidential Decree.

(3) The Minister of Communications shall notify the result of the confirmation as referred to in Paragraph (1) to the Minister of Public Information.

**Article 20**   (Use of Transmission Line Facilities)

(1) The comprehensive cable television broadcasting station shall use the transmission line facilities installed by the transmission network businessman.

(2) The transmission network businessman shall prepare an agreement concerning the charge for use of the transmission line facilities and other conditions of use (hereinafter referred to as "agreement on use") under the conditions as prescribed by the Presidential Decree to obtain the approval of the Minister of Communications. This provision shall also apply in case where he desires to modify it.

(3) If the Minister of Communications desires to grant an approval under Paragraph (2), he shall examine whether it is conformed to the following criteria:

   1. The charge for use should be proper;

   2. Matters concerning the responsibility of the transmission network businessman and the transmission line users should be impartial and clear; and

   3. Specified persons should not be discriminated unreasonably.

(4) In case where the Minister of Communications desires to approve the agreement on use or any modification thereof under Paragraph (2), he shall consult in advance with the Minister of Public Information on matters concerning the charge for use of the transmission line facilities.

**Article 21**   (Cancellation, etc. of Permission)

(1) If a comprehensive cable television broadcasting station falls under any of the following subparagraphs, the Minister of Public Information may cancel the permission or order to suspend the whole or part of affairs thereof with a period not exceeding three months fixed:

   1. Where it has obtained a permission, permission on modification or repermission by a deceitful or other unlawful way under Article 7 (1), 10 (1) or 12 (1);

   2. Where it violates the prohibition of a concurrent operation as prescribed in Article 4 (1) to (4);

   3. Where a large-scale enterprise as prescribed in Article 4 (5) to (7), its interrelated ones, etc. operate the comprehensive cable television broadcasting station;

   4. Where it receives any contribution of property in contravention of the provisions of Article 6;

   5. Where it fails to undergo an inspection on completion of the comprehensive cable television broadcasting station facilities by the time limit as prescribed in Article 9 (1) (in case where it has the time limit extended under Article 9 (2), the time limit so extended);

   6. Where it gives an advertising broadcast in contravention of the provisions of Article 26 (1), (2) or (4);

   7. Where it violates the order of correction as prescribed in Article 47;

   8. Where it violates the order to improve facilities under Article 48 (1); and

   9. Where it fails to give the comprehensive cable television broadcast for more than the hours as determined by the Presidential Decree.

(2) If a program supplier falls under any of the following subparagraphs, the Minister of Public Information may cancel the permission or order to suspend the whole or part of the affairs with a period not exceeding three months fixed:

1. Where he has obtained the permission as prescribed in Article 13 (1) by a deceitful or other unlawful way;
2. Where he violates the prohibition of a concurrent operation as prescribed in Article 4 (1);
3. Where he has any property contributed in contravention of the provisions of Article 6;
4. Where he supplies the broadcasting programs in any field other than the supply fields designated under Article 14;
5. Where he refuses to supply any broadcasting program without any justifiable reason in contravention of the provisions of Article 15 (1);
6. Where he imports any foreign broadcasting program, relays any broadcast of a foreign country, or produces jointly any broadcasting program with a foreign programmer without obtaining the approval as prescribed in Article 16;
7. Where he violates any order of correction as prescribed in Article 47; and
8. Where he has no actual result of supply of the broadcasting programs for a period as determined by the Presidential Decree.

(3) If a transmission network businessman falls under any of the following subparagraphs, the Minister of Communications may cancel the designation or order to suspend the whole or part of the business with a period not exceeding three months fixed:

1. Where he is designated under Article 17 (1) by a deceitful or other unlawful way;
2. Where he fails to obtain the confirmation by the time limit as prescribed in Article 19 (1) (in case where the time limit is extended under Article 19 (2), by the extended time limit); and
3. Where he violates the order to improve facilities under Article 48 (1).

(4) If the Minister of Public Information desires to take the disposition as referred to in Paragraph (1), he shall hear the opinion of the city/province governor, and, as referred to in Paragraph (2), the opinion of the Comprehensive Cable Television Broadcasting Committee, respectively.

(5) If the Minister of Communications has canceled a designation under Paragraph (3), he shall notify it to the Minister of Public Information.

(6) In case where a comprehensive cable television broadcasting businessman falls under any of subparagraphs of Paragraphs (1) to (3) and should have been subject to a disposition of business suspension, but if such suspension of business might give a great inconvenience to receivers of the comprehensive cable television broadcast or be detrimental to the public interest, the Minister of Public Information or Communications may impose on him a penalty not exceeding twenty million Won in lieu of such business suspension.

(7) The categories of offenses for which the penalty as referred to in Paragraph (6) is imposed, the amount of penalty, and other necessary matters shall be determined by the Presidential Decree.

(8) If a person liable for payment of the penalty as referred to in Paragraph (6) fails to pay it by the time limit for payment, the Minister of Public Information or Communications shall collect it according to the example of a disposition of the national taxes in arrears.

## CHAPTER III. OPERATION OF COMPREHENSIVE
## CABLE TELEVISION BROADCAST

**Article 22** (Constitution and Operation of Channels)

(1) The channel of a comprehensive cable television broadcasting station shall be constituted and operated so as to embody the diversity of broadcasting fields and not to be overemphasized on specified field.

(2) The comprehensive cable television broadcasting station shall reserve any channel to be used for any public purpose by the State under the conditions as prescribed by the Presidential Decree.

(3) The comprehensive cable television broadcasting station may operate a regional channel to transmit any regional information, information on broadcasting programs, official announcement, etc. which are made by itself under the conditions as prescribed by the Presidential Decree.

(4) No channel of the comprehensive cable television broadcasting station may be lent to, or allowed to be used by, another person onerously or gratuitously.

**Article 23** (Freedom of and Responsibility for Programming)

(1) No person may regulate or interfere in the programming of a comprehensive cable television broadcast without complying with the conditions as prescribed by this Act.

(2) The head of a comprehensive cable television broadcasting station shall designate persons responsible for the programming and advertisement and publish their names once or more times each day in the broadcasting hours, and if they are unable to perform their duties, he shall immediately designate those who act for them.

**Article 24** (Criteria for Programming) In making broadcasting programs, the head of a comprehensive cable television broadcasting station shall make them conformed to the following criteria:

1. To be conformed to the criteria for deliberation as prescribed in Article 41;
2. Not to distort the fact; and
3. Not to violate the provisions of this Act.

**Article 25** (Programming of Foreign Broadcast) The radio of broadcasting programs imported from foreign countries to the whole broadcasting programs shall not exceed that as determined by the Presidential Decree.

**Article 26** (Advertising Broadcast)

(1) The advertising broadcast shall be distinguished clearly from a broadcasting program so as not to be confused with the later.

(2) The time, frequency, etc. of the advertising broadcast shall be determined by the Presidential Decree to the extent that it does not impede in the programming and operation of the comprehensive cable television broadcast.

(3) In case of a channel exclusively giving the advertising broadcast for the features of the comprehensive cable television broadcast, the provisions of Paragraphs (1) and (2) shall not be applicable.

(4) The comprehensive cable television broadcasting station shall broadcast noncommercial advertisements for public interests which are produced for the purpose of promoting the public interest at the rate more than that as determined by the Presidential Decree.

**Article 27** (Simultaneous Retransmission of Cable Televisionless Broadcast)

(1) The comprehensive cable television broadcasting station shall retransmit simultaneously any broadcast (excluding the radio broadcast) given by the cable televisionless

broadcasting station as designated by the Presidential Decree except in case where the broadcasting zone of the comprehensive cable television broadcasting station is not included in that of the cable televisionless broadcasting station, in which the broadcast is to be retransmitted simultaneously.

(2) In the case of a simultaneous retransmission as referred to in Paragraph (1), the provisions of Article 69 of the Copyright Act concerning the right to simultaneous relay broadcast, which the cable televisionless broadcasting station has, shall not be applicable.

**Article 28** (Liability for Furnishing Service and Approval on Agreement)

(1) No comprehensive cable television broadcasting station shall refuse to furnish services of the comprehensive cable television broadcast in the comprehensive cable television broadcasting zone under its control without any justifiable reason.

(2) The comprehensive cable television broadcasting station shall prepare an agreement relating to the fee and other services under the conditions as prescribed by the Ordinance of the Prime Minister to obtain the approval of the Minister of Public Information. This provision shall also apply in case where it desires to modify it.

(3) If the Minister of Public information desires to grant an approval as referred to in Paragraph (2), he shall examine whether or not the following criteria are met:

    1. The fee shall be proper;

    2. Matters concerning the responsibility of both the comprehensive cable television broadcasting station and receiving persons shall be impartial and clear; and

    3. Unreasonable discrimination shall not be made against a specified person.

(4) If the Minister of Public Information desires to approve the agreement or modified one as referred to in Paragraph (2), he shall hear the opinion of the Comprehensive Cable Television Broadcasting Committee.

**Article 29** (Report on Activities) The comprehensive cable television broadcasting station shall report to the Minister of Public Information the following matters concerning services to be furnished through the comprehensive cable television broadcast not later than two months before the station begins its operation under the conditions as prescribed by the Presidential Decree and notify it to the Comprehensive Cable television Broadcasting Committee. This provision shall also apply in case where it desires to modify and of such matters:

    1. Kinds and conditions of services to be furnished (including the simultaneous retransmission service);

    2. Particulars of the constitution and operation of channels;

    3. Criteria for programming, broadcasting hours and programs;

    4. Estimated number of persons having entered into a receiving contract;

    5. Estimate of earnings and expenses by services;

    6. Facilities and frequency to be used;

    7. Predetermined date at which the comprehensive cable television broadcasting station starts its service; and

    8. Other matters as prescribed by the Ordinance of the Prime Minister.

**Article 30** (Recording and Keeping Contents of Broadcast)

(1) The comprehensive cable television broadcasting station shall keep a broadcasting diary to record the broadcast matters and submit periodically the result of broadcasting to the Minister of Public Information and the Comprehensive Cable Television

Broadcasting Committee, respectively, under the conditions as prescribed by the Presidential Decree.

(2) The comprehensive cable television broadcasting station shall keep the original or copy of the broadcasting programs produced by itself under Article 22 (3) for one month after broadcasting them.

(3) The program supplier shall keep the original or copy of the broadcasting programs supplied to the comprehensive cable television broadcasting stations for one month after broadcasting them.

**Article 31**   (Report on Discontinuance and Suspension of Business)

(1) If a comprehensive cable television broadcasting station desires to discontinue its business, it shall report it without delay to the Minister of Public Information under the conditions as prescribed by the Presidential Decree.

(2) Any comprehensive cable television broadcasting station may discontinue its business only in case where there is any uncontrollable reason, such as natural disaster, terrestrial upheaval, etc. In this case, the comprehensive cable television broadcasting station shall report it without delay to the Minister of Public Information under the conditions as prescribed by the Presidential Decree.

**Article 32**   (Establishment of Branch Office, etc.)

(1) If a comprehensive cable television broadcasting station or a program supplier desires to establish a branch office or station in a foreign country, he shall obtain the approval of the Minister of Public Information under the conditions as prescribed by the Presidential Decree. This provision shall also apply in case where he desires to change it.

(2) If a foreign cable television broadcasting businessman desires to establish a branch office or station in Korea, he shall obtain the permission of the Minister of Public Information under the conditions as prescribed by the Presidential Decree. This provision shall also apply in case where he desires to change it.

(3) If a branch office or station permitted under Paragraph (2) falls under any of the following subparagraphs, the Minister of Public Information may cancel the permission:

1. Where it obtains the permission by a deceitful or other unlawful manner;
2. Where it violates the conditions of permission; and
3. Where the cable television broadcasting businessman as referred to in Paragraph (2) puts the Constitution of the Republic of Korea into disorder or damages the prestige thereof.

**Article 33**   (Technical Standards of Comprehensive Cable Television Broadcasting Station Facilities) Matters concerning the establishment and maintenance of comprehensive cable television broadcasting station facilities and the boundary lines, etc. of transmission line facilities shall be conformed to the technical standards as determined by the Ordinance of the Ministry of Communications (hereinafter referred to as "technical standards").

## CHAPTER IV. COMPREHENSIVE CABLE
## TELEVISION BROADCASTING COMMITTEE

**Article 34**   (Establishment of Comprehensive Cable Television Broadcasting Committee)

(1) In order to promote the publicness and morality of the comprehensive cable television broadcast and the qualitative improvement of the broadcasting contents, the Compre-

hensive Cable television Broadcast Committee (hereinafter referred to as "Committee") shall be established.

(2) The Committee shall be composed of seven to eleven members including a chairman and a deputy chairman.

(3) The chairman and the deputy chairman shall be elected from among members.

(4) The Committee may appoint three or less permanent members including the chairman.

(5) The members shall be appointed by the Minister of Public Information from among those as prescribed by the Presidential Decree, such as experts in broadcasting field, those qualified for lawyer, etc.

(6) The chairman shall represent the committee and take charge of the general affairs thereof, and if he is absent by any accident, the deputy chairman shall act for him.

(7) Manners necessary for the composition, operation, etc. of the committee shall be prescribed by the Presidential Decree.

**Article 35** (Term of Member)

(1) The term of the members including the chairman and the deputy chairman shall be three years.

(2) If any vacancy occurs in members, it shall be filled under Article 34, and the term of the person appointed to fill the vacancy shall be the remaining period of his predecessor.

**Article 36** (Disqualification for Member) No person who falls under any of the following subparagraphs may be a member of the Committee:

1. Public officials (excluding educational public officials and judicial officer);
2. Members of political parties as prescribed by the Political Party Act;
3. Those who are engaged in the comprehensive cable television broadcasting business; and
4. Those who fall under any of subparagraphs of Article 33 of the National Civil Service Act.

**Article 37** (Independence in Performance of Duties and Guarantee of Status of Member)

(1) No member shall be subject to any external direction or interference in the course of carrying out his duties during his tenure of office.

(2) No member shall be released from his office against his intention, except in any of the following cases:

1. Where he is sentenced to a punishment heavier than the imprisonment without hard labor; and
2. Where he is unable to carry out his duties due to a mental or physical disability for a long time.

**Article 38** (Function of Committee)

(1) The committee shall deliberate and decide the following manners:

1. Manners concerning the publicness and morality of the contents of the comprehensive cable television broadcast;
2. Manners concerning the presentation of opinion by the committee under Articles 13 (3), 21 (4) and 28 (4);
3. Matters concerning the survey on complaints and suggestions of those who receive the broadcast; and
4. Matters concerning the enactment, amendment and repeal of the Committee Regulations.

(2) In deliberating and deciding matters as referred to in subparagraphs of Paragraph (1), the Committee may deliberate and decide whether or not any of the following broadcasting materials are broadcast before broadcasting them:
  1. Dramatic movies and cartoon films (including video products) for broadcasting;
  2. Foreign broadcasting programs (excluding those as to relay and report on athletic sports, etc.); and
  3. Advertising broadcast.

(3) If the contents of a comprehensive cable television broadcast is contrary to the criteria for deliberation as prescribed in Article 41, the Committee may order the comprehensive cable television broadcasting station or program supplier a warning, explanation, apology, rectification, or suspension of the advertising broadcast or broadcasting program (hereinafter referred to as "measure for correction").

(4) If the Committee desires to order any measure for correction, it shall give in advance the party or his representative an opportunity to state his opinion, except in case where the party or his representative fails to comply with it without any justifiable reason, or it is impossible to give him an opportunity to state his opinion due to the obscurity of his address, etc.

(5) Any comprehensive cable television broadcasting station or program supplier shall, upon receiving the order as referred to in Paragraph (3), comply with the order within fourteen days and report the result to the Committee.

(6) The Committee shall, upon issuing the order as referred to in Paragraph (3) or receiving the report as referred to in Paragraph (5), notify it without delay to the Minister of Public Information.

**Article 39** (Quorum Required for Decision) The proceedings of the Committee shall be decided with the attendance of more than two-thirds of all members and by a concurrent vote of a majority of members present.

**Article 40** (Establishment of Deliberative Working Organ)

(1) In order to assist affairs concerning the deliberation as prescribed in Subparagraph 1 of Paragraph (1) and Paragraph (2) of Article 38, the committee may appoint a deliberative working organ.

(2) Manners necessary for the organization and operation of the deliberative working organ shall be determined by the Committee Regulations.

**Article 41** (Criteria for Deliberation) In order to deliberate manners as referred to in Subparagraph 1 of Article 38 (1), the committee shall enact and promulgate by the Committee Regulations the criteria for deliberation including the following matters:
  1. Matters concerning the maintenance of the fundamental democratic order and the respect of human rights in the Constitution;
  2. Manners concerning the sound home life and the proper guidance of children and youths;
  3. Matters concerning the elimination of lewdness, decadence, and violence, and the encouragement of public morality and social ethics;
  4. Matters concerning the prevention of international friendship from damaging;
  5. Manners concerning the cultivation of the national identity;
  6. Manners concerning the creative development of the national culture;
  7. Manners concerning the impartiality of news and comments; and
  8. Matters concerning the measure for correction as prescribed in Article 38.

**Article 42** (Secretariat)

(1) The Committee shall set up a secretariat to assist affairs of the Committee.

(2) A secretary-general and necessary personnel shall be assigned to the secretariat, and they shall be appointed by the chairman. In this case, the appointment of the secretary-general shall be approved by the Committee.

(3) The organization and operation of the secretariat, the remuneration of employees of the secretariat, and other necessary matters shall be determined by the Committee Regulations.

**Article 43**  (Committee Regulations) The chairman may enact the regulations relating to the operation of the committee through a resolution of the Committee.

**Article 44**  (State Subsidy) The State may grant the State subsidy to the Committee in the limit of the budget.

## CHAPTER V. REMEDY AGAINST INFRINGEMENT

**Article 45**  (Claim for Correction Report)

(1) Any person who has been aggrieved by a factual allegation published through a comprehensive cable television broadcast (hereinafter referred to as "aggrieved person") may make in writing a claim for broadcasting a correction report to the head of the comprehensive cable television broadcasting station or person responsible for the programming within thirty days after such publication is made.

(2) The written claim for correction report shall include the signature, seal and address of the aggrieved person or his representative, and the contents of the report against which the objection is made, and the written correction report requesting the broadcast shall be appended thereto.

(3) The head of the comprehensive cable television broadcasting station or the person responsible for the programming shall, upon receiving a request for correction report, broadcast it gratis without delay after consulting with the aggrieved person or his representative about the contents, etc. of such correction report: Provided that if the aggrieved person has no rightful interest in the exercise of the claim for correction report, or the contents of the requested correction report is obviously contrary to the fact, or the claim aims only at a commercial advertisement, the broadcast thereof may be refused.

(4) The correction report shall be limited to the factual statement and any explanation required to communicate it distinctly and may not include any unlawful contents.

(5) The number of words in the written correction report may not exceed that of the published contents against which the objection is made.

(6) Any correction report made by the head of the comprehensive cable television broadcasting station or the person responsible for the programming shall be made by the same channel in the same time zone and by any manner to produce the same effect as the publication thereof is made.

(7) If a program supplier is also connected with the claim for a correction report as referred to in Paragraph (1), the program supplier shall discharge the liability for making the correction report in such manner as referred to in Paragraph (6).

(8) The provisions of Paragraphs (1) to (7) shall not be applicable in case of any factual broadcast on any public meeting of the State, local government or public organization, and any public trial procedure of the court.

(9) With respect to matters concerning the arbitration of disputes and the proceeding thereof, caused by a claim for correction report on a comprehensive cable television broadcast, and those concerning the decision on a case of claim for correction report,

and those concerning the claim for further report, the provisions of Articles 17 to 20 of the Act Relating to Registration, etc. of Periodicals shall be applicable.

## CHAPTER VI. SUPPLEMENTARY PROVISIONS

**Article 46**  (Report and Inspection)

(1) If it is deemed necessary for the qualitative improvement of the comprehensive cable television broadcast and the establishment of the sound order, the Minister of Public Information may have any comprehensive cable television broadcasting businessman make a necessary report, or a public official concerned enter any office, business place, etc. to inspect relevant documents, etc., under the conditions as prescribed by the Presidential Decree.

(2) The Minister of Communications may have any comprehensive cable television broadcasting station and transmission network businessman make any necessary report on the comprehensive cable television broadcasting facilities, or any public official concerned enter such facilities, business place, etc. to inspect such facilities, equipment, etc., under the conditions as prescribed by the Presidential Decree.

(3) Any public official who conducts the inspection under Paragraphs (1) and (2) shall carry with him a certificate indicating his competence and show it to interested persons.

**Article 47**  (Order of Correction) If a comprehensive cable television broadcasting businessman falls under any of the following subparagraphs, the Minister of Public Information may order him to correct it:

1. Where it is deemed that he violates this Act or any permitted condition; and
2. Where it is deemed that manners concerning services of the comprehensive cable television broadcast infringe unreasonably the interest of receiving persons.

**Article 48**  (Order to Improve Facilities)

(1) If it is found as a result of the inspection as prescribed in Article 46 (2) that the comprehensive cable television broadcasting facilities are unconformed to the technical standards as prescribed in Article 33 or those as prescribed in Article 25 of the Basic Telecommunication Act, the Minister of Communications may order any repair, improvement or moving of such facilities or other necessary measures (hereinafter referred to as "facilities improvement order").

(2) When the Minister of Communications has issued the facilities improvement order under Paragraph (1), he shall notify it without delay to the Minister of Public Information.

**Article 49**  (Comprehensive Cable Television Broadcasting Association)

(1) In order to promote a balanced development of the comprehensive cable television broadcasting business and drive forward any survey and research on the comprehensive cable television broadcast and the development of manpower and technology, the comprehensive cable television broadcasting businessmen shall establish the Comprehensive Cable Television Broadcasting Association (hereinafter referred to as "Association").

(2) The Association shall be a juristic person.

(3) Any comprehensive cable television broadcasting businessman shall be a member of the Association.

(4) Expenses needed for activities of the Association shall be covered with the membership fee, business proceeds, etc.

(5) Manners necessary for the establishment, operation, etc. of the Association shall be determined by the Presidential Decree.

(6) Except as provided by this Act, the provisions of the Civil Code concerning the incorporated body shall be applicable to the Association.

**Article 50** (Hearing) In the following cases, the Minister of Public Information or Communications shall give in advance the person who is subject to the disposition or his representative an opportunity to state his opinion under the conditions as prescribed by the Presidential Decree, except in case where the person or his representative fails to comply with it without any justifiable reason, or it is impossible to give him an opportunity to state his opinion due to an obscurity of his address, etc.:

1. Where a repermission as prescribed in Article 12 is refused;
2. Where the permission or designation as prescribed in Article 21 is canceled, or a disposition of business suspension or imposition of penalty is taken; and
3. Where the permission as prescribed in Article 32 (3) is canceled.

**Article 51** (Fee) Any person who applies for a permission, permission on change, repermission or designation under this Act or who desires to undergo an inspection of the completion for comprehensive cable television broadcasting facilities shall pay the fee under the conditions as prescribed by the Ordinance of the Prime Minister. In this case, he shall consult with the Minister of Communications on the designation application fee and the completion inspection fee of comprehensive cable television broadcasting facilities.

**Article 52** (Delegation and Entrustment of Authority) The Minister of Communications may delegate the authority to conduct the inspection of completion as prescribed in Article 9 (1) to the director of the communication Office, or entrust it to the Radio Station Management and Business Association as prescribed by the Radio Waves Control Act under the conditions as prescribed by the Presidential Decree.

## CHAPTER VII. PENAL PROVISIONS

**Article 53** (Penal Provisions) Any person who falls under any of the following subparagraphs shall be punished by imprisonment for not more than three years or a fine not exceeding twenty million Won:

1. Person who has obtained the permission, repermission or designation as prescribed in Article 7 (1), 12 (1), 13 (1) or 17 (1) by any deceitful or other unlawful manner and has operated the comprehensive cable television broadcasting business; and
2. Person who has operated the comprehensive cable television broadcasting business without obtaining the permission, repermission or designation as prescribed in Article 7 (1), 12 (1), 13 (1) or 17 (1).

**Article 54** (Penal Provisions) Any person who falls under any of the following subparagraphs shall be punished by imprisonment for not more than one year or a fine not exceeding ten million Won:

1. Person who violates the prohibition of concurrent operation of businesses as prescribed in Article 4 (1) to (4);
2. Person who operates a comprehensive cable television broadcasting station or owns the stocks or quotas thereof, in contravention of the provisions of Article 4 (5) or (7);
3. Person who receives any contribution of property in contravention of the provisions of Article 6;

4. Person who obtains a permission on change as prescribed in Article 10 (1) by any deceitful or other unlawful manner and operates a comprehensive cable television broadcasting station;
5. Person who operates a comprehensive cable television broadcasting station without obtaining the permission on change as prescribed in Article 10 (1);
6. Person who imports any foreign broadcasting program, relays any foreign broadcast, or produces jointly a broadcasting program with a foreign programmer without obtaining the approval as prescribed in Article 16;
7. Person who regulates or interferes with the programming of a comprehensive cable television broadcast as prescribed in Article 23 (1);
8. Person who sets up a branch office or station in Korea without the permission or permission on change as prescribed in Article 32 (2);
9. Person who violates the order as prescribed in Article 38 (3); and
10. Person who produces and distributes any obscene materials which might be remarkably detrimental to the public order and good morals in contravention of the criteria for deliberation as prescribed in Article 41.

**Article 55** (Joint Penal Provisions) If a representative of a juristic person, or an agent, serviceman or employee of a juristic person or an individual commits an offense as prescribed in Article 53 or 54 in connection with affairs of the juristic person or individual, the fine as prescribed in the respective Article shall be imposed on such juristic person or individual, in addition to the punishment of the offender.

**Article 56** (Fine for Negligence)

(1) Any person who falls under any of the following subparagraphs shall be punished by a fine for negligence not exceeding five million Won:

1. Person who fails to notify publicly or submit the property situation of a comprehensive cable television broadcasting station as prescribed in Article 4 (9);
2. Person who fails to make a report as prescribed in Article 9 (3), 10 (1) (proviso), 29, or 31;
3. Person who refuses to supply any broadcasting program without any justifiable reason in contravention of the provisions of Article 15 (1);
4. Person who lends to another person, or has another person use, any channel of a comprehensive cable television broadcasting station in contravention of the provisions of Article 22 (4);
5. Person who draws up broadcasting programs imported from foreign countries in excess of the programming rate as prescribed in Article 25;
6. Person who fails to record the broadcasting diary as prescribed in Article 30 (1) or makes a false record;
7. Person who fails to keep the original or copy of a broadcasting program as prescribed in Article 30 (2) or (3);
8. Person who sets up any branch office or station in any foreign country without obtaining the approval or approval on change as prescribed in Article 32 (1); and
9. Person who fails to make a report as prescribed in Article 46, or makes a false report or who refuses, interferes with, or evades the inspection.

(2) The fine for negligence as referred to in Paragraph (1) shall be imposed and collected by the Minister of Public Information or Communications (hereinafter referred to as "imposing authority") under the conditions as prescribed by the Presidential Decree.

(3) Any person who is dissatisfied with the disposition of the fine for negligence as referred to in Paragraph (2) may make an objection against the imposing authority within thirty days after he is informed of such disposition.

(4) If a person who is subject to a disposition of the fine for negligence under Paragraph (2) makes an objection under Paragraph (3), the imposing authority shall notify it without delay to the competent court, which shall, upon receiving the notification, bring the case of fine for negligence to a trial under the Non-Contentious Case Procedure Act.

(5) If no objection is made, and no fine for negligence is paid, in the period as referred to in Paragraph (3), it shall be collected according to the example of the disposition of the national taxes in arrears.

## ADDENDA

(1) (Enforcement Date) This Act shall enter into force as of July 1, 1992: Provided that the provisions of Chapter IV (Articles 34 to 44) shall enter into force as of the date of its promulgation.

(2) (Special Case Concerning Beginning of Comprehensive Cable Television Broadcast) Any comprehensive cable television broadcasting station permitted under Article 7 may start any comprehensive cable television broadcast (including any test broadcast) after January 1, 1993, except in case of a test broadcast in operation at the time this Act is promulgated.

(3) Omitted.

## ADDENDUM (Law No. 4737, Jan. 7, 1994)

This Act shall enter into force as of March 1994.

# APPENDIX   G

# Copyright Act

(Wholly Amended by Law No. 3916, Dec. 31, 1986)
(Amended by Law No. 4183, Dec. 30, 1989)
(Amended by Law No. 4268, Dec. 27, 1990)
(Amended by Law No. 4352, Mar. 8, 1991)
(Amended by Law No. 4541, Mar. 6, 1993)
(Amended by Law No. 4717, Jan. 7, 1994)
(Amended by Law No. 4746, Mar. 24, 1994)

## CHAPTER I. GENERAL PROVISIONS

**Article 1**  (Purpose) The purpose of this Act is to contribute to the improvement and development of culture by protecting the right of authors and the rights neighboring thereto, and by promoting fair use of the copyrighted works.

**Article 2**  (Definition) The definition of terms used in this Act shall be as follows:

1. "Works" means original literary, scientific or artistic works;
2. "Authors" means those who have created works;
3. "Public performance" means to present a work to the general public by staging, musical performance, singing, reciting, screening or by other means, and it shall include to present a work to the general public by playing recordings or videotapes of a public performance, broadcasting or stage performance;
4. "Stage performance" means to express a work by acting, dancing, musical performance, singing, reciting or other artistic way, and it shall include to express something other than a work, done in a similar way;
5. "Stage performers" means those who conduct a stage performance and those who direct, produce or supervise a stage performance;
6. "Phonograph record" means a tangible medium in which sound is fixed (excluding medium in which sound is fixed together with some visual images);
7. "Phonograph record maker" means a person who has initially fixed sound in phonograph records;
8. "Broadcasting" means to transmit voices, sounds or images, etc. by radio or wire communication methods for the purpose of enabling the general public to receive it (excluding to amplify or transmit merely sounds within the same unintercepted area);
9. "Broadcaster" means a person who carries on broadcasts as industry;

10. "Cinematographic works" means creative works in which a series of images (regardless of whether or not accompanied by sound) are collected and which can be seen or seen and heard by playing on mechanical or electronic devices;

11. "Cinematographic producer" means a person who controls and is responsible for the whole production of cinematographic works;

12. "Computer program" means that which is expressed in the forms of a series of instructions and commands used directly or indirectly in a device having the information processing capacity, such as computers, in order to obtain specific results;

13. "Joint work" means a work created jointly by two or more persons in which the contribution of each person may not be separately exploited;

14. "Reproduction" means to reproduce works into tangible mediums of expression by printing, photographing, copying, sound recording, videotaping or by any other means; in the case of architectural work, it means to execute a construction work in accordance with drawings or models for construction thereof; and in the case of play, musical score or other similar works, it includes the recording and videotaping of a public performance, broadcast or stage performance of the works;

15. "Distribution" means to transfer or lend the original or reproductions of a work to the general public with or without compensation therefor;

16. "Publication" means to reproduce and distribute a work for the demand of the general public; and

17. "Release" means to present a work to the general public through public performance, broadcasting, display or by any other means, and to publish a work.

**Article 3**   (Foreigners' Works)

(1) Foreigners' works shall be protected under treaties which the Republic of Korea has entered into or signed: Provided that foreigners' works published prior to the effective date of the treaty concerned are not protected.

(2) Notwithstanding the provisions of Paragraph (1), works of a foreigner who resides at all times in the Republic of Korea (including foreign juristic persons having the principal office in the Republic of Korea; hereinafter the same shall apply) and foreigners' works which are first published in the Republic of Korea (including works published in the Republic of Korea within thirty days after publication in a foreign country) shall be protected under this Act.

(3) Even when a foreigner's works is to be protected under Paragraphs (1) and (2), if the foreign country concerned does not protect works of the nationals of the Republic of Korea, the protection under treaties and this Act may be restricted correspondingly.

## CHAPTER II. RIGHTS OF AUTHOR

### Section 1. Works

**Article 4**  (Examples of Works)

(1) The following shall be the examples of work referred to in this Act:

1. Novels, poems, thesis, lectures, recitations, plays and other linguistic and literary works;

2. Musical works;

3. Theatrical works including dramas, ballet, dance, pantomimes, etc.;

    4. Art works including paintings, calligraphy, designs, sculptures, crafts, applied fine art works and other art works;

    5. Architectural works including buildings, architectural models and design drawings for architecture;

    6. Photographic works including those prepared by such means of photographs and other similar production methods;

    7. Cinematographic works;

    8. Maps, charts, design drawings, sketches, models and other diagrammatic works; and

    9. Computer program works.

(2) Matters necessary for the protection, etc. of computer program works under Subparagraph 9 of Paragraph (1) shall be provided in a special law.

**Article 5** (Derivative Works)

(1) Any creative work produced by translation, arrangement, changing, dramatization, cinematography, etc. of an original work (hereinafter referred to as "derivative work") shall be protected as an independent work. (Amended by Law No. 4717, Jan. 7, 1994)

(2) The protection of a derivative work shall not prejudice the rights of the author of the original work.

**Article 6** (Compilation Works)

(1) Any compilation which is of a creative nature in the selection or arrangement of subject matters (hereinafter referred to as "compilation work") shall be protected as an independent work.

(2) The protection of a compilation work shall not prejudice the rights of the author of the work which constitutes the compilation work.

**Article 7** (Works, etc. not protected) No work which falls under any of the following subparagraphs shall be protected under this Act:

    1. Laws and Regulations;

    2. Notices, public notifications, directions and other similar work of the State or local public organization;

    3. Judgments, decisions, decrees or rulings of courts, or resolutions, decisions, etc. made in the course of the administrative appeal procedure or other similar procedures;

    4. Compilations or translations of works as referred to in Subparagraphs 1 to 3, which are produced by the State or local public organization;

    5. Current news reports merely transmitting facts; and

    6. Speeches delivered at an open session of a court, the National Assembly or a local council.

## Section 2. Authors

**Article 8** (Presumption of Author, etc.)

(1) Any person who falls under any of the following subparagraphs shall be presumed to be an author:

    1. A person whose real name (hereinafter referred to as "real name") or well known stage or screen name, pseudonym, abbreviation, etc. (hereinafter referred to as "alias") is indicated as an author in a general way on the original or reproduction of a work; and

    2. A person whose real name or well-known alias indicated as an author in a public performance or broadcasting of a work.

(2) For a work on which the author under the subparagraphs of Paragraph (1) is not indicated, the person who is indicated as publisher or performer shall be presumed to have the copyright.

**Article 9**  (Author of Work in Organization's Name) Except as otherwise provided in the agreement or the service regulations, etc. the author of a work which is prepared on duty by a person working for a juristic person under the direction of a corporation, organization or other employer (hereinafter referred to as "juristic person, etc." in this Article) and which is published in the name of the juristic person, etc. (hereinafter referred to as "work in organization's name") shall be the juristic person, etc. unless otherwise provided by employment or independent agreement.

**Article 10**  (Copyrights)

(1) Authors shall have the rights prescribed in Articles 11 to 13 (hereinafter referred to as "author's personal rights") and the rights prescribed in Articles 16 to 21 (hereinafter referred to as "author's property rights").

(2) The copyright shall commence from the time of completing a work regardless of the fulfillment of any procedure or formality.

## Section 3. Author's Personal Rights

**Article 11**  (Right to Release)

(1) The author shall have the right to decide whether or not to release his work.

(2) If an author has transferred his property rights to his unpublished work under Article 41 or given his consent to the use under Article 42, he shall be presumed to have given the other party his consent to the release of the work.

(3) If an author has transferred the original of unpublished art, architectural or photographic work (hereinafter referred to as "art work, etc."), he shall be presumed to have given the other party his consent to its release in the normal way of display of the original.

(4) If a derivative or compilation work is released with the consent of the original author, the original work shall also be considered to have been released.

**Article 12**  (Right to indicate Name)

(1) The author shall have the right to indicate his real name or alias on the original or reproduction of his work, the same shall apply in case of releasing author's work.

(2) Any person who uses a work shall indicate the real name or alias of the author under the conditions as indicated by the latter unless he manifests otherwise.

**Article 13**  (Right to maintain Identity)

(1) The author shall have the right to maintain the identity of contents, form and title of his work.

(2) The author shall not make an objection to a modification falling under any of the following subparagraphs unless essential contents are changed:

1. In the case of a work being used under Article 23, a modification of expression within limits as deemed inevitable for the purpose of school education;
2. Expansion, remodelling and other forms of transformation of a building; and
3. Other modifications within limits as deemed inevitable in view of the nature of a work or the object or form of its use.

## Section 4. Nature, Exercise, etc. of Author's Personal Rights

**Article 14**  (Exclusiveness of Author's Personal Right)

(1) The author's personal right shall belong exclusively to the author himself.

(2) Any person who uses a work after the death of its author shall not do any act that might prejudice the author's personal right had he been alive, except in a case where it is deemed that, in view of the prevailing community standards and in consideration of the nature and extent of the act, such act does not defame the dignity of the author.

**Article 15** (Author's Personal Right of Joint Work)

(1) The author's personal right of a joint work may not be exercised without unanimous agreement of all the authors concerned. In this case, no coauthor may unreasonably refuse to make such agreement.

(2) Authors of a joint work may designate one of them who is to exercise the author's personal right as their representative.

(3) If any restriction is imposed on the power of a representative who exercises the author's personal right under Paragraph (2), such restriction shall not be effective against a *bona fide* third person.

**Section 5. Author's Property Rights**

**Article 16** (Right to Reproduce) The author shall have the right to reproduce his work.

**Article 17** (Right to Perform Publicly) The author shall have the right to perform his work publicly.

**Article 18** (Right to Broadcast) The author shall have the right to broadcast his work.

**Article 19** (Right to Display) The author shall have the right to display the originals or reproduction of art work, etc.

**Article 20** (Right to Distribute) The author shall have the right to distribute the original or reproduction of his work.

**Article 21** (Right to Produce Derivative Works, etc.) The author shall have the right to produce and use a derivative work the original of which is his work or a compilation work the constituent of which is his work.

**Section 6. Restrictions on Author's Property Rights**

**Article 22** (Reproduction in Judicial Proceedings, etc.) If it is necessary for the judicial proceedings or as internal material for legislative or administrative purposes, any work may be reproduced for such purposes unless it infringes unreasonably the interest of the author's property right owner in the light of the nature of the work and numbers and forms of the reproduction.

**Article 23** (Use for Purpose of School Education)

(1) The released works may be inserted in textbooks to the degree necessary for the educational purposes at schools of lower level than high schools or the equivalent thereto.

(2) Any educational institution established under a special law or the Education Act or operated by the State or local government may, if the released work is deemed necessary for educational purposes, broadcast or reproduce the releases work.

(3) Any person who desires to use a work under Paragraphs (1) and (2) shall pay to the author's property right owner the compensation as determined and announced officially by the Minister of Culture and Sports according to the criteria for compensation prescribed in Subparagraph I of Article 82 or shall deposit the same as provided by the Presidential Decree: Provided that in cases of broadcasting or reproduction conducted at the schools of the level lower than the high schools and the equivalent thereto under Paragraph (2), no compensation shall be paid. (Amended by Law No.

4183, Dec. 30, 1989; Law No. 4268, Dec. 27, 1990; Law No. 4541, Mar. 6, 1993; Law No. 4717, Jan. 7, 1994)

**Article 24** (Use for Current News Report) In a case of reporting current news through broadcasting, motion pictures, newspapers or other means, any work which is viewed or listened to in the course of such report may be reproduced, distributed, performed publicly or broadcast within the limits proper for such purposes.

**Article 25** (Quotation from Released Works) Released works may be quoted for report, criticism, education, research, etc. within the reasonable limit in conformity with fair practice.

**Article 26** (Nonprofit Public Performance and Broadcasting)

(1) If it is not for profit or for receiving any compensation in whatever form from an audience, spectators or a third person, any released work may be performed publicly or broadcast unless an ordinary remuneration is paid to the stage performer.

(2) If any compensation for a public performance is not charged on an audience or spectators, the phonograph records or cinematographic works for sale may be played for the general public, except in cases as prescribed by the Presidential Decree.

**Article 27** (Reproduction for Private Use) In a case where a released work is used individually and without commercial purposes or within the confines of a private residence or the equivalent thereto, the user may reproduce it.

**Article 28** (Reproduction in Libraries, etc.) In libraries which are prescribed by the Library Promotion Act and in the facilities in which books, documents, records and other materials are provided for the use of the general public and which are designated by the Presidential Decree (hereinafter referred to as "libraries, etc."), reproducing a work using materials in the custody of such libraries shall be allowed in the following cases; (Amended by Law No. 4352, Mar. 8, 1991)

1. Where only one partial reproduction of a released work is given to a user upon his request for research and study purposes;
2. Where it is necessary to the libraries, etc. for their own conservation of the materials; and
3. Where the reproduction of a work of scarce existence due to out-of-print or other similar reasons is done upon the request of other libraries, etc. and for the conservation purpose thereof.

**Article 29** (Reproduction for Examination Purposes) If it is required for an entrance examination to schools or for any other examination testing scholastic achievements or vocational skills, released works may be reproduced within the limits proper for such purposes: Provided that it is not for commercial purposes.

**Article 30** (Reproduction in Braille)

(1) Released works may be reproduced in braille for the blind.

(2) In facilities established for the promotion of the welfare of the blind and designated by the Presidential Decree, released works may be recorded in order to provide for use of the blind.

**Article 31** (Ephemeral Recording or Videotaping by Broadcasters)

(1) Broadcasters may record or videotape a work by their own means and for their own broadcasting purposes, except in a case where contrary to the intention of the person having the broadcasting right to the work.

(2) Recordings or videotapes made under Paragraph (1) may not be kept for a period exceeding one year from the date of recording or videotaping unless they are kept as materials for public records in a place as prescribed by the Presidential Decree.

**Article 32** (Display or Reproduction of Fine Art Works, etc.)

(1) The owner of the originals of fine art works, etc. or a person who has obtained the owner's consent may display the work in their original forms: Provided that if it is displayed at all times at a street, park, outer side of the wall of a building or other place open to the general public, the consent of the owner of its copyright shall be obtained.

(2) Fine art works, etc. displayed at all times at an open place as referred to in the proviso of Paragraph (1) may be reproduced in any way, except in the following cases:

　　1. Where a building is reproduced in another one;

　　2. Where a sculpture or painting is reproduced in another one;

　　3. Where the reproduction is made in order to display at all times at an open place, etc. under the proviso of Paragraph (1); and

　　4. Where the reproduction is made for commercial purposes.

(3) Any person who displays fine art works, etc. under Paragraph (1) or who desires to sell originals of fine art works, etc. may reproduce them in a pamphlet in the form of catalogue describing or introducing such works and distribute them.

(4) A portrait or a similar photographic work made by contract for hire may not be displayed or reproduced without the consent of the entrusting person.

**Article 33** (Use through Translation, etc.)

(1) In a case of using a work under Article 23, 26 or 27, the work may be used by translating, arranging or adapting it.

(2) In a case of using a work under Article 22, 24, 25, 29 or 30, the work may be used by translating it.

**Article 34** (Specification of Sources)

(1) Except as provided for in Articles 26 to 29 and 31, any person who uses a work under this Section shall specify its sources.

(2) The specification of sources shall be made in a reasonable method according to the situation in which a work is used, and in the case of a work on which the real name or alias of the author is indicated, such real name or alias must be specified.

**Article 35** (Relation with Author's Personal Right) Nothing in the Articles of this Section shall be construed to have an effect on the author's personal right.

### Section 7. Protection Period of Author's Property Right

**Article 36** (Principles of Protection Period)

(1) Except as provided otherwise in this Section. the author's property rights shall not be extinguished for the lifetime of the author and fifty years thereafter: Provided that the author's property rights in a work released after forty years and before fifty years after the author's death shall not be extinguished for ten years from the date of its release.

(2) The author's property rights of a joint work shall not be extinguished for fifty years after the death of the last surviving coauthor.

**Article 37** (Protection Period of Anonymous or Pseudonymous Work)

(1) The author's property right of a work anonymously done or indicated by an alias not well-known shall not be extinguished for fifty years from the date of its release.

(2) The provisions of Paragraph (1) shall not apply to any of the following cases:

    1. Where the real name or well-known alias of the author is revealed during the period as referred to in Paragraph (1); and

    2. Where the real name of the author is registered under Article 51 (1) during the period as referred to in Paragraph (1).

**Article 38** (Protection Period of Works in Organization's Name) The author's property rights of a work in the name of an organization shall not be extinguished for fifty years from the date of its release: Provided that if it is not released within ten years from the date of its creation, it shall be valid for fifty years from the date of its creation.

**Article 39** (Release Time of Serial Publications, etc.)

(1) For works which are released in independent volumes, issues or sequels, the time of release as prescribed in the proviso of Article 36 (1), Articles 37 (1) and 38 shall be the date when each independent volume, issue or sequel is published, and for the works which by their nature can be completed only in serials, the time of release shall be the date when the last part of the serial is released.

(2) In a case of a work to be completed wholly by a serial order, if a part to be continued is not released within after three years from the release of the latest serial, the latest part released shall be considered as the last part under Paragraph (1).

**Article 40** (Commencement of Protection Period) The protection period of the author's property right as prescribed in this Section and Article 77 shall commence from the next year following the death of the author or creation or release of the work.

### Section 8. Transfer, Exercise and Extinguishment of Author's Property Right

**Article 41** (Transfer of Author's Property Rights)

(1) The author's property rights may be transferred in whole or in part.

(2) In the case where the author's property rights are transferred in whole, the right to prepare a derivative or compilation work as prescribed in Article 21 shall be presumed not to be included therein, unless otherwise agreed.

**Article 42** (Consent to Use of Work)

(1) The author's property right owner may give his consent to the use of his work by others.

(2) Any person who has obtained consent under Paragraph (1) may use the work in such manners and within the limits of such conditions as agreed.

(3) The right to use a work by consent as referred to in Paragraph (1) shall not be transferred to a third person without the consent of the author's property right owner.

**Article 43** (Offer of Work for Transaction) If the original or reproduction of a work is offered for transaction by means of sale with the consent of the owner of the distribution right, it may be distributed continuously.

**Article 44** (Exercise of Pledge Right on Author's Property Right) The right to pledge the object of which is the author's property rights may be exercised even against money or other things (including compensation for the publication right) to be paid to the owner of the author's property right due to the transfer of the author's property rights or the use of the work: Provided that the right to such payments shall be garnished before payment of the money or delivery of things.

**Article 45** (Exercise of Author's Property Rights on Joint Works)

(1) The author's property right of a joint work may not be exercised without the unanimous consent of all the co-owners, and none of them may transfer his share or put into pledge without consent of the rest. In this case, each of the author's property right owner may not unreasonably prevent an agreement or refuse consent.

(2) Profits accrued from the use of a joint work shall be distributed to each coauthor according to the extent of his contribution to the creation of the work unless otherwise agreed among them. In this case, if the extent of their respective contribution are unclear, they shall be presumed to be equal.

(3) The author's property right owner to a joint work may renounce his share therein, and if he renounces his share or if he is deceased without an heir, his share shall be distributed among other author's property right owners in proportion to their shares.

(4) The provisions of Article 15 (2) and (3) shall apply *mutatis mutandis* to the exercise of the author's property rights of a joint work. In such cases, the author's personal rights shall be considered as the author's property rights.

**Article 46** (Extinguishment of Author's Property Right) If the author's property right falls under any of the following subparagraphs, it shall be extinguished:

    1. Where the author's property right owner is deceased without an heir, and his right is reverted to the State under the Civil Code and other laws; and

    2. Where the author's property right owner who is a juristic person or organization is dissolved, and its right is reverted to the State under the Civil Code and other laws.

**Section 9. Legal Approval for Use of Works**

**Article 47** (Use of Works When Author's Property Right Owner is Unknown)

(1) If it is impossible to obtain consent to the use of a released work because the author's property right owner or his residence is not known notwithstanding considerable efforts of search, any person may use it with the approval of the Minister of Culture and Sports under the conditions as prescribed by the Presidential Decree and after depositing the compensation as determined by the Minister of Culture and Sports based on the criteria for compensation as prescribed in Subparagraph 1 of Article 82. (Amended Law No. 4183, Dec. 30, 1989; Law No. 4541, Mar. 6, 1993)

(2) Any person who uses a work under Paragraph (1) shall indicate the content and the date of approval.

**Article 48** (Broadcasting of Released Works) If a broadcaster who desires to broadcast a released work for the necessity of public interest has conferred with the author's property right owner but failed to reach an agreement, he may broadcast it with the approval of the Minister of Culture and Sports under the conditions as prescribed by the Presidential Decree and after paying to the author's property right owner the compensation as determined by the Minister of Culture and Sports based on the criteria for compensation under Subparagraph 1 of Article 82, or depositing the compensation. (Amended by Law No. 4183, Dec. 30, 1989; Law No. 4541, Mar. 6, 1993)

**Article 49** (Translation and Publication of Released Works)

(1) Any person who desires to translate and publish in the Korean language a foreign language work protected under this Act may translate and publish it when he obtains the approval of the Minister of Culture and Sports under the conditions as prescribed by the Presidential Decree and pays the compensation as determined by the Minister of Culture and Sports based on the criteria for the compensation under Subparagraph 1 of Article 82 to a person having the right to translate (hereinafter referred to as "owner of the translation right") or deposits the compensation and if the following requirements are met: (Amended by Law No. 4183, Dec. 30, 1989; Law No. 4541, Mar. 6, 1993)

1. That the work was published in a foreign country and at least seven years have passed since its publication, and its Korean version has not been released, or if it has been, it is out of print; and
2. That he has conferred with the owner of the translation right to translate and publish the work in the Korean language but failed to reach any agreement, or it is impossible to obtain the consent of the owner of the translation right because his identity or domicile is unknown even after considerable efforts are made.

(2) Any person who translates and publishes a foreign language work under Paragraph (1) shall indicate the title of the work and the name of its author on all translated reproductions.

(3) If a person who desires to get consent to a translation or publication under Paragraph (1) desires to translate a work written in a foreign language into Korean for the purpose of education, study and research, the term "seven years" in Paragraph (1) shall be read as "one year".

**Article 50** (Manufacture of Phonograph Records for Sale) In a case where a phonograph record is on sale for the first time in the Republic of Korea, and three years have passed thereafter, if a person who desires to manufacture other phonograph records for sale by recording a work recorded on the phonograph record has conferred with its author's property right owner but failed to reach an agreement, he may manufacture other phonograph records for sale with the approval of the Minister of Culture and Sports under the conditions as prescribed by the Presidential Decree and after paying to the author's property right owner the compensation as determined by the Minister of Culture and Sports based on the criteria for compensation under Subparagraph 1 of Article 82, or depositing the compensation. (Amended by Law No. 4183, Dec. 30, 1989; Law No. 4541, Mar. 6, 1993)

### Section 10. Registration

**Article 51** (Registration, etc. in Real Name)

(1) The author of an anonymous work or a work on which his alias is indicated may register his real name regardless of the present ownership of its author's property rights.

(2) In a case where the author is deceased without making his intention clear, a person designated by his will or his heir may make a registration as referred to in Paragraph (1).

(3) The author's property right owner may register the first publication or release date of the work.

(4) Any person whose real name is registered under Paragraphs (1) and (2) shall be presumed to be the author of such registered work; and for a work the first publication or release date of which is registered, its first publication or release shall be presumed to have occurred on the date of its registration.

**Article 52** (Effect of Registration) The following matters may not be claimed against a third party unless they are registered:

1. Transfer (excluding inheritance and other cases of general succession) or restriction on disposal of the author's property rights; and
2. Establishment, transfer, modification, extinguishment or restriction on disposal of the pledge right having the author's property rights for its object.

**Article 53** (Procedure, etc. of Registration) The registration as prescribed in Articles 51 and 52 shall be made by the Minister of Culture and Sports in the register book of copyrights under the conditions as prescribed by the Presidential Decree. (Amended by Law No. 4183, Dec. 30, 1989; Law No. 4541, Mar. 6, 1993)

## CHAPTER III. RIGHT OF PUBLICATION

**Article 54**  (Establishment of Publication Right)

(1) Any person who has the right to reproduce and distribute a work (hereinafter referred to as "owner of the reproduction right") may establish a right to publish the work (hereinafter referred to as "right to publish the work") for the person who desires to publish it in the form of document of drawing in print or by other similar means.

(2) Any person for whom the right to publish the work has been established under Paragraph (1) (hereinafter referred to as "holder of the right to publish the work") shall be entitled to publish the work which is the object of such right, in its original form, under the conditions as provided for in the act of establishment .

(3) If a pledge the object of which is the right to reproduce a work is established, the person having the right of reproduction may establish a right to publish the work only with the consent of the pledgee.

**Article 55**  (Obligations of Holder of Right to Publish the Work)

(1) If there is no special agreement in the establishment act, the holder of the right to publish the work shall publish manuscripts or the equivalent thereto, which are necessary for reproducing a work which is the object of the right to publish the work within nine months from date on which they have been received.

(2) If there is no special agreement in the establishment act, the holder of the right to publish the work shall keep on publishing the work according to the customary practice.

(3) Unless otherwise agreed, the holder of the right to publish the work shall indicate his emblem on each publication under the conditions as prescribed by the Presidential Decree.

**Article 56**  (Revision, Addition and Reduction of Work)

(1) In a case where the holder of the right to publish republishes a work which is the object of his right, the author may revise, add or reduce contents of the work within proper limits.

(2) In every case where the holder of the right to publish desires to republish a work which is the object of his right, unless otherwise agreed, he shall inform such fact to the author in advance whenever the case occurs.

**Article 57**  (Duration, etc. of Right to Publish)

(1) Unless otherwise agreed at the time of establishment, the right to publish shall not be extinguished for three years from the day of its first publication.

(2) If the author of a work which is the object of the right to publish is deceased during the duration of such right to publish, the holder of the right to reproduce may, notwithstanding the provisions of Paragraph (1), include the work in the complete works or other compilations for the author or separate the work which is part of such complete works or compilations and publish it separately.

**Article 58**  (Notice of Extinguishment of Right to Publish)

(1) If the holder of the right to publish has violated the provisions of Article 55 (1) or (2), the holder of the right to reproduce may demand him to fulfill his obligation in a prescribed period of no shorter than six months, and if he fails to fulfill his obligation during such period, the holder of the right to reproduce may give him the notice to the effect that his right to publish has been extinguished.

(2) In case it is impossible for the holder of the right to publish a work or in case it is obvious that he has no intention to publish a work, the owner of the right to reproduce may, notwithstanding the provisions of Paragraph (1), give him an immediate notice to the effect that his right to publish has been extinguished.

(3) In case a notice of the extinguishment of the right to publish has been given under Paragraph (1) or (2), the right to publish shall be considered to have been extinguished at the time the holder of such right receives the notice.

(4) In such events as might arise under Paragraph (3), the holder of the right to reproduce may demand the holder of the right to publish for the compensation of the damage by way of restitution or cessation of publication.

**Article 59** (Distribution of Publication after Extinguishment of Right to Publish) In case the right to publish has been extinguished due to the expiration of its duration or for any other reason, a person who has held the right to publish may not distribute a publication prepared during such period, except in the following cases:

1. Where special agreement has been made at the time of the establishment of the right to publish; and

2. Where the royalties for the right to reproduce have, during the publication right, been paid to the holder of such right in exchange for the right to distribute the number of copies equivalent to the royalties.

**Article 60** (Transfer, Restriction, etc. of Right to Publish)

(1) The right to publish may not be transferred or put in pledge without the consent of the holder of the right to reproduce.

(2) The provisions of Articles 22, 23 (1) and (2), 24, 25, 27 to 30, 32 (2) and (3) shall apply *mutatis mutandis* to the reproductions of works which are the objects of the right to publish. In such cases, the term "author's property right owner" in Article 22 shall be considered as "holder of the right to publish".

(3) The provisions of Articles 52 and 53 shall apply *mutatis mutandis* to the registration of the right to publish. In such cases, the term "author's property right" in Article 52 shall be considered as "right to publish," "register of copyrights," and as "register of the rights to publish," respectively.

## CHAPTER IV. NEIGHBORING RIGHTS

### Section 1. General Rules

**Article 61** (Neighboring Rights) Stage performances, phonograph records and broadcasting which fall under any of the following subparagraphs shall be protected as neighboring rights under this Act:

1. Stage performances
   a. Stage performances conducted by the nationals of the Republic of Korea (including juristic persons established under the laws and regulations of the Republic of Korea and foreign juristic persons holding their main office in the Republic of Korea; hereinafter the same shall apply).
   b. Stage performances fixed in phonograph records as referred to in Subparagraph 2; and
   c. Stage performances transmitted by broadcasting as referred to in the items prescribed in Subparagraph 3 (excluding those recorded or videotaped before transmission);
2. Phonograph records

   a. Phonograph records produced by a national of the Republic of Korea;
   b. Phonograph records in which sounds are initially fixed in the Republic of Korea;
   c. Phonograph records protected by treaties signed or entered into by the Republic of Korea;
3. Broadcasting
   a. Broadcasting conducted by a broadcaster who is a national of the Republic of Korea;
   b. Broadcasting made by broadcasting facilities in the Republic of Korea.

**Article 62**  (Relation to Copyrights) Nothing in the articles of this Chapter shall be construed to have any effects on the copyright.

### Section 2. Rights of Stage Performers

**Article 63**  (Right to Record, Videotape, etc.) Any stage performer shall have the right to record, videotape or to photograph his stage performance.

**Article 64**  (Right to Broadcast Stage Performance) Any stage performer shall have the right to broadcast his stage performance, except in the case where the stage performance is recorded by someone else with his consent.

**Article 65**  (Compensation by Broadcaster to Stage Performer)

(1) In a case where a broadcaster broadcasts phonograph records on commercial channels on which a stage performance is recorded, he shall pay reasonable compensation to the stage performer.

(2) Those who are entitled to exercise the right to receive compensation as referred to in Paragraph (1) shall be an organization consisting of persons engaged in the stage performing business in the Republic of Korea and designated by the Minister of Culture and Sports shall obtain in advance the consent of such organization. (Amended by Law No. 4183, Dec. 30, 1989; Law No. 4541, Mar. 6, 1993)

(3) The organization as referred to in Paragraph (2) shall, upon request of a person who is not its member but is entitled to the compensation (hereinafter referred to as "right holder"), not refuse to exercise the right for him. In this case, the organization is entitled to perform in its own name a judicial or nonjudicial act to the right.

(4) The amount of compensation which an organization as referred to in Paragraph (2) may claim for a right holder shall be determined each year by the agreement between the organization and the broadcaster.

(5) If the organization or broadcaster fails to reach an agreement under Paragraph (4), it or he may request arbitration to the Copyright Deliberation and Conciliation Committee under the conditions as prescribed by the Presidential Decree.

(6) Matters necessary for designation, etc. of the organization as referred to in Paragraph (2) shall be determined by the Presidential Decree.

**Article 65-2**  (Permission of Stage Performer on Lending of Phonograph Records)

(1) Any stage performer shall have the right to permit a lending of any phonograph record for sale on which his stage performance is recorded with the intention of making any profits.

(2) The provisions of Article 65 (2), (3) and (6) shall be applicable to the exercise, etc. of the stage performer's right as referred to in Paragraph (1). (Newly Inserted by Law No. 4717, Jan. 7, 1994)

**Article 66**  (Joint Stage Performers)

(1) In a case where two or more persons perform jointly in a chorus, concert, drama, etc., the rights of stage performer as prescribed in this Section shall be exercised by a representative(s) chosen by the joint stage performers: Provided that if such representative(s) is (are) not chosen, the director of producer, etc. shall exercise the rights.

(2) In exercising the rights of a stage performer under Paragraph (1), if a vocal or instrumental solo had been accompanied to the stage performance, the consent of such vocalist or soloist shall be obtained.

## Section 3. Rights of Phonorecord Makers

**Article 67** (Right to Reproduce and (or) Distribute) Any phonorecord maker shall have the right to reproduce and (or) distribute his phonograph records.

**Article 67-2** (Permission of Offer for Transaction and Lending of Phonograph Records)

(1) The provisions of Article 43 shall be applicable to the distribution of phonograph records and permission on lending of records for sale by the phonograph record makers.

(2) The provisions of Article 65 (2), (3) and (6) shall be applicable to the exercise, etc. of the phonograph record maker's right as referred to in Paragraph (1). (Newly Inserted by Law No. 4717, Jan. 7, 1994)

**Article 68** (Compensation to Phonorecord Maker by Broadcaster)

(1) In case a broadcaster broadcasts phonograph records on a commercial channel, he shall pay a reasonable compensation to such phonorecord maker.

(2) The provisions of Article 65 (2) to (6) shall apply *mutatis mutandis* to the amount of compensation and claim procedure therefor as prescribed in Paragraph (1). In such cases, the term "stage performance" in Article 65 (2) shall be taken as "phonorecord making".

## Section 4. Rights of Broadcaster

**Article 69** (Right to Reproduce and Simulcast) Any broadcaster shall have the right to reproduction or simulcast by means of recording, videotaping, photographing or similar means. He shall also have the right to broadcast live.

## Section 5. Period of Protection

**Article 70** (Period of Protection) Neighboring rights shall commence from the time which falls under any of the following subparagraphs, and survive for fifty years from the following year: (Amended by Law No. 4717, Jan. 7, 1994)

1. For a stage performance, when it is conducted;
2. For a phonograph record, when the sound is initially fixed thereon; and
3. For broadcasting, when it is made.

## Section 6. Restriction, Transfer, Exercise, etc. of Rights

**Article 71** (Restriction on Neighboring Rights) The provisions of Articles 22, 23 (2), 24 to 29, 30 (2), 31, 33 and 34 shall apply *mutatis mutandis* to the use of stage performances, phonograph records or broadcasts which are the object of the neighboring rights.

**Article 72** (Transfer, Exercise, etc. of Neighboring Rights) The provisions of Article 41 (1) shall apply *mutatis mutandis* to a transfer of neighboring rights; the provisions of Article 42, to consent to the use of stage performances, phonograph records or broadcasts; the provisions of Article 44, to an exercise of the pledge right established on a neighboring right; and the provisions of Article 46, to an extinguishment of neighboring rights, respectively. (Amended by Law No. 4717, Jan. 7, 1994).

**Article 73** (Registration of Neighboring Rights) The provisions of Articles 52 and 53 shall apply *mutatis mutandis* to a registration of neighboring rights. In this case, the term "register of copyright" as provided in Article 53 means "register of neighboring rights".

## CHAPTER V. SPECIAL PROVISIONS CONCERNING CINEMATOGRAPHIC WORKS

**Article 74** (Cinematization of Works)

(1) In a case where the author's property right owner gives another person his consent to the cinematization of his work, unless otherwise agreed between them, such consent shall be considered to include the following acts:

1. To dramatize a work for production as a cinematographic work;
2. To reproduce and distribute the cinematographic work;
3. To play publicly the cinematographic work;
4. To broadcast a cinematographic work designed for broadcasting; and
5. To use a translation of a cinematographic work in the same way as the cinematographic work.

(2) In a case where the author's property right owner consents to a cinematization of his work, unless otherwise agreed, he may consent to a cinematization of the work in another cinematographic work after five years from the day of such consent.

**Article 75** (Rights to Cinematographic Works)

(1) If a person who has agreed to cooperate in the production of a cinematographic work acquires the copyright to the cinematographic work, the right necessary for the use of such cinematographic work shall be considered to have been transferred to the producer.

(2) The author's property rights to a novel, play, fine art work or musical work used for the production of cinematographic work shall not be affected by the provisions of Paragraph (1).

(3) The rights to record, videotape, etc. as prescribed in Article 63 relating to the use of a cinematographic work of a stage performer who has agreed to cooperate in the production of the cinematographic work and right to broadcast stage performance as prescribed in Article 64 shall be considered to have been transferred to the cinematographic producer unless there is any special contract. (Amended by Law No. 4717, Jan. 7, 1994)

**Article 76** (Rights of Cinematographic Producer) Any cinematographic producer shall have the right to reproduce, distribute or use for a public screening or broadcasting videotapes in which a cinematographic work is included to transfer or to offer such rights for a pledge.

**Article 77** (Protection Period of Cinematographic Works) The author's property rights of a cinematographic work shall not be extinguished for fifty years from the date of its release: Provided that if it is not released within ten years after its creation, it shall survive for fifty years from the date of its creation.

## CHAPTER VI. COPYRIGHT AGENCY BUSINESS

**Article 78** (Permit, etc. of Copyright Agency Business)

(1) Any person who desires to operate a business as an agent, mediator or trustee for a person holding rights protected under this Act (hereinafter referred to as "copyright agency business") shall obtain a permit from the Minister of Culture and Sports under the conditions as prescribed by the Presidential Decree. Provided that a person who

desires to operate the copyright agency business only as agent or mediator, shall report it to the Minister of Culture an Sports under the conditions as prescribed by the Presidential Decree. (Amended by Law No. 4183, Dec. 30, 1989; Law No. 4541, Mar. 6, 1993; Law No. 4717, Jan. 7, 1994)

(2) No person falling under any of the following categories shall be eligible for the copyright agency business under Paragraph (1):

1. A person judicially declared as incompetent to quasi-incompetent;
2. A person whose legal capacity has not been restored following bankruptcy;
3. A person who is within a one-year period following the execution of criminal penalty more severe than a fine imposed for the violation of this Act or the final decision to suspend the execution of the sentence, or who is in a probation period following a criminal sentence to the effect;
4. A person who has no domicile in the Republic of Korea; and
5. A juristic person or organization in which a person falling under any of Subparagraphs 1 to 4 is a representative or director.

(3) Any person who has obtained a license for, or make the reportion, a copyright agency business under Paragraph (1) (hereinafter referred to as "copyright agent") may collect fees for his service from the author's property right owner or other interested persons. (Amended by Law No. 4717, Jan. 7, 1994)

(4) The rates or amounts of the fees as referred to in Paragraph (3) shall be determined by the copyright agents with the approval of the Minister of Culture and Sports.

**Article 79** (Supervision)

(1) The Minister of Culture and Sports may require the copyright agents to report of his business. (Amended by Law No. 4183, Dec. 30, 1989; Law No. 4541, Mar. 6, 1993)

(2) In order to promote the protection of author's interests and the convenient use of works, the Minister of Culture and Sports may issue necessary and proper orders regarding activities of a copyright agent. (Amended by Law No. 4183, Dec. 30, 1989; Law No. 4541, Mar. 6, 1993)

**Article 80** (Cancellation, etc. of Permission)

(1) If a copyright agent commits acts prescribed in any of the following subparagraphs, the Minister of Culture and Sports may order the suspension of business for a specified period of no longer than six months: (Amended by Law No. 4183, Dec. 30, 1989; Law No. 4541, Mar. 6, 1993)

1. Where he has received fees in excess of the approved amount in violation of the provisions of Article 78 (3);
2. Where he fails to file a report as prescribed in Article 79 (1) without good cause or he makes a false report; and
3. Where he has received an order as prescribed in Article 79 (2) but fails to obey it without any good cause.

(2) If a copyright agent commits acts prescribed in any of the following subparagraphs, the Minister of Culture and Sports may cancel his permission for, or to order to close, the copyright agency business: (Amended by Law No. 4183, Dec. 30, 1989; Law No. 4541, Mar. 6, 1993; Law No. 4717, Jan. 7, 1994)

1. Where the copyright agent has obtained a permit by a fraudulent or unlawful means; and
2. Where the copyright agent continues to conduct the business after receiving an order of suspension under Paragraph (1).

(3) If the Minister of Culture and Sports intends to take measures under Paragraphs (1) and (2), he shall give the party against whom the measure is taken or his representative a timely opportunity to present his case under the conditions as prescribed by the Presidential Decree, except in cases where the party or his representative fails to comply it without any justifiable reason, or it is impossible to give him an opportunity to present his case because his whereabouts are unknown, etc. (Amended by Law No. 4183, Dec. 30, 1989; Law No. 4541, Mar. 6, 1993)

## CHAPTER VII. DELIBERATION ON COPYRIGHTS AND CONCILIATION OF DISPUTES

**Article 81**  (Copyright Deliberation and Conciliation Committee)

(1) In order to deliberate matters concerning the copyright and conciliate disputes concerning the rights protected under this Act (hereinafter referred to as "disputes"), the Copyright Deliberation and Conciliation Committee (hereinafter referred to as "Committee") shall be established.

(2) The Committee shall consist of more than fifteen but less than twenty deliberation and conciliation members (hereinafter referred to as "members") including one Chairman and two vice-chairmen.

(3) Members shall be selected by the Minister of Culture and Sports from among persons of highly reputable knowledge and experience in copyright matters, and the Chairman and vice-chairmen shall be elected from among the members. (Amended by Law No. 4183, Dec. 30, 1989; Law No. 4541, Mar. 6, 1993)

(4) The term of members shall be three years but it shall be renewable.

(5) In case a vacancy arises in the Committee, a substitute shall be elected in the same manner as prescribed in Paragraph (3) and serve for the remaining period of his predecessor's term. A substitute may not be selected in cases where the total number of the incumbent members exceeds fifteen.

**Article 82**  (Function) In addition to the conciliation of disputes, the Committee shall deliberate on the following matters: (Amended by Law No. 4183, Dec. 30, 1989; Law No. 4541, Mar. 6, 1993)

1. Matters concerning the criteria for compensation as prescribed in Articles 23 (3) (text), 47 (1), 48, 49 (1) and 50;

2. Matters concerning the rates or amounts of the fee chargeable by the copyright agents as prescribed in Article 78 (3); and

3. Matters as referred by the Minister of Culture and Sports or jointly by three or more members.

**Article 83**  (Arbitration Division) In order to carry out effectively the disputes arbitration affairs of the Committee, an arbitration division consisting of three members, including at least one member qualified as a lawyer, shall be established in the Committee.

**Article 84**  (Request, etc. for Conciliation)

(1) Any person who desires to have a dispute conciliated may request the Committee to conciliate the dispute with the tenor and cause of the request specified.

(2) The conciliation of disputes under Paragraph (1) shall be carried out by the arbitration division as prescribed in Article 83.

(3) The Committee shall reach conciliation about the dispute within three months from the day on which the conciliation has been requested and if no conciliation has been reached during said period, the conciliation shall be considered to have failed.

**Article 85**  (Demand for Attendance)

(1) If it is deemed necessary for the conciliation of dispute, the Committee may demand a person concerned, his representative or an interested person thereto attend hearings for conciliation purposes or to present relevant documents.

(2) If the person concerned fails to comply with the demand for attendance under Paragraph (1) without any justifiable reason, the conciliation shall be considered to have failed.

**Article 86**  (Effectuation of Conciliation)

(1) The conciliation shall be effectuated by signing on a protocol specifying terms of agreement reached between the parties.

(2) The protocol as referred to in Paragraph (1) shall have the same effect as a judicial conciliation unless it is concerned with matters which are outside the scope of autonomy of the concerned parties.

**Article 87**  (Failure of Conciliation) In case no agreement has been reached between the parties in conciliation or if conciliation is considered to have failed under Article 84 (3) or 85 (2), such facts shall be stated in a protocol.

**Article 88**  (Costs of Conciliation)

(1) The costs of conciliation shall be borne by the requesting party: Provided that in case conciliation is reached, they shall be borne by both parties in equal share, unless otherwise agreed.

(2) The amount of conciliation costs as referred to in Paragraph (1) shall be determined by the Committee.

**Article 89**  (Organization, etc. of Committee) The organization and operation of the Committee, procedures of conciliation, methods of payments of the conciliation costs and other matters necessary for the operation of the Committee shall be determined by the Presidential Decree.

**Article 90**  (Subsidy for Expenses) The State may subsidize the expenses needed for the operation of the Committee within the limits of the budget.

## CHAPTER VIII. REDRESS FOR INFRINGEMENT OF RIGHTS

**Article 91**  (Demand for Withdrawal from Infringement, etc.)

(1) Any person holding a copyright of any other right protected under this Act (excluding the rights to be compensated under Articles 65 and 68; hereinafter the same shall apply in this Article) may demand a person infringing on his rights to withdraw from such act or demand a person likely to infringe on his rights to take preventative measures or deposit securities therefore.

(2) In a case where any person holding a copyright or other rights protected under this Act makes a demand under Paragraph (1), he may demand the disposal of goods procured by infringing acts or other measures necessary for the correction.

(3) In such events as might arise under Paragraphs (1) and (2) or in a case where a criminal indictment under this Act has been filed, upon request of the plaintiff or accuser, the court may, with or without imposing securities therefor, issue orders to the effect that the acts complained of be stopped temporarily or the products procured by the acts complained of be seized or to some other effects deemed proper.

(4) In cases of as referred to in Paragraph (3), if a final judgment has been made to the effect that no infringement had been done to the copyrights and other rights protected under this Act, the complainant shall compensate for the damages caused thereby.

**Article 92**  (Acts Considered as Infringement)

(1) Any act falling under any of the following subparagraphs shall be considered to be an infringement on the copyrights and other rights protected under this Act:

    1. An act of importing, for the purpose of distribution in the Republic of Korea, goods which would infringe on the copyrights or other rights protected under this Act, had they been made in the Republic of Korea at the time of import; and

    2. An act of distributing goods made by an act infringing on the copyrights or other rights protected under this Act where the distributor has knowledge thereof (including imported goods as referred to in Subparagraph 1).

(2) Any act of using a work in a manner likely to defame its author's dignity shall be considered to be an infringement on the author's personal right.

**Article 93** (Claim for Damages)

(1) Any person holding the author's property rights or other rights protected under this Act (excluding the author's personal rights) (hereinafter referred to as "author's property right owner, etc.") may demand a person who has infringed on his rights deliberately or with negligence for the compensation of the damages caused thereby.

(2) In a case where the owner of the author's property rights owner, etc. makes a demand under Paragraph (1), if the tort-feasor had gained profits by his tortious acts the amount of such profit shall be presumed to be the amount of damages sustained by the author's property right owner, etc.

(3) The author's property right owner, etc. may claim as compensation for damages the amount equivalent to that he could have earned by the ordinary exercise of his rights, in addition to the amount of damages as referred to in Paragraph (2).

**Article 94** (Presumed Number of Copies of Illegal Publications) In a case where a work is published without the consent of the author's property right owner, if it is difficult to discern the number of illegal publications, it shall be presumed to be 5,000 copies for the published works, and 10,000 for phonorecords respectively.

**Article 95** (Demand for Restoration of Reputation, etc.) An author may demand a person who has infringed intentionally or negligently on his author's personal right to take measures necessary for the restoration of his reputation instead of or in addition to the compensation for damages.

**Article 96** (Protection of Author's Personal Right after Author's Death) After the death of an author, his family (the spouse, children, parents, grandchildren, grandparents or siblings of the deceased) or an executor may make demand under Article 91 against a person who has violated or is likely to violate the provisions of Article 14 (2) with respect to the work concerned and demand for the restoration of reputation, etc. under Article 95 against a person who has infringed intentionally or negligently on the author's personal right, or who violated the provisions of Article 14 (2).

**Article 97** (Infringement on Rights or Joint Works) Each coauthor or co-owner of the author's property rights of a joint work may demand without the consent of the rest under Article 91 and claim or demand the compensation of damages under Article 93 based on his own share in the joint work with respect to the infringement of the author's property right.

## CHAPTER IX. PENAL PROVISIONS

**Article 98** (Infringement of Rights) Any person who falls under any of the following subparagraphs shall be punished by imprisonment for not more than three years or a fine not exceeding three million Won or both: (Amended by Law No. 4717, Jan. 7, 1994)

1. A person who has infringed on an author's property rights or other property right protected under this Act by means of reproduction, public performance, broadcast, display, etc.;
2. A person who has infringed on an author's personal rights and thereby defamed the dignity of the author; and
3. A person who has fraudulently made a registration as prescribed in Articles 51 and 52 (including a case where these provisions are applied *mutatis mutandis* under Article 60 (3) or 73).

**Article 99** (Illegal Publication, etc.) Any person who falls under any of the following subparagraphs shall be punished by imprisonment for not more than one year or a fine not exceeding one million Won:

1. A person who has released a work under the real name or alias of a person other than the author;
2. A person who has violated the provisions of Article 14 (2);
3. A person who has operated a copyright agency business without obtaining a permit under Article 78; and
4. A person who has committed an act considered to be an infringement under Article 92.

**Article 100** (Offense, etc. of Incompliance with Specification of Source) Any person who falls under any of the following subparagraphs shall be punished by a fine not exceeding five million Won:

1. Person who fails to specify the source in contravention of the provisions of Article 34 (including the case where it is applicable under Article 71);
2. Person who fails to make a mark that he is the person entitled to reproduce in contravention of the provisions of Article 55 (3); and
3. Person who carries on the copyright agency business only as agent or mediator without making the report as prescribed in the proviso of Article 78 (1) or who continues to operate the business after he receives an order to close it under Article 80 (2). (Wholly Amended by Law No. 4717, Jan. 7, 1994)

**Article 101** (Confiscation) Reproductions which are made by infringing on copyright or other rights protected under this Act in the domain of the infringer, printer, distributor or public performer shall be confiscated.

**Article 102** (Accusation) Except as provided in Subparagraph 3 of Article 98 and Subparagraphs 1 to 3 of Article 99 and Subparagraph 3 of Article 100, crimes as prescribed in this Chapter shall be prosecuted only on accusation of the victim. (Amended b y Law No. 4717, Jan. 1994)

**Article 103** (Joint Penal Provisions) If a representative of a juristic person, or an agent, employee or other employed person of a juristic person or an individual has committed a crime a prescribed in this Chapter with respect to affairs of the juristic person or individual respectively, the fine as prescribed in Articles concerned shall be imposed on such juristic person or individual, in addition to the punishment of the offender.

## ADDENDA

**Article 1** (Enforcement Date) This Act shall enter into force as of July 1, 1987.

**Article 2** (Interim Measures Concerning Scope of Application)

(1) This Act shall not apply to that portion of copyright works, which, as of the date of enforcement of this Act, has been extinguished wholly or partly or which is not protected by the previous Act. Such matters shall be governed by the previous Act.

(2) The following works released pursuant to the previous Act before the enforcement of this Act shall be governed by the previous Act:
1. Musical performance, song, dramatic production, phonograph record or cinematographic work as prescribed in Article 2 of the previous Act;
2. Ownership and use of the copyrights of joint works as prescribed in Article 12 of the previous Act;
3. Ownership of the copyrights of works by contract as prescribed in Article 13 of the previous Act;
4. Ownership of the copyrights of photographs as prescribed in Article 36 of the previous Act; and
5. Ownership of the copyrights of motion pictures as prescribed in Article 38 of the previous Act.

**Article 3** (Interim Measures Concerning Protection Period of Works) The protection period of works which are released before the enforcement of this Act and which do not fall under Article 2 (1) of this Addenda shall be as follows:
1. When the protection period as prescribed in the previous Act is longer than that as prescribed in this Act, the previous Act shall apply; and
2. When the protection period as prescribed in the previous Act is shorter than that as prescribed in this Act, this Act shall apply.

**Article 4** (Interim Measures Following Transaction in Rights) The copyrights (including established right to publish) which had been created or were disposed of by transfer or other means pursuant to the provisions of the previous Act before the enforcement of this Act shall be considered to have been created or disposed of by transfer or other means under this Act.

**Article 5** (Interim Measures Concerning Registration of Copyrights) Any registration made pursuant to the provisions of the previous Act before the enforcement of this Act shall be considered as made under this Act.

**Article 6** (Interim Measures Concerning Failure to Disclose Sources) Notwithstanding the provisions as prescribed in Article 34 (1), in case of a use of work under Article 23 (1), the user may not disclose the sources for five years following the enforcement of this Act.

**Article 7** (Interim Measures Concerning Infringement on Rights) Remedies for infringement of copyrights under the Chapter IV of the previous Act (including an act infringing the established right to publish the work) committed before the enforcement of this Act shall be governed by the provisions of the previous Act.

**Article 8** (Interim Measures Concerning Penal Provisions) As for the criminal acts committed before the enforcement of this Act, the provisions of the previous Act shall apply.

### ADDENDA (Law No. 4183, Dec. 30, 1989)

**Article 1** (Enforcement Date) This Act shall enter into force as of the date of its promulgation. (Proviso omitted) Articles 2 to 6 omitted.

### ADDENDA (Law No. 4268, Dec. 27, 1990)

**Article 1** (Enforcement Date) This Act shall enter into force as of the date of its promulgation. (Proviso omitted) Articles 2 to 10 omitted.

### ADDENDA (Law No. 4352, Mar. 8, 1991)

**Article 1**   (Enforcement Date) This Act shall enter into force at the expiration of one month after its promulgation. Articles 2 to 6 omitted.

### ADDENDA (Law No. 4541, Mar. 6, 1993)

**Article 1**   (Enforcement Date) This Act shall enter into force as of the date of its promulgation. (Proviso omitted)

**Articles 2 to 5 Omitted.**

### ADDENDA (Law No. 4717, Jan. 7, 1994)

(1) (Enforcement Date) This Act shall enter into force as of July 1, 1994.

(2) (Interim Measures Concerning Lending Right) With respect to a lending of phonograph records for sale including works published before this Act enters into force, the previous provisions shall apply.

(3) (Interim Measures Concerning Neighboring Right to Literary Work) The protection period of neighboring right to literary work, which is acquired before this Act enters into force, shall be subject to the previous provisions.

(4) (Interim Measures Concerning Compensation for Books for Curricula) Notwithstanding the provisions of Article 23 (3) concerning the payment of compensation or deposit, in case where a work to which the Minister of Education holds the copyright or which is published on a book used for the curricula and authorized by the Minister of Education is inserted, the said provisions shall not apply for five years after this Act enters into force.

(5) (Interim Measures Concerning Right to Cinematographic Works) The revised provisions of Article 75 (3) shall not apply for five years after this Act enters into force.

### ADDENDA (Law No. 4746, Mar. 24, 1994)

**Article 1**   (Enforcement Date) This Act shall enter into force at the expiration of four months after its promulgation.

**Article 2 to 7 Omitted.**

# A P P E N D I X   H

# Press Ethics Code

The social mission of Korean journalists is extremely important, all the more so because the nation is confronted with the task of reconstructing the homeland into a democratic, unified, independent country.

Thoroughly aware of this, Korean journalists have organized the Korean Newspaper Editors Association chiefly among the editors of daily newspapers and news agencies across the country and have adopted the Press Ethics Code in order to rectify press ethics and firmly uphold their journalistic integrity. Journalists have pledged themselves to be faithful to the Code and to fulfill the people's expectations of good journalism.

Not only editors but all engaged with the press shall abide by this Code. Since this Code calls for voluntary implementation, there is no authoritative organization which enforces it.

However, if newspapers and journalists are unfaithful to the Code, they will surely lose public support and thereby endanger their very survival.

## FREEDOM

Freedom of the press, one of the most basic rights of human beings, must be protected so as to satisfy the people's right to know. The press has complete freedom to report and comment. Although any violation of public interest is subject to control under general law, there can be no law restricting or interfering with the freedom of the press. Freedom of the press, of course, includes freedom to criticize and to oppose any such law.

## RESPONSIBILITY

The press, being a social instrument, has a special public position, and journalists command a unique social standing. However, this position results only if the press gives the public a true picture of affairs and the public uses this picture as the basis for their judgments.

Therefore, the most important responsibility of the press is to faithfully serve the public interest based on the realization that the public relies upon the press. This responsibility also constitutes the most important reason for preserving the press' special public position.

The press displays its special position concretely by being always dauntless in the pursuit of justice, courageous in opposing justice and in siding with and speaking for the weak.

## REPORTING AND COMMENTING

The speedy and faithful dissemination of facts is vital to reporting. Therefore, the facts subject to reporting must be limited to those whose value can be verified in terms of their source and content.

In commenting, a journalist's independent beliefs and opinions should be expressed fairly and courageously in particular; any prejudice that deliberately distorts or evades the truth should be guarded against.

Journalists should be sincere toward the public by being as thorough and correct in reporting and commenting as possible.

## INDEPENDENCE

The press should stand on the principle that all persons are equal before the law and should not be swayed by any political, economic or other social prejudices. At the same time, the press cannot be used privately for individual interests running counter to the public interest or for worthless or immoral purposes. Journalists cannot escape responsibility simply because others ordered or requested special treatment.

## HONOR AND FREEDOM

The press should respect the honor of others and cannot violate individual rights or sentiments out of curiosity or evil intent. In parallel with the demand for the freedom of the press, the press should have the magnanimity to recognize the freedom claimed by others.

## DIGNITY

A high degree of dignity and pride is required of the press because of its public position. In particular, vulgar conduct or any activity resulting in vulgarity cannot be tolerated.

## GUIDELINES FOR REPORTING

[1] Interpretation of the provisions of Articles 3 and 4, Chapter "Honor and Freedom of Others," Guidelines for Implementation of the Press Ethics Code (October 13, 1961):

1. Offenders caught in the very act shall be excepted from the "principle that in reporting criminal cases, the accused shall be treated as not guilty until convicted," Article 3, Chapter "Honor and Freedom of Others," Guidelines for Implementation of the Press Ethics Code.

2. The term "minor" mentioned in Article 4, Chapter "Honor and Freedom of Others," Guidelines for Implementation of the Press Ethics Code, means those who are more than one day, up to 20 in age.

3. In the provision that the name and picture of minor suspects and the accused and sexually assaulted women shall not be disclosed, Article 4, Chapter "Honor and Freedom of Others," Guidelines for Implementation of the Press Ethics Code, no number of home address in the case of Seoul and other cities nor name of village in other provincial areas can be disclosed.

4. In giving addresses, no number, "tong and "pan" in Seoul and other cities, nor village "pan" and number in other provincial areas can be disclosed. (Supplement, May 26, 1965)

[2] Notice in Reporting Sexually Assaulted Women (No. 3768, Korean Press Ethics Commission, October, 2, 1979):

Regarding sexually assaulted women, the Commission made the ruling on May 26, 1965, that "in giving address, no number, 'tong' and 'pan' in Seoul and other cities, nor village, 'pan' and number in other provincial areas can be given." Again on October 2, 1978, the Commission ruled that even if an address is not given directly, any information leading to the inference of victim's address, such as a case in which the culprit is identified with the remark, "he assaulted a woman of his village," or in which the location of the victim's office is given or the names of her relatives are identified, is also subject to control.

[3] Interpretation of the Provisions of Articles 1 and 2, Chapter "Honor and Freedom of Others," Guidelines for Implementation of Press Ethics Code (February 15, 1963):

1. No individual honor shall be damaged unless so doing is for the sake of public interest.
2. Even if it is for public interest, no undue personal attacks or low language can be used.
3. The same is true for individuals, public officials, offices or organizations, and of juridical persons, nonjuridical persons or groups.

[4] Reporting of Suicides (January 8, 1967):

In consideration of the effect the reports of suicide have on society, the Commission makes the following rules as the criteria for such reports, based on the spirit of the provisions of Article 3, Chapter "Independence," Guidelines for Implementation of the Press Ethics Code.

1. The name and amount of the lethal dose of the medicine used in suicide shall not be given. However, such may be reported in incidents related with crime or carrying a special social significance.
2. Cruel methods of suicide shall not be described.
3. Since the words "group suicide" can be an inaccurate expression in case it involves children and other family members not willing to die, accurate expression shall be used depending on the incident.

   At no time should such incidents be reported in a way that caters to the public's curiosity; nor should they be beautified.

[5] Notice on Reports about Stimulants (No. 3744, Korea Press Ethics Commission, April 19, 1979):

Since the giving of the names of stimulants such as Sekonal and adhesive glue in reporting the cases of adolescents using stimulants is apt to influence innocent adolescents into making similar mistakes, an instruction was handed out not to make public the names of such medicine or material.

[6] Report on Kidnapping Incident (August 30, 1967):

1. Reports on kidnappings should be made with an emphasis on the return of kidnapped victim. Such reports shall in principle be withheld so long as the victim remains in the hands of the abductor.

   However, reports may be made when such reporting is considered necessary for the rescue of the victim.

2. The whole picture of the kidnapping incident may be made once the incident has come to a solution.

[7] Reports on Suspects (September 6, 1967):

1. Excepting those caught in the act or those against whom evidence is salient, the address, name picture, and occupation of suspects shall not be disclosed.
2. No reports that prompt the assumption that suspects are guilty shall be made without any express evidence.
3. No picture of the brutal scene of an on-the-spot investigation of a criminal case shall be released.

[8] Reports on Protection of Surrendered Agents and Those Informing on Communist Agents (February 14, 1968):

1. In reports about those who have reported espionage agents and communist guerrillas, pseudonyms shall be used and their pictures, workshops and addresses shall not be made public. Address, however, down to city, country or ward can be disclosed.
2. The provision of the preceding paragraph shall also be applied to surrendered espionage agents and communist guerrillas. However, if government authorities make official announcements or if there exists the need to inform the people, they shall be made public.

[9] Reports without Credits (July 26, 1964):

The following violates the provisions of Article 4, Chapter "Dignity," Guidelines for Implementation of the Press Ethics Code:

1. Use of distributed articles after replacing its by-line name with that of one's own correspondent.
2. Use of the whole of distributed articles without giving any credit.
3. Use of distributed articles after altering (plagiarizing) leads.
4. Use of plagiarized part of wire service articles in one's own article.

[10] Children's Newspapers or Columns and Advertisement on Medicine for Venereal Diseases (June 1, 1966):

In newspapers where advertisements for medicines for venereal disease are carried, no children's column shall be used.

# NOTES

## CHAPTER 1

1. For a detailed discussion of South Korea, see *South Korea: A Country Study* (Andrea Matles Savada and William Shaw eds., 4th ed. 1992). *See also A Handbook of Korea* (10th ed. 1994).

2. Sung Moon Pae, *Korea Leading Developing Nations: Economy, Democracy and Welfare* 3 (1992).

3. *See* "Treaty of Annexation Between Korea and Japan, Proclamation, and Accompanying Documents" (1910), *translated in* Woonsang Choi, *The Fall of the Hermit Kingdom* 135–39 (1967). Article 1 of the treaty read: "His Majesty the Emperor of Korea makes complete and permanent cession to his Majesty the Emperor of Japan of all rights of sovereignty over the whole of Korea."

4. *See* "Convention Between Japan and Korea Providing for Control of Korean Foreign Relations by Japan" (1905), *translated in* Choi, *op. cit.*, pp. 134–35. Article 1 of the convention read: "The Government of Japan ... will hereafter have control and direction of the external relations and affairs of Korea, and the diplomatic and consular representatives of Japan will have the [sic] charge of the subjects and interests of Korea in foreign countries."

5. Sungjoo Han, *The Failure of Democracy in South Korea* 7 (1974).

6. *See generally* C.I. Eugene Kim and Han-Kyo Kim, *Korea and the Politics of Imperialism 1876–1910*, at 150–56 (1967).

7. David I. Steinberg, *The Republic of Korea: Economic Transformation and Social Change* 41 (1989).

8. Ibid., p. 42.

9. *See* "Declaration of Korean Independence," March 1, 1919, *translated in* Choi, *op. cit.*, pp. 139–41 ("We herewith proclaim the independence of Korea and the liberty of the Korean people").

10. More than 6,000 Koreans were killed and about 15,000 wounded, in addition to 50,000 others arrested by the Japanese police. *See Korea Annual 1990*, at 320 (27th ed. 1990).

11. Among the reforms adopted by the "liberal and righteous" Japanese colonialists in the wake of the independence movement of 1919 were non-discrimination between Japanese and Koreans, respect for Korean culture and customs, and freedom of speech and the press. *See* Government-General of Chosen, *Annual Reports on Administration of Chosen, 1936–37*, at 7–8, *cited in* Andrew J. Grajdanzev, *Modern Korea* 57 (1944).

12. Steinberg, *Republic of Korea, op. cit.*, p. 45.

13. *See generally* Carter J. Eckert et al., *Korea Old and New: A History* 254–326 (1990).

14. Ibid., p. 345.

15. Pae, *op. cit.*, p. xiii.

16. Choi Chang Yoon, "Korea: An Emerging Democratic Power," in *Democracy in Korea: The Roh Tae Woo Years* 1 (Christopher J. Sigur ed., 1992).

17. Eckert et al., *op. cit.*, p. 348.

18. Sung-joo Han, "An Assessment of the Ho Chong and Chang Myon Governments," 22 *Korea Journal* 7 (May 1982). For a detailed discussion of South Korea's brief experiment with a parliamentary democracy during the Chang Myon era in 1960–1961, see Han, *Failure of Democracy, op. cit.*

19. Ibid., p. 4.

20. Donald S. Macdonald, "Korea's Transition to Democracy," in *Democracy in Korea, op. cit.*, p. 21 n.3, *quoting* Park Chung Hee, *The Country, the Revolution and I* 184 (2d ed. 1970).

21. For General Chun Doo Hwan's rise to power in Korea, see Harold C. Hinton, *Korea Under New Leadership: The Fifth Republic* (1983). *See also* Chong-Sik Lee, "South Korea in 1980: The Emergence of a New Authoritarian Order," 21 *Asian Survey* 125–43 (January 1981); Dae-Sook Suh, "South Korea in 1981: The First Year of the Fifth Republic," 22 *Asian Survey* 107–15 (January 1982).

22. Jerome Alan Cohen and Edward J. Baker, "U.S. Foreign Policy and Human Rights in South Korea," in *Human Rights in Korea: Historical and Policy Perspectives* 196 (William Shaw ed., 1991).

23. Kun Yang, Freedom of Expression and Regulation of Mass Media in Korea: Changes in Law and Reality 1 (1994) (research paper presented at the Law and Society Association convention in Phoenix, Ariz.).

24. Roh's statement is officially known as "Grand National Harmony and Progress Towards a Great Nation: Special Declaration on June 29, 1987," *translated in* Roh Tae Woo, *Korea in the Pacific Century: Selected Speeches, 1990–1992,* at 293–97 (1992).

25. Editorial, "Breakthrough in Seoul," *New York Times*, June 30, 1987, p. 30. For a discussion of the "democratization" of Korea in 1987, see generally Han Sung-Joo, "South Korea in 1987: The Politics of Democratization," 28 *Asian Survey* 52–61 (January 1988).

26. David I. Steinberg, "Korean Democracy Today," in *Democracy in Korea, op. cit.*, p. 55.

27. Donald Gregg, "Roh Tae Woo: Setting the Stage for Current Democratic Reforms," in *Continuity and Change in Contemporary Korea* 10–11 (Christopher J. Sigur ed., 1994).

28. Steinberg, "Korean Democracy Today," *op. cit.*, pp. 53–55.

29. Seung-Soo Han, "Kim Young Sam's Reform Policies and Korea-U.S. Relations," in *Continuity and Change, op. cit.*, p. 19.

30. Myoung-Soo Kim, "Governmental Reform in the Republic of Korea," in *Continuity and Change, op. cit.*, p. 34.

31. *See* ibid., pp. 35–39.

32. Wonmo Dong, "Civilian Democracy and the Politics of Leadership Change in Korea," in *Continuity and Change, op. cit.*, p. 51.

33. Myoung-Soo Kim, *op. cit.*, p. 39.

34. *A Handbook of Korea* 120 (9th ed. 1993).

35. Kang Sang-hyon, "The Press Coverage of Reform," in *The Korean Press 1994*, at 38 (1994).

36. *A Handbook of Korea, op. cit.*, p. 508.

37. *The Korean Press 1993*, at 8 (1993).

38. Eric W. Allen, "International Origins of the Newspapers: The Establishment of Periodicity in Print," 7 *English Journalism* 310 (1930).

39. Otto Groth, editor of the *Frankfurter Zeitung* in Germany, established the criteria for distinguishing a "true" newspaper from other publications:

A true newspaper must be:

1. *Periodical* in publication, and, in practice, of a frequency not less than weekly. It must be regular.
2. *Mechanical* in its reduplication. This bars the handwritten newsletters, but admits the possible radio and screen newspapers.
3. *Available* to all comers who are willing to pay the price. Its circulation must not be exclusive or esoteric.

And its *contents* must be:

4. *Miscellaneous*, varied, catholic, universal, complete, including every occurrence that is publicly interesting, so long as this interest is:
5. *General* in its appeal. The newspaper ideally should not include such matter that is interesting only to small groups. It should appeal to the public *as a public*.

And so long as the material is:

6. *Timely*. The German word for this quality is *actualitat*, and it is, of course, fundamental.

Passing from content to organization, the newspaper should possess an

7. *Effective Organization*. It should be a going concern. Its continuity should be reasonably provided for. Organization and continuity become the seat of policy and influence—the power of the press.

Allen, "International Origins of the Newspapers," *op. cit.*, p. 311, quoting Otto Groth, "Die Zeitung—Ein System des Zeitungskunde (Journalistik)," J. Bensheimer Mannheim 1 (1928): 21 et seq.

40. John A. Lent, "A Reluctant Revolution Among Asian Newspapers," in *Mass Communications: A World View* (Alan Wells ed., 1974) (footnote omitted).

41. Bong-Ki Kim, 1 *History of Korean Journalism* 9 (1967).

42. Among the eight regulations of the Yi Dynasty relating to publication of *Hansung Sunbo*, *reprinted in* Choe Chun, *A Discourse on Korean Newspaper History* (Korean) 21 (1982), was that official pronouncements should be given a top priority.

43. *Hansung Sunbo* was published entirely in Chinese characters until December 1884, when it was forced out of business during a political reform movement, notwithstanding its initial policy of using Chinese "for the time being." *See* the *Hansung Sunbo* regulations, *op. cit.* ("[*Hansung Sunbo*] shall, for the time being, be printed in Chinese characters only").

44. Chun Chhoe, "Characteristics of Korea [sic] Press," 2 *Korea Journal* 6 (May 1962).

45. *UNESCO Korea Survey* 481 (Korean National Commission for UNESCO comp., 1960). *See also* Kim, 1 *History of Korean Journalism, op. cit.*, p. 17 (noting that *Tongnip Shinmun* left "a revolutionary record in the history of the Korean press"). The *Tongnip Shinmun*'s stature as the first private newspaper in Korea is nonpareil in that the Korean press annually commemorates April 7, the date of the paper's founding, as its Newspaper Day.

46. Bae-ho Hahn, *Communication Policies in the Republic of Korea* 19 (1978).

47. *See* the "mission" of *Tongnip Shinmun* as stated in the editorial published in the inauguration issue of the paper, *reprinted in* Yi Hae-chang, *A Study of Korean Press History* (Korean) 30–31 (rev. ed. 1983).

48. Isabella Bird Bishop, *Korea and Her Neighbors* 440 (3d ed. 1897). *See also* Homer B. Hulbert, *The Passing of Korea* 152 (reprinted ed. 1969) (noting that "[f]rom the first [Tongnip Shinmun] exerted a powerful influence among the Koreans").

49. For a detailed discussion of *Tongnip Shinmun*, see Choe, *Korean Newspaper History, op. cit.*, pp. 42–105.

50. Michael Edson Robinson, *Cultural Nationalism in Colonial Korea, 1920–1925*, at 28–29 (1988).

51. *See* Yi, *A Study of Korean Press History, op. cit.*, pp. 34–67 passim.

52. Kim, 1 *History of Korean Journalism, op. cit.*, p. 24.

53. Yi, *A Study of Korean Press History, op. cit.*, p. 41.

54. According to one study on the Korean press, 22 daily newspapers were published in 1910, when Korea was colonized by Japan. Jae-won Lee, "South Korea," in 1 *World Press Encyclopedia* 581 (George Thomas Kurian ed., 1982).

55. Seong-hi Yim, "Constitution Guarantees Freedom of Press in ROK [Republic of Korea]: Its Thorny Past and Bright Future," 3 *Korean Report* 21 (September 1963).

56. Kim, 1 *History of Korean Journalism, op. cit.*, p. 74.

57. Yim, *op. cit.*, p. 22. For a discussion of the impact of the March 1 Independence Movement upon the Japanese colonial government's policy toward the Korean press, see Choe, *Korean Newspaper History, op. cit.*, pp. 312–54.

58. Robinson, *op. cit.*, p. 51.

59. *The Korean Press 1984*, at 12 (1984).

60. Min-Hwan Kim, "The Centennial Traces of Korean Journalism," in *Elite Media Amidst Mass Culture: A Critical Look at Mass Communication in Korea* 34 (Chie-woon Kim and Jae-won Lee eds., 1994).

61. Michael Robinson, "Mass Media and Popular Culture in 1930s Korea: Cultural Control, Identity, and Colonial Hegemony," in *Korean Studies: New Pacific Currents* 74 (Dae-Sook Suh ed., 1994).

62. Jong Geun Kang and Won Yong Kim, "A Survey of Radio and Television: History, System and Programming," in *Elite Media Amidst Mass Culture, op. cit.*, p. 126.

63. Ibid., p. 127.

64. Grajdanzev, *op. cit.*, p. 273.

65. *See generally* Hugh Borton, "Korea Under American and Soviet Occupation, 1945–7," in *Survey of International Affairs, 1939–1946: The Far East, 1942–46*, at 428–73 (Arnold Toynbee ed.,1955).

66. Kyu Ho Youm, "Press Law in the Republic of Korea," 6 *New York Law School Journal of International and Comparative Law* 669 (1986).

67. Under the "libertarian" press theory, the press functions to inform, entertain, and sell. The press's main purpose, however, is to uncover and present the truth. The press often serves as a Fourth Estate, supplementing the executive, legislative, and judicial branches of government. Press freedom in a libertarian society is a right of citizens, not a special privilege to be accorded by the government to a limited segment of society. Anyone who can pay for it may operate a communication medium and say whatever he likes, except perhaps for personal defamation, obscenity, invasion of privacy, wartime sedition, and the like. For a detailed discussion of the "libertarian" press theory, see Fred S. Siebert et al., *Four Theories of the Press* 39–71 (1956).

68. Hahn, *Communication Policies, op. cit.*, p. 19.

69. For a discussion of Ordinance No. 88, see chap. 4 *infra*.

70. *The Korean Press 1984, op. cit.*, p. 12.

71. Kang and Kim, *op. cit.*, p. 128 (footnotes omitted).

72. Ibid. (footnotes omitted).

73. Dong-Chol Kim, "Korean Newspapers: Past and Present," 2 *Korean Report* 22 (September–October 1962).

74. Kim, 2 *History of Korean Journalism, op. cit.*, p. 35.

75. Choe Chun, *A History of Korean Newspapers* (Korean) 380 (1960).

76. *A Handbook of Korea, op. cit.*, p. 514.

77. Kyu Kim, Won-Yong Kim, and Jong-Geun Kang, *Broadcasting in Korea* 47 (1994).

78. Ibid.

79. *The Korean Press 1984, op. cit.*, p. 13.

80. Ibid., p. 48.

81. D. Wayne Rowland, "The Press in the Korean Republic: Its Status and Problems," 35 *Journalism Quarterly* 451 (1958).

82. *The Korean Press 1984, op. cit.*, p. 13.

83. Haruko Watanabe, "South Korean Press, 1945–," 119 *Freedom of Information Center Publication* 4 (1964).

84. *The Korean Press 1984, op. cit.*, p. 14.

85. For a discussion of freedom of the Korean press during the Chang Myon government (1960–1961), see Yu Pyong-mu, "A Study of Freedom of the Press in Korea," 10 *Journalism Quarterly* (Korean) 85–106 (Autumn 1976).

86. Kim, Kim, and Kang, *op. cit.*, p. 49.

87. *Military Revolution in Korea* 29 (1961).

88. Chang Yong, *The Press and Human Rights* (Korean) 159 n.185 (1969).

89. Sunwoo Nam, "Newspapers Under Tribulation: The Present-Day Korean Press?" 27 *Gazette* 110 (1978) (footnote omitted).

90. Kim, Kim, and Kang, *op. cit.*, p. 49.

91. Nam, *op. cit.*, p. 110.

92. Lee, "South Korea," *op. cit.*, p. 582.

93. Ibid.

94. Chin Sok Chong, "The South Korean Press," in *Korea Briefing, 1992*, at 126 (Donald N. Clark ed., 1992).

95. *Human Rights in Korea* 289 (1986).

96. Lee, "South Korea," *op. cit.*, p. 585.

97. Suh, "South Korea in 1981," *op. cit.*, p. 107. *See also Index on Censorship,* December 1980, p. 71.

98. Won Ho Chang, *Mass Communication and Korea: Toward a Global Perspective for Research* 40 (1988).

99. For a discussion of the history of Korean news agencies including the establishment of Yonhap News Agency in January 1981, see Paeng Won-sun, A Study of the Structural Characteristics of Korean News Agencies (Korean) 175–221 (1982) (Ph.D. dissertation, Seoul National University).

100. *Facts About Korea* 143 (17th ed. 1983).

101. *Korea Annual 1984*, at 227 (21st ed. 1984).

102. 2 *The Europa Year Book 1984: A World Survey* 1876 (1984).

103. For a discussion of the "press guidelines" issued by the Korean government to the press, see chap. 4 *infra*.

104. Kyu Ho Youm, "Press Freedom Under Constraints: The Case of South Korea," 26 *Asian Survey* 882 (August 1986).

105. "South Korea," in Jon Vanden Heuvel and Everette E. Dennis, *The Unfolding Lotus: East Asia's Changing Media* 13 (1993).

106. Ibid., p. 10.

107. "Status of Periodical Registrations," *Newspapers and Broadcasting* (Korean), January 1995, p. 166.

108. *A Handbook of Korea, op. cit.*, p. 516.

109. Gwang-jub Han, "Promises and Myths of Cable Television and Telecommunications Infrastructure in Korea," in *Elite Media Amidst Mass Culture, op. cit.*, p. 137. *See also* Gwang-jub Han and Jong G. Kang, "Development of Cable Television," in Kim, Kim, and Kang, *op. cit.*, p. 137.

110. Sohn Tae-soo, "Start of CATV Service March 1 to Spur Cultural Impact," *Korea Herald*, January 1, 1995, p. 1 (supplement).

# CHAPTER 2

1. Constitution, amended in 1987, art. 40, *translated in* 1 *Current Laws of the Republic of Korea* 1–24 (1994) [hereinafter *ROK Current Laws*].

2. Ibid., art. 66 (4).

3. Ibid., art. 101 (1).

4. *Facts About Korea* 29 (rev. ed. 1994). *See also* Boo-Whan Han, "Major Features of the Constitution of the Sixth Republic of Korea and Its Two-Year's Implementation," 23 *Justice* 99 (1990) (noting that "[u]nder the Sixth Republic, the independence of Judiciary has been remarkably strengthened by the self-awareness of judges and popular sentiment as well as by the 9th Amendment").

5. *See* Gregory Henderson, "Constitutional Changes from the First to the Six Republics: 1948–1987," in *Political Change in South Korea* 22–43 (Ilpyong J. Kim and Young Whan Kihl eds., 1988).

6. *Judicial System of Korea* 5 (1991).

7. Dae-Kyu Yoon, *Law and Political Authority in South Korea* 170 (1990).

8. Hahm Pyong-Choon, *The Korean Political Tradition and Law* 165 (1967).

9. Yoon, *op. cit.*, p. 17.

10. For a thoughtful discussion of the sources of press law in Korea, see Kim Taek-hwan, *Korean Press Laws: Their Status and Issues* (Korean) 11–17 (1993).

11. The "civil-law" system followed in Korea, Japan, Germany, and France is distinguished from the Anglo-American "common-law" tradition: "Civil-law systems depend heavily upon written codes of private law ... as primary sources for authoritative statements of the law. Judicial decisions are less important than they are in common-law jurisdictions. While a line of judicial decisions establishing a particular legal proposition ... does carry substantial weight, the common-law rule of binding precedent ... is not recognized in traditional civil-law systems." George Dargo, "Civil Law," in *The Oxford Companion to the Supreme Court of the United States* 147 (Kermit L. Hall ed., 1992).

12. [Sang Hyun Song], "Special Problems in Studying Korean Law," in *Introduction to the Law and Legal System of Korea* 16 (Sang Hyun Song ed., 1983) [hereinafter *Law and Legal System*].

13. *See generally* Kang Kyong-gun, *An Exposition on Constitutional Law* (Korean) 11–24 (1993).

14. Lawrence Ward Beer, *Freedom of Expression in Japan* 129–30 (1984).

15. Song, *op. cit.*, p. 16.

16. Ibid.

17. *See* Supreme Court Rule No. 1003 (1988), revised by Supreme Court Rule No. 1180 (1991), *reprinted in Compendium of Codes* (Korean) 1667–68 (1994).

18. Song, *op. cit.*, p. 16.

19. For a discussion of "stare decisis" in the civil- and common-law systems, see Helen Silving, "'Stare Decisis' in the Civil and in the Common Law," 6 *Seoul Law Journal* 15–50 (1964).

20. Ibid., pp. 17–18 (emphasis added).

21. *Stare decisis* is defined as:

[A] doctrine that, when [a] court has once laid down a principle of law as applicable to a certain state of facts, it will adhere to that principle, and apply it to all future cases, where facts are substantially the same; regardless of whether the party and property are the same. Under [the] doctrine a deliberate or solemn decision of court made after argument on question of law fairly arising in the case, and necessary to its determination, is an authority, or binding precedent in the same court, or in other courts of equal or lower rank in subsequent cases where the very point is again in controversy.

*Black's Law Dictionary* 978 (6th ed. 1991).

22. Song, *op. cit.*, p. 18.

23. Ibid., p. 18.

24. Interview with Justice Han Pyong-chae of the Constitution Court of Korea, August 2, 1994.

25. *See* State v. Yi Sang-gwan, 65 Ko 8762, Taegu District Court, October 18, 1967, *Law Times* (Korean), November 6, 1967, p. 6; *Journalists Association of Korea Newsletter* (Korean), October 15, 1967, p. 2. For a discussion of the *Yi Sang-gwan* case, see chap. 11 *infra*.

26. 249 U.S. 47 (1919).

27. Song, *op. cit.*, p. 17.

28. In preparing this section, the author is deeply indebted to Attorney Woong-Shik Shin for his excellent article, "Judicial Organization in Korea," in *Business Laws in Korea* 107–42 (Chan-Jin Kim ed., 2d ed. [1988]).

29. Constitution, art. 110 (1).

30. Ibid., art. 110 (2).

31. Ibid., art. 101 (1).

32. Court Organization Act, Law No. 3992 (1987), revised by Law No. 4300 (1990), art. 14, *translated in* 1 *ROK Current Laws*, *op. cit.*, pp. 301–18.

33. Code of Criminal Procedure, Law No. 341 (1954), revised by Law No. 3955 (1987), art. 383, *translated in* 3 *Laws of the Republic of Korea* X-103 to X-165-1 (4th ed. 1994) [hereinafter *ROK Laws* (1994)].

34. Code of Civil Procedure, Law No. 547 (1960), revised by Law No. 4423 (1991), art. 394, *translated in* 3 *ROK Laws* (1994), *op. cit.*, pp. IX-44 to IX-45.

35. Shin, *op. cit.*, p. 110.

36. Code of Criminal Procedure, art. 372.

37. Code of Civil Procedure, art. 360.

38. Court Organization Act, art. 4.

39. Ibid., art. 7.

40. Ibid.

41. Ibid.

42. Ibid.

43. *Judicial System of Korea*, *op. cit.*, p. 8.

44. Yun Chin-su, "An Introduction to Practice of Law," in *Report on the '94 Symposium for Court Reporters* (Korean) 16 (1994).

45. Supreme Court of Korea, *Statutes Relating to Reforms in the Judicial System* (Korean) 112 (1994).

46. For the text of the proposed Special Act on Appeal Procedures, see *Statutes Relating to Reforms in the Judicial System*, *op. cit.*, pp. 111–18.

47. "Special Act on Appeal Procedures," *op. cit.*, arts. 2, 4.

48. Court Organization Act, art. 8 (emphasis added).

49. Shin, *op. cit.*, pp. 108–109.

50. *Law and Legal System, op. cit.*, p. 260.

51. Yoon, *op. cit.*, p. 163.

52. Song, *op. cit.*, p. 18.

53. Tscholsu Kim and Sang Don Lee, "The Influence of U.S. Constitutional Law Doctrines in Korea," in *Constitutional Systems in Late Twentieth Century Asia* 313 (Lawrence W. Beer ed., 1992).

54. Constitution, art. 111.

55. Ibid., art. 107 (2).

56. Code of Administrative Procedure, Law No. 3754 (1984), revised by Law No. 4017 (1988), art. 9, *reprinted in Compendium of Codes, op. cit.*, pp. 1617–73.

57. Court Organization Act, art. 28.

58. Code of Criminal Procedure, art. 361-5.

59. Court Organization Act, art. 7 (3).

60. Ibid., art. 27 (3).

61. Ibid., art. 6 (2) ("The Chief Justice of the Supreme Court may have a judge of a District Court or Family Court act for a judge of a High Court or other District Court or Family Court").

62. *Explanatory Sources on the Proposed Acts on Reforms in the Judicial System* (Korean) 36 (1994).

63. Shin, *op. cit.*, p. 123.

64. Court Organization Act, art. 7 (4), (5).

65. Ibid., art. 32 (1).

66. Ibid., art. 32 (2).

67. Ibid., art. 28.

68. Ibid., art. 14-2.

69. Shin, *op. cit.*, p. 135.

70. Court Organization Act, arts. 7 (5), 14 (2).

71. Ibid., art. 14-2.

72. *Explanatory Sources, op. cit.*, p. 42.

73. Constitution, art. 109; Court Organization Act, art. 56.

74. Ibid.; Court Organization Act, art. 57 (1).

75. Court Organization Act, art. 59.

76. For a concise discussion of how to find and cite Korean law, see Song, *op. cit.*, pp. 18–21.

77. Song, *op. cit.*, p. 20.

78. Ibid., p. 21.

79. *See Broadcasting Handbook 1994* (Korean) (1994).

80. Ibid., pp. 32–72.

81. Song, *op. cit.*, pp. 15–16.

82. *See The Bluebook: A Uniform System of Citation* (15th ed. 1991) (not a single reference to Korean law is found in this most widely used guide for legal citations in the United States, whereas citation systems in the Constitution, statutes, and court cases of China and Japan are provided).

83. "Introduction" to *Laws of the Republic of Korea* (4th ed. 1983).

84. The author has relied upon the English translations of a number of Korean statutes in *Current Laws of the Republic of Korea* and *Laws of the Republic of Korea* insofar as they are substantially

accurate. On occasion, however, he has used his own translations when the translations in the two sources are not close to the original Korean-language texts of the statutes.

85. *See* 4 *ROK Current Laws, op. cit.*, pp. 2561–2563-10.

86. *See* 3 *ROK Laws, op. cit.*, pp. X-64 to X-70-1, X-103 to X-165-1, X-49 to X-50, respectively.

87. *See The Korean Criminal Code* (Paul Ryu trans., Gerhard O.W. Mueller ed., 1960).

88. Ibid., pp. 1–29.

89. *See The Korean Press 1995*, at 135–45, 146–59, 159–83, 183–203 (1995), respectively. Appendixes D–G are the reprints of the English translations of the Korean press statutes in *The Korean Press 1995*, pp. 135–203.

90. Ibid., pp. 130–31, 131–34, 134–35, respectively.

91. Song, *op. cit.*, p. 19.

92. Ibid.

93. Ibid.

94. Ibid.

95. Donald M. Gillmor et al., *Mass Communication Law* xxxi (5th ed. 1990).

96. Donald M. Gillmor, *Power, Publicity and the Abuse of Libel Law* 129 (1992), *quoting* Cynthia Bolbach, managing editor of *Media Law Reporter*.

97. Song, *op. cit.*, p. 18.

98. Kim Chol-su, *Casebook on Constitutional Law* (Korean) (rev. ed. 1980).

99. Ibid., pp. 284–303.

100. Pak Won-sun, 1 *Study of National Security Laws* (Korean) 20 (1989).

101. Professor Song does not include the names of the parties in case citations. *See* Song, *op. cit.*, p. 19.

102. Yosiyuki Noda, *Introduction to Japanese Law* 232 n.12 (Anthony H. Angelo trans. and ed., 1976).

# CHAPTER 3

1. John C. Merrill and S. Jack Odell, *Philosophy and Journalism* 151–52 (1983).

2. *See* William A. Hachten, *The World News Prism* 16 (3d ed. 1992).

3. Raymond B. Nixon, "Factors Related to Freedom in National Press Systems," 37 *Journalism Quarterly* 13 (1960).

4. Donald M. Gillmor, "Freedom in Press Systems and the Religious Variable," 39 *Journalism Quarterly* 26 (1962).

5. *See* Doo-hun Kim, "Confucian Influences on Korean Society," 3 *Korea Journal* 17 (September 1963) (noting that "in every facet of Korean civilization and thought Confucian elements are to be deeply observed, although there have [sic] been a little difference in the degree of the influence according to the trends of any given time").

6. Woo-keun Han, *The History of Korea* 61 (Lee Kyung-shik trans., Grafton K. Mintz ed., 1970).

7. Vipan Chandra, "Korean Human-Rights Consciousness in an Era of Transition: A Survey of Late-Nineteenth-Century Developments," in *Human Rights in Korea: Historical and Policy Perspectives* 78 (William Shaw ed., 1991).

8. Rhoda E. Howard and Jack Donnelly, "Introduction," in *International Handbook of Human Rights* 20 (Jack Donnelly and Rhoda E. Howard eds., 1987).

9. Chandra, *op. cit.*, pp. 78–79.

10. Pak Yong-sang, "A History of Korean Press Law," *Newspaper Research* (Korean), Winter 1980, p. 9.

11. Choe Chun, *A History of Korean Newspapers* (Korean)18–19 (new ed. 1990).

12. Ibid., p. 19. It is significant that Li Hung-chang took note of the greater credibility of *Hansung Sunbo*, a government paper, and its more harmful impact on the prestige of China, in comparison with the credibility and impact of private newspapers. According to one recent study of American libel law, source credibility affects reputational harm. *See* Kenneth R. Blake, Explaining Link Between Source Credibility and Reputational Harm: Effects of Publication Type on Belief of Unfavorable Statements 22 (1995) (paper presented at the Southeast Colloquium of the Association for Education in Journalism and Mass Communication in Gainesville, Fla.).

13. Bong-Ki Kim, 1 *History of Korean Journalism* 13 (1967).

14. Editorial, *Tongnip Shinmun*, April 7, 1896, *reprinted in* Yi Hae-chang, *A Study of Korean Press History* 30 (rev. ed. 1983); *translated in part in* Kim, 1 *History of Korean Journalism, op. cit.*, pp. 17–20.

15. Chun Chhoe, "Characteristics of Korea [sic] Press," 2 *Korea Journal* 6 (May 1962).

16. Chong Chin-sok, *A History of the Korean Press* (Korean) 161 (1990).

17. Ibid.

18. After the abortive Kapshin coup d'etat in 1884, So went to the United States in 1895 after a short sojourn in Japan. During the next 10 years, he earned a doctorate in medicine from George Washington University in Washington, D.C.. So married an American woman and became an American citizen. He returned to Korea in December 1895 and was appointed advisor to the Privy Council of the Yi Dynasty. So published *Tongnip Shinmun* as a U.S. citizen with the financial support from the Korean government. Chong, *A History of the Korean Press, op. cit.*, pp. 158–59.

19. So recalled later: "Some advised me to slacken the tempo of reformation because too rapid a reform would prove prejudicial to my personal safety, and some tried to bribe me to stop printing certain articles. Also some threatened me with personal injury in case I should print their shady political activities." Kim, 1 *History of Korean Journalism, op. cit.*, p. 20.

20. Pak, "A History of Korean Press Law," *op. cit.*, p. 19.

21. Yi, *A Study of Korean Press History, op. cit.*, p. 30.

22. The royal cabinet of the Yi Dynasty deleted three of the 36 provisions in the original bill. The bill, which almost paralleled the Japanese Publication Law of 1893, was revised because Korea was different from Japan in its politics, customs, and language. *See* Choe, *A History of Korean Newspapers, op. cit.*, p. 84. The Japanese Publication Law, translated in *The Press Laws of Foreign Countries with an Appendix Containing the Press Laws of India* 153–57 (Montague Shearman and O.T. Rayner eds., 1926), was composed of 35 articles.

23. Choe, *A History of Korean Newspapers, op. cit.*, p. 84.

24. Ibid., p. 84.

25. Chin-Sok Chong, *The Korean Problem in Anglo-Japanese Relations 1904–1910: Ernest Thomas Bethell and His Newspapers, the Daehan Maeil Sinbo and the Korea Daily News* 124 n.81 (1987).

26. Ibid.

27. Ibid.

28. Law No. 1 (July 24, 1907), *reprinted in Complete Collection of Korean Press Laws, 1945–1981* (Korean), at 15–16 (Chong Chin-sok ed., 1982) [hereinafter *Korean Press Laws*]; *translated in* Kim, 1 *History of Korean Journalism, op. cit.*, pp. 53–59.

29. Hahm Pyong-Choon, *Korean Jurisprudence, Politics and Culture* 135 (1986) (the law was promulgated to deal with the Korean press "which had been increasingly anti-Japanese").

30. Newspaper Law (1907), arts. 1, 4.

31. Ibid., art. 6.

32. Ibid., art. 10.

33. Ibid., art. 11.

34. Ibid., art. 13.

35. Ibid., art. 15.

36. Ibid., art. 12.

37. Ibid., art. 14.

38. Ibid., arts. 21, 34.

39. Ibid., arts. 25–37.

40. Kim, 1 *History of Korean Journalism, op. cit.*, p. 52.

41. Sukhyon Kim Moon, Aspects of Korean Press Development: From Its Beginnings to the Present 93 (1988) (Ph.D. dissertation, University of Maryland) (noting that the Japanese Resident-General "pressured" the Korean royal cabinet to amend the law "so that newspapers published by foreigners and Koreans abroad were also subject to the law").

42. Law No. 8 (1908), art. 34, *reprinted in Korean Press Laws, op. cit.*, p. 18.

43. Ibid., arts. 35, 36.

44. Hahm, *op. cit.*, p. 144.

45. Law No. 6 (February 23, 1909), *reprinted in* Yi, *A Study of Korean Press History, op. cit.*, pp. 412–14.

46. Ibid., art. 11.

47. Professors John Merrill and Jack Odell find the "forced slave" status of the press when it is a "forced instrument of government." They argue that the forced slave press "is controlled, directed, dictated to, censored [by the government], and its desires and aspirations are ignored. This is the ultimate totalitarian or ultra-authoritarian situation." Merrill and Odell, *op. cit.*, p. 152.

48. Yi Sang-chol, a communication professor at Chungang University in Seoul, divides the Japanese colonial era into three segments from the perspective of the Korean press: (1) the dark period between 1910 and 1919; (2) the semi-daylight period between 1920 and 1939; and (3) the dark period between 1940 and 1945. *See* Yi Sang-chol, *A History of Communications Development* (Korean) 164–75 passim (1982).

49. *See* "Detailed Report of the Shooting and Killing of Stevens," *translated in* Chong, *Korean Problem, op. cit.*, pp. 331–33. The translation of the *Maeil Sinbo* article of April 17, 1909, was part of the evidence presented to the court for a trial relating to the story. Ibid., p. 331.

50. Chong, *Korean Problem, op. cit.*, p. 256.

51. Chang Yong, *The Press and Human Rights* (Korean) 115 (1969).

52. Choe, *A History of Korean Newspapers, op. cit.*, p. 175. *See also* Edward J. Baker, *The Role of Legal Reforms in the Japanese Annexation and Rule of Korea, 1905–1919*, at 33 n.122 (1979) (noting that under the revised Newspaper Law, a total of 52,062 copies of 110 editions of foreign and domestic newspapers were seized in 1911, including 50,497 copies of 70 editions of Japanese newspapers).

53. Ibid., p. 330.

54. Ibid, p. 210.

55. Chong Chin-sok, *A History of the Struggle by the Korean Press Under Japanese Rule* (Korean) 72–73 (1982).

56. Choe, *A History of Korean Newspapers, op. cit.*, p. 206.

57. Pak, "A History of Korean Press Law," *op. cit.*, p. 23.

58. A Korean journalism scholar has characterized the Peace Maintenance Law as "[a] legal base for the totalitarian control of the press, both in Japan and abroad under the Japanese control." Moon, *op. cit.*, p. 110. Under the law, the Minister of Home Affairs was authorized to dissolve any association

or forbid any gathering he deemed necessary in order to preserve peace and order. *1909 Annual Report, op. cit.*, p. 49.

59. Chong, *Struggle by the Korean Press, op. cit.*, p. 115–16.

60. Yi, *Communications Development, op. cit.*, p. 173.

61. Yi, *A Study of Korean Press History, op.cit.*, p. 147.

62. *The Korean Press 1984*, at 12 (1984).

63. Kun Yang, "Law and Society Studies in Korea: Beyond the Hahm Theses," 23 *Law and Society Review* 897 (1989).

64. Ibid.

65. Haruko Watanabe, "South Korean Press, 1945–," 119 *Freedom of Information Center Publication* 1 (1964). *See also Introduction to the Law and Legal System of Korea* 4 (Sang Hyun Song ed., 1983) (describing the Japanese colonial rule as "very oppressive").

66. *See* ibid.

67. Moon, *op. cit.*, p. 112.

68. Myung Shik Koh, A History of Korean Journalism Under U.S. Military Government, 1945–1948, at 18–19 (1967) (M.A. thesis, University of Iowa) (footnote omitted).

69. Jae-won Lee, "South Korea," in 1 *World Press Encyclopedia* 582 (George Thomas Kurian ed., 1982).

## CHAPTER 4

1. Henry Steele Commager, *Crusaders for Freedom* 16 (1962). *See also* Palko v. Connecticut, 302 U.S. 319, 326–27 (1937) (characterizing protection of speech and the press as a "fundamental" liberty in part because "our history, political and legal," recognized "freedom of thought and speech" as "the matrix, the indispensable condition, of nearly every other form of freedom").

2. Under the "authoritarian" theory of press freedom, the press is to support and advance the policies of the government in the main capacity of a governmental propaganda agency. The authoritarian press system, usually adopted by many a strongman" type of government, is based upon the proposition that freedom of the press is a special privilege to be granted by the State, not one of the basic political and civil liberties of individuals. The authoritarian press, although functioning as private enterprise within the individual country, owes its existence to the State. Thus, the press has as much freedom as the government allows it to have. For a detailed discussion of the authoritarian theory of the press, see generally Fred S. Siebert et al., *Four Theories of the Press* 9–37 (1956).

3. Jae-kyoung Lee, A Crisis of the South Korean Media: The Rise of Civil Society and Democratic Transition 6 (1993) (paper presented at the Association for Education in Journalism and Mass Communication convention in Kansas City, Mo.).

4. D. Wayne Rowland, "The Press in the Korean Republic: Its Status and Problems," 35 *Journalism Quarterly* 454 (1958).

5. E. Grant Meade, *American Military Government in Korea* 7 (1951).

6. Myung Shik Koh, A History of Korean Journalism Under U.S. Military Government, 1945–1948, at 40 (1967) (M.A. thesis, University of Iowa), citing *The Maeil Shinbo*, September 12, 1945.

7. Ibid., pp. 40–41.

8. Sir William Blackstone, the oracle of the common law in the minds of the American framers, stated: "The *liberty of the press* is indeed essential to the nature of a free state; but this consists in laying no *previous* restraints upon publications, and not in freedom from censure for criminal matter when published." Sir William Blackstone, 4 *Commentaries on the Laws of England*, 151–52 (London, 1765–69), *quoted in* Leonard W. Levy, *Emergence of a Free Press* 12 (1985).

9. Chong Tae-chol, "The Press Policy of the American Military Government and the Press Reality," in *Modern Society and Freedom of the Press* (Korean) 510 (Committee on Publication of Research Papers in Honor of Dr. Paeng Won-Sun's 61st Birthday ed., 1989), *citing Maeil Shinbo*, October 11, 1945.

10. Ordinance No. 11 (1945).

11. Among the Japanese colonial laws and regulations abolished by Ordinance No. 11 were the Publication Law, Law No. 6 (February 22, 1909), and the Publication Rules, Residency-General Decree No. 20 (1910), *reprinted in* Yi Hae-chang, *A Study of Korean Press History* (Korean) 412–15 (rev. ed. 1983).

12. Ordinance No. 11, § II.

13. Hahm Pyong-Choon, *Korean Jurisprudence, Politics and Culture* 147 (1986). For a discussion of the Publication Law of 1909 and other repressive laws enforced by Japanese colonialists, see Edward J. Baker, *The Role of Legal Reforms in the Japanese Annexation and Rule of Korea, 1905–1919*, at 28–34 (1979).

14. Sunwoo Nam, "Newspapers Under Tribulation: The Present-Day Korean Press?" 27 *Gazette* 120 (1978). One American journalism professor wrote in 1958: "In Seoul, almost overnight, there were 24 dailies and uncounted publications of irregular frequency, but little resembling responsible journalism." Rowland, *op. cit.*, p. 450. For detailed statistical data on newspapers and other periodicals published in 1945–1948, see *Summation of United States Army Military Activities in Korea*, No. 12 (September 1946): 78; No. 19 (April 1947): 65; No. 22 (July 1947): 100 [hereinafter *USAMAIK Summation*]; *South Korean Interim Government Activities*, No. 24 (September 1947): 128; No. 34 (July–August 1948): 240 [hereinafter *SKIG Activities*].

15. Koh, *op. cit.*, pp. 42–43.

16. Ibid., p. 43 (emphasis added) (footnotes omitted).

17. *USAMAIK Summation, op. cit.*, No. 13 (October 1946): 26.

18. Ibid., p. 82.

19. Ibid.

20. *SKIG Activities, op. cit.*, No. 34 (July–August 1948): 239. *See also USAMAIK Summation, op. cit.*, No. 13 (October 1946): 82–83.

21. *SKIG Activities, op. cit.*, No. 31 (April 1948): 167.

22. Ibid.

23. Meade, *op. cit.*, p. 224.

24. *The Korean Press 1985*, at 11 (1985).

25. William A. Hachten, *The World News Prism* 16 (3d ed. 1992) (emphasis deleted).

26. Meade, *op. cit.*, p. 31, *quoting* General Hodge.

27. Hakjoon Kim, "The American Military Government in South Korea, 1945–1948: Its Formation, Policies, and Legacies," 12 *Asian Perspective* 80 (Spring–Summer 1988).

28. Ordinance No. 19 (October 30, 1945), *translated in A Complete Compilation of Laws and Ordinances of the U.S. Army Military Government in Korea* 75–78 (1971) [hereinafter *USAMGIK Laws and Ordinances*].

29. Ibid., § V.

30. On October 10, 1945, General Arnold "order[ed] the Korean press to publicize his statement" that the USAMGIK was the "only government" in South Korea. Professor Leonard Hoag noted:

> The request to print this statement "with the force of an order" provoked a protest from Korean correspondents who tended to regard the action as a violation of the freedom of the press. They insisted that the language, when translated into Korean, was particularly insulting and created a lost [sic] of face for everyone. But the order stood. Some members of the staff

questioned the wisdom of ordering such a publication in a country where Americans were trying to teach the freedom of the press.

C. Leonard Hoag, *American Military Government in Korea: War Policy and the First Year of Occupation, 1941–1946*, at 273 (1970) (draft manuscript produced under the auspices of the Office of the Chief of Military History, Department of the Army, Washington, D.C.).

31. Bruce C. Cumings, *The Origins of the Korean War* 148 (1981).

32. Professor Bruce Cumings of the University of Chicago, criticizing the investigation, wrote: "The purpose of this investigation was to discover some flaw which could be used as a legitimate reason for controlling the paper if it seemed advisable. 'It was like getting Al Capone for his income tax,' said one of the officers charged with the investigation." Ibid., p. 194.

33. Ibid. (footnote omitted).

34. Choe Chun, *A History of Korean Newspapers* (Korean) 331–32 (new ed. 1990).

35. Ibid., p. 332.

36. Hahm, *op. cit.*, p. 150.

37. Cumings, *op. cit.*, p. 531 n.131.

38. The First Amendment to the U.S. Constitution reads: "Congress shall make no law respecting an establishment of religion, or prohibiting the free exercise thereof, or abridging the freedom of speech, or of the press, or the right of the people peaceably to assemble, and to petition the Government for a redress of grievances." U.S. CONST. amend. I.

39. *See* Ordinance No. 55, *reprinted in SCAP [Supreme Commander for the Allied Powers] Summation*, No. 5 (February 1946) and USAMGIK, *Official Gazette*, February 23, 1946, *cited in* Cumings, *op. cit.*, p. 531 n.128.

40. USAMGIK, *Official Gazette*, May 4, 1946, *cited in* Cumings, *op. cit.*, pp. 246–47.

41. *SKIG Activities, op. cit.*, No. 9 (June 1946), p. 19. The Ordinance was formally abolished in April 1948. *See SKIG Activities, op. cit.*, No. 31 (April 1948), p. 166.

42. Hahm, *op. cit.*, p. 150.

43. Martin H. Redish, *Freedom of Expression: A Critical Analysis* 5 (1984). One leading authority on freedom of the press in the United States has observed: "American constitutional law holds few principles dearer than the idea that prior restraints on publication are inconsistent with freedom of expression.... [E]ven the most niggardly views of freedom of expression have accepted that principle since well before the drafting of the First Amendment." Marc A. Franklin and David A. Anderson, *Mass Media Law* 61 (4th ed. 1990).

44. Ordinance No. 88 (May 29, 1946), § I, *translated in USAMGIK Laws and Ordinances, op. cit.*, pp. 189–91.

45. As a USAMGIK report stated, the Ordinance was aimed at placing "a check on the small, fly-by-night propaganda sheets which were printed without authority in one building after another." *SKIG Activities, op.cit.*, No. 34 (July–August 1948): 240.

46. Kim Dong-jin, A Study of the Public Interest of Broadcasting (Korean) 160 (1986) (Ph.D. dissertation, Yonsei University (Seoul)), Appendix 3. The Broadcasting Regulation Rule also stipulated: "Stations shall approve or disapprove broadcasting of public announcements or news reports on the basis of whether they are for public interest, convenience, concern and necessity, and at the same time they are for truth, fairness, and justifiable ends; stations shall not air advertisements of political parties which did not register [with the USAMGIK] in compliance with Ordinance No. 55." Ibid.

47. Dong-Jin Kim, "Development of the Concept of Public Interest in Korean Broadcasting," 14 *Korean Social Science Journal* 161 (1988). *See* Communications Act of 1934, § 303, 48 Stat. 1064, 47 U.S.C.A. § 303 (West Supp. 1994) (the Federal Communications Commission "as public interest, convenience, or necessity requires, shall ... have authority to make special regulations applicable to radio stations engaged in chain broadcasting").

48. Ibid.

49. Bong-Ki Kim, 2 *History of Korean Journalism* 10 (1969).

50. Ordinance No. 88, § IV.

51. George M. McCune and Arthur L. Grey, *Korea Today* 86 (1950). *But cf.* Pak Won-sun, "History of Enforcement of National Security Act Against the Press," in *Collection of Research Papers in Honor of Mr. Yi Yong-hi's 61st Birthday* (Korean) 498 (Committee on Publication of Research Papers in Honor of Mr. Yi Yong-hi's 61st Birthday ed., 1989) (noting that nearly all leftist and/or anti-USAMGIK newspapers disappeared around the end of 1947 due to the "press massacre" by the American military government) (footnote omitted).

52. The Legislative Council was the legislative branch of the South Korean Interim Government (SKIG) organized by the USAMGIK in late 1946. Half of its members were elected by the popular vote and the other half were appointed by the U.S. miliary governor. Donald Stone Macdonald, *The Koreans: Contemporary Politics and Society* 48 (2d ed. 1990).

53. The Law Governing Newspapers and Other Periodicals (September 19, 1947), arts. 2, 6, *reprinted in Complete Collection of Korean Press Laws, 1945–1981* (Korean) 20 (Chong Chin-sok ed., 1982) [hereinafter *Korean Press Laws*]; *translated in* Kim, 2 *History of Korean Journalism, op. cit.*, pp. 12–15.

54. Ibid., art. 6.

55. Ibid., art. 8.

56. Kim, 2 *History of Korean Journalism, op. cit.*, p. 16.

57. *SKIG Activities, op.cit.*, No. 25 (October 1947): 125.

58. U.S. Army Military Government in Korea, *Official Gazette*, No. 7 (October 18, 1947): 618. Haebang News Agency was the only news agency in South Korea under American military rule that carried Tass. Five other news agencies were in operation in 1945–1948. *See* Choe, *A History of Korean Newspapers, op. cit.*, pp. 375–76.

59. Law No. 1 (July 1, 1907). The Newspaper Law prohibited publication of several categories of news stories, some of which were: (1) articles profaning the dignity of the royal family, undermining the Constitution, or detrimental to international amicability; (2) articles distorting crimes or justifying and protecting criminal defendants; and (3) false reports intended to defame others. Ibid., arts. 11, 13, 15.

60. The Newspaper Law was enacted "to control the press which had been becoming increasingly anti-Japanese." Hahm, *op. cit.*, p. 135.

61. State v. Kim Kwang-su, Hyongsang 369, Seoul High Court, April 7, 1948, *Korean Press Annual 1968* (Korean) 515 (1968).

62. Ibid.

63. Kim Kwang-su v. State, Pisang 1, Supreme Court, May 21, 1948, *Korean Press Annual 1968, op. cit.*, p. 515.

64. Ibid.

65. Dai-Kwon Choi, "The Development of Law and Legal Institutions in Korea," in Bong Duk Chun et al., *Traditional Korean Legal Attitudes* 87 (1980). *See also* Dae-Kyu Yoon, *Law and Political Authority in South Korea* 27 (1990) (noting that "[a] sudden lifting of all forms of political constraints created an atmosphere of total freedom, which soon turned into undisciplined license").

66. Robert T. Oliver, *Syngman Rhee and American Involvement in Korea, 1942–1960*, at 16 (1978). *See also* Soon Sung Cho, *Korea in World Politics 1940–1950*, at 61 (1967) ("[The United States] was completely unprepared and it has paid dearly for this error"); Joungwon Alexander Kim, *Divided Korea: The Politics of Development, 1945–1972*, at 53 (1975) ("Korean policy ... very poorly coordinated"); Won Sul Lee, *The United States and the Division of Korea, 1945*, at 92 (1982) ("United States forces ... had practically no preparations").

67. Chilton R. Bush, "foreword" to William J. Coughlin, *Conquered Press: The MacArthur Era in Japanese Journalism* (1952).

68. One authority on South Korea characterized General Hodge as the "key figure dominating both American policies and means of implementing them in South Korea." Oliver, *op. cit.*, p. 74.

69. Chang Yong, *The Press and Human Rights* (Korean) 128 (1969).

70. J. Franklin Ray, Jr., "Reorganization of Education System," *Voice of Korea*, August 30, 1947, pp. 214–16.

71. Koh, *op. cit.*, p. 106.

72. Kyu Ho Youm and Michael B. Salwen, Press Freedom and Social and Economic Progress in the Far East: The Case of South Korea (1988) (paper presented at the Association for Education in Journalism and Mass Communication convention in Portland, Ore.) (available on ERIC (ED 297 329)) (1989).

73. Choe, *A History of Korean Newspapers, op. cit.*, p. 342.

74. Ibid.

75. Constitution of Korea, art. 13, ordained and promulgated in 1948, *translated in* 2 *Constitutions of Nations* 549–59 (Amos J. Peaslee ed., 2d ed. 1956).

76. Tscholsu Kim and Sang Don Lee, "The Influence of U.S. Constitutional Law Doctrines in Korea," in *Constitutional Systems in Late Twentieth Century Asia* 306 (Lawrence W. Beer ed., 1992).

77. Young Ho Lee, The Political Culture of Modernizing Society: Political Attitudes and Democracy in Korea 33 (1969) (Ph.D. dissertation, Yale University), *quoting* Gabriel A. Almond and G. Bingham Powell, Jr., *Comparative Politics: A Developmental Approach* (1966).

78. Yi, *A Study of Korean Press History, op. cit.*, p. 154.

79. Andrew C. Nahm, *A History of the Korean People, Tradition and Transformation* 424 (1988).

80. For the history of the National Security Act of 1948, see Pak Won-sun, 1 *A Study of National Security Laws* 75–105 (1989).

81. National Security Act, Law No. 10 (1948), *reprinted in Korean Press Laws, op. cit.*, p. 760.

82. Nahm, *op. cit.*, pp. 424–25.

83. One section of Article 4 of Ordinance No. 88 read: Newspapers and other periodicals shall have their licensees revoked and suspended "when they violate laws." Ordinance No. 88, art. 4 § 3.

84. Choe, *A History of Korean Newspapers, op. cit.*, p. 354.

85. Ibid., p. 355.

86. Ibid., p. 356.

87. Ibid., p. 367.

88. Ibid.

89. Yi Hae-chang, "Changes in Press Control in Korea," 16 *Journal of Korean Cultural Research Institute* (Korean) 101 (June 1970).

90. Choe, *A History of Korean Newspapers, op. cit.*, p. 372.

91. Ibid., p. 376.

92. Bong-gi Kim, "Korea," in *The Asian Newspapers' Reluctant Revolution* 97 (John A. Lent ed., 1971).

93. *See* Upper House Election Act, Law No. 469 (1958), and Lower House Election Act, Law No. 470 (1958), *reprinted in Korean Press Laws, op. cit.*, pp. 813–17.

94. Lower House Election Act, art. 73; Upper House Election Act, art. 157.

95. *See* Lower House Election Act, art. 72.

96. Law No. 500 (1958), *reprinted in Korean Press Laws, op. cit.*, pp. 760–64.

97. For a discussion of the National Security Act of 1958, see Pak, 1 *Study of National Security Laws*, *op. cit.*, pp. 129–59.

98. National Security Act (1958), art. 1.

99. Ibid., art. 11.

100. Ibid., art. 4.

101. Ibid., art. 12 (1).

102. Ibid., art. 12 (2).

103. Ibid., art. 17 (5).

104. Ibid., art. 22.

105. Nahm, *op. cit.*, p. 435.

106. John Kie-Chiang Oh, *Korea: Democracy on Trial* 58 (1968).

107. Kim, 2 *History of Korean Journalism*, *op. cit.*, p. 66.

108. Dong-Chol Kim, "Korean Newspapers: Past and Present," 2 *Korean Report* 23 (September–October 1962).

109. Constitution of Korea, amended in 1960, art. 13, *translated in Military Revolution in Korea* 115–48 (1961).

110. Ibid., art. 28.

111. Gregory Henderson, "Constitutional Changes from the First to the Sixth Republics: 1948–1987," in *Political Change in South Korea* 30 (Ilpyong J. Kim and Young Whan Kihl eds., 1988).

112. Kim and Lee, *op. cit.*, p. 311.

113. Act on Registration of Newspapers and Political Parties, Law No. 553 (1960), *reprinted in Korean Press Laws*, *op. cit.*, pp. 21–22.

114. Ibid., art. 1.

115. National Security Act, Law No. 549 (1960), revised by Law No. 1151 (1962), *translated in Laws of the Republic of Korea* 1314–20 (2d ed. 1969). A new provision on "special aggravated penalties for second-time offenders" was added to the National Security Act through its revision in 1962. *See* National Security Act, revised in 1962, art. 10-2.

116. For a discussion of the revised National Security Act of 1960, see Pak, 1 *Study of National Security Laws*, *op. cit.*, pp. 160–68.

117. Kim Bong-gi, "Korea," *op. cit.*, p. 99.

118. Oh, *Democracy on Trial*, *op. cit.*, p. 90 (footnote omitted).

119. Chin Sok Chong, "The South Korean Press," in *Korea Briefing, 1992*, at 117 (Donald N. Clark ed.,1992).

120. *See* Haruko Watanabe, "South Korean Press, 1945–," 119 *Freedom of Information Center Publication* 4 (1964).

121. Oh, *Democracy on Trial*, *op. cit.*, pp. 90–91 (footnote omitted).

122. Seong-hi Yim, "Constitution Guarantees Freedom of the Press in ROK [Republic of Korea]: Its Thorny Past and Bright Future," 3 *Korean Report* 23 (September 1963).

123. Decree No. 1 (1961), *reprinted in Korean Press Laws*, *op. cit.*, p. 780.

124. Ibid.

125. Decree No. 4 (1961), *reprinted in Korean Press Laws*, *op. cit.*, p. 781.

126. Edward W. Wagner, "Failure in Korea," 40 *Foreign Affairs* 130 (October 1961).

127. Decree No. 11 (1961), *reprinted in Korean Press Laws*, *op. cit.*, p. 781.

128. Oh, *Democracy on Trial*, *op. cit.*, pp. 123–24.

129. Chang, *The Press and Human Rights*, *op. cit.*, p. 159 n.186.

130. Kim, 2 *History of Korean Journalism*, *op. cit.*, p. 97.

131. Dong-Chol Kim, "Korean Newspapers: Past and Present," 2 *Korean Report* 12 (November–December 1962).

132. For the text of the written arraignment of the *Minjok Ilbo* case, see *Korean Press Annual 1968*, *op. cit.*, pp. 529–32.

133. Cho Yong-su v. State, Hyoksang 3, Prosecution Ministry of the Military Revolutionary Government, October 31, 1961, *Korean Press Annual 1968, op. cit.*, p. 532.

134. Constitution of Korea, art. 18 (1), amended in 1962, *translated in Laws of the Republic of Korea* 1–20 (2d ed. 1969).

135. Ibid.

136. Yim, "Constitution Guarantees Freedom of the Press in ROK," *op. cit.*, p. 24.

137. Kwang-kil Kay, "Press Ethics Commission," 5 *Korea Journal* 13 (February 1965).

138. Om Ki-hyong, *A Discourse on Press Ethics* (Korean) 138 (1982).

139. Press Ethics Commission Act, Law No. 1652 (1964), art. 1, *reprinted in Korean Press Laws*, *op. cit.*, pp. 37–39.

140. The ethics code of the Korean press was modeled after U.S. codes of press ethics. One commentator said: "The Code of the Korean Press Ethics Commissions was drafted by two leading members of the Kwanhun Club, Kwon-sang Park and Yong-gu Kim. Both of them went to the United States as grantees of the U.S. State Department and continued their study at Northwestern University. They collected materials and observed the operation of press codes in the United States. On the basis of these, they drafted the Korean code." Sukhyon Kim Moon, Aspects of Korean Press Development: From Its Beginnings to the Present 134 (1988) (Ph.D. dissertation, University of Maryland). For an English translation of the code of press ethics in Korea, see *The Korean Press 1995*, at 130–31 (1995).

141. Press Ethics Commission Act, art. 3 (2).

142. Ibid., art. 14.

143. Ibid., art. 19.

144. Of the 26 newspapers then in Korea, 21 supported the enforcement of the Press Ethics Commission Act, four opposed it and one took a neutral stand. Om, *op. cit.*, p. 144 (1982).

145. Jae Cheon Yu, The Current Problems of Press Freedom in Korea 27–28 (1972) (M.A. thesis, University of Minnesota).

146. *See* Song Kon-ho, *A Modern History of the Korean Press* (Korean) 139–44 (1990).

147. Chie-woon Kim and Tae-sup Shin, "The Korean Press: A Half Century of Controls, Suppression and Intermittent Resistance," in *Elite Media Amidst Mass Culture: A Critical Look at Mass Communication in Korea* 52 (Chie-woon Kim and Jae-won Lee eds., 1994).

148. Raymond B. Nixon, "Freedom in the World's Press: A Fresh Appraisal with New Data," 42 *Journalism Quarterly* 12 (Winter 1965).

149. Park Chung Hee, *Our Nation's Path: Ideology of Social Reconstruction* 26–27 (1962).

150. Choe Chong-ho, "The Modernization of Korea and Communication Culture of Two Decades," 22 *Korea Journal* 31 (March 1982).

151. *See generally* J. Herbert Altschull, *Agents of Power: The Media and Public Policy* 229–37 (2d ed. 1995); Hachten, *op. cit.*, pp. 34–37.

152. *Major Speeches by Korea's Park Chung Hee* 99 (Shin Bum Shik comp., 1970). Professor Yunshik Chang of the University of British Columbia noted: "[Park's] idea of the press ... was that it should not be a critic, but a participant in the government program of rebuilding the nation.... He had little tolerance for opposition party media, and was determined either to have the entire media on his side or to silence those not favorably inclined to the government." Yunshik Chang, "From Ideology to Interest: Government and Press in South Korea, 1945–1979," in *Korean Studies: New Pacific Currents* 253 (Dae-Sook Suh ed., 1994).

153. John C. Merrill et al., *The Foreign Press: A Survey of the World's Journalism* 264 (1974).

154. The Declaration of State of National Emergency (1971), *reprinted in Korean Press Laws, op. cit.*, p. 786.

155. Jae-won Lee, "South Korea," in 1 *World Press Encyclopedia* 586 (George Thomas Kurian ed., 1982).

156. Henderson, "Constitutional Changes," *op. cit.*, p. 33.

157. *See* Martial Law Decree No. 1 (1972), *reprinted in Korean Press Laws, op. cit.*, p. 786; *translated in* "Decree No. 1," *Korea Times*, October 18, 1972, p. 1.

158. Ibid.

159. *See* Press Policy Guidelines Issued Under Martial Law Decree No. 1, *reprinted in Korean Press Laws, op. cit.*, p. 787.

160. Additions to News Stories Banned from Being Broadcast or Published (1972), *reprinted in Korean Press Laws, op. cit.*, p. 787.

161. Constitution of Korea, amended in 1972, art. 18, *translated in Laws of the Republic of Korea* 1–7 (3d ed. 1975).

162. Ibid., art. 32 (2).

163. Jerome Alan Cohen and Edward J. Baker, "U.S. Foreign Policy and Human Rights in South Korea," in *Human Rights in Korea, op. cit.*, p. 176.

164. William P. Cheshire, "Outlawing Dissent Leads to Violence," *Arizona Republic*, January 8, 1995, p. D1.

165. *See generally* William J. Butler, "Political Repression in South Korea—1974," *ICJ [International Commission of Jurists] Review*, no. 13 (December 1974): 37–44.

166. Presidential Emergency Measure No. 1 (1974), *translated in Documents on the Struggle for Democracy in Korea* 89 (Emergency Christian Conference on Korean Problems ed., 1975); *Emergency Measures Proclaimed by the President of the Republic of Korea Under Article 53 of the Constitution* 12 (1974).

167. Presidential Emergency Measure No. 4 (1974), *translated in Struggle for Democracy, op. cit.*, pp. 124–26.

168. Ibid.

169. Decree No. 9 (1975), *reprinted in Korean Press Laws, op. cit.*, p. 78; *translated in* "Presidential Decree No. 9," *Korea Herald*, May 14, 1975, p. 2.

170. *Index on Censorship*, September–October 1979, p. 70.

171. *Index on Censorship*, March–April 1978, p. 63.

172. *Index on Censorship*, February 1980, p. 73.

173. *Index on Censorship*, Autumn 1975, p. 86.

174. *Index on Censorship*, Winter 1973, p. vii.

175. *Index on Censorship*, Summer 1972, p. 96.

176. Law No. 239 (1953), revised by Law No. 2745 (1975), art. 104-2, *translated in 3 ROK Laws* (1983), *op. cit.*, X-1 to X-44.

177. Peter T. White, "South Korea: What Next?" 148 *National Geographic* 427 (September 1975).

178. Cohen and Baker, *op. cit.*, p. 186.

179. *Index on Censorship*, Spring 1973, p. 95.

180. *Index on Censorship*, November–December 1978, p. 65.

181. Nam, "Newspapers Under Tribulation," *op. cit.*, p. 119.

182. *Struggle for Democracy, op. cit.*, pp. 213–16.

183. Ibid., p. 216.

184. *Dong-A Ilbo* carried 10,931 advertisements of encouragement from January 1, 1975, to April 8, 1975. Kim Chin-hong, *Politics of Press Control* (Korean) 91 (1983).

185. *IPI [International Press Institute] Report*, December 1975, p. 16. *See also* Robert Crabbe, "S. Korea's Secret Police Cancel Ads in Dong-A Ilbo," *Editor & Publisher*, February 15, 1975, p. 13.

186. *Journalists Association of Korea Newsletter* (Korean), February 14, 1975, p. 1.

187. Moon, *op. cit.*, p. 140.

188. Lee, "South Korea," *op. cit.*, p. 583.

189. Nam, "Newspapers Under Tribulation," *op. cit.*, p. 110.

190. John A. Lent, "A Reluctant Revolution Among Asian Newspapers," in *Mass Communications: A World View* 117–18 (Alan Wells ed., 1974).

191. Nam, "Newspapers Under Tribulation," *op. cit.*, p. 120.

192. *IPI Report*, October 1980, p. 12.

193. Constitution, amended in 1980, art. 20 (1)–(2), *translated in* 1 *ROK Laws* (1983), *op. cit.*, pp. I-1 to I-19.

194. Lent, "Reluctant Revolution," *op. cit.*, p. 113.

195. Basic Press Act, Law No. 3347 (1980), *translated in* 1 *Laws of the Republic of Korea* III-112 to III-135 (4th ed. 1983).

196. Sang-won Lim, The Press Law of Korea (South) 2 (1982) (paper prepared for Journalism 425: Control of Information at the University of Missouri-Columbia School of Journalism).

197. Basic Press Act, Law No. 3347 (1980), arts. 6, 8, *translated in* 1 *ROK Laws* (1983), *op. cit.*, pp. III-122 to III-135.

198. Article 3 of the Basic Press Act stipulated: (1) The press shall respect dignity and value of human beings and the basic democratic order; (2) The press shall perform its public duties by contributing to the formation of democratic public opinions concerning matters of public interest by means of news reports, commentary, and other methods; (3) The press shall not infringe upon the personal honor or rights of an individual, or public morality or social ethics; (4) The press shall not encourage or praise violence and other illegal actions which disrupt public order. Ibid., art. 3 (1)–(4).

199. "Standards for Implementation of the Press Policy," *reprinted in Korean Press Laws, op. cit.*, p. 784.

200. Basic Press Act, art. 21.

201. Ibid., art. 20.

202. Ibid., art. 24 (1) (emphasis added).

203. Law No. 3313 (1980), revised by Law No. 3492 (1981), art. 2, *translated in* 1 *ROK Laws* (1983), *op. cit.*, pp. II-165 to II-168.

204. *Chayu Shinmun* (Korean), June 3, 1983, p. 8.

205. *IPI Report*, November 1985, pp. 1, 16.

206. Ibid., p. 16.

207. *IPI Report*, December 1985, p. 6.

208. *IPI Report*, November 1985, p. 1.

209. Tim Shorrock, "Korea," *Progressive*, February 1986, p. 25.

210. Ibid.

211. *See* "Conspiracy Between Power and the Press: Press Guidelines, Secret Messages Sent by the Power to the Press," *Mal* (Korean), special issue, September 6, 1986, *partially translated in How Mass Media Are Controlled in South Korea: Pre-Censorship by "Instructions to the Press"* 2–13 (1986).

212. Lek Hor Tan, "South Korea: 'Guiding' the Press," *Index on Censorship*, May 1987, pp. 28–29.

213. For a discussion of the Chun government's heavy-handed control of the Korean press through its daily guidelines, see Council for Democratic Press Movement, *Press Guidelines* (Korean) 10–63 (1988).

214. *How Mass Media Are Controlled in Korea, op. cit.,* passim.

215. Patrick Oster, "'Political Freedom': A Hollow Phrase for S. Koreans," *Chicago Sun-Times,* April 11, 1983, p. 26. For a discussion of the strong-arm press policy of the Chun Doo Hwan government, see Hak Soo Kim and James F. Larson, "Communication and Martial Law in the Republic of Korea, 1979–1988," *Canadian Journal of Communication,* Fall 1988, pp. 87–91 (special issue).

216. Sung-joo Han, "South Korea: Politics in Transition," in *Democracy in Developing Countries: Asia* 292 (Larry Diamond et al. eds., 1989).

217. Peter Galliner, "World Press Freedom Review," *IPI Report,* December 1988, p. 26.

218. Constitution, amended in 1987, art. 21 (2), *translated in* 1 *ROK Current Laws, op. cit.,* pp. 1–24.

219. Constitution, amended in 1980, art. 20, *translated in 1 ROK Laws* (1983), *op. cit.,* pp. I-1 to I-19.

220. Constitution, amended in 1987, art. 21 (3).

221. Law No. 3347 (1980), revised by Law No. 3786 (1984), *translated in The Korean Press 1986, op. cit.,* at 207–24.

222. "Grand National Harmony and Progress Towards a Great Nation; Special Declaration on June 29, 1987," *translated in* Roh Tae Woo, *Korea in the Pacific Century: Selected Speeches, 1990–1992,* at 293–97 (1992).

223. Law No. 3979 (1987), revised by Law No. 4441 (1991), *translated in The Korean Press 1995, op. cit.,* pp. 135–45.

224. Law No. 3978 (1987), revised by Law No. 4441 (1991), *translated in The Korean Press 1995, op. cit.,* pp. 146–59.

225. Law No. 239 (1953), revised by Law No. 2745 (1975), art. 104-2, *translated in* 1 *ROK Laws* (1983), *op. cit.,* pp. X-1 to X-44.

226. *June 29 Declaration and Legislative Reforms* (Korean) 67 (1989).

227. Law No. 3318 (1980), revised by Law No. 4373 (1991), *translated in* 3 *ROK Laws, op. cit.,* pp. X-64 to X-70-1.

228. For a discussion of the Constitution Court's ruling on the National Security Act of 1980, see chap. 5 *infra.*

229. James M. West and Edward J. Baker, "The 1987 Constitutional Reforms in South Korea: Electoral Processes and Judicial Independence," in *Human Rights in Korea, op. cit.,* p. 237.

230. Larry Diamond et al., "Democracy in Developing Countries: Facilitating and Obstructing Factors," in Raymond D. Gastil, *Freedom in the World: Political Rights and Civil Liberties* 246 (1988).

231. Dennis L. Wilcox, "Black African Press," in *Press Control Around the World* 222 (Jane Leftwich Curry and Joan R. Dassin eds., 1982).

232. David I. Steinberg, "Law and Development in Korean Society," in *Introduction to the Law and Legal System of Korea* 68 (Sang Hyun Song ed., 1983).

233. Mark Clifford, "Making Justice Blind," *Far Eastern Economic Review,* August 11, 1988, p. 16.

234. For a discussion of the Korean "judicial crisis" in mid-1988, see Han Chin-su, "Full Story of Judicial Crisis," *Shin Dong-A* (Korean), August 1988, pp. 202–15.

235. Clifford, *op. cit.,* p. 17.

236. "Dramatic Improvement," *IPI Report,* September–October 1988, p. 11.

237. *CPJ [Committee to Protect Journalists] Update,* March 1989, p. 17.

238. The Korean government was not limited to the news media in stationing its agents for surveillance. The National Assembly and the Supreme Court were also its targets of surveillance. *See*

Mark Clifford, "Law and Liberty," *Far Eastern Economic Review*, March 2, 1989, p. 26; "Judges Move to Take Second Action for Sweeping Reforms," *Korea Times*, June 19, 1988, p. 3.

239. Galliner, *op. cit.*, p. 27.

240. Han Sung-Joo, "South Korea in 1988: A Revolution in the Making," 29 *Asian Survey* 31 (January 1989).

241. Ibid., p. 29.

242. For similar changes in the press systems in the Philippines and Taiwan, see John A. Lent, "The Press Under Aquino," *Index on Censorship*, August 1986, pp. 8–9; Margot Cohen, "Taiwan's Press Breaks Loose," *Columbia Journalism Review*, September–October 1988, p. 16; "Democratic Changes in Taiwan Brings Livelier Newspapers," *Korea Times*, June 9, 1988, p. 5.

243. In June 1985, the Chun administration approved the registration of the *Daily Sports Seoul* as a "special daily newspaper" to concentrate on sports, leisure, and culture in preparation for the 1986 Asian Games and the 1988 Olympics in Seoul. Throughout its seven-year rule, however, the Chun regime did not register a new "general daily newspaper," maintaining its basic press policy of structurally minimizing critical media coverage of the government. The Basic Press Act distinguished a general from a special daily newspaper in that the former would deal primarily with news of sociopolitical interest, while the latter would be limited to apolitical topics such as sports, religion, science, etc.

244. Kyu Ho Youm and Michael B. Salwen, "A Free Press in South Korea: Temporary Phenomenon or Permanent Fixture?" 30 *Asian Survey* 318 (March 1990) (footnote omitted).

245. Ibid.

246. Oles Gadacz, "Korean Press Freedom Issues Loom," *Advertising Age*, January 4, 1988, p. 23.

247. "Inaugural Statement," *Han-kyoreh Shinmun* (Korean), May 15, 1988, p. 1.

248. *The Han-kyoreh Shinmun* (n.d.).

249. Ibid.

250. *Freedom of Expression in the Republic of Korea* 65 (1988).

251. *Han-kyoreh Shinmun* (Korean) 6 (1989).

252. Ibid., p. 4.

253. *See* Kim Soo-Mi, "Truth or Consequences?" *Business Korea*, December 1988, p. 77; "Pusan Ilbo Elects News Chief Editor," *Korea Times*, July 20, 1988, p. 3.

254. *The Korean Press 1993*, at 21 (1993).

255. In March 1974, the first press labor union was organized by the *Dong-A Ilbo* reporters. But it was short-lived because the newspaper's management at the behest of the Park Chung Hee regime forced it out of existence by dismissing those involved in the labor union. *See How the Dong-A Committee for Struggle for Protection of Press Freedom Fought* (Korean) 6–7 (1987).

256. Youm and Salwen, "A Free Press in South Korea," *op. cit.*, p. 320.

257. Ibid., citing *Hankuk Ilbo* (Korean), March 6, 1989, p. 10 (U.S. ed.).

258. Ibid., citing *Han-kyoreh Shinmun* (Korean), November 4, 1989. *See also* Kim Chu-on, "Let's Not Accept *Chonji*," *Wolgan Chosun* (Korean), June 1989, pp. 446–49. A Korean journalism scholar estimated that typical *chonji* would range from US$100 to US$200. Youngchul Yoon, Political Transition and Press Reform in South Korea 27 n.18 (1989) (paper presented at the International Communication Association convention in San Francisco).

259. Lee, "South Korea," *op. cit.*, p. 586.

260. *Pseudo-Journalists as Seen Through Actual Cases* (Korean) 6–7 (1989) (noting public concern about the increasing violence of "pseudo-journalists" and governmental action to address the concern).

261. Youm and Salwen, "A Free Press in South Korea," *op. cit.*, p. 320. For a collection of reports on more than 200 cases involving "pseudo-journalists" from July 1985 to May 1989, see *Pseudo-Journalists, op. cit.*, pp. 11–66.

262. Ibid., p. 321, citing *Chosun Ilbo*, October 24, 1989.

263. Ibid.

264. *See* "At Loggerheads in South Korea," *Time*, March 27, 1989, p. 36 (Pacific ed.); "Kim Dae-Jung Attacks Leading Newspaper over Tour Story," Associated Press, March 8, 1989; "Korean Paper Calls for International Support for Press Freedom," Japan Economic Newswire, April 25, 1989.

265. Ibid.

266. Youm and Salwen, "A Free Press in South Korea," *op. cit.*, p. 321, citing *Chosun Ilbo* (Korean), March 9, 1989.

267. Ibid. (footnote omitted).

268. Ibid.

269. Ibid.

270. Sanford J. Ungar, "Seoul Promises to Loosen News Straitjacket," *CPJ [Committee to Protect Journalists] Update*, July–August 1987, p. 3.

271. "South Korea," in Jon Vanden Heuvel and Everette E. Dennis, *The Unfolding Lotus: East Asia's Changing Media* 13 (1993).

272. Ibid., p. 10.

273. "Status of Periodical Registrations," *Newspapers and Broadcasting* (Korean), January 1995, p. 166.

274. Sang Hoon Bang, The Korean Press: New Challenges in a Changing World (1992) (speech delivered at the International Press Institute convention, Budapest, Hungary) (text on file with author).

275. David E. Halvorsen, *Confucianism Defies the Computer: The Conflict Within the Korean Press* 3 (1992). *Confucianism Defies the Computer* is a most penetrating report on the Korean press. It is the "best non-Korean look at the Korean press in recent memory." Edward Neilan, "Korean Press Conflict," *Korea Herald*, October 17, 1992, p. 6.

276. David E. Halvorsen, "How Koreans Squander Press Freedom," *Asian Wall Street Journal*, September 22, 1992, p. 10.

277. In the "equal contender" relationship, the press is an autonomous entity operating independent of government. On the other hand, the "antagonist or adversary" press looks at its primary function as a watchdog checking on the government as an adversary. *See* John C. Merrill and S. Jack Odell, *Philosophy and Journalism* 152 (1983).

278. While the "voluntary servant" press is an instrument of government in *voluntarily* cooperating with the government policy, the "forced slave" status of the press is found when the press is *involuntarily* controlled by the government. Ibid.

279. John C. Merrill, *The Dialectic in Journalism* 34–35 (1989).

280. C. Edwin Baker, *Human Liberty and Freedom of Speech* 253, 254 (1989). *See also* Thomas Gibbons, "Freedom of the Press: Ownership and Editorial Values," *Public Law*, Summer 1992, pp. 279–99.

281. Ibid.

282. *The Korean Press 1989*, at 11 (1989).

283. *But cf.* Yong-Whan Cho, Korea at the Crossroads: Violation of Freedom of Expression and Its Implications for Democracy 9 (1995) (unpublished research manuscript, on file with author). Human rights lawyer Yong-Whan Cho claimed:

> The ANSP [Agency for National Security Planning] maintains the guideline for the press report related to north Korea. Even though this guideline does not have the legal binding, the press is forced to follow the guideline because of the threat of prosecution under the National Security Law in the case of its breach. This guideline contains many broad and vague restrictions on reporting matters which are related with "national security," and thereby leads the press to reflect the views of the government. This has given the government ample room for manipulating

the information for its benefit while infringing the right of the press and the right to information of the people.

Ibid.

284. Kyu Ho Youm, "Korean Journalist, Research Scholar Chooses Cronkite School," *ASU [Arizona State University] Journalist*, Winter 1995, p. 12 ("Korean journalists do not enjoy the kind of press freedom that their American counterparts do. The Korean press is often asked to 'cooperate' with its government in coping with a host of problems facing South Korea in transition"), quoting Byung-Joon Ahn, assistant foreign desk editor of the *Seoul Shinmun*.

285. Hans Verploeg and Tony Wilton, *Press Freedom in Korea: The Search for Professionalism* 15 (1991).

286. David E. Halvorsen, Talking Straight About Ethics 2 (English text of David E. Halvorsen, "If Cash Gifts Are Justifiable, Why Not Tell Your Readers?" 21 *Journalism* (Korean) 144–47 (March 1991) (on file with author).

287. Ibid.

288. Halvorsen, "Koreans Squander Press Freedom," *op. cit.*, p. 10. The corrupting impact of *kijadan* on the Korean press is similar to the self-censoring influence of "kisha clubs" on the Japanese press. For a discussion of the press clubs in Japan, see "Japan," in Heuvel and Dennis, *op. cit.*, pp. 83–84. *See also* Jonathan Alter, "The Media Gap," *Newsweek*, July 19, 1993, p. 20.

289. Yi Hyo-song, *Criticism of the Press* (Korean) 79 (1990).

290. *Chonji* journalism in Korea has attracted international attention. *See* Michael Breen, "'Scoop' Has Different Meaning for S. Korean Reporters," *Washington Times*, April 8, 1991, p. A10; Sam Jameson, "Media: Payoffs, Politics and Korea's Press," *Los Angeles Times*, April 2, 1991, p. 2; Peter Leyden and David Bank, "The Web of Bribery That Envelopes South Korea News Media," *San Francisco Chronicle*, April 16, 1990, p. A22; Peter Leyden and David Bank, "Reform Bears a Price for Korean Journalists," *Chicago Tribune*, April 15, 1990, p. 15; C.S. Manegold, "Envelopes of 'Good Will,'" *Newsweek*, April 23, 1990, p. 49 (Pacific ed.). *See also* Kyu Ho Youm, "Korea's *Chonji* Journalism," *Grassroots Editor*, Spring 1993, pp. 7–8.

291. Halvorsen, *Confucianism Defies Computer*, *op. cit.*, pp. 22–23 (footnote omitted).

292. Halvorsen, "Talking Straight About Ethics," *op. cit.*, p. 3.

293. Kwon-sang Park, "Slouching Toward Press Freedom in Korea," in Heuvel and Dennis, *op. cit.*, p. 11.

294. Bang, *op. cit.*

295. "South Korea," in Heuvel and Dennis, *op. cit.*, p. 20.

296. Letter to W.T. Barry, August 4, 1822, *quoted in* Environmental Protection Agency v. Mink, 410 U.S. 73 (1973) (Douglas, J., dissenting). One recent study argues that the Madison quote meant not "a right of access to government documents and other collection of data" but "education," which was the common 19th century sense of information. Paul H. Gates, Jr. and Bill F. Chamberlin, Madison Misinterpretation: Historical Presentism Skews Scholarship 1 (1995) (paper presented at the Southeast Colloquium of the Association for Education in Journalism and Mass Communication in Gainesville, Fla.)

297. For a discussion of the emerging recognition of access to information as a right in Korean law, see chap. 12 *infra*.

298. Eric Archer, "Opening the Doors to Government Proceedings: The Citizen as Critic," 19 *Connecticut Law Review* 561 (1989).

299. Don R. Pember, *Mass Media Law* 318 (1996 ed. 1996).

300. Basic Press Act, art. 8.

301. Lee, "South Korea," *op. cit.*, p. 892 (emphasis added).

302. "News Media Should Be Prudent Against Violation of Rights: Kim [Young Sam]," *Korea Herald*, June 18, 1993, p. 2.

303. "Joongang Daily Reporter Arrested on Libel Charges," *Korea Herald*, June 15, 1993, p. 3.

304. "Defense Minister Files Libel Suit Against Joongang Daily," *Korea Herald*, June 12, 1993, p. 3.

305. *See* "Chapter XXXIII: Crimes Against Reputation" of the Criminal Code, Law No. 293 (1953), revised by Law No. 4040 (1988), *translated in* 2 *ROK Current Laws* (1991), *op. cit.*, pp. 761–812.

306. "Joongang Daily Reporter Arrested on Libel Charges," *op. cit.*, p. 3.

307. "Joongang Reporter to Be Released as Defense Minister Revokes Suit," *Korea Herald*, June 20, 1993, p. 3.

308. Criminal Code, art. 312 (2) ("The crimes of Articles 307 and 309 shall not be prosecuted over the express objection of the complainant").

309. Chong Chae-hon was the first journalist in Korea to be arrested for publishing a news story since 1980. *See* "Joongang Daily Reporter Arrested on Libel Charges," *op. cit.*, p. 3.

310. Yi Kwang-jae, "The Conflict Between the New Administration and the Press Revealed," *Newspapers and Broadcasting* (Korean), December 1993, p. 10.

311. Ibid.

312. Kim, "American Military Government," *op. cit.*, p. 80 (noting that "the greatest legacy that South Koreans received from the American Military Government was the spirit of freedom"). *See also* Han Mu Kang, The United States Military Government in Korea, 1945–1948: An Analysis and Evaluation of Its Policy 254–55 (1970) (Ph.D. dissertation, University of Cincinnati) ("[USAMGIK] ... helped to establish important elements of democratic thought and procedure theretofore unknown in Korea"); Chong, "The Press Policy of the American Military Government," *op. cit.*, pp. 508–509 (noting that the press policy of the USAMGIK became "a critical factor in drawing a paradigm about the development of the Korean press").

313. Meade, *op. cit.*, p. 74.

314. *See* ibid., p. 7; McCune and Grey, *op. cit.*, p. 72.

315. Frederick Seaton Siebert, *Freedom of the Press in England, 1476–1776*, at 10 (1952).

316. Jeffery A. Smith, "Further Steps Toward a Theory of Press Control," 8 *Journalism History* 94 (Autumn–Winter 1981).

317. Raymond D. Gastil, "The Comparative Survey of Freedom," *Freedom at Issue,* January–February 1983, p. 5.

318. IPI [International Press Institute], *Government Pressures on the Press* 26 (1955).

319. Shim Jae Hoon, "Watching the Watchdog," *Far Eastern Economic Review*, August 23, 1990, p. 24, quoting Professor Yu Jae-chon of Sogang University.

320. *The Japanese Press 1993*, at 19 (1993), quoting Yasunobu Fukuya, reporter for the *Asahi Shimbun*.

## CHAPTER 5

1. The profound significance of judicial review for constitutionalism has been demonstrated in the emerging democracies in Eastern Europe and the former Soviet Union, which have established tribunals with authority to invalidate legislation inconsistent with constitutional principles. *See* Herman Schwartz, "The New East European Constitutional Courts," 13 *Michigan Journal of International Law* 741–85 (1992).

2. *See generally* Horace H. Lurton, "A Government of Law or a Government of Men?" 193 *North American Review* 9 (January 1911), *reprinted in Judicial Review and American Democracy* 104 (Albert P. Melone and George Mace eds., 1988).

3. *See* Lawrence W. Beer, "Introduction: Constitutionalism in Asia and the United States," in *Constitutional Systems in Late Twentieth Century Asia* 8–10 (Lawrence W. Beer ed., 1992) [hereinafter *Constitutional Systems*]." Beer argues that human rights constitutionalism offers "the most persuasive set of normative standards by which to assess the quality of a constitutional system and its day-to-day operation," is distinctive from "democracy," "documentary constitutionalism," and "non-constitutionalism." Ibid., p. 8. According to Beer, human rights constitutionalism applies to a government that recognizes the following principles: (1) the separation of powers among the basic governmental organs; (2) an independent judiciary; (3) "regularized" limits on office terms; (4) government power limited by the international norms of human rights; (5) government involvement in meeting the basic social and economic needs of citizens as human beings, especially where the private section fails to meet these needs; (6) legal protection of freedom of expression; (7) legal tolerance and support for expression of beliefs, unless such expression is disrespectful of others "in the circumstances of the specific society"; (8) self-governance of regions which respects the human rights claims of other regions; (9) procedural rights of citizens to equality before law; (10) acceptance by the people of the constitution as the supreme law of the state. Ibid., pp. 9–10.

4. Archbald Cox, *The Court and the Constitution* 372 (1987).

5. "Rule of law" is distinguished from "rule by law." One Korean constitutional law scholar explains: "In form as well as by law, the [rule-by-law] government is divided into several separate branches, yet in practice the executive branch invariably gains the upper hand, and law is made and applied pretty much the way the executive branch wants; little or no countervailing force is at work. Under the rule-*of*-law, the government has been differentiated into branches so that one branch restrains another, and the judiciary remains independent, with the result that law is not abused by politics." Dae-Kyu Yoon, *Law and Political Authority in South Korea* 87 (1990) (footnotes omitted).

6. Tscholsu Kim and Sang Don Lee, "The Influence of U.S. Constitutional Law Doctrines in Korea," in *Constitutional Systems, op. cit.*, p. 327.

7. The year 1987 was such a critical turning point in Korea's political history that it is often described as "the year of a constitutional miracle" in Korea. Ibid., p. 322.

8. Under the Constitution of Korea, which was amended in 1987, the Constitution Court is a tribunal empowered to review the constitutionality of statutes, as distinguished from administrative decrees, regulations, or actions. Constitution, amended in 1987, art. 111 (1), *translated in* 1 *Current Laws of the Republic of Korea* 1–24 (1994).

9. James M. West and Dae-Kyu Yoon, "The Constitutional Court of the Republic of Korea: Transforming the Jurisprudence of the Vortex?" 40 *American Journal of Comparative Law* 115 (1992). *See also* Kun Yang, "Judicial Review and Social Change in the Korean Democratizing Process," 41 *American Journal of Comparative Law* 2 (1993) (noting the "significant role" of the Constitution Court in Korean politics).

10. James M. West and Edward J. Baker, "The 1987 Constitutional Reforms in South Korea: Electoral Processes and Judicial Independence," in *Human Rights in Korea: Historical and Policy Perspectives* 243 (William Shaw ed., 1991).

11. *See generally* Kyu Ho Youm, "Press Law in the Republic of Korea," 6 *New York Law School Journal of International and Comparative Law* 667–702 (1986).

12. Yoon, *op. cit.*, p. 151.

13. The historical overview of judicial review in Korea prior to 1987 is more extensively discussed in Yoon, *op. cit.*, pp. 151–70; Dai-Kwon Choi, Law and Social Change: The Korean Experience 209–66 (1976) (Ph.D. dissertation, University of California (Berkeley)).

14. Constitution, ordained and proclaimed in 1948, art. 81, *translated in* 2 *Constitutions of Nations* 549–59 (Amos J. Peaslee ed., 2d ed. 1956).

15. Ibid., art. 81 (1).

16. Ibid., art. 81 (3).

17. Ibid., art. 81 (4).

18. Yoon, *op. cit.*, p. 156. The Constitution of the Second Republic was adopted two months after the First Republic was overthrown by the Students Uprising in April 1960. One Korean legal scholar has termed the Constitution of the Second Republic the "most liberal democratic" in Korean political history. Choi, *op. cit.*, p. 216.

19. Constitution, amended in 1960, art. 83-3, 83-4, *translated in Military Revolution in Korea* 115–48 (1961). Under the Constitution of the First Republic (1948–1960), the Constitution Committee operated on an ad-hoc basis, holding its sessions only when called upon to act. Choi, *op. cit.*, p. 211.

20. Choi, *op. cot.*, p. 216.

21. Constitution, amended in 1960, art. 83-4 (4).

22. The Constitution of 1962 reflected "more of an 'American flavor'" than any of its predecessors. Kim and Lee, *op. cit.*, p. 312. According to Kim and Lee, in the course of drafting the Constitution, the Korean government invited Professor Thomas I. Emerson of Yale Law School and a New York University professor for consultation. Ibid. The two American professors allegedly visited Korea in 1962. Ibid., p. 328 n.12. Contrary to Kim and Lee's assertions, Emerson "never went to Korea." Mrs. Thomas Emerson has stated: "I don't believe he had anything to do with advising about a new Constitution for South Korea." Letter from Ruth Emerson to the author (March 1, 1993) (on file with author). Professor Emeritus Gisbert H. Flanz of New York University, who was incorrectly identified as "Professor Frantz" by Kim and Lee, ibid., p. 312, said that he and the late Professor Rupert Emerson, a political scientist at Harvard University, not legal scholar Thomas Emerson of Yale University, had visited South Korea in October 1962 as American advisors to the Constitution Deliberation Committee of Korea. Telephone Interview with Gisbert H. Flanz, professor emeritus of New York University (October 4, 1993). Flanz has discussed the 1962 amendment of the Constitution of South Korea from his perspective as a consultant to the Korean government. *See* Gisbert Flanz, "Korea and Vietnam: Two Constitutional Experiments," 42 *St. John's Law Review* 18–37 (1967).

23. Constitution, amended in 1962, art. 102, *translated in Laws of the Republic of Korea* 1–30 (2d ed. 1969).

24. Choi, *op. cit.*, p. 222.

25. Yoon, *op. cit.*, p. 159 (footnote omitted).

26. Constitution, amended in 1972, art. 109 (1), *translated in Laws of the Republic of Korea* 1–7 (3d ed. 1975).

27. Yoon, *op. cit.*, p. 165.

28. Constitution, amended in 1980, art. 108 (emphasis added), *translated in* 1 *Laws of the Republic of Korea* I-1 to I-19 (4th ed. 1983).

29. For an excellent analysis of the judicial review system under the current Constitution of Korea, see generally West and Yoon, *op. cit.*

30. *See generally* Manwoo Lee, *The Odyssey of Korean Democracy: Korean Politics, 1987–1990* (1990); *Political Change in South Korea* (Ilpyong J. Kim and Young Whan Kihl eds., 1988).

31. For a discussion of the sociopolitical context of the constitutional amendment in 1987, see West and Baker, *op. cit.*

32. Constitution, amended in 1987, art. 21 (2).

33. Ibid., art. 67 (1).

34. Ibid., art. 70.

35. Ibid., art. 104 (2).

36. Ibid., art. 61 (1).

37. West and Baker, *op. cit.*, p. 241.

38. West and Yoon, *op. cit.*, p. 75 (footnote omitted).

39. Constitution, amended in 1987, art. 111 (1).

40. This structure of judicial review promotes checks and balances between the judiciary and the legislature because judges can request the Constitution Court to rule on the constitutionality of any law passed by lawmakers. See *Judicial System of Korea* 5 (1991).

41. Constitution, amended in 1987, art. 107 (2) ("The Supreme Court shall have the power to make a final review of the constitutionality or legality of administrative decrees, regulations or actions, when their constitutionality or legality is at issue in a trial").

42. Ibid. The Constitution Court Act of 1988 elaborates thus: "Any person who is infringed on his basic right guaranteed by the Constitution due to exercise or non-exercise of the public power, may request to the Constitution Court an adjudgment on constitutional petition excluding a trial of the court: Provided, That if any procedure of relief is provided by other laws, no request shall be made without passing through such procedure." Constitution Court Act, Law No. 4017 (1988), revised by Law No. 4408 (1991), art. 68 (1), *translated in* 1 *ROK Current Laws, op. cit.*, pp. 91–92.

43. *Constitution: The Republic of Korea* (1987), *quoted in* West and Baker, *op. cit.*, p. 242.

44. Yoon, *op. cit.*, p. 169.

45. Constitution Court Act, art. 1.

46. Ibid., art. 41 (1).

47. Ibid., art. 41 (5).

48. Constitution, amended in 1987, art. 107 (1).

49. Constitution Court Act, art. 41 (1).

50. West and Yoon, *op. cit.*, p. 89.

51. Constitution Court Act, art. 41 (1).

52. Ibid., art. 68 (2).

53. West and Yoon, *op. cit.*, p. 89.

54. [Constitution Court of Korea], "Caseload of the Constitutional Court," [February 1995] (on file with author).

55. Yoon, *op. cit.*, p. 154.

56. Ibid., p. 158.

57. Ibid., p. 197.

58. Ibid., pp. 166, 168. *See also* West and Baker, *op.cit.*, p. 242.

59. *See, e.g.,* Han Chang-u v. Chon Sung-chon, 4292 Haengsang 110, Supreme Court, February 5, 1960, *reprinted in Korean Press Annual 1968* (Korean), at 528 (1968).

60. Law No. 3318 (1980), *translated in* 3 *Laws of the Republic of Korea* X-64 to X-70 (4th ed. 1983) [hereinafter *ROK Laws* (1983)]. This version of the National Security Act was revised by Law No. 4373 (1991), *translated in* 3 *Laws of the Republic of Korea* X-64 to X-70-1 (4th ed. 1994) [hereinafter *ROK Laws* (1994)]. The National Security Act at issue in the April 1990 decision was that of 1980, Law No. 3318.

61. For the Korean government's position on the National Security Act, see *Human Rights in Korea: Facts and Fiction* 25–51 (1990). For a criticism of the National Security Act, see Marcia Greenberg and Helet Merkling, *Broken Promises, Unfulfilled Dreams: Human Rights and Democracy in South Korea* 11–18 (Kerry Kennedy Cuomo et al. eds. [1992]).

62. 89 Honga 113, Constitution Court, April 2, 1990, 2 *Constitution Court Case Report* (Korean) 49 (1990) [hereinafter National Security Act Judgment].

63. Ibid., pp. 62–63, 65.

64. Ibid., pp. 65–66.

65. Ibid., p. 63.

66. Ibid.

67. Ibid., p. 67 (Pyon Chong-su, J., dissenting). Though Justice Pyon cites no sources for his version of the "bad tendency" test, he was probably influenced by U.S. constitutional theory on freedom of expression. This is also evident from his discussion of "clear and present danger." The "bad tendency" test, also known as the "reasonable tendency" test, is no longer recognized as a First Amendment principle in the United States. First Amendment commentator Anthony Lewis has criticized the vagueness of the bad tendency test: "Speech with a 'bad tendency' was speech that might someday have undesirable social consequences. The rule did not define either the time frame or the kind of consequences with any specificity." Anthony Lewis, *Make No Law: The Sullivan Case and the First Amendment* 68 (1991).

68. Ibid., p. 63.

69. Ibid. (parentheses in original). The "clear and present danger" test was developed by the U.S. Supreme Court in 1919 as a replacement for the bad tendency test. For a lucid discussion of the clear and present danger test as part of the evolving continuum of the bad tendency test for present-day First Amendment protection in the United States, see Rodney A. Smolla, *Free Speech in an Open Society* 114–16 (1992).

70. 90 Honga 11, Constitution Court, June 25, 1990, *Official Gazette* (Korean), July 26, 1990, pp. 20–21.

71. 89 Honga 104, Constitution Court, February 25, 1992, *Domestic and Foreign Legal News* (Korean), July 15, 1992, p. 5 [hereinafter Military Secrets Protection Act Judgment].

72. Law No. 2387 (1972), revised by Law No. 3492 (1981), *reprinted in Compendium of Codes* (Korean) 2265–66 (1991).

73. Military Secrets Protection Act Judgment, *op. cit.*, p. 5.

74. Ibid., p. 12.

75. Ibid. This ruling contrasts with the Korean Supreme Court's application in 1972 of the National Security Act, in which the Supreme Court held that information, even though published in newspapers or broadcast through radio and television, was protected by the National Security Act as a classified state secret if it was found useful to North Korea. *See* Yim Chong-jo v. State, 72 To 1514, Supreme Court, September 12, 1972, *Monthly Court Case Report* (Korean), November 1972, pp. 76–77.

76. Ibid., p. 9. The Constitution Court cited Article 37 (2) of the Constitution, which states: "The freedoms and rights of citizens may be restricted by law only when necessary for national security, the maintenance of law and order or for public welfare. Even when such restriction is imposed, no essential aspect of the freedom or right shall be violated." Ibid.

77. Ibid., p. 10.

78. *See* 88 Honma 22, Constitution Court, September 4, 1988, *Official Gazette* (Korean), October 6, 1989, p. 50 [hereinafter Right to Know Judgment].

79. Military Secrets Protection Act Judgment, *op. cit.*, p. 11. While the Constitution Court provides no citation, its discussion of values related to the right to know, i.e., freedom of the press and speech, is strikingly identical to the values that the late Professor Thomas Emerson of Yale Law School identified with freedom of expression. *See* Thomas I. Emerson, *Toward a General Theory of the First Amendment* 3–15 (1966).

80. Ibid. Although Vincent Blasi looked at the "checking value" theory on freedom of the press in the United States as an institutional concept, *see* Vincent Blasi, "The Checking Value in First Amendment Theory," *American Bar Foundation Journal* 521–649 (1977), the Constitution Court is broader than Blasi's in its view of the right to know in Korea. The Court has noted the individual and social value of the right to know, in addition to the institutional "watchdog" notion.

81. Ibid.

82. Right to Know Judgment, *op. cit.*, p. 50.

83. Ibid., p. 55.

84. Ibid.

85. Ibid.

86. Ibid.

87. 90 Honma 133, Constitution Court, May 13, 1991, 3 *Constitution Court Case Report* (Korean) 234, 237–38 (1992).

88. Ibid., p. 238.

89. Ibid. The United Nations Universal Declaration of Human Rights states: "Everyone has the right to freedom of opinion and expression; this right includes freedom to hold opinions without interference and to seek, receive and impart information and ideas through any media and regardless of frontiers." Universal Declaration of Human Rights, G.A. Res. 217A (III), U.N. GAOR, art. 19, U.N. Doc. A/810 (1948).

90. Ibid., p. 246.

91. Ibid.

92. Ibid.

93. Ibid.

94. Ibid., p. 249. The Court reasoned that the duty of the State to comply with the request for access to governmental information by way of freedom of expression, i.e., right to know, was derived from Article 10 of the Constitution, which states in part: "It shall be the duty of the State to confirm and guarantee the fundamental and inviolable human rights of individuals."

95. Ibid.

96. Law No. 3979 (1987), revised by Law No. 4411 (1991), *translated in The Korean Press 1995*, at 135–45 (1995).

97. For a discussion of the "claim for correction of reports" provisions of the Periodicals Act, see chap. 7.

98. 89 Honma 165, Constitution Court, September 16, 1991, 3 *Constitution Court Case Report* (Korean) 518 (1992) [hereinafter Right of Reply Judgment].

99. Ibid., p. 526.

100. Ibid.

101. Ibid.

102. The Court noted Article 10 ("All citizens shall be assured of human worth and dignity and have the right to pursue happiness"), Article 17 ("The privacy of no citizen shall be infringed"), and Article 21 (4) ("Neither speech nor the press shall violate the honor or rights of other persons nor undermine public morals or social ethics. Should speech or the press violate the honor or rights of other persons, claims may be made for the damage resulting therefrom"). Ibid., pp. 526–27.

103. Ibid., p. 527.

104. Ibid. The Court's view is analogous to the "marketplace of ideas" concept, one of the first doctrines used by the U.S. Supreme Court in interpreting the First Amendment. The doctrine was articulated by Justice Holmes in 1919: "The best test of truth is the power of the thought to get itself accepted in the competition of the market." Abrams v. United States, 250 U.S. 616, 624 (1919) (Holmes, J., joined by Brandeis, J., dissenting).

105. The petitioner's argument that imposing a statutory obligation on a newspaper to publish a reply would be an invalid interference with editorial freedom parallels the First Amendment position of the *Miami Herald* on freedom of the press, which the U.S. Supreme Court accepted in 1974. *See* Miami Herald Publishing Co. v. Tornillo, 418 U.S. 241 (1974). Retraction is considered more preferable to a right of reply in protecting the editorial freedom of the press. American media law scholars stated: "From the point of view of those for whom editorial freedom is the primary value…the fact that the editor loses control over the subject matter of the reply is the principal defect of right of reply legislation. It allows someone to be published whom the editor would not otherwise publish. At least the retraction is prepared

by the newspaper staff. If a newspaper is willing to take the consequences, a retraction does not have to be published." Donald M. Gillmor et al., *Fundamentals of Mass Communication Law* 230–31 (1996).

106. Right of Reply Judgment, *op. cit.*, pp. 529–30.

107. Ibid., p. 530.

108. *See* Article 16 (1) of the Periodicals Act.

109. *See* Article 16 (3) of the Periodicals Act.

110. *See* Article 16 (1) of the Periodicals Act.

111. *See* Article 16 (4), (5) of the Periodicals Act.

112. *See* Article 19 (1) of the Periodicals Act.

113. Right of Reply Judgment, *op. cit.*, p. 531.

114. *See* Article 19 (3) of the Periodicals Act.

115. Right of Reply Judgment, *op. cit.*, p. 532.

116. Ibid., p. 534. What would be the result if the media organizations are forced to publish a reply in compliance with the district court's ruling, but appeal and win? Thus far, there has been no statutory or judicial clarification of this issue. Chief Judge Pak Yong-sang of the Seoul High Court in Korea, the premier authority on the right of reply in Korean press law, has noted:

> [I]f the court's order to publish a reply is set aside or altered when challenged by a media defendant, the enforced publication of the reply will be considered illegal. Accordingly, a court order should be issued for payment of damages to the media organization in compensation for the financial loss resulting from the enforcement of the now illegal reply. The amount of damages cannot be based on the advertising rates that might be charged for the space devoted to the reply. Instead, the costs of the printing and production of the reply should be used.

Pak Yong-sang, "Exercising the Right to Claim Corrected Reports: Requirements and Procedures," *Press Arbitration Quarterly*, Winter 1991, p. 84.

117. 90 Honga 23, Constitution Court, June 26, 1992, 4 *Constitution Court Case Report* 300 (1993) [hereinafter Registration of Periodicals Judgment].

118. *See* Article 7 of the Periodicals Act.

119. Registration of Periodicals Judgment, *op. cit.*, p. 302.

120. Ibid., p. 304. It is noteworthy that the distinction between media licensing and registration is recognized by several international agreements including the European Convention on Human Rights (ECHR). Attorney Sandra Coliver, law program director of ARTICLE 19 in London, has stated: "Licensing requirements, by which government approval is necessary before a new entity may begin publishing, although not expressly prohibited by the ECHR are widely held to be prohibited implicitly.... In contrast, registration requirements, which require registration of the names and addresses of those legally responsible for a publication, are permitted under the ECHR and are present in several European countries." Sandra Coliver, "Press Freedom Under the European Convention on Human Rights," in *Press Law and Practice: A Comparative Study of Press Freedom in European and Other Democracies* 223–24 (Sandra Coliver ed., 1993).

121. Ibid., p. 305.

122. Ibid.

123. Ibid., p. 306. The Court referred to national security, the maintenance of law and order, and public welfare as constitutional justifications for limiting freedom of the press.

124. Ibid.

125. Ibid., p. 307.

126. Ibid.

127. Ibid.

128. Ibid., p. 309.

129. Ibid., p. 313.

130. Ibid., p. 317 (Pyon Chong-su, J., dissenting).

131. *See* Article 7 (3) of the Periodicals Act.

132. Registration of Periodicals Judgment, *op. cit.*, pp. 317–18.

133. Ibid., pp. 319–20. Article 11 of the Constitution provides: "All citizens shall be equal before the law, and there shall be no discrimination in political, economic, social or cultural life on account of sex, religion or social status." Constitution, amended in 1987, art. 11 (1).

134. 90 Honba 26, Constitution Court, June 26, 1992, 4 *Constitution Court Case Report* (Korean) 362 (1993) [hereinafter Delivery of Copies Judgment].

135. Periodicals Act, art. 10.

136. Article 24 states: "[A person who fails to deliver copies under Article 10 (1)] shall be punished by a fine for negligence not exceeding 1 million *won* [US$1,250]." Periodicals Act, art. 24.

137. Delivery of Copies Judgment, *op. cit.*, p. 365.

138. Ibid., pp. 367–68.

139. Ibid., pp. 370–71 (emphasis added).

140. Ibid., p. 371.

141. Ibid.

142. Ibid., pp. 371–72.

143. Ibid., pp. 373–74.

144. Civil Code, Law No. 471 (1958), revised by Law No. 4199 (1990), art. 764, *translated in* 2 *ROK Current Laws*, *op. cit.*, pp. 401–556.

145. *See, e.g.*, Kwon In-suk v. Seoul Munhwasa, 90 Kahap 15896, Seoul Civil District Court, January 17, 1991, *Press Arbitration Quarterly*, Autumn 1991, pp. 152–55; Kim Song-hi v. Yi Kap-sop, 89 Na 8158, Seoul High Court, November 29, 1989, *Korean Press Cases* (Korean) 284–95 (1990); Cho Ha-mun v. Yowonsa, 88 Kahap 17151, Seoul District Court (East Branch), April 21, 1989, *Korean Press Cases* (Korean) 295–301 (1990); Kim Song-hi v. Dong-A Ilbosa, 88 Kahap 31161, Seoul Civil District Court, July 25, 1989, *Korean Press Cases* (Korean) 301–11 (1990).

146. 89 Honma 160, Constitution Court, April 1, 1991, *Press Arbitration Quarterly* (Korean), Summer 1991, pp. 162–66 [hereinafter Notice of Apology Judgment].

147. *See* Kim Song-hi v. Dong-A Ilbosa, *op. cit.*

148. 89 Ka 33299, Seoul Civil District Court, July 10, 1989, *Press Arbitration Quarterly* (Korean), Summer 1991, pp. 166–67 [hereinafter Petition for Review].

149. Article 19 of the Constitution states: "All citizens shall enjoy freedom of conscience." Constitution, amended in 1987, art. 19.

150. Petition for Review, *op. cit.*, p. 167.

151. Ibid. In addition to the press freedom clause of the Constitution, the Seoul district court invoked Article 37 (2) in arguing that freedom of speech and the press is limited.

152. Ibid.

153. Notice of Apology Judgment, *op. cit.*, p. 164.

154. Ibid.

155. Ibid. The Constitution Court noted the United Nations Universal Declaration of Human Rights of 1948, which Korea ratified in 1990, for its guarantee of freedom of thought and conscience. The Declaration reads in pertinent part: "Everyone has the right to freedom of thought, conscience and religion; this right includes freedom to change his religion or belief, and freedom either alone or in community with others and in public or private, to manifest his religion or belief in teaching, practice, worship and observance." Universal Declaration of Human Rights, G.A. Res. 217A(III), U.N. GAOR, art. 18, U.N. Doc.A/810 (1948).

156. Ibid.

157. Ibid., pp. 164–65.

158. Ibid., p. 165.

159. Ibid.

160. Ibid.

161. Ibid. In this context, the apology sanction is more punitive than compensatory, as under the Civil Code. *See* Yu Il-sang, *A Discourse on Press Ethics and Law* (Korean) 277 (1991).

162. More often than not, Korean courts thus far have applied a penal servitude and/or a fine to criminal libel under the Criminal Code. *See* State v. Yi Ik-sun, 93 To 1732, Supreme Court, September 24, 1993, *Press Arbitration Quarterly* (Korean), Winter 1994, pp. 155–56; State v. Chang Kon-sop, 89 To 1744, Supreme Court, November 14, 1989, *Korean Press Cases* (Korean) 330–31 (1990); Ham Yun-sik v. Song Ki-hyon, 91 Kodan 8793, Seoul Criminal District Court, September 14, 1992, *Press Arbitration Quarterly* (Korean), Winter 1992, pp. 165–66; State v. Yi Ik-sun, 91 Kodan 6158, Seoul Criminal District Court, May 26, 1992, *Press Arbitration Quarterly* (Korean), Autumn 1992, pp. 158–59.

163. Notice of Apology Judgment, *op. cit.*, p. 165.

164. Ibid. The Constitution Court obviously shares Professor Lawrence Beer's view on the public apology requirement under Japanese libel law. Beer has stated: "When apology is ordered, the [Japanese] courts may tend to refrain from awarding substantial damages which might be more likely to dissuade the media from future violation." Lawrence Ward Beer, *Freedom of Expression in Japan* 315 (1984).

165. Ibid. For a discussion of the compulsory public apology for libel under the Civil Code of Japan, see Kyu Ho Youm, "Libel Laws and Freedom of the Press: South Korea and Japan Reexamined," 8 *Boston University International Law Journal* 68–70 (1990).

166. The Constitution Court discussed the libel laws of England, the United States, Germany, France, and Switzerland. The Court found that in England and the United States, damages are awarded as a rule while a voluntary apology by the defendant is recognized as a mitigating factor in reducing the damage award. In Germany, France, and Switzerland, courts order a retraction of the defendant's statement, rule on the truth of defamation, or award damages. For a succinct discussion of libel laws in England, Germany, and France, see Michael J. Calvey et al., "Foreign Defamation Law," in *LDRC [Libel Defense Resource Center] 50-State Survey 1987: Current Developments in Media Libel and Invasion of Privacy* xvi–xxxi, 1xi–1xxi, 1xxi–1xxx (Henry R. Kaufman ed.,1987). For a concise discussion of libel laws in Switzerland and the United States, see Peter F. Carter-Ruck et al., *Carter-Ruck on Libel and Slander* 378–79, 383–90 (4th ed. 1992).

167. Notice of Apology Judgment, *op. cit.*, p. 166.

168. Ibid.

169. Yoon, *op. cit.*, p. 170.

170. Republic of Korea, *Consideration of Reports Submitted by States Parties Under Article 40 of the Covenant* 2 (1991). This was submitted to the Secretary-General of the United States as an initial report of the Korean government on "the progress made in the guarantees of the fundamental human rights provided for in the International Covenants on Civil and Political Rights, and in the enjoyment of these rights." Ibid., p. 1.

171. *See* James West, "Laying Down the Law," *Far Eastern Economic Review*, July 23, 1992, p. 13 (arguing that "efforts to enhance the independence of judicial institutions have encountered tenacious resistance").

172. West and Yoon, *op. cit.*, p. 107. For a discussion of the National Security Act, as revised in 1991, see chap. 11 *infra*.

173. Greenberg and Merkling, *op. cit.*, p. 2 (describing the revision as "weak and ineffective").

174. Editorial, "How to Complete Democracy in Korea," *New York Times*, April 18, 1992, p. 18. *See generally* Yong-Whan Cho, Korea at the Crossroads: Violation of Freedom of Expression and Its Implications for Democracy 15–23 (1995) (unpublished research manuscript, on file with author).

175. "In definitional balancing, courts define the outer limit of free speech before the balancing test is applied in individual cases." Kent R. Middleton and Bill F. Chamberlin, *The Law of Public Communication* 39 (3d ed. 1994).

176. According to Professor Won-Soon Paeng, no Korean court has defined the essential aspect of press freedom under the Korean Constitution. Won-Soon Paeng, "Press Law in Korea," 3 *Sungkok Journalism Review* 6 (1992).

177. As the U.S. Supreme Court stated in 1989: "If there is a bedrock principle underlying the First Amendment, it is that the Government may not prohibit the expression of an idea simply because society finds the idea itself offensive or disagreeable." Texas v. Johnson, 491 U.S. 391, 414 (1989) (citations omitted).

178. Ibid. (citations omitted).

179. *See* Enforcement Decree of the Periodicals Act, Presidential Decree No. 12422 (1988), revised by Presidential Decree No. 13783 (1992), *reprinted in Compendium of Codes* (Korean) 2939–40 (1994).

180. Ibid., art. 6.

181. No Mu-hyon v. Chosun Ilbosa, 91 Kahap 82923, Seoul Civil District Court, December 4, 1992, *reprinted in Newspapers and Broadcasting* (Korean), February 1993, p. 107.

182. Ibid.

183. Ibid., pp. 107–10.

184. West and Yoon, *op. cit.*, p. 115.

185. Pnina Lahav, "Conclusion: An Outline for a General Theory of Press in Democracy," in *Press Law in Modern Democracies: A Comparative Study* 333–34 (Pnina Lahav ed., 1985).

# CHAPTER 6

1. David E. Halvorsen, *Confucianism Defies the Computer: The Conflict Within the Korean Press* 35–36 (1992). Ambassador Donald Gregg has termed the Korean press since 1987 "a jack-in-the-box that has just been released and is springing about in all directions." Donald P. Gregg, Future of American and Korean Relations (1991) (lecture delivered at East-West Center, Honolulu), *quoted in* ibid., p. 35.

2. *See generally* Raymond D. Gastil, *Freedom in the World: Political Rights and Civil Liberties, 1988–1989*, at 413–14 (1989); Department of State, *Country Reports on Human Rights Practices for 1988*, at 842–54 (1989); Department of State, *Country Reports on Human Rights Practices for 1989*, at 885–99 (1990).

3. Raymond D. Gastil, "The Comparative Survey of Freedom: 1989," *Freedom at Issue*, January–February 1989, p. 47. *See also* Leonard R. Sussman, *Power, the Press and the Technology of Freedom* 278–80 (1989).

4. Prior to the Korean National Assembly's legislative action, Roh's proposal for sweeping political changes led to constitutional reform. The October 1987 amendments to the Constitution of Korea guarantees freedom of speech and the press thus:

1. All citizens shall enjoy freedom of speech and the press...;
2. Licensing or censorship of speech and the press ... shall not be recognized;
3. The standards of news service and broadcast facilities and matters necessary to ensure the functions of newspapers shall be determined by law;
4. Neither speech nor the press shall violate the honor or rights of other persons nor undermine public morals or social ethics. Should speech or the press violate the honor or rights of other persons, claims may be made for the damage resulting therefrom.

Constitution of Korea, amended in 1987, art. 21, *translated in* 1 *Current Laws of the Republic of Korea* 1–24 (1994) [hereinafter *ROK Current Laws*]. For a concise background and other explanatory notes on the amended Constitution of Korea, see *Constitution: The Republic of Korea* 45–62 (1987).

5. Law No. 3979 (1987), revised by Law No. 4441 (1991), *translated in* 4 *ROK Current Laws, op. cit.*, pp. 2541–52; *The Korean Press 1995*, at 135–45 (1995).

6. Law No. 3978 (1987), revised by Law No. 4441 (1991), *translated in* 4 *ROK Current Laws, op. cit.*, pp. 2571–2571.12; *The Korean Press 1995, op. cit.*, pp. 146–59.

7. The Basic Press Act was enacted to replace the Act on Registration of Newspapers, News Services and Others, Law No. 1486 (1963), *reprinted in Complete Collection of Korean Press Laws, 1945–1981* (Korean) 24–26 (Chong Chin-sok ed., 1982) [hereinafter *Korean Press Laws*]; Press Ethics Commission Law, Law No. 1652 (1964), *reprinted in Korean Press Laws, op. cit.*, pp. 37–39; and Broadcasting Act, Law No. 1535 (1963), revised by Law No. 2535 (1973), *reprinted in Korean Press Laws, op. cit.*, pp. 290–92, then in effect. *See* Basic Press Act, Addenda, art. 2.

8. Peter Galliner, "World Press Freedom Review," *IPI [International Press Institute] Report*, December 1988, p. 3.

9. Kyu Ho Youm, "Press Freedom in 'Democratic' South Korea: Moving from Authoritarian to Libertarian?" 43 *Gazette* 59 (1989).

10. *See, e.g., Freedom of Expression in the Republic of Korea* 33–37 (1988) [hereinafter *Freedom of Expression*]; Association for Study of Korean Laws, *Democratic Progress and Legislative Reforms* (Korean) 203–47 (1989); Yi Kang-su, "Press Policy During the Era of a Free Press," in *Modern Society and Freedom of the Press* (Korean) 27–55 (Committee on Publication of Research Papers in Honor of Dr. Paeng Won-sun's 61st Birthday ed.,1989); Paeng Won-sun, *A New Discourse on Press Law* (Korean) 228–41 (1989).

11. Paeng Won-sun, "Comments: Characteristics and Problems of the New Press Laws," *Newspapers and Broadcasting* (Korean), December 1987, p. 35.

12. Ibid., p. 38.

13. Kim Chae-kon, "Regulatory Press Laws and News Reporters," *Newspaper Research* (Korean), Winter 1987, p. 80.

14. For a detailed discussion of the libertarian versus authoritarian theories of the press, see generally Fred S. Siebert et al., *Four Theories of the Press* 9–71 (1956).

15. On January 1, 1990, the Ministry of Culture and Information (MOCI) was reorganized into the Ministry of Public Information (MOPI) and the Ministry of Culture. *The Korean Press 1990*, at 28 (1990)

16. Basic Press Act, art. 1. Article 1 of the Basic Press Act read: "This law is aimed at promoting the dignity and value of man and serving to realize the public good by safeguarding the people's freedom of expression and their right to know and ensuring the function of the press to form public opinion."

17. Periodicals Act, art. 1. Article 1 of the Periodicals Act reads: "The purpose of this Act is to strive for a sound development of the press by providing for matters concerning periodically published newspapers, news services, magazines, and other publications."

18. Won-Soon Paeng, "Main Characteristics of Korea's Press Law," 20 *Journal of Korean Society for Journalism and Communication Studies* 36 (1985) (footnote omitted).

19. In the American context of "press responsibility" provisions of the several state constitutions, it is accepted that the effect of the "responsibility" language is restrictive, not expansive, of freedom of the press. For example, the Supreme Court of California stated:

> This [responsibility of the press] provision makes clear that the right to speech is not unfettered and reflects a considered determination that the individual's interest in reputation is worthy of constitutional protection. The federal Constitution, by contrast, contains no express provision imposing responsibility for abuse of the right of free speech. This difference refutes defendants' policy argument that our state Constitution weighs in favor of a standard of fault higher than that required under the federal Constitution.

Brown v. Kelly Broadcasting Co., 48 Cal. 3d 711, 746 (1989).

20. Characterizing the "public responsibility" requirement of the Basic Press Act as a regulatory concept particularly appealing to the Korean government which never ceased emphasizing the "public-ness" or the "public responsibility" of its press, one Korean commentator noted: "While this [public responsibility of the press] theory was developed by some German constitutional scholars beginning in the 1920s, it was first used by the Nazi regime as the theoretical underpinning of a positive law in enacting 'Schriftleitergesetz' [of February 4, 1933] to restrict the press." Paeng, *New Discourse, op. cit.*, p. 246. Indeed, the "öffentliche Aufgabe der Presse" notion is still statutorily recognized as a concept of press freedom in nine states of West Germany. *See Press Laws: Documents of Politics and Society in the Federal Republic of Germany* (Sigrid Born ed., Martin Fry trans., 3d ed. 1994); Urs Schwarz, *Press Law for Our Times: The Example of the German Legislation* (1966). For a discussion of press law in West Germany, *See* Helmut Kohl, "Press Law in the Federal Republic of Germany," in *Press Law in Modern Democracies: A Comparative Study* 185 (Pnina Lahav ed.,1985).

21. Article 3 of the Basic Press Act stipulated:

1. The press should respect human dignity and values, and democratic fundamental order;
2. Through its contribution to molding democratic public opinion by means of covering, reporting, and commenting on matters of public interest or by other means the press shall perform its public mission;
3. The press should not infringe upon the honor or right of citizens, nor should it violate public morality or social ethics;
4. The press should not encourage or praise illegal acts which disrupt public order, including acts of violence.

22. Basic Press Act, art. 6. Article 6 of the Basic Press Act read: "The State, local governments, and public organizations should supply information on matters of public interest when so requested by the publishers of a newspaper or a news service, the chief of a broadcasting station or their agents."

23. Ibid., art. 8. Article 8 of the Basic Press Act read: "Journalists may refuse to disclose the identity of the writer and informer of, or the possessor of the material for, the published matter, and to state the facts basic to the contents of the published matter."

24. Paeng Won-sun, *A Theory of Mass Communication Law* (Korean) 298–300, 333–36 (rev. ed. 1988).

25. The statutory provisions concerning the protection of secrets are found in the Military Penal Code, Law No. 1003 (1962), revised by Law No. 4685 (1993), *reprinted in Compendium of Codes* (Korean) 2554–58 (1994); Military Secrets Protection Act, Law No. 4616 (1993), *reprinted in Compendium of Codes, op. cit.*, pp. 2552–53; National Security Planning Agency Act, Law No. 3313 (1980), revised by Law No. 3492 (1981), *translated in* 1 *ROK Laws, op. cit.*, pp. II-165 to II-164; and National Security Act, Law No. 3318 (1980), revised by Law No. 4373 (1991), *translated in* 3 *ROK Laws, op. cit.*, pp. X-64 to X-70-1, among others.

26. Basic Press Act, revised by Law No. 3786 (1984), art. 6. When the Basic Press Act was partially revised in 1984, the fourth exemption was deleted. The deleted exemption said that the request for information might not be filled if and when it "[c]auses serious impediment to the normal performance of official duties on account of the demand for an excessive amount and scope of the requested information." *See* Basic Press Act, art. 6 (4), as enacted in 1980.

27. Paeng, "Korea's Press Law," *op. cit.*, p. 42. *But cf.* Pak Yong-sang, "Basic Press Act," in *Laws Relating to Politics* (Korean) 155–56 (Kim Chol-su ed., 1983) (expressing optimism about the positive impact of the access on information provision of the Basic Press Act upon the Korean press).

28. Ibid. *See also* Han Pyong-gu, *A Theory of Press Law* (Korean) 216–17 (1987).

29. The shield was denied when a particular publication disclosed contents which would constitute a crime, subject to imprisonment of more than one year, with an exception for the journalist punished for publishing a story based on the confidential information; when the information was obtained through a criminal act which might carry an imprisonment of more than one year; or when it was clear from the

contents of the published material that the writer, informer, or possessor of the material had committed a crime listed in Article 2 of the Social Safety Act. Basic Press Act, art. 8.

30. Pak, *op. cit.*, pp. 154-56.

31. Paeng, *New Discourse, op. cit.*, p. 236.

32. Periodicals Act, art. 2-1.

33. Basic Press Act, art. 5-2.

34. Ibid., art. 5-9. Korean journalist Kwon-sang Park's experience with the "journalist" provision of the Basic Press Act is illustrative. Park has claimed: "Under the Basic Press Law [sic] drawn by the military government in the 1980's, I was forbidden to practice journalism, i.e., I was 'cleansed' from the media. The government invalidated my IPI [International Press Institute] membership because, it said, I did not meet the criteria of a 'journalist,' which it described as 'anyone who is engaged in reporting and commentary on current events and also who is a member of an organization of news media'." Kwon-sang Park, "Slouching Toward Press Freedom in Korea," in Jon Vanden Heuvel and Everette E. Dennis, *The Unfolding Lotus: East Asia's Changing Media* 8 (1993).

The statutory approach to definition of "professional" journalists is conceptually related to the licensing of journalists by governments in a number of authoritarian countries. *See* "Licensing: Improving the Profession, Destroying Their Freedom," in *The Press and the State* 468 (Walter M. Brasch and Dana R. Ulloth eds., 1986), quoting media scholar John C. Merrill. Leonard Sussman of Freedom House cites three arguments for governmental licensing of journalists:

> The extreme argument: Journalists should operate under a governmental umbrella in order to perform according to a code, also officially inspired. The moderate position: Newspersons have a quasi-public mission; like doctors or engineers, they should be licensed to protect the public from quacks. The self-serving factor put forth by some journalists themselves: Anyone who can write his name may compete as a reporter; therefore, to reduce competition, particularly from unskilled, journalists should be formally certified.

Sussman, *op. cit.*, p. 181. The Inter-American Court of Human Rights (IACHR) in 1985 ruled governmental licensing of journalists incompatible with freedom of speech and the press as a basic human right. IACHR stated: "Such a law [on licensing of journalists] would contain restrictions to freedom of expression … and would consequently be in violation of only the right of each individual to seek and impart information and ideas through any means of his choice, but also the right of the public at large to receive information without any interference." Inter-American Court of Human Rights (IACHR), San Jose, Advisory Opinion of November 13, 1985, No. OC-5/85—Compulsory membership in an association prescribed by law for the practice of journalism (Arts. 13 and 29 American Convention on Human Rights)—requested by the Government of Costa Rica, *reprinted in* "Decisions and Reports," 7 *Human Rights Law Journal* 91 (1986). For a discussion of governmental licensing of journalists from an international-law perspective, see Kyu Ho Youm, "Licensing of Journalists Under International Law," 46 *Gazette* 113–24 (1990).

35. Periodicals Act, art. 9 (1)-3, 4. With respect to disqualifications for being publishers or editors, Article 9 (1) of the Periodicals Act reads:

> 3. A person who was sentenced to imprisonment without hard labor or more severe punishment for committing a crime as prescribed in Articles 87 to 90, 92 to 101 of the Criminal Code, Articles 5 to 8, 9 (2), 11 to 16 of the Military Penal Code or Articles 3 to 9 of the National Security Act, and the execution of such punishment is not terminated, or non-execution of it does not become definite, or the period for stay of execution is not terminated; and
> 4. A person who is subject to execution of a disposition for security under the Social Security Act or a disposition for protection under the Social Protection Act.

36. Ibid., art. 9 (1)-1, 2. This regulation is not applied to in-house publications. Ibid., art. 9 (3). In-house publications refer to the periodicals published "for the purpose of being disseminated to the members of an organization only."

37. *See* Basic Press Act, art. 12.

38. For a discussion of the theoretical basis for the similar provisions of the Basic Press Act, see Pak, *op. cit.*, pp. 143–45, 167–69.

39. Periodicals Act, art. 3 (1).

40. Ibid., art. 3 (2).

41. Ibid., art. 3 (3). *Compare with* Basic Press Act, art. 12 (1).

42. *Compare* Periodicals Act, art. 4, *with* Basic Press Act, art. 14.

43. Ibid.

44. Periodicals Act, art. 7 (1). *Compare* Periodicals Act, art. 7 (1), *with* Basic Press Act, art. 20 (1). Article 20 (1) of the Basic Press Act provided for the registration requirements for the print thus:

> (1) A party with intention to publish a periodical is required to register the following matters with the Minister of Culture and Information as stipulated in presidential decrees. The same is required when change occurs in matters so registered. Exemptions are made of such periodicals as are published either by the State, local governments or organizations, and agencies specified by presidential decrees for distribution among their staff members, and such periodicals devoted wholly to commercial advertisement:
>
> > 1. Title;
> > 2. Classification and frequency of publication;
> > 3. Permanent domicile, present address, name and date of birth of the publisher, the editor and the printer (in case the publisher or the printer is a juridical person or an organization, its name, location of its head office and the permanent domicile, present address, name and date of birth of its representative should be provided);
> > 4. Address of the place of publication;
> > 5. Style of print;
> > 6. Used language;
> > 7. Purpose and contents of publication;
> > 8. Means of circulation, main audience and prospective area of circulation;
> > 9. Facilities required under the provisions of Article 21.
>
> (2) The Minister of Culture and Information may delegate to chiefs of local government authorities the power over registration of periodicals published by an enterprise or a purely fraternal society for limited circulation among its members;
>
> (3) No periodical can register under a title so similar to an already registered one as to cause confusion.

45. Ibid.

46. Ibid., art. 7 (3).

47. *The Han-Kyoreh Shinmun* (n.d.).

48. Oles Gadacz, "Korean Press Freedom Issues Loom," *Advertising Age*, January 4, 1988, p. 23.

49. Periodicals Act, art. 7 (4).

50. Ibid., art. 12 (2). In September 1990, for example, the MOPI requested the Taegu District Court for a ruling on cancellation of registration of *Kyongbuk Ilbo* newspaper, claiming that the newspaper submitted false receipts and records of bank deposits as documentary evidence of the required printing facilities in violation of Article 12 (2) of the Periodicals Act. "Public Information Office Asks for Court Decision on Cancellation of Registration for Kyongbuk Ilbo," *Joongang Ilbo* (Korean), September 28, 1990, p. 2 (U.S. ed.).

51. Basic Press Act, art. 24.

52. Ibid., art. 24 (1).

53. Periodicals Act, art. 12 (2)-1.

54. Ibid., art. 12 (2)-2.

55. Ibid., art. 12 (2).

56. Ibid., art. 12 (1).

57. Ibid., art. 13. The new requirement that the MOPI give the publisher an opportunity to "state his opinions" about the MOPI's pending action against him seems to do little to thwart the government's power.

58. Constitution, amended in 1987, art. 37 (2) ("The freedoms and rights of citizens may be restricted by law only when necessary for national security, the maintenance of law and order or for public welfare. Even when such restriction is imposed, no essential aspect of the freedom or right shall be violated").

59. For a discussion of the *Silchon Munhak* cancellation, see Paeng Won-sun, "The Basic Press Act Should Be Revised," *Shin Dong-A* (Korean), October 1985, pp. 226–32. *See also* So Chung-sok, "5-Minute Interview," *Shin Dong-A* (Korean), March 1987, pp. 291–92.

60. For a discussion of the MOCI's cancellation of *Changjak Kwa Pipyong, See* Cho Yong-rae, "The Changjak Kwa Pipyong Case and Freedom of Publication," *Shin Dong-A* (Korean), January 1986, pp. 496–503; Ko Un, "Deploring the Changjak Kwa Pipyong Case," *Shin Dong-A* (Korean), February 1986, pp. 270–79.

61. Article 24 (1)-2 provided for a ground for cancellation of registration of a periodical thus: "A periodical has been published with changes in matters required to be registered with the proper authorities as provided for in Paragraph 1 of Article 20." Basic Press Act, art. 24 (1)-2. Article 20 (1) read in part: "A party with intention to publish a periodical is required to register the following matters with the MOCI as stipulated in the presidential decrees. The same is required when change occurs in matters so registered. ...: 1. title; 2. classification and frequency of publication." Ibid., art. 20 (1).

62. A "non-regular" periodical is a publication which appears on an intermittent basis.

63. The MOPI suspended three monthlies for violating of Article 12 (2) 2 of the Periodicals Act because they carried "titillating and decadent" pictures and stories, not the kind of contents specified at the time of their registration with the MOPI. *See* "Three Periodicals Including Monthly Miso Suspended from Publication for Two Months," *Hankuk Ilbo* (Korean), March 6, 1990, p. 16 (U.S. ed.). *See also* Council for Movement for Publishing Culture in Korea, *The Sixth Republic and Its Suppression of Publications* (Korean) 15–16 (1990) (discussing the MOPI's suspension of *Nodong Haebang Munhak* (Labor Liberation Literature), a progressive monthly, from publication for three months on the grounds that the periodical published the kind of articles not specified at the time of its registration with the MOPI). *Nodong Haebang Munhak* reportedly challenged the legality of the MOPI's action early in 1990. *See* "Nodong Haebang Munhak Filing Administrative Suit," *Han-kyoreh Shinmun* (Korean), January 30, 1990, p. 14 (U.S. ed.) (challenging the MOPI's suspension of *Nodong Haebang Munhak* for the magazine's alleged violation of Article 12 (2) 2 of the Periodicals Act).

64. *Compare* Periodicals Act, art. 6, *with* Basic Press Act, art. 21.

65. Periodicals Act, art. 6 (3) 1. The "annexed printing facilities," as stipulated by Article 6 of the Periodicals Act refers to typesetting and platemaking facilities. *See* Decree on Implementation of the Periodicals Act, No. 12422 (1988), revised by Decree No. 13783 (1992), art. 5, *reprinted in Compendium of Codes, op. cit.*, pp. 2939–41.

66. *See, e.g., Democratic Progress and Legislative Reforms, op. cit.*, pp. 215–16.

67. *See Military Revolution in Korea* 29 (1961). Professor John Kie-Chiang Oh has noted: "The abuse of freedom tended to be carried to the extreme by the press. It might be recalled that the amended Constitution of the Second Republic made it impossible for the government to restrict the freedom of the press with the provisions of law. The number of newspapers and periodicals suddenly jumped from about 600 to nearly 1,600 by April, 1961, employing some 160,000 reporters." John Kie-Chiang Oh, *Korea: Democracy on Trial* 90–91 (1968).

68. *See* Decree No. 11, *reprinted in Korean Press Laws, op. cit.*, p. 781. The Decree eventually served as the underpinnings of the Standards for Implementation of the Press Policy enforced by the Supreme Council for National Reconstruction in 1962, *reprinted in Korean Press Laws, op. cit.*, pp. 784–85.

69. *Freedom of Expression, op. cit.*, pp. 62-63; Paeng, *New Discourse, op. cit.*, pp. 248–49. For a discussion of the Constitution Court's ruling on the registration requirement of the Periodicals Act, see chap. 5 *supra.*

70. Periodicals Act, art. 14.

71. Ibid., art. 15 (1).

72. Ibid., art. 15 (2).

73. Ibid., art. 15 (2)-3. Other conditions for the MOPI's cancellation of a branch office of foreign periodicals are as follows:

> 1. When it is discovered that permission for the establishment of a branch office of foreign periodicals has been obtained by deceit or other unlawful means;
> 2. When the terms and conditions of the permission as originally granted by the MOPI have been violated.

Ibid., art. 15 (2)-1 and 2.

74. Criminal Code, Law No. 239 (1953), revised by Law No. 2745 (1975), art. 104-2, *translated in* 3 *ROK Laws, op. cit.*, pp. X-1 to X-44. The crime of anti-State defamation provision of the Criminal Code was abolished in 1988. For a discussion of Article 104-2 of the Criminal Code, see chap. 9 *infra.*

75. Basic Press Act, art. 28 (2)-4.

76. A Korean constitutional jurist noted that the Basic Press Act derived its basic framework from German press law. *See* Yang Sam-sung, "Analysis of Trends in Court Decisions on the Press," *Press Arbitration Quarterly* (Korean), Spring 1990, p. 31. In this context, the German notion of "correction" of factual reports is noteworthy:

> [N]either the inaccuracy or untruth of the original publication nor the correctness and truthfulness of the answer need affect the granting of the right to reply. No decision is made between truth or untruth: so long as certain formal conditions are fulfilled, the answer must be published. For this reason the laws, led by Hesse and Bavaria, do not use the word "correction" but introduce the much more appropriate word "Gegendarstellung" (which is used in this translation for "reply" and which means, roughly, putting the opposite view).

Schwarz, *op. cit.*, p. 82 (parentheses in original).

77. Periodicals Act, art. 16 (1). This provision is identical to Article 49 of the Basic Press Act, except that claim for correction of news stories disseminated by the broadcasting media is no longer stipulated by the Periodicals Act. *Compare* Periodicals Act, art. 16 (1), *with* Basic Press Act, art. 49.

78. As Article 16 (4) states, "Any corrected report shall be limited to factual statements and an explanation necessary for transmitting it clearly...." Ibid., art. 16 (4). With respect to a policy justification for the Korean press law's limitation on correction of news reports to statements of facts, one commentator reasons that it derives from a similar German law aimed at preventing the press from being chilled in its role as a critic of matters of public concern. Paeng, *Mass Communication Law, op. cit.*, p. 179 (footnote omitted). For a succinct discussion of the "right of reply" concept in German press law, see Schwarz, *op. cit.*, pp. 81–85.

79. An Chae-ran v. Korean Federation for Education, Supreme Court of Korea, 85 Taka 1973, January 28, 1986, *Press Arbitration Quarterly* (Korean), Spring 1986, p. 171.

80. Periodicals Act, art. 16 (3). The Basic Press Act gave the offending periodical seven days to print the correction. Basic Press Act, art. 49 (3).

81. Ibid., art. 16 (6). In connection with Article 16 (6) of the Periodicals Act, it is noteworthy that the mayor of Pusan in March 1990 advised the administrative agencies of Pusan City to request press

arbitration commissions for "correction of news reports." He stated: "When the credibility of the city government is damaged by inaccurate news stories by way of falsehoods, exaggeration, or bias, there should be a recovery for the damage. Unless prompt response to the damage is taken, it aggravates the public's distrust of the city government. Thus, the press arbitration commissions should be actively utilized to the maximum possible extent." *See* "Request Correction of Reports When the Reports Are Inaccurate," *Hankuk Ilbo* (Korean), March 29, 1990, p. 8 (U.S. ed.).

82. Ibid., art. 17 (1).

83. Ibid., art. 17 (1).

84. Ibid., art. 19 (1) ("No claim for a corrected report shall be requested to the court without passing through an arbitration of the Arbitration Commissions"). For a discussion of implementation by press arbitration commission of the claim for correction of news reports, *See* Yi Hye-bok, "Reporting on Accidents and Violations of Personal Interests: An Examination," in *Press Arbitration Quarterly* (Korean), Autumn 1990, pp. 16–34. *See also Public Interest of the Press and Press Regulation* (Korean) 29 (Oh In-hwan ed., 1991).

85. Article 48 of the Basic Press Act stated: "Courts should adjudicate a lawsuit instituted for damages caused by the press prior to any other cases."

86. Periodicals Act, art. 20 (1).

87. As Professor Stephen Holmes of the University of Chicago has stated, "[O]bligatory speech is not very different from forbidden speech." Stephen Holmes, "Liberal Constraints on Private Power?: Reflections on the Origins and Rationale of Access Regulation," in *Democracy and the Mass Media* 47 (Judith Lichtenberg ed., 1990). The U.S. Supreme Court, rejecting "obligatory speech," has noted its harmful impact upon the editorial freedom of the news media:

> Compelling editors or publishers to publish that which "'reason' tells them should not be published" is what is at issue in this case [Miami Herald Publishing Co. v. Tornillo].
>
> ...
>
> A newspaper is more than a passive receptacle or conduit for news, comment, and advertising. The choice of material to go into a newspaper, and the decisions made as to limitations on the size and content of the paper, and treatment of public issues and public officials—whether fair or unfair—constitute the exercise of editorial control and judgment. It has yet to be demonstrated how governmental regulation of this crucial process can be exercised consistent with First Amendment guarantees of a free press as they have evolved to this time.

Miami Herald Publishing Co. v. Tornillo, 418 U.S. 241, 256 (1974).

88. Periodicals Act, arts. 22-24.

89. The MOPI informed the prosecutory authorities of an alleged violation by three pornographic magazines of the Periodicals Act in continuing with publication notwithstanding the MOPI's suspension order against their publication. *See* "Three Pornographic Magazines Reported to Prosecution for Continuous Publication in Violation of Suspension Orders," *Joongang Ilbo* (Korean), October 1, 1990, p. 19 (U.S. ed.).

90. Periodicals Act, art. 22.

91. Ibid., art. 23.

92. Article 7 (4) stipulates: "Any person who has registered a periodical ... shall publish the registered periodical within six months (one year in case of biannual and annual publication) after it is registered." Ibid., art. 7 (4).

93. Ibid., art. 24. Other penal provisions stipulate punishment of those who fail to comply with the MOPI's request for information pertinent to the statutory prohibition of concurrent operation of the mass media, as required by Article 3 (5); those who fail to insert such "obligatory" information as the number and date of registration, title, classification by publication, publisher, editor, printer, publishing office and date of publication, etc., into their publications, as required by Article 8; those who fail to "immediately" deliver two copies of their publication to the MOPI, as required by Article 10; and those

who fail to notify the MOPI of the fact in case their publication is suspended from publication or discontinues their operation, as required by Article 11.

94. *Compare* Periodicals Act, art. 22, *with* Basic Press Act, art. 52.

95. Basic Press Act, art. 57.

96. *The Korean Press 1988*, at 33 (1988).

97. Broadcast Act, art. 1.

98. *Compare* Broadcast Act, art. 3 (1) ("The freedom of broadcast programming shall be guaranteed"), *with* Basic Press Act, art. 29 ("Unless otherwise specified in this Act or any other law, no one can regulate or interfere with the work of drawing up broadcasting programs").

99. *Compare* Broadcast Act, art. 3 (2) ("No person shall regulate or interfere with the drawing up or making of a broadcasting program or operation of broadcasting station without complying with the conditions as prescribed by this Act or other Acts), *with* Basic Press Act, art. 29 ("Unless otherwise specified in this Act or any other law, no one can regulate or interfere with the work of drawing up broadcasting programs").

100. Basic Press Act, art. 3.

101. Broadcast Act, art. 4.

102. Ibid., art. 5. One commentator has drawn a parallel between Article 5 of the Broadcast Act and the now abolished "Fairness Doctrine" of the United States. Deanna Campbell Robinson, "South Korean Communication in Transition," in *Modern Society and Freedom of the Press, op. cit.*, p. 223. The analogy is partially correct in that the Fairness Doctrine required broadcasters to devote a reasonable percentage of air time to the discussion of public issues, in addition to presentation of contrasting views in the case of controversial issues of public importance. *See* "In the Matter of the Handling of Public Issues Under the Fairness Doctrine and the Public Interest Standards of the Communications Act," 48 F.C.C.2d 1, 7, 9–11, 30 P and F Rad. Reg.2d 1261, 1273, 1276–78 (1974).

103. Basic Press Act. art. 34.

104. Broadcast Act, art. 11.

105. Ibid., art. 14 (1).

106. Ibid., art. 12 (1).

107. Ibid., art. 12 (2).

108. *See* Paeng, *New Discourse, op. cit.*, pp. 237–38.

109. For a discussion of the restructuring of the Korean government since early 1988, see Myung-soon Shin, "Democratization in Korean Politics: Presidential and Parliamentary Aspects," in Sejong Institute, *Democracy and Political Institutions*, Seminar Series 88-03 (1988); James M. West and Edward J. Baker, "The 1987 Constitutional Reforms in South Korea: Electoral Processes and Judicial Independence," in *Human Rights in Korea: Historical and Policy Perspectives* 221–52 (William Shaw ed.,1991).

110. Robinson, *op. cit.*, p. 227.

111. Broadcasting Act, art. 17 (1).

112. Ibid., art. 17 (2).

113. Ibid., art. 17 (3). The Broadcast Act reads: "Matters as referred to in Subparagraphs 2 to 4 of Paragraph (2) of Article 17 shall be deliberated and decided before they are broadcast by a broadcasting station." Ibid. Subparagraphs 2 to 4 of Paragraph (2) of Article 17 provides:

> 2. Matters on whether or not the television dramatic films and cartoon films for broadcast are televised under Article 12 (4) of the Cinema Act;
> 3. Matters on whether or not the television films and cartoon films for broadcast imported by a broadcasting station are televised;

4. Matters on whether or not advertising matters which the Korea Broadcasting Advertisement Corp. desires to broadcast by entrusting it to a broadcasting station under Article 15 of the Korea Broadcasting Advertisement Corp. Act are televised.

Ibid., art. 17 (2)-2, 3, 4.

114. Ibid., art. 19 (1).

115. Ibid., art. 20 (2).

116. Ibid., art. 21 (1).

117. Ibid., art. 21 (2).

118. Ibid., art. 21 (3).

119. Ibid., art. 21 (5).

120. Ibid., arts. 6–8. *Compare with* Basic Press Act, arts. 11, 12, 14.

121. Ibid., art. 9. The disqualification provisions of the Broadcast Act are almost identical to those of the Periodicals Act, except that the former explicitly disallows a representative of a corporation or organization, who is not a Korean national or does not have a domicile in Korea, from being in charge of broadcast programming, while the latter does not. *Compare* Broadcast Act, art. 9, *with* Periodicals Act, art. 9.

122. Ibid., arts. 25-29. The Broadcast Act provides for payment of television broadcast reception fee thus: "Any person who has a television receiver … in order to receive the television broadcast, shall register the TV set with the Broadcasting Commission under the conditions as prescribed by the Presidential Decree, and pay the television broadcast reception fee: provided, that with respect to TV sets as prescribed by the Presidential Decree the registration may be exempted or the whole or part of the reception fee may be reduced or exempted." Ibid., art. 25.

One Korean media law scholar has argued that the statutory change in collection of TV reception fees originated from an "impure" desire of the Korean government to prevent recurrence of the widespread protest of the Korean public in 1986 against the allegedly biased news reports of the then government-controlled Korean Broadcasting System (KBS) in the form of its refusal to pay the fees. Paeng, *New Discourse, op. cit.*, p. 239. For a discussion of the campaign against TV reception fees, see Kang Chun-man, *A History of Movement for Broadcasting Democratization in Korea* (Korean) 8–27 (1990).

123. Ibid., art. 30.

124. Ibid., art. 30 (4). The Basic Press Act, which did not require that the head of a broadcasting network follow the Broadcasting Advisory Committee's advice on the broadcasting program, stated: "The Advisory Committee may deliberate on matters related to broadcasting programming, present its opinions to the head of a broadcasting network on the basis of its deliberations, or recommend to him that correction be made when necessary." Basic Press Act, art. 45 (3).

125. *Compare* Broadcast Act, arts. 33–35, *with* Basic Press Act, arts. 42–44.

126. Broadcast Act, art. 40 (1).

127. Ibid., art. 40 (2).

128. Ibid., art. 41.

129. Ibid., art. 42.

130. Ibid., art. 43.

131. Ibid., art. 44.

132. *Freedom of Expression, op. cit.*, p. 36.

133. Paeng, "Korea's Press Law," *op. cit.*, p. 48.

134. The Fifth Republic under President Chun Doo Hwan, employing the similar provision of the Basic Press Act, accepted no application for registration of new "general" daily newspapers throughout its seven-year rule (1981–1987), in line with its basic press policy of "structurally minimizing critical media coverage of the government." In June 1985 the Chun regime approved the registration of the

*Supochu Seoul* (Daily Sports Seoul) as a "special daily newspaper," which was prohibited from dealing with topics of sociopolitical interest. Kyu Ho Youm and Michael B. Salwen. "A Free Press in South Korea: Temporary Phenomenon or Permanent Fixture?" 30 *Asian Survey* 318 n.15 (March 1990).

135. *See* "Onron Nobo's Failure at Registration Blamed on MOCI," *Han-kyoreh Shinmun* (Korean), November 30, 1989, p. 20 (U.S. ed.) (*Onron Nobo*, a weekly published by the Federation of Unions of Media Employees without a then MOCI-issued certification of registration, claiming that the MOCI "unlawfully" refused to issue the certification to the publication). *See* also "Onoryon, Confronting the Surrounding Attack by the Ministry of Labor and the MOCI, Determined to Continue with Administrative Litigation," *Han-kyoreh Shinmun* (Korean), November 30, 1989, p. 16 (U.S. ed.).

136. According to the Korean Press Institute's 1990 annual survey on the Korean press, periodicals registered with the MOPI as of the end of 1989 totaled 4,400 including 68 dailies, two wire services, and 819 weeklies. Compared with June 1987, the report said, the number of periodicals, increased by 2,162, including 38 dailies and 618 weeklies. *The Korean Press 1990, op. cit.*, p. 48.

137. "Deliberative Rules" are the rules of the Broadcasting Deliberation Committee related to deliberation of broadcasts. The rules focus on the following matters:

1. Matters concerning the impartiality of news and comments;
2. Matters concerning the promotion of free democracy and the respect of human rights;
3. Matters concerning the cultivation of national identity;
4. Matters concerning creative enlightenment and development of national culture;
5. Matters concerning the proper guidance of children and youth;
6. Matters concerning the purity of family life;
7. Matters concerning the promotion of the public morality and social ethics; and
8. Other matters proscribed by this Act.

Broadcast Act, art. 20 (2).

138. Pnina Lahav, "Conclusion: An Outline for a General Theory of Press Law in Democracy," in *Press Law in Modern Democracies, op. cit.*, p. 347.

139. Ibid., p. 349.

## CHAPTER 7

1. The term "claim for corrected reports," first used in the Basic Press Act, is a misnomer in that the 1980 press statute in effect provided for the right of an injured person to respond to incorrect news reports, not the correction by the news media of their erroneous news stories.

2. Basic Press Act, Law No. 3347 (1980), art. 49, revised by Law No. 3786 (1984), *translated in The Korean Press 1986*, at 207–24 (1986). The Basic Press Act was abolished in 1987, when the Korean National Assembly enacted the Periodicals Act and the Broadcast Act to replace the 1980 act.

3. Yang Sam-sung, "News Reporting on Accidents and Issues in Law and Ethics," 36 *Press Arbitration Quarterly*, Autumn 1990, pp. 13–14. The right of reply was originated in Europe "as a means to resolve libel disputes." *See* Charles Danziger, "The Right of Reply in the United States and Europe," 19 *New York University Journal of International Law and Politics* 183 (1986).

4. Basic Press Act, art. 50.

5. Pak Yong-sang, "Basic Press Act," in *Laws Relating to Politics* (Korean) 211 (Kim Chol-su ed., 1983).

6. The right of reply is statutorily recognized in at least 13 countries in Europe. Danziger, *op. cit.*, p. 183 (footnote omitted). For a comprehensive discussion of the right of reply adopted by European countries, see *Das Gegendarstellungsrecht in Europa: Möglichkeiten der Harmonisierung* (The Right of Reply in Europe: Possibilities of Harmonization) (Martin Löffler et al. eds., 1974) [hereinafter *Right of Reply in Europe*]. For an earlier discussion of the right of reply as recognized by a number of countries including those in Europe and South America, see Richard C. Donnelly, "The Right of Reply: An

Alternative to an Action for Libel," 34 *Virginia Law Review* 884–91 (1948). *See also* Ignaz Rothenberg, *The Newspaper: A Study in the Workings of the Daily Press and Its Laws* 114–40 (1946). The United States and England have yet to accept the right of reply in toto. It should be noted, however, that while the U.S Supreme Court in 1974 ruled mandatory right of reply statutes governing the print media unconstitutional, *see* Miami Herald Publishing Co. v. Tornillo, 418 U.S. 241 (1974), the Communications Act provides for the "personal attack" and "political editorial" rules on the broadcasting media, *see* 47 C.F.R. 73.1920 (1989) and 47 C.F.R. 73.1930 (1989). For a recent discussion of the right of reply in American law, see Jerome A. Barron, "The Right of Reply to the Media in the United States: Resistance and Resurgence," 15 *Hastings Communications and Entertainment Law Journal* 1–20 (1992). In England a right of reply bill was introduced to the House of Commons in the 1988–1989 session of the Parliament, *see* Tony Worthington, "Right of Reply Bill," 10 *Journal of Media Law and Practice* 78–82 (1989); Tony Worthington, "The Right of Reply," 9 *Franco British Studies* 7–18 (1990), but it was "talked out" in April 1989, *see* "Privacy Inquiry Set up as Right of Reply Bill Fails in the Commons," *The Times* (London), April 22, 1989, p. 6. For the text of the "Right of Reply" bill as presented by its key sponsor, Tony Worthington, to the House of Commons in 1989, contact the author.

7. Rudolf B. Schlesinger et al., *Comparative Law* 10 (5th ed. 1988).

8. Constitution Court, 89 Honma 165: Constitutional Petition for Review of Periodicals Act, arts. 16 (3) and 19 (3), September 16, 1991, *Press Arbitration Quarterly*, Autumn 1991, pp. 169–77 [hereinafter Constitutional Petition].

9. Basic Press Act, Law No. 3347 (1980), revised by Law No. 3786 (1984), art. 49.

10. *See* Act Relating to Registration of Periodicals (Periodicals Act), Law No. 3979 (1987), revised by Law No. 4441 (1991), art. 16, *translated in The Korean Press 1995*, at 135–45 (1995), and Broadcast Act, Law No. 3978 (1987), revised by Law No. 4441 (1991), art. 41, *translated in The Korean Press 1995, op. cit.*, pp. 146–59.

11. Constitution, art. 10 ("All citizens shall be assured of human worth and dignity and have the right to pursue happiness. It shall be the duty of the State to confirm and guarantee the fundamental and inviolable human rights of individuals").

12. Constitutional Petition, *op. cit.*, p. 172.

13. Ibid.

14. Pak Yong-sang, "Legislative Proposals for Improvement of the Right of Claim for Corrected Reports and Press Arbitration System," *Press Arbitration Quarterly*, Autumn 1991, p. 11.

15. Periodicals Act, art. 16 (1) (emphasis added). *See also* Broadcast Act, art. 41.

16. *See* Yang Sam-sung, "Right to Claim Corrected Reports: A Legal Perspective," *Press Arbitration Quarterly*, Winter 1982, p. 14.

17. One Korean Press Institute report on the right of reply complaints in Korea states: "[C]omplaints submitted for arbitration to the Korean Press Arbitration Commission during 1990 reached 159 cases.... This number shows a 31% increase over the previous year of 1989. Of the total, 136 complaints (86%) were on libel and violation of privacy, and the remaining 23 cases on infringement on property rights." *The Korean Press 1991*, at 18 (1991).

18. "Factual" is not related to the "truth" of the stories. It is a term of art to make a distinction between objective facts and subjective opinions.

19. The fact-opinion distinction under the Korean press statutes is derived from the press law of Baden-Württemberg in Germany. *See* Pak, "Legislative Proposals," *op. cit.*, p. 13.

20. The Periodicals Act defines "periodicals" as "newspapers, communication, magazines, and other publications which are published continuously under the same title more than once a year." Periodicals Act, art. 2.

21. The Broadcast Act defines "broadcasts" as "a transmission of wireless communication operated by a broadcasting station for the purpose of propagating to the general public, news, comments, and

public opinion on politics, economy, society, culture, current events, etc., and education, music, entertainment, etc." Broadcast Act, art. 2.

22. Periodicals Act, art. 16 (3).

23. Ibid.

24. Ibid.

25. Ibid., Broadcast Act, art. 41 (3).

26. Ibid., art. 16 (6); Broadcast Act, art. 41 (7).

27. The "fair report privilege" doctrine allows the media to publish stories on government proceedings and records without fear of a libel suit, "provided that they give a fair and accurate account." Wayne Overbeck, *Major Principles of Media Law* 108 (1994 ed. 1995).

28. Periodicals Act, art. 16 (4); Broadcast Act, art. 41 (4).

29. Ibid., Broadcast Act, art. 41 (5).

30. Ibid., art. 17 (1). The Broadcast Act incorporates Articles 17 to 20 of the Periodicals Act with respect to arbitration of right of reply disputes in toto. *See* Broadcast Act, art. 42.

31. Ibid., art. 18.

32. Ibid., art. 19 (2).

33. Ibid., art. 19 (1).

34. Ibid., art. 19 (3).

35. Ibid.

36. Ibid., art. 20 (1). One Korean jurist traces the *ex post facto* provision of the new press laws to the Austrian press law of 1982. *See* Pak Yong-sang, "Press Arbitration System Under the New 'Act Relating to Registration, etc. of Periodicals,'" *Press Arbitration Quarterly* (Korean), Winter 1987, p. 67.

37. Ibid., art. 20 (2).

38. According to a 1988 study of the governmental "inclination to control" the press in 58 countries, Germany, then West Germany, was ranked third among the countries surveyed. John C. Merrill, "Inclination of Nations to Control Press and Attitudes on Professionalization," 65 *Journalism Quarterly* 843 (1988).

39. Under the Basic Law of Germany, press powers "are limited ... by the right to inviolability of personal honour." Basic Law of Germany, promulgated in 1949 and amended in 1990, art. 5 (1). For an English translation of the Basic Law of Germany, as amended in 1990, see "Germany" in *Constitutions of the Countries of the World* 79–89 (Binder V) (Albert P. Blaustein and Gisbert H. Flanz eds., 1995). The German Constitution is still known as the Basic Law (Grundgesetz), although the term "basic law" was originated "to underscore the temporary nature of the constitution pending the reunification of Germany." Donald P. Kommers, "The Jurisprudence of Free Speech in the United States and the Federal Republic of Germany," 53 *Southern California Law Review* 659 n.6 (1980).

40. Michael J. Calvey et al., "Foreign Defamation Law," in *LDRC [Libel Defense Resource Center] 50-State Survey 1987: Current Developments in Media Libel and Invasion of Privacy Law* 1xii (Henry R. Kaufman ed., 1987).

41. Article 1 of the Basic Law of Germany states in pertinent part:

    (1) The dignity of man shall be inviolable. To respect and protect it shall be the duty of all state authority;

    (2) The German people therefore acknowledge inviolable and inalienable human rights as the basis of every community, of peace and of justice in the world.

Article 2 provides as follows:

    (1) Everyone shall have the right to the free development of his personality in so far as he does not violate the rights of others or offend against the constitutional order or the moral code;

(2) Everyone shall have the right to life and to inviolability of this person. The liberty of the individual shall be inviolable. These rights may only be encroached upon pursuant to a law.

42. Basic Law of Germany, art. 5 (2).

43. Ibid., art. 19 (2).

44. Urs Schwarz, *Press Law for Our Times* 81 (1966).

45. Ibid., pp. 81–82. The German press law of 1874 provided for right of "correction" thus:

The responsible editor of a periodical publication is bound to exhibit, without additions or omissions, at the request of any public authority who may be concerned therein, or of a private person, a *correction* of a statement which has appeared in his paper, in so far as such *correction* is signed by its contributor, does not contain anything which constitutes a punishable offence, and confines itself to a statement of *actual facts*.

The printing of the *correction* must be undertaken in the number immediately following its reception, provided that such number is not already set up in type, and must appear in the same portion of the publication and in the same type as the article which it *corrects*.

Such insertion shall be gratis in so far as the correction does not occupy more space in the journal than the announcement which it *corrects*; for each line in excess thereof the usual costs for the insertion of advertisements must be paid.

Press Law, art. 11 (1874) (emphasis added), *reprinted in The Press Laws of Foreign Countries with an Appendix Containing the Press Laws of India* 103–109 (Montague Shearman and O.T. Rayner eds., 1926).

46. In this regard, German press law on the right of reply is distinctive from the Korean press law, whose right of reply provisions are purported both to protect individuals from being falsely injured in their reputation *and* to increase the public access to the news media.

47. Helmut Kohl, "Press Law in the Federal Republic of Germany," in *Press Law in Modern Democracies: A Comparative Study* 214 (Pnina Lahav ed., 1985).

48. Martin Löffler, "The 'Gegendarstellungsrecht' in the Federal Republic of Germany," in *Right of Reply in Europe, op. cit.*, p. 190.

49. Hamburg Press Law, enacted in 1965, *translated in* Schwartz, *Press Law for Our Times, op. cit.*, pp. 103–12; *Press Laws: Documents on Politics and Society in the Federal Republic of Germany* 17–24 (Sigrid Born ed., Martin Fry trans., 3d ed. 1994).

50. Kohl, "Press Law," *op. cit.*, p. 203.

51. Hamburg Press Law, para. 11 (1) (emphasis added).

52. For a discussion of the French right of reply (Le Droit de Reponse), see Danziger, *op. cit.*, pp. 184–90; Franklyn S. Haiman, *Citizen Access to the Media: A Cross-Cultural Analysis of Four Democratic Societies* 12–19 (1987); Emmanuel Derieux, The Right of Reply in France (1992) (paper presented at the Association for Education in Journalism and Mass Communication convention in Montreal, Canada).

53. Löffler, "'Gegendarstellungsrecht,'" *op. cit.*, p. 190.

54. Hamburg Press Law, para. 7 (4).

55. Ibid., para. 11 (2).

56. Ibid.

57. Ibid.

58. Ibid., para. 11 (3).

59. Ibid.

60. Ibid., para. 11 (6).

61. Ibid.

62. Ibid.

63. Ibid.

64. Ibid., para. 11 (5).

65. Schwartz, *Press Law for Our Times, op. cit.*, p. 83.

66. Löffler, "'Gegendarstellungsrecht,'" *op. cit.*, p. 191.

67. Hamburg Press Law, para. 11 (4).

68. Ibid.

69. Schwartz, *Press Law for Our Times, op. cit.*, pp. 84–85.

70. Ignace Rothenberg, "The Right of Reply to Libels in the Press," 23 *Journal of Comparative Legislation and International Law* 59 (1941).

71. Hamburg Press Law, para. 11 (4).

72. *See* An Chae-ran v. Korean Federation of Education, 85 Taka 1973, Supreme Court, January 28, 1986, *Collection of Korean Press Cases* (Korean) 71–73 (1990) [hereinafter *Korean Press Cases*].

73. Ibid., pp. 71–73.

74. Ibid., p. 73, *quoted with approval* in Dong-A Ilbosa v. Yi Kyu-ho, 90 Taka 25468, January 15, 1991, *Press Arbitration Quarterly* (Korean), Spring 1991, pp. 173–74.

75. Ibid.

76. Ibid. The Court said: "([T]he title of the right, i.e., claim for corrected report, is not an accurate expression. It is correct that the title should have been a right to claim a reply to reports)." Ibid. (parentheses in original).

77. Ibid.

78. An Chae-ran v. Korean Federation of Education, 84 Ka 1598, Seoul Civil District Court, May 25, 1984, *Korean Press Cases* (Korean), *op. cit.*, pp. 64–68.

79. Ibid., p. 66.

80. Ibid. *See also* Yi Ui-hyang v. Dong-A Ilbosa, 82 Ka 27454, Seoul Civil District Court, November 4, 1982, *Korean Press Cases* (Korean), *op. cit.*, pp. 44–49; Dong-A Ilbosa v. Yi Ui-hyang, 82 Na 4188, Seoul High Court, November 17, 1983, *Korean Press Cases* (Korean), *op. cit.*, pp. 50–56.

81. *See* Korean Federation of Education v. An Chae-ran, 82 Na 2524, Seoul High Court, August 16, 1985, *Korean Press Cases* (Korean), *op. cit.*, pp. 68–70.

82. 90 Taka 25468, Supreme Court, January 15, 1991, *Press Arbitration Quarterly* (Korean), Spring 1991, pp. 172–74.

83. Ibid., p. 174.

84. Yi Kyu-ho v. Dong-A Ilbosa, 89 Ka 52256, Seoul Civil District Court, December 29, 1989, *Korean Press Cases* (Korean), *op. cit.*, pp. 186–87.

85. During the presidential election of 1987, the plaintiff, then the Minister of Construction, made derogatory remarks about the Cholla people, who often tend to be sympathetic to the opposition parties while vociferously critical of the ruling authorities. Ibid., p. 187.

86. The plaintiff made the statement quoted in the story at issue in the context of his argument that violence should be stopped in the campaign speech sites. Ibid.

87. *See* Yi Kyu-hyo v. Dong-A Ilbosa, 90 Na 484, Seoul High Court, July 3, 1990, *Press Arbitration Quarterly* (Korean), Spring 1991, pp. 174–77.

88. *Yi Kyu-hyo*, Supreme Court, p. 174.

89. Ibid. The media defendant argued that the plaintiff's comment related to a matter of public interest and thus should not be subject to a claim for reply by the plaintiff.

90. Though not in the right of reply context, Anglo-American libel law follows the common law rule that "one who repeats or otherwise republishes defamatory matter is subject to liability as if he had originally published it." *Restatement (Second) of Torts* § 578 (1977).

91. 83 Ka 9145, Seoul Civil District Court, August 19, 1983, *Korean Press Cases* (Korean), *op. cit.*, pp. 31–35.

92. Ibid., p. 32.

93. Ibid., p. 34. *See also* World Association for Christian Unification and Spirits v. Christian News, 83 Ka 9146, Seoul Civil District Court, August 19, 1983, *Korean Press Cases* (Korean), *op. cit.*, pp. 35–39.

94. 89 Ka 11518, Seoul Civil District Court, July 7, 1989, *Korean Press Cases* (Korean), *op. cit.*, pp. 157–60, *aff'd,* Yi Chong-ja v. Han-kyoreh Shinmunsa, 89 Na 30506, Seoul High Court, February 6, 1990, *Korean Press Cases* (Korean), *op. cit.*, pp. 161–164.

95. Ibid., p. 158.

96. 89 Ka 5999, Seoul District Court (South Branch), November 7, 1989, *Korean Press Cases* (Korean), *op. cit.*, pp. 175–80.

97. Ibid., p. 176.

98. 87 Ka 40175, Seoul Civil District Court, December 11, 1987, *Korean Press Cases* (Korean), *op. cit.*, pp. 131–34.

99. Ibid., p. 133.

100. Ibid., pp. 132–33.

101. One authority explains "colloquium" thus:

A publication may clearly be defamatory as to somebody, and yet on its face make no reference to the individual plaintiff. In such a case the plaintiff must sustain the burden of pleading and proof, by way of "colloquium," that the defamatory meaning attached to him.... He need not, of course, be named, and the reference may be an indirect one, with the identification depending upon circumstances known to the hearers, and it is not necessary that every listener understand it, so long as there are some who reasonably do; but the understanding that the plaintiff is meant must be a reasonable one, and if it arises from extrinsic facts, it must be shown that these were known to those who heard.

W. Page Keeton et al., *Prosser and Keeton on the Law of Torts* 783 (5th ed. 1984) (footnotes omitted).

102. 86 Na 4096, Seoul High Court, March 18, 1987, *Korean Press Cases* (Korean), *op. cit.*, pp. 127–31, *aff'g,* Chin Pu-ja v. Joongang Ilbosa, 86 Ka 28755, Seoul Civil District Court, September 26, 1986, *Korean Press Cases* (Korean), *op. cit.*, pp. 121–25.

103. *Chin Pu-ja* began when *Joongang Women*, a monthly magazine owned by the media defendant, published a "reader's story of experience" focusing on a suicide by a high school student under pressure to be at the top of his class. The story, written by the student's "mother," depicted her remorse over her pushing her children to excel academically. The name of the mother, as given in the story, was "fictional." Ibid., p. 128.

104. *Joongang Ilbo*, a daily newspaper owned by the defendant, previously reported that one of the plaintiff's twin children "fell to death" from the veranda of her apartment. Ibid.

105. Ibid.

106. Ibid., p. 129. *See also* Yim Hyong-sin v. Kyonghyang Shinmun, 82 Ka 1863, Seoul Civil District Court, September 3, 1982, *Korean Press Cases* (Korean), *op. cit.*, pp. 13–17.

107. 89 Ka 46152, Seoul Civil District Court, December 29, 1989, *Korean Press Cases* (Korean), *op. cit.*, pp. 180–85.

108. Ibid., p. 183.

109. Ibid. In the story in question in *Yon Song-man*, the plaintiff was reported to have been involved in making arrangements for the illegal visit by a dissident Korean student to North Korea in violation of the National Security Act.

110. Ibid.

111. Article 48 of the Code of Civil Procedure states: "An association or foundation which is not a juristic person, but which is provided with a representative or administrator, may become a party of a suit in its name." Code of Civil Procedure, Law No. 547 (1960), revised by Law No. 4423 (1991), art. 48, *translated in* 2 *ROK Current Laws, op. cit.*, pp. 753–754.

112. Yi Chin-kyu v. Na Un-mong, 83 Ka 22003, Seoul Civil District Court, November 25, 1983, *Korean Press Cases* (Korean), *op. cit.*, pp. 56–62.

113. Ibid., p. 58.

114. Ibid.

115. 89 Ka 28545, Seoul Civil District Court, September 22, 1989, *Korean Press Cases* (Korean), *op. cit.*, pp. 167–72.

116. Ibid., p. 169. The plaintiff, a prominent dissident leader in South Korea, was quoted in the story as saying, "To be frank with you, I do not want to return [to South Korea]," at a news conference during his stopover in Beijing, China, from his illegal visit to Pyongyang, capital of North Korea. In the story he was reported to have made the statement in response to a reporter's question about the possibility that he might be arrested by the South Korean government on his return to South Korea.

117. Ibid., pp. 169–70.

118. 89 Ka 28984, Seoul Civil District Court, May 25, 1990, *Press Arbitration Quarterly* (Korean), Winter 1990, pp. 160–63.

119. Ibid., p. 161.

120. Ibid. Finding that the statements "Experts point out that these [consulting] clubs could not find that much advertising revenue unless they were fraudulent" and "[i]t was indicated that they would inflict serious harm upon new investors in the provinces" were not factual assertions, the court stated that they were nothing but quotations of others' *comments* on the facts underlying the foregoing stories.

121. Supreme Court, 86 Taka 818, December 23, 1986, *Korean Press Cases* (Korean), *op. cit.*, pp. 118–20, *aff'g,* Kim Tong-yol v. Joongang Ilbosa, 85 Na 3140, Seoul High Court, February 25, 1986, *Korean Press Cases* (Korean), *op. cit.*, pp. 114–18.

122. Ibid., p. 119. The Supreme Court said the "no proper interest" limitation on the right of reply was to "prevent the news media from being crippled or weakened by the unlimited guarantee of the claim for corrected reports." Ibid.

123. Ibid., pp. 119–20.

124. 88 Ka 62228, Seoul Civil District Court, August 18, 1989, *Korean Press Cases* (Korean), *op. cit.*, pp. 164–67.

125. Ibid., p. 166.

126. Ibid.

127. 84 Ka 35089, Seoul Civil District Court, November 30, 1984, *Korean Press Cases* (Korean), *op. cit.*, pp. 91–95.

128. Ibid., p. 93.

129. Ibid.

130. 84 Ka 34374, Seoul Civil District Court, November 30, 1984, *Korean Press Cases* (Korean), *op. cit.*, pp. 82–86.

131. Ibid., p. 82. In the advertisement, the plaintiff was described as having illegally disrupted a religious meeting and beaten a member of the church sponsoring the meeting. The advertisement also stated that he distorted the incident in a story published in his *Modern Religion* magazine, while intentionally challenging the hierarchy of the church. Ibid.

132. Ibid., p. 83. For its application of the right of reply provision to the facts in the case, the court considered the plaintiff's request for corrective advertisement as a corrected report as defined by the Basic Press Act.

133. Ibid., pp. 83–84. *See also* Tak Myong-hwan v. Church Federation News, 84 Ka 34375, Seoul Civil District Court, November 30, 1984, *Korean Press Cases* (Korean), *op. cit.*, pp. 87–88.

134. Ibid.

135. 83 Ka 7933, Seoul Civil District Court, May 24, 1983, *Korean Press Cases* (Korean), *op. cit.*, pp. 28–31.

136. Ibid., p. 30.

137. Ibid. For example, the court found truthful the assertions in the story that the plaintiff raised his fist and shouted "action, action"; that he had claimed that an intelligence agent was watching; that the meeting was video-taped; and that a resolution adopted separately from the meeting was printed and circulated.

138. Ibid.

139. 84 Na 3255, Seoul High Court, January 18, 1985, *Korean Press Cases* (Korean), *op.cit.*, pp. 78–82, *aff'g*, Seoul District Court, 84 Ka 17261, July 13, 1984, *Korean Press Cases* (Korean), *op. cit.*, pp. 75–78.

140. Article 49 (7) of the Basic Press Act stated: "The provisions of this Article [on claim for corrected reports] shall not apply to a faithful factual report ... of the open trial proceedings of a court of justice."

141. *Yi Ui-hyang*, Seoul High Court, p. 80. The *Hankuk Ilbo* newspaper published a story about the plaintiff in a libel case in which he lost to the newspaper defendant. The plaintiff argued that the story misled readers into believing that he had lost in the right of reply cases originating from the same story that led to the libel suit.

142. For a discussion of the "moral rights" of an author under the Copyright Act of Korea, see chap. 12 *infra*.

143. 83 Ka 17754 Seoul Civil District Court, August 26, 1983, *Korean Press Cases* (Korean), *op. cit.*, pp. 39–43.

144. Ibid., pp. 41–42.

145. Ibid., p. 42.

146. Ibid. The court *parenthetically* noted the author's moral rights in his work as applied to the plaintiff's claim. The Copyright Act of 1957, in effect at the time of the court ruling in *Kim Yong-so*, provided for the "copyright holder's right of maintenance of status quo" in pertinent part thus: "Without relation to the property right to works or after transfer of their rights in such works, the authors of such works shall have the right to raise objections to persons who damage the authors' honor and reputation by revising, cutting or making alterations to the content or title of the works." Copyright Act, Law No. 432 (1957), art. 16, *translated in* 1 *Laws of the Republic of Korea* III-136 to III-143 (4th ed. 1983).

The Copyright Act of 1957 was "[w]holly amended" in 1986. The new Copyright Act of 1986 stipulates the author's right to originality of his work thus: "An author may demand a person who has infringed intentionally or negligently on his author's personal right, to take measures necessary for the restoration of his reputation instead of or in addition to the compensation for damages." Copyright Act, Law No. 3916 (1986), revised by Law No. 4541 (1993), art. 95, *translated in* 4 *ROK Current Laws, op. cit.*, pp. 2561–64.

147. 81 Ka 36289, Seoul Civil District Court, October 21, 1982, *Korean Press Cases* (Korean), *op. cit.*, pp. 17–21.

148. Ibid., pp. 20–21.

149. Ibid., p. 21.

150. The "Rule on Judgment on Claims for Corrected News Reports," as set forth by the Supreme Court of Korea in 1988, states: "Court judgments on claims for corrected news reports or for *ex post facto* reports shall not be appealed for suspension of their execution, except that they may be objected against or appealed in accordance with Article 703 of the Code of Civil Procedure." Rule on Judgment on Claims for Corrected News Reports, Supreme Court Rule No. 1003 (1988), revised by Supreme

Court Rule No. 1180 (1991), art. 8, *reprinted in Compendium of Codes* (Korean) 1667–68 (1994). Article 703 of the Code of Civil Procedure reads:

(1) A debtor may raise an objection against a ruling for provisional attachment;

(2) The objection under Paragraph (1) shall explicitly state the reasons of demanding revocation or alteration of the provisional attachment;

(3) The raising of objection does not suspend the execution of the provisional attachment.

Code of Civil Procedure, art. 703.

151. The Code of Civil Procedure provides: "In cases where the nature of a claim permits compulsory performance, the court of the suit of the first instance shall, upon application of a creditor, fix an appropriate period to make performance, and shall order, in cases where the debtor defaults the performance within the period, to make reparation of a certain amount in proportion to the period of delay or an immediate reparation." Code of Civil Procedure, art. 693.

152. *See* Yi Ui-hyang v. Dong-A Ilbosa, 82 Ka 27454, Seoul Civil District Court, November 4, 1982, *Korean Press Cases* (Korean), *op. cit.*, pp. 44–49.

153. Yi Ui-hyang v. Dong-A Ilbosa, 82 Ta 20095, Seoul Civil District Court, December 10, 1982, *Korean Press Cases* (Korean), *op. cit.*, pp. 49–50.

154. Ibid., p. 50.

155. *See* Yi Chin-kyu v. Na Un-mong, 83 Ta 20389, Seoul District Court, January 12, 1984, *Korean Press Cases* (Korean), *op. cit.*, pp. 62–63. The defendant was given two weeks to comply with the order and was ordered to pay 500,000 *won* (US$625) per day to the plaintiff after the two-week period.

156. *See* Chin Pu-ja v. Joongang Ilbosa, 86 Ta 24988, Seoul Civil District Court, December 18, 1986, *Korean Press Cases* (Korean), *op. cit.*, pp. 125–26 (publish the reply in the first issue of the defendant's magazine following the order or pay 10 million *won* (US$12,500) per day after publication of the issue); Pasteur Milk Co. v. Joongang Ilbosa, Seoul Civil District Court, 89 Tagi 1608, February 28, 1989, *Korean Press Cases* (Korean), *op. cit.*, p. 151 (publish the reply in the defendant's newspaper within five days beginning the day of receipt of the order or pay 5 million *won* (US$6,250) a day after the five-day period); Yi Chong-ja v. Han-kyoreh Shinmun, 89 Tagi 11984, Seoul Civil District Court, August 21, 1989, *Korean Press Cases* (Korean), *op. cit.*, pp. 160–61 (publish the reply in the first issue of the defendant's paper not yet camera-ready after receipt of the order or pay 30 million *won* (US$37,500) per day after publication of the issue).

157. Plaintiffs prevailed in 35 cases out of 54 from 1981 through 1994.

158. Between 1981 and 1994, a total of 93 reported court decisions involved publication of allegedly harmful stories in the Korean news media.

## CHAPTER 8

1. Arthur B. Hanson, 1 *Libel and Torts* 1 (1969). *See also* Peter F. Carter-Ruck et al., *Carter-Ruck on Libel and Slander* 1 (4th ed. 1992) (noting that libel has been recognized "as a wrongful act from the very earliest times and as an actionable wrong in nearly every modern system of law").

2. Robert C. Post, "The Social Foundations of Defamation Law: Reputation and the Constitution," 74 *California Law Review* 702 (1986) (footnote omitted).

3. Noting that in the United States "reputation interest" is seen primarily from the perspective of the individual, one American sociologist wrote: "Our tendency to think of reputation in individualistic terms is rooted in our cultural emphasis on the autonomy, independence, and achievements of individuals." Robert N. Bellah, "The Meaning of Reputation in American Society," 74 *California Law Review* 743 (1986).

4. Young C. Kim, *Japanese Journalists and Their World* 71 (1981).

5. Paeng Won-sun, *A Theory of Mass Communication Law* (Korean) 155 (rev. ed. 1988).

6. Lawrence Ward Beer, *Freedom of Expression in Japan* 314 ( 1984).

7. Frederick Schauer, "Social Foundations of the Law of Defamation: A Comparative Analysis," 1 *Journal of Media Law and Practice* 3 (May 1980).

8. One commentator noted: "American constitutional law is distinguished by its protection of defamers, rather than the defamed." Oscar S. Gray, "Constitutional Protection of Freedom of Expression in the United States as It Affects Defamation Law," 38 *American Journal of Comparative Law* 463 (1990).

9. Schauer, *op. cit.*, p. 18.

10. For a discussion of libel litigation against American media in foreign countries, see Kyu Ho Youm, "Suing American Media in Foreign Courts: Doing an End-run Around U.S. Libel Law?" 16 *Hastings Communications and Entertainment Law Journal* 235–64 (1994). It is noteworthy, however, that foreign libel judgments against American media may not be enforced in the United States because they are considered by American courts to be incompatible with the First Amendment. *See generally* Kyu Ho Youm, "U.S. Media and Libel Law: An International Perspective," 55 *Gazette* 185–205 (1995).

11. David A. Anderson, "Is Libel Law Worth Reforming?" in *Reforming Libel Law* 2 (John Soloski and Randall P. Bezanson eds., 1992). *See also* Kent R. Middleton and Bill F. Chamberlin, *The Law of Public Communication* 70 (3d ed. 1994) (characterizing defamation as "one of the most important issues" in U.S. media law).

12. *See* "Chapter XXXIII: Crimes Against Reputation" of the Criminal Code, Law No. 293 (1953), revised by Law No. 4040 (1988), *translated in* 2 *Current Laws of the Republic of Korea* 761–812 (1994) [hereinafter *ROK Current Laws*].

13. *See* "Chapter V: Unlawful Act" of the Civil Code, Law No. 471 (1958), revised by Law No. 4199 (1990), *translated in* 2 *ROK Current Laws, op. cit.*, pp. 401–556.

14. By mid-1984, a total of 35 libel cases had been adjudicated." *See* Kyu Ho Youm, "The Libel Law of the Republic of Korea," 35 *Gazette* 193 (1985).

15. According to a 1985 study, 10 libel cases involved the press "in one way or another." *See* ibid.

16. Hamid Mowlana and Chul-Soo Chin, "Libel Laws of Modern Japan and South Korea Are Compared," 48 *Journalism Quarterly* 330 (1971).

17. The number of media cases is based on the court rulings reported in *Collection of Korean Press Cases* (Korean) (1990) and in *Press Arbitration Quarterly* (Korean) from winter 1990 through winter 1994. *Collection of Korean Press Cases* [hereinafter *Korean Press Cases*] is a complete collection of the court decisions on the Korean press published in *Press Arbitration Quarterly* from Winter 1981 through Autumn 1990. Among the 99 media cases are the Constitution Court's rulings on the right of reply provisions of the Korean press law in September 1991 and on the public-apology requirement under the Civil Code in April 1991.

18. Kyu Ho Youm, "Libel Laws and Freedom of the Press: South Korea and Japan Reexamined, " 8 *Boston University International Law Journal* 78–79 (1990).

19. For a discussion of the Korean press as a powerful institution, see Kim Chong-tak, *The Press Republic* (Korean) 235–52 (1991).

20. For constitutional guarantees of freedom of speech and the press in various countries, see *Constitutions of the Countries of the World* (Albert P. Blaustein and Gisbert H. Flanz eds., 1995).

21. Ibid., art. 20 (2).

22. Ibid., art. 10.

23. Criminal Code, art. 307 (emphasis added). The amount of fines imposed under the Criminal Code has been changed by the Temporary Act on Fines, Law No. 216 (1951), revised by Law No. 4296 (1990), *reprinted in Compendium of Codes* (Korean) 1827 (1994). Article 4 (1) of the Temporary Act on Fines provides: "When the provisions of fines in the Criminal Code are to be applied, such fines shall be fixed in the amount equivalent to 40 times those specified in the provisions; provided, however, that where the monetary unit *hwan* appears in the provisions, it shall be regarded as *won*."

24. Rather than following the once-prevalent Anglo-American common law maxim, "The greater the truth, the greater the libel," *see* Rodney A. Smolla, *Law of Defamation* 5-2 (1995), the Korean Criminal Code recognizes truth as a mitigating factor in determining liability. *See* Criminal Code, art. 307 (2).

25. Criminal Code, art. 309 (emphasis added).

26. As one American media attorney noted, "Defamatory statements made in a television or radio broadcast usually qualify as libel because, like writings, they have broader and longer exposure than the fleeting spoken word." Neil J. Rosini, *The Practical Guide to Libel Law* 3 (1991) (footnote omitted).

27. One authority defines "malice" as "[t]he intentional doing of a wrongful act without just cause or excuse, with an intent to inflict an injury or under circumstances that the law will imply an evil intent." It adds that in libel law, malice "consists in intentionally publishing, without justifiable cause, any written or printed matter which is injurious to the character of another." *Black's Law Dictionary* 660 (6th ed. 1991).

28. Criminal Code, art. 310 (emphasis added).

29. For a discussion of libel of the dead in Korean law, see Son Tong-gwon, "Press Reports and Libel of the Dead," *Press Arbitration Quarterly* (Korean), Spring 1992, pp. 6–11. Anglo-American law does not recognize liability for defamation of the dead, either to the estate of the deceased or to the deceased's descendants or relatives. For a discussion of libel of the dead under American law, see Kyu Ho Youm, "Survivability of Defamation as a Tort," 66 *Journalism Quarterly* 646–52, 669 (1989).

30. Criminal Code, art. 308 (emphasis added).

31. *See* ibid., art. 312 (1) ("The crimes of Article 308 and the preceding Article shall be prosecuted only upon complaint").

32. Ibid., art. 312 (2) ("The crimes of Articles 307 and 309 shall not be prosecuted over the express objection of the complainant").

33. "Trade libel" is defined as "[i]ntentional disparagement of quality of property, which results in pecuniary damage to plaintiff." Personal libel is distinguished from trade libel in that "the former concerns the person or reputation of plaintiff and the latter relates to his goods." *Black's Law Dictionary*, *op. cit.*, p. 1038.

34. Criminal Code, art. 313.

35. Ibid., art. 314.

36. Civil Code, art. 751.

37. Ibid., art. 764.

38. *But cf.* 89 Honma 160, Constitution Court, April 1, 1991, *Press Arbitration Quarterly* (Korean), Summer 1991, p. 162 (ruling that compulsory apology for libel under the Civil Code is unconstitutional).

39. *See* Kim O-su, "Types of Compensations by the Press for Liabilities," *Press Arbitration Quarterly* (Korean), Spring 1983, p. 39; Yang Sam-sung, "News Reporting on Accidents and Issues in Law and Ethics," *Press Arbitration Quarterly* (Korean), Autumn 1990, p. 13.

40. *See* Code of Criminal Procedure, Law No. 341 (1954), revised by Law No. 3955 (1987), art. 249, *translated in* 3 *Laws of the Republic of Korea* X-103 to X-165-1 (4th ed. 1994) ("Public prosecutions shall expire after lapse of the following terms … 4. Five years for crimes punishable with penal servitude or imprisonment for a maximum term of less than 10 years; 5. Three years for crimes punishable with penal servitude or imprisonment for a maximum term of less than five years, or suspension of qualifications for a maximum term of 10 years or more, or fines of 10,000 *won* or more").

41. Civil Code, art. 766 (1) ("The right to claim damages which has arisen from an unlawful act shall elapse by prescription if not exercised within three (3) years from the time when the injured party or his legal representative becomes aware of such damage and of the identity of the person who caused it"). For a judicial interpretation of Article 766 (1), see Yi Hak-ki v. Kwangmyong Remikon, 92 Ta 42583, Supreme Court, *Monthly Court Case Report*, April 1993, pp. 111–13.

42. Paeng, *op.cit.*, p. 151.

43. 4287 Hyongsang 36, Supreme Court, April 22, 1955, 1 *Collection of Supreme Court Decisions* (Korean) 428–29 (1964) [hereinafter *Supreme Court Decisions*].

44. Ibid., p. 429.

45. 4293 Hyongsang 244, Supreme Court, November 16, 1960, *Law Times* (Korean), December 12, 1960, pp. 3–4.

46. 4294 Hyongsang 12, Supreme Court, May 17, 1962, *Law Times* (Korean), May 28, 1962, p. 3.

47. State v. Ko Chong-hun, 4293 Hyongkong 3959, Seoul District Court, September 20, 1960, *Law Times* (Korean), October 10, 1960, p. 3.

48. 4294 Hyongsang 451, Supreme Court, November 16, 1961, *Law Times* (Korean), December 11, 1961, p. 3.

49. Song Un v. State, [docket number not provided], Taejon District Court, March 20, 1961, *Korean Newspaper Editors Association Newsletter* (Korean), April 5, 1961, pp. 4–5.

50. *Song Un*, Supreme Court, p. 3. The Supreme Court of Korea can quash the original judgment of the lower courts and render a direct judgment on the appealed case. *See* Code of Criminal Procedure, Law No. 341 (1954), art. 396, revised by Law No. 3955 (1987), *translated in* 3 *ROK Laws* (1994), *op. cit.*, pp. X-103 to X-165-1.

51. 67 No 631, Seoul Criminal District Court, January 21, 1969, *Law Times* (Korean), January 19, 1970, p. 6; January 26, 1970, p. 6.

52. Supreme Court, March 31, 1970, *General Digest of Court Cases* (Korean) 612–17 (1981).

53. 68 Ka 11886, Seoul Civil District Court, June 20, 1969, September 14, 1970, *Law Times* (Korean), September 14, 1970, pp. 6–7; September 21, 1970, p. 6.

54. Ibid., *Law Times* (Korean), September 21, 1970, p. 6.

55. 77 Kodan 681, Seoul Criminal District Court, October 5, 1977, *Monthly Court Case Report* (Korean), April 1978, pp. 107–108.

56. Ibid., p. 108.

57. 72 To 1798, Supreme Court, September 26, 1972, 26(3) *Supreme Court Decisions* (Korean) 19–20 (1969).

58. Ibid.

59. Ibid.

60. "Publication" in libel law requires that at least one third person other than the plaintiff was exposed to a precipitating defamatory statement. *Black's Law Dictionary, op. cit.,* p. 854.

61. *See* Yi Song-chun v. State, 79 To 1517, Supreme Court, August 14, 1979, 27 (2) *Supreme Court Decisions* (Korean) 77–79 (1979); Hwang Chang-yon v. State, 81 To 149, Supreme Court, August 25, 1981, *Official Gazette of Courts* (Korean), October 15, 1981, pp. 14313–14.

62. *See, e.g.*, Pak Kum-gyu v. State, 66 To 787, Supreme Court, May 16, 1967, 15(2) *Supreme Court Decisions* (Korean) 3–4 (1967); State v. Ku Yong-hwa, 75 To 473, Supreme Court, April 25, 1978, *Monthly Court Case Report* (Korean), October 1978, p. 85.

63. 66 To 179, Supreme Court, April 19, 1966, *slip opinion* (Korean).

64. 70 To 704, Supreme Court, May 26, 1970, *slip opinion* (Korean).

65. State v. Kim Tok-won, 70 To 1266, Supreme Court, July 21,1970, *slip opinion* (Korean).

66. 89 To 1744, Supreme Court, November 14, 1989, *Korean Press Cases* (Korean), *op. cit.*, pp. 330–31.

67. Originally the picture was that of the special airborne troopers who killed armed espionage agents from North Korea in 1969. State v. Chang Kon-sop, 88 Kodan 8891, Seoul Criminal District Court, March 29, 1989, *Korean Press Cases* (Korean), *op. cit.*, pp. 325–27.

68. Ibid.

69. Chang Kon-sop v. State, 89 No 2338, Seoul High Court, July 14, 1989, *Korean Press Cases* (Korean), *op. cit.*, pp. 327–30.

70. *Chang Kon-sop*, Supreme Court, p. 331.

71. Ibid.

72. 89 Kodan 3303, Seoul District Court (East Branch), May 16, 1990, *Korean Press Cases* (Korean), *op. cit.*, pp. 332–34. *See also* State v. Choi Myong-jae, 90 Kodan 108, Chunchon District Court, February 26, 1991, *Press Arbitration Quarterly* (Korean), Summer 1991, pp. 168–71 (ruling that the defendant interfered with the business of the Korean Institute for Protection of Consumers by damaging its credibility through false allegations on the institute).

73. Ibid. p. 333.

74. Of the 42 media libel actions, the Civil Code was applied in 31 cases.

75. 93 Na 31886, Seoul Civil District Court, Appellate Division, March 30, 1994, *Press Arbitration Quarterly* (Korean), Autumn 1994, pp. 152–56.

76. The cutline, which read "'slaves to money': students at Ehwa Women's University," and the picture ran as part of the cover story of *Newsweek*, Pacific edition, on November 11, 1991. The story focused on the notorious spending spree of Koreans. *See* Tony Emerson, "Too Rich, Too Soon," *Newsweek*, November 11, 1991, p. 12 (Pacific ed.).

77. Kwon Sun-jong v. Newsweek, Inc., 92 Kadan 57989, Seoul Civil District Court, July 8, 1993, *Newspapers and Broadcasting* (Korean), September 1993, p. 130. The plaintiffs claimed:

3. ...The content of the Article and the caption of the Photo give misleading impression that Plaintiffs, as the Article or the caption of the Photo describes or implies, spend too much and are slaves to money. The Magazine were [sic] widely distributed in Korea and in other countries and stirred sensational attention due to the Article and the Photo. The Photo also appeared at Korean newspapers.

4. Defendant, by taking the Photo without the consent of Plaintiffs and publishing it at the Magazine at its will, infringed upon Plaintiffs' rights of portrait and of privacy.

5. And Defendant by publishing the Photo at its will also damaged Plaintiffs' reputation feeling and caused social appreciation of Plaintiffs to be degraded, thus damaging the reputation of Plaintiffs.

6. Due to the above-mentioned torts committed by Defendant, each of Plaintiffs has suffered mental and physical pains incalculable in terms of money; and their social activities have been impaired to a great extent.

Plaintiffs' Complaint in Kwon Sun-jong v. Newsweek, Inc., 92 Kadan 57989: Damages, Seoul Civil District Court (filed, May 1992). The complaint was translated into English by Attorney Seungduk Koh, who represented the plaintiffs in *Kwon Sun-jong*. The author's quotation is from the English-language translation of the plaintiffs' complaint as filed with the Seoul Civil District Court in May 1992.

78. Ibid., p. 131.

79. *Newsweek, Inc.,* Seoul Civil District Court, Appellate Division, p. 152. Newsweek, Inc. did not appeal the decision of the Seoul Civil District Court, Appellate Division, to the Supreme Court of Korea. Letter from Kim Song-yong, attorney for Newsweek, Inc., to the author (May 28, 1994) (on file with author).

80. 82 Kahap 4734, Seoul Civil District Court, April 11, 1984, *Korean Press Cases* (Korean), *op. cit.*, pp. 229–35.

81. Ibid., p. 233 (emphasis added). This case originated from a story published in the *Dong-A Ilbo* newspaper, which claimed that Yi, who operated an institute for the handicapped, embezzled public funds. The news reporter prepared the story after being convinced that his story was truthful after interviewing several handicapped people staging a sit-in against Yi, after checking on the complaint filed with police against Yi, and after attempting unsuccessfully to contact Yi for his responses to the complaint. Ibid., pp. 232–33.

82. Ibid.

83. Ibid., p. 234.

84. 85 Taka 29, Supreme Court, October 11, 1988, *Korean Press Cases* (Korean), *op. cit.*, pp. 224–28.

85. Ibid., p. 227 (emphasis added).

86. Ibid., p. 228. The memoir at issue in *Yi Il-jae* was written by a person who retained Yi as an attorney. Yi was described as immoral, unethical, and dubious as a lawyer. The memoir was published in *Chubu Saenghwal* (Housewife Life), owned by Hakwonsa. Ibid., p. 225.

87. Ibid., p. 227.

88. The Supreme Court's reasoning in *Yi Il-jae* relating to the nature of news as an actionable factor is identical to the standard of liability as recognized by American courts, *see* Associated Press v. Walker, 388 U.S. 130 (1967) and Rosenbloom v. Metromedia, Inc., 403 U.S. 29 (1971). As media attorney Bruce Sanford succinctly noted:

> [C]ourts evaluating whether a libel defendant exercised due care must consider the time constraints under which the defendant operated. If the publication at issue constituted "hot news"—*i.e.*, information of immediate news value requiring prompt dissemination—courts have excused news organizations from any obligation to undertake extensive efforts at verification.

Bruce W. Sanford, *Libel and Privacy* 430 (2d ed. 1996) (footnotes omitted).

89. 89 Na 8158, Seoul High Court, November 29, 1989, *Korean Press Cases* (Korean), *op. cit.*, pp. 284–95, *aff'g*, 88 Kahap 20604, Seoul Civil District Court, January 18, 1989, *Korean Press Cases* (Korean), *op. cit.*, pp. 274–84.

90. 83 Kadan 7668, Seoul Civil District Court, October 15, 1984, *Korean Press Cases* (Korean), *op. cit.*, pp. 241–44.

91. One authority on libel law defines "colloquium" as the "proof of extrinsic facts … to establish that a libelous statement is about or understood to be about ('of and concerning') a particular plaintiff." Robert D. Sack and Sandra S. Baron, *Libel, Slander, and Related Problems* 136 (2d ed. 1994).

92. *Yi Tu-sik, op. cit.*, p. 243.

93. 91 Na 27320, Seoul High Court, September 25, 1991, *Press Arbitration Quarterly* (Korean), Winter 1991, pp. 166–70.

94. Ibid., p. 169. The story complained of in the case asserted that the plaintiff was the actual assassin of Yuk Yong-su, the first lady of President Park Chung Hee, in 1974.

95. For a comparative analysis of the fair report privilege in English and U.S. libel law, see Kyu Ho Youm, "Fair Report Privilege *versus* Foreign Government Statements: United States and English Judicial Interpretations Compared," 40 *International and Comparative Law Quarterly* 124–50 (1991).

96. In the United States, the common law "fair report privilege" protects the news media from libel suits for providing their readers and viewers "a fair and true account of defamatory statements made in the course of legislative, judicial, or other official proceedings if those proceedings are open or available to the public and relate to a matter of public concern." Slade R. Metcalf, 1 *Rights and Liabilities of Publishers, Broadcasters and Reporters* 1–187 (1994).

97. 87 Kahap 3739, Seoul Civil District Court, April 29, 1988, *Korean Press Cases* (Korean), *op. cit.*, pp. 262–66.

98. Ibid., pp. 265–66. Each of the six newspapers respectively owned by the six individual defendants published a false story stating, on the basis of police information, that the plaintiff had been convicted seven times, instead of once. The plaintiff sued the Korean government and the six news media organizations for libel.

99. Ibid., p. 266.

100. 89 Kahap 18505, Seoul District Court (South Branch), October12, 1990, *Press Arbitration Quarterly* (Korean), Spring 1991, pp. 164–72.

101. Ibid., p. 171. The *Labor Union of Munhwa Broadcasting Corp.* case began when *Dong-A Ilbo* published a story and an editorial about the sit-in strike by the labor union of the Munhwa Broadcasting Corporation in Seoul in September 1989. The strike related to a dispute between the management and labor of the broadcasting company. Ibid., p. 165.

102. Ibid. (emphasis added).

103. 90 Kahap 15896, Seoul Civil District Court, January 17, 1991, *Press Arbitration Quarterly* (Korean), Autumn 1991, pp. 152–55.

104. *Kwon In-suk* involved an unauthorized publication in *Umon Sensu* (Woman Sense) magazine of parts of the plaintiff's memoir entitled "Climbing Over a Wall," which described how she was sexually assaulted by a policeman while under custody in connection with her civil rights activities during the mid-1980s. The plaintiff demanded publication of an apology in the defendant's magazine in compensation for injury to her reputation. Ibid., p. 153.

105. Ibid., p. 154.

106. Ibid.

107. *See, e.g.*, Kim Song-hi v. Dong-A Ilbosa, 89 Na 36528, Seoul High Court, May 4, 1990, *Press Arbitration Quarterly* (Korean), Summer 1991, pp. 155–62, *aff'g*, 88 Kahap 31161, Seoul Civil District Court, July 25, 1989, *Korean Press Cases* (Korean), *op. cit.*, pp. 301–11; Kim Song-hi v. Yi Kap-sop, 89 Na 8158, Seoul High Court, November 29, 1989, *Korean Press Cases* (Korean), *op. cit.*, pp. 284–294, *aff'g*, 88 Kahap 20604, Seoul Civil District Court, January 18, 1989, *Korean Press Cases* (Korean), *op. cit.*, pp. 274–84; Cho Ha-mun v. Yowonsa, 88 Kahap 17151, Seoul District Court (East Branch), April 14, 1989, *Korean Press Cases* (Korean), *op. cit.*, pp. 295–301.

108. 89 Na 36528, Seoul High Court, May 4, 1990, *Press Arbitration Quarterly* (Korean), Summer 1991, pp. 155–62, *aff'g*, 88 Kahap 31161, Seoul Civil District Court, July 25, 1989, *Korean Press Cases* (Korean), *op. cit.*, pp. 301–11.

109. The *Yosong Dong-A* story, "Clarification of Truth on 500 million *won* Suit for Story 'Rumor on Affair with Chon Kyong-hwan'—Truth Ignored to Attract Curiosity," was a spin-off of a 1989 libel case, Kim Song-hi v. Yi Kap-sop, 88 Kahap 20604, Seoul Civil District Court, January 18, 1989, *Korean Press Cases* (Korean), *op. cit.*, pp. 274–80.

110. Kim Song-hi v. Dong-A Ilbo, 89 Na 36528, Seoul High Court, p. 159.

111. Ibid., p. 158.

112. Ibid., p. 160.

113. 89 Honma 160, Constitution Court, April 1, 1991, *Press Arbitration Quarterly* (Korean), Summer 1991, pp. 166–67. For a detailed commentary on the Constitution Court's decision on compulsory apology for defamation under Korean law, see Song Nak-in, "Advertising Notice of Apology for Libel and the Constitution Court's Ruling," *Press Arbitration Quarterly* (Korean), Spring 1992, pp. 27–42.

114. For a discussion of the Constitution Court's ruling on the apology for libel requirement under the Civil Code, see chap. 5 *supra*.

115. The Korean Press Ethics Commission, established as a *voluntary* organization operating "with a strong support" of Korean news media since 1961, "acts on libelous comment and reporting and other irregularities" and "[i]ts decisions range from mere warnings to orders for retraction and public apology." Mowlana and Chin, *op. cit.*, p. 330. For a discussion of the Korean Press Ethics Commission, see Bong-Ki Kim, 2 *History of Korean Journalism* 155–80 (1969).

116. Yu Chae-chon, *Korean Press and Media Culture* (Korean) 171–74 (1986).

117. Youm, "Libel Law," *op. cit.*, p. 194.

118. Ibid., p. 193. For a comprehensive analysis of human rights in Korea, see *Human Rights in Korea: Historical and Policy Perspectives* (William Shaw ed., 1991).

119. Ibid. *See also* Han Ki-chan, "From Freedom to Responsibility: Reforming Is Valuable When It's Voluntary," *Newspapers and Broadcasting* (Korean), February 1995, p. 62 (noting that "suing a powerful media organization is easier said than done").

120. *See generally* Yi Hyok-chu and Kim Chang-su, *Judge and Trial* (Korean) (1986).

121. Youm, "Libel Law," *op. cit.*, p. 193. Journalist David Halvorsen, who studied the Korean press as a Fulbright scholar and participated in various journalism workshops throughout South Korea over the years, has observed: "The [Korean] journalists consider themselves a part of the ruling class.... A top official of the Korean Federation of Newspaper Unions looked me in the eye and said exactly that: 'We are part of the ruling class.'" David E. Halvorsen, The Korean Press: Free, but Is It Responsible? (1991) (lecture delivered at the Korean Journalists Workshop in Honolulu, Hawaii) (text on file with author).

122. Yi Hye-bok, "Reporting on Accidents and Violations of Personal Interests: An Examination," *Press Arbitration Quarterly* (Korean), Autumn 1990, pp. 16–17.

123. Ibid., p. 17.

124. Ibid., pp. 17–18. *See also* Hans Verploeg and Tony Wilton, *Press Freedom in Korea: The Search for Professionalism* 14–17 (1991).

125. Ibid., p. 18.

126. *See* Yi Ui-hyang v. Dong-A Ilbosa, 82 Ka 27454, Seoul Civil District Court, November 4, 1982, *Korean Press Cases* (Korean), *op. cit.*, pp. 44–49; Dong-A Ilbosa v. Yi Ui-hyang, 82 Na 4188, Seoul High Court, November 17, 1983, *Korean Press Cases* (Korean), *op. cit.*, pp. 50–56.

127. Kyu Ho Youm and Michael B. Salwen, "A Free Press in South Korea: Temporary Phenomenon or Permanent Fixture?" 30 *Asian Survey* 316 (1990).

128. Ibid.

129. Ibid., pp. 316–17 (footnote omitted).

130. Ibid.

131. Dae-Kyu Yoon, Law and Political Authority: A Study on the Rule of Law in Korea 290 (1987) (Ph.D. dissertation, University of Washington (Seattle)).

132. For a detailed background on the Korean Army officers' assault on a Korean newspaper editor, see Chon Pyong-dok, "Oh Hong-gun Incident Typifies Right-Wing Terrorism: Thorough Investigation of Its Cause Urgently Needed," *Chugan Hankuk* (Korean), September 15, 1988, p. 4. *See also* "Announcement of the Results of the Ministry of Defense Investigation (Full Text)," in Oh Hong-gun, *Dear Mr. President* (Korean) 286–91 (1989).

133. Youm and Salwen, *op. cit.,* p. 317 (footnote omitted). For the text of the Military Court's opinion in the Oh Hong-gun case, see Oh, *Dear Mr. President, op. cit.*, pp. 292–94.

134. Chong Chin-sok, "Changes in Media Environment and Press Arbitration System," *Press Arbitration Quarterly* (Korean), Spring 1991, p. 14.

## CHAPTER 9

1. Anthony Lewis, *Make No Law: The Sullivan Case and the First Amendment* 52 (1991).

2. Norman Rosenberg, "Seditious Libel," in *The Oxford Companion to the Supreme Court of the United States* 766 (Kermit L. Hall ed., 1992).

3. ARTICLE 19, *World Report 1991: Information, Freedom and Censorship* 413 (1991).

4. Law No. 239 (1953), revised by Law No. 2745 (1975), art. 104-2, *translated in* 3 *Laws of the Republic of Korea* X-1 to X-44 (4th ed. 1983) [hereinafter *ROK Laws* (1983)].

5. "Curb on Criticism Is Voted in Seoul," *New York Times*, March 20, 1975, p. 6.

6. Criminal Code, art. 104-2.

7. Kyu Ho Youm, "Press Freedom in 'Democratic' South Korea: Moving from Authoritarian to Libertarian?" 43 *Gazette* 62 (1989).

8. *The American Heritage Dictionary of the English Language* 1434 (3d ed. 1992).

9. Namgung Ho-gyong, "An Examination of the Crime of Defaming the State," 33 *Seoul Law Journal* (Korean) 182 (September 1992).

10. Ibid., p. 183.

11. For a discussion of libel and insults as a crime under the Criminal Code of Korea, see chap. 8 *supra*.

12. Kwak Kwi-ja v. State, 87 To 739, Supreme Court, May 12, 1987, *Official Gazette of Courts* (Korean), July 1, 1987, p. 83 (emphasis added). *See also* Cho Ku-hyon v. State, 85 To 1629, Supreme Court, October 22,1985, *Official Gazette of Courts* (Korean), December 15, 1985, p. 74.

13. Robert D. Sack and Sandra S. Baron, *Libel, Slander, and Related Problems* 93 (2d. 1994).

14. Ibid., p. 574 (footnote omitted).

15. Namgung, *op. cit.*, p. 190, quoting Yu Ki-chon (footnote omitted).

16. Ibid., p. 191.

17. Ibid., pp. 191–92.

18. For a discussion of the Anti-Communist Act and the National Security Act, see chap. 11 *infra*.

19. Namgung, *op. cit.*, p. 194.

20. For a discussion of the Supreme Court rulings on anti-State defamation, see *infra* notes 32–66 and accompanying text.

21. The seditious libel clause of the Criminal Code was abrogated in December 1988 to "remove the possible grounds for suppressing sound criticism conducive to national development." *Human Rights in Korea: Facts and Fiction* 79 (1990).

22. Namgung, *op. cit.*, p. 180.

23. Ibid., pp. 180–81.

24. Nicholas D. Kristof, "A 'Moderate' Tells Why Students in Korea Fight," *New York Times*, August 2, 1987, § 4, p. 3.

25. *Freedom of Expression in the Republic of Korea* 42 (1988).

26. *Assessing Reform in South Korea* 49 (1988).

27. Criminal Code, Law No. 293 (1953), revised by Law No. 4040 (1988), art. 107 (2), *translated in* 2 *ROK Current Laws, op. cit.*, pp. 761–812.

28. Ibid., art. 108 (2).

29. Ibid., art. 105.

30. Ibid., art. 107.

31. Ibid., art. 109.

32. 83 To 515, Supreme Court (en banc), June 14, 1983, 2 *Collection of Supreme Court Decisions* (Korean) 440–55 (1978–87) [hereinafter *Supreme Court Decisions*].

33. "Re-Appeal of Defamation of the State, Prosecutor Recommending Three Years in Prison," *Joongang Ilbo* (Korean), November 25, 1983, p. 11.

34. Kim Chol-gi v. State, 82 To 6161, Seoul Criminal District Court, February 11, 1983, *reprinted in Kim Chol-gi*, Supreme Court, *op. cit.*, p. 455.

35. Ibid.

36. Ibid., p. 454.

37. Ibid.

38. Ibid.

39. Ibid.

40. *See* "Reasons for the Appeal," *reprinted in Kim Chol-gi*, Supreme Court, *op. cit.*, pp. 451–53.

41. Ibid., p. 452.

42. Ibid.

43. Ibid.

44. Ibid., pp. 452–53.

45. Ibid., p. 453.

46. *Kim Chol-gi*, Supreme Court, *op. cit.*, pp. 445–46 (emphasis added).

47. Ibid., p. 446.

48. Ibid.

49. Ibid., p. 447.

50. Ibid.

51. Ibid., pp. 447–48.

52. Ibid., p. 450.

53. Ibid., p. 448.

54. Ibid., pp. 448–49.

55. Ibid., p. 449.

56. Ibid.

57. Ibid.

58. Ibid., p. 450.

59. Ibid.

60. 86 To 1209, Supreme Court, August 19, 1986, 34(2) *Supreme Court Decisions* (Korean) 486–89 (1986).

61. Kim Pyong-gon v. State, 86 No 973, Seoul Criminal District Court, May 14, 1986, 2 *Lower Court Decisions* (Korean) 434 (1986).

62. Ibid.

63. Ibid., p. 430, citing *Kim Chol-gi*, Supreme Court, *op. cit.*

64. Ibid.

65. 86 To 1209, Supreme Court, August 19, 1986, 34(2) *Supreme Court Decisions* (Korean) 486 (1986).

66. Ibid., pp. 487–88.

67. Harry Kalven, Jr., "The New York Times Case: A Note on 'the Central Meaning of the First Amendment,'" *Supreme Court Review* 205 (1964).

68. David I. Steinberg, "Law, Development and Korean Society," 13 *Koreana Quarterly* 67–68 (Fall 1971).

69. Hak-Kyu Sohn, *Authoritarianism and Opposition in South Korea* 1–3 (1989).

## CHAPTER 10

1. Richard F. Hixson, *Privacy in a Public Society: Human Rights in Conflict* 3 (1987).

2. United Nations Universal Declaration of Human Rights, November 10, 1948, art. 12, *reprinted in The Human Rights Reader* 197–202 (Walter Laqueur and Barry Rubin eds., rev. ed. 1989).

3. Griswold v. Connecticut, 381 U.S. 479, 509 (1965).

4. Franklyn S. Haiman, *Speech and Law in a Free Society* 61 (1981).

5. Dan Rosen, "Private Lives and Public Eyes: Privacy in the United States and Japan," 6 *Florida Journal of International Law* 144 (1990). Professor Lawrence Beer stated: "The individuals [sic] great

concern for face in Japan may in part result from the weak societal protection of the individual's privacy within the group, as well as strong group insistence upon the individual's loyal maintenance of the group's good name before society. In this context, good name and privacy are viewed as important values primarily in terms of interaction taking place in the group or in the group's relations with society, not in terms of the individual's rights as a member of society." Lawrence W. Beer, "Defamation, Privacy, and Freedom of Expression in Japan," 5 *Law in Japan: An Annual* 196 (1972).

6. Jisuk Woo, "The Personal Data Protection Regime Emerging in Korea," in *Pacific Telecommunications Conference Proceedings* 93 (1993).

7. Samuel D. Warren and Louis D. Brandeis, "The Right to Privacy," 4 *Harvard Law Review* 195 (1890).

8. Charles Fried, "Privacy," 77 *Yale Law Journal* 482 (1968). *See also* Alan F. Westin, *Privacy and Freedom* 7 (1967) (defining privacy as "the claim of individuals, groups, or institutions to determine for themselves when, how, and to what extent information about them is communicated to others").

9. Olmstead v. United States, 277 U.S. 438, 478 (1928) (Brandeis, J., dissenting).

10. Donald M. Gillmor et al., *Mass Communication Law* 478 (5th ed. 1990).

11. *See* Hakwonsa v. Yi Il-jae, 85 Taka 29, Supreme Court, October 11, 1988, *Official Gazette of Courts* (Korean), November 15, 1988, pp. 30–32; *Press Arbitration Quarterly* (Korean), Winter 1988, pp. 167–70.

12. Rodney A. Smolla, *Free Speech in an Open Society* 120 (1992).

13. Kim Tong-chol, "Information Society and Privacy," in *A General Discourse on Press Law* (Korean) 154 (Han Pyong-gu ed., 1990) (footnote omitted).

14. Kim Tong-chol, *A Study of Free Press Law* (Korean) 185 (1987).

15. Constitution, amended in 1980, art. 16, *translated in* 1 *Laws of the Republic of Korea* I-1 to I-19 (4th ed. 1983). For a discussion of Article 16 of the Constitution on privacy, see Chae Won-sik, "The Relationship Between Right of Privacy and Legislation," 14 *Lawyer* (Korean) 402–403 (1984).

16. Constitution, amended in 1987, art. 17, *translated in* 1 *Current Laws of the Republic of Korea* 1–16 (1994) [hereinafter *ROK Current Laws*].

17. Ibid., art. 10.

18. *Compare with* Constitution of 1980, art. 9.

19. Constitution of 1987, art. 14.

20. Ibid., art. 16.

21. Ibid., art. 17.

22. Ibid., art. 21 (4).

23. Ibid., art. 36 (1) ("Marriage and family life shall be entered into and sustained on the basis of individual dignity and equality of the sexes, and the State shall do everything in its power to achieve that goal").

24. Kim Sang-yong, "Invasion of Right of Character and Civil Liberty," *Monthly Court Case Report* (Korean), November 1993, p. 56.

25. Woo, *op. cit.*, p. 939.

26. Civil Code, Law No. 471 (1958), revised by Law No. 4199 (1990), art. 750, *translated in* 2 *ROK Current Laws, op. cit.*, pp. 401–556.

27. Ibid., art. 751 (1).

28. Ibid., art. 766.

29. Ibid., art. 243. The provision is obviously borrowed from Article 235 of the Civil Code of Japan, which reads: "A person who constructs at a distance of less than one meter from the boundary line a window or veranda which overlooks the garden of another person shall put a screen thereto." *See* Lawrence Ward Beer, *Freedom of Expression in Japan* 325 (1984).

30. Criminal Code, Law No. 293 (1953), revised by Law No. 4040 (1988), art. 316, *translated in* 2 *ROK Current Laws, op. cit.*, pp. 761–812 (1994).

31. Ibid., art. 317.

32. Postal Services Act, Law No. 542 (1960), revised by Law No. 3602 (1982), art. 3, *translated in* 6 *ROK Current Laws, op. cit.*, pp. 3761–71.

33. Criminal Code, art. 319 (1).

34. Law No. 3979 (1987), revised by Law No. 4441 (1991), *translated in The Korean Press 1995*, at 135–45 (1995).

35. Law No. 3978 (1987), revised by Law No. 4441 (1991), *translated in The Korean Press 1995*, *op. cit.*, pp. 146–59.

36. Law No. 4494 (1991), revised by Law No. 4737 (1994), *translated in The Korean Press 1995*, *op. cit.*, pp. 183–203.

37. *See* Periodicals Act, art. 16; Broadcast Act, art. 41; Cable Television Act, art. 45.

38. For the text of the Act on Protection of Personal Information of Government Agencies (Personal Information Act), see *Compendium of Codes* (Korean) 5500–5501 (1994).

39. Personal Information Act, art. 1.

40. Ibid., art. 4.

41. Ibid., art. 5 (1).

42. Ibid., art. 6 (2).

43. Ibid., art. 10.

44. Ibid., art. 12.

45. Ibid., art. 13.

46. Rosen, *op. cit.*, p. 161 (footnote omitted).

47. Paeng Won-sun, *A Theory of Mass Communication Law* (Korean) 245 (rev. ed. 1988). *See also* Chae, *op. cit.*, p. 409.

48. Ibid.

49. Kim, "Right of Character and Civil Liability," *op. cit.*, p. 55.

50. Robert D. Sack and Sandra S. Baron, *Libel, Slander, and Related Problems* 551 (2d ed. 1994) (footnote omitted).

51. William L. Prosser, "Privacy," 48 *California Law Review* 383 (1960).

52. Rodney A. Smolla, *Law of Defamation* 10–3 (1995).

53. Kim, "Right of Character and Civil Liability," *op. cit.*, pp. 60, 65.

54. In American law, the "right of publicity" recognizes the "commercial value of the picture or representation of a prominent person or performer and protects his proprietary interest in the profitability of his public reputation or persona." Ali v. Playgirl, Inc., 447 F. Supp. 723 (S.D.N.Y. 1978).

55. *Chosanggwon* is identical to what is known as *Shozoken* or "a right not be photographed without consent" in Japanese law. *See* Beer, *Freedom of Expression in Japan, op. cit.*, p. 325.

56. 93 Na 31886, Seoul Civil District Court, Appellate Division, March 30, 1994, *Press Arbitration Quarterly* (Korean), Autumn 1994, pp. 152–56.

57. For a discussion of factual background in *Newsweek, Inc. v. Kwon Sun-jong*, see chap. 8 *supra*.

58. *Newsweek, Inc.*, Seoul Civil District Court, Appellate Division, *op. cit.*, p. 154.

59. Ibid., p. 155.

60. Ibid.

61. Ibid.

62. 87 Kahap 6032, Seoul Civil District Court, September 9, 1988, *Korean Press Cases* (Korean) 270–74 (1990).

63. Ibid., p. 273.

64. Ibid.

65. Ibid.

66. 87 Kahap 6175, Seoul Civil District Court, May 11, 1988, *Korean Press Cases* (Korean), *op. cit.*, pp. 267–70.

67. Ibid., p. 268.

68. Ibid.

69. Ibid.

70. Ibid.

71. Ibid.

72. 4294 Minsang 1028, Supreme Court, March 8, 1962, 10(1) *Supreme Court Decisions* (Korean) 184–86 (1962).

73. Ibid., p. 184.

74. Sigman L. Splichal, The U.S. Supreme Court and the Practical Obscurity Doctrine: Judicial Recognition of "Forgive and Forget" 16–17 (1995) (paper presented at the Southeast Colloquium of the Association for Education in Journalism and Mass Communication in Gainesville, Fla.).

75. Woo, *op. cit.*, p. 939.

## CHAPTER 11

1. Urban C. Lehner, "Korean Presidential Race Puts Twist on U.S. Script," *Asian Wall Street Journal Weekly*, December 14, 1992, p. 12.

2. Sang Hoon Bang, The Korean Press: New Challenges in a Changing World (1992) (speech delivered at the International Press Institute convention in Budapest, Hungary) (text on file with author).

3. Dennis v. United States, 341 U.S. 494, 520 (1951) (Frankfurter, J., concurring).

4. *See* Hong Song-dam v. State, 90 To 1586, Supreme Court, September 25, 1990, 38(3) *Supreme Court Decisions* (Korean) 353–64 (1990); *Monthly Court Case Report* (Korean), February 1991, pp. 184–89.

5. Rodney P. Katz, "National Security," in *South Korea: A Country Study* 303 (Andrea Matles Savada and William Shaw eds., 4th ed. 1992).

6. Lee Sung-yul, "Korean Situation Remains 'Tense,'" *Korea Herald*, January 20, 1995, p. 3.

7. Donald Stone Macdonald, *The Koreans: Contemporary Politics and Society* 239 (2d ed. 1990). *See also* Pak Chol-on, The Study on the Collision and Harmony of the Freedom of the Press and National Security (Korean)145 (Ph.D. dissertation, [Hanyang University, Seoul], 1989).

8. Constitution, amended in 1987, art. 37 (2), *translated in* 1 *Current Laws of the Republic of Korea* 1–24 (1994) [hereinafter *ROK Current Laws*].

9. *See Complete Collection of Korean Press Laws, 1945–1981* (Korean) 2–3 (Chong Chin-sok ed., 1982) (noting that more than 360 laws and regulations relating to the Korean press were enforced between 1945, when Korea was liberated from its Japanese colonial rule, and 1982).

10. Law No. 3979 (1987), revised by Law No. 4441 (1991), *translated in* 4 *ROK Current Laws*, *op. cit.*, pp. 2541–52.

11. Law No. 3978 (1987), revised by Law No. 4441 (1991), *translated in* 4 *ROK Current Laws*, *op. cit.*, pp. 2571–72.

12. Law No. 4688 (1993), *reprinted in Compendium of Codes* (Korean) 2941–42 (1994).

13. *See* Periodicals Act, art. 12 (1), (2).

14. Article 9 (1) of the Periodicals Act provides:

Any person who falls under any of the following Subparagraphs, shall not be a publisher or editor of a periodical:

....

3. A person who was sentenced to imprisonment without hard labor or more severe punishment for committing a crime as prescribed in Articles 87 to 90, 92 to 101 of the Criminal Code, Articles 5 to 8, 9 (2), 11 to 16 of the Military Penal Code or Articles 3 to 9 of the National Security Act, and the execution of such punishment is not terminated, or non-execution of it does not become definite, or the period for stay of execution is not terminated; and

4. A person who is subject to execution of a disposition for security under the Social Security Act or a disposition for protection under the Social Protection Act.

15. Broadcast Act, art. 9.

16. Foreign Periodicals Act, arts. 7, 8.

17. Ibid., art. 7.

18. Ibid., art. 8.

19. Law No. 3318 (1980), revised by Law No. 4373 (1991), *translated in* 3 *Laws of the Republic of Korea* X-64 to X-70-1 (4th ed. 1994) [hereinafter *ROK Laws*].

20. Law No. 643 (1961), revised by Law No. 1997 (1968), *translated in Laws of the Republic of Korea* 776–80 (3d ed. 1975). The Anti-Communist Act was repealed by the National Security Act in 1980.

21. Law No. 10 (1948), *reprinted in* Pak Won-sun, 1 *Study of National Security Laws* (Korean) 227 (1989). For a succinct discussion of the history of the National Security Act, see Lawyers for a Democratic Society and National Council of Churches in Korea, *Human Rights in South Korea: Counter Report to the Human Rights Committee on the Initial Report Submitted by the Republic of Korea Under Article 40 of the International Covenant on Civil and Political Rights* 36–37 (May 1992).

22. William Shaw, "Government and Politics," in *South Korea: A Country Study, op. cit.,* p. 245.

23. *See* Yi Pom-yol, "National Security Act Abused for Political Security," *Shin Dong-A* (Korean), March 1988, pp. 262–68. *See also* Jerome Alan Cohen and Edward J. Baker, "U.S. Foreign Policy and Human Rights in South Korea," in *Human Rights in Korea: Historical and Policy Perspectives* 184–85 (William Shaw ed., 1991).

24. David I. Steinberg, "Law, Development and Korean Society," in *Introduction to the Law and Legal System of Korea* 61 (Sang Hyun Song ed., 1983).

25. Anti-Communist Act, art. 4 (1).

26. Cohen and Baker, *op. cit.,* p. 184.

27. Steinberg, *op. cit.,* p. 61 n.57.

28. Ibid.

29. National Security Act, Law No. 3318 (1980), art. 7 (1), (5), *translated in* 3 *ROK Laws, op. cit.,* pp. X-64 to X-70 (4th ed. 1983).

30. Ibid., art. 1 (1).

31. Ibid.

32. The Constitution Court in 1990 held that the National Security Act was constitutional insofar as it was properly interpreted without risking the overbroad application of the law in violation of the basic human rights as guaranteed under the Constitution. *See* Constitution Court, 89 Honga 113, *Official Gazette* (Korean), May 1, 1990, p. 27. For a discussion of the Constitution Court's interpretation of the National Security Act, see chap. 5 *supra.*

33. "Reasons for Revision of the National Security Act," *Official Gazette* (Korean), May 31, 1991, p. 20.

34. National Security Act, revised in 1991, art. 1 (2). For a discussion of several major provisions of the National Security Act, as revised in 1991, see Amnesty International, *South Korea: Prisoners Held for National Security Reasons* 6–8 ([1991]).

35. Ibid.

36. Ibid.

37. Ibid., art. 7 (1) (emphasis added).

38. Ibid., arts. 6, 8.

39. Republic of Korea, *Consideration of Reports Submitted by States Parties Under Article 40 of the Covenant* 57 ([1991]).

40. Marcia Greenberg and Helet Merkling, *Broken Promises, Unfulfilled Dreams: Human Rights and Democracy in South Korea* 17 (Kerry Kennedy Cuomo et al. eds., [1992]). *See also* Lawyers for a Democratic Society and National Council of Churches in Korea, *op. cit.,* pp. 37–38.

41. Constitution, art. 76 (2).

42. Ibid., art. 77 (1).

43. Ibid., art. 77 (3).

44. *See* Martial Law, Law No. 3442 (1981), *translated in* 1 *ROK Laws, op. cit.,* pp. II-154 to II-156.

45. Ibid., art. 9 (1).

46. Customs Act, Law No. 1976 (1967), revised by Law No. 4743 (1994), *translated in* 3 *ROK Current Laws, op. cit.,* pp. 1701–1795-18.

47. Ibid., art. 146.

48. Ibid.

49. Ibid., art. 179.

50. Dae-Kyu Yoon, *Law and Political Authority in South Korea* 170 (1990).

51. 4289 Hyongsang 80, Supreme Court, May 8, 1956, *Law Times* (Korean), June 25, 1956, p. 3; *Korean Press Annual 1968* (Korean) 518–19 (1968).

52. Ibid.; *Korean Press Annual 1968* (Korean), *op. cit.,* p. 519.

53. The Korean government under President Syngman Rhee opposed the cease-fire of the Korean War in the belief that any kind of cease-fire would be nothing but a defeat of the South Korean side by North Korea, which provoked the war.

54. *See* State v. Choe Sok-chae, [no docket number provided], Taegu District Court, December 6, 1955, *Korean Press Annual 1968* (Korean), *op. cit.,* p. 517; 3 *Korean Press Chronology, 1951–1955* (Korean) 1334–35 (Kye Hun-mo ed., [1993]); State v. Choe Sok-chae, Hyonggong 832, Taegu High Court, January 27, 1956, *Korean Press Annual 1968* (Korean), *op. cit.,* pp. 517–18; 3 *Korean Press Chronology* (Korean), *op. cit.,* pp. 1335–37.

55. Pak Won-sun's three-volume study entitled "Study of National Security Laws" is by far the most comprehensive and in-depth analysis of various national security laws in Korea since 1948. *See* Pak Won-sun, *Study of National Security Laws* (Korean), 3 vols. (1989, 1992).

56. Pak, 3 *Study of National Security Laws* (Korean), *op. cit.,* p. 60 (1992).

57. 4291 Hyonggong 74, Seoul Criminal District Court, April 3, 1958, *Law Times* (Korean), July 28, 1958, p. 3.

58. Ibid.

59. 4291 Hyongsang 559, Supreme Court, February 27, 1959, 25 *General Digest of Court Cases: Constitutional Law* (Korean) 1:13–14 (1982).

60. The Supreme Court of Korea's recognition in the *Progressive Party* case of the "preferred position" concept relating to political expression is particularly noteworthy. In this connection, the Pusan High Court stated: "Expressive acts in a political forum usually take on the form of opinion and are usually allowed as expressions of opinion under the Constitution. It can be stated that a preferred freedom

principle applies to expressive acts in the course of election campaigns because they are performed under the circumstances in which political opinions reach their climax in their intensity." Kim Kyong-sop v. State, 92 No 215, Pusan High Court, June 17, 1992, 2 *Lower Court Decisions* (Korean) 514 (1992). The constitutional law of the United States holds that freedom of expression is in a "preferred position" because it is "so essential to the exercise of other basic freedoms" that it "needs to be weighted by the 'judicial thumb' in the balancing of interests process." Harry W. Stonecipher, "Safeguarding Speech and Press Guarantees: Preferred Position Postulate Reexamined," in *The First Amendment Reconsidered* 90 (Bill F. Chamberlin and Charlene J. Brown eds., 1982). The "clear and present danger" rule is "the most visible vehicle" through which the preferred position doctrine has been implemented in U.S. law. Martin Shapiro, *Freedom of Speech: The Supreme Court and Judicial Review* 115 (1966).

61. Article 4 (1) of the Anti-Communist Act of 1961 read: "Any person who has benefitted the anti-State organizations by praising, encouraging or siding with or through other means the activities of an anti-State organization or their components or the communist organizations outside the Republic of Korea shall be punished by imprisonment at hard labor for not more than seven years. The same shall apply to the person who has organized or affiliated with the organizations for the purpose of committing such acts." Anti-Communist Act, Law No. 634 (1961), revised by Law No. 1997 (1968), *translated in Laws of the Republic of Korea* 1321–28 (2d ed. 1969).

62. 64 Ko 7902, Seoul Criminal District Court, August 31, 1964, *Journalism Review* (Korean), October 1964, p. 2 of the List of Contents.

63. Ibid.

64. Ibid.

65. 64 Ko 1811, Seoul Criminal District Court, April 30, 1965, *Law Times* (Korean), May 17, 1965, p. 6.

66. Professor Dae-Kyu Yoon stated: "The language of the provision—such as praising, encouraging and supporting—is so broad in scope and vague in meaning as to be open to possibilities that prosecutors or judges might interpret to suit their own purposes. A case thus can be made against the provision that it runs counter to the principle of criminal legality, and thus it leads to infringement of free speech and academic freedom." Dae-Kyu Yoon, "Judicial Review in the Korean Political Context," 17 *Korean Journal of Comparative Law* 154 (1989).

67. Ibid.

68. *Hwang Yong-ju*, Seoul Criminal District Court, *Law Times* (Korean), May 17, 1965, p. 6.

69. The Supreme Court stated: "It was proper to regard the defendant's actions as those prohibited by the Anti-Communist Act, article 4 (1). It was with good reason that the lower court decided that the Anti-Communist Act, article 4 (1), is not against the Constitution which guarantees the principle of criminal legality and freedom of speech." Yoon, "Judicial Review," *op. cit.*, p. 154 (footnote omitted).

70. Ibid., p. 156 (footnote omitted).

71. 65 Ko 2047, Seoul Criminal District Court, December 8, 1965, *Law Times* (Korean), January 10, 1966, p. 6; January 24, 1966, p. 6; January 31, 1966, p. 6.

72. Ibid., *Law Times* (Korean), January 31, 1966, p. 6.

73. 66 Ko 141, Seoul Criminal District Court, December 27, 1966, *Law Times* (Korean), January 9, 1967, p. 6; January 16, 1967, p. 6; January 23, 1967, p. 6.

74. In *Schenck v. United States*, Justice Oliver Wendell Holmes, Jr., writing for the U.S. Supreme Court, set forth the "clear and present danger" test in determining when the constitutionally guaranteed freedom of speech and the press can be restricted by the government. Justice Holmes defined the test:

[T]he character of every act depends upon the circumstances in which it is done.... The most stringent protection of speech would not protect a man in falsely shouting fire in a theatre and causing a panic.... The question in every case is whether the words used are used in such circumstances and are of such a nature as to create a clear and present danger that they will bring about the substantive evils that Congress has a right to prevent. It is a question of proximity and degree.

Schenck v. United States, 249 U.S. 47, 52 (1919).

75. *So Min-ho*, Seoul Criminal District Court, *Law Times* (Korean), January 9, 1967, p. 6.

76. Ibid., *Law Times* (Korean), January 16, 1967, p. 6.

77. Ibid.

78. Ibid., *Law Times* (Korean), January 23, 1967, p. 6.

79. Ibid., *Law Times* (Korean), January 9, 1967, p. 6.

80. Ibid.

81. Ibid.

82. Ibid., *Law Times* (Korean), January 16, 1967, p. 6.

83. Ibid.

84. Ibid., *Law Times* (Korean), January 23, 1967, p. 6.

85. Ibid.

86. 66 Ko 2067, Taejon District Court, May 18, 1967, *Law Times* (Korean), September 11, 1967, p. 6; September 18, 1967, p. 6.

87. Ibid., *Law Times* (Korean), September 18, 1967, p. 6.

88. 66 Ko 14198, Seoul Criminal District Court, June 28, 1967, *Law Times* (Korean), August 7, 1967, p. 6; August 14, 1967, p. 6; August 21, 1967, p. 6.

89. Ibid., *Law Times* (Korean), August 21, 1967, p. 6.

90. 65 Ko 8762, Taegu District Court, October 18, 1967, *Law Times* (Korean), November 6, 1967, p. 6.

91. Ibid. (emphasis added).

92. Ibid.

93. *See* State v. Yi Sang-gwan, 68 No. 451, Taegu District Court, November 7, 1969, *Journalists Association of Korea Newsletter* (Korean), November 21, 1969, p. 2.

94. Pak, 2 *Study of National Security Laws* (Korean), *op. cit.*, pp. 75–76.

95. *Journalists Association of Korea Newsletter* (Korean), November 21, 1969, p. 2.

96. 68 Ta 1631, Supreme Court, April 29, 1969, *Law Times* (Korean), May 26, 1969, p. 4.

97. Ibid.

98. 68 Ko 21972, Seoul Criminal District Court, June 15, 1970, *Law Times* (Korean), August 17, 1970, p. 6; August 24, 1970, p. 6.

99. Ibid., *Law Times* (Korean), August 24, 1970, p. 6.

100. Ibid.

101. 71 To 2264, Supreme Court, February 29, 1972, *Law Times* (Korean), March 20, 1972, p. 4.

102. 72 To 1514, Supreme Court, September 12, 1972, *Monthly Court Case Report* (Korean), November 1972, pp. 76–77.

103. Pnina Lahav, "The Press and National Security," in *National Security and Democracy in Israel* 180 (Avner Yaniv ed., 1993).

104. 67 Ko 10961, Seoul Criminal District Court, April 17, 1972, *Law Times* (Korean), May 1, 1972, p. 6.

105. Ibid.

106. Ibid.

107. Ibid.

108. 72 To 1730, Supreme Court, September 26, 1972, 26(3) *Supreme Court Decisions* (Korean) 16–18 (1972).

109. Ibid., p. 17.

110. 72 Kahap 315, Seoul Criminal District Court, September 27, 1972, *Journalists Association of Korea Newsletter* (Korean), September 29, 1972, p. 4; October 6, 1972, p. 6.

111. 68 To 1118, Supreme Court, October 22, 1968, *slip opinion* (Korean); Supreme Court Ruling Card no. 3412.

112. Ibid.

113. Ibid.

114. *See* Pak Kyu-sin v. State, 74 To 3488, Supreme Court, January 28, 1975, 23(1) *Supreme Court Decisions* (Korean) 3–6 (1975); *Official Gazette of Courts* (Korean), April 15, 1975, p. 34.

115. 76 To 3446, Supreme Court, December 28, 1976, *Law Times* (Korean), February 14, 1977, p. 4.

116. Ibid.

117. *See* Kim Sok-chu v. State, 74 To 2755, Supreme Court, November 26, 1974, *Official Gazette of Courts* (Korean), February 15, 1975, pp. 18–19.

118. 76 To 3097, Supreme Court, December 14, 1976, *Law Times* (Korean), December 27, 1976, pp. 4–5.

119. Ibid., p. 5.

120. 68 Ko 1080, Seoul Criminal District Court, February 6, 1969, *Law Times* (Korean), February 24, 1969, p. 6.

121. Ibid.

122. 69 To 80, Supreme Court, May 12, 1970, 18(2) *Supreme Court Decisions* (Korean) 1–2 (1970).

123. 70 Ko 45085, Seoul Criminal District Court, February 11, 1971, *Monthly Court Case Report* (Korean), April 1971, pp. 78–80.

124. 82 To 716, Supreme Court, May 25, 1982, 20(2) *Supreme Court Decisions* (Korean) 20–27 (1982); *Law Times* (Korean), June 21, 1982, p. 6. *See also* State v. Son Hak-kyu, 74 To 1236, Supreme Court, July 13, 1976, *Official Gazette of Courts* (Korean), September 1, 1976, pp. 17–18; *Monthly Court Case Report* (Korean), December 1976, pp. 75–76.

125. *But cf.* Chong Chae-hong v. State, 82 To 269, Supreme Court, June 8, 1982, *Monthly Court Case Report* (Korean), November 1982, pp. 128–29.

126. 78 To 2254, Supreme Court, October 31, 1978, 26(3) *Supreme Court Decisions* (Korean) 82–85 (1978).

127. Ibid., pp. 83–84. *See also* Pyo Ul-kyong v. State, 78 To 2243, Supreme Court, December 13, 1978, 26(3) *Supreme Court Decisions* (Korean) 131–40 (1978).

128. 78 To 2706, Supreme Court, January 16,1979, 21(1) *Supreme Court Decisions* (Korean)1–6 (1979).

129. Ibid., p. 6.

130. Ibid., p. 3.

131. 71 To 466, Supreme Court, May 24, 1971, *Monthly Court Case Report* (Korean), August 1971, p. 95.

132. Ibid.

133. *See* State v. An Song-gun, 71 To 745, Supreme Court, June 22, 1971, 19(2) *Supreme Court Decisions* (Korean) 33–35 (1971); *Monthly Court Case Report* (Korean), September 1971, pp. 101–102.

134. *See* State v. Cho Tok-son, 77 To 1360, Supreme Court, July 12, 1977, *Law Times* (Korean), August 15, 1977, p. 7; State v. Han Sang-kyun, 73 To 3392, Supreme Court, December 9, 1975, 23(3) *Supreme Court Decisions* (Korean) 49–52 (1975); *Official Gazette of Courts* (Korean), February 15, 1976, p. 27.

135. State v. Yi Sin-bom, 70 Ko 11034, Seoul Criminal District Court, February 15, 1971, *Monthly Court Case Report* (Korean), April 1971, pp. 80–81. *See also* State v. Hong Yun-ok, 70 To 1486, Supreme Court, August 31, 1970, 18(2) *Supreme Court Decisions* (Korean) 99–101 (1970); *Monthly Court Case Report* (Korean), November 1970, p. 73.

136. 71 To 2022, Supreme Court, December 28, 1971, 19(3) *Supreme Court Decisions* (Korean) 78–80 (1971).

137. Ibid., p. 79.

138. Pak Chong-duk v. State, 73 To 2602, Supreme Court, December 11, 1973, 21(3) *Supreme Court Cases* (Korean) 59–61 (1973); *Monthly Court Case Report* (Korean), March 1974, pp. 28–29.

139. 76 To 3603, Supreme Court, December 14, 1976, *Monthly Court Case Report* (Korean), May 1975, pp. 84–85.

140. *See* State v. Paek Sang-gi, 75 To 982, Supreme Court, November 25, 1975, *Monthly Court Case Report* (Korean), February 1976, pp. 70–72.

141. *See* Yi Che-bong v. State, 76 No 11699, Seoul Criminal District Court, February 16, 1977, *Law Times* (Korean), March 7, 1977, p. 9.

142. *See* State v. Kim Chong-ho, 73 To 2045, Supreme Court, February 12, 1974, *Monthly Court Case Report* (Korean), May 1974, pp. 78–79; Yon Hak-hum v. State, 76 To 2671, Supreme Court, September 28, 1976, *Law Times* (Korean), October 18, 1976, p. 4.

143. 70 To 1325, Supreme Court, September 29, 1970, *Monthly Court Case Report* (Korean), December 1970, pp. 80–81.

144. Ibid., p. 80.

145. 73 To 166, Supreme Court, March 13, 1973, *Monthly Court Case Report* (Korean), May 1973, p. 78.

146. Ibid.

147. Ibid.

148. 74 To 846, Supreme Court, July 16, 1974, *Monthly Court Case Report* (Korean), December 1974, pp. 88–89.

149. Ibid., p. 88.

150. Ibid., p. 89.

151. 86 To 1786, Supreme Court, November 11, 1986, *Official Gazette of Courts* (Korean), January 1, 1987, p. 48.

152. Ibid. *See also* Choe Un-yong v. State, 92 No 633, Seoul Criminal District Court, August 5, 1992, 2 *Lower Court Decisions* (Korean) 449–60 (1992).

153. 86 To 1784, Supreme Court, October 28, 1986, *Official Gazette of Courts* (Korean), December 15, 1986, pp. 84–87.

154. Ibid., p. 85. *See also* Yi Chong-ju v. State, 87 To 1081, Supreme Court, July 21, 1987, *Official Gazette of Courts* (Korean), September 15, 1987, pp. 74–75.

155. Ibid. *See also* Yi Pu-yong v. State, 90 To 450, Supreme Court, January 29, 1993, 41(1) *Supreme Court Decisions* (Korean) 639–53 (1993); State v. Chong Hyong-bae, 92 To 2068, Supreme Court, October 27, 1992, *Monthly Court Case Report* (Korean), March 1993, pp. 235–39; Choe Un-yong v. State, 92 No 633, Seoul Criminal District Court, August 5, 1992, 2 *Lower Court Decisions* (Korean) 449–60 (1992); Hwang Chun-ung v. State, 89 To 251, Supreme Court, July 24, 1990, *Monthly Court Case Report* (Korean), December 1990, pp. 174–76; Yang Tong-Hwa v. State, 86 To 1429, Supreme Court, September 23, 1986, 34(3) *Supreme Court Decisions* (Korean) 528–46 (1986); Yi Kwang-chol v. State, 83 To 2528, Supreme Court, November 22, 1983, *Official Gazette of Courts* (Korean), January 15, 1984, pp. 66–67; Choe Song-un v. State, 87 To 388, Supreme Court, April 14, 1987, *Official Gazette of Courts* (Korean), June 1, 1987, pp. 82–83; Ko Kyong-dae v. State, 87 To 434, Supreme Court, April 28, 1987, *Official Gazette of Courts* (Korean), June 15, 1987, pp. 83–84; Sim Han-sik v. State, 87 To

929, Supreme Court, September 22, 1987, *Official Gazette of Courts* (Korean), November 15, 1987, pp. 67–69; Yi Kwang-ung v. State, 83 To 2379, Supreme Court, December 27, 1983, *Official Gazette of Courts* (Korean), February 15, 1984, pp. 43–45; Chong Chin-tae v. State, 83 To 2755, December 27, 1983, *Official Gazette of Courts* (Korean), February 15, 1984, pp. 51–52; Ku Myong-u v. State, 87 To 432, Supreme Court, May 26, 1987, *Official Gazette of Courts* (Korean), July 15,1987, pp. 87–90.

156. Ibid., p. 86. *See also* Yi Pu-yong v. State, 90 To 450, Supreme Court, January 29, 1993, 41 (1) *Supreme Court Decisions* (Korean) 639–53 (1993).

157. Ibid.

158. 81 To 1145, Supreme Court, December 27, 1983, *Official Gazette of Courts* (Korean), February 15, 1984, pp. 36–37.

159. Ibid., p. 36.

160. Ibid.

161. 84 To 2310, Supreme Court, November 27, 1984, *Official Gazette of Courts* (Korean), January 15, 1985, pp. 68–69.

162. Ibid., p. 69.

163. Ibid.

164. 90 To 2033, Supreme Court, March 31, 1992, 40(1) *Supreme Court Decisions* (Korean) 691–718 (1992).

165. *See* Kim Sang-myong v. State, 90 No 515, Masan District Court, August 9, 1990, *reprinted in* 40(1) *Supreme Court Decisions* (Korean) 718 (1992).

166. *See* "Reasons for Appeal," *reprinted in* ibid., p. 716.

167. Ibid., p. 696.

168. Ibid.

169. Ibid., p. 697.

170. Ibid., pp. 697–98 (Yi Hoe-chang, Yi Chae-song, and Pae man-un, JJ., dissenting).

171. Ibid., p. 698 (emphasis added).

172. Ibid.

173. Ibid., pp. 698–99.

174. Ibid., p. 700.

175. Ibid., p. 701.

176. Ibid.

177. Ibid., p. 702.

178. Ibid. The "concrete and probable danger" test is comparable to U.S. Judge Learned Hand's test, "whether the gravity of the 'evil,' discounted by its improbability, justifies such invasion of free speech as is necessary to avoid the danger," which was adopted in *Dennis v. United States*, 341 U.S. 494, 510 (1951).

179. Ibid., pp. 702–703.

180. Ibid., p. 703.

181. Ibid.

182. Ibid., p. 704 (emphasis added).

183. Ibid.

184. Ibid., pp. 704–705 (emphasis added).

185. Ibid.

186. Ibid., p. 707.

187. Ibid., p. 708.

188. Ibid., p. 710.

189. Ibid. The dissenting opinion seems to be drawn from the U.S. Supreme Court's holding in *Yates v. United States*, 354 U.S. 298 (1957), which made a distinction between advocacy of abstract doctrine and advocacy of unlawful action.

190. Ibid., p. 711.

191. Ibid., p. 713.

192. Ibid., pp. 713–14.

193. 92 To 1211, Supreme Court, August 14, 1992, 40(2) *Supreme Court Decisions* (Korean) 717–26 (1992).

194. Ibid., pp. 725–26.

195. 92 To 1711, Supreme Court, February 9, 1993, *Official Gazette of Courts* (Korean), October 1, 1994, pp. 241–44.

196. Ibid., p. 244.

197. Ibid. *See also* Ham Un-gyong v. State, 86 To 403, Supreme Court, June 24, 1986, 34(2) *Supreme Court Decisions* (Korean) 385–91 (1986).

198. State v. Yi _____ (appellee's full name not provided), 94 To 135, Supreme Court, October 20, 1994, *Law Times* (Korean), October 20, 1994, p. 10.

199. Ibid.

200. Ibid.

201. Bang, *op. cit. See also* Yoon, *Law and Political Authority, op. cit.*, p. 172 (noting that the Anti-Communist Act and the National Security Act "have inevitably placed some restriction on civil liberties, especially freedom of expression. Alleging that the government authorities have reacted excessively to violations of these laws, their constitutionality has been repeatedly challenged").

202. 87 Kodan 503, Seoul Criminal District Court, June 3, 1987, *Press Guidelines* (Korean) 230–39 (Council for Democratic Press Movement ed., 1988).

203. For a discussion of the press guidelines issued by the Korean government under President Chun Doo Hwan in 1980–1987, see chap. 4 *supra*.

204. *Kim Tae-hong*, Seoul Criminal District Court, *Press Guidelines* (Korean), *op. cit.*, p. 237.

205. Ibid., p. 229.

206. Kim Tae-hong v. State, 88 No 781, Seoul Criminal District, July 5, 1994, *slip opinion* (Korean).

207. Ibid., p. 8 (emphasis added). The court defined the "threat" and "harm" to the State under the National Security Act:

> To threaten the existence and security of the State means to threaten and attack the independence of the Republic of Korea and to invade its territory and to destroy and paralyze the functions of the Constitution and laws or the constitutional organs. To harm the fundamental order of our liberal democracy means to make it difficult to maintain the rule of law based on the principle of citizens' autonomy, freedom, and equality determined by the majority of people to the exclusion of a violent and arbitrary rule, i.e., a one-man or one-party anti-State dictatorship. To be more concrete, it means to destroy and change our internal system, which comprises a respect for basic human rights, separation of powers, parliamentary system, multi-party system, election systems, the market system recognizing private property and market economy as its essence, or the independent judiciary.

Ibid., pp. 8–9, citing 89 Honga 113: Ruling on Constitutionality of Article 7 of the National Security Act, Constitution Court, April 2, 1990, *Official Gazette* (Korean), May 1, 1990, pp. 25–27.

208. Ibid., p. 9. *See also* Choe Un-yong v. State, 92 No 633, Seoul Criminal District Court, August 5, 1992, 2 *Lower Court Decisions* (Korean) 449–60 (1992).

209. Ibid., p. 10.

210. *See Human Rights in Korea: Facts and Fiction, op. cit.*, pp. 32–33.

211. 89 Kodan 3509, Seoul Criminal District Court, September 25, 1989, *slip opinion* (Korean). Yi had already spent 160 days in jail since his arrest. Chin Sok Chong, "The South Korean Press," in *Korea Briefing, 1992*, at 139 (Donald N. Clark ed., 1992).

212. Yi Yong-hi v. State, 89 No 5990, Seoul Criminal District Court, February 2, 1993, *slip opinion* (Korean).

213. Ibid., pp. 3–4.

214. Ibid., p. 4.

215. 92 No 6354, Seoul Criminal District Court, January 20, 1993, 1 *Lower Court Decisions* (Korean) 412–20 (1993).

216. Ibid., p. 414.

217. Ibid., p. 415.

218. Ibid.

219. "MOCI: Telephone Conversation by News Media with Miss Yim in NK Prohibited by National Security Act," *Chosun Ilbo* (Korean), July 4, 1989, p. B16.

220. Bradley Martin, "A Party in Pyongyang," *Newsweek*, July 17, 1989, p. 35.

221. Department of State, *Country Reports on Human Rights Practices for 1993*, at 667 (February 1993).

222. Editorial, "Legal Idealists and Rigors of Reality," *Korea Herald*, January 20, 1995, p. 6.

223. For a discussion of the authoritarian politics of South Korea through repressive emergency decrees in 1973–1975, see Hak-Kyu Sohn, *Authoritarianism and Opposition in South Korea* 65–88 (1989).

224. 76 To 876, Supreme Court, May 11, 1976, *Monthly Court Case Report* (Korean), October 1975, pp. 92–93.

225. Ibid., p. 93. *See also* Yi Chang-jun v. State, 77 To 3984, Supreme Court, March 14, 1978, *Official Gazette of Courts* (Korean), May 1, 1978, pp. 29–30; *Monthly Court Case Report* (Korean), August 1978, pp. 92–92; Hwang Chu-hong v. State, 76 To 3905, Supreme Court, February 22, 1977, *slip opinion* (Korean).

226. 76 To 3638, Supreme Court, January 11, 1977, *slip opinion* (Korean).

227. Ibid.

228. 78 To 2203, November 28, 1978, *Official Gazette of Courts* (Korean), March 1, 1979, p. 39.

229. Ibid.

230. 79 To 2391, Supreme Court, December 28, 1979, *Official Gazette of Courts* (Korean), February 15, 1980, p. 12506.

231. Ibid.

232. 81 To 543, Supreme Court, April 14, 1981, *Law Times* (Korean), May 18, 1981, p. 6.

233. Ibid.

234. Kim Taek-hwan, *Korean Press Laws: Their Status and Issues* (Korean) 57–58 (1993).

235. Lahav, "The Press and National Security," *op. cit.*, pp. 175, 176.

236. Leonard W. Levy, *Emergence of a Free Press* 130 (1985).

237. Editorial, "Legal Idealists and Rigors of Reality," *op. cit.*, p. 6.

## CHAPTER 12

1. Lawrence Ward Beer, *Freedom of Expression in Japan* 362 (1984).

2. Sandra Coliver, "Comparative Analysis of Press Law in European and Other Democracies," in *Press Law and Practice* 255 (Sandra Coliver ed., 1993).

3. ARTICLE 19, *World Report 1991: Information, Freedom and Censorship* 423 (1991).

4. Law No. 4688 (1993), *reprinted in Compendium of Codes* (Korean) 2941–42 (1994).

5. Ibid., art. 1.

6. Ibid., art. 3 (1).

7. Ibid., art. 5 (1).

8. Ibid., art. 2 (1) 4.

9. Implementation Decree of the Act Relating to Import and Distribution of Foreign Periodicals, Presidential Decree No. 14056 (1993), art. 2 (1), *reprinted in Compendium of Codes* (Korean), *op. cit.*, pp. 5508–5509. The Decree stipulates that "designated" foreign periodicals do not include:

1. Those which, though published in North Korea, are deemed not to be political or ideological in their contents;
2. Those which, though containing information about North Korea, are deemed to be negligible in political propaganda and to carry a value as introductory or research material;
3. Those which, though carrying the contents on the origin, revolutionary tactics, and revolutionary movement or revolutionaries of communism, are deemed to have little impact on our society;
4. Those which, though carrying the contents critical of capitalism, are deemed to be negligible in denouncing our system;
5. Those which, though carrying the contents distorting historical facts, are deemed negligible in impacting on our society.

Ibid., art. 2 (2).

10. Ibid., art. 3.

11. Ibid., art. 7. In this regard, the *Newsweek* magazine episode of the late 1960s is a case in point. In a 1968 issue, *Newsweek* erroneously used Japanese names for Korean cities on a map pertaining to its cover story. The Ministry of Culture and Information of the Korean government ordered *Newsweek*'s local distributor to blacken the "offending" portion of the map in all copies of the issues designated for distribution. Sunwoo Nam, A Comparative Study of Freedom of the Press in Korea, Taiwan, and the Philippines in the 1960's, at 56 (1969) (Ph.D. dissertation, University of Wisconsin (Madison)).

12. Ibid., art. 9.

13. Ibid., art. 16.

14. Law No. 1976 (1967), revised by Law No. 4351 (1991), *translated in* 3 *Current Laws of the Republic of Korea* 1701–96 (1994) [hereinafter *ROK Current Laws*].

15. Ibid., art. 146.

16. Ibid.

17. Ibid., art. 179.

18. Ibid., art. 185.

19. Coliver, *op. cit.*, p. 285.

20. Criminal Code, Law No. 2745 (1975), revised by Law No. 4040 (1988), art. 243, *translated in* 2 *ROK Current Laws*, *op. cit.*, pp. 761–812.

21. Ibid., art. 244.

22. Law No. 834 (1961), revised by Law No. 4351 (1991), *reprinted in Compendium of Codes* (Korean), *op. cit.*, p. 960.

23. Ibid., art. 2-2.

24. Law No. 904 (1961), revised by Law No. 4541 (1993), *reprinted in Compendium of Codes* (Korean), *op. cit.*, p. 2966.

25. Ibid., art. 5-2 (5).

26. 73 To 409, Supreme Court, August 21, 1973, 21(2) *Supreme Court Decisions* (Korean) 47–49 (1973).

27. 73 To 2178, Supreme Court, October 23, 1973, 21(3) *Supreme Court Decisions* (Korean) 25–29 (1973).

28. Ibid., p. 25.

29. 74 To 976, Supreme Court, December 9, 1975, 23(3) *Supreme Court Decisions* (Korean) 52–57 (1975). For a discussion of *State v. Yom Chae-man*, see Yi Kon-ho, "The 'Revolting Slaves' Case and Obscenity," 3 *Study of Case Law* (Korean) 269–79 (1978).

30. Ibid., p. 53. *See also* Yi Kun-suk v. State, 91 To 1550, Supreme Court, September 10, 1991, 39(3) *Supreme Court Decisions* (Korean) 854 (1991); State v. Chong Chun-gyo, 90 To 1485, Supreme Court, October 16, 1990, *Monthly Court Case Report* (Korean), March 1991, p. 197.

31. Ibid.

32. 93 No. 446, Seoul Criminal District Court, July 13, 1994, *slip opinion* (Korean).

33. Ibid., pp. 5–6.

34. Ibid., pp. 4–5.

35. Sin Sang-chol v. State, 70 To 1879, Supreme Court, October 30, 1970, 1 *Supreme Court Decisions* (Korean) 1 (1971). For a discussion of *Sin Sang-Chol v. State*, see Kwon Mun-taek, "Obscene Work of Art," 20 *Lawyers Association Journal* (Korean) 1–16 (January 1971).

36. Ibid.

37. 78 To 2327, Supreme Court, November 14, 1978, 26(3) *Supreme Court Decisions* (Korean) 100–103 (1978).

38. Ibid., p. 101.

39. 69 Ko 27460, Seoul Criminal District Court, December 15, 1969, Kim Chol-su, *Casebook on Constitutional Law* (Korean) 336 (1980).

40. Constitution, ordained and promulgated in 1948, art. 14, *translated in* 2 *Constitutions of Nations* 549–59 (Amos J. Peaslee ed., 2d ed. 1956).

41. Copyright Act, Law No. 432 (1957), *translated in Laws of the Republic of Korea* 806–13 (3d ed. 1975).

42. Constitution, amended in 1987, art. 22, *translated in* 1 *ROK Current Laws, op. cit.*, pp. 1–16.

43. Law No. 3916 (1986), revised by Law No. 4746 (1994), *translated in The Korean Press 1995*, at 159–83 (1995). For a discussion of the Copyright Act, as revised in 1986, see Han Sung-hon. *Copyright Law and Practice* (Korean) (1988); Song Yong-sik, "Problems with the Current Copyright Act (I), " 19 *Lawyer* (Korean) 181–200 (1989); "Problems with the Current Copyright Act (II), " 21 *Lawyer* (Korean) 339–54 (1991).

44. Ibid., art. 1.

45. Ibid., art. 36.

46. Ibid.

47. Ibid., art. 9. Article 9 reads: "[T]he author of a work which is prepared on duty by a person working for a juristic person under the direction of a corporation, organization or other employer ... and which is published in the name of the juristic person, etc. ..., shall be the juristic person, etc., unless otherwise provided by employment or independent agreement."

48. Ibid., art. 38.

49. Ibid., art. 3. For a discussion of copyright protection of foreigners under the Copyright Act, see William Enger, "Korean Copyright Reform," 7 *UCLA Pacific Basin Law Journal* 199–213 (Spring 1990).

50. Ibid., art. 4.

51. Ibid., art. 7.

52. Cho Su-bi v. Yonbang Film Co., 91 Ra 79, Seoul High Court, September 5, 1991, 3 *Lower Court Decisions* (Korean) 269–70 (1991).

53. *See* Baker v. Seldon, 101 U.S. 99 (1879) (making a distinction between protected expressions and unprotected ideas under copyright law).

54. Kim Son-gi v. Sin Sa-hun, 93 Ta 3073, 3080, Supreme Court, June 8, 1993, 41(2) *Supreme Court Decisions* (Korean)104 (1993) (emphasis added). For a discussion of *Kim Son-gi v. Sin Sa-hun*, see Sim Chang-sop, "Copyright Owner in the Case of Producing Applicational Art Work by Order," 19(2) *Commentaries on Supreme Court Decisions* (Korean) 390–408 (1993).

55. Ibid., p. 105 (emphasis added).

56. *Yi Chong-suk*, Supreme Court, p. 10.

57. The "fair use" concept under the copyright law is "[a] privilege in others than the owner of a copyright to use the copyrighted material in a reasonable manner without the owner's consent, notwithstanding the monopoly granted to the owner." *Black's Law Dictionary, op. cit.*, p. 415.

58. Copyright Act, art. 22.

59. Ibid., art. 23 (1). The "released works" means works presented to the public "through performance, broadcasting, display, or by any other means...." Ibid., art. 2.

60. Ibid., art. 24. *See Yi Chong-suk*, Supreme Court, p. 11 (copyrighted pictures used for an entertainment purpose, not for news, and thus not a fair use).

61. Ibid., art. 25. The Seoul Civil District Court ruled in 1994 that quotations must be complementary, explanatory, or illustrative or reference material relating to the quoting work and that it must not affect the market demand for the quoted work. *See* Irand Co. v. Sim Chae-jong, 94 Kahap 2072, Seoul Civil District Court, April 14, 1994, *slip opinion* (Korean), p. 3.

62. Ibid., art. 26.

63. Ibid., art. 27.

64. Ibid., art. 28.

65. *See* ibid., art. 29 (reproduction of copyrighted works for examination purposes); art. 30 (reproduction in Braille); art. 31 (ephemeral recording or videotaping by broadcasters); art. 32 (display or reproduction of fine art works); and art. 33 (use through translation).

66. Ibid., art. 35.

67. An authority on copyright defines the "moral rights" of an author to his work as the rights "to prevent others from falsely attributing to him the authorship of work which he has not in fact written; to prevent others from making deforming changes in his work; to withdraw a published work from distribution if it no longer represents the views of the author; and to prevent others from using the work or the author's name in such a way as to reflect on his professional standing." Melville B. Nimmer et al., *Cases and Materials on Copyrights and Other Aspects of Entertainment Litigation Including Unfair Competition, Defamation, Privacy Illustrated* 602 (4th ed. 1991).

68. Copyright Act, art. 14 (1).

69. Ibid., art. 14 (2) ("Any person who uses a work after the death of its author, shall not do any act that might prejudice the author's personal right had he been alive...").

70. Ibid., art. 95.

71. Ibid., art. 98.

72. 92 Na 35846, Seoul High Court, September 29, 1994, *Press Arbitration Quarterly* (Korean), Winter 1994, pp. 161–71.

73. Han Sang-jin v. Korean Broadcasting Corp., 90 Kaham 1404, Seoul District Court (South Branch), May 14, 1992, *Press Arbitration Quarterly* (Korean), Summer 1992, p. 169.

74. Ibid., p. 170. Professor Han Sang-jin of Seoul National University, an authority on what he has termed the "middle class theory," gave a lecture entitled "South Korea in the 21st Century: A Sociological Perspective." According to Han's theory, the now progressive middle class, the progressive

part of the working class and youth/students will be at the forefront of social change in Korea. *See* "Road to Establishing a Middle Class Society," in Han Sang-jin, *Korea: Searching for the Third Road* (Korean) 333–57 (1992). "Road to Establishing a Middle Class Society" is the "reorganized" transcript of Han's original lecture taped for the KBS program.

75. Han Sang-jin v. KBS, 89 Seoul Chungjae 73, *Press Arbitration Quarterly* (Korean), Summer 1990, pp. 111–12.

76. Ibid., p. 112.

77. Ibid. *But cf.* Kang Hyon-du, "Broadcasters' Editorial Freedom: Its Ethics and Limits," *Newspapers and Broadcasting* (Korean), March 1991, pp. 50–51.

78. *Han Sang-Jin*, Seoul District Court (South Branch), p. 169.

79. Ibid.

80. Ibid., p. 172.

81. *Han Sang-jin*, Seoul High Court, p. 165.

82. Ibid.

83. Ibid., p. 165.

84. Ibid., p. 170.

85. 90 Taka 8845, Supreme Court, October 23, 1990, 38(3) *Supreme Court Decisions* (Korean) 7–20 (1990).

86. Yi Chae-gil v. Yi Chong-suk, 89 Na 32908, Seoul High Court, February 13, 1990, 1 *Lower Court Decisions* (Korean) 262–74 (1990).

87. *Yi Chong-suk*, Supreme Court, p. 14.

88. Gwang-jub Han, "The Cable Television Development Planning in Korea: A Critique," 5 *Sungkok Journalism Review* 23 (Fall 1994).

89. Law No. 4494 (1991), revised by Law No. 4737 (1994), *translated in The Korean Press 1995*, *op. cit.*, pp. 183–203.

90. Law No. 3978 (1987), revised by Law No. 4441 (1991), *translated in The Korean Press 1995*, *op. cit.*, pp. 146–59.

91. Ibid., art. 1.

92. Ibid., art. 23.

93. Ibid., art. 4 (1), (2), (3),(4).

94. Ibid., art. 4 (5).

95. Ibid., art. 4 (6).

96. Ibid., art. 5. *Compare with* Broadcast Act, art. 9.

97. *Compare* Cable Television Act, art. 6, *with* Broadcast Act, art. 8.

98. Ibid., art. 7 (2).

99. Ibid., art. 11.

100. Decree of Enforcement of the Comprehensive Cable Television Broadcast Act, Presidential Decree No. 13682 (1992), revised by Decree No. 13842 (1993), art. 10, *reprinted in Compendium of Codes* (Korean), *op. cit.*, pp. 2950–52.

101. Cable Television Act, art. 12 (2).

102. Ibid., art. 12 (3).

103. Ibid., art. 50.

104. Ibid., art. 13.

105. Presidential Enforcement Decree of the Cable Television Act, art. 13.

106. Ibid., art. 16.

107. Ibid., art. 14 (2).

108. Ibid., art. 24.

109. Han, "Cable Television Development," *op. cit.*, p. 27, citing "Revised Presidential Decree 14221" of April 22, 1994.

110. Among the grounds that the MOPI may cite for revoking the license of a cable broadcasting station or for suspending its operation are: (1) The station has obtained a permission, permission on modification or repermission by a deceitful or other unlawful way; (2) It violates the prohibition of a concurrent operation; (3) It is operated by a business conglomerate; (4) It receives contribution from a foreign source; (5) It broadcasts advertising in violation of the relevant provisions of the Act; (6) It violates the governmental order of correction or to improve facilities as stipulated by the Act. Ibid., art. 21 (1).

111. Ibid., art. 21 (3).

112. Ibid.

113. *See* 47 U.S.C. § 531 (1988).

114. Ibid.

115. Cable Television Act, art. 22 (1).

116. Ibid., art. 22 (2), (3), (4).

117. Ibid., art. 24.

118. Ibid., art. 34.

119. Ibid., art. 34 (2), (5).

120. Ibid., art. 35 (1). The Presidential Decree of the Cable Television Act prescribes those eligible for appointment to the Cable Television Broadcast Commission thus:

> 1. Those who have been employed in media organizations such as broadcasting for more than 10 years;
> 2. Those who have served in the positions of judge, attorney, or prosector for more than five years;
> 3. Those who have held the positions of associate professor or higher for more than three years at universities established under the Education Act;
> 4. Those who the Minister of Public Information considers have sufficient knowledge and experience in their specialties [relating to cable broadcasting programming].

Presidential Decree of the Cable Television Act, art. 32.

121. Ibid., art. 38 (1) 1.

122. Ibid., art. 38 (2).

123. Ibid., art. 41.

124. Ibid., art. 45. *Compare with* Broadcast Act, arts. 41–42, and Periodicals Act, art. 16–19, *translated in The Korean Press 1995, op. cit.*, pp. 135–59.

125. Ibid., art. 45 (9).

126. Ibid., art. 56.

127. Ibid., art. 53.

128. Ibid., art. 54.

129. Kyu Ho Youm and Michael B. Salwen, "A Free Press in South Korea: Temporary Phenomenon or Permanent Fixture?" 30 *Asian Survey* 324 (1990).

130. *See* Basic Press Act, art. 6 ("The State, local governments and public organizations shall supply information on matters of public interest when so requested by the publishers of a newspaper or a news service, the chief of a broadcasting station or their agents"). Basic Press Act, Law No. 3347 (1980), revised by Law No. 3786 (1984) (repealed in 1987), art. 6, *translated in The Korean Press 1986*, at 207–24 (1986).

131. For a discussion of the Constitution Court's interpretation of the right to know under the Constitution of Korea in 1992, see chap. 5 *supra*.

132. The right of access to information in the United States is firmly grounded in the First Amendment which gives the press its roles as the "watchdog" of the government. Constitutional law scholar Laurence Tribe has noted:

> [I]t is important to keep in mind that government affects public opinion as much by what it *does not* say as by what it *does* say.... The resulting need is to impose pressure on government to speak—and truth—through judicially recognizing and enforcing rights of access to certain governmental institutions and proceedings, legislatively enacting suitably designed freedom of information statutes, and undertaking both legislative and executive de-classification of documents needlessly deemed secret.

Laurence H. Tribe, *American Constitutional Law* 813–14 (2d ed. 1988) (footnotes omitted).

133. "DP [Democratic Party] Calls for Elimination of 'Poisonous Clause' from Military Secrets Bill," *Korea Herald*, August 7, 1992, p. 2.

134. Ibid.

135. Editorial, "Military Secrets vs. Right to Know," *Korea Herald*, August 7, 1992, p. 6.

136. *See* Military Secrets Protection Act, Law No. 4616 (1993), *reprinted in Compendium of Codes, op. cit.*, pp. 2552–53.

137. Ibid., art. 2. *Compare with* Military Secrets Act, Law No. (1981), art. 2 (defining "military secrets" as information "which, if disclosed, will create a harmful consequence for the national security").

138. Ibid., art. 9.

139. Ibid., art. 7.

140. Ibid., art. 8.

141. Ordinance on Release of Administrative Information of Chongju City. It went into force on July 1, 1992, *reprinted in Newspapers and Broadcasting* (Korean), August 1992, p. 99.

142. Ibid., art. 3.

143. 5 U.S.C. § 552 (1988).

144. FOIA exempts matters "specifically exempted from disclosure by statute (other than section 552b of this title) provided that such statute (A) requires that the matters be withheld from the public in such a manner as to leave no discretion on the issue, or (B) establishes particular criteria for withholding or refers to particular types of matters to be withheld." 5 U.S.C. § 552(b)(3) (1989).

145. Ordinance on Administrative Information, *op. cit.*, art. 5 (1) 1.

146. Ibid., art. 5 (2) 2. Article 5 (2) 2 disallows disclosure of information on the birthplace, ideology, religion, career, etc., of an individual that might violate the individual's right of privacy. It also recognizes an exemption for information involving business secrets and property of an individual, an association, or a corporate body, which, if disclosed, would cause serious loss of benefits to those involved or which deserve protection from release. *Compare with* FOIA, which exempts trade secrets and financial information obtained from any person, and privileged or confidential" and "personnel and medical files and similar files the disclosure of which would constitute a clearly unwarranted invasion of privacy." 5 U.S.C. § 552(b)(4), (6) (1989).

147. Ibid., art. 5 (1) 3.

148. Ibid., art. 8.

149. Ibid., art. 11 (1).

150. Ibid., art. 11 (2).

151. Ibid., art. 15.

152. Mayor of Chongju v. City Council of Chongju, 92 Chu 17, Supreme Court, June 23, 1992, *Newspapers and Broadcasting* (Korean), August 1992, pp. 97–98.

153. Ibid.

154. Ibid., p. 97.

155. Ibid.

156. Ibid., p. 98.

157. Ibid.

158. Donald M. Gillmor et al., *Mass Communication Law* 457 (5th ed. 1990) (emphasis deleted) (quoting Wellford v. Hardin, 315 F. Supp. 768 (D.C.C. 1970)).

159. 90 Kodan 3615, Seoul Criminal District Court, September 6, 1993, *slip opinion* (Korean).

160. The Criminal Code prohibits disclosure of official secrets. Article 127 states: "A public official or former public official who divulges official secrets obtained in the course of performing his duties and classified by law as secret shall be punished by penal servitude or imprisonment for not more than two years or suspension of qualifications for not more than five years." Criminal Code, revised in 1988, art. 127.

161. *Yi Mun-ok*, pp. 2–3.

162. Ibid., pp. 3–4.

163. Ibid., p. 3. The Seoul district court gave the following definition of "official secrets": "Official secrets under law are not necessarily limited to those statutorily designated secrets. Also included among the secrets is the information that is kept secret for political, military, economic, or social necessities, and also the information the government, administrative offices, or the general public has a considerable interest in keeping confidential from an objective and general perspective." Ibid. (citing 89 To 2822, Supreme Court, June 22, 1982).

164. Ibid., p. 5 (emphasis added).

165. *See* 5 U.S.C. § 2302(b) (8) (1993):

> (b) Any employee who has authority to take, direct others to take, recommend, or approve any personnel action, shall not, with respect to such authority ... (8) take or fail to take, or threaten or fail to take, a personnel action with respect to any employee or applicant for employment because of—
>> (A) any disclosure of information by an employee or applicant which the employee or applicant reasonably believes evidences—
>>> (i) a violation of any law, rule, or regulation, or
>>> (ii) gross mismanagement, a gross waste of funds, an abuse of authority, or a substantial and specific danger to public health or safety, if such disclosure is not specifically prohibited by law and if such information is not specifically required by Executive order to be kept secret in the interest of national defense or the conduct of foreign affairs....

# SELECTED BIBLIOGRAPHY

## Books and Monographs (in English)

Altschull, J. Herbert. *Agents of Power: The Media and Public Policy*. 2d ed. White Plains, N.Y.: Longman Publishers USA, 1995.

Amnesty International. *South Korea: Prisoners Held for National Security Reasons*. New York: Amnesty International USA, 1991.

ARTICLE 19. *World Report 1991: Information, Freedom and Censorship*. Chicago: American Library Association, 1991.

*Assessing Reform in South Korea: A Supplement to the Asia Watch Report on Legal Process and Human Rights*. New York: Asia Watch, 1988.

Baker, C. Edwin. *Human Liberty and Freedom of Speech*. New York: Oxford University Press, 1989.

Baker, Edward J. *The Role of Legal Reforms in the Japanese Annexation and Rule of Korea, 1905–1919*. Cambridge: Harvard Law School, 1979.

———. *South Korea's New Constitution: The Emperor's New Clothes*. Washington, D.C.: North American Coalition for Human Rights in Korea, 1980.

Bedeski, Robert E. *The Transformation of South Korea: Reform and Reconstruction in the Sixth Republic Under Roh Tae Woo, 1987–1992*. London: Routledge, 1994.

Beer, Lawrence W., ed. *Constitutional Systems in Late Twenties Century Asia*. Seattle: University of Washington Press, 1992.

Beer, Lawrence Ward. *Freedom of Expression in Japan: A Study in Comparative Law, Politics, and Society*. Tokyo: Kodansha International Ltd., 1984.

Bishop, Isabella Bird. *Korea and Her Neighbors: A Narrative of Travel, with an Account of the Recent Vicissitudes and Present Position of the Country*. 3d ed. New York: Fleming H. Revell Co., 1897.

Blaustein, Albert P., and Gisbert H. Flanz, eds. *Constitutions of the Countries of the World*. 20 binders. Dobbs Ferry, N.Y.: Oceana Publications, 1995.

Born, Sigrid, ed. and Fry, Martin, trans. *Press Laws: Documents of Politics and Society in the Federal Republic of Germany*. 3d ed. Bonn: INTER NATIONES, 1994.

Boyle, Kevin, ed. *ARTICLE 19 World Report 1988: Information, Freedom and Censorship*. New York: Times Books, 1988.

Brasch, Walter M., and Dana R. Ulloth. *The Press and the State: Sociohistorical and Contemporary Studies*. Lanham, Md.: University Press of America, 1986.

Carter, T. Barton, Marc A. Franklin, and Jay B. Wright. *The First Amendment and the Fourth Estate: The Law of Mass Media*. 6th ed. Westbury, N.Y.: Foundation Press, 1994.

Carter-Ruck, Peter F., Richard Walker, and Harvey N.A. Starte. *Carter-Ruck on Libel and Slander*. 4th ed. London: Butterworths, 1992.

Chamberlin, Bill F., and Charlene J. Brown, eds. *The First Amendment Reconsidered: New Perspectives on the Meaning of Freedom of Speech and Press*. New York: Longman, 1982.

Chandra, Vipan. *Imperialism, Resistance, and Reform in Late Nineteenth-Century Korea: Enlightenment and the Independence Club*. Berkeley: Center for Korean Studies, University of California, 1988.

Chang, Won Ho. *Mass Communication and Korea: Toward a Global Perspective for Research*. Seoul: Sungkok Foundation for Journalism, 1988.

Cho, Soon Sung. *Korea in World Politics 1940–1950: An Evaluation of American Responsibility*. Berkeley: University of California Press, 1967.

Choi, Woonsang. *The Fall of the Hermit Kingdom*. Dobbs Ferry, N.Y.: Oceana Publications, 1967.

Chong, Chin-Sok. *The Korean Problem in Anglo-Japanese Relations 1904–1910: Ernest Thomas Bethell and His Newspapers, the Daehan Maeil Sinbo and the Korea Daily News*. Seoul: Nanam Publications, 1987.

Chu, Godwin C., Jae-won Lee, Won-yong Kim, and Yanan Ju. *Modernization vs. Revolution: Cultural Change in Korea and China*. Seoul: Sung Kyun Kwan University Press, 1993.

Chun, Bong Duck, William Shaw, and Dai-Kwon Choi. *Traditional Korean Legal Attitudes*. Berkeley: Center for Korean Studies, University of California, 1980.

Chun, Shin-yong, ed. *Legal System of Korea*. Seoul: Si-sa-yong-o-sa Publishers, 1982.

Chung, Kyung Cho. *Korea: The Third Republic*. New York: Macmillan Co., 1971.

Clark, Donald N., ed. *Korea Briefing, 1992*. Boulder, Colo.: Westview Press, 1992.

Coliver, Sandra, ed. *The ARTICLE 19 Freedom of Expression Handbook: International and Comparative Law, Standards and Procedures*. London: ARTICLE 19, 1993.

————. *Liberty and Secrecy: National Security, Freedom of Expression and Access to Information*. London. Forthcoming.

————. *Press Law and Practice: A Comparative Study of Press Freedom in European and Other Democracies*. London: ARTICLE 19, 1993.

Commager, Henry Steele. *Crusaders for Freedom*. Garden City, N.Y.: Doubleday & Co., 1962.

*A Complete Compilation of Laws and Ordinances of the U.S. Army Military Government in Korea*. Seoul: Korean Legislation Research Association, 1971.

*Constitution: The Republic of Korea*. Seoul: Korean Overseas Information Service, 1987.

Cooper, Thomas W. *Communication Ethics and Global Change*. White Plains, N.Y.: Longman, 1989.

Cotton, James, ed. *Korea Under Roh Tae-woo: Democratisation, Northern Policy and Inter-Korean Relations*. Canberra, Australia: Allen & Unwin, 1993.

Coughlin, William J. *Conquered Press: The MacArthur Era in Japanese Journalism*. Palo Alto, Calif.: Pacific, 1952.

Cox, Archibald. *The Court and the Constitution*. Boston: Houghton Mifflin Co., 1987.

*Criminal Prosecution System in Korea*. Seoul: Supreme Public Prosecutor's Office, 1992.

Cumings, Bruce C. *The Origins of the Korean War: Liberation and the Emergence of Separate Regimes, 1945–1947*. Princeton, N.J.: Princeton University Press, 1981.

*Current Laws of the Republic of Korea*. 6 vols. Seoul: Korea Legislation Research Institute, 1994.

Curry, Jane Leftwich, and Joan R. Dassin, eds. *Press Control Around the World*. New York: Praeger Publisher, 1982.

*Democracy and Political Institutions*. Seoul: Sejong Institute, [1988].

*Democracy in South Korea: A Promise Unfulfilled*. New York: International League for Human Rights, 1985.

Department of State. *Country Reports on Human Rights Practices for 1994*. Washington, D.C.: U.S. Government Printing Office, 1995.

————. *Country Reports on Human Rights Practices for 1993*. Washington, D.C.: U.S. Government Printing Office, 1994.

————. *Country Reports on Human Rights Practices for 1989*. Washington, D.C.: U.S. Government Printing Office, 1990.

———. *Country Reports on Human Rights Practices for 1988.* Washington, D.C.: U.S. Government Printing Office, 1989.

———. *Country Reports on Human Rights Practices for 1987.* Washington, D.C.: U.S. Government Printing Office, 1988.

———. *Country Reports on Human Rights Practices for 1982.* Washington, D.C.: U.S. Government Printing Office, 1983.

———. *Country Reports on Human Rights Practices for 1980.* Washington, D.C.: U.S. Government Printing, 1981.

———. *Country Reports on Human Rights Practices for 1979.* Washington, D.C.: U.S. Government Printing Office, 1980.

———. *Country Reports on Human Rights Practices for 1977.* Washington, D.C. U.S. Government Printing, 1978.

Dewind, Adrian W., and John Woodhouse. *Persecution of Defense Lawyers in South Korea.* Geneva, Switzerland: International Commission of Jurists, 1979.

Diamond, Larry., Juan J. Linz, and Seymour Martin Lipset, eds. *Democracy in Developing Countries: Asia.* Boulder, Colo.: Lynne Rienner Publishers, 1989.

Donnelly, Jack, and Rhoda E. Howard, eds. *International Handbook of Human Rights.* New York: Greenwood Press, 1987.

Eckert, Carter J., Ki-baik Lee, Young Ick Lew, Michael Robinson, and Edward W. Wagner. *Korea Old and New: A History.* Seoul: Ilchokak Publishers, 1990.

Elder, David A. *Defamation: A Lawyer's Guide.* Deerfield, Ill.: Clark Boardman Callaghan, 1993.

Emergency Christian Conference on Korean Problems, ed. *Documents on the Struggle for Democracy in Korea.* Tokyo: Shinkyo Shuppansha, 1975.

Emerson, Thomas I. *Toward a General Theory of the First Amendment.* New York: Random House, 1966.

———. *The System of Freedom of Expression.* New York: Vintage Books, 1970.

*The Europa Year Book 1984: A World Survey.* 2 vols. London: Europa Publications Ltd., 1984.

*Facts About Korea.* Rev. and condensed ed. Seoul: Korean Overseas Information Service, 1994.

*Facts About Korea.* Rev. and condensed ed. Seoul: Korean Overseas Information Service, 1993.

*Facts About Korea.* Rev. and condensed ed. Seoul: Korean Overseas Information Service, 1991.

*Facts About Korea.* 17th ed. Seoul: Korean Overseas Information Service, 1983.

*Facts About Korea.* 16th ed. Seoul: Korean Overseas Information Service, 1981.

Farr, Ronald T., and John D. Stevens. *Mass Media and the National Experience: Essays in Communications History.* New York: Harper & Row, 1971.

Franklin, Marc A., and David A. Anderson. *Mass Media Law.* 5th ed. Westbury, N.Y.: Foundation Press, 1995.

———. *Mass Media Law.* 4th ed. Westbury, N.Y.: Foundation Press, 1990.

*Freedom of Expression in the Republic of Korea.* New York: Asia Watch, 1988.

*The Frozen Clock and the Detained Conscience: Long-Term Political Prisoners and Ideological Conversion in South Korea.* Albany, Calif.: Stop Torture in Korea, [1992].

Gastil, Raymond D. *Freedom in the World: Political Rights and Civil Liberties 1988–1989.* West Port, Conn.: Greenwood Press, 1989.

———. *Freedom in the World: Political Rights and Civil Liberties.* West Port, Conn.: Greenwood Press, 1988.

Gertz. Elmer. *Gertz v. Robert Welch, Inc.: The Story of a Landmark Libel Case.* Carbondale, Ill.: Southern Illinois University Press, 1992.

Gillmor, Donald M. *Power, Publicity and the Abuse of Libel Law.* New York: Oxford University Press, 1992.

Gillmor, Donald M., Jerome A. Barron, Todd F. Simon, and Herbert A. Terry. *Fundamentals of Mass Communication Law.* St. Paul, Minn.: West Publishing Co., 1996.

———. *Mass Communication Law.* 5th ed. St. Paul, Minn.: West Publishing Co., 1990.

Gleason, Timothy W. *The Watchdog Concept: The Press and the Courts in Nineteenth-Century America.* Ames, Iowa: Iowa State University Press, 1990.

Goldstein, Joseph, Alan M. Dershowitz, and Richard D. Schwartz, eds. *Criminal Law: Theory and Process*. New York: Free Press, 1974.

*Government Pressures on the Press*. Zurich: International Press Institute, 1955.

Grajdanzev, Andrew J. *Modern Korea*. New York: Institute of Pacific Relations, 1944.

Greenberg, Marcia, and Helet Merkling. *Broken Promises, Unfulfilled Dreams: Human Rights and Democracy in South Korea*. Edited by Kerry Kennedy Cuomo, Joseph P. Manguno, Helet Merkling, and Edward W. Poitras. New York: Robert F. Kenney Memorial Center for Human Rights, [1992].

Hachten, William A. *The World News Prism: Changing Media of International Communication*. 3d ed. Ames, Iowa: Iowa State University Press, 1992.

Hahm, Pyong-Choon. *Korean Jurisprudence, Politics and Culture*. Seoul: Yonsei University Press, 1986.

———. *The Korean Political Tradition and Law: Essays in Korean Law and Legal History*. 2d ed. Seoul: Royal Asiatic Society, Korea Branch, 1971.

Hahn, Bae-ho. *Communication Policies in the Republic of Korea*. Paris: UNESCO, 1978.

Haiman, Franklyn S. *Citizen Access to the Media: A Cross-Cultural Analysis of Four Democratic Societies*. [Evanston, Ill.]: Institute for Modern Communications, Northwestern University, 1987.

———. *Speech and Law in a Free Speech*. Chicago: University of Chicago Press, 1981.

Hall, Kermit L., ed. *The Oxford Companion to the Supreme Court of the United States*. New York: Oxford University Press, 1992.

Halloran, Richard. *The Tiger and the Eagle*. New York: Carnegie Council on Ethics and International Affairs, [1994].

Halvorsen, David E. *Confucianism Defies the Computer: The Conflict Within the Korean Press*. Honolulu: East-West Center, 1992.

Han, Sungjoo. *The Failure of Democracy in South Korea*. Berkeley: University of California Press, 1974.

Han, Sung-Joo, and Robert J. Myers, eds. *Korea: The Year 2000*. Lanham, Md.: University Press of America, 1987.

Han, Woo-keun. *The History of Korea*. Translated by Lee Kyung-shik and edited by Grafton K. Mintz. Seoul: Eul-yoo Publishing Co., 1970.

*A Handbook of Korea*. 10th ed. Seoul: Korean Overseas Information Service, 1994.

*A Handbook of Korea*. 9th ed. Seoul: Korean Overseas Information Service, 1993.

Hanson, Arthur B. *Libel and Related Torts*. 2 vols. New York: American Newspaper Publishers Association Foundation, 1969.

Hasiung, James C. *Human Rights in East Asia: A Cultural Perspective*. New York: Paragon House Publishers, 1995.

Hester, Al, and Kristina White, eds. *Creating a Free Press in Eastern Europe*. Athens, Ga.: James M. Cox. Jr. Center for International Mass Communication Training and Research, Henry W. Grady College of Journalism and Mass Communication, University of Georgia, 1993.

Heinke, Rex S. *Media Law*. Washington, D.C.: Bureau of National Affairs, 1994.

Heuvel, Jon Vanden, and Everette E. Dennis. *The Unfolding Lotus: East Asia's Changing Media*. New York: Freedom Forum Media Studies Center, Columbia University, 1993.

Hinton, Harold C. *Korea Under New Leadership: The Fifth Republic*. New York: Praeger Publishers, 1983.

Hixon, Richard F. *Privacy in a Public Society: Human Rights in Conflict*. New York: Oxford University Press, 1987.

Horton, Philip C., ed. *The Third World and Press Freedom*. New York: Praeger Publishers, 1978.

*How Mass Media Are Controlled in South Korea: Pre-Censorship by "Instructions to the Press."* Tokyo: International Labor Movement Institute, 1986.

Hulbert, Homer B. *The Passing of Korea*. Reprint, Seoul: Yonsei University Press, 1969.

*Human Rights in Korea*. New York: Asia Watch, 1986.

*Human Rights in Korea: Facts and Fiction*. Seoul: Korean Overseas Information Service, 1990.

*Human Rights Violations Under the National Security Laws in Asian Countries*. Seoul: Korea NGOs' Network for the U.N. World Conference on Human Rights, 1993.

Hurst, G. Cameron, III. *Korea 1988: A Nation at the Crossroads*. Lawrence, Kan.: Center for East Asian Studies, University of Kansas, 1988.

*An Introduction to the Press Arbitration Commission*. Seoul: [Press Arbitration Commission, n.d.].

IPI [International Press Institute]. *Government Pressures on the Press*. Zurich: International Press Institute, 1955.

*JAK [Journalists Association of Korea] in Brief*. Seoul: Journalists Association of Korea, [1982].

*The Japanese Press 1993*. Tokyo: Japanese Press Institute, 1993.

*Judicial System of Korea*. Seoul: Supreme Court of Korea, 1991.

Kalven, Harry, Jr. *A Worthy Tradition: Freedom of Speech in America*. Edited by Jamie Kalven. New York: Harper & Row, 1988.

Kang, Hyeon-Dew, ed. *Changing International Order in North-East Asia and Communications Policies*. Seoul: Nanam Publishing House, 1992.

———. *International Communications in North-East Asia*. Seoul: Nanam Publishing House, 1994.

Karpen, Ulrich, ed. *The Constitution of the Federal Republic of Germany: Essays on the Basic Rights and Principles of the Basic Law with a Translation of the Basic Law*. Baden-Baden, Germany: Nomos Verlagsgesellschaft, 1988.

Kaufman, Henry R., ed. *LDRC [Libel Defense Resource Center] 50-State Survey 1987: Current Developments in Media Libel and Invasion of Privacy Law*. New York: Libel Defense Resource Center, 1987.

*KBC: Korean Broadcasting Commission 1989*. Seoul: Korean Broadcasting Commission, 1989.

Keeton, W. Page, Dan B. Dobbs, Robert E. Keeton, and David 'T. Owen. *Prosser and Keeton on the Law of Torts*. 5th ed. St. Paul, Minn.: West Publishing Co., 1984.

Kelly, Sean. *Access Denied: The Politics of Press Censorship*. The Washington Papers, no. 55. Beverly Hills, Calif.: Sage Publications, 1978.

Kim, Bong-Ki. *History of Korean Journalism*, 2 vols. Seoul: Korea Information Service, 1967, 1969.

Kim, Chan-Jin, ed. *Business Laws in Korea*. 2d ed. Seoul: Panmun Book Co., [1988].

Kim, Chie-woon, and Jae-won Lee, eds. *Elite Media Amidst Mass Culture: A Critical Look at Mass Communication in Korea*. Seoul: Nanam Publishing House, 1994.

Kim, C.I. Eugene, and Han-Kyo Kim. *Korea and the Politics of Imperialism, 1876–1910*. Berkeley: University of California Press, 1967.

Kim, Dae-jung. *Korea and Asia: A Collection of Essays, Speeches, and Discussions*. Seoul: Kim Dae-jung Peace Foundation Press, 1994.

Kim, Ilpyong J., and Young Whan Kihl, eds. *Political Change in South Korea*. New York: Korean PWPA, Inc., 1988.

Kim, Joungwon Alexander. *Divided Korea: The Politics of Development, 1945–1972*. Cambridge: East Asian Research Center, Harvard University, 1975.

Kim, Kyu, Won-Yong Kim, and Jong-Geun Kang. *Broadcasting in Korea*. Seoul: Nanam Publishing House, 1994.

Kim, Young C. *Japanese Journalists and Their World*. Charlottesville, Va.: University Press of Virginia, 1981.

Kim, Young C., and Abraham M. Halpern, eds. *The Future of the Korean Peninsula*. New York: Praeger, 1977.

*Korea Annual 1994*. 31st annual ed. Seoul: Yonhap News Agency, 1994.

*Korea Annual 1990*. 27th annual ed. Seoul: Yonhap News Agency, 1990.

*Korea Annual 1984*. 21st annual ed. Seoul: Yonhap News Agency, 1984.

Korean Association of IVR, ed. *Philosophy of Law and Social Philosophy East and West*. Seoul: Bobmun Publishing Co., 1990.

Korean Branch of International Association of Constitutional Law, ed. *Constitutional and Political Laws of the Republic of Korea*. Seoul: Korean Constitutional Law Institute, 1995.

Korean National Commission for UNESCO, comp. *UNESCO Korea Survey*. Seoul: Dong-A Publishing Co., 1960.

*The Korean Press 1995*. Seoul: Korean Press Institute, 1995.

*The Korean Press 1994*. Seoul: Korean Press Institute, 1994.

*The Korean Press 1993*. Seoul: Korean Press Institute, 1993.
*The Korean Press 1991*. Seoul: Korean Press Institute, 1991.
*The Korean Press 1990*. Seoul: Korean Press Institute, 1990.
*The Korean Press 1989*. Seoul: Korean Press Institute, 1989.
*The Korean Press 1988*. Seoul: Korean Press Institute, 1988.
*The Korean Press 1987*. Seoul: Korean Press Institute, 1987.
*The Korean Press 1986*. Seoul: Korean Press Institute, 1986.
*The Korean Press 1985*. Seoul: Korean Press Institute, 1985.
*The Korean Press 1984*. Seoul: Korean Press Institute, 1984.
*Korea's History*. Seoul: Korean Overseas Information Service, n.d.
Ku, Dae-yeol. *Korea Under Colonialism: The March First Movement and Anglo-Japanese Relations*. Seoul: Seoul Computer Press, 1985.
Kurian, George Thomas, ed. *World Press Encyclopedia*. 2 vols. New York: Facts on File, Inc., 1982.
Lahav, Pnina, ed. *Press Law in Modern Democracies: A Comparative Study*. New York: Longman, 1985.
Laqueur, Walter, and Barry Rubin, eds. *The Human Rights Reader*. Rev. ed. New York: New American Library, 1989.
*Laws of the Republic of Korea*. 4th ed. 3 vols. Seoul: Korean Legal Center, 1994.
————. 3d ed. Seoul: Korean Legal Center, 1975.
————. 2d ed. Seoul: Korean Legal Center, 1969.
Lawyers for a Democratic Society and National Council of Churches in Korea. *Human Rights in South Korea: Counter Report to the Human Rights Committee on the Initial Report Submitted by the Republic of Korea Under Article 40 of the International Covenant on Civil and Political Rights*. Seoul: Lawyers for a Democratic Society and Human Rights Committee of the National Council of Churches in Korea, 1992.
Lee, Han-Been. *Korea: Time, Change, and Administration*. Honolulu: East-West Center Press, 1968.
Lee, Ki-baik. *A New History of Korea*. Translated by Edward W. Wagner with the assistance of Edward J. Shultz. Seoul: Ilchokak Publishers, 1984.
Lee, Manwoo. *The Odyssey of Korean Democracy: Korean Politics, 1987–1990*. New York: Praeger, 1990.
Lee, Won Sul. *The United States and the Division of Korea, 1945*. Seoul: Kyung Hee University Press, 1982.
Leng, Shao-chuan, ed. *Coping with Crises: How Governments Deal with Emergencies*. Lanham, Md.: University Press of American, Inc., 1990.
Lent, John A., ed. *The Asian Newspapers' Reluctant Revolution*. Ames, Iowa: Iowa State University Press, 1971.
Levy, Leonard W. *Emergence of a Free Press*. New York: Oxford University Press, 1985.
Lewis, Anthony. *Make No Law: The Sullivan Case and the First Amendment*. New York: Random House, 1991.
Lichtenberg, Judith, ed. *Democracy and the Mass Media: A Collection of Essays*. Cambridge: Cambridge University Press, 1990.
Löffler, Martin, Heribert Golsong, and Götz Frank. *Das Gegendarstellungsrecht in Europa: Möglichkeiten der Harmonisierung* (The Right of Reply in Europe: Possibilities of Harmonization), Mönich: C.H. Beck'sche Verlagsbuchhandlung, 1974.
London, Martin, and Barbara Dill. *At What Price?: Libel Law and Freedom of the Press*. [New York]: Twentieth Century Fund Press, 1993.
Lyman, Albert, comp. and ed. *Selected Legal Opinions of the Department of Justice, United States Army Military Government in Korea: Opinions Rendered in the Role of Legal Adviser to the Military Government of Korea, and Covering a Period from March 1946, to August 1948*. 2 vols. Seoul: Department of Justice, Headquarters, United States Army Military Government in Korea, 1948.
Macdonald, Donald Stone. *The Koreans: Contemporary Politics and Society*. 2d ed. Boulder, Colo.: Westview Press, 1990.
Marsh, Norman S., ed. *Public Access to Government-Held Information: A Comparative Symposium*. London: Stevens & Son, 1987.

McCune, George M., and Arthur L. Grey. *Korea Today*. Cambridge: Harvard University Press, 1950.

McWhirter, Darien A. *Freedom of Speech, Press, and Assembly*. Phoenix: Oryx Press, 1994.

Meade, E. Grant. *American Military Government in Korea*. New York: King's Crown Press, 1951.

Melone, Albert P., and George Mace, eds. *Judicial Review and American Democracy*. Ames, Iowa: Iowa State University Press, 1988.

Merrill, John C. *A Handbook of the Foreign Press*. Baton Rouge, La.: Louisiana State University Press, 1959.

———. *The Dialectic in Journalism: Toward a Responsible Use of Press Freedom*. Baton Rouge, La.: Louisiana State University Press, 1989.

———. *The Imperative of Freedom: A Philosophy of Journalistic Autonomy*. New York: Freedom House, 1990.

———, ed. *Global Journalism: Survey of International Communication*. 3d ed. White Plains, N.Y.: Longman Publishers USA, 1995.

Merrill, John C., Carter R. Bryan, and Marvin Alisky. *The Foreign Press: A Survey of the World's Journalism*. Baton Rouge, La.: Louisiana State University Press, 1974.

Merrill, John C., and S. Jack Odell. *Philosophy and Journalism*. New York: Longman, 1983.

Metcalf, Slade R. *Rights and Liabilities of Publishers, Broadcasters and Reporters*. Shepard's/McGraw-Hill, Inc., 1994.

Middleton, Kent R., and Bill F. Chamberlin. *The Law of Public Communication*. 3d ed. New York: Longman, 1994

*Military Revolution in Korea*. Seoul: The Secretariat, Supreme Council for National Reconstruction, 1961.

Min, Kwan-Shik. "Personal Reflections on Democracy in Korea." *Center for Korean Studies Colloquium Paper*, no. 3. Honolulu: Center for Korean Studies, University of Hawaii, 1975.

Ministry of Court Administration, comp. *Justice in Korea*. Seoul: Supreme Court of the Republic of Korea, 1981.

Mueller, Gerhard O.W., ed. *The Korean Criminal Code*. American Series of Foreign Penal Codes, no. 2. Translated by Paul Ryu. South Hackensack, N.J.: Fred B. Rothman & Co., 1960.

Nahm, Andrew C. *A History of the Korean People: Tradition and Transformation*. Seoul: Hollym, 1988.

Nimmer, Melville B., Paul Marcus, and David Myers. *Cases and Materials on Copyrights and Other Aspects of Entertainment Litigation Including Unfair Competition, Defamation, Privacy Illustrated*. 4th ed. St. Paul, Minn.: West Publishing Co., 1991.

Nimmo, Dan, and Michael W. Mansfield. *Government and the News Media: Comparative Dimensions*. Waco, Texas: Baylor University Press, 1982.

Noam, Eli, Seisuke Komatsuzaki, and Douglas A. Conn. *Telecommunications in the Pacific Basin: An Evolutionary Approach*. New York: Oxford University Press, 1994.

Noda, Yosiyuki. *Introduction to Japanese Law*. Translated and edited by Anthony H. Angelo. Tokyo: University of Tokyo Press, 1976.

Oh, John Kie-Chiang. *Korea: Democracy on Trial*. Ithaca, N.Y.: Cornell University Press, 1968.

Oliver, Robert T. *Syngman Rhee and American Involvement in Korea, 1942–1960: A Personal Narrative*. Seoul: Panmun Book Co., 1978.

O'Neil, Patrick, ed. *The Media and Global Democratization*. Forthcoming.

Overbeck, Wayne. *Major Principles of Media Law*. 1994 ed. Fort Worth: Harcourt Brace, 1995.

Pae, Sung Moon. *Korea Leading Developing Nations: Economy, Democracy and Welfare*. Lanham, Md.: University Press of America, 1992.

Park, Chung Hee. *Our Nation's Path: Ideology of Social Reconstruction*. Seoul: Dong-A Publishing Co., 1962.

Peaslee, Amos J., ed. *Constitutions of Nations*. 2d ed. 3 vols. The Hague: Martin Nijhoff, 1956.

Pember, Don R. *Mass Media Law*. 1996 ed. Dubuque, Iowa: Brown & Benchmark, 1996.

*Progress in Democracy: The Pacific Basin Experience*. Seoul: Ilhae Institute, [1987].

Redden, Kenneth Robert. *Modern Legal Systems Cyclopedia*. Buffalo, N.Y.: Williams S. Hein & Co., 1989.

Redish, Martin H. *Freedom of Expression: A Critical Analysis*. Charlottesville, Va.: Michie Co., 1984.

Reporters Sans Frontiers. *1992 Report: Freedom of the Press Throughout the World*. London: John Libbey & Co., 1992.

Republic of Korea. *Consideration of Reports Submitted by States Parties Under Article 40 of the Covenant*. [Seoul: Ministry of Justice, 1991].

*Retreat from Reform: Labor Rights and Freedom of Expression in South Korea*. New York: Human Rights Watch, 1990.

Robinson, Michael Edson. *Cultural Nationalism in Colonial Korea, 1920–1925*. Seattle: University of Washington Press, 1989.

Robinson, Thomas W. *Democracy and Development in East Asia: Taiwan, South Korea and the Philippines*. Washington, D.C.: AEI Press, 1991.

Roh, Tae Woo. *Korea, a Nation Transformed: Selected Speeches of Roh Tae Woo, President of the Republic of Korea*. Oxford: Pergamon Press, 1990.

————. *Korea in the Pacific Century: Selected Speeches, 1990–1992*. Lanham, Md.: University Press of America, 1992.

Rosen, Philip T., ed. *International Handbook of Broadcasting Systems*. New York: Greenwood Press, 1988.

Rosini, Neil J. *The Practical Guide to Libel Law*. New York: Praeger, 1991.

Rothenberg, Ignaz. *The Newspaper: A Study in the Workings of the Daily Press and Its Laws*. New York: Staples Press, 1946.

Sack, Robert D., and Sandra S. Baron. *Libel, Slander, and Related Problems*. 2d ed. New York: Practising Law Institute, 1994.

Sanford, Bruce W. *Libel and Privacy*. 2d ed. Englewood Cliffs, N.J.: Prentice Hall Law & Business, 1996.

Savada, Andrea Matles, and William Shaw, eds. *South Korea: A Country Study*. 4th ed. Washington, D.C.: Headquarters, Department of the Army, 1992.

Schlesinger, Rudolf B., Hans W. Baade, Mirjan R. Damaska, and Peter E. Herzog. *Comparative Law*. 5th ed. Mineola, N.Y.: Foundation Press, 1988.

Schwarz, Urs. *Press Law for Our Times: The Example of the German Legislation*. Zurich: International Press Institute, 1966.

Shapiro, Martin. *Freedom of Speech: The Supreme Court and Judicial Review*. Englewood Cliffs, N.J.: Prentice-Hall, 1966.

Sharp, Eugene W. "The Censorship and Press Laws of Sixty Countries." *The University of Missouri Bulletin*, vol. 37 no. 24. [Columbia: University of Missouri], November 1, 1936.

Shaw, William, ed. *Human Rights in Korea: Historical and Policy Perspectives*. Cambridge: East Asian Legal Studies Program of the Harvard Law School and the Council on East Asian Studies, Harvard University, 1991.

Shearman, Montague, and O.T. Rayner, eds. *The Press Laws of Foreign Countries with an Appendix Containing the Press Laws of India*. London: His Majesty's Stationery Office, 1926.

Shin, Bum Shik, comp. *Major Speeches by Korea's Park Chung Hee*. Seoul: Hollym Corp., 1970.

Shin, Woong Shik. *Comparative Analysis of Korean and American Judicial System*. Chicago: American Judicature Society, 1974.

Siebert, Fred S., Theodore Peterson, and Wilbur Schramm. *Four Theories of the Press*. Urbana, Ill.: University of Illinois Press, 1956.

Siebert, Frederick Seaton. *Freedom of the Press in England, 1476–1776*. Urbana: University of Illinois Press, 1952.

Sigur, Christopher J., ed. *Continuity and Change in Contemporary Korea*. New York: Carnegie Council on Ethics and International Affairs, 1994.

————. *Democracy in Korea: The Roh Tae Woo Years*. New York: Carnegie Council on Ethics and International Affairs, 1992.

————. *Korea's New Challenges and Kim Young Sam*. New York: Carnegie Council on Ethics and International Affairs, 1993.

Smolla, Rodney A. *Free Speech in an Open Society*. New York: Alfred A. Knopf, 1992.

————. *Law of Defamation*. Deerfield, Ill.: Clark Boardman Callaghan, 1995.

————. *Suing the Press*. New York: Oxford University Press, 1986.

Sohn, Hak-Kyu. *Authoritarianism and Opposition in South Korea*. London: Routledge, 1989.

Soloski, John, and Randall P. Bezanson, eds. *Reforming Libel Law*. New York: Guilford Press, 1992.

Song, Sang Hyun, ed. *Introduction to the Law and Legal System of Korea*. Seoul: Kyung Mun Sa Publishing Co., 1983.

*South Korea: Violations of Human Rights*. London: Amnesty International Publications, 1986.

Sprinzak, Ehud, and Larry Diamond. *Israeli Democracy Under Stress*. Boulder, Colo.: Lynne Rienner Publishers, 1993.

Steinberg, David I. *The Republic of Korea: Economic Transformation and Social Change*. Boulder, Colo.: Westview Press, 1989.

*A Stern, Steady Crackdown: Legal Process and Human Rights in South Korea*. [New York]: Asia Watch Committee, 1987.

*The Structure for Democracy: Round Table for Journalists and Media Unions*. [Seoul: Korean Federation of Press Unions and Journalists Association of Korea, 1993].

Suh, Dae-Sook, and Chae-Jin Lee, *Political Leadership in Korea*. Seattle: University of Washington Press, 1976.

Suh, Dae-Sook, ed. *Korean Studies: New Pacific Currents*, Honolulu: Center for Korean Studies, University of Hawaii, 1994.

Sussman, Leonard R. *Power, the Press and the Technology of Freedom: The Coming Age of ISDN*. New York: Freedom House, 1989.

Toynbee, Arnold, ed. *Survey of International Affairs, 1939–1946: The Far East, 1942–46*. London: Oxford University Press, 1955.

Tribe, Laurence H. *American Constitutional Law*. 2d ed. Mineola, N.Y.: Foundation Press, 1988.

U.S. House Subcommittee on Asian and Pacific Affairs of the Committee on Foreign Affairs. *Developments in Korea*. September 17, 1987.

————. *Update on Political Developments in Korea*. June 30, 1987.

Verploeg, Hans, and Tony Wilton. *Press Freedom in Korea: The Search for Professionalism*. Brussel: International Federation of Journalists, 1991.

Watanabe, Haruko. "South Korean Press, 1945–." *Freedom of Information Center Publication*, no. 119. Columbia, Mo.: School of Journalism, University of Missouri, March 1964.

Wells, Alan, ed. *Mass Communications: A World View*. Palo Alto, Calif.: National Press Books, 1974.

Westin, Alan F. *Privacy and Freedom*. New York: Atheneum, 1967.

Woo, Jisuk. "The Personal Data Protection Regime Emerging in Korea." In *Pacific Telecommunications Conference Proceedings*. Honolulu: Pacific Telecommunications Association, 1993.

"World Press Freedom, 1967," *Freedom of Information Center Report*, no. 201. Columbia, Mo.: School of Journalism, University of Missouri, 1968.

Wright, Edward Reynolds, ed. *Korean Politics in Transition*. Seattle: University of Washington Press, 1975.

Yaniv, Avner, ed. *National Security and Democracy in Israel*. Boulder, Colo.: Lynne Rienner Publishers, 1993.

Yim, Seong Hi. *The Impacts on the Korean Society*. Seoul: Nutinamoo Publishing Co., 1990.

Yoon, Dae-Kyu. *Law and Political Authority in South Korea*. Boulder, Colo.: Westview Press, 1990.

Youm, Kyu Ho. "The Impact of *People v. Croswell* on Libel Law." *Journalism Monographs*, no. 113. Columbia, S.C.: Association for Education in Journalism and Mass Communication, 1989.

————. "Libel Law and the Press in South Korea: An Update." *Occasional Paper/Reprints Series in Contemporary Asian Studies*, no. 110. Baltimore, Md.: School of Law, University of Maryland, 1992.

## Unpublished Material (in English)

Bang, Sang Hoon. "The Korean Press: New Challenges in a Changing World." Speech delivered at the International Press Institute convention, Budapest, Hungary, May 1992 (text on file with author).

Blake, Kenneth R. "Explaining Link Between Source Credibility and Reputational Harm: Effects of Publication Type on Belief of Unfavorable Statements." Paper presented at the Southeast Colloquium of the Association for Education in Journalism and Mass Communication, Gainesville, Florida, March 1995.

Chang, Hosoon. "National Security v. First Amendment Freedoms: U.S. Supreme Court Decisions on Anti-Communist Regulations, 1919–1974." Ph.D. diss., University of North Carolina-Chapel Hill, 1993.

Chang, Won Ho, and Young-Khee Kim. "Media Reform in Korea." Paper presented at the western conference of the Association for Asian Studies, Long Beach, Calif., October 1989.

Cho, Yong-Whan. "Korea at the Crossroads: Violation of Freedom of Expression and Its Implications for Democracy." Research manuscript, Seoul, 1995 (on file with author).

Choi, Dai-Kwon. "Law and Social Change: The Korean Experience." Ph.D. diss., University of California-Berkeley, 1976.

Derieux, Emmanuel. "The Right of Reply in France." Paper presented at the Association for Education in Journalism and Mass Communication convention, Montreal, Canada, August 1992.

Engardio, Pete. "Constraints Against Western Standards in South Korean Journalism: A Case Study of the Korea Herald." Research report prepared at the University of Missouri-Columbia School of Journalism, November 1983.

"A Fragile Peace: North and South Korea." ABC television broadcast, November 10, 1983 (transcript on file with author).

Gates, Paul H., Jr., and Bill F. Chamberlin. "Madison Misinterpretation: Historical Presentism Skews Scholarship." Paper presented at the Southeast Colloquium of the Association for Education in Journalism and Mass Communication, Gainesville, Fla., March 1995.

Halvorsen, David E. "The Korean Press: Free, but Is It Responsible?" Lecture delivered at the Korean Journalists Workshop, Honolulu, Hawaii, July 1991 (text on file with author).

———. "Talking Straight About Ethics." English text of David E. Halvorsen, "If Cash Gifts Are Justifiable, Why Not Tell Your Readers?" *Journalism* (Korean) 21 (March 1991): 144–47.

Han, Byoung-ku. "The Kyunghyang-Shinmun and Its Struggles with the Rhee Regime." Master's thesis, University of Missouri-Columbia, 1965.

Han, Gwang-jub, and Jae-chul Shim. "Telecommunication Policy in Korea: A Case of Cable TV Development Planning." Paper presented at the Association for Education in Journalism and Mass Communication conference, Kansas City, Mo., August 1993.

Hoag, C. Leonard. "American Military Government in Korea: War Policy and the First Year of Occupation 1941–1946." Draft manuscript produced under the auspices of the Office of the Chief of Military History, Department of the Army, Washington, D.C., 1970.

Hong, Chong-in. "The March of Korean Journalism: A Brief History of Early Korean Journalism." Paper presented at the World Media conference, Seoul, Korea, October 1982.

"JFK Assassination: Conspiracy Theories." ABC television broadcast, November 11, 1983 (transcript on file with author).

Jung, Tae Chul. "The Media, Social Conflict and Change in South Korea: A Critical Analysis." Ph.D. diss., University of Missouri-Columbia, August 1989.

Kang, Han Mu. "The United States Military Government in Korea, 1945–1948: An Analysis and Evaluation of Its Policy." Ph.D. diss., University of Cincinnati, Cincinnati, Ohio, 1970.

Kang, Myungkoo. "From Watchdog to Power: Journalists' Career Movement Toward Political Power." Paper presented at the Association for Education in Journalism and Mass Communication convention, Kansas City, Mo., August 1993.

Kim, Chong-Chol. "The Freedom of Press and the Related Laws in Korea." Lecture delivered in the Arizona State University Walter Cronkite School of Journalism and Telecommunication, Tempe, Ariz., June 1994 (text on file with author).

"Kim Dae Jung's Return: What Happened & Why?" ABC television broadcast, February 11, 1985 (transcript on file with author).

Kim, Jong-ki. "The Consequences of South Korea's Political Communication for the Political System in Transition During Two Successive Authoritarian Regimes (1972–79 and 1979–88)." Paper presented at the International Association for Mass Communication Research convention, Seoul, South Korea, July 1994.

Kim, Keun Tae. "Prospects and Tasks of Democracy in Korea." Paper prepared for the Transformation in the Korean Peninsula Toward the 21st Century: Peace, Unity and Progress conference, East Lansing, Mich., July 1993.

Kim, Ki Hee. "National Aspects Which Influence the Development of Modern Mass Media in the Republic of Korea (South)." Master's thesis, University of Texas-Austin, 1971.

Kim, Pyung Woo. "Mass Communication in Korea." Paper presented at the Law of the World convention, Seoul, September 1987.

Kline, Karen E. "Exploring the Possibilities of an International Right of Correction." Paper presented at the Association for Education in Journalism and Mass Communication convention, Boston, Mass., August 1991.

Koh, B.C. "Democratization and External Relations." Paper presented at the Korea's Democratic Experiment convention, Seoul, Korea, June 1991.

Koh, Myung Shik. "A History of Korean Journalism Under U.S. Military Government, 1945–1948." Master's thesis, University of Iowa, 1967.

Ku, Bon-Hak. "Libel Laws and Regulations: United States and South Korea Compared." Research paper prepared at the Columbia University Graduate School of Journalism, 1994.

Lee, Jae-Jin. "Korean Libel Laws in Transition: 1981–1993." Master's thesis, University of Iowa, 1995.

Lee, Jae-kyoung. "A Crisis of the South Korean Media: The Rise of Civil Society and Democratic Transition." Paper presented at the Association for Education in Journalism and Mass Communication convention, Kansas City, Mo., August 1993.

———. "Manufacturing American Patronage: Korean Military Regime's Management of U.S.-Related News in the 1980s." Paper presented at the International Association for Mass Communication Research convention, Seoul, July 1994.

Lee, Young Ho. "The Political Culture of Modernizing Society: Political Attitudes and Democracy in Korea." Ph.D. diss., Yale University, 1969.

Lim, Sang-won "The Press Law of Korea (South)." Research paper prepared for Journalism 425: Controls of Information at the University of Missouri-Columbia School of Journalism, 1982.

Macdonald, Donald S. "Soldiers Run a Country: Organization of U.S. Military Government in Korea." Paper presented at the Association for Asian Studies convention, Los Angeles, Calif., March 1993.

Manheim, Jarol B. "Culture in Conflict: External Communications and U.S.-Korean Relations." Paper presented at the International Communication Association convention, New Orleans, La., June 1988.

Moon, Sukhyon Kim. "Aspects of Korean Press Development: From Its Beginnings to the Present." Ph.D. diss., University of Maryland, 1988.

Moore, Roy L. "A Comparative Analysis of Press and Telecommunications Law in the United States and the Federal Republic of Germany." Paper presented at the Southeast Colloquium of the Association for Education in Journalism and Mass Communication convention, Athens, Ga., March 1985.

Nam, Sunwoo. "A Comparative Study of Freedom of the Press in Korea, Taiwan, and the Philippines in the 1960's." Ph.D. diss., University of Wisconsin-Madison, 1969.

"1984: Secrecy, Security and the Media." ABC television broadcast, January 19, 1984 (transcript on file with author).

Novak, Robert. "The Press: Protector of Freedom or Violator of Privacy." Paper presented at the Reforms in Korean Society convention, Seoul, Korea, September 1993.

Park, Hong-Kyu. "Development Dictatorship and Human Rights: Human Rights Violations and National Security Ideology in Asia, esp. Korea." Paper presented at the International Conference on National Security Laws in the Asia-Pacific, Seoul, Korea, November 1995.

Park, Yong-Sang. "The Korean Press Under the Park Regime." Research paper prepared for Journalism 425: Controls of Information at the University of Missouri-Columbia School of Journalism, [April 1980].

Robinson, Deanna Campbell, Won Woo-hyun, and Yoon Sun-hee. "The Productive Context in South Korea: An Historical Analysis." Paper presented at the Pacific Telecommunications conference, Honolulu, Hawaii, January 1992.

Salwen, Michael B. "Press Freedom in the Republic of Korea: Coping with the Authoritarian Structure." Paper presented at the International Communication Association convention, New Orleans, La., May 1988.

Splichal, Sigman L. "The U.S. Supreme Court and the Practical Obscurity Doctrine: Judicial Recognition of 'Forgive and Forget.'" Paper presented at the Southeast Colloquium of the Association for Education in Journalism and Mass Communication, Gainesville, Florida, March 1995.

Yang, Hwee-Boo. "The Government's Authority over the News Media in South Korea." Research paper prepared for Journalism 425: Controls of Information at the University of Missouri-Columbia School of Journalism, Winter 1983.

Yang, Kun. "Freedom of Expression and Regulation of Mass Media in Korea: Changes in Law and Reality." Paper presented at the Law and Society Association convention, Phoenix, Ariz., June 1994.

Yoo, Kum Soon. "Syngman Rhee and His Press Relations, 1948–1960." Master's thesis, Indiana University, 1965.

Yoon, Dae-Kyu. "Law and Political Authority: A Study on the Rule of Law in Korea." Ph.D. diss., University of Washington, 1987.

Yoon, Youngchul. "Political Transition and Press Ideology in South Korea." Ph.D. diss., University of Minnesota, 1989.

———. "Political Transition and Press Reform in South Korea." Paper presented at the International Communication Association convention, San Francisco, Calif., May 1989.

Youm, Kyu Ho. "Freedom of the Press in South Korea, 1945–1983: A Sociopolitical and Legal Perspective." Ph.D. diss., Southern Illinois University-Carbondale, 1985.

———. "The Innocent Construction Rule as a Libel Defense: Its Strengths, Weaknesses, and Uncertain Future." Master's thesis, Southern Illinois University-Carbondale, 1982.

———. "Press Freedom in South Korea: A Process of Ebb and Flow." Paper presented at the Third World Studies convention, Omaha, Neb., October 1988.

Youm, Kyu Ho, and Michael B. Salwen. "Press Freedom and Social and Economic Progress in the Far East: The Case of South Korea." Paper presented at the Association for Education in Journalism and Mass Communication convention, Portland, Ore., July 1988.

Yu, Jae Cheon. "The Current Problems of Press Freedom in Korea." Master's thesis, University of Minnesota, 1972.

## Journal Articles (in English)

Allen, Eric W. "International Origins of the Newspapers: The Establishment of Periodicity in Print." English Journalism 7 (1930): 307–19.

Alter, Jonathan. "The Media Gap." Newsweek. July 19, 1993, p. 20.

Altman, Albert A. "Korea's First Newspaper: The Japanese Chosen shinpo." Journal of Asian Studies 43 (August 1984): 685–96.

"The Amended Constitution of South Korea." ICJ [International Commission of Jurists] Review, no. 26 (1981): 17–23.

Archer, Eric. "Opening the Doors to Government Proceedings: The Citizen as Critic." Connecticut Law Review 19 (1989): 561–87.

Barron, Jerome A. "Access to the Press—A New First Amendment Right." Harvard Law Review 80 (1967): 1641–78.

———. "The Right of Reply to the Media in the United States: Resistance and Resurgence." Hastings Communications and Entertainment Law Journal 15 (1992): 1–20.

Beer, Lawrence W. "Defamation, Privacy, and Freedom of Expression in Japan." Law in Japan: An Annual 5 (1972): 192–208.

―――. "Freedom of Expression: The Continuing Revolution in Japan's Legal Culture." *Law and Contemporary Problems* 53 (Spring 1990): 39–69.

Bellah, Robert N. "The Meaning of Reputation in American Society." *California Law Review* 74 (1986): 743–51.

Blasi, Vincent. "The Checking Value in First Amendment Theory." *American Bar Foundation Journal* (1977): 521–649.

Bratt, Eyvind. "Government and the Press: A Comparative Analysis." *Journalism Quarterly* 21 (1944): 185–99.

Butler, William J. "Political Repression in South Korea—1974." *ICJ [International Commission of Jurists] Review*, no. 13 (1974): 37–44.

Cate, Fred H. "The First Amendment and the International 'Free Flow' of Information." *Virginia Journal of International Law* 30 (1990): 371–420.

Chang, Chun-ha. "Freedom Reappraised." *Korea Journal* 2 (March 1962): 10–11.

Chhoe, Chun. "Characteristics of Korea [sic] Press." *Korea Journal* 2 (May 1962): 6–7.

―――. "Politics and the Press in Korea." *Korean Affairs* 3 (December 1964): 296–303.

Cho, Kyu-ha. "Korean Press Inaugurates Ethics Commission to Further Freedom." *Korea Journal* 1 (October 1961): 25–26.

Choe, Chung-ho. "The Modernization of Korea and Communication Culture of Two Decades." *Korea Journal* 22 (March 1982): 26–32.

Choi, Chongko. "Constitution and Democracy in Korea." *Seoul Law Journal* 34 (February 1993): 128–35.

―――. "The Judiciary Needs Reform." *Korea Focus* 1 (1993): 79–80.

―――. "Legal Philosophy and Theory in Korea: A Survey." *Seoul Law Journal* 32 (December 1991): 61–70.

Chong, Chin-sok. "E.T. Bethell and the Taehan Maeil Shinbo." *Korea Journal* 24 (April 1984): 39–44.

"Chun Regime Purged 717 Journalists." *IPI [International Press Institute] Report*, January 1989, p. 23.

Clark, William, Jr. "Korea: Moving Quickly Toward Democracy." *Department of State Bulletin* 87 (November 1987): 29–31 [statement by William Clark, Jr., Deputy Secretary for East Asian and Pacific Affairs, before the Subcommittee on Asian and Pacific Affairs of the House Foreign Affairs Committee, September 17, 1987].

Clifford, Mark. "Land of the Bribe." *Far Eastern Economic Review*, February 28, 1991, pp. 8–9.

―――. "Law and Liberty." *Far Eastern Economic Review*, March 2, 1989, pp. 24, 26.

―――. "Making Justice Blind." *Far Eastern Economic Review*, August 11, 1988, p. 16.

―――. "Read and in the Black." *Far Eastern Economic Review*, June 24, 1993, pp. 62–63.

Cohen, Margot. "Taiwan's Press Breaks Loose." *Columbia Journalism Review*, September–October 1988, p. 16.

Crabble, Robert. "S. Korea's Secret Police Cancel Ads in Dong-A Ilbo." *Editor & Publisher*, Feb. 15, 1975, p. 13.

Danziger, Charles. "The Right of Reply in the United States and Europe." *New York University Journal of International Law and Politics* 19 (1986): 171–201.

Desmond, Edward W. "A Step Toward Conciliation." *Time*, June 1, 1987, p. 30 (Pacific. ed.).

Donnelly, Richard C. "The Right of Reply: An Alternative to an Action for Libel." *Virginia Law Review* 34 (1948): 867–900.

Doronila, Amando. "The Role of Media in Strengthening Democracy." *Democratic Institutions* 1 (1992): 39–47.

"Dramatic Improvement." *IPI [International Press Institute] Report*, September–October 1988, p. 11.

Emerson, Tony. "Too Rich, Too Soon." *Newsweek*, November 11, 1991, p. 12 (Pacific ed.).

Enger, William. "Korean Copyright Reform." *UCLA Pacific Basin Law Journal* 7 (Spring 1990): 199–213.

Ensor, Paul. "A Closed Cartel, but with Fierce Competition." *Far Eastern Economic Review*, August 22, 1985, pp. 26–28.

―――. "Government-Owned TV Reflects Official View." *Far Eastern Economic Review*, August 22, 1985, pp. 28–29.

Flanz, Gisbert. "Korea and Vietnam: Two Constitutional Experiments." *St. John's Law Review* 42 (1967): 18–37.

Fried, Charles. "Privacy." *Yale Law Journal* 77 (1968): 475–93.

Gadacz, Oles. "Korean Press Freedom Issues Loom." *Advertising Age*, January 4, 1988, p. 23.

Galliner, Peter. "World Press Freedom Review." *IPI [International Press Institute] Report*, December 1988, pp. 1–3.

Gastil, Raymond D. "The Comparative Survey of Freedom 1983." *Freedom at Issue*, January–February 1983, pp. 3–14.

———. "The Comparative Survey of Freedom 1984." *Freedom at Issue*, January–February 1984, pp. 3–15.

———. "The Comparative Survey of Freedom: 1989." *Freedom at Issue*, January–February 1989, pp. 46–52.

Gibbons, Boyd. "The South Koreans." *National Geographic* 174 (August 1988): 232–57.

Gibbons, Thomas. "Freedom of the Press: Ownership and Editorial Values." *Public Law*, Summer 1992, pp. 279–99.

Gillmor, Donald M. "Freedom in Press Systems and the Religious Variable." *Journalism Quarterly* 39 (1962): 15–26.

Gray, Oscar S. "Constitutional Protection of Freedom of Expression in the United States as It Affects Defamation law." *American Journal of Comparative Law* 38 (1990): 463–55.

Greenberg, Bradley S. "Additional Data on Variables Related to Press Freedom." *Journalism Quarterly* 38 (1961): 76–78.

Griffith, Thomas. "It's News, but Is It Reality?" *Time*, May 27, 1994, p. 67.

Hamburger, Philip. "The Development of the Law of Seditious Libel and the Control of the Press." *Stanford Law Review* 37 (1985): 661–765.

Han, Boo-Whan. "Major Features of the Constitution of the Sixth Republic of Korea and Its Two-Year's Implementation." *Justice* 23 (1990): 99–111.

Han, Gwang-jub. "The Cable Television Development Planning in Korea: A Critique." *Sungkok Journalism Review* 5 (Fall 1994): 23–64.

Han, Sung-joo. "An Assessment of the Ho Chong and Chang Myon Governments." *Korea Journal* 22 (May 1982): 4–13.

Han, Sung-Joo. "Korea's Democratic Experiment: 1987–1991." *Democratic Institutions* 1 (1992): 63–78.

———. "South Korea in 1987: The Politics of Democratization." *Asian Survey* 28 (January 1988): 52–61.

———. "South Korea in 1988: A Revolution in the Making." *Asian Survey* 29 (January 1989): 29–38.

Han, Tai Yun. "Constitutional Development in Korea." *Koreana Quarterly* 5 (1963): 45–55.

Harvey, Pharis J. "The Honey and the Rod: Controlling Journalism in South Korea." *CPJ [Committee to Protect Journalists] Update*, November–December 1984, pp. 2–3.

Hill, Alfred. "Defamation and Privacy Under the First Amendment." *Columbia Law Review* 76 (1976): 1205–1313.

Hong, I-sop. "Political Philosophy of Korean Confucianism." *Korea Journal* 3 (September 1963): 12–16, 37.

Hwang, Woo Yea. "Efforts to Expedite Judicial Process in Korea." *Korean Journal of Comparative Law* 18 (1990): 174–85.

Hyun, Soong-jong. "The Traditional Laws of Korea and the Modern Laws of the West." *Korea Journal* 15 (October 1975): 11–17.

Im, Yung-Ho. "Media and the Politics of Citizens' Press Movement in Korea, 1985–1993." *Sungkok Journalism Review* 6 (Fall 1995): 71–86.

"The Independent Served Pioneer in Korean Journalism." *Korea Journal* 2 (May 1962): 17.

Josephs, Hilary K. "Defamation, Invasion of Privacy, and the Press in the People'sRepublic of China." *UCLA Pacific Basin Law Journal* 11 (1993): 191–215.

Kalven, Harry, Jr. "The New York Times Case: A Note on 'the Central Meaning of the First Amendment.'" *Supreme Court Review* (1964): 191–221.

Kang, Hyeon-Dew. "Development of Early Journalism and Its Reference to the Outside World in Nineteenth Century in Korea." *Sungkok Journalism Review* 2 (Fall 1991): 217–26.

Kang, Joon-Mann. "Reporters and Their Professional and Occupational Commitment in a Developing Country." *Gazette* 40 (1987): 3–20.

Karantnycky, Adrian. "Democracies on the Rise, Democracies at Risk." *Freedom Review*, January–February 1995, pp. 5–10.

Kay, Kwang-kil. "Press Ethics Commission." *Korea Journal* 5 (February 1965): 13–14.

Kent, Kurt E. "Freedom of the Press: An Empirical Analysis of One Aspect of the Concept." *Gazette* 28 (1972): 65–79.

Kihl, Young Whan. "Korea's Fifth Republic: Domestic Political Trends." *Journal of Northeast Asian Studies* 1 (June 1982): 37–55.

———. "South Korea in 1989: Slow Progress Toward Democracy." *Asian Survey* 30 (January 1990): 67–73.

Kim, C.I. Eugene. "Emergency, Development, and Human Rights: South Korea." *Asian Survey* 18 (April 1978): 363–78.

———. "Korea at the Crossroads: The Birth of the Fourth Republic." *Pacific Affairs* 46 (1973): 211–31.

Kim, Chin. "Constitution and Obscenity: Japan and the U.S.A." *American Journal of Comparative Law* 23 (1975): 255–83.

Kim, Dae Jung. "Is Culture Destiny?: The Myth of Asia's Anti-Democratic Values." *Foreign Affairs* 73 (November–December 1994): 189–94.

"Kim Dae-Jung Attacks Leading Newspaper over Tour Story." Associated Press, March 8, 1989.

Kim, Dong-Chol. "Korean Newspapers: Past and Present." *Korean Report* 2 (September–October 1962): 21–23; 2 (November–December 1962): 10–12.

Kim, Dong-Jin. "Development of the Concept of Public Interest in Korean Broadcasting." *Korean Social Science Journal* 14 (1988): 158–72.

Kim, Doo-hun. "Confucian Influences on Korean Society." *Korea Journal* 3 (September 1963): 17–21, 40–41.

Kim, Hakjoon. "The American Military Government in South Korea, 1945–1948: Its Formation, Policies, and Legacies." *Asian Perspective* 12 (Spring–Summer 1988): 51–83.

———. "The Influence of the American Constitution on South Korean Constitutional Government Since 1948." *Asian Perspective* 16 (Fall–Winter 1992): 25–42.

Kim, Hak Soo, and James F. Larson, "Communication and Martial Law in the Republic of Korea, 1979–1988." *Canadian Journal of Communication*, Fall 1988, pp. 87–91 (special issue).

Kim, Joungwon Alexander. "The Republic of Korea: A Quest for New Directions." *Asian Survey* 11 (January 1971): 92–103.

Kim, Ki-Bom. "Certain Features of the Constitution." *Korean Affairs* 3 (April 1964): 20–28.

———. "Revisions of the Korean Constitution." *Korea Journal* 14 (July 1974): 4–13; (August 1974): 18–24.

Kim, Kyu. "South Korean Protest Movements Discover New Ways to Communicate." *Media Development* 35 (1988): 8–9.

Kim, Kyu-whan. "The Past and Present of Journalism in Korea." *Korean Affairs* 1 (1962): 261–66.

Kim, Sang-hyop. "Practice and Ideal of Korean Democracy." *Korea Journal* 7 (March 1967): 8–12.

Kim, Soo-Mi. "Truth or Consequences?" *Business Korea*, December 1988, pp. 76–77.

Kim, Woo-Hyung. "Freedom of Political Speech vs. National Security in Korea: A Historical Survey." *International Lawyer* 5 (1971): 488–510.

Koh, Myung-shik. "Development of the Korean Press." *Korea Journal* 8 (January 1968): 5–9.

Kommers, Donald P. "The Jurisprudence of Free Speech in the United States and the Federal Republic of Germany." *Southern California Law Review* 53 (1980): 657–95.

"Korea—Purge on the Press." *IPI [International Press Institute] Report*, October 1980, pp. 12–13.

"Korean TV Reporters Protest over 'Biased' Election Coverage." *IPI [International Press Institute] Report*, January 1989, p. 2.

Kuo, Peter. "Taiwan's News Media: Its Democratization." *World Affairs* 155 (Winter 1993): 109–116.

Lahav, Pnina. "American Influence on Israel's Jurisprudence of Free Speech." *Hastings Constitutional Law Quarterly* 9 (Fall 1981): 21–108.

Lee, Byung Soo. "Press Freedom During Korea's 5th and 6th Republic." *Sungkok Journalism Review* 1 (Fall 1990): 15–35.

Lee, Chae-Jin. "South Korea in 1983: Crisis Management and Political Legitimacy." *Asian Survey* 24 (January 1984): 112–21.

Lee, Chong–Sik. "South Korea in 1980: The Emergence of a New Authoritarian Order." *Asian Survey* 21 (January 1981): 125–43.

Lee, Dong-Heub. "The Influence of the American Constitution on Korean Constitutional Law." *Justice* 20 (1980): 167–73.

Lee, Ha-Woo. "Human Rights in Korea: The Crisis of Relevance." *Korea Observer* 8 (Summer 1977): 119–42.

Lee, Han-Key. "Constitutional Developments in South Korea." *Hong Kong Law Journal* 4 (1974): 41–51.

Lee, Hyo-Seong. "Political Manipulation and Mass Media During the Sixth Republic in Korea." *Sungkok Journalism Review* 4 (Fall 1993): 93–107.

Lee, Jae-kyoung. "Press Freedom and National Development: Toward a Re-Conceptualization." *Gazette* 48 (1991): 149–63.

Lee, Suk Tae. "South Korea: Implementation and Application of Human Rights Covenants." *Michigan Journal of International Law* 14 (1993): 705–38.

Lent, John A. "Freedom of Press in East Asia." *Human Rights Quarterly* 3 (1981): 137–49.

———. "The Press Under Aquino." *Index on Censorship*, August 1986, pp. 8–9.

———. "Press Freedom in Asia: The Quiet but Completed Revolution." *Gazette* 24 (1978): 41.

———. "Press and Government in East Asia: An Overview." *Asia Quarterly*, no. 2 (1980): 129–37.

Lim, Hy-Sop. "A Study on Legal Values in Korea: An Analysis of Attitude Toward Law." *Social Science Journal* 2 (1974): 59–79.

"At Loggerheads in South Korea." *Time*, March 27, 1989, p. 36 (Pacific ed.).

Manegold, C.S. "Envelopes of 'Good Will.'" *Newsweek*, April 23, 1990, p. 49 (Pacific ed.).

Markin, Terrence C. "South Korea in Transition: Establishing a Better Benchmark to Measure Progress." *Journal of Northeast Asian Studies* 7 (Fall 1988): 44–58.

Massing, Michael. "The Libel Chill: How Cold *Is* It out There?" *Columbia Journalism Review*, May–June 1985, pp. 31–43.

McBeth, John. "Judicial Generosity." *Far Eastern Economic Review*, June 18, 1987, p. 24.

———. "Not Yet Democracy." *Far Eastern Economic Review*, December 15, 1989, p. 29.

McCune, George M. "Post-War Government and Politics of Korea." *Journal of Politics* 9 (1947): 605–23.

McGovern, Melvin P. "Early Western Presses in Korea." *Korea Journal* 7 (July 1967): 21–23.

Merrill, John C. "Inclination of Nations to Control the Press and Attitudes on Professionalization." *Journalism Quarterly* 65 (1988): 839–44.

Min, Bok Ki. "Legally Viewed Anti-Communist Attitude of Korea." *Popcho* [Lawyers Association Journal] 18 (May 1969): 5–10.

Mowlana, Hamid, and Chul-Soo Chin. "Libel Laws of Modern Japan and South Korea Are Compared." *Journalism Quarterly* 48 (1971): 326–30, 348.

Nagel, Robert F. "How Useful Is Judicial Review in Free Speech Cases?" *Cornell Law Review* 69 (1984): 302–40.

Nam, Sunwoo. "The Flow of International News into Korea." *Gazette* 25 (1976): 14–26.

———. "The Korean Press After Park." *Gazette* 26 (1980): 259–66.

———. "Newspapers Under Tribulation: The Present-Day Korean Press?" 27 *Gazette* (1978): 109–20.

———. "The Taming of the Korean Press." *Columbia Journalism Review*, March–April 1978, pp. 43–45.

"The News from Seoul." *Harper's Magazine*, August 1987, pp. 13–14.

Ni, Yen-yuan. "State-Media Relations Under Authoritarian Regimes in South Korea and Taiwan." *Issues & Studies* 31 (October 1993): 99–117.

Nixon, Raymond B. "Factors Related to Freedom in National Press Systems." *Journalism Quarterly* 37 (1960): 13–28.

———. "Freedom in the World's Press: A Fresh Appraisal with New Data." *Journalism Quarterly* 42 (Winter 1965): 3–14, 118–19.

Nord, David Paul. "First Steps Toward a Theory of Press Control." *Journalism History* 4 (Spring 1977): 8–13.

Ogan, Christine L. "Development Journalism/Communication: The Status of the Concept." *Gazette* 29 (1982): 3–13.

Oh, Eugene J. "The Practice of Law in Korea: A Canadian Lawyer's Perspective." *The Advocate* 48 (1990): 751–50.

Oh, Jin-hwan. "Toward a Practical Approach to Journalism in Developing Countries: The Case of South Korea." *Korea Journal* 15 (March 1975): 13–26.

Okonogi, Masao. "South Korea's Experiment in Democracy." *Japan Review of International Affairs* (Spring–Summer 1988): 24–41.

Oliver, Robert T. "Present-Day Newspapers in the Republic of Korea." *Journalism Quarterly* 34 (1957): 85–86.

Paeng, Won-Soon. "Main Characteristics of Korea's Press Law." *Journal of Korean Society for Journalism and Communication Studies* 20 (1985): 35–50.

———. "Press Law in Korea." *Sungkok Journalism Review* 3 (Fall 1992): 5–12.

Paisley, Ed. "Dominance, Submission." *Far Eastern Economic Review*, June 24, 1993, p. 64.

Park, Chong-Min. "Authoritarian Rule in South Korea: Political Support and Governmental Performance." *Asian Survey* 31 (August 1991): 743–61.

Park, Kiljun. "Problems Concerning the Reform of Legal Education in Korea." *Korean Journal of Comparative Law* 6 (1978): 55–98.

Park, Kwon-Sang. "How the Threat Was Met." *IPI [International Press Institute] Report*, October 1964, pp. 1–2.

———. "Papers Still Guilty of Bias." *IPI [International Press Institute] Report*, June–July 1993, pp. 41–42.

Pearce, Alan. "Korea—Purge on the Press." *IPI [International Press Institute] Report*, October 1980, pp. 12–13.

"Persecution of Lawyers in South Korea: Report of DeWind Mission." *CIJL [Center for the Independence of Judges and Lawyers] Bulletin*, October 1979, pp. 24–55.

Picard, Robert G. "Revisions of the 'Four Theories of the Press' Model." *Mass Comm Review* (Winter–Spring 1982–83): 25–28.

Post, Robert C. "The Social Foundations of Defamation Law: Reputation and the Constitution." *California Law Review* 74 (1986): 691–721.

"Press Restrictions Ease After Five Years of Clamps." *IPI [International Press Institute] Report*, September 1985, p. 8.

"Press Under Aquino." *Index on Censorship*, August 1986, pp. 8–9.

Prosser, William L. "Privacy." *California Law Review* 48 (1960): 383–423.

Ray, J. Franklin, Jr. "Reorganization of Educational System." *Voice of Korea*, August 30, 1947, pp. 214–16.

"Renovating a Government Mouthpiece." *Business Korea*, December 1988, p. 79.

"The Revised Constitution of Republic of Korea." *Korean Affairs* 2 (1963): 11.

Rosen, Dan. "Private Lives and Public Eyes: Privacy in the United States and Japan." *Florida Journal of International Law* 6 (1990): 141–75.

Rothenberg, Ignace. "The Right of Reply to Libels in the Press." *Journal of Comparative Legislation and International Law* 23 (1941): 38–59.

Rowland, D. Wayne. "The Press in the Korean Republic: Its Status and Problems." *Journalism Quarterly* 35 (1958): 450–54.

Sanger, David E. "Living-Room Welcome for New 'Invasion.'" *IPI [International Press Institute] Report*, May 1991, pp. 16–17.

Scalapino, Robert A. "Asia at the End of the 1970s." *Foreign Affairs* 58 (1980): 693–737.

————. "Asia: An Uneven Course." *Freedom at Issue*, January–February 1985, pp. 34–37.

Schauer, Frederick. "Social Foundations of the Law of Defamation: A Comparative Analysis." *Journal of Media Law and Practice* 1 (May 1980): 3–23.

Schwartz, Herman. "The New East European Constitutional Courts." *Michigan Journal of International Law* 13 (1992): 741–85.

"Seoul Charges Four in Press Guidelines Link." *IPI [International Press Institute] Report*, August 27, 1987, p. 13

Shim, Jae Hoon. "Foreign Media and Government Enjoy More Relaxed Relations." *Far Eastern Economic Review*, August 22, 1985, pp. 24–25.

————. "An Impatient Public Spurs the Media to Be Bolder." *Far Eastern Economic Review*, August 22, 1985, pp. 23–25.

————. "Paper Under Pressure." *Far Eastern Economic Review*, July 27, 1989, p. 22.

————. "Speciality Magazines Thrive on Increased Influence." *Far Eastern Economic Review*, August 22, 1985, p. 30.

————. "Watching the Watchdog." *Far Eastern Economic Review*, August 23, 1990, pp. 24–26.

Shorrock, Tim. "Korea." *Progressive*. February 1986, pp. 25–28.

Silving, Helen. "'Stare Decisis' in the Civil and in the Common Law." *Seoul Law Journal* 6 (1964): 15–50.

Smith, Ellen M. "Reporting the Truth and Setting the Record Straight: An Analysis of U.S. and Japanese Libel Laws." *Michigan Journal of International Law* 14 (1993): 871–904.

Smith, Jeffery A. "Further Steps Toward a Theory of Press Control." *Journalism History* 8 (Autumn–Winter 1981): 93–95.

Smolla, Rodney A. "Let the Author Beware; The Rejuvenation of the American Law of Libel." *University of Pennsylvania Law Review* 132 (1983): 1–94.

Sochurek, Howard. "South Korea: Success Story in Asia." *National Geographic* 135 (March 1969): 301–44.

"South Korea." *ICJ [International Commission of Jurists] Review* 20 (1978): 19.

"South Korea's Newspaper Boom." *World Press Review*, September 1990, p. 68.

Sowle, Kathryn Dix. "Defamation and the First Amendment: The Case for a Constitutional Privilege of Fair Report." *New York University Law Review* 54 (1979): 469–545.

Steinberg, David I. "Law, Development and Korean Society." *Koreana Quarterly* 13 (Fall 1971): 43–80.

Suh, Dae-Sook. "South Korea in 1981: The First Year of the Fifth Republic." *Asian Survey* 22 (January 1982): 107–15.

Tan, Lek Hor. "South Korea: Cabbage Pickle and Press Pay-Offs." *Index on Censorship*, October 1990, pp. 10–13.

————. "South Korea: 'Guiding' the Press." *Index on Censorship*, May 1987, pp. 28–36.

Thorpe, Norman. "S. Korea and the Press." *Editor & Publisher*, April 12, 1975, p. 56

"Transfer of Judges Threatens Independence of the Judiciary." *CIJL [Center for the Independence of Judges and Lawyers] Bulletin*, October 1985, pp. 21–23.

Ungar, Sanford J. "Seoul Promises to Loosen News Straitjacket." *CPJ [Committee to Protect Journalists] Update*, July–August 1987, pp. 1–3.

————. "Unchaining South Korean Journalists." *U.S. News & World Report*, August 10, 1987, p. 31.

Wagner, Edward W. "Failure in Korea." *Foreign Affairs* 40 (October 1961): 128–35.

Warren, Samuel D., and Louis D. Brandeis. "The Right to Privacy." *Harvard L. Review* 4 (1890): 193–220.

West, James. "Laying down the Law." *Far Eastern Economic Review*, July 23, 1992, p. 13.

West, James M., and Edward J. Baker. "The 1987 Constitutional Reforms in South Korea: Electoral Processes and Judicial Independence." *Harvard Human Rights Yearbook* 1 (Spring 1988): 135–77.

West, James M., and Dae-Kyu Yoon. "The Constitutional Court of the Republic of Korea: Transforming the Jurisprudence of the Vortex?" *American Journal of Comparative Law* 40 (1992): 73–119.

White, Peter T. "South Korea: What Next?" *National Geographic* 148 (September 1975): 394–427.

Whitton, John B. "An International Right of Reply." *American Journal of International Law* 44 (1950): 141–45.

Won, Woo-Hyun. "Korean Mass Media Today and Its Role in Democratic Development: An Analysis of the Political Role of Mass Media Within Korea's Changing Political Environment." *Sungkok Journalism Review* 2 (Fall 1991): 27–32.

———. "The Social and Cultural Impact of Satellite Broadcasting in Korea." *Media Asia* 20 (1993): 15–20.

Worthington, Tony. "The Right of Reply." *Franco British Studies* 9 (1990): 7–18.

———. "Right of Reply Bill." *Journal of Media Law and Practice* 10 (1989): 78–82

Yang, Joon-Mo. "Judicial Supremacy in the Korean Constitution." *Korean Affairs* 3 (December 1964): 346–63.

Yang, Kun. "Judicial Review and Social Change in the Korean Democratizing Process." *American Journal of Comparative Law* 41 (1993): 1–8.

———. "Law and Society Studies in Korea: Beyond the Hahm Theses." *Law and Society Review* 23 (1989): 891–901.

Yim, Seong-hi. "Constitution Guarantees Freedom of Press in ROK [Republic of Korea]: Its Thorny Past and Bright Future." *Korean Report* 3 (September 1963): 21–24.

Yoon, Dae-Kyu. "Constitutional Amendment in Korea." *Korean Journal of Comparative Law* 16 (1988): 1–13.

———. "Constitutional Change in Korea: Retrospect and Prospects." *Asian Affairs* 25 (1994): 178–86.

———. "Judicial Review in the Korean Political Context." *Korean Journal of Comparative Law* 17 (1989): 133–78.

Youm, Kyu Ho. "Breach of Confidence and News Sources: English and U.S. Press Laws Compared." *Anglo-American Law Review* 22 (1993): 421–46.

———. "Fair Report Privilege *versus* Foreign Government Statements: United States and English Judicial Interpretations Compared." *International and Comparative Law Quarterly* 40 (1991): 124–50.

———. "Korean Journalist, Research Scholar Chooses Cronkite School." *ASU [Arizona State University] Journalist*, Winter 1995, p. 12.

———. "Korea's *Chonji* Journalism." *Grassroots Editor* 34 (Spring 1993): 7–8.

———. "The Libel Law of the Republic of Korea." *Gazette* 35 (1985): 183–96.

———. "Libel Laws and Freedom of the Press: South Korea and Japan Reexamined." *Boston University International Law Journal* 8 (1990): 53–83.

———. "Libel and the Press: U.S. and South Korea Compared." *UCLA Pacific Basin Law Journal* 13 (1995): 231–64.

———. "Licensing of Journalists Under International Law." *Gazette* 46 (1990): 113–24.

———. "Press Freedom in 'Democratic' South Korea: Moving from Authoritarian to Libertarian." *Gazette* 43 (1989): 53–71.

———. "Press Freedom Under Constraints: The Case of South Korea." *Asian Survey* 26 (August 1986): 868–82.

———. "Press Freedom and Judicial Review in South Korea." *Stanford Journal of International Law* 30 (1994): 1–40.

———. "Press Law in the Republic of Korea." *New York Law School Journal of International and Comparative Law* 6 (1986): 667–702.

———. "Press Policy of the U.S. Military Government in Korea: A Case of Failed 'Libertarian' Press Theory?" *American Journalism* 8 (Spring–Summer 1991): 161–77.

———. "Right of Reply Under Korean Press Law: A Statutory and Judicial Perspective." *American Journal of Comparative Law* 41 (1993): 49–71.

———. "South Korea: Press Laws in Transition." *Columbia Human Rights Law Review* 22 (1991): 401–35.

———. "Suing American Media in Foreign Courts: Doing an End-run Around U.S. Libel Law?" *Hastings Communications and Entertainment Law Journal* 16 (1994): 235–64.

———. "Survivability of Defamation as a Tort." *Journalism Quarterly* 66 (1989): 646–52, 669.

————. "U.S. Media and Libel Law: An International Perspective." *Gazette* 55 (1995): 185–205.

Youm, Kyu Ho, and Michael B. Salwen. "A Free Press in South Korea: Temporary Phenomenon or Permanent Fixture?" *Asian Survey* 30 (March 1990): 312–25.

Zimmerman, Diane Leenheer, "False Light Invasion of Privacy: The Light That Failed." *New York University Law Review* 64 (1989): 364–453.

## Books and Monographs (in Korean)

*Abridged Compendium of Codes.* 1994 ed. Seoul: Codes Publishing Co., 1994.

*Abridged Compendium of Codes.* 1995 ed. Seoul: Hyonamsa, 1995.

An, Yong-gyo. *Korean Constitution.* Completely revised ed. Seoul: Kosiyongusa, 1992.

Association for Study of Korean Laws. *Democratic Progress and Legislative Reforms.* Seoul: Saram Kwa Saenggaksa, 1989.

Association for Study of Korean Society and Press, ed. *Capitalistic Press and Democracy.* Seoul: Hanul, 1993.

Association of Lawyers for a Democratic Society. *Opinions on Revision and Abolition of Anti-Democratic Evil Laws.* Seoul: Yoksa Pipyongsa, 1989.

*Broadcasting Handbook 1994.* Seoul: Korean Broadcasting Commission, 1994.

Chang, Yong. *The Press and Human Rights.* Seoul: Sonmyong Munhwasa, 1969.

Chong, Chin-sok. *A History of the Korean Press,* Seoul: Nanam, 1990.

————. *A History of the Struggle by the Korean Press Under Japanese Rule.* Seoul: Chonumsa, 1982.

————, ed. *Complete Collection of Korean Press Laws, 1945-1981.* Seoul: Sinyong Research Fund of Kwanhun Club, 1982.

Choe, Chun. *A Discourse on Korean Newspaper History.* Seoul: Iljogak, 1982.

————. *A History of Korean Newspapers.* Seoul: Iljogak, 1960.

————. *A History of Korean Newspapers.* New ed. Seoul: Iljogak, 1990.

Choe, Sok-chae. *Sequence: A Fighting Chapter of the Commoners.* Seoul: Hyongsol Chulpansa, 1990.

*Collection of Constitution Court Rulings,* 6 vols. Seoul: Korean Constitution Court, 1989-1994.

*Collection of Korean Press Cases.* Seoul: Press Arbitration Commission, 1990, 1995.

Committee on Publication of Research Papers in Honor of Dr. Paeng Won-sun's 61st Birthday, ed. *Modern Society and Freedom of the Press.* Seoul: Nanam, 1989.

Committee on Publication of Research Papers in Honor of Professor Han Pyong-gu's 61st Birthday, ed. *Legal Control of the Press.* Seoul: Nanam, 1989.

Committee on the Chosun Struggle for Protection of a Free Press. *A Free Press: The Banner That Cannot Be Lowered.* Seoul: Ture Chulpansa, 1993.

Committee on Publication of Research Papers in Honor of Professor Kim Tong-chol's Retirement, ed. *Issues in Press and Communication.* Seoul: Nanam, 1993.

Committee on Publication of Research Papers in Honor of Mr. Ko Chae-uk's 61st Birthday, ed. *Nation, Freedom, and the Press.* Seoul: Iljogak,1963.

Committee on Publication of Research Papers in Honor of Mr. Yi Yong-hi's 61st Birthday, ed. *Collection of Research Papers in Honor of Mr. Yi Yong-hi's 61st Birthday.* Seoul: Ture,1989.

*Compendium of Codes.* Seoul: Hyonamsa, 1994.

*Compendium of Codes.* Seoul: Codes Publishing Co., 1991.

Corporation for Promotion of Broadcasting Culture, *Korean Broadcasting: A Comprehensive Look.* Seoul: Nanam, 1991.

Council for Democratic Press Movement, ed. *Press Guidelines.* Seoul: Ture, 1988.

Council for Movement for Publishing Culture in Korea. *The Sixth Republic and Its Suppression of Publications.* Seoul: Council for Movement for Publishing Culture in Korea, 1990.

*Democratization in South Korea the World Was Watching.* Seoul: Overseas Information Service, Ministry of Information, 1992.

*Explanatory Sources on the Proposed Acts on Reforms in the Judicial System.* Seoul: [1994].

Han, Dong-won, ed. *Inaccurate Reporting and Corrections.* Seoul: Korean Press Institute, 1990.

————. *Korean Press II.* Seoul: Korean Press Institute, 1992.

————. *Korean Press I.* Seoul: Korean Press Institute, 1991.

Han, Ki-hae. *National Security Law.* Seoul: Kongdongchae, 1989.

Han, Pyong-chae. *A Discourse on Judicial Review.* Seoul: Kosigye, 1994.

Han, Pyong-gu. *A Theory of Press Law.* Seoul: Nanam, 1987.

————, ed. *A General Discourse on Press Law.* Seoul: Nanam, 1990.

Han, Sung-hon. *Copyright Law and Practice.* Seoul: Samminsa,1988.

*How the Dong-A Committee for Struggle for Protection of Press Freedom Fought.* Seoul: Dong-A Committee for Struggle for Protection of Press Freedom, 1987.

*June 29 Declaration and Legislative Reforms.* Seoul: Ministry of Legislation, 1989.

Kang, Chun-man. *Dancing Press and Shaking Elections.* Seoul: Achim,1992.

————. *Is the Press Chameleon?* Seoul: Toso Chulpan Konggan, 1993.

————. *A History of Movement for Broadcasting Democratization in Korea.* Seoul: Taeam, 1990.

————. *Korean Press and a Crisis in Democracy.* Seoul: Achim, 1992.

Kang, Hyon-du. *Popular Culture in the Electronic Age.* Seoul: Hyonamsa, 1984.

Kang, Kyong-gun. *An Exposition on Constitutional Law.* Seoul: Ilsinsa, 1993.

Kang, Myong-gu. *Sociology of Professionalism of the Korean Press.* Seoul: Nanam, 1993.

Kim, Chin-hong. *Politics of Press Control.* Seoul: Hongsongsa,1983.

Kim, Chol-su. *Casebook on Constitutional Law.* Revised ed. Seoul: Popmunsan, 1980.

————. *Korean Constitution.* Expanded ed. Seoul: Popyongsa, 1992.

————, ed. *Laws Relating to Politics.* Seoul: Pakyongsa, 1983.

Kim, Chong-chan. *Press Manipulation During the Six Republic.* Seoul: Achim, 1991.

Kim, Chong-tak. *The Press Republic.* Seoul: Sodam Chulpansa, 1991.

Kim, Min-nam, Kim Yu-won, Pak Chi-dong, Yu Il-sang, Yim Tong-uk, and Chong Tae-su. *A Newly Written History of Korean Press.* Seoul: Achim, 1993.

Kim, Ok-cho. *Reporting and Libel.* Seoul: Korean Press Institute, 1994.

Kim, On-ho. *Publication Movement: Its Situation and Logic.* Seoul: Hankilsa, 1987.

Kim, Taek-hwan. *Korean Press Laws: Their Status and Issues.* Seoul: Korean Press Institute, 1993.

Kim, Tong-chol. *A Study of Free Press Law.* Seoul: Nanam, 1987.

Kim, Tong-min, ed. *Theory and Reality of Press Law.* Seoul: Hannarae, 1993.

Korean Bar Association, ed. *Human Rights Report.* Seoul: Yoksa Pipyongsa, 1987, 1988, and 1989.

————. *Human Rights Report.* Seoul: Korean Bar Association, 1990, 1991, and 1992.

Korean Christian Research Institute of Social Affairs. *The Press and Society.* Seoul: Minjungsa, 1983.

*Korean Newspapers and Broadcasting Annual 1994.* Seoul: Korean Press Institute, 1994.

*Korean Newspapers and Broadcasting Annual 1993.* Seoul: Korean Press Institute, 1993.

*Korean Newspapers and Broadcasting Annual 1992.* Seoul: Korean Press Institute, 1992.

*Korean Newspapers and Broadcasting Annual 1991.* Seoul: Korean Press Institute, 1991.

*Korean Newspapers and Broadcasting Annual 1990.* Seoul: Korean Press Institute, 1990.

*Korean Newspapers and Broadcasting Annual 1989.* Seoul: Korean Press Institute, 1989.

*Korean Press Annual 1968.* Seoul: Korean Press Institute, 1968.

*The Korean Press in Transition.* Seoul: Korean Newspaper Editors Association, 1990.

Ku, Pyong-sak. *An Introductory Discourse on the New Constitution.* Completely revised ed. Seoul: Pakyongsa, 1993.

Kwon, Yong-song. *An Introductory Discourse on the New Constitution.* Seoul: Popmunsa, 1994.

Kye, Hun-mo, ed. *Korean Press Chronology, 1951-1955.* Seoul: [1993].

*Law, Order, and Human Rights.* Seoul: Ministry of Justice, 1990.

Oh, Hong-gun. *Dear Mr. President.* Seoul: Hwangto, 1989.

Oh, In-hwan, ed. *Public Interest of the Press and Press Regulation: A. Collection of the Late Professor Kim Tong-jin's Research Papers.* Seoul: Department of Mass Communication, Yonsei University, 1991.

Oh, Se-kyong, ed. *Compendium of Court Decisions.* Seoul: Codes Publishing Co., 1991.

Oh, Se-ung. *So Jae-pil's Reform Movement and Today's Tasks.* Seoul: Koryowon, 1993.

Om, Ki-hyong. *A Discourse on Press Ethics.* Seoul: Iljisa,1982.

Paeng, Won-sun. *A Discourse on Korean Press Law.* Seoul: Popmunsa, 1994.

————. *A New Discourse on Press Law*. Seoul: Nanam, 1989.

————. *A Theory of Mass Communication Law*. Seoul: Popmunsa,1984.

————. *A Theory of Mass Communication Law*. Revised ed. Seoul: Popmunsa, 1988.

Pak, Chol-on. *The Press and National Security*. Seoul: Korean Press Institute, 1986.

Pak, Kwon-sang. *A Proposition for a Free Press*. Seoul: Chonyewon, 1983.

Pak, Won-sun. *Study of National Security Laws*. 3 vols. Seoul: Yoksa Pipyongsa, 1989, 1992.

Pak, Yong-sang. *A Discourse on Broadcasting Law*. Seoul:Kyobomungo, 1988.

————. *A Legislative Examination of the Broadcasting Commission*. Seoul: Broadcasting Commission, 1990.

————. *Press Freedom and Public Duty*. Seoul: Kyobomungo, 1982.

Pang, Chong-bae. *A Discourse on Reforms in the Korean Press*. Seoul: Nanam, 1991.

*Pseudo-Journalists as Seen Through Actual Cases*. Seoul: Ministry of Culture and Information, 1989.

*Report on the '94 Symposium for Court Reporters*. Seoul: 1994.

So, Chin-un, Pak Chong-guk, and Chi Kyu-chol. *A Concise Discourse on the New Constitution*. Seoul: Tongbang Toso, 1993.

So, Chong-u, Cha Bae-kun, and Choe Chang-sop. *A Theory on Press Control*. Revised ed. Seoul: Popmunsa, 1983.

Social Science Research Institute, ed. *Ideology and Informationalizing Society*. Seoul: Sungkyunkwan University Press, 1990.

Son, Chu-hwan. *The Scene of a Free Press*. Seoul: Nanam, 1988.

Song, Kon-ho. *A Modern History of Korean Press*. Seoul: Samminsa, 1990.

Song, Kon-ho, Yim Chae-chong, Kim Hak-chon, Kim Chong-chol, Yi Tae-ho, Chong Yon-chu, Chong Dae-su, Kang Tae-in, Kim Tae-hong, and Ko Sung-u. *Populace and Free Press*. Seoul: Achim, 1984.

Songkok Press Culture Foundation, ed. *The Korean Press in the '90s: Its Directions and Prospects*. Seoul: Songkok Press Culture Foundation, 1990.

Supreme Court of Korea. *Statutes Relating to Reforms in the Judicial System*. Seoul: 1994.

*Theory and Practice of Public-Information Affairs*. Seoul: Ministry of Information, 1993.

*Toward a New Pacific Era*. Seoul: Overseas Information Service, Ministry of Information, 1993.

*Unabridged Compendium of Codes*. Seoul: Chongrimgak, 1982.

Won, U-hyon. *Mass Media and Cultural Development*. Seoul: Pommusa, 1984.

Yang, Kon. *An Argument in Defense of Constitutionalism*. Seoul: Kosikye, 1987.

Yi, Chin-bok. *Human Rights and National Security Policy in Korea*. Seoul: Ilwolsogak, 1987.

Yi, Hae-chang. *A Study of Korean Press History*. Revised ed. Seoul: Songmungak, 1983.

Yi, Hyo-song. *Criticism of the Press*. Seoul: Iron Kwa Silchon, 1990.

————. *Korean Society and the Press*. Seoul: Achim, 1993.

————. *Press Freedom and Democratic Politics*. Seoul: Research Institute of Media and Culture, Sogang University, 1989.

Yi, Hyok-chu, and Kim Chang-su. *Judge and Trial*. Seoul: Kosikye, 1986.

Yi, Pyong-guk. *President and the Press*. Seoul: Nanam, 1987.

Yi, Sang-chol. *A History of Communications Development*. Seoul: Iljisa, 1982.

Yi, Sang-hyon. *Press Embargo I*. Seoul: Chongum, 1987.

————. *Press Embargo II*. Seoul: Chongum, 1987.

Yi, Yon. *The Role of the Chosun Central Information Committee During the Japanese Rule*. Seoul: Research Institute of Media and Culture, Sogang University, 1989.

Yu, Chae-chon. *Korean Press and Media Culture*. Seoul: Nanam,1986.

Yu, Il-sang. *A Discourse on Press Ethics and Law*. Seoul: Achim,1991.

————. *Naked Korean Press*. Seoul: Mundoksa,1990.

## Unpublished Material (in Korean)

"Collection and Management of Information and Protection of Privacy." Research report prepared by the Korean Society of Public Law, Seoul, December 1989.

Kim, Chin-hong. "Evaluation of the Credibility of the Korean Newspapers in Transition and Study of Readers' Cognizance of Press Guidelines." Paper presented at the Korean Society for Journalism and Communication Studies convention, n.p., Autumn 1988.

Kim, Chong-sun, Kang Myong-gu, and Yi Chin-bok. "Election and Broadcasting." Research report prepared for the Corporation for Promotion of Broadcasting Culture, Seoul, 1993.

Kim, Chun-sik. "An Empirical Study of Press Guidelines as a Factor of Press Control: Focusing on the Fifth Republic." Master's thesis, Hankuk University of Foreign Studies, Seoul, 1989.

Kim, Dong-jin. "A Study of Legal Control of a Free Press." Master's thesis, Yonsei University, Seoul, 1977.

———. "A Study of the Public Interest of Broadcasting." Ph.D. diss., Yonsei University, Seoul, 1986.

Kim, Pok-su. "A Study of the Korean Press Under the U.S. Military Rule." Ph.D. diss., Hanyang University, Seoul, 1991.

Paeng, Won-sun. "A Study of Libel as a Tort." Master's thesis, Sungkyunkwan University, Seoul, 1977.

———. "A Study of the Structural Characteristics of Korean News Agencies." Ph.D. diss., Seoul National University, Seoul, 1982.

Pak, Chol-on. "The Study on the Collision and Harmony of the Freedom of the Press and National Security: Focusing on Restrictions on the Access to National Secrets." Ph.D. diss. [Hanyang University, Seoul], 1989.

Yi, Chae-jin. "A Study on the Conflict Between Press Freedom and Right of Character." Master's thesis, Seoul National University, Seoul, 1991.

Yim, Tu-bin. "An Introduction to Laws Governing the Press." Lecture prepared for the Korean Press Institute, Seoul, n.d. (text on file with author).

———. "Mass Communication and Privacy." Lecture prepared for the Korean Press Institute, Seoul, n.d. (text on file with author).

Yu, Il-sang. "A Comparative Study of Korean and U.S. Statutory and Case Law on Obscene Expression." Paper presented at the Korean Society for Journalism and Communication Studies convention, Seoul, 1995.

## Journal Articles (in Korean)

"Act Relating to Remedies for Press Infringements (Proposed)." *Press Arbitration Quarterly* 13 (Winter 1993): 33–54.

An, Kwang-sik. "Ethical Responsibility of the Press in Transition." *Press Arbitration Quarterly* 11 (Autumn 1991): 63–64.

———. "Free Competition and Ethical Responsibility of the Press." *Press Arbitration Quarterly* 10 (Winter 1990): 38–43.

An Yong-gyo. "Concept and Meaning of the Right of Image." *Press Arbitration Quarterly* 2 (Summer 1982): 6–13.

Cha, Hyong-kun. "Petition to the Constitution Court on the Constitutionality of Article 764 of the Civil Code." *Study of Case Law* 5 (1992): 29–34.

———. "An Examination of the Broadcast Act." *Lawyer* 23 (1993): 111–27.

Cha, Pae-gun. "Press Dysfunctions and the Need for a Press Arbitration System." *Press Arbitration Quarterly* 5 (Autumn 1985): 35–37.

Chang, Yong-su. "An Introduction to the Structure for Achieving Freedom of the Press." *Press Arbitration Quarterly* 14 (Summer 1994): 19–35.

———. "An Overview of Recent Court Rulings on the Press." *Press Arbitration Quarterly* 13 (Autumn 1993): 33–43.

Chi, Hong-won. "Violation of the Right of Character." *Collection of Discourses on Judicature* 10 (1979): 213–40.

Cho, Yong-rae. "The Changjak Kwa Pipyong Case and Freedom of Publication." *Shin Dong-A*, January 1986, pp. 496–503.

Choe, Chang-sop. "TV Investigative Programs and Human Rights." *Press Arbitration Quarterly* 14 (Summer 1994): 6–12.

Choe, U-chan. "A Criminal Law Examination of Justification of Defamation." *Press Arbitration Quarterly* 12 (Spring 1992): 12–18.

Choe, Won-sik. "The Relationship Between Right of Privacy and Legislation." *Lawyers* 14 (1984): 399–411.

Chon, Kwan-u. "The National Security Act and the Anti-Communist Act Should Be Revised." *Journalism Review* 38 (Autumn 1971): 13–16.

Chon, Pyong-dok. "Oh Hong-gun Incident Typifies Right-Wing Terrorism: Thorough Investigation of Its Case Urgently Needed." *Chugan Hankuk*, September 15, 1988, p. 4.

Chon, Pyong-tae. "Freedom of Expression and Privacy." *Press Arbitration Quarterly* 14 (Winter 1994): 71–73.

Chong, Chae-hwang. "Constitution Court Case Law on Freedom of Speech and the Press." *Civil Examination Society*, March 1994, pp. 64–81.

———. "Judgment on the Constitutionality of Article 7 (1) of the Act Relating to Registration of Periodicals." *Operational Status and Revitalization of Constitutional Litigation*, December 12, 1993, pp. 3–9.

———. "Judgment on the Constitutionality of Article 6 of the Military Secrets Act." *Development of the Constitution Court*, December 1992, pp. 384–89.

Chong, Chin-sok. "Changes in the Legal and Ethical Environment of the Korean Press." *Press Arbitration Quarterly* 10 (Spring 1990): 6–14.

———. "Changes in Media Environment and Press Arbitration System." *Press Arbitration Quarterly* 11 (Spring 1991): 10–15.

———. "Classification of Press Infringements According to Eras." *Press Arbitration Quarterly* 2 (Autumn 1982): 53–61.

———. "The Full-scale War Between the Press and the Park Chung Hee Regime: An Occasion in Which Management Takes an Upper Hand over Editors." *Newspapers and Broadcasting*, March 1995, pp. 34–43.

———. "Past Changes and Future Directions in Remedies for Press Infringements." *Press Arbitration Quarterly* 11 (Summer 1991): 34–35.

———. "The Press and Right of Reply." *Press Arbitration Quarterly* 14 (Winter 1994): 7–15.

———. "The Reality of Remedies for Press Infringement and the Audience Movement." *Press Arbitration Quarterly* 11 (Winter 1991): 11–22.

"Conspiracy Between Power and the Press: Press Guidelines, Secret Messages Sent by the Power to the Press." *Mal*, September 6, 1986 (special issue).

"Discussion of Improvement of Press-Related Laws." *Newspapers and Broadcasting*, December 1988, p. 15.

Han, Chin-su. "Full Story of Judicial Crisis." *Shin Dong-A*, August 1988, pp. 202–15.

Han, Ki-chan. "From Freedom to Responsibility: Reforming Is Valuable When It's Voluntary." *Newspapers and Broadcasting*, February 1995, pp. 60–63.

Han, Pyong-gu. "A Reconsideration of Limits of Press Freedom and Media Ethics." *Press Arbitration Quarterly* 11 (Winter 1991): 50–51.

———. "Status of Right of Reply Laws in Various Countries Around the World." *Press Arbitration Quarterly* 2 (Summer 1982): 67–77.

———. "Types of Defamation and Remedies." *Press Arbitration Quarterly* 3 (Autumn 1983): 26–35.

Han, Sang-bom. "News Reporting and Public Figures and Celebrities." *Press Arbitration Quarterly* 66 (Summer 1986): 16–22.

———. "Photo-Reporting and Right of Image." *Press Arbitration Quarterly* 2 (Summer 1982): 14–20.

Han, Tae-yol. "National Interest and the Reality of News Reporting." *Press Arbitration Quarterly* 11 (Summer 1991): 27–33.

Han, Wi-su. "Court Reporting as Observed by a Judge: Issues and Suggestions." *Press Arbitration Quarterly* 14 (Autumn 1994):18–26.

Ho, Yong. "On the Constitutionality of Article 7 of the National Security Act." *Development of Constitutional Litigation*, December 1991, pp. 333–39.

Hwang, Sok-yon. "A Study of the Basic Press Act." *Lawyer* 13 (1983): 123–65.

Kang, Hyon-du. "Broadcasters' Editorial Freedom: Its Ethics and Limits." *Newspapers and Broadcasting,* March 1991, pp. 50–51.

Kang, Ku-jin. "The Functions of Law in Korean Society." *Seoul Law Journal* 15 (June 1974): 135–57.

Kang, Kyong-gun. "Judicial Limitations on Reporting on National Interests." *Press Arbitration Quarterly* 11 (Summer 1991): 19–26.

———. "Practice of Right of Reply and Press Arbitration System." *Press Arbitration Quarterly* 14 (Winter 1994): 16–37.

Kim, Chae-kon. "Regulatory Press Laws and News Reporters." *Newspaper Research,* Winter 1987, pp. 74–81.

Kim, Chol-su. "Concept of Human Rights and Meaning of the Press." *Press Arbitration Quarterly* 2 (Spring 1982): 6–14.

———. "An Introduction to the Impact of the U.S. Constitution on the Korean Constitution." *Seoul Law Journal* 26 (December 1985): 22–68.

Kim, Chong-so. "An Examination of Issues in Right to Correction of News Reports." *Press Arbitration Quarterly* 15 (Spring 1995): 6–23.

Kim, Chong-so. "Legal Status and Rights of the Viewing and Listening Audience." *General Commentaries on Constitutional Law* 4 (1993): 427–83.

Kim, Chong-su. "Right of Privacy." *Lawyer* 1 (1969): 108–23.

Kim, Chu-on. "Let's Not Accept *Chonji*." *Wolgan Chosun,* June 1989, pp. 446–49.

Kim, Il-su. "On the Constitutionality of Article 6 of the Military Secrets Act." *Development of the Constitutional Court System,* December 1992, pp. 155–207.

Kim, Kwang-ok. "Release of Information and Right to Know." *Press Arbitration Quarterly* 9 (Summer 1989): 6–10.

Kim, Kyu-hwan. "The Korean Press's Struggle for Its Freedom." *Newspaper Review* 8 (November–December 1964): 16–18.

Kim, O-su. "Types of Compensations by the Press for Liabilities." *Press Arbitration Quarterly* 3 (Spring 1983): 32–43.

Kim, Pyong-guk. "Access to Information and Defamation." *Press Arbitration Quarterly* 9 (Summer 1989): 23–28.

Kim, Sang-chol. "The Basic Press Act: A Legalistic Perspective." *Newspaper Research,* Summer 1987, pp. 22–29.

Kim, Sang-hyon. "Chongju 'Public Servants' Rejecting the Tradition of Administrative Control of Information." *Sisa Journal,* April 8, 1993, p. 33.

Kim, Sang-yong. "Invasion of Right of Character and Civil Liability." *Monthly Court Case Report,* November 1993, pp. 50–65.

Kim, Song-nam. "A Legal Examination of the Press Arbitration System." *Press Arbitration Quarterly* 9 (Autumn 1989): 7–14.

———. "Press Infringement and Remedies." *Press Arbitration Quarterly* 8 (Autumn 1988): 50–58.

Kim, Tong-chol. "Civil and Criminal Liability for Press Infringement." *Press Arbitration Quarterly* 3 (Spring 1983): 19–31.

———. "Controversy over Denial of Access to Arrest Warrants and Right to Know." *Press Arbitration Quarterly* 12 (Winter 1992): 13–21.

———. "Ethics of and Legal Problems with News Photos." *Press Arbitration Quarterly* 7 (Spring 1987): 19–37.

———. "Freedom of Expression and Obscenity." *Press Arbitration Quarterly* 5 (Winter 1985): 9–21.

———. "Right of Access and Opinion Advertising." *Press Arbitration Quarterly* 3 (Winter 1983): 60–73.

———. "Right to Know and Privacy." *Press Arbitration Quarterly* 5 (Summer 1985): 6–17.

Kim, Tong-hwan. "Injury to a Company's Credit and Its Recovery." *Press Arbitration Quarterly* 5 (Autumn 1985): 15–24.

Kim, Un-ryong. "Legal Problems with Publicity on Suspected Crimes." *Press Arbitration Quarterly* 2 (Autumn 1982): 6–14.

———. "News Reporting and Defamation." *Press Arbitration Quarterly* 3 (Autumn 1983): 17–25.

Ko, Sung-dok. "Law and Judicial Proceedings Applicable to International Libel Litigation." *Press Arbitration Quarterly* 13 (Autumn 1993): 14–32.

Ko, Un. "Deploring the Changjak Kwa Pipyong Case." *Shin Dong-A*, February 1986, pp. 270–79.

Ku, Pyong-sak. "The Legal Theory and Applicational Trends of Protection of Military Secrets." *General Commentaries on Constitutional Law* 2 (1991): 135–75.

———. "A New Reflection on Freedom of the Press." *Newspaper Research*, Summer 1987, pp. 8–16.

Kwon, Mun-taek. "Obscene Work of Art." *Lawyers Association Journal* 20 (January 1971): 1–16.

Kwon, O-gon. "Future Directions for the Current Press Arbitration System." *Press Arbitration Quarterly* 14 (Autumn 1994): 43–44.

Kwon, O-sung. "Meaning of Reputation and Types of Libel." *Press Arbitration Quarterly* 3 (Autumn 1983): 6–16.

Kwon, Yong-sol. "Freedom of the Press and an Issue of Public Interest." *Press Arbitration Quarterly* 4 (Autumn 1984): 16–26.

Kwon, Yong-song. "The Constitutional Review System in Korea." *Seoul Law Journal* 29 (December 1988): 39–45.

———. "Meaning of Privacy and Its Historical Development." *Press Arbitration Quarterly* 3 (Summer 1983): 6–14.

Namgung, Ho-gyong. "An Examination of the Crime of Defaming the State." *Seoul Law Journal* 33 (September 1992): 180–97.

Oh, Se-tak. "Ethical Responsibility of the Press and Press Arbitration System." *Press Arbitration Quarterly* 13 (Summer 1993): 43–44.

Oh, So-baek. "Protection of Human Rights and Press Responsibility." *Press Arbitration Quarterly* 2 (Spring 1982): 32–37.

———. "Weeklies and Violation of Right of Character." *Press Arbitration Quarterly* 3 (Spring 1983): 70–78.

Oh, Taek-sop. "Problems with Reporting on Juvenile Crimes." *Press Arbitration Quarterly* 2 (Winter 1982): 80–87.

Paeng, Won-sun. "The Basic Press Act Should Be Revised." *Shin Dong-A*, October 1985, pp. 226–32.

———. "Comments: Characteristics and Problems of the New Press Laws." *Newspapers and Broadcasting*, December 1987, pp. 35–38.

———. "Freedom of News Reporting and Fair Trial." *Press Arbitration Quarterly* 5 (Spring 1985): 7–13.

———. "Obscenity in Mass Media in Korea: Its Actual Situation and Regulatory Status." *Press Arbitration Quarterly* 5 (Winter 1985): 34–46.

———. "Press Freedom and National Interests." *Press Arbitration Quarterly* 11 (Summer 1991): 6–11.

———. "Reporting on Privacy of Political Candidates and Legal and Ethical Problems." *Press Arbitration Quarterly* 13 (Spring 1993): 18–26.

———. "Right of Reply: Its Historical Development." *Press Arbitration Quarterly* 2 (Summer 1982): 47–55.

Pak, Chong-kyu. "Regulations and Freedom as Viewed Through Press History." *Press Arbitration Quarterly* 8 (Summer 1988): 6–15.

Pak, Chong-su. "Ethics and Self-Regulation of the Korean Press." *Press Arbitration Quarterly* 13 (Summer 1993): 6–17.

Pak, Ki-sun. "Right of Access and Reader Contributions." *Press Arbitration Quarterly* 3 (Winter 1983): 74–85.

Pak, Tong-hi. "Economic Reporting and Protection of a Corporate Credit." *Press Arbitration Quarterly* 5 (Autumn 1985): 8–14.

———. "Suggestions for Revitalizing Various Laws and Systems to Protect Human Rights." *Justice* 23 (1990): 74–87.

Pak, Won-sun. "A Study of the Original National Security Act." *Lawyer* 19 (1989): 263–90.

Pak, Yong-sang. "A General Examination of the Press Arbitration System." *Press Arbitration Quarterly* 9 (Autumn 1989): 51–63.

———. "Exercising the Right to Claim Corrected Reports: Requirements and Procedures," *Press Arbitration Quarterly* 11 (Winter 1991): 55–86.

———. "A History of Korean Press Law." *Lawyers Association Journal* 32 (1983): 13–29.

———. "A History of Korean Press Law." *Lawyers Association Journal* 32 (1983): 24–43.

———. "A History of Korean Press Law." *Newspaper Research*, Winter 1980, pp. 8–44.

———. "A History of Korean Press Law." *Newspaper Research*, Winter 1983, pp. 150–77.

———. "A Legislative Background and Issues with Revision of the Basic Press Act." *Newspaper Research*, Summer 1987, pp. 36–47.

———. "Legislative Proposals for Improvement of the Right of Claim for Corrected Reports and Press Arbitration System." *Press Arbitration Quarterly* 11 (Autumn 1991): 9–44.

———. "News Reporting and Right to Correction of News Reports." *Press Arbitration Quarterly* 3 (Summer 1983): 36–47.

———. "Press Arbitration in Korea." *Press Arbitration Quarterly* 1 (Winter 1981): 18–25.

———. "Press Arbitration System Under the 'New Act Relating to Registration, etc. of Periodicals.'" *Press Arbitration Quarterly* 7 (Winter 1987): 61–89.

———. "The Reality of the Right of Claim for Corrected News Report as Examined in Court Decisions." *Press Arbitration Quarterly* 11 (Spring 1991): 22–33.

Pang, Chong-bae. "Public Interest of the Press Reconsidered." *Press Arbitration Quarterly* 3 (Summer 1983): 66–75.

"Publicity on Suspected Crimes: Its Practice and Limitation." *Press Arbitration Quarterly* 2 (Autumn 1982): 34–45.

Pyon Chae-ok. "Development of Information Industry and Privacy." *Press Arbitration Quarterly* 5 (Summer 1985): 18–27.

Sim, Chang-sop. "Copyright Owner in the Case of Producing Applicational Art Work by Order." *Commentaries on Supreme Court Decisions* 19(2) (1993): 390–408.

———. "Parameters for Literary Works to Be Protected by Copyright." *Commentaries on Supreme Court Decisions* 19(2) (1993): 379–89.

Sin, Pong-gi. "Theory of and Case Law on Freedom of Speech and the Press." *Press Arbitration Quarterly* 12 (Winter 1992): 32–43.

Sin, Pyong. "Reporting on Judicial Proceedings: Its Problems and Impact." *Press Arbitration Quarterly* 5 (Spring 1985): 25–35.

So, Chong-u. "News Reporting and Invasion of Privacy." *Press Arbitration Quarterly* 3 (Summer 1983): 15–23.

———. "Remedial System for Press Infringements in Our Country." *Press Arbitration Quarterly* 13 (Autumn 1994): 56–57.

———. "Responsibility of the Korean Press Entering the Free Competition Era." *Press Arbitration Quarterly* 8 (Summer 1988): 30–37.

So, Chung-sok. "5-Minute Interview." *Shin dong-A*, March 1987, pp. 291–92.

Son, Chang-yol. "Crime Reporting and Violation of Human Rights: A Criminal Law Perspective." *Prosecurator* 1 (1990): 362–467.

Son, Tong-gwon. "Press Reports and Libel of the Dead." *Press Arbitration Quarterly* 12 (Spring 1992): 6–11.

Son, Yong. "TV Dramas and Actors' Reputation." *Press Arbitration Quarterly* 4 (Summer 1984): 23–29.

Song, Nak-in. "Advertising Notice of Apology for Libel and the Constitution Court's Decision." *Press Arbitration Quarterly* 12 (Spring 1992): 27–42.

———. "Characteristics of and Problems with Korean Press Laws." *Press Arbitration Quarterly* 14 (Spring 1994): 6–20.

———. "Enactment of Laws on Protection of Private Information and Release of the Information, and the Press." *Press Arbitration Quarterly* 15 (Spring 1995): 36–46.

———. "Governmental Protection of Privacy: Focusing on Laws on Public Agencies' Protection of Privacy." *Study of Public Law* 22 (June 1994): 1–46.

———. "The Press and Press Arbitration in an Information Age." *Press Arbitration Quarterly* 12 (Winter 1992): 44–45.

Song, Yong-sik. "News Reports of Public Interest and Limitations on Defamation." *Journalism Review* 1 (April 1964): 33–35.

———. "Problems with the Current Copyright Act I." *Lawyer* 19 (1989): 181–200.

———. "Problems with the Current Copyright Act II." *Lawyer* 21 (1991): 339–54.

"Status of Periodical Registrations." *Newspapers and Broadcasting*, January 1995, p. 166.

"Status of Photo-Reporting and Its Task." *Press Arbitration Quarterly* 2 (Summer 1982): 30–46.

"Types of Press Infringement and Its Remedies." *Press Arbitration Quarterly* 1 (Winter 1981): 26–33.

"Women's Magazines and Obscenity." *Press Arbitration Quarterly* (Autumn 1983): 57–65.

Won U-hyon. "The Modern Meaning of Right of Access and Its Exercise." *Press Arbitration Quarterly* 3 (Winter 1983): 49–59.

Yang, Kon. "Exercise of the Right of Reply: Its Current Status." *Press Arbitration Quarterly* 3 (Summer 1982): 56–66.

Yang, Sam-sung. "The Actual Situation of Press Infringement as Examined Through Press Arbitration Cases." *Press Arbitration Quarterly* 11 (Winter 1991): 23–33.

———. "Analysis of Trends in Court Decisions on the Press." *Press Arbitration Quarterly* 10 (Spring 1990): 30–38.

———. "News Reporting on Accidents and Issues in Law and Ethics." *Press Arbitration Quarterly* 10 (Autumn 1990): 7–15.

———. "Proposals for Reforming the Press Arbitration System." *Press Arbitration Quarterly* 12 (Autumn 1992): 7–22.

———. "Proposed Reforms in Claims for Correction of News Reports and in Press Arbitration System." *Press Arbitration Quarterly* 13 (Winter 1993): 7–20.

———. "Rationale for Revitalizing the Press Arbitration System." *Press Arbitration Quarterly* 7 (Autumn 1987): 40–44.

———. "Right to Claim Corrected Reports: A Legal Perspective." *Press Arbitration Quarterly* 2 (Winter 1982): 10–29.

———. "A Study of Article 764 of the Civil Code (on Special Measures on Defamation)." *Press Arbitration Quarterly* 13(Autumn 1993): 6–13.

Yang, Sung-du. "Citizens' Right Consciousness and the Remedial System for Press Infringement." *Press Arbitration Quarterly* 9 (Winter 1989): 36–43.

———. "Koreans' Consciousness of Human Rights." *Press Arbitration Quarterly* 2 (Spring 1982): 15–22.

Yi, Chae-sang. "Publication of Defamation." *Monthly Court Case Report*, May 1986, pp. 60–62, 74.

Yi, Chu-hung. "Notification on Outdoor Assembly Under the Act on Assembly and Demonstration." *Commentaries on Supreme Court Decisions* 14 (1990): 433–45.

Yi, Hae-chang. "Changes in Press Control in Korea." *Journal of Korean Cultural Research Institute* 16 (June 1970): 81–107.

Yi, Hae-jin. "Freedom of Conscience and Notice of Apology Under the Constitution." *Lawyer* 22 (1992): 7–22.

Yi, Hye-bok. "Fair News Reporting and Press Ethics." *Press Arbitration Quarterly* 11 (Winter 1991): 45–46.

———. "The Era of Civilian Government and Press Responsibility." *Press Arbitration Quarterly* 13 (Autumn 1993): 44–45.

———. "Press Freedom and Arbitration System." *Press Arbitration Quarterly* 9 (Summer 1989): 38–39.

———. "Press Freedom and Citizens' Rights." *Press Arbitration Quarterly* 9 (Winter 1989): 67–68.

———. "Press Responsibility in an Era of Free Competition." *Press Arbitration Quarterly* 8 (Autumn 1988): 41–42.

———. "Reporting on Accidents and Individuals' Rights." *Press Arbitration Quarterly* 7 (Summer 1987)): 7–30.

———. "Reporting on Accidents and Violations of Personal Interests: An Examination." *Press Arbitration Quarterly* 10 (Autumn 1990): 16–34.

Yi, Hyong-ha. "Conflict and Accommodation Between Freedom of Speech and the Press and Copyright." *General Commentaries on Constitutional Law* 2 (1991): 279–320.

Yi, Kang-hyok. "Confidentiality of News Sources and Its Legal Protection." *Press Arbitration Quarterly* 9 (Summer 1989): 11–16.

———. "Public Disclosure of Information and Its Structural Mechanism." *Monthly Court Case Report*, June 1993, pp. 5–8.

Yi, Kon-ho. "The 'Revolting Slaves' Case and Obscenity." *Study of Case Law* 3 (1978): 269–79.

Yi, Kwan-gu. "All Media People, Stand Up in Revising and Abolishing the Restrictive Press Laws and Regulations." *Journalism Review* 38 (Autumn 1971): 2–6.

Yi, Kwang-jae. "The Conflict Between the New Administration and the Press Revealed." *Newspapers and Broadcasting*, December 1993, pp. 7–10.

———. "Publicity on Suspected Crimes and Accident Reporting." *Press Arbitration Quarterly* 2 (Autumn 1982): 15–25.

Yi, Kwang-yol. "Defamation and Publication." *Commentaries on Supreme Court Decisions* 10 (1988): 520–29.

Yi, Pom-ho. "Case Notes on Supreme Court Decisions on the Obscenity of Literary Works." *Study of Case Law* 3 (1978): 261–67.

Yi, Pom-yol. "National Security Act Abused for Political Security." *Shin Dong-A*, March 1988, pp. 262–68.

Yi, Sang-chol. "A Theoretical Basis for Broadcasting Regulation." *Press Arbitration Quarterly* 4 (Summer 1984): 6–13.

Yi, Sang-don. "Issues in Pre-Trial Coverage and Remedies for Infringement." *Press Arbitration Quarterly* 5 (Spring 1985): 14–24.

Yi, Sang-hoe. "Press Arbitration System and Freedom of Reporting." *Press Arbitration Quarterly* 6 (Summer 1986): 45–47.

———. "Press Arbitration System and Right to Correction of News Reports." *Press Arbitration Quarterly* 4 (Spring 1984): 58–61.

Yi, Sang-hyon. "News Gathering Environment of Court Reporting and Access to Information." *Press Arbitration Quarterly* 14 (Autumn 1994): 8–17.

Yi, Sang-kyong. "A Study of Assessment of Damages in Defamation Suits for News Reporting." *Press Arbitration Quarterly* 12 (Spring 1992): 43–61.

Yi, Sok-yon. "Legal Theory and Application of Defamation Under Criminal Code." *Press Arbitration Quarterly* 12 (Winter 1992): 6–12.

Yi, Su-jong. "Basic Press Act: A View on the Spirit of Its Enactment." *Press Arbitration Quarterly* 1 (Winter 1981): 38–46.

Yi, Sung-u. "A Case Note on the Constitution Court's Decision on Article 6 of the Military Secrets Act." *Operational Status and Revitalization of Constitutional Litigation*, December 1993, pp. 10–24.

———. "A Case Note on the Constitution Court's Decision on People's 'Right to Know.'" *Development of Constitutional Litigation*, December 1991, pp. 314–25.

Yi, Taek-hwi. "The Press and the Press Arbitration in a Rapidly Changing Society." *Press Arbitration Quarterly* 9 (Summer 1989): 43–44.

Yi, Taek-su. "Right to Know and Limitation of News Reporting." *Press Arbitration Quarterly* 12 (Autumn 1992): 34–39.

Yi, U-se. "Notice of Court Judgments and Claim for *ex post facto* Reporting." *Press Arbitration Quarterly* 12 (Spring 1992): 19–26.

Yim Tu-bin. "Right of Image and Photo-Taking in Courtroom." *Press Arbitration Quarterly* 2 (Summer 1982): 21–29.

Yu, Chae-chon. "Evaluation of Investigative Stories in Magazines." *Press Arbitration Quarterly* 8 (Winter 1988): 12–17.

———. "An Examination of Press Ethics and Self-Regulations of Media Companies." *Press Arbitration Quarterly* 10 (Winter 1990): 6–14.

———. "A Plan for Revitalizing the Press Arbitration System." *Press Arbitration Quarterly* 9 (Autumn 1989): 23–33.

———. "Professional Ethics of the Press and the Press Arbitration System." *Press Arbitration Quarterly* 11 (Autumn 1991): 68–69.

———. "Release of Information and Privacy." *Press Arbitration Quarterly* 9 (Summer 1989): 17–22.

———. "Reporting Tendencies of the Korean Press and Violations of Human Rights." *Press Arbitration Quarterly* 2 (Spring 1982): 23–31.

———. "Social Responsibility of the Press and the Press Arbitration Quarterly." *Press Arbitration Quarterly* 9 (Winter 1989): 62–63.

Yu, Il-sang. "Elections and Reporting on Public Opinion Surveys." *Press Arbitration Quarterly* 12 (Winter 1992): 22–31.

———. "Ethical and Legal Responsibilities of Reportage Stories." *Press Arbitration Quarterly* 10 (Autumn 1990): 12–20.

———. "Media Law Research: Its Characteristics and Methodology." *Press Arbitration Quarterly* 14 (Spring 1994): 34–46.

Yu, Kang-hwan. "Mass Culture and Pornography." *Press Arbitration Quarterly* 5 (Winter 1985): 22–33.

Yu, Kun-il. "The Basic Press Act: A Realistic Perspective of the Press." *Newspaper Research*, Summer 1987, pp. 18–21.

Yu, Pyong-mu. "A Study of Freedom of the Press in Korea." *Journalism Quarterly* 10 (Autumn 1976): 85–106.

Yu, Sung-sam. "Reporting with Actual Names and Human Rights." *Press Arbitration Quarterly* 12 (Summer 1992): 28–37.

Yun, Chin-su. "On the Notice of Apology and the Constitutionality of Article 764 of the Civil Code." *Development of the Constitution Court*, December 1992, pp. 290–322.

# INDEX

This index is alphabetized word-by-word. In indexing Korean names, if a name is in Korean order especially as it is in Korean-language publications, it is left as is, with no inversion and no comma; if in Western order as usually the case with authors writing in English, the name is inverted, with a comma, like a Western European name.